DISCOVERING AMERICA'S PAST

CUSTOMS, LEGENDS, HISTORY & LORE Of Our Great Nation

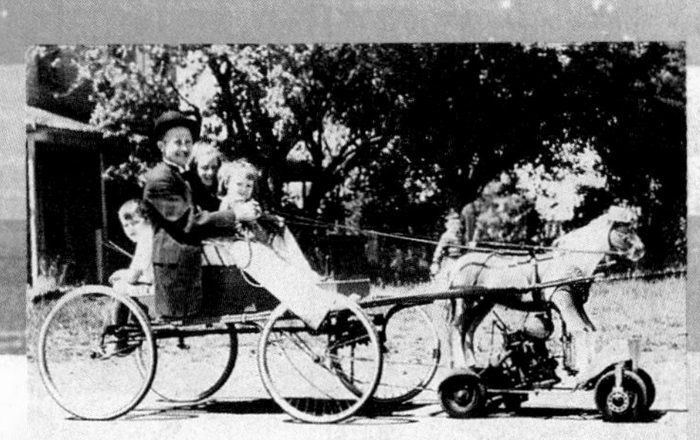

THE READER'S DIGEST ASSOCIATION, INC., PLEASANTVILLE, NEW YORK / MONTREAL

Library of Congress Cataloging in Publication Data
Discovering America's past: customs, legends, history & lore of our great nation
p. cm.
Includes index.
ISBN 0-89577-520-4

1. United States—History—Anecdotes. 2. United States—Social life and customs—Anecdotes. 3. United States—Biography—Anecdotes. I. Reader's Digest Association.
E178.6.D57 1993
973—dc20 93-3508

Printed in the United States of America

Front cover: *Hats* Enid Kotschnig; *mansion* SuperStock; *Southern costume* Virginia Division of Tourism; *ship* New York Public Library, Rare Book Division; *"Join or Die"* Library of Congress; *covered wagon* Charles Henry Carter; *"Amazing Stories"* private collection; *"McClure's"* Culver Pictures; *Cord automobile* Picturama Publications/Henry Rasmussen; *lingerie model* New York Public Library Picture Collection; *frontiersmen* Edward Vebell; *campaign buttons* Culver Pictures. Back cover, counterclockwise from upper left: NewYork State Historical Association, Cooperstown, N.Y.; The Bettmann Archive; Culver Pictures; Culver Pictures; UPI/Bettmann; UPI/Bettmann Newsphotos; Levi Strauss.

DISCOVERING AMERICA'S PAST

Project Editor: Richard L. Scheffel
Project Art Editor: Kenneth Chaya

Senior Associate Editors: Judith Cressy, Melanie Hulse

Art Associate: Angel Weyant
Art Assistant: Jason L. Peterson
Associate Picture Editor: Marion Bodine

Senior Editor, Research: Hildegard B. Anderson
Research Associate: Linda Ingroia

Editorial Assistant: Dolores Damm

Contributors:
Writers: Rita Christopher, Thomas Christopher, Martha Fay, Wendy Murphy
Artists: Sylvia Bokor, Jill Enfield, Chuck Schmidt, Neil Shigley, Bill Shortridge, Robert Villani
Researchers: Jill McManus, Sara Solberg
Picture Researchers: Linda Patterson Eger, Sue Israel
Copy Editor: Mel Minter
Indexer: Sydney Wolfe Cohen

TABLE OF CONTENTS

DISCOVERING AMERICA'S PAST

LUCIE

Chapter 1

FAMILY AFFAIRS

A FAMILY ALBUM

Leonard Dakin photographed his extended family at a summer reunion in 1886.

American Views

While still in his twenties in the 1880's, Leonard Dakin polished his skills as an amateur photographer — using his family as models — during leisurely summers in Cherry Valley, New York. Their relaxed self-confidence as they romped for the camera typifies, for many, what the American family looked like in the Victorian era. As part of a new and flourishing middle class, they could afford to live comfortably. Among other things, that meant indulging in new-fangled hobbies like photography, and leaving the city each summer for vacations in the country.

But many "typical" family situations existed in the 1880's. By the end of the decade, a third of the country's population was urban. Both recent immigrants — nearly 800,000 in 1882 alone — and the rural poor flocked to the cities, where factory work promised a living, if not much of a life. Whole families labored for long hours and even then could afford nothing better to live in than crowded tenements. For them, lawn tennis and lakeside picnics were unthinkable luxuries.

At the same time, other families lived the way Americans did a century earlier. Much of the West remained sparsely populated, and settlers

The photographer posed solemnly in a studio at age seven in 1865 (left), but 25 years later he recorded a more relaxed view of his young cousins (above).

Amateur photographers were few in 1888, and informal shots like this — stopping action in midair and exposing a few ankles — were rare indeed.

Dakin's female cousins were obviously more athletic than most, but even so, women of their class wore their bustles, petticoats, hats, and veils even while they played.

By the end of the 1880's Dakin was focusing his camera on his fiancée as much as he was on his family.

As members of a flourishing middle class, the Dakin family could enjoy leisurely vacations and spend sultry summer afternoons picnicking in the shade.

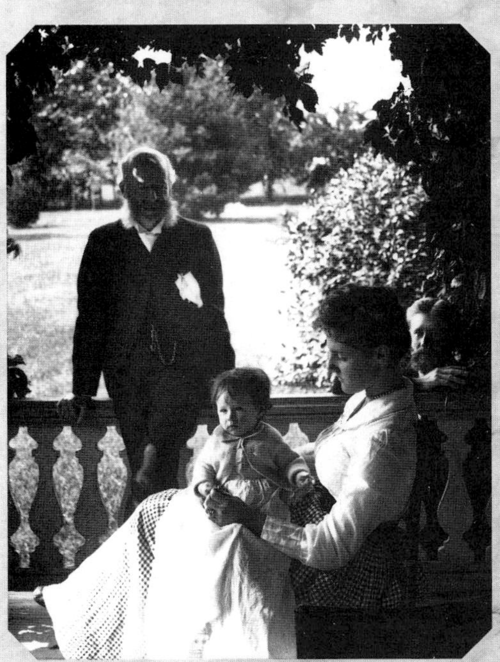

In 1890 Dakin portrayed three generations of his family — father, brother, wife, and son.

who could not reach their western destinations by rail in the 1880's still transported their household goods by wagon train. Making do in log cabins or sod houses, many such pioneering families had to wait a long time before experiencing any civilized comforts, a neighbor, or a school near enough for their children to attend.

At the other extreme from the struggling poor were families living in unimaginable ease. Until a federal income tax was instituted in 1913, those who established America's major new industries, such as railroads and steel, enjoyed boundless wealth. They lived in mansions, entertained lavishly, and married their daughters off to European nobility. If not exactly "typical," they were a breed of family unique to the era.

The trailblazing amateur pursued his hobby long enough to catch his children growing up. This delightful shot of his second son was his favorite.

LOVE AND MARRIAGE

Marriages, particularly second marriages in the late 18th century, often had more to do with money than with romance. Prenuptial agreements read like mergers between businesses, and dowries were as sumptuous as families could afford. This painting by J. L. G. Ferris depicts Sarah Richardson, a bride literally worth her weight in gold, stepping on the scales to measure out her dowry in 1771.

Judge Sewall Woos the Widows

Shortly after his wife died in 1717, Judge Samuel Sewall of Boston, Massachusetts, confided to his diary that he was "Wandering in my mind whether to live a Single or a Married Life." And well he might: since Puritan America frowned on the unmarried, a widow or widower usually hastened to recommit to a suitable companion. A proposal, in fact, might be offered within weeks, or even days, of a spouse's death.

In Sewall's case, thanks to his voluminous, minutely detailed diaries, we have an unusually complete record of one widower's return to wedlock. Following a brief but unsuccessful overture to Widow Winthrop, Sewall entered serious negotiations with Widow Denison. On the day of Mr. Denison's funeral Sewall had impulsively confided to his diary that he hoped "to keep house" with the widow. Their courtship was affectionate, but the pension of 250 pounds a year that he offered her, should he die, was no match for the estate left by the late Mr. Denison — a portion of which she would forfeit if she remarried. With regret on both sides, their dalliance ended in the winter of 1718.

Success came at last to Sewall on Thanksgiving Day in 1719, when he married Widow Tilley. His bride, however, fell ill and died the following May. Single once again, the judge's attention returned to Widow Winthrop. But she, having once "done very generously . . . in giving up her Dower" and stung, perhaps, by the judge's earlier abandonment, was anything but encouraging. After months of persistent pursuit on his part and an unrelenting cold shoulder on hers, Sewall gave up the chase.

Following a flurry of interest in three more prospective mates, Sewall eventually proposed to Widow Gibbs. "Aged, feeble, and exhausted as I am," he wrote to his intended, "your favourable Answer . . . will much oblige." Her reply, though favorable, was followed by some sharp prenuptial bargaining; but on April 1, 1722, the indefatigable suitor Sewall at last "sat with my wife in her pew."

Singular Problems

Marriage may be an honorable state, but throughout our history it took the law or public censure to persuade many Americans to indulge.

Be married, or be fined. So said the city council of Fort Dodge, Iowa, when, in 1907, it passed a law requiring everyone between the ages of 25 and 45 to wed — or else.

As extreme as the measure seemed at that late date, however, it would have been entirely normal in Colonial America, where public censure ensured that unmarried adults remained a rarity. In 17th-century New England, "antient maids" of 25 were labeled a "dismal spectacle." And in North Carolina, one newspaper declared them "never-to-be-pleased, good for nothing creatures." Single women usually had no choice but to live with relatives, where they might spend their lives spinning flax and wool for the family; hence the name *spinster.* The epithets *thornback, stale Maid,* and *antique virgin* also were commonly applied.

Bachelors fared every bit as badly. Viewed as suspect or even criminal, they were spied upon by the local constabulary and penalized to make sure they would enjoy less freedom as bachelors than they would if married. Unattached men were taxed in Maryland and Connecticut. And in 1695 the (evidently) bird-infested burg of Eastham, Massachusetts, required that "every unmarried man in the township shall kill six blackbirds or three crows while he remains single." On the other hand, town fathers in New England sometimes sweetened the deal for bachelors, offering them free home sites if they succumbed to wedlock.

The Wait for a Mate

A young man of the Amana sect who went courting in the late 19th century faced as many trials as a knight on a quest. Unlike other utopian sects, the Society of the True Inspirationists, as this group called themselves, did not forbid courtship and marriage; they just made getting there so difficult that only the most determined would succeed.

Children were warned that the opposite sex possessed a "magical fire." Young people who were drawn to one another despite this warning could apply to the community's Great Council for permission to marry. If the young man was 24 years old and the woman 20, the minimum ages required for marriage, they were examined for "spiritual, mental, or physical" suitability and advised that marrying would lower their spiritual standing in the community. If deemed suitable, the man spent a year in another of the Amana villages that dotted a six-mile stretch along the Iowa River. Finally, if the couple's affection withstood this separation, the man returned to his home, a wedding date was set — sometimes for as much as a year in the future — and permission was granted for Sunday courtship calls.

Despite these trials — or maybe because of them — marriage flourished and Amana thrived.

Under-cover Courtship

A bundling couple went to bed, / With all their clothes from foot to head, / That the defence might seem complete, / Each one was wrapped in a sheet." Thus one 18th-century song bandied the pros and cons of bundling — a curious custom that allowed a clothed couple to carry on their courting in bed.

Although the practice created a hailstorm of controversy, many upright and God-fearing colonists defended bundling on purely practical grounds. In rural areas especially, where a suitor might have to travel many miles to visit his sweetheart, an overnight stay made perfect sense. Besides, it was felt, allowing the young pair to whisper in the dark saved valuable candles and fuel after everyone else had gone to bed. In large households, moreover, the young woman's bed might, in fact, be the only place that a couple could find a little privacy. And it was surely the coziest place to visit on a winter night.

Since all was done openly, with family members sometimes helping the young woman by knotting her securely in her clothes, it was assumed that such courtships would remain chaste. The problem was, however, that young couples often could not resist temptation. As the numbers of premarital pregnancies rose in the 18th century, some people maintained that bundling was at least partially to blame, and railed against it: "Down deep in hell there let them dwell, / And bundle on that bed; / There burn and roll without control, / 'Till all their lusts are fed." Accordingly, it was only a matter of time before bundling was scorned as lower class. "'Tis a method of proceeding, / As much abhor'd, by those of breeding," sniffed yet another ditty.

Between such admonitions, and the fact that homes were gradually being equipped with improved lighting, parlor stoves, and comfortable furniture, bundling faded from practice. By the early 1800's only couples in the most remote rural areas were still courting beneath an eiderdown.

"Bed and board" had a different meaning for couples who courted in New England in the 1700's. Swathed in individual linens and separated by a board or bolster, sweethearts pitched their woo while snug in bed.

Dear Dorothy

For more than half a century, a demure Southern matron was the world's friend and confidante, the oracle that some 60 million people turned to for advice.

"It came to me that everything in the world had been written about women and for women, except the truth," Dorothy Dix recalled when asked how she hit upon the unique style of her newspaper advice column. "They had been celebrated as angels. They had been pitied as martyrs. . . . It was time . . . to come down to hardpan and be sensible, useful people."

Dorothy Dix was the pen name of Elizabeth Meriwether Gilmer. Born in 1870 to a genteel but impoverished Tennessee family, she married George Gilmer when she was 18. It soon became evident, however, that her husband was mentally unstable, and while coping with his illness, Dix herself suffered a breakdown. As a recuperative exercise, she began writing stories.

A New Orleans neighbor, who happened to own *The Daily Picayune,* read some of Dix's tales and was charmed by her refreshingly direct, unadorned style. In 1896 she hired the young woman to write "Sunday Salad," an advice column for "womankind" full of "crisp, fresh ideas . . . a dressing mixed of oil of kindness, vinegar of satire, salt of wit." Gilmer chose a new name — "Dorothy" because she liked its dignity, and "Dix" to honor a former slave who had helped the family during the Civil War — and set to work dispensing the compassionate, realistic advice that would be her trademark for the next half-century.

Her column, renamed "Dorothy Dix Talks," caught the attention of publisher William Randolph Hearst, and in 1901 he lured Dix to his *New York Journal.* There, in addition to her three-times-a-week advice column, she covered some of the most sensational murder trials of the era. But Dix wearied of working the crime beat; helping people with their own private fears and joys was what she did best, and in that she proved indefatigable.

Dix prized a good sense of humor and advised against marrying any man who lacked one. Her own sense of humor shone through in her writing. When a young woman asked if she should tell her beau that she had false teeth, Dix replied, "No, marry him and keep your mouth shut." In answer to a new bride who wanted to know what it meant when her husband criticized her cooking, she replied: "It means you have married a man instead of an archangel."

But Dix also scolded women for being vain,

Queen of Hearts

Esther Howland was a valentine visionary. Inspired by some fancy lace-covered English valentines that her father sold in his stationery store, the 19-year-old graduate of Mt. Holyoke Female Seminary's class of 1847 decided to make some of her own.

Using what she knew of the family's stationery business — and her own considerable artistic ability — she went to work with paste, paper, and paint and created an array of sample valentines. One of her brothers was skilled in penmanship, and she persuaded him to inscribe sentiments in the cards. Another brother was a salesman for the family business, and he agreed to try to get some orders for next season's trade.

When her brother returned with an astonishing $5,000 in orders, Howland promptly set up shop in her parents' house. She hired four friends to help her and adopted a revolutionary assembly-line approach. Seated at a long table, one worker cut out small colored lithographs of sentimental subjects, the next laid them on brilliantly glazed paper backgrounds, a third assembled the layers of lace paper that framed the central design, and the fourth pasted down a printed sentiment, typically inside the card or under a flap where only the recipient could see it.

self-pitying, nagging, or profligate. With practical compassion she urged that women not be too quick to abandon husbands guilty of occasional infidelities. Idealistic young men were advised to "find out what was inside of a girl's head . . . instead of being content just to admire the outside scenery," and they were bluntly told that anyone who was taken in by a gold digger "deserved all he got." She also coached them on the best time to propose marriage — not when the intended was feeling "on top of the world," but rather when she needed a lift after a fight with her boss.

Her hard-headed, big-hearted philosophy was often attributed to the difficulties of her own marriage. But as Dix once commented, "I never once thought of divorce. I could not say to others 'Be strong' if I did not myself have strength to endure."

Dorothy Dix did more than endure. Her life spanned America's past from the Civil War to World War II. And her career reflected the changes in courtship concerns from "Should I help a gentleman on with his coat?" to "Is it all right for me to spend a week end in Atlantic City with a boy friend?" When Dix died in 1951 at the age of 81, her advice column had appeared in a total of 273 newspapers and influenced millions of readers around the world.

Flirting With Flowers

To those versed in the rules of 19th-century flirtation, flowers were "the alphabet of angels." Each blossom had its symbolic meaning, and a carefully selected bouquet could speak "the softest impressions . . . without offence."

Did the sender wish to initiate a friendship? An iris says "My compliments." A bolder appeal — "Will you return my affection?" — was offered by a jonquil. Whole sentences were composed by tying individual blooms in a silk cord then rolling them into a bouquet. When unscrolled, the message appeared. A floral phrase composed of ivy, blue convolvulus, and straw pleaded "Let the bonds of marriage unite us." After consulting her lexicon, the recipient might send welcome peach blossoms ("My heart is thine"), a coy sprig of apple ("Temptation"), or a disheartening snapdragon ("No"). Senders were cautioned "Tie your bouquets more accurately!" to avoid lapses in communication.

How-to manuals listed the flowers, their meanings, and rules for their presentation. A rosebud presented upright indicated "I hope, but I fear." If returned stripped of its leaves, the bud meant "There is everything to fear," but stripped of its thorns, it promised "There is everything to hope."

At a time when Americans who wanted to send someone a love token had to make one by hand or buy one of the few rather witless and plain commercial offerings available, Howland's sentimental creations were a tremendous innovation. Despite their high cost — many of the cards sold for $5 to $10 each, and some truly extravagant ones, bedecked with ribbons, satin, and silk, cost up to $30 — the business boomed.

Howland sold her business to a former employee in 1880 and retired to take care of her aging father. Although she herself never married, she gave wings to the romantic fancies of countless other Americans.

As many as seven layers of paper and lace were assembled to create the exquisite missives (opposite and above) that earned Esther Howland her fortune. Her success sparked an industry (left) and inspired many imitators.

Elisha Buchanan (above) sat for his miniature likeness in 1840. At that date hair jewelry also was in vogue; often the hair of several loved ones was combined in a single ornament (above right).

Tokens of Affection

As even the most tongue-tied suitors have learned, eloquence comes easier when sentiments are expressed with love tokens. No one can know how many hearts have been won with such courtship gifts, but from Colonial times, Americans have been among those willing to give the technique a try.

Their choices have ranged from the sentimental to the witty and the wildly original. One pragmatic 18th-century gent presented only useful gifts such as shoe buckles, raisins and almonds, and even writing paper and sealing wax (in hope, perhaps, of a letter in return). But other sorts of tokens became customary offerings, much the way that red roses are today.

One of the most enduring gestures was to exchange miniature portraits that could be worn around the neck or kept in a pocket. Often a lock of hair was hidden on the back, though by the mid-1800's women wore brooches that featured their intended's hair plaited into an elaborate love knot.

Less costly, though no less valued were the hand-painted love knots, inscribed with verses, that appeared on notes and valentines. Other suitors folded and cut paper, snowflake style, into lacy pictures and decorated them with hearts and flowers. And school children, particularly, were fond of making "puzzle purses" — pieces of paper that were decorated on both sides and then folded to form a sort of envelope. If the folds were undone in the correct sequence, the successive lines of a verse were revealed and a little picture found in the center.

But it was homesick sailors who created some of the most personal love tokens. Those with a talent for carving made scrimshaw trinkets from whalebone and ivory, then engraved them with symbols of love. But those who could not carve might still bring home a gift: they needed only to stop at Barbados and buy one of the handmade seashell mosaics that came to be known as sailor's valentines.

Sailors were fond of making scrimshaw busks to stiffen the corsets of their lady friends back home. Few, however, were as pretty as this whalebone example. Its hearts, flowers, whaling ship, and circled stars were far too charming to hide under layers of clothes.

The puzzle purse (below) was given as a valentine in the 1790's. On its reverse, parts of a verse were written along the diagonal lines, then the whole was neatly folded into a puzzle square. The Pennsylvania-German cutwork love letter (right) was made by Christian Strenge around 1800. Decorating it with watercolors, he included 16 heart-felt messages.

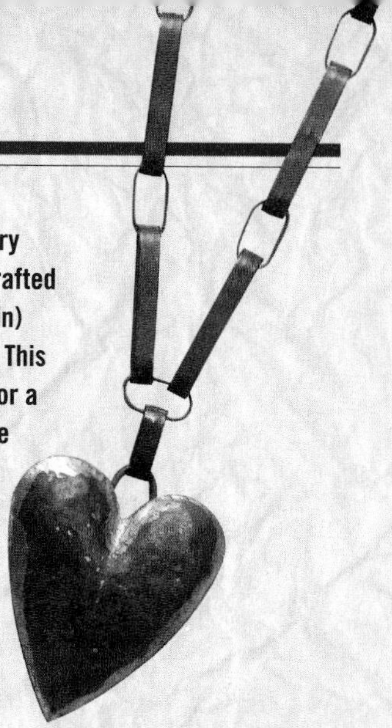

Nineteenth-century tinsmiths often crafted whimsical 10th (tin) anniversary gifts. This heart was made for a sentimental spouse to present around 1840.

The sailor who carved the scrimshaw courtship scene (above) obviously had more on his mind than whaling while he was at sea. Throughout the 19th century many mariners brought sailor's valentines home from the West Indies (left). Framed as shadow boxes, each half was 10 or 12 inches in diameter, and the shell mosaics could be customized with hearts, anchors, flowers, and verses.

Lonely Bachelors, Mail-Order Brides

Commenting on one of Iowa's burning issues in 1838, a local newspaper reported, "So anxious are our settlers for wives that they never ask a single lady her age. All they require is *teeth.*" And Iowa was not alone with the problem. Even as late as 1865 the ratio of men to women was 3 to 1 in California, 8 to 1 in Nevada, and 20 to 1 in Colorado. Once they had staked their claims or established their homesteads, all those bachelor frontiersmen who had headed west on their own were more than ready for a little female companionship, or more importantly — wives.

Many means were devised for filling the need, but the most efficient solution was the "mail-order bride." Some men advertised for a wife in the personals columns of what were called "heart-and-hand" newspapers, and proposed after a brief courtship by correspondence. "I love to think of thee and think that thare is a day a coming when wee will be hapy together," wrote one young man in 1853, who then added, "I live a lonsom and desolate life."

Where whole groups of men wanted wives, a "jobber" might be hired to send a "bulk shipment" of suitable feminine candidates from back East or from overseas. Romance was hardly considered in these transactions. The woman who answered an ad for such a roundup had usually resigned herself to spinsterhood if she remained at home. She went off knowing full well that she would have to settle for whatever was offered, including the possibility of a man with "vile wilderness habits" who might also be twice her age, and living conditions of extreme hardship.

Judging from one contemporary description of a meeting that took place in Dubuque, Iowa, in 1844, the matchups that resulted from these bulk shipments could be haphazard to say the least. Reporting on the arrival of a contingent of 41 single women aboard a Mississippi River steamboat, the writer recounted the unusual way in which "paying addresses" and getting "hitched" took place. Even before the women had the chance to disembark, it seemed, gentlemen on shore had begun calling out through speaking trumpets: "Miss with blue ribbon on your bonnet, will you take me?" or "Hallo thar, gal with a cinnamon-colored shawl! if agreeable we will jine."

The Clevelands' wedding — the only presidential nuptials ever held in the White House — took place in a flower-bedecked Blue Room, as depicted in *Puck* magazine (above). Frances Cleveland (right) was more tolerant of the press than her husband, and the public, in turn, adored her.

A White House Wedding

Immensely private, somewhat abrasive, and a portly 300 pounds, President Grover Cleveland was not most people's idea of a romantic leading man. But, as a 49-year-old bachelor in the White House, he nevertheless had mothers throughout America busily plotting schemes for introducing their daughters to him. Cleveland, however, paid no mind: when asked about his marriage plans, he simply replied, "I'm waiting for my wife to grow up."

Little did anyone suspect that Cleveland was serious, for he was in fact courting lovely Frances Folsom — 27 years his junior, and the daughter of his former law partner in Buffalo, New York. Frances had been 11 when her father died, and Cleveland, who adminstrated the estate, also took on the role of her guardian. It was a duty he undertook with the utmost propriety. But in time, his avuncular concerns for his young ward ripened into abiding affection.

Given their considerable age difference and Cleveland's prominence, he pursued the relationship with great delicacy and secrecy, mostly by mail. Waiting until she had graduated from college and made the grand tour of Europe, Cleveland stunned America with the announcement on May 28, 1886, that he would marry Frances at the White House within the week. By marrying quickly, he hoped, the opportunities for gossip and "keyhole journalism" would be kept to a minimum. But that was not to be.

The couple's simple Blue Room wedding (at which Frances wore an ivory satin gown with a 15-foot train) was duly covered by the press. But when the Clevelands left by rail for a remote honeymoon cottage in the foothills of Maryland's Blue Ridge Mountains, they were trailed by a second train loaded with newsmen, who set up camp nearby.

With the aid of fieldglasses, the reporters went to work telling the world every intimate detail of the couple's activities. As the days went by, Cleveland became increasingly outraged by what he termed the "newspaper nuisances" and their "colossal impertinence." In truth, however, the public's hunger for news of the pair was inspired not by malice but by affection. The president had captured the nation's heart by falling in love. Frances turned out to be one of the most popular first ladies ever to preside in the executive mansion, and their January-and-June marriage remains among the more celebrated of all presidential matches.

If not exactly welcome, a noisy horde of uninvited guests could nonetheless be expected on one's wedding night in rural America. Artist John Stokes pictured a shivaree in the making in his 1872 painting *Wedding in the Big Smoky Mountains.*

Shivaree Nights

Imported, perhaps, by French settlers, the Old World custom of serenading newlyweds with a cacophony of horns, gunfire, caterwauling, cowbells, and tin-pan tympani grew into one of the more notorious amusements of rural and small-town life in 19th-century America. These tumultuous entertainments, known originally as charivari (Latin for "headache") and later corrupted into shivaree, were the poor man's wedding reception. But instead of the couple throwing the party, it was the frolickers — often a noisy mob of thirsty bachelors — who did the deed. Usually, they had no more than mischief in mind.

By general custom a shivaree was staged on the wedding night, when newlyweds presumably wanted nothing more than to retreat to the privacy of their nuptial bed. Consequently, the raucous partyers gathered right under the bedroom window, the better to annoy. If the couple tried to ignore the hooting and hollering, the level of noise simply rose until even the most tolerant was unable to bear it any longer. Eventually, the groom descended to the yard, a jug of whiskey or hard cider in hand, to join his old friends in celebration. His new wife, meanwhile, was expected to do her part in providing food and drink.

If the couple was lucky, the crowd grew tired and went home before dawn. But it was not uncommon for them to abduct the groom, toss him into an icy stream, ride him on a rail, or detain him till daybreak — just for the fun of it.

The Bare Necessities of Married Life

One of the odder customs brought over by New England's earliest settlers was the "smock wedding." According to English common law, anyone who married a widow became liable for her late husband's debts if she brought any of the deceased's property with her. Since women owned nothing in their own right, not even their homemade clothing, it became customary for indebted widows to get married in their underwear, or smocks.

Thus the smock wedding was part marriage ceremony, part bankruptcy proceeding, and part investiture, since the unfrocked bride then received a new set of clothes from her new husband.

In theory the ceremony was held on a public highway, for all to see. But in practice many smock weddings moved indoors. When Major Moses Joy married Widow Hannah Ward of Newfane, Vermont, in 1789, she took the vows while standing in a closet, her hand extended through a hole cut in the door. But just to be sure no one forgot the underlying symbolism, Hannah went through the proceedings stark naked. She then slipped into a fine new set of clothes and, within moments, emerged from her closet in style, to the general admiration of the assembled.

Betsy Bonaparte, Duchess of Baltimore

Had it not been for Napoleon Bonaparte, Betsy Patterson of Baltimore might have borne a royal title. Visiting Maryland, the last stop of an American tour, in 1803, Napoleon's youngest brother, Jérôme, was so smitten by Betsy that he married her. Napoleon, newly crowned as emperor of France, however, had other plans. He intended to marry his siblings off to royalty, install them on their own thrones, and create a transcontinental, imperial family. Jérôme's rash marriage was not part of that grand plan, and Napoleon demanded that he return to Europe — alone.

Betsy Patterson was as celebrated for her beauty as she was for her marriage. In this portrait, artist Georges D'Almaine depicted her in triplicate.

Trusting that his brother would relent once he met Betsy, Jérôme sailed home with his bride. But when his ship landed in Portugal, he was ordered to proceed to France without her. Betsy — six months pregnant — traveled on to London, where she gave birth to a son, Jérôme Napoleon Bonaparte, known as Bo, and eventually returned to the United States.

Once the marriage had been annulled, Jérôme was wed to a German princess. Betsy, on the other hand, never remarried. Having once been married to the brother of an emperor, she haughtily explained, "I had not the meanness of spirit to descend from such an elevation to the deplorable condition of being the wife of an American." Fellow Baltimoreans snidely referred to her as "the duchess," but she ignored them.

Betsy petitioned Napoleon for a title and a pension, and though he refused her the title, he did pay her 60,000 francs a year until his abdication in 1814. Investing the money carefully, Betsy lived in comfort with Bo on both sides of the Atlantic and later put her son through Harvard. In her old age she was still shrewdly tending her investments. "Once I had everything but money," she quipped at 90. "Now I have nothing *but* money."

The Dollar Princesses

Some marriages are made in heaven. But for the turn-of-the-century American heiresses whose weddings united New World money with Old World aristocracy, marriage was made in the countinghouse. When the Duke of Marlborough married Consuelo Vanderbilt in 1895, he acquired not only an American wife but $2.5 million in cash and 50,000 shares of railroad stock. Their prenuptial contract stipulated that the Duke would retain his income for life, regardless of his marital status. This proved extraordinarily foresightful since the couple's troubled and loveless union eventually ended in divorce.

Not all the "dollar princesses," as the press dubbed these well-heeled Americans, were condemned to unhappy marriages. According to Englishman George Curzon, when he proposed to Mary Leiter, daughter of a wealthy Chicago merchant, she confessed to having "waited for nearly three years since the time when we first met, rejecting countless suitors. . . ." Curzon quickly made plain to Mary exactly what he was looking for in a wife: "Give me a girl that knows a woman's place and does not yearn for trousers,"

This 1895 cartoon, depicting American girls as they looked over a motley display of available European titles, was not the only one to lampoon the growing trend. By 1915 an edition of *Titled Americans* listed more than 450 women who were married to foreign aristocrats.

he wrote her shortly after their engagement. Mary's place turned out to be a decidedly exalted one. In 1899 Lord Curzon was appointed Viceroy of India, and as his consort, Mary stood near the very apex of British imperial society.

Ironically, one of the best-known brides of the period — Virginian Nancy Langhorne Shaw — brought no fortune with her. Instead, she acquired one when she married Waldorf Astor, a naturalized English citizen and heir to the immense fortune accumulated in the American fur trade by his great-great-grandfather John Jacob Astor.

Nancy might simply have lived the life of a wealthy society matron, but when her husband's father, a viscount, died in 1919, Waldorf inherited the peerage from him and, as a result, had to give up his seat in the House of Commons. Nancy in turn decided to run for for her husband's vacated seat. Her victory made her the first woman ever to sit in Parliament.

During the 26 years she served in office, Lady Astor habitually wore a white-trimmed black dress and a black three-cornered hat. Her trademark outfit was so well known that on the rare occasions when she wore anything different, her male colleagues would shout, "Bravo, Nancy." Not that she ever let male opinions intimidate her. In an address to a women's rights organization, Lady Astor gave a sample of the straight-talking feminism that was the hallmark of her personal and political life. "We are not asking for superiority," she declared, "for we have always had that. All we ask is equality."

Brides by the Boatload

Awash with war brides, this ship arrived in San Francisco in 1944 with nearly 300 foreign-born wives of American soldiers on board. Seventy-two of them had babies less than a year old, and many more were on the way.

"Overpaid, oversexed — and over here." So said many a resentful Englishman of the American GI's stationed in Great Britain during World War II. And indeed, some 70,000 Americans in England did marry local girls during the course of the war. In addition, more than twice that many GI's married European women between 1944 and 1950, and perhaps as many as 100,000 Asian women wed American soldiers stationed in the Far East.

After an initial outbreak of "quickie" marriages early in the war, the War Department instituted strict regulations designed to discourage such unions. Beginning in June 1942, soldiers wishing to marry had to request permission in writing, and some prospective brides underwent interviews with senior military personnel. One woman recalled that her husband's commanding officer "remarked that he should wait until he was back in the U.S. and marry an American girl." When the GI demurred, he was broken in rank.

Nor did all the objections come from American officers. "Father thought it terrible to go to the colonies!" recalled one English war bride. Another concerned parent warned his daughter that America was filled with "nothing but hoodlums with guns or cowboys and Indians."

And when they finally arrived in this country, the new brides sometimes were met with anger. An Australian woman remembered getting off a ship in San Francisco to catcalls of "You stole our husbands. You stole our boyfriends." But not everyone showed such hostility. One bride recalled how, en route by train to meet her husband, her loneliness was instantly dispelled when the conductor greeted her with a warm "Welcome to America, young lady. You will be a great addition to our country, I'm sure."

AND BABY MAKES THREE

House Calls and Home Deliveries

Well into the 19th century, the midwife served America's rural communities as obstetrician, visiting nurse, pharmacist, and comforter.

As a midwife in Hallowell, Maine, Martha Ballard was no stranger to hardship and drama. They were, in fact, a regular part of her routine. An entry in her diary in April 1789, for instance, records that she was called out in a storm by Ebenezer Hewin, whose wife was about to give birth. In order to get to his house, the pair crossed a river by boat, then used floating logs as stepping stones to get across a stream. As they proceeded on horseback, Ballard wrote, "a large tree blew up by the roots before me which caused my horse to spring back and my life was spared." But the trip was not yet over. Coming to another stream, where the bridge was gone, she noted, "Mr. Hewin took the reins, waded through and led the horse. Assisted by the same almighty power I got safe through and arrived unhurt, Mrs. Hewin safe delivered at 10 in the evening of a daughter."

Ballard, 54 years old at the time, had been on call in her community for the past four years. (She began her career as a midwife after her own nine children were grown.) Schooled in midwifery and herbal medicine through years of informal apprenticeship, Ballard, like others in her trade, preferred to specialize in childbirth. Between 1785 and 1812 she presided over more than 800 deliveries. But her nursing duties ranged far beyond ushering the newborn into the world. Just as she was from time to time thrown from her horse or forced to wade through mud while racing night or day to her neighbors' aid, her diary tells us that she tended sufferers with everything from "canker rash," or scarlet fever, to swollen feet, fits, shingles, abcesses, dysentery, and numerous other complaints. As a midwife, she had to be familiar with a roster of traditional cures and reliefs for specific ailments, but in many instances — often emergencies — she relied solely on common sense in drawing from a selection of such homegrown remedies as tinctures, purges, and plasters.

Though often working alone, at childbirth Ballard and other midwives were assisted by six or more of the woman's female relatives or neighbors. While one might ply the laboring mother with rum to relax muscles, the others distracted her with cheerful conversation, bawdy jokes, and words of sympathy. At such moments technical skills were only part of the midwife's arsenal of assistance. Being calm and reassuring through the ordeal was just as important, for suffering and even death often went hand in hand with childbirth. (One tract written for mothers-to-be solemnly urged them to be particularly pious during their pregnancy for "they may perchance need no other linnen shortly than a Winding Sheet, and have no other chamber but a grave, no neighbors but worms.")

Ballard's standard fee for a birth was a modest six shillings, with no surcharge for arduous travel or extended care. Even so, payment was often long in coming, and then not in cash. Thus, one father paid her with "1½ Bushl of apples in the fall not very good," and another settled his account with "2 lb coffee, 1 yd ribbon, and a cap border." Midwife Ballard was never heard to complain, however, for she and the community saw her trade as offering rewards beyond mere money.

WHAT·IS·IT

They may look like baked potatoes wrapped in foil but they are aluminum mittens meant to be tied over a baby's hands. The mitts were sure guards against thumbsucking — and other acts that, as one 19th-century expert put it, might cause infants to "inflict evils on themselves, which not infrequently terminate in disease, delirium, and death."

Bringing Up Baby

In Colonial days, many Americans believed that children were born with an evil nature, and that the naughtiest ones were "infinitely more hateful than vipers." They were seen as pint-sized adults and dressed accordingly, and the only route to their salvation was thought to be through constant correction with rod or switch. Changes in attitude began to occur when Englishman John Locke's 1693 book, *Some Thoughts Concerning Education,* reached the Colonies. Locke was one of the first to suggest that goodness might exist in children, but he too had his puritanical side. Even while advocating that youngsters be allowed to run free in fresh air, for instance, he argued that they should be made to wear "shoes so thin that they might leak and let in water" in order to strengthen youthful constitutions.

Between the times of Locke and Spock, Americans have been offered countless theories on child rearing by writers — from mothers to doctors — whose ideas have been as effective as political upheavals in changing the way we live. Following the Revolution, the country's new freedoms trickled all the way down to children. No longer were babies regarded as being born bad; rather, parents were seen as key influences in their development. Corporal punishment would remain part of household discipline for quite some time, but parents in the late 18th century were warned not to break a youngster's will; the child should be led to develop self-control, they were told, "so that his will may be his strong point."

The new crop of writers on child rearing urged parents to nurture children with tenderness, tolerance, and selective reinforcement of positive behavior. Whereas fathers had previously been judged the proper masters of their offspring, mothers now were judged better able to reach the child's heart, and so manipulate his behavior for the better.

Turning to a book for advice in the early 1800's, a mother might find information on such things as bathing a child or teaching good manners. By the second quarter of the century, however, there was a growing list of titles that offered "what to do — if" information and physicians' advice. When Dr. William P. Dewees published his child-care manual in 1825, he stressed the very modern ideas of keeping nursing bottles clean and keeping babies in dry diapers (wet diapers had earlier been thought advantageous for toughening the infant).

By the last decades of the century attitudes toward child rearing had changed completely. Childhood was seen as a golden time, and children deserving of protection against complex adult concerns. Manuals, consequently, became far more permissive in tone than they had been in the past.

As depicted by Tompkins Matteson in ***Caught in the Act,*** in the 1860's a tug on the ear could serve as stiff punishment.

Among the most widely read contemporary writers were Catharine Beecher and her sister, Harriet Beecher Stowe, whose book *The American Woman's Home* was brimming with maxims. "It is very injurious and degrading to any mind to be kept under the constant fear of penalties," the sisters warned in the spirit of the day. "*Love* and *hope* are the principles that should be mainly relied on, in forming the habits of childhood."

However painful it may appear, this scene of Dad with a shingle aimed at junior's posterior was meant to amuse. It was posed for a stereograph slide and given the title "Meeting of the Board of Education."

Davy Crockett's Growing Pains

Even as a boy, Davy Crockett was better known for his exploits than for his interest in books. For his family, however, his adventures could be worrisome. Born and raised in Tennessee, Crockett was 13 when he first attended school in 1799. But he did not stay for long: within four days he argued with a classmate over a spilled bottle of ink and attacked the student "like a wildcat, scratched his face like a flitter-jig, an' made him cry fur quarter."

Fearing he would be punished at home, Crockett ran away, joining a cattle drover headed for Virginia. There, he teamed up with a waggoner and traveled all the way to Baltimore, Maryland, where the sight of ships in the harbor made him dream of sailing to England. Unable to collect his wages from the waggoner, however, Crockett decided to return to Tennessee. He walked most of the distance, earning a few dollars by doing odd jobs along the way.

The runaway was nearly 16 when he finally reappeared at his family's door. And he had changed his mind about the three Rs. Exchanging his labors for lessons, Crockett learned enough to carry him through his later careers as congressman and "king of the wild frontier."

Sacajawea's Well-Traveled Son

After spending the first winter of their western expedition in Fort Mandan, North Dakota, Meriwether Lewis and William Clark set out again in the spring of 1805. And among the 30-odd soldiers and civilians traveling with them was a newborn baby boy. The son of the expedition's guide, Sacajawea, a Shoshone woman, and her French-Canadian husband, Toussaint Charbonneau, who served as interpreter, the baby was named Jean-Baptiste but was fondly called Pomp.

From the start little Pomp proved an engaging child, traveling most of the distance to the Pacific on his mother's back. He so thoroughly won his way into William Clark's heart, in fact, that the leader begged the parents to let him take Pomp to St. Louis to receive an education. Eventually, they yielded, and the boy came under the combined care of Clark and a Baptist preacher.

At age 18 young Charbonneau's life took another unusual turn when he was introduced to the touring Prince Paul of Württemberg and accompanied the prince back to Germany. After six years of traveling in Europe and learning the gentlemanly arts of hunting and conversation, Pomp returned to the land and life of his ancestors, but not to obscurity. Spending his time as trapper, trader, and genial mountain host, he seems to have been everywhere, for his name is mentioned in many journals, often in the company of such notables as Jim Bridger. Then in 1846 he led the Mormon Battalion across the southwestern deserts to San Diego, where he was named administrator of one of the settlements. But he was accused of showing favoritism to Indians and forced to resign.

Lured north by the California Gold Rush of 1849, Pomp apparently prospected with a modicum of success until 1866, when it is believed that he died en route to the gold fields of Montana.

Visitors attending the baby show cast votes for their favorites. This illustration from *Frank Leslie's Illustrated Newspaper* showed a tyke being poked for plumpness.

Bedlam in Babyland

The American penchant for showmanship took a peculiar turn in the late 19th century when toddlers became the draw for curiosity-seeking crowds. One such event, touted as the "Prize Baby Show," was staged in New York at the appropriately named Midget Hall in 1877.

Lured by the promise of cash and jewelry if they won, and unspecified consolation prizes if they merely stayed the course, over a hundred mothers flocked to enter their little champions in one of more than two dozen categories of competition. There would be prizes for twins and triplets, "fattest" (58 pounds at 11 months), "smallest" (1½ pounds), and "novelty" (a catchall category that included a newborn with teeth, and an infant rescued from a burning house). "Prettiest," "noisiest," "smartest," and "homeliest" also had their contenders, with the last category going easily to a tot described as a "little creature closely resembling a monkey."

For two weeks, the mothers and their offspring returned each day to be examined by 30,000 visitors, who cast ballots to determine the winners. When all the votes were tallied, however, the majority of mothers discovered that as "also rans" they would not get so much as a free ticket to the closing ceremonies, much less the promised consolation prizes. Furious at the way they had been used, the mothers rioted, causing the police to come running and a crowd of amused spectators to join the fray.

With the losers locked out, the *New York World* reported, the awards ceremony took place before an audience of empty chairs. Even so, an orchestra played and a soloist sang before the show's manager appeared on stage to announce the winners. The first was called up to receive a gold watch for being the handsomest mother. "She looked very charming," said the *World*, "and . . . also rather sorry that there was nobody there to see her."

Families Before the Footlights

Probably no one ever was really born in a trunk, but many American children were raised in dressing rooms and followed their parents out on stage.

Evolving in the last quarter of the 19th century as a sanitized version of the saloon variety show, vaudeville entertainment, unlike its bawdy predecessor, welcomed families both in front of the lights and behind them. Many of the most famous performing troupes on the circuit were, in fact, composed of children and their parents. Working together was part of their audience appeal, and while social workers and truant officers often dogged their heels, vaudevillians prided themselves on the uncommon closeness of their family acts. The Four Cohans, the Mortons, the Marx Brothers, the Four Diamonds, the Three Keatons, the Musical Cuttys, Eddie Foy and the Seven Little Foys, and the 10-member Bell Family were just some of the best-known audience pleasers.

Keeping a family intact while living in cheap hotels and on trains required a good deal of patience and ingenuity. Recalling his own early years in vaudeville, Fred Allen wrote that the small-time vaudeville mother had to have "the endurance of a doorknob." Often her babies were born all but unassisted on a train or in a dressing room, and she was expected to go back on stage within a day or two, or risk having the family act dropped from the line-up. Frequently, the top drawer of her theatrical trunk had to double as the baby's bassinet, laundry was washed in the dressing-room sink, and meals were cooked over a Sterno flame.

Vaudeville children, it was said, were weaned on applause and raised on popcorn. And they began learning the family trade as soon as they could walk. Buster Keaton was a preschooler when his father literally tossed him into his no-holds-barred acrobatic act, and Sammy Davis, Jr., began dancing in his father's act at about the same age. For all the hardships, many of the children who grew up in vaudeville saw their life as one of peculiar privilege and diversion. As one performer fondly remembered, "If I was spoiled, blame the Spanish wirewalkers, the German jugglers, the sister teams, the animal trainers. . . . They all petted, spoiled, and flattered the one child among them."

Before they became known simply by their last name, Harpo, Groucho, and Zeppo Marx (from the top, above) were teamed with Leo Lerner (bottom) in a vaudeville act called the Four Nightingales.

One of vaudeville's best-known acrobatic acts was the Three Keatons — Joe, Myra, and little Buster. Barely beyond the toddler stage when he began his career, Buster Keaton attended school for only one day in his life.

Fit to Be Tied: The Small Set Suits Up

For the Colonial child, fashion offered few options. Until the end of the 18th century, newborns were routinely swaddled (bound to a board or rod that kept the neck and back straight), a practice thought to be beneficial to both the child's moral and its physical character. The ties were not loosened until the toddler stage, when, regardless of sex, the baby was put into an ankle-length dress.

A grown-up look for little people

Then, between the ages of four and five, dresses were exchanged for the garments of adulthood. In what approached the solemnity of an initiation rite, boys were "breeched" when they put on their first pair of britches. As one Massachusetts father described his newly breeched son, "he struts, and swells, and puffs, and looks as important as a Boston Committeeman." The sons of laboring men were destined for loose-fitting pants and shirts, but boys born to the upper ranks wore the embroidered waistcoats, lace-trimmed shirts, and powdered wigs of their fathers. (If a boy did not wear a wig, then on formal occasions his hair might be dressed with curling iron, powder, and pomade.) Shoes, which were identical for right and left feet, were typically sturdy boots with silver or brass buckles.

Similarly, little girls of wealthier families graduated overnight from unisex dresses to stays and corsets, hooped petticoats, and tight-waisted dresses of fine materials. Their shoes, like their mothers', were of soft leather, with a pretty heel and an ornamental bow at the instep.

Revolutionary changes

It was not until after the American Revolution, that clothing designed specifically for children — rather than miniature adults — began to appear. The change reflected the growing conviction that children ought to be allowed greater freedom, and that the restraints of earlier fashions were unnatural. Swaddling gave way to soft, loose baby garments. And when boys graduated to gender-specific clothes, they were likely to wear what was called a skeleton suit, consisting of comfortable pants that buttoned onto a matching shirt. The 1830's saw the beginning of a vogue for imaginative "fancy dress," including the sailor suit, which has remained popular for young boys ever since. At the opposite extreme was the velvet, lace-collared Fauntleroy suit of the 1880's, which made mothers proud but little boys miserable.

Among fashion's innocent victims at the turn of the century were the three lads pictured here. The two at the top wear modified versions of the Fauntleroy suit. The toddler (above) has yet to be breeched and still wears a lace dress.

Introduced in the early 1800's, pantalets were a practical addition to children's wardrobes. As can be seen in this 1843 portrait, they were worn by both girls and boys.

With the introduction of the Empire dress in the early 1800's, girls were freed for several decades from the constraints of corsets. The graceful new style was soft, thin, high-waisted, and often worn over pantalets that revealed just a suggestion of ankle. Then, for the remainder of the century, as reformers and fashion arbiters argued back and forth and emancipating bloomers came and went, well-bred little girls were generally the losers. Trussed up once again in bustles, bows, and bonnets, they had little choice but to stand on the sidelines, scarcely able to play.

In Their Own Words

"They braced My Aunt against a board
To make her straight and tall,
They laced her up, they starved her down,
To make her light and small.
They pinched her feet, they singed her hair,
They screwed it up with pins,
Oh, never mortal suffered more
In penance for her sins."

— Oliver Wendell Holmes, 1831

The Game of the Name

Falling in and out of favor over the decades, American given names often offer clues as to when — and sometimes even where — a person was born.

Steeped in religion as Colonial New Englanders were, they almost always turned to the Bible when it came time to christen their children. Names of Old Testament characters were most popular, with girls tagged Rachel, Abigail, Esther, and the like. Biblical names for boys ranged from the familiar — Moses, Noah, and Isaiah — to the obscure — Shearjashub, Mahershalalhashbaz, and Zerubbabel. Christian hopes and admonitions supplied names that were equally appropriate for girls and boys, including Mindwell, Kill-sin, and Fly-fornication — none of which were considered outlandish at the time. The fact that a name appeared in the Bible at all, apparently, mattered more than the character's importance. New Englanders also encouraged virtue in their sons by christening them Experience, Increase, or Rejoice. In the less Calvinistic South, however, Colonial lads were more likely to receive conventional English monikers such as Edward, George, and James.

After America's independence, many parents, inspired by the ideals of democracy, looked toward ancient Greece and Rome when naming their children. The classical tradition was revived in such names as Minerva, Cassandra, and Portia for girls, and Horatio, Ulysses, and Homer for boys. Other parents commemorated American heroes: thus hundreds of youngsters had two-part givens like George Washington, Thomas Jefferson, and Benjamin Franklin, a custom that coincidentally helped institutionalize the middle name. Girls had no such pantheon on which to draw, but in 1814 one father who recognized no limits on the wellsprings of creativity when it came to names christened his youngest daughter Encyclopedia Britannica Dewey.

An Elusive Formula

Since Colonial times, Americans have searched for a suitable infant formula — and the most convenient means for getting it into baby's mouth.

Weaned from mother's milk but not yet able to take solid food, an infant in the 1780's might be propped on its nurse's lap and fed with the aid of a pap boat — a shallow dish with a broad spout used for pouring liquid food into the child's mouth. The food itself was apt to be a brew such as bread boiled in water, flour and water, or weak beer. Earlier in the 18th century, cow's milk was frowned on as an alternative since it was thought to give children a bovine nature. But by century's end the increasingly favored method of "hand-rearing" was to give the infant watered-down cow's milk, using a primitive sort of nursing bottle.

This was a risky business at best, since milk was unpasteurized and everything about the bottles seemed designed to harbor bacteria. Lozenge-shaped and holding about 16 ounces of fluid, they were made of pewter, pottery, or blown glass. The baby fed through a spout at one end, with a nipplelike device controlling the flow. The nipple itself might be fashioned from a bit of sponge, rag, or chamois, though some mothers preferred to use a calf's teat, which could be purchased (pickled in spirits) in apothecary shops. All were difficult to keep clean, with the result that in the 1800's the mortality rate among babies bottle-fed on milk was about 7 out of 10.

Rubber nipples, which were first introduced in the 1840's, were more easily washed than earlier varieties, but knowledge of sterilization was still a long way off. One baby bottle, called the turtle, was actually responsible for increasing infant mortality rates in the latter part of the century. The turtle-shaped bottle and its nipple came packaged with a special scrub brush. The two parts, however, were connected by a narrow rubber hose that could not be cleaned at all and so was an ideal breeding ground for disease.

Mothers, meanwhile, had been given many more choices as to what to put in the bottles. By the mid-19th century, researchers developed a "formula" for making cow's milk more like mother's milk. Packaged formula could be purchased and prepared at home: if fresh milk was not always at hand, condensed and evaporated milk were newly available. At the same time, products called lactated foods — cereals mixed with whole or dried milk — appeared in stores and could also be ordered through the mail. Because they were slightly sweet in flavor, infants literally drank them up. And mothers loved the new products since they promised to produce plump babies.

As shown by the advertisement (top), babies could barely resist lactated food, which was sure to make them healthy, happy, and hearty. One of the nursing innovations in the 1860's was the turtle bottle (above). Although frequently lethal, it remained popular until the 20th century.

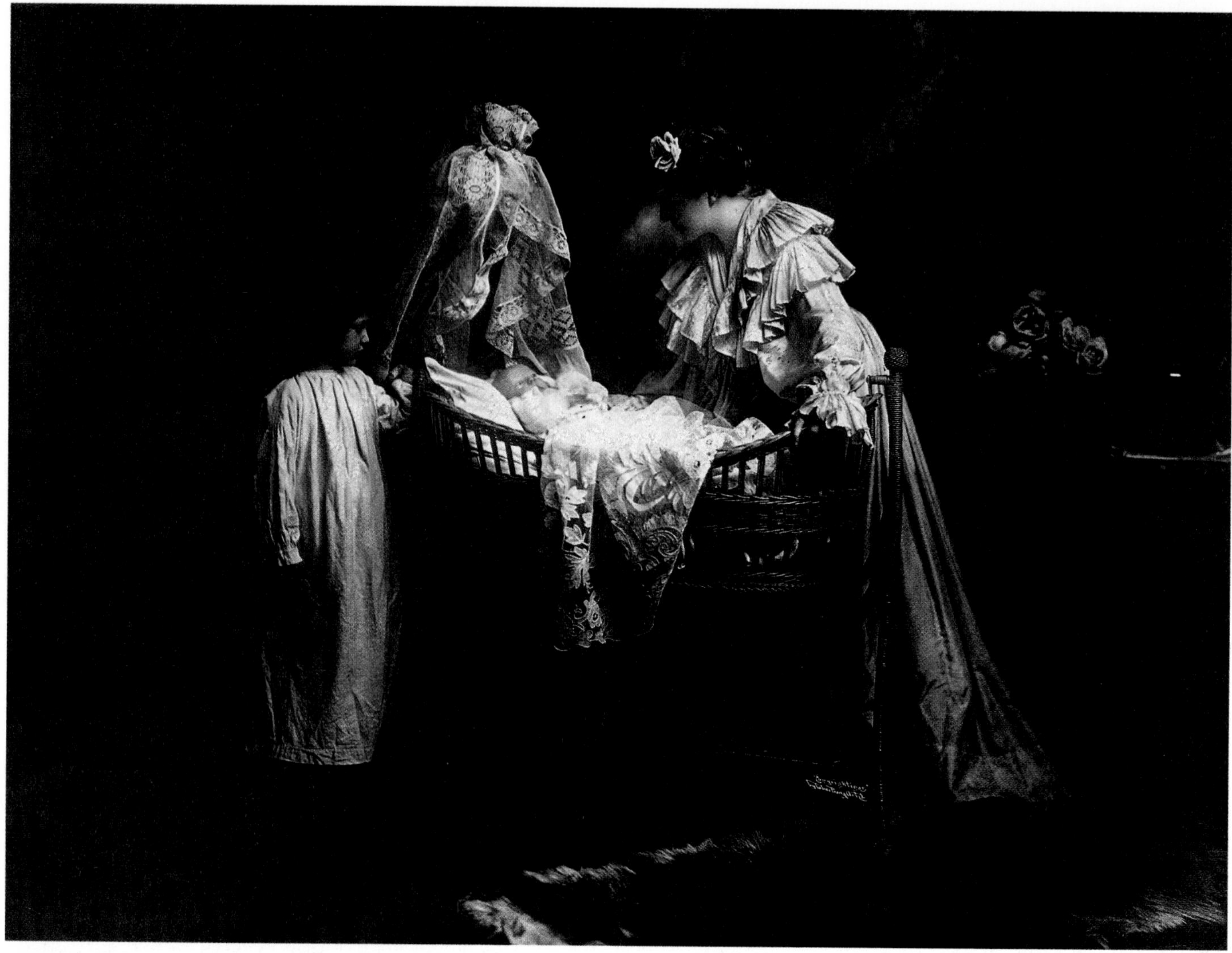

Children's furniture often reflects the attitude of its owners. A lace-draped Victorian cradle isolated the child in a shrine of cherished innocence (above). But a cradle with cut-out handholds (below) could be moved about so that the baby was always in the company of its family.

Cradles of Contentment

Born aboard the *Mayflower,* Peregrine White spent the first nights of his life being lulled to sleep by the motion of the Atlantic. After the ship landed at Plymouth, however, the infant was lulled by the gentle rocking of the cradle that had been packed in anticipation of his birth and brought along to the New World.

Peregrine's cradle was the first in America. But as time went on, ingenious inventors dreamed up all sorts of variations on the rockered baby boxes. Between 1790 and 1873, some 78 patents were granted for cradle designs. Some could be unfolded to become swings, cribs, playpens, or carriages. There was even a "hydrostatic steam cradle," which presumably was self-rocking.

Wicker was a popular material for cradles, being both light and sturdy, but in frosty New England concerned parents generally favored the draft-deflecting properties of solid wood. Some cradles had the further cold-beating refinements of hoods and pegged or pierced walls that allowed parents to securely lace the child in place beneath its blankets. In the 19th century, when a passion for fresh air and exercise swept the country, child-care authorities began advocating slatted cradle walls and looser blanketing.

Medical opinion, however, was sharply divided on the effects of rocking itself. One expert claimed that the motion induced "fatuity, by constantly shaking the brain." Others blamed rocking for an array of disorders that ranged from indigestion to "deranged" nervous systems. Some sages approved — provided the little ones were not "jumbled about like travellers in a mailcoach." And one endorsed rocking as "the most gentle and certain anodyne."

By the early 20th century cribs and bassinets had pretty much replaced cradles, which by then were curiosities more often used to store wood by the fireplace than to soothe infants to sleep.

The Lullaby That Rocked the Nation

Rock-a-bye baby, on the treetop, / When the wind blows, the cradle will rock. / When the bough breaks, the cradle will fall, / And down will come baby, cradle and all."

So goes America's best-known lullaby, the creation of a girl of just 15. In 1872 Effie Crockett, a descendant of frontiersman Davy Crockett, was minding a fussy baby when, to calm the child, she began humming an old nursery rhyme to an improvised tune. The child was charmed to sleep and "Rock-a-bye Baby" was born.

Crockett was given a banjo for Christmas that year and soon learned to plunk out her tune on the instrument. The result so pleased her music teacher that he referred her to a Boston music publisher. Equally captivated by the lullaby, the man asked for permission to publish it. Crockett composed three additional verses for her song, and the lullaby became a smash hit.

Fearful of her family's reaction to her artistic effort, Crockett used her grandmother's name — Canning — as a pseudonym for the published version. "It was not until the song began to sweep the country that I told Father I wrote it," she later confessed.

Whatever her father's misgivings, Crockett's simple ditty, composed on the spur of the moment, has soothed restless children for generations.

A Baby Parade at the Promenade

Once upon a sunny day in 1848, Mrs. Charles Burton appeared on the promenade at New York City's Battery Park and caused a small sensation. She was pushing a miniature carriage that her ingenious husband had devised, with their new baby securely ensconced inside the canopied, three-wheeled conveyance. Envious mothers with babes in arms were agape; many stopped and asked where they could obtain such a carriage.

Concluding from the women's reaction that he was on to a good thing, Burton, an Englishman, disassembled his invention, packed up, and headed home to Britain. Hoping to make his fortune, he settled in London near Kensington Palace and quickly developed a thriving carriage trade throughout the Old World. Queen Victoria bought three for her royal progeny. Queen Isabella II of Spain ordered one for her son, the future King Alfonso XII. Even an Egyptian pasha purchased a patented Burton baby buggy.

But the women of America were not to be denied. Despite the defection of the inventor, a demand for baby carriages swept the country and industrious imitators set to work to supply them. Among the entrepreneurs were a pair of cousins, F. W. and F. A. Whitney, who set up shop in Leominster, Massachusetts.

In 1858, their first year in business, they produced 75 two-wheeled carriages; later designs added a third, and then a fourth, wheel for stability. The Victorian passion for ornamentation led to some elaborately woven wickerwork bodies, upholstered in richly hued fabrics and topped with fringe-festooned silk parasols — the perfect setting for the family's crown jewel.

The Whitney family's reputation for excellent craftsmanship generated orders from the four corners of the world. One carriage, sent to a missionary's wife in Turkey, drew so many admirers that crowds slowed its progress on the street: every Turkish mother wanted to let her baby lie for just a minute in the exotic rolling baby basket from America.

Around 1906, low-priced, mass-produced carriages began to replace the handcrafted marvels of the 19th century. Burton's baby carriage — and its innumerable offspring — had become an indispensible part of child rearing.

The 19th-century fashion for fresh air gave a boost to the baby carriage industry. Parents bundled their babies into the newfangled prams (above) — some of which were elaborate fantasies of lace, silk, and wicker (top) — and proudly paraded through the public parks.

Sunday Toys

In Colonial times — when laughing on the Lord's Day could land a person in stocks in the public square — Sundays meant dreary afternoons for children. Stuck in the family parlor, forbidden to run, whittle, whistle, or otherwise while away the time, even the most dutiful tykes grew cranky and restless. So it was that doting parents devised "Sunday toys" to lighten the long hours.

Inspired by religious themes, Sunday toys were also teaching tools. A "biblical museum," for example, was a box of tiny specimens of plants and minerals mentioned in the scriptures. Board games, such as The Game of Christian Endeavor, demonstrated the rewards of virtue and the penalties for vice. Music boxes that played hymns and building-block churches were allowed. But the favorite Sunday toys were the hand-carved Noah's Ark sets that began appearing in the 17th century.

Some sets may have been carved by fond fathers during long evenings at the fireside, but many sprang from the genius of professional carvers. Two by two, every species known to the craftsmen — and many that were purely imaginary — marched into the boat-shaped toy chests. Exotic jungle beasts paraded peaceably with barnyard cows and dogs; bugs and birds hopped along behind elephants and gnus. And presiding over all was Noah, clad perhaps in a loincloth — or a respectable bowler and topcoat, depending on the carver's whim.

Each Sunday-toy ark contained a cavalcade of animals that was limited only by the carver's creativity. The only constant in these early teaching toys was the dove that signified the end of Noah's trial and the salvation of humanity through his and his family's faith.

One ad for Lionel Lines electric trains showed Bob Butterfield, the engineer of the famed 20th Century Limited, in front of his train holding the Lionel model.

The Little Engines That Could

Operating a good train layout is one of the greatest challenges I know," exclaimed Joshua Lionel Cowen. And he would know, for Cowen was the driving force behind the Lionel Corporation, which, in 1954, was the world's preeminent producer of electric toy trains.

Cowen's inventiveness had literally explosive beginnings. In 1887, when he was seven, Cowen built a small steam engine that he used to power a toy train he had carved. The thing unfortunately blew up in his mother's kitchen. At 18 he patented a fuse that would reliably ignite photographer's flash powder. The navy saw its potential for mine detonation and quickly hired the young inventor. Bored with fuses, Cowen's ingenuity struck again when he put a dry cell in a metal tube and attached a small light bulb. Seeing no immediate profit in the idea, he gave it to a friend, who promptly founded the Eveready Flashlight Company.

Fascinated with miniaturization and electricity, Cowen brought the two together in the summer of

Oh, You Beautiful Doll

Considered "as American as patchwork quilts and corn pone," rag dolls were cherished companions that charmed both the young and the young at heart.

In 1915 John Gruelle gave his daughter Marcella a rag doll that had been in the attic. The doll was dubbed Raggedy Ann after The Raggedy Man and Little Orphant Annie, two characters created by James Whitcomb Riley, a family friend and neighbor. To amuse the ailing Marcella, Gruelle began making up stories starring the doll. Three years later Gruelle, a cartoonist for an Indianapolis newspaper, published *The Raggedy Ann Stories,* an illustrated collection of his tales. A Raggedy Ann doll was offered for sale along with the book, and one of the best-loved characters of American childhood was born.

But Ann and her brother Andy, who appeared in 1920, were only part of a long line of cloth charmers that had delighted children for generations. Lovingly created from scraps of calico, bits of yarn or fur, and sometimes leather, most rag dolls had painted or embroidered faces. Some had shiny buttons for eyes, and noses built up with cloth or wood chips.

Laura Ingalls Wilder, author of *Little House on the Prairie,* recalled how her mother had restored a doll that had been left out in the rain by removing the original face and replacing it with a new one. Many cloth dolls were renewed this way, receiving different "facelifts" as suited their owners' fancies. But the Amish took the commandment forbidding graven images to heart: their dolls had no faces at all. Another variation, the "topsy-turvy" doll, doubled the fun by being two dolls in one. It was two heads and torsos sewn together at the waist.

As for Raggedy Ann, in 1977 the 1918 doll, whose imitators captivated thousands of youngsters, was given the key to the city of Indianapolis. She still wears it on her apron, next to her heart.

The homemade heart-stealers (above, left) were fashioned in imitation of the 1918 Raggedy Ann doll. The jauntily garbed knitted doll (above) was made in 1892.

A handcar pumped by the ubiquitous Mickey and Minnie Mouse delighted many a young collector in the 1930's —and helped keep Lionel going during the Depression.

1900, when he built another toy train. It was intended as a window display, but when "the first customer who saw it bought the advertisement instead of the goods," the store's owner ordered six more trains and Cowen was on his way.

In 1903 he issued a catalog of products that included an electric trolley and a suspension bridge; in 1907 he introduced a realistic replica of a Baltimore & Ohio locomotive. Business boomed. Soon there was a whole fleet of model trains and track, plus layout accessories such as tunnels and signal towers; depots and ticket offices; lampposts, flagpoles, and shrubbery.

By the early 1920's other toy train companies were competing in the race through America's living rooms. Over the years some of them fell on hard times and a couple were bought by Lionel. In a flash of righteous arrogance Cowen, who considered one competitor's work "inartistic," cast its dies into the Connecticut River.

Cowen's genius as an inventor was matched by his genius as a promoter. His catalogs unblushingly appealed both to a man's nostalgia for boyhood and a boy's eagerness for manhood. Despite their expense the chuffing miniatures became the must-have toys of their time and they have been handed down from father to son since the beginning. For many families, no Christmas is complete without the ritual of setting up a track and running the tiny locomotives.

Inspired by the authenticity of the cars, some collectors go to great lengths to create elaborate landscapes — complete with weather — as settings for their prized engines. The Lionel company helped one hobbyist simulate a storm and explained to another how to create an aurora borealis.

SEVERED TIES

American Spirits of Independence

Though divorce in early America was far from common, the colonists were much more willing than their English counterparts to dissolve unhappy unions. Just how liberal divorce laws were, however, varied depending on which Colony you happened to be in.

While even the English recognized adultery as ground for divorce, for instance, in New England, where such suits were generally considered civil matters, divorce was also allowed in cases of desertion, bigamy, impotence, nonsupport, and cruelty. Connecticut granted divorce as well when a mate's religious views were judged too eccentric. In the southern Colonies divorce was not available, and in the middle Colonies, at least for a time, each case required a special act by the legislature.

By the early 19th century one general agreement among state legislatures was a distinction between partial, or "bed and board," divorce and absolute divorce. Far more easily come by, partial divorce allowed a couple to separate on a number of grounds, including "extreme cruelty and other misconduct", but forbade remarriage. Absolute divorce usually required a decision by the legislature and resulted in total annulment of the first marriage with permission to remarry. The one remarkable exception was South Carolina, which continued to hold that marriages contracted in its boundaries were "indissoluble by any means," a position it did not relinquish until the end of the 19th century.

By 1879 divorce laws were liberal enough to provoke this cartoon, in which prospective suitors inspect a divorcée's "matrimonial tree" along with her other features.

The Reluctant First Lady

The untidiness of divorce laws in the 19th century was at times the cause of heartbreak. Such was the case of Andrew Jackson and Rachel Donelson, who married in 1791 only to learn years later that Donelson's first marriage had never been fully dissolved. Jackson's political opponents seized the opportunity to humiliate him while accusing Rachel of adultery. Although the harried pair promptly went through a second ceremony to correct the technical mistake, Rachel remained deeply wounded by the charges, and Jackson repeatedly engaged in skirmishes to reclaim her honor. In one duel in 1806 he took a near-fatal bullet in the chest before killing his opponent with a return shot.

For her part Rachel wanted nothing more than to remove herself and her husband from the limelight and to live in seclusion at their plantation in Tennessee. But Jackson's celebrity as a military leader and politician made that impossible. Matters came to a climax in 1828 when he was named Democratic candidate for president. With her reputation once again besmirched in the partisan debate, Rachel protested that she would rather be a doorkeeper in the house of God than dwell in "that palace in Washington." Then, when Jackson won the election, a friend noted that the first lady–elect's "energy subsided, her spirits drooped, and her health declined. . . . She has been heard to speak but seldom since." On December 17, 1828, Rachel suffered an apparent heart attack and died five days later. Her husband buried her in the white satin gown that she was to have worn at his inauguration.

Divorce Rights and Wrongs

In the 19th century a man's claim on his wife did not necessarily end with their divorce. Abby McFarland, for instance, had been married for several years to her husband, Daniel — an often abusive alcoholic — before she decided to flee for safety. A neighbor, Albert Richardson, helped Abby arrange a trip to Indiana, where she lived for 16 months in order to obtain the divorce she could not get in New York.

Meanwhile, Abby's friendship with the widowed Richardson deepened through months of letter writing, and when she returned to New York City in October 1869, it was the pair's intention to be married. Still vengeful, however, McFarland got wind of the plan, stalked Richardson, and shot him. Richardson lived just long enough to marry Abby from his deathbed, and McFarland was charged with murder.

But many New Yorkers agreed with McFarland's lawyer that his client's actions were perfectly justified since the dead man had interfered with a husband's God-given right to possess his wife, whatever her complaints. This, said the lawyer, was "the law of the Bible; for one of the two parties is superior and the other inferior."

Women's rights activists, led by Elizabeth Cady Stanton, demanded that McFarland either be hanged or confined to an insane asylum. In a scathing denunciation of New York's divorce laws, Stanton declared that "no matter what the character of the husband . . . the woman shall continue to be his wife . . . though her flesh crawl and her soul sicken every time he enters her presence." But her words did no good. McFarland left the courtroom not only free and cleared but with custody of the couple's older son.

Western Disunion

By the 1850's Westward-ho had become the battle cry for many Americans hoping to break the bonds of marriage, with Indiana among the first of the divorce havens. Not only was a residence requirement practically nonexistent, but its courts could grant a divorce for any cause deemed "proper." Some Indianans disapproved: "We are overrun by a flock of ill-used, and ill-using, petulant, libidinous, extravagant, ill-fitting husbands and wives," declared one local paper.

After the Civil War Indiana tightened its laws, but many other rough-and-ready western territories were eager to step into the breach. California, for example, recognized adultery, cruelty, desertion, felony conviction, alcoholism, and nonsupport as grounds for divorce. And because of the mobility of the population there, residency requirements were short and informally applied.

Other states courted out-of-state divorce trade through advertisements in eastern cities. Utah thus gained brief celebrity as a divorce mill in the 1870's, followed by the Dakotas. Sioux Falls, where most of South Dakota's divorce business centered, installed a handsome young judge who specialized in dealing with female divorcées; for male clients it boasted several gambling houses and a bevy of ladies for hire. When South Dakota's conservative element campaigned successfully to tighten divorce laws, Oklahoma and Wyoming eagerly took up the slack.

Finally, after the turn of the century, Nevada, and particularly the city of Reno, gained ascendancy as the place for "quickee divorces." Nevada's magic formula: easy divorce laws, a six-month residency requirement, and lots of amusements to keep people busy while they waited.

Arkansas Preparing To Compete with Reno
HOT SPRINGS OFFERS
A Divorce After 90 Days' Residence
Sunday Theaters, Three Swell Night Clubs, Fine Hotels
Famous Baths, Mountain Trails, Golf, Tennis, Swimming, Boating, Fishing
A Plan to Legalize Horse Racing
NEVADA
RENO
ARK.
HOT SPRINGS
WHAT RENO OFFERS—
A Divorce After 90 Days' Residence
A Plan to Cut This to Six Weeks and Secrecy As to Details
Swanky Gambling Casinos, Horse Racing
Dude Ranches, Swimming, Golf, Winter Sports Amid Mountains
Gay Night Life, Fine Hotels, Theaters
MEXICO
(DIVORCES BY MAIL)

Both Reno, Nevada, and Hot Springs, Arkansas, stressed their recreation facilities in order to attract divorcées when the item (above) appeared in the news in 1931. In 1932 two happy, and newly divorced, society matrons (right) were photographed as they prepared to toss their wedding rings into Reno's Truckee River.

ALTERNATIVE LIFE-STYLES

Naughty and Nice

Earthiness yielded to restraint as a rising middle class in American society tried to develop new rules for the mating game.

The earliest Puritan settlers in New England had a punishment to fit every sexual transgression: whip lashings for fornication, scarlet A's for adultery, confinement in stocks or pillory for newly married couples whose children were born less than nine months after the wedding. Yet despite these severities, some estimates conclude that fully one-third of the children born in late 18th-century New England were conceived out of wedlock.

In the long run, however, changing social customs achieved what stocks and pillory could not. Sexual squeamishness, in fact, became a mark of social refinement in 19th-century America. It also spawned a flourishing business in books for all ages and both sexes on avoiding temptation. In *Mother's Help and Child's Best Friend,* Carrica Le Favre attributed the emergence of a child's sexual awareness to between-meal snacks, which, she wrote, bring blood to the stomach "thereby developing abnormally the lower instincts." She suggested flying kites as an uplifting alternative.

The author of *The Science of a New Life* urged women to eschew chignons because "this great pressure of hair on the small brain . . . causes an unusual flow of the blood to amativeness." Sylvester Graham warned young men that "overstimulation" would lead to "a shocking state of debility and excessive irritability." And some thought that not even the sanction of marriage should lift restrictions on amorousness. In 1840 Dr. William Andrus Alcott cautioned newlyweds against frequent sex, explaining "that one indulgence to each lunar month is all that the best health of the parties can possibly require."

The Victorian passion for prudery was less than universal. Some were so straitlaced that they clothed naked piano legs in frilled pantalets. But others frankly delighted in illustrations of scantily clad, generously proportioned women performing acrobatic feats.

Sex Among the Sects

"Everybody has a perfect right to do everything," claimed Josiah Warren, founder of Modern Times, a utopian settlement in what is now Brentwood, Long Island, in 1851. In contrast to the many communes that embraced a Shaker-like standard of celibacy, his and many another mid-19th-century group were definitely of a freewheeling frame of mind.

The leaders of such communities often clad their theories in quasi-religious trappings. Thomas Lake Harris, for one, in 1851 organized the Mountain Cove Community in Fayette County, Virginia, which he claimed was the site of the Garden of Eden. Harris urged celibacy on his flock, but he also taught that one's "spiritual spouse" might reside in the body of another or might flit willy-nilly from body to body. Celestial unions were made through the agency of the "Lily Queen," the female aspect of Harris's dual-sexed deity. He also shared with his female followers the startling news that fairies inhabited their breasts — agents of "Divine Love" in the left breast and of "Divine Truth" in the right. Ultimately a disaffected female acolyte told a reporter lurid tales of life at the settlement, and the resulting scandal led to its dissolution.

Even stranger were the reputed goings-on at Cyrus Spragg's mid-19th-century New Jerusalem in Illinois. Spragg had previously experimented with communal living — including a nudist colony in Michigan that failed, in part because of the inhospitable climate. After settling in Illinois, Spragg decreed himself "the Eternal and Invisible Presence" and retired to a temple that his followers had built. Messages were transmitted from temple to community by a succession of virgins who spent the night with Spragg inside the temple. (A different applicant was sent in nightly.) Among the messages from Spragg was the revelation that one of these young women would give birth to the Messiah and she would become "the modern Madonna."

The irate suitor of one woman eventually invaded the temple and fired several shots at Spragg. But the virgin who visited the next night reported that Spragg, who had always received his guests in total darkness, was unharmed. All seemed normal for a time, until Spragg's daughter-in-law revealed that her husband and his brother had taken Spragg's place in the chamber. Despite the brothers' cries of sacrilege, the temple was investigated and the "Eternal and Invisible Presence" was found to be gone. Lacking its charismatic leader and disillusioned by the deception, the community disbanded.

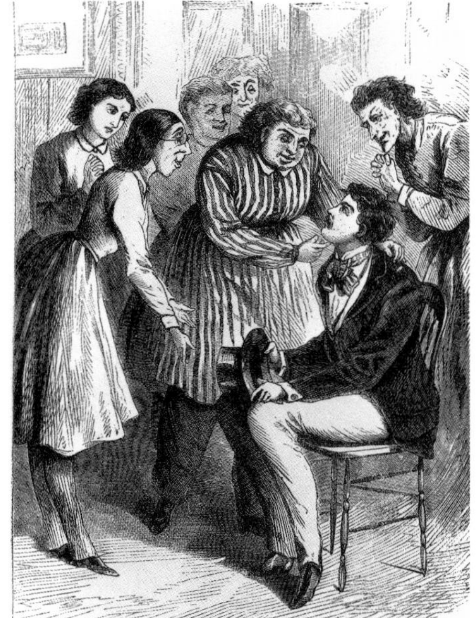

Communal living inevitably sparked speculation among outsiders. Trying to imagine what qualifications New York's Oneida Community might require of applicants, one artist also guessed at who would comprise the board of review.

Bewitching Broker

At a time when most Americans were so modest that they referred to womens' underwear as "white-sewing," it is unlikely that Victoria Claflin Woodhull resorted to such euphemisms. Delicacy — euphemistic or otherwise — was not part of her stock in trade.

Born in 1838 to a family of eccentrics, she maintained that she began to have visions at an early age. A spiritualist (she claimed Demosthenes as her familiar), suffragist, and stockbroker by turns, Woodhull was a dazzlingly persuasive personality. Her notoriety blossomed from her power as a public speaker — and her advocacy of free love.

When, in the midst of an 1871 speech in New York City, a member of the crowd demanded "Are you a free lover?" Woodhull did not flinch. "Yes! I am," she declared. "I have an inalienable, constitutional, and natural right to love whom I may, to love as long or as short a period as I can, to change that love every day if I please!"

Though Woodhull did not change loves every day, her domestic arrangements nevertheless scandalized her contemporaries. At one time her household included both her ailing ex-husband and her new lover, a fast-talking huckster named Col. James Blood. Also among her admirers was Commodore Vanderbilt, who provided Woodhull and her sister with enough money to open a brokerage firm. They later started a small newspaper, *Woodhull & Claflin's Weekly.* In speech and in print, Woodhull aired causes as diverse as vegetarianism, women's suffrage, Marxism — and of course, free love.

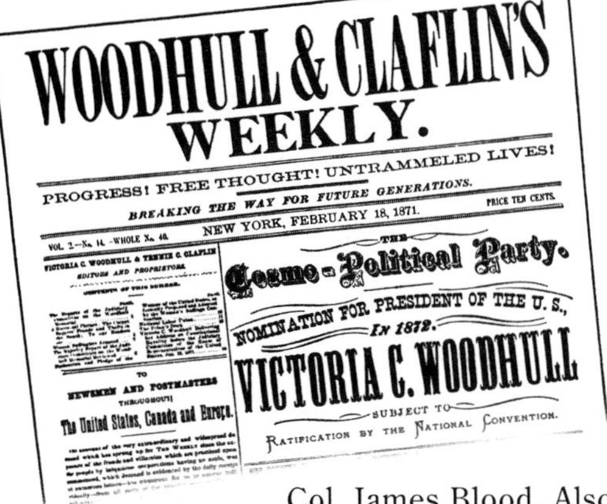

WOODHULL & CLAFLIN'S
WEEKLY.
PROGRESS! FREE THOUGHT! UNTRAMMELED LIVES!
BREAKING THE WAY FOR FUTURE GENERATIONS.
NEW YORK, FEBRUARY 18, 1871.
PRICE TEN CENTS.
THE
Cosmo-Political Party.
NOMINATION FOR PRESIDENT OF THE U. S.,
IN 1872.
VICTORIA C. WOODHULL
SUBJECT TO
RATIFICATION BY THE NATIONAL CONVENTION.
TO
NEWSMEN AND POSTMASTERS
THROUGHOUT
The United States, Canada and Europe.

Woodhull considered herself "a woman of destiny"; others thought her a crank and a crook. But in many ways she was a herald with legitimate concerns whom Horace Greeley once endorsed by saying, "This is a spirit to respect, perhaps to fear, certainly not to be laughed at."

Believing that "if a Victoria could rule England, it was time for one to run the United States," Woodhull declared herself a presidential candidate in 1872.

DEALING WITH DEATH

Grave and Spirited Ceremonies

The loss of friends and family was as common an occurrence for our ancestors, but funerals in the past were not necessarily solemn occasions.

Throughout America's Colonial period, life expectancy was brief and death at any age was accepted as a matter of fact. Following the death of one of his daughters, the Puritan diarist Samuel Sewall wrote of spending Christmas day in the family tomb. "'Twas an awful yet pleasing Treat," he recalled. By the mid-18th century, some people even waxed poetic on the subject. In the 1740's, traveling evangelist George Whitefield composed a hymn for use at his own funeral. "Ah! Lovely appearance of death, / No sight upon earth is so fair; / Not all the gay pageants that breathe, / Can with a dead body compare," it went in part. (He had to wait nearly three decades before his paean was sung.)

Preparing for burial

During the early years of settlement, funerals were stark, though social, affairs. Burial generally took place on family land with friends and neighbors present. The women prepared the corpse, clothing the body in its Sunday best, and slipping it into a shroud made of waxed linen or alum-soaked wool. At first this was the only covering used at burials, but by the late 1600's funerals were increasingly taking place in churchyards, and shrouded bodies were laid out in coffins. These plain, unpadded pine boxes were made to measure by local carpenters and might feature a sectional lid so that the upper torso could be viewed when friends came to pay their final respects.

Beginning in the 1830's customers wanting something finer could choose from ready-made patented coffins. Many of these were touted as offering special advantages, including such "superior" materials as metal, marble, and cast cement. In the 1840's — by which time funerals took place in cemeteries rather than churchyards — patents were being awarded for specialty models. One called the "torpedo coffin," for example, exploded when tampered with, presumably to discourage body snatchers and grave robbers.

Lively local customs

Getting to the burial site required the services of bearers and, later, hearses. The bearers were of two types: the pallbearers, who managed the pall, or cloth covering on the coffin, and the underbearers, who did the heavy work of carrying the box itself. The earliest hearses were simple wheeled "dead wagons," which might be pulled by men or a horse. As fashions changed, they became elaborate, with curtained windows and funerary urns and tasseled swags as decorations. The grandest hearses required two horses, preferably matched pairs of black high-steppers.

Although solemn sermons and prayers traditionally marked the services at church and graveside, funerals otherwise could be relatively upbeat occasions. Depending on the community and religion, attendees might be given souvenirs such as dead-cakes (a kind of cookie with the deceased's initials baked in), a bottle of wine, a ring, a scarf, or gloves. Memorial rings and gloves were particular favorites, and ministers often accumulated them by the hundreds. One thrifty Boston parson resold his for extra cash.

Alcoholic refreshment, dispensed with lavish abandon by a grog committee after the interment, could leave a family in debt for months. Nathaniel Hawthorne found it odd that his New England ancestors were most comfortable celebrating when it involved the "grisly jollity" of a funeral. But Southerners also followed funerals with bibulous receptions and sent the departed off in style with volleys of gun salutes at graveside.

Customs everywhere changed considerably in the late 1800's, as professional undertakers took over the business of burial. The coffins of old were replaced by caskets with quilted velvet interiors, heavy silver hardware, and rare woods that were said to outlast the "lapse of ages" and mitigate "the harsh realities of the grave."

WHAT·IS·IT

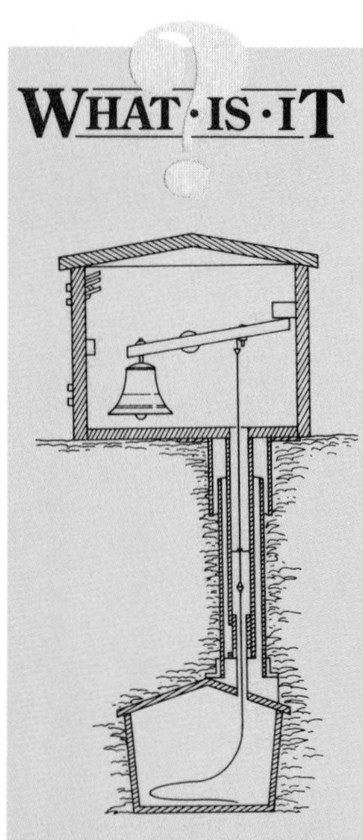

"Saved by the bell" had a special meaning to the user of this elaborate device. Patented in 1893, it was one of many "grave alarms" designed by Victorian inventors in response to people's fears of being buried alive — not an unfounded concern at that time.

In this example a cord connected the "deceased" in his or her subterranean chamber with an alarm bell aboveground. Other coffins featured flags that unfurled and lids that sprang open, allowing the body to be rescued from a fate worse than death.

The Ultimate Beauty Rest

For Bostonians in the mid-19th century, a fine day was excuse enough to visit Mount Auburn Cemetery. On any given weekend the number of mourners found there was apt to pale next to the throngs of sightseers, trysting couples, and families out for a spin in the carriage. Their interest was hardly morbid, for Mount Auburn's grounds were truly idyllic. "A glance at this beautiful cemetery," wrote one visitor, "almost excites a wish to die."

Established in 1831 on 72 wooded acres just outside the city proper, Mount Auburn was the first cemetery of its kind in America. Previously, graveyards — or boneyards, as they were known — were small and dismal plots often located next to churches. By the early 1800's they were denounced as a blight on urban life and were described as "festering charnel

When the Saints Go Marching In

On the way to the cemetery, New Orleans's traditional brass bands would play a funeral march or a slow hymn like *Nearer My God to Thee.* After the graveside ceremony, however, participants would dance along as the pace picked up and the band roared out such lively tunes as *When the Saints Go Marching In.*

A tradition unique to New Orleans, the brass band funeral flourished between the 1880's and 1920's. "That's just the way it was in those days," one musician recalled decades later. "You'd march to the graveyard playing very solemn and very slow, then on the way back all hell would break loose!"

"All hell" was generated by the band itself, which usually included trumpet, trombone, tuba, and clarinet, along with snare and bass drums. Marching along with the band were "second liners," a crowd of townspeople who joined the procession on the way to the cemetery.

While the graveside solemnities were under way, the band and second liners waited respectfully outside the cemetery gates. Then, when the family and other primary mourners finally left, the band's grand marshal turned to the expectant crowd and asked: "Are you still alive?" And the roar went up: "YEAH!" "Do we like to live?" "YEAH!" "Do you want to dance?" "YEAH!" With that the band swung into a medley of ragtime, Dixieland, and jazzed-up popular tunes, the second-liners broke into exuberant dancing and singing, and the whole rollicking procession wended its way back to town.

This laughing in the face of death was far from cynical: it helped reaffirm the joy of living, reminding all who participated of the hope of resurrection. More to the point, in the words of jazzman Jelly Roll Morton, the celebration provided "the end of a perfect death."

grounds, injurious to health." Forming what came to be known as the rural cemetery movement, people argued that burial should take place outside of cities, and that simple monuments should mark graves, reflecting the young republic's democratic ideals.

Mount Auburn set the style for all such cemeteries to come. Within four years of its founding, the grounds had been expanded to 110 acres and landscaped with lawns, meandering lanes, and over 1,300 ornamental trees. At the urging of the local press, which suggested the site should be "as remarkable for the treasures of art collected there, as it now is for its scenery," the country's finest sculptors were commisioned to design its marble and granite monuments. More beautiful than ever today, Mount Auburn is the resting place of over 90,000 people, whose names form a who's who of Massachusetts's history.

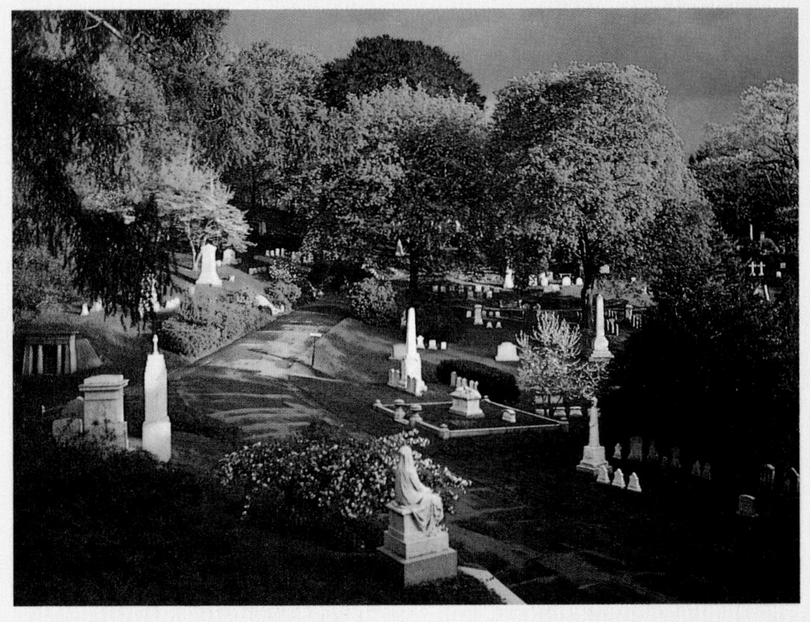

Mourning Becomes Eclectic

For 19th-century Americans the death of a loved one could affect the the way a person dressed, socialized, and otherwise behaved for years.

From the moment of death and often for many months thereafter, the activities and dress of people close to the deceased were governed by strict rules during the Victorian era. Customs defining the length of mourning and the type and color of clothing to be worn had been established by the early 1800's, but the rituals grew more complex as the century wore on. To know what to do and when to do it, however, one simply turned to the family's shelf of etiquette books.

Rules for women

A woman went into deep mourning immediately following a death and, except to attend the funeral and church, did not leave the house for at least a month. If she lost her husband, she might remain in deep mourning for two years; the loss of a parent or child required one year; grandparents, siblings, and anyone else who left an inheritance got six months; and aunts, uncles, nieces, and nephews, three.

Black was the customary color for a widow's mourning weeds during the first year, with crepe, serge, and alpaca the fabrics of choice. In the second year she could lighten up a bit by switching to a glossy fabric such as silk in shades of dark purple or gray. She also replaced her usual hat with a black bonnet and was expected to wear a veil over her face during the first three months, then trail it down the back of the bonnet for another nine. Ornament was out of the question while in deep mourning, but jet, woven hair, and other mourning jewelry were worn when the appropriate amount of time had passed.

America's mourning customs had already been firmly established when this silk memorial picture was embroidered in 1807. The wearing of black clothing bound a family together in its grief, while setting it apart from the rest of society.

And customs for others

Though men displayed their grief for somewhat shorter periods than women, they too wore suit, tie, hat band, and even shirt studs and cuff buttons in basic black. If the man used a walking stick, he might tie a bit of black ribbon around it as well, as a symbol of his mourning. Children under twelve wore white in summer and gray in winter, but whatever the season, the clothes were trimmed with black buttons, ruffles, belts, and ribbons.

Families also had to observe a host of rules about the house. A typical prescription for mourning behavior appeared in the 1882 edition of *Our Deportment, or the Manners, Conduct and Dress of the Most Refined Society:* "There should be no loud talking or confusion while the body remains in the house. All differences and quarrels must be forgotten . . . , and personal enemies who meet at a funeral must treat each other with respect and dignity."

Toward the end of the century the rules finally eased somewhat. According to one authority on etiquette, modern taste dictated that mourners "make no one else gloomy because they, themselves, suffer." In the same spirit a bicycle company produced an all-black two-wheeler suitable for mourners who wished to get their exercise without scandalizing the neighborhood. And the prescribed period for wearing black veils was curtailed. Expressing the new freedom of the age, Annie Randall White, the author of a guide for polite society, suggested that the veil endangered health, "for it is laden with arsenic, and is dangerous to the eyes and skin, besides being excessively hot and cumbersome."

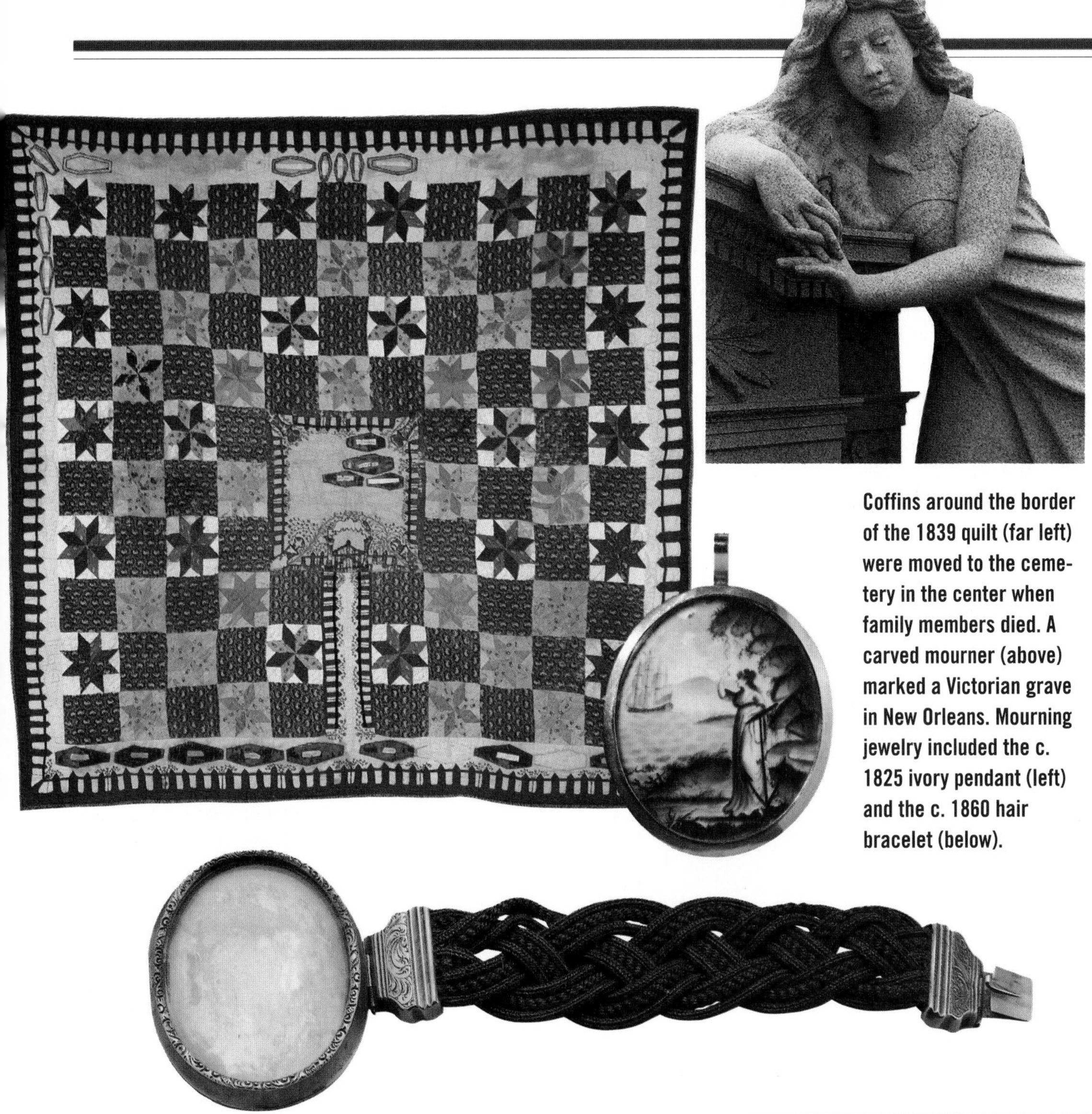

Coffins around the border of the 1839 quilt (far left) were moved to the cemetery in the center when family members died. A carved mourner (above) marked a Victorian grave in New Orleans. Mourning jewelry included the c. 1825 ivory pendant (left) and the c. 1860 hair bracelet (below).

When This You See, Remember Me

While the Colonists certainly did not forget loved ones after laying them in their graves, few would have spent time romanticizing the loss. But as life in America changed after the Revolution, so did attitudes toward death. Beginning with George Washington's death in 1799, when the whole country joined in a long and solemn period of mourning, and for most of the 19th century, sentimental memorials were very much the fashion.

Mourning pictures — embroidered in silk, painted in watercolor, or stenciled on velvet — were among the most popular forms of memorials in the early 1800's. Made primarily by teenaged girls who learned such artistry at school, the pictures were highly symbolic. Typically they depicted weeping mourners in a garden that featured a willow tree (regeneration), an evergreen (everlasting life), a flowing stream (absolution), and an urn or tombstone (the spirit of the departed).

Artists painted similar scenes in miniature on ivory, to be worn as mourning jewelry. In some instances the deceased's hair was ground and used as pigment for the paint. Or a lock of hair might be preserved inside a locket.

By midcentury many people switched to wearing bracelets or other pieces made of plaited hair. These were so popular that women's magazines published do-it-yourself instructions. Anyone interested could also turn to a professional "hair jeweler" such as the enterprising Mrs. C. S. Wilbur, who advertised her skill at making "Elaborate Necklaces, Broaches, Rings, Gentlemen's Guard and Fob Chains, Charms and Ear Rings" of the deceased's hair —items, she ventured, that "no person of good taste will venture to deny."

Many portrait artists, if called in quickly enough, would paint likenesses of the dead as if still alive. Daguerreotypists were not so concerned with achieving a "living" image, however, since one of the quirkier aspects of mourning during the Victorian era was a vogue for photographs of the dead reposing in their coffins.

NATIVE TONGUE

DEATH-DEFYING FEATS OF LANGUAGE

Death is a subject that many have traditionally tried their best to avoid. What rested in the coffin or, rather, casket in the funeral home or parlor (late-19th-century euphemisms for a very unhomelike place) was not a corpse. The body, instead, was referred to as the deceased or dear departed who had gone to glory, passed away, or met his or her Maker. In a classic gaffe one graveside preacher is said to have pointed to the late lamented and solemnly pronounced, "This is only the shell. The nut is gone."

But there have always been plain speakers as well, those, for example, who do not hesitate to call a corpse a stiff. And in contrast to such circumlocutions as "taken from this earthly garden," others get right down to basics with phrases like "pushing up daisies" and "food for worms." Soldiers don't mince words either. The rich store of military terms for stone cold dead ranges from such expressions as "stopped a bullet" to "answered the last muster."

Occupations, in fact, have had a way of following the dead to their graves. Sailors "give up the ship" and go to "Davy Jones's locker"; cowboys "die with their boots on"; gamblers, when their number is up, are likely to "cash in their chips"; farmers "lay down their shovels"; and as for theatrical folk, when their time comes, "it's curtains."

LINES OF DESCENT

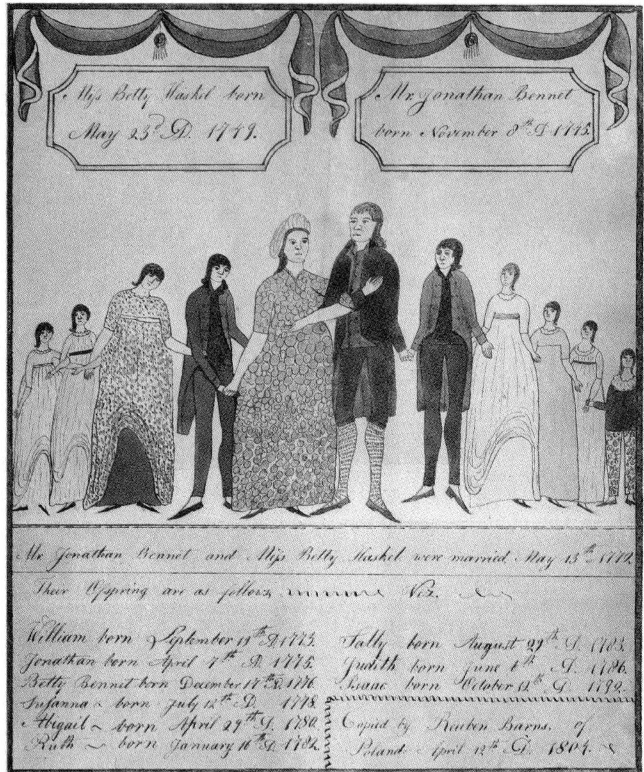

The marriage of Mr. Jonathan Bennet and Miss Betty Haskel in 1772 was an opportunity to commemorate their family histories. This genealogy, dated April 12, 1804, is a watercolor copy by Reuben Barns.

Who Was Who

Whether one's forebears were settlers, soldiers, or sovereigns, there seems to be a hereditary club to commemorate their existence. The Daughters of the American Revolution, the Order of First Families of Virginia, and the Society of the Cincinnati are perhaps the best known of these organizations. But others abound. There are, for instance, nearly 100 organizations that unite members who share a common surname, if not a common lineage. One is so egalitarian that it publishes a newsletter titled *Gresham — Any Way You Spell It.*

Members of Flagon and Trencher are descended from men and women who ran "a tavern, inn, or other type of hostelry on, or prior to, July 4, 1776." The Sons of Sherman's March to the Sea still get together, too — although they probably don't socialize with the descendants of Hood's Texas Brigade, which fought with Robert E. Lee.

Proof of royal descent isn't enough to ensure membership in the Order of the Crown in America — one must be invited to join its select circle of 400. But if your highness came from the wrong side of the sheets, there is the Descendants of the Illegitimate Sons and Daughters of the Kings of Britain, who irreverently call themselves the Royal Bastards. And if you are a "male descendant of witches or persons accused . . . as witches," you can be an official Son of a Witch.

Roots and Branches

Shake any American family tree, and a *Mayflower* passenger may well fall out. According to the General Society of Mayflower Descendants, somewhere between 5 and 20 million people can probably count one of the original Pilgrims among their forebears.

But there may be even more. Founded in 1897 "to perpetuate to a remote posterity the memory of our Pilgrim Fathers," the society accepts the documented offspring of only 24 of the 41 men who signed the Mayflower Compact and the sons of 2 others — far fewer than the 100 or so who were passengers on the ship. And a single Pilgrim union — that of John Alden and Priscilla Mullins — produced 10 children, at least 68 grandchildren, and nearly 400 great-grandchildren. Today there may be millions of Alden descendants alone.

Some of those millions might also be descended from the poet Henry Wadsworth Longfellow, who immortalized his ancestors' romance in *The Courtship of Miles Standish;* or from President John Adams, who had the Aldens in his pedigree.

None of the original Pilgrims was rich, titled, or particularly well educated. One historian, in fact, wryly noted that "a group of English immigrants more socially insignificant could hardly be imagined." One preening Puritan descendant seemed to support that assessment when she sniffed that her family "sent our servants" over on the *Mayflower.* But it is doubtful that any *Mayflower* descendants would trade their Pilgrim forebears for a more aristocratic background. The Pilgrim belief in the equality of all people strongly influenced the development of our relatively classless society and forms the backbone of our government.

And scattered among the millions of *Mayflower* descendants are many worthy servants of the commonweal. Seven presidents — both Adamses, Grant, Taylor, both Roosevelts, and Taft — were of Pilgrim lineage, as were Mrs. Ralph Waldo Emerson, financier J. P. Morgan, painter Grandma Moses, and Adm. Alan Shepherd, the only person to play golf on the moon.

A Bang-up Bash

On New Year's Eve and New Year's Day in 1950, 632 relatives from the French, English, Italian, Swiss, and American branches of the family of Pierre Samuel du Pont de Nemours gathered to celebrate his landing in America 150 years before.

Du Pont and his family had fled revolution-torn France in the autumn of 1799 and, after a ghastly three-month journey aboard the barely seaworthy *American Eagle*, landed in Rhode Island on January 1, 1800. Casting about for welcome, the family, which had subsisted on game pies during the voyage, happened upon a farmhouse. No one answered their knock, but the determined group entered anyway and found a table set for breakfast and heaped with johnnycake. Famished, the du Ponts fell to, left some gold to pay for their serendipitous meal, and departed.

The du Ponts would never again need to filch a meal — nor ever lack the means to pay for one. In 1802 one of Pierre's sons, Eleuthère Irénée, built a gunpowder mill on the Brandywine River in Delaware. Business boomed. By the 20th century the company was also producing Lucite, nylon, and an array of other products. And the du Ponts had become one of America's wealthiest families.

Past, present, and future

In preparation for the gala family reunion, the 40 members of the Sesquicentennial Committee had spent 17 months interviewing caterers, collecting memorabilia, and organizing diversions. There were movies and buffet meals for the children, dinner and dancing for the adults, and a grand photo session at 11 P.M. on New Year's Eve. On New Year's Day, 1950, the whole clan gathered for a reunion luncheon. The guest list was limited to those who could show permits for burial in the family cemetery, and color-coded name tags identified the various branches of the family tree. To honor the du Ponts' beginnings in America, game pies — made from the old family recipe — and johnnycake were included on the reunion menu.

During the party traditions were honored, family ties were renewed, and the future was affirmed. The youngest du Pont descendant, sixth-generation Rose Lee Bigelow, however, was unable to attend the party: she had just been born that New Year's morning.

On New Year's morning in 1950 four generations of du Ponts gathered in the greenhouses of Longwood Gardens to celebrate the 150th anniversary of their family's arrival in America.

One need not be rich and famous to enjoy a family reunion. Shaded by trees, at least one umbrella, and a huge American flag, the Carr-Todd family of Cooperstown, New York, gathered for an informal picnic in 1914.

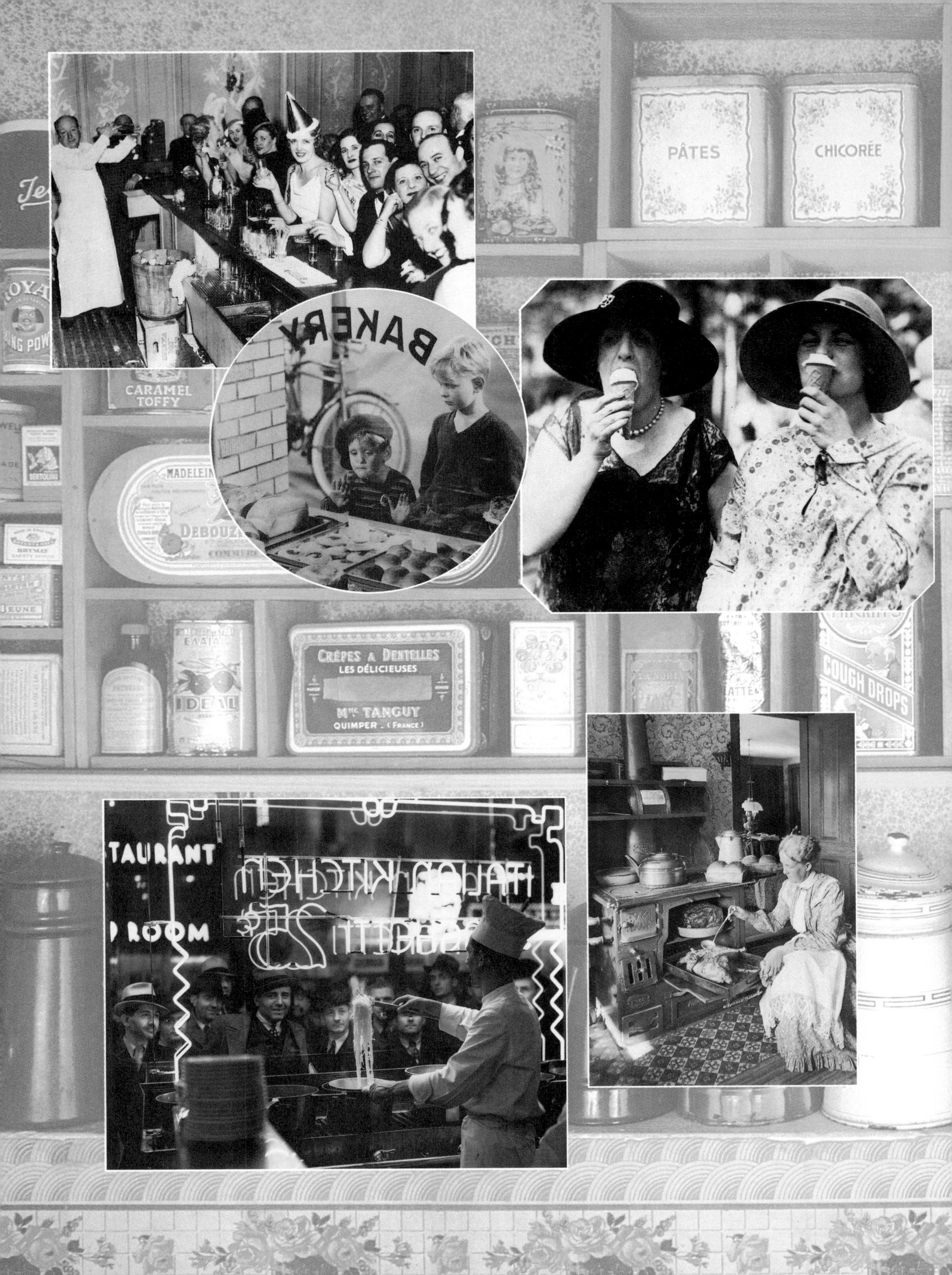
PÂTES
CHICORÉE
BAKERY
CARAMEL
TOFFY
CRÊPES A DENTELLES
LES DÉLICIEUSES
Mlle TANGUY
QUIMPER . (FRANCE)
IDEAL
COUGH DROPS

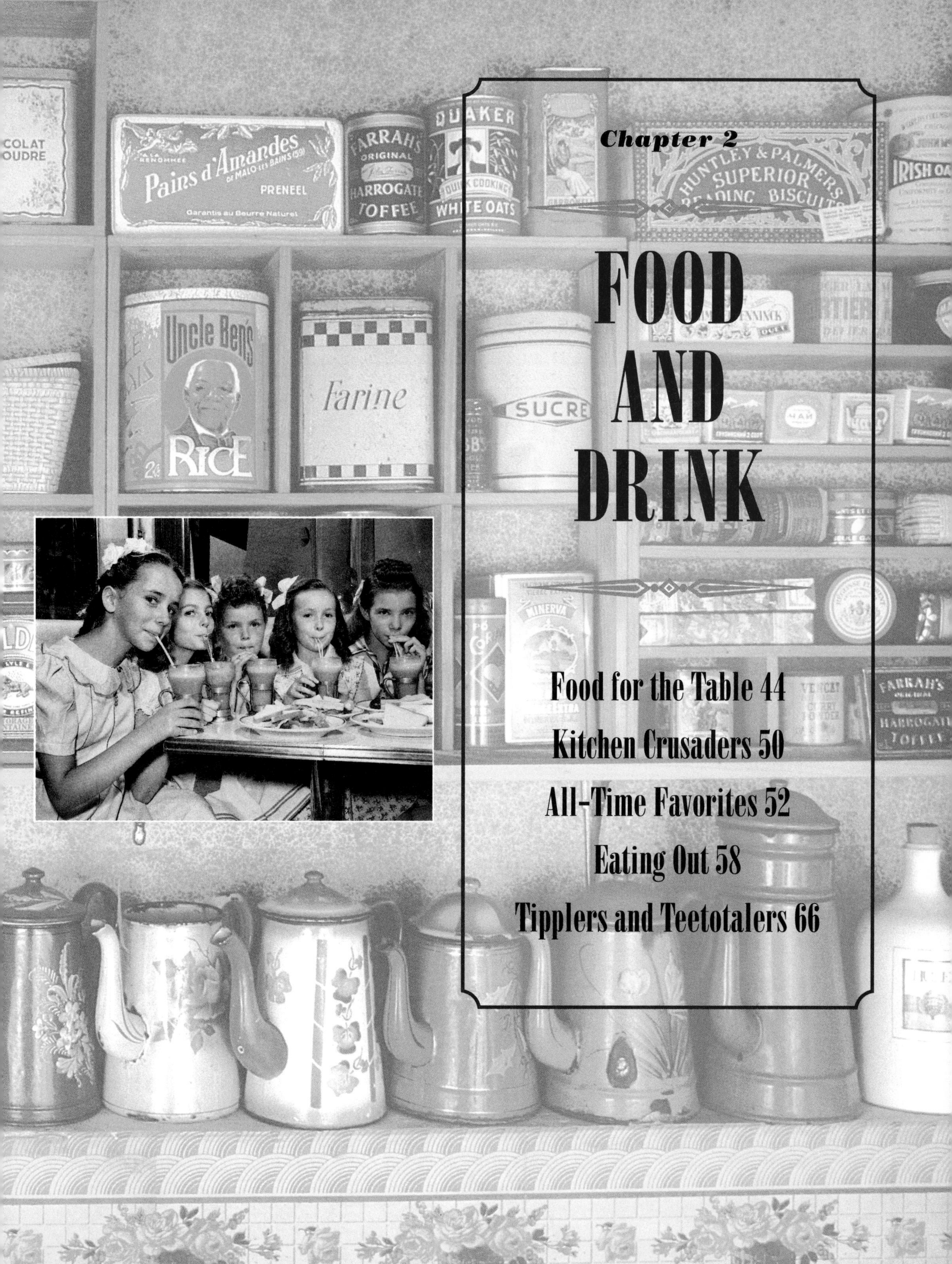

Chapter 2

FOOD AND DRINK

FOOD FOR THE TABLE

The Food That Kept America Growing

Although early Americans lived with uncertain harvests, their bountiful new land was amply supplied with finned, furred, and feathered fare. Indeed, one writer claimed that "game made the settlement of America possible."

Some colonists suffered a surfeit of seafood. In 1622 the Pilgrims bemoaned the fact that they could offer newcomers nothing but lobster (some of which weighed 25 pounds). And Captain John Smith observed, "He is a very bad fisher who cannot kill in one day one, two, or three hundred cod."

In later centuries the abundance of game on the frontier was equally astonishing. On a wagon trip west from Missouri, one boy wrote that "frequently my father killed three deer before breakfast." Countless settlers made meals of the then-ubiquitous passenger pigeon. The birds (now extinct — in part as a result of overhunting) flew in flocks so vast that they darkened the sky. A single blast of buckshot could fell as many as 125. In 1736 the birds were so prolific that farmers fed them to their pigs, and city dwellers could buy a half-dozen for a penny.

Those with more refined palates dined on the delectable canvasback duck — a treat praised by the hard-to-please English novelist Frederick Marryat. Describing the "countless profusion" at American markets, Marryat wrote that he had seen "nearly three hundred head of deer, with quantities of bear, raccoons . . . and every variety of bird. Bear I abominate," he cautioned, but "raccoon is pretty good."

Another observer, however, noted that a companion enjoyed bear meat "so passionately that he would growl like a Wild-Cat over a Squirrel." Other native delicacies included beaver tail, moose (especially the nose), and terrapin.

LEGEND —AND— LORE

Gib Morgan, a Texas oilman known for his tall tales, claimed that he fished using a tree for his fishing pole and a ship's anchor baited with a steer for his hook. Once when he yanked a whopping catfish ashore, crowed Morgan, the water level in the river dropped a full two feet.

Heaven on the Half Shell

He was a valiant man," King James I opined, "who first adventured on eating of oysters." But in America, where sailors found oyster beds large enough to capsize ships, the courageous and cowardly alike gulped them with gusto. River oysters in fact, helped the Jamestown settlers survive their winter of starvation in 1609.

The tasty bivalves soon became a staple in the diets of many, with recipes from the Gilded Age calling for oysters by the hundreds. They were sold by the piece and by the barrel; eaten at shops, stands, and bars; and shipped inland on wagons and canal boats. The prodigious heaps of shells left behind were sometimes used as landfill.

All this manic munching of mollusks was almost their doom. But conservation efforts, which began in the 17th century, have ensured that oysters continue to grace our tables.

The Victorians introduced an air of elegance to oyster eating. Poised for the palate, the tasty morsels were served on special plates (above) with carefully crafted depressions that cradled the individual mollusks. Many oyster bars, on the other hand, did not bother with plates (right). The shucker shucked, the customer slurped, and the tab was tallied by counting the number of empty shells that piled up.

To Market, to Market

In the days before refrigeration, meat made its way to market in its original state — as living cattle, sheep, geese, and turkeys, which were then slaughtered for sale. By the early 19th century the demand was so great that herds of steers were often driven hundreds of miles to sate the avid appetites in distant cities. Produce got there in wagons, traveling from field to market stall in enormous loads hauled by straining teams of as many as eight horses.

All this movement was accomplished by teamsters and drovers, who came to be known as the Gentry of the Whip. For teamsters, 25 or 30 miles was considered a good day's journey. Drovers, on the other hand, had to make their way on foot with meandering flocks and herds, and so might cover only 13 miles a day, in the course of which they might run about 30. Heavy traffic and bad weather could slow progress even further, to as little as three or four miles a day. Traffic jams—punctuated by bawling cattle, squawking fowl, and swearing teamsters—were common. Tolls began to be collected to repair roads damaged by the pounding from sharp-hoofed herds.

Taverns grew up along the roadsides, complete with corrals and pastures to contain the animals while their guides rested overnight. (The drovers, who usually smelled as bad as the animals they herded, were often asked to sleep in the barn.)

The advent of the refrigerated car in the 1870's caused a major change in the movement of goods. As trains — and eventually trucks — supplanted the long hoof-and-wagon trek to market, the whip-cracking teamsters were forced to retire their teams.

The City's Pantry

Noisy, smelly, sometimes filthy, and always crowded, city markets were nevertheless an indispensible feature of 19th-century America. Urbanites depended on them for their daily sustenance, and farmers found a thriving livelihood in the cavernous buildings with their hundreds of vendors' stalls.

Ideally, a market was situated where it was easily accessible to street, rail, and ship traffic. In a port city it might be right on the waterfront.

While the city slept, the gaslit market was a hive of activity. Teams of butchers, knives flashing, went about the task of slaughtering, skinning, and gutting cattle. For practiced hands, dressing an ox took a mere 15 minutes. Hogs took roughly one-third the time, and an efficient slaughterhouse could process as many as 7,000 in a day.

Special trains sped goods from the surrounding countryside and far-flung farms. Milk trains brought in milk by the thousands of gallons as well as cheese, butter, and eggs. A single run of New Jersey's "Pea Line" brought 80,000 baskets of strawberries to New York.

Ships discharged fragile cargoes of fish and exotic fruit, much of which was sold directly from the pier. The fish was packed in ice, then transferred to trains and transported inland. Canneries took the bulk of the fruit — one bought half a million pineapples a year. Vendors haggled for the remainder and hurried to their stalls to sort and stack it for sale.

Also in the rabbits' warren of the market were sellers of housewares and notions such as crockery, shoelaces, and tobacco; offices for the merchants (some with telegraph machines to track the latest prices); and even restaurants.

Savvy and well-to-do shoppers flocked to the stalls at daybreak, well aware that quality — and prices — would drop steadily as the day wore on. Enterprising restaurateurs filled lines of hackneys with delicacies for the evening's expected crowds of diners. Basket-toting housewives haggled with merchants for fruit and vegetables. Pandemonium reigned until the sold-out merchants began to leave — sometimes as late as midnight. This is when the city's poor obtained their meager provisions from the shopworn fowl and discarded produce remaining at day's end. Finally, the stalls closed — and the market's feverish cycle of supply began anew.

Pigs were not merely a source of food in the 19th century. In lieu of garbage collection, they roamed the streets freely, scavenging all the while. Rowdy boys sometimes taunted the stout animals into stampeding — with confusion and crisis as the inevitable result. Around 1850 an anonymous watercolorist depicted such a scene at the Jersey Market Terminus in Philadelphia.

America's Age of Ice

Keeping vegetables crisp and ice cream frozen is no problem today, but in America's first 300 years chilling food was a lot of work.

Ice and ingenuity served Americans for three centuries in the search for fresh food. Beginning with the Jamestown settlement, colonists dug pits to store ice along with meat and butter. By the late 18th century wealthy citizens were building elaborate ice houses as they adopted the French craze for iced desserts. George Washington spent several seasons developing an efficient ice house at Mount Vernon; for his friend James Madison, Thomas Jefferson designed one with a garden pavilion on top.

In the 1840's New Yorker Nicolino Calyo painted an iceman (above) delivering supplies from a lake north of the city. Workers (below) harvest ice from the Milwaukee River. Once cut, the blocks, packed in sawdust, were stored in enormous ice houses.

In 1803, Maryland farmer Thomas Moore developed the first "refrigerator" — a tin tub within a cedar tub, packed with ice and insulated with rabbit skins. "Every housekeeper may have one in his cellar," he wrote in his pamphlet, *An Essay on the Most Eligible Construction of Ice-Houses; Also, a Description of the Newly Invented Machine Called the Refrigerator.*

Moore was concerned with bringing firm, chilled butter from his farm to market. Some of his readers, however, had bigger ideas. Among them was Bostonian Frederic Tudor, who became known as the "Ice King." Tudor was determined to turn ice storage and delivery into a profitable industry, though it would take him — and others — some time to do so. Harvesting ice, after all, was a cumbersome business. Workers hacked and sawed lake ice into chunks and hauled them to shore by sleigh. The uneven blocks were hard to ship, hard to store, and melted quickly no matter how they were insulated.

The situation began to change when, in 1824, Tudor hired Nathaniel Wyeth, who streamlined the process with a series of ingenious inventions. Among the most important was his ice cutter, a sleigh with sawlike runners that sliced parallel grooves two to three inches deep across a frozen lake. Run crosswise over the original grooves, the cutter produced neat rectangular blocks that were easy to stack in an ice storage plant. From there the blocks could be moved by conveyor belt to waiting railroad cars. The cost of harvesting ice soon dropped from 30 cents to 10 cents a ton.

An ice box in every kitchen

Wyeth's inventions arrived just in time, for America's interest in ice really burgeoned by midcentury. While a mere 1,900 tons of ice were shipped out of Boston in 1827, the numbers exceeded

43,000 tons in 1848 and topped 97,000 by 1860.

One reason for the increased use of ice was the rapid growth of America's cities, which prompted a constant demand for fresh provisions. There also were new products. Great quantities of ice were used in brewing lager, which was introduced here by German beer makers in the 1840's. Ice cream became an institution too: an 1850 *Godey's Lady's Book* called it "one of the necessary luxuries of life."

Meanwhile, iceboxes had gained a place in the average home. An 1838 newspaper noted that they were as much a household necessity as a dining table. Two decades later, cookbook writers were taking refrigeration for granted.

Keeping those myriad iceboxes chilled was the job of icemen, who became a familiar part of the American scene: by 1880 one Philadelphia ice company employed 800 of them. Delivering door to door, an iceman made his rounds six or seven days a week in a brightly painted horse-drawn wagon. Often surrounded by children begging for ice chips, he used iron tongs to hoist a 60-pound block to a leather blanket on his shoulder, and then carried it inside to the icebox. The sound of melted ice dripping from the box to a pan below it was common to every kitchen.

By the 1930's mechanical refrigeration had replaced the need for home delivery, and the colorful ice wagons soon were gone. But the iceman — and the vast industry he represented — remain an unforgettable part of the nation's past.

When American men went overseas to serve in World War I, many women took on jobs they otherwise would never have tried. This pair teamed up to keep their neighbors' ice boxes chilled.

Swift Supplies for the Nation's Tables

"There are gigantic days in every man's life, Annie," meat packer Gustavus Swift confided to his wife in the fall of 1877. "This," he added, "is one of mine." They were standing in a Chicago freight yard as a train pulled out for Boston hauling refrigerated cars filled with beef.

Until that day Swift and other meat suppliers had had to ship live animals to eastern markets since existing refrigerated cars, when effective at all, were only so in winter. Fed up with the expense and inefficiency of such a system, Swift approached several railroad lines and tried to convince them to produce a better car. Since the railroads had large investments in cattle cars and stockyards, however, they had no interest in changing the way things were done.

Not one to be put off, Swift hired an engineer to design a system for circulating cold air and had the cars built himself. Introduced on the Grand Trunk Railway — the one line with few ties to the meat business — Swift's new cars ultimately revolutionized the way that food supplies reached America's tables.

A Swift and Company advertising card from the late 19th century fancifully extolled the glories of dressed meat. Because of Swift's innovations in railroad car refrigeration, "Western" beef — produced by Chicago's packers — was in plentiful supply in eastern restaurants and butcher shops by the 1880's. Once he had conquered the domestic market, Swift used refrigerator ships to make American beef an export product.

As American as "Pompkin Pie"

If Amelia Simmons had not been an orphan, she might not have written the first American cookbook. But according to Simmons, an orphan had to "have an opinion and determination of her own." And what she determined to do, in 1796, was write a manual "for the improvement of the rising generation of Females in America."

Featuring native ingredients such as cornmeal and cranberries, and New World recipes like that for "pompkin pie," the book made clear that in gastronomy as well as politics, the former British colonies had developed tastes of their own.

Simmons was also full of practical advice. She instructed housewives on how to dress a turtle: "about 9 o'clock hang up your Turtle by the hind fins"; noted that one should buy veal that had been brought to market in baskets rather than "flouncing on a sweaty horse"; and that garlic "tho' used by the French," was "better adapted to the uses of medicine than cookery."

Some of Simmons's New England staples, like Indian pudding and johnnycakes, are still prepared today. Few modern cooks, however, would want to follow her recipe for the drink known as syllabub: "Sweeten a quart of cyder with double refined sugar, grate nutmeg into it, then milk your cow into your liquor."

Measuring Up With Fannie Farmer

Like most Victorian ladies, Fannie Farmer always carried a fresh handkerchief. But unlike the others, she used hers to carry tidbits of tasty dishes out of restaurants so that she could analyze the recipes at home.

A graduate of the Boston Cooking School in the 1880's, Farmer objected to the casual way that the cookbooks of her day listed recipe measurements. "A nut of butter," they might suggest. Or, perhaps, a handful of flour, a pinch of salt, a glass of wine. Farmer fervently believed in bringing a laboratorylike precision to the kitchen. "Scientific cookery," she preached, ". . . means the elevation of the human race."

When she became director of her alma mater in 1891, and five years later when she published the *Boston Cooking-School Cook Book*, Farmer insisted on something no one had ever stressed before: the use of standardized measurements. Her instructions left little doubt as to what the standard was: "A cupful is measured level," she informed her readers. "A tablespoonful is measured level." To make sure that would-be cooks got the amounts just right, Farmer urged them to purchase newfangled kitchen utensils like "tin measuring cups and tea and table spoons of regulation sizes."

Fannie Farmer's cookbook made her a culinary celebrity. She founded a cooking school that bore her own name, wrote food columns in women's magazines, and lectured widely not only to housewives but also to such unexpected audiences as the students at Harvard Medical School. The preparation of food for invalids was one of Farmer's pet subjects, since as a teenager, she herself had been bedridden for several years with what may have been polio. "Never serve a patient custard scooped out from a large pudding dish," she told one medical group. "He wants to feel that he is being particularly looked out for, and the individual custard suits him."

Compared to modern concepts of taste and nutrition, many of Farmer's original recipes now seem cloying. Her exotic Tango Salad, for instance, featured avocados whose centers were filled with orange sections and then covered with a cooked dressing made of condensed milk, whipped cream, and orange juice.

But Farmer's contemporaries literally ate up her creations. By the time she died in 1915, over 360,000 copies of her book had been sold. Continually revised and updated, Fannie Farmer's cookbook remains a kitchen standby, encouraging novice cooks to do what her precise instructions first made possible: "If reliable recipes are at hand, try them, and you will be repaid a thousand times by family praise."

By eliminating guesswork in recipes, Fannie Farmer ensured both novice and experienced chefs perfect results and consequently earned herself the moniker Mother of Level Measurements.

WHAT·IS·IT

Call it what you will, this 1870's gizmo made short work of shelling corn. But its inventor, Pennsylvanian Anthony Iske, had more than one thing in mind when he made it. Depending on how you held it, his gadget could also serve as bootjack, hammer, tack puller, pot lifter, or wrench.

Winning Ways at the Dinner Table

World War II was fought not just on the battlefields of Europe and in the Pacific, but on American dinner tables as well. With the troops overseas consuming 20,000 tons of food a day, the government had little choice but to enforce conservation at home.

But while food rationing severely curtailed supplies of staples such as meat, canned vegetables, sugar, coffee, and tea, home economists and food authorities rallied to the cause. In cookbooks and promotional pamphlets they were apt to sound a lot like military leaders cheering their troops. "American Housewives — Generals at home in Defense — I salute you!" wrote the author of *Thrifty Cooking for Wartime*. "Hail to the women of America!" the fictional but nonetheless authoritative Betty Crocker addressed her readers in *Your Share.*

Many new recipes, devised to accommodate shortages, made clear by their very names that to use them was to support the war effort. The evening meal became a Victory Dinner, which might start with a Civilian Defense Cocktail — a concoction of cold water, evaporated milk, and tomato juice — or, perhaps, a bowl of Boot Camp Spud Soup. Precious supplies of beef were ground and turned into V-for-Victory Hamburgers or Military Meatballs. Victory gardens, which by 1943 produced half the country's fresh vegetables, provided the makings for Kitchen Patrol Carrots or Home Front Vegetable Plate with Hot Cheese Sauce. And rationing could not spoil Wartime Cake, a dessert made without eggs, milk, or butter.

In addition to recipes, the cookbooks provided homemakers with advice on subjects that ranged from getting the most out of their rationing coupons, to convincing their families to eat liver. The books, moreover, pointed out how sensible habits translated into patriotic support. "Make sure none of one's ration is being wasted," exhorted the author of *Wartime Meals,* revealing that undissolved sugar in the bottom of coffee cups wasted three-and-a-half tons of sugar a day in New York City alone. "Now that . . . our allies are pleading for food with which to sustain themselves for our common battle," she insisted, "waste is the unforgivable kitchen sin."

Settting aside their studies, students at Mount Holyoke College were ready to dig in at the college victory garden in the fall of 1942. By 1943 over 20 million such plots had been planted in the United States.

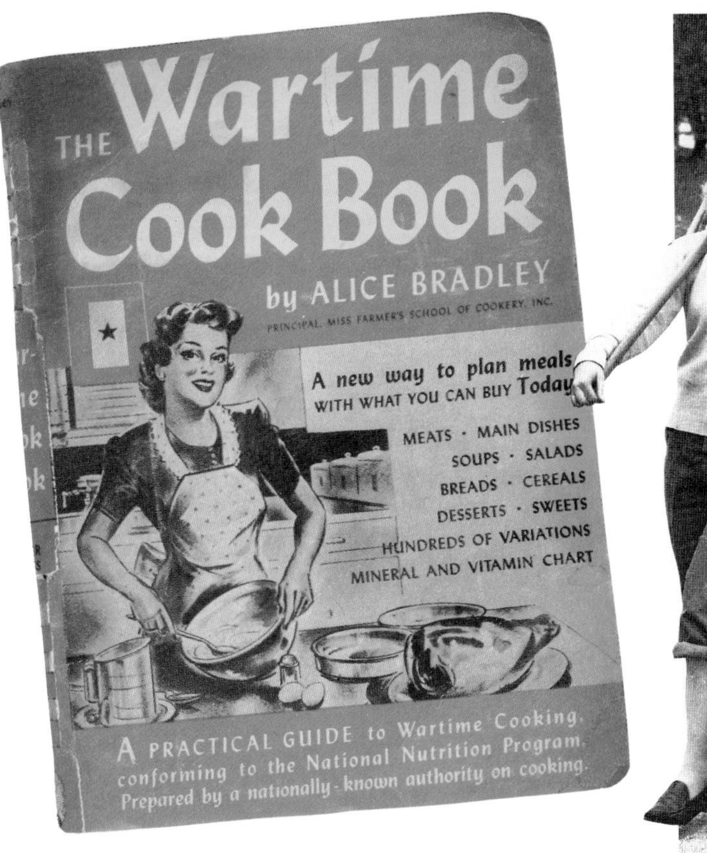

Wartime cookbooks typically promoted a spirit of goodwill. Even if shortages existed at the grocery store, the books seem to suggest, they need not be felt at the dinner table.

KITCHEN CRUSADERS

The Apostle of Bran

Graham crackers, now thought of as cookies, were created by "the poet of bran bread and pumpkins" as a healthful alternative to 19th-century junk food.

When Sylvester Graham, a frail and disgruntled early-19th-century Connecticut cleric, went searching for the root of all evil, he came up with a long list of possibilities. At the very top was the American diet. Embracing his new calling as a nutritional moralist, Graham traveled the country inveighing against red meat, fats, alcohol, salt, sweets, condiments, tobacco, and white bread. Graham alleged that these substances were not merely unhealthful, but downright immoral. Among their ill effects, he contended, were sexual excesses, family conflict, disease, and insanity.

Graham's recommendations were a mixture of asceticism and practicality. He advocated tooth brushing, frequent bathing, looser clothing, exercise, a vegetarian diet, clean air and pure drinking water, laughter as a digestive aid, and temperance in everything — all radical ideas in his day.

Fortunately his zealotry contained several kernels of sound, albeit intuitive, advice. Graham's "Treatise on Bread and Bread-Making," written in 1837, made a persuasive case for what is now known as a high-fiber diet. And his assertion that whole-grain dark bread was preferable to bread made from refined white flour was later borne out by the 20th-century discovery of vitamins.

Even so, Graham's lecture tours were often dogged by riot and dissent. His reformist arguments attracted considerable ridicule and violent protests — especially from professional bakers and butchers.

Graham's bran crusade influenced many — including such prominent individuals as Horace Greeley and Mother Ellen Harmon White, spiritual leader of the burgeoning Seventh-Day Adventists — and sparked sweeping changes in America's eating habits. In a time when many started the day with heaping platters of meat and potatoes, he ate a daily ration of dry, crumbled, whole wheat biscuits — the original Graham crackers. Ironically, health "expert" Graham never attained the vigor he promised others. He took his last righteous meal in the fall of 1851 — dying at the early age of 57.

POSTUM
POSTUM
POSTUM
Miss Nervis Hedake: "I wonder if it really is Coffee that keeps me sallow, skinny and sick most of the time."
Miss Comfort: "I used to do a bit of wondering, too, until I tried it out by quitting Coffee and using Postum."
"THERE'S A REASON" for POSTUM
Postum Cereal Co., Ltd., Battle Creek, Mich., U. S. A.

Ads for Post products often contrasted robust, attractive consumers of those products with frail nonconverts. Other ads used testimonials obtained from Post-sponsored contests in obscure magazines. Cash prizes were offered for the best responses to requests such as "Give name and account of one or more coffee drinkers who have been hurt by it and who have been induced to quit and use Postum."

Welcome to Wellville

Among the many philosophical heirs of Sylvester Graham was Charles W. Post, a traveling salesman and sometime venture capitalist. Chronically bedeviled by digestive disorders and other health problems, Post tried a number of "cures," with little success. In 1884 he found his way to the Battle Creek Sanitarium, a widely touted health spa directed by John Harvey Kellogg, M.D.

Patient Post endured a variety of treatments and some curious regimens at Kellogg's "San," including the Grahamite diet and instruction in the "Chewing Song," a ditty Kellogg had composed to encourage thorough mastication. He came away after nine months no stronger than when he had gone in. "Given up on by the doctors," as he would later claim, Post took his troubles to a Battle Creek Christian Science practitioner. Within two days his appetite and strength returned. Post was convinced that he owed his recovery to a combination of natural foods and positive mental suggestion, and that there were untold marketing opportunities in such an approach. He opened his own spa and began experimenting with ways to prepare more palatable health foods. In 1895 he launched a bran, wheat, and molasses-based no-caffeine coffee substitute called Postum. Grape-Nuts, a gritty "scientific" formulation that had neither grapes nor nuts in its cereal mix, appeared in 1898. These were followed in 1906 by "Elijah's Manna," an earnest entry in the cornflakes sweepstakes, later rechristened Post Toasties.

Post's new products, marketed with some of the most persuasive advertising ever devised, brought him great wealth. But he never lost his conviction that "Sickness is man-made," and that people would choose a healthier way if only shown how. To this end he published "The Road to Wellville," a prescriptive pamphlet that explained how to maximize health by consuming Post products — and thoughtfully enclosed a copy in every package.

Chew, Chew Training

"Nature will castigate those who don't masticate," scolded Horace Fletcher. Denied life insurance in 1895 because he was both overweight and dyspeptic, Fletcher was jolted into reforming his habits. He developed, by his own account, a new, "progressive" way to live and resolved to share his health-promoting discoveries with others.

According to Fletcher bad health was traceable to the pernicious habit of bolting meals. To attain "economic digestion," followers were to eat only so long as hunger dictated, and to masticate — that is, chew — every bite until the last nuance of taste was extracted and the food reduced to a creamy pulp. He noted that 30 chews per mouthful usually did the trick. But some particularly resilient foods, such as green onions, might need as many as 700 chews before being subdued.

The fad swept the country and everyone from the cadets at West Point to the renowned Harvard philosopher William James was dutifully, endlessly chewing. James however, probably spoke for many when he later confessed, "I had to give it up, it nearly killed me."

The Great Begatsby

"The man who is looking for health, but does not want muscles, will search in vain," proclaimed publisher and fitness guru Bernarr Macfadden at the turn of the century. The brawny five-foot-six Macfadden bounded onto the health scene touting a combination of nutrition and "kinesitherapy," or weight lifting. In books and magazines, published by his own Physical Culture Publishing Company, Macfadden gleefully explained how to perfect everything from the scalp (controlled hair-pulling) to the toes (walking barefoot). Dismissing pure vegetarianism as too pallid to produce optimum vigor, he nonetheless warned that man's appetite for animal flesh often led to overindulgence, and prescribed a periodic purgative of fasting.

Macfadden startled his readers with frank and quirky practices to tone up the sexual organs, often with devices sold through his magazines. And his third wife, 26 years his junior, publicly called her husband "the Great Begatsby" in tribute to his "powers."

For all his eccentricities, Macfadden deserved his lifelong celebrity for feats of stamina and derring-do. When well into his seventies, he was still lecturing while standing on his head, and still hiking in his own annual Macfadden-sponsored 325-mile long "Cracked Wheat Derby." He died at 87, apparently as the result of a routine three-day fast.

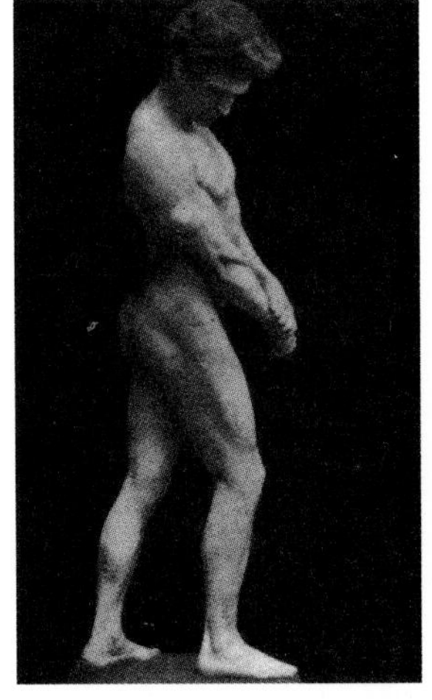

Macfadden was unabashed about displaying his carefully crafted physique in support of his cause (above). He celebrated his 75th birthday by giving an interview while standing on his head, and marked his 83rd with a parachute jump over the Hudson River (left).

ALL-TIME FAVORITES

Candy-Coated Popcorn, Peanuts, and a Prize

A prize in every box! That is what generations of kids have looked forward to whenever they asked for Cracker Jack. But even before the popcorn, peanut, and molasses treat became identified with hidden treasure, it was one of America's favorite snacks.

First finding popularity in 1871 when Frederick Rueckheim concocted the confection and sold it from his Chicago popcorn stand, it met with even wider acclaim when Rueckheim and his brother introduced it at the 1893 World's Columbian Exposition. By 1899 Cracker Jack was distributed in snack-size boxes, and in 1908 it was immortalized in the song "Take Me Out to the Ball Game." When prizes were tucked into every package in 1912, Cracker Jack's success was assured.

From the beginning the prizes were remarkably inventive. There were whistles, watches, watch fobs, and even Cracker Jack piggybanks that held five pennies — just enough to buy the next box. With prizes numbering in the thousands, a child could expect a surprise with each new box he opened.

Cracker Jack sales soared in 1912 when prizes like these were first packed in the boxes.

In 1890's slang anything that was "crackerjack" was pretty darn good. Sailor Jack and his dog, Bingo, joined the distinctive red, white, and blue Cracker Jack label in 1918.

Prior to the use of plastic in the 1940's, the most durable prizes were molded from tin. But some of the most interesting were made of paper. Sports fans could collect several series of baseball cards, including one for the short-lived Federal League. Elaborate paper cutouts included an "Indian" headdress that, unfolded, was almost two feet long. Other prizes bore the likenesses of Sailor Jack and his dog, Bingo, the snack's mascots. Modeled after Rueckheim's grandson, Jack debuted on the logo in 1918, and he and Bingo appear to this day on every box of Cracker Jack.

A Sweet and Edible Kingdom

If the kids cannot go to the circus, bring the circus to the kids — this seems to have been the idea behind the introduction of animal crackers in 1902. Although animal-shaped cookies had long existed, it was the National Biscuit Company that took them out of bins and tins and put them into compact, colorful boxes. Initially the sweet treats were produced only at holiday time, but the string handle on each box, meant for hanging it on a Christmas tree, was soon deemed perfect for tyke-sized wrists, and animal crackers gained year-round popularity. Over the years the menagerie has taken the form of 37 animals. Up to 18 different beasts — produced at a rate of over half a million animals per hour — may inhabit each box, including the ever-popular lions, tigers, and bears, as well as hyenas, camels, and seals.

Biscuits by the Bowlful

It was breakfast time at a Nebraska hotel one morning in 1892 when lawyer Henry Perky noticed a man eating a bowlful of boiled wheat and milk. Helps my indigestion, the stranger explained. A fellow sufferer, Perky tried some himself, and so, legend has it, a cereal was born.

Back in his hometown of Denver, Perky built a machine that could shred moist wheat and fold the filaments into spongy, pillow-shaped biscuits. The biscuits tended to spoil quickly, but Perky found that baking preserved them. Believing the invention would make his fortune, Perky tried marketing his machine but soon discovered that no one wanted equipment for an unknown product. Undaunted, he decided to sell the cereal itself, peddling the biscuits door-to-door from a wagon.

Searching for a national market, Perky traveled east with his cereal and, in 1901, built a bakery at Niagara Falls. The move was a marketing coup. Thousands of tourists, still damp from the falls, visited the sparkling new plant and took home free samples. Before long, Shredded Wheat was a breakfast standard.

WHAT'S THAT SIZZLING SOUND I HEAR?
GET UP! IT'S SPAM AND EGGS, MY DEAR!

As a new product in the 1930's, SPAM was advertised (left) as ideal for everything from SPAM and eggs and baked SPAM, to the famous SPAMwich. Because it needed no refrigeration, SPAM was a staple during World War II. Members of one air force squadron (below) evidently got their fill and so named their post SPAMville.

A Slice of America

Innovate, don't imitate." That was Minnesota meat packer George Hormel's advice to his employees. So when the company that bears his name found itself with several thousand pounds of leftover pork shoulder, they transformed some of it into a unique product, a canned, minced pork and ham loaf that required no refrigeration. To market the product, Hormel offered a $100 prize for a catchy name, and the winning entry — SPAM — has since become a genuine slice of American folklore.

Introduced in 1937, SPAM by the tens of millions of pounds was shipped abroad during World War II. Many GIs remember it as the "ham that didn't pass its physical." No less a figure than Gen. Dwight D. Eisenhower, European Commander-in-Chief, ate his share of it too. "I'll even confess to a few unkind remarks about it," he joked some 20 years later, adding that of course they were "uttered during the strain of battle."

Today Hormel boasts that Americans use nearly four 7-ounce cans of SPAM a second. But not all of that is for eating. Austin, Texas, hosts an annual SPAM Olympics featuring a SPAM toss in which pairs of contestants toss a greased can between them until someone fumbles. At a 50th birthday party Hormel gave for itself in 1987, one celebrant carved a SPAM model of Auguste Rodin's "The Thinker." And entries in a SPAM sculpture contest in Seattle, Washington, included replicas of Uncle SPAM, FrankenSPAM, and a model of England's famous circle of Druidic stones — SPAMhenge.

American ingenuity, it seems, has known no bounds when it has come to finding uses for SPAM. One wag even dared to suggest "SPAM-on-a-Rope," for people who get hungry in the shower.

Spice of Life

When Edmund McIlhenny returned to his Avery Island, Louisiana, home at the end of the Civil War, he found little left of his family's sugarcane plantation and salt-mining operation. Casting about for some new way to make a living, McIlhenny focused on a patch of exotic red-pepper plants in the kitchen garden. Natives of Mexico, the peppers had an astonishingly hot taste that, McIlhenny hoped, would pique the interest of Louisiana's Creole cooks.

Chopping up the pepper pods, McIlhenny mixed them with Avery Island salt, then set the mash to age in oak barrels. When it had ripened to his liking, he added vinegar, decanted the brew into an assortment of old cologne bottles, and gave samples to friends. McIlhenny's fiery red sauce, which he called Tabasco — the name of a Mexican river — was an immediate success. In 1872 he patented the process for his pyrotechnic condiment and shortly after opened a London office to handle the swelling tide of foreign business. And his descendants are still making Tabasco on Avery Island, at the red-hot pace of about 180,000 bottles a day.

TIME TABLE

BRAND-NAME DEBUTS

1842 *Whitman's chocolate is marketed in Philadelphia.*

1857 *Gail Borden peddles sweetened condensed milk from a pushcart in Manhattan.*

1867 *Underwood recommends deviled ham as a sandwich spread.*

1868 *Fleischmann revolutionizes baking with the first standardized yeast.*

1868 *Libby McNeill & Libby sell their first meat products.*

1869 *Canned Campbell's soups appear in stores.*

1869 *Heinz produces pickled horseradish, the first of more than 57 varieties.*

1870 *Hires root beer is advertised as a temperance drink.*

1877 *Quaker Oats devises the Quaker trademark for its breakfast cereal.*

"Foreign" Foods From Next Door

When Americans visiting France in the 1940's first asked for "Vichyssoise," French chefs were puzzled. One restaurateur tried to oblige by serving a Vichy-style carrot-based concoction, astonishing the diners who expected leek and potato soup — a specialty, they thought, of the French town. But Vichyssoise is purely American, invented at New York's Ritz-Carlton Hotel and glamorized with a continental title.

Indeed, some of the most exotic fare on American menus comes not from far corners of the globe, but from not-so-faraway corners of the country. Pungent Liederkranz cheese, for instance, was created accidently when Emil Frey, a cheesemaker in Monroe, New York, was trying to make another kind entirely. His felicitous failure so delighted friends who sampled it at the Liederkranz singing society that the cheese was given their name.

Fiery chili con carne is another imposter. True, it is spiced with Mexican *chile ancho*. But one Mexican dictionary writes it off as "a detestable food with a false Mexican title which is sold in the United States." Texans, however, proudly claim the "bowl of red" as their own. Thought to have been invented in San Antonio during the late 1800's, the dish gained popularity after 1902, when a German immigrant figured out how to turn chili peppers into chili powder, allowing the spice to travel.

Other familiar foods took names from garbled foreign words. Chinese laborers building this country's railroads in the 1800's, for example, dubbed their usual fare — a mix of vegetables and meat over rice — *tsa sui*, meaning odds and ends. *Tsa sui* became chop suey, and it remains one of the homegrown exotics that brings lively and welcome flavors to American tables.

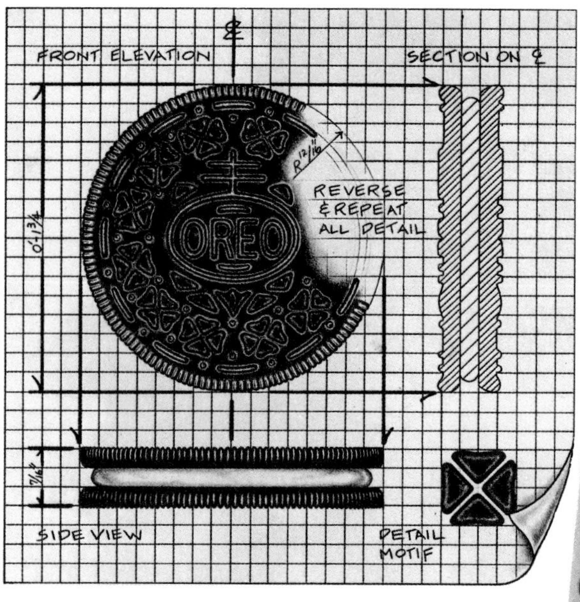

Oreo's simple schematic design (above left) has been reproduced more than 200 billion times since 1912. Popular with tea in the early years, the cookies were also served as a dessert with dinner (above).

The Little Cookie That Could

On March 6, 1912, a New Jersey grocer, S. C. Thuesen, made history when he purchased a 9¼-pound tin of chocolate-sandwich cookies. Little did Thuesen know that he was the first person ever to buy what would become the best-selling cookie in the world: Oreos, which now sell at a rate of some 6 billion cookies a year. It is estimated, in fact, that if all the Oreos produced since Thuesen's time could be stacked, there would be enough to reach the moon four times.

Conceived as one of a trio of English-style tea cookies (the others were Veronese and Mother Goose biscuits), Oreos are the only one of the three still produced. Since the beginning, their design has been round and flat, with embossed decoration and a creamy filling. But the size of Oreos has varied considerably. The familiar 1¾-inch two-bite size produced today is about halfway between the large chocolate sandwich of 1912 and a later, tiny, pop-in-the-mouth version. Curiously, while many of the facts and figures connected with the cookies' past are a matter of record, no one remembers how or why Oreos got their name.

"Don't these guys ever eat anything but Baby Ruth?"
Well, Soldier, anywhere and anytime you do "fatigue" duty, you'll think the same . . .
Because wherever our fighters go, Baby Ruth goes too. And so do many other fine foods produced and packaged by Curtiss Candy Company.
Our big food plants are working day and night to keep pace with the demands of the Armed Forces . . . and the home front as well.
Active, hard-working people realize that Baby Ruth and Butterfinger are *great* candy bars, rich in dextrose sugar, providing real food energy to help folks fight fatigue, to carry on their work and play.
While we are not always able to keep all dealers supplied with Baby Ruth and Butterfinger we promise you our best efforts to produce both the quantity you demand and the quality you expect of these great American Candy Bars.
Baby Ruth
BUY U. S. WAR BONDS AND STAMPS
When you don't find BABY RUTH on the candy counter, remember . . . Uncle Sam's needs come first with us as with you.
CURTISS CANDY COMPANY • Producers of Fine Foods • CHICAGO, ILLINOIS

Otto Schnering, the man who brought us Baby Ruth, Butterfinger, and other treats from the Curtiss Candy Company, loved a good advertising gimmick. In the 1920's he hired biplanes (above) to bombard 40 cities with Baby Ruth bars fitted with little parachutes. The campaign was so successful that by 1926 Schnering's chocolate-covered peanut bar was the best-selling brand in America. The sales pitch at the left appeared during World War II.

America's Sweetest Success Stories

After three failures in as many cities, Milton Hershey had finally made it big in the candy business. His delicious caramels had made him one of the wealthiest citizens of Lancaster, Pennsylvania. But as he strolled through Chicago's 1893 World's Columbian Exposition, Hershey saw something that changed his life: chocolate-making machinery.

Before long, Hershey was churning out chocolate cigars, flowers, and similar novelties. All this was a mere prelude, however, to the creation that would make mouths water at the mention of Hershey's name — the candy bar.

In 1894 Hershey introduced his milk chocolate and chocolate-and-almond bars. Then, selling the caramel business for $1 million in 1900, he built a chocolate factory in southeastern Pennsylvania. An entire town grew up around the industry. Saddled at first with the name Hersheykoko, the town came to be called simply Hershey.

Although Hershey was the undisputed chocolate king, he did have competitors, only some of whom identified their products with their own names. Several, however, chose to name their candy bars and bonbons after other people. Leo Hirschfield's daughter, for instance, lent her nickname, Tootsie, to his chewy, chocolaty "rolls" in 1896. When Otto Schnering launched a new peanutty candy bar called Baby Ruth in 1920, the tribute was not to the hard-hitting Babe of baseball, but to President Grover Cleveland's daughter, who had charmed the nation as a toddler. Then, in the 1930's, Philip Silverstein gave his sweet block of chocolate the same pet name that he used for his chubby little granddaughter — Chunky. The candy itself, which was chockablock full of nuts and raisins, more than adequately fit the description.

While girls seemed to predominate, at least one chocolate bar was named for a young man. The fellow in question was a frequent visitor at George Williamson's Chicago candy shop, where he liked to flirt with the candymakers. He showed up so often, in fact, that the women began asking him to do odd jobs, inevitably starting their requests with "Oh, Henry." When Williamson needed a name for a new candy bar (Baby Ruth's rival) in 1921, Oh Henry! came easily to mind.

1890 *Aunt Jemima ready-mix pancakes are introduced as a new breakfast fare.*

1891 *Fig Newtons (named after Newton, Massachusetts) become one of America's favorite cookies.*

1891 *Del Monte begins to can fruits and vegetables.*

1894 *Our Pet evaporated milk with its cow logo appears on the market.*

1895 *C. W. Post invents Postum, a no-caffeine breakfast drink.*

1897 *A popular gelatin dessert is dubbed Jell-O.*

1907 *Kellogg's Toasted Corn Flakes are marketed as a breakfast food.*

1911 *Crisco is chosen as the winning entry in a product-naming contest sponsored by Procter & Gamble.*

1912 *Lifesavers is adopted as the name for little mints with holes in their centers.*

1916 *Planters Nut and Chocolate Company introduces Mr. Peanut.*

1921 *Betty Crocker is invented to answer questions from customers at Gold Medal Flour.*

1928 *Gerber Baby Food markets its first five varieties at 15 cents a can.*

1947 *Miss Chiquita, the animated banana, begins her singing and dancing career.*

Dipped in chocolate, baked in crusts, popped on sticks, or straight from the cone — the cool richness of ice cream delights kids of all ages.

I Scream, You Scream

Velvety smooth and delectably cold, ice cream was an exotic treat before an inventive New Jersey woman turned her hand to making it.

Nancy Johnson could have made a fortune. Instead, she made ice cream. In 1846 Johnson invented the simple hand-cranked freezer that allowed ice cream to be made at home with relative ease. Inexplicably, she never patented, and thus never profited from, her creation.

Before the advent of Johnson's brainchild, ice cream was laboriously made by filling a bowl with cream, nesting it in a second bowl filled with ice, then whipping the cream energetically while shaking the whole assembly up and down. The luscious dessert that resulted had long been a favorite of George Washington. Over the course of the summer of 1790, the first president avidly ate his way through $200 worth of ice cream imported from New York. To further satisfy his sweet tooth, Mount Vernon's kitchen included "two pewter ice cream pots." After a visit to Philadelphia he brought back a contraption described as a "Cream Machine for Making Ice."

Thomas Jefferson had also turned the light of his prodigious ingenuity on the frosty confection and came up with an 18-step process for its manufacture — and a recipe for something similar to Baked Alaska. His version seems to have been only moderately successful. After sampling it, one guest grumbled: "Ice cream very good, crust wholly dried crumbled into thin flakes."

With the rise of commercial ice production, the ice cream industry really boomed. Street vendors hawked it with the popular cry "I Scream, Ice Cream." The appeal of the frozen dessert was lost on Ralph Waldo Emerson, however. "We dare not trust our wit for making our house pleasant to our friends," he sniffed. "So we buy ice cream." But temperance advocates touted it as the perfect treat for diverting an alcohol-dulled palate. And that indispensable household adviser, *Godey's Lady's Book,* opined: "A party without ice cream would be like a breakfast without bread or a dinner without roast."

Over the years an astonishing array of flavors had arisen to tempt the taste buds. Flowers such as rose and violet made brief appearances; various fruits, including persimmons and casaba melons, were tried. One adventurous manufacturer combined root beer and horseradish; another came up with a sauerkraut sherbet, but they didn't catch on. Vanilla quickly emerged as the most sought-after flavor.

From the Civil War forward, the military used ice cream to boost morale. During World War I, it was declared an "essential foodstuff" and escaped rationing restrictions. In World War II American bomber crews based in England went to great heights for it. They mixed all the ingredients for ice cream in sealed cans and placed them in the rear compartment of their airplanes. Once aloft, the plane's vibrations churned the mixture and the high altitude chilled it so that one of the rewards of a safe landing was a dish of perfectly blended ice cream.

Fizz Kings

The American passion for sparkling water dates back at least to 1825 when Elié Magliore Durand opened a drugstore in Philadelphia that counted soda water among its wares. Created in imitation of nature's effervescent waters, the fizzy elixir was touted as a health drink and compared to the waters of European spas.

In the mid-1830's John Matthews came up with a new method for making the needed gas. By combining sulfuric acid with marble chips left over from the construction of St. Patrick's Cathedral in New York City, he bubbled up some 25 million gallons of water.

Matthews also developed a crate-sized apparatus that could be placed on a pharmacist's counter to dispense carbonated water. This simple fountain quickly metamorphosed into exuberant assemblages of mirrors, marble, and metal such as the one James Tufts operated at the Philadelphia Centennial Exposition in 1876. Tufts paid $50,000 to be the fair's sole source of sodas, which he dispensed from a 30-foot-tall fountain that was decorated with "statues, globes, and every attraction money can command."

But however fanciful, some of the dispensers had a practical side as well. One manufacturer, A. D. Puffer and Sons of Boston, Massachusetts, boasted that each of its fountains came with a hose that transformed the apparatus into the "best fire annihilator ever made."

Another innovation, the great marriage of soda and ice cream, happened by chance in 1874 when soda fountain operator Robert Green ran out of the cream he used to flavor his drinks. He hastily obtained some vanilla ice cream, slipped it into his sodas, and hoped his customers wouldn't notice the difference. They did — and sales soared from $6 to $600 a day. When Green died, "Originator of the Ice Cream Soda" was inscribed as his epitaph.

Soda jerks delighted customers with their acrobatic style and creative concoctions.

Soda fountains were endorsed by temperance societies as wholesome alternatives to taverns. Some clergymen, however, railed against "sucking soda" on the Sabbath, and in some places selling soda water on Sunday was outlawed. But the drink itself may not have been the real object of their ire. "Young people do not go for country walks in America," wrote a foreign observer, "They chiefly consort in ice cream parlors."

By the early decades of the 20th century, soda water was completely divorced from its heritage as a health beverage. Some soda fountains became huge, tiled palaces — a few seated as many as 1,000 people. Armed with siphon and scoop, white-jacketed soda jerks (so called from the sharp pull they exercised on the fountain levers) created malteds, floats, and whipped ice cream drinks. Overwhelmed by the elaborate potions, one consumer complained, "I freeze in vari-colored gobs of ice cream.... Floods of syrup engulf me." But thousands more happily trooped to their corner stores and made sipping soda a time-honored American tradition.

The splashy three-story soda fountain James Tufts took to the Philadelphia Centennial featured a fern-bedecked fountain of perfumed water as well as the more mundane dispensers devoted to soda and syrups.

The Bean and the Bottle

"We need a bottle which a person will recognize as a Coca-Cola bottle even when he feels it in the dark! The Coca-Cola bottle should be so shaped that, even if broken, a person could tell at a glance what it was." This challenge, offered by the Coca-Cola Company in 1913, was met by the glass makers at the Root Company in Terre Haute, Indiana. Inspired by the plump, rippled cocoa bean pod, the Root team came up with the unmistakable silhouette in pale green glass that has meant "Coke" to generations of thirsty folks since 1916.

EATING OUT

An English cartoonist lampooned American diners as the "Minute Men of 1880."

Gobble, Gulp, and Go

The speed with which Americans eat is sometimes seen as a reaction to the quickening pace of the 20th century. But in fact we have always been a nation of gobblers.

The habit may well have begun with the Puritans. Condemning all sensual pleasures as sinful indulgences, they wolfed down their meals in dour silence. Nor had the practice changed much by the mid-1800's, when one amazed observer commented: "I'll be d——d if ever I saw a Yankee that didn't bolt his food whole like a Boa Constrictor."

Yankees were not the only ones to be singled out. A writer for the New York *World* described the western dining style as, "Dab, dab, peck, peck, grunt, growl, snort!" And an eastern critic declared that when Americans ate, it was with "one undistinguishable flash of knife and fork." In most hotels and many households, after all, it was customary to put all the food on the table at the same time. He who helped himself first — and fastest — left with the fullest belly.

Europeans also marveled at the energetic spectacle of the mealtime in America. In the 1820's the Italian Count Carlo Vidua described a family dinner at which "each enters the room, says not a word . . . devours in a few instants the few ill-cooked dishes, and . . . without waiting till the others have finished, rises, takes his hat and is off." Another foreign observer was even more to the point: the nation's motto, he wrote, seemed to be "Gobble, gulp, and go."

Eating on the Run

For travelers in the early years of railroads, there was virtually no such thing as a civilized meal. Even after the appearance of the first dining car in 1868, many passengers brought their own box lunches, which they bolted down as they rattled along. "The bouquet from those lunches hung around all day," reported one disgruntled rider, "and the flies wired ahead for their friends to meet them at each station."

Eating at the station was hardly an improvement: some of the worst food in the country was served at depot lunchrooms. And the facilities worsened as the train went westward. By the time one Connecticut passenger had reached the Great Plains, he described the dining rooms (called "quick-lunches") as "miserable shanties, with tables dirty, and waiters not only dirty but saucy."

By Easterners' standards the food was often exotic. At one Nebraska stop, passengers discovered that the "chicken stew" served for breakfast was in fact prairie dog. Other menus routinely included buffalo steaks and antelope chops. But whatever the fare, it did not vary much from one stop to the next. Wrote one New Yorker, "It was necessary to look at one's watch to tell whether it was breakfast, dinner or supper we were eating."

Trains usually stopped in stations for a mere 15 minutes. Hundreds of hungry passengers seized the opportunity and stampeded the depot restaurant, where cooks stood ready with heaping platters. Everyone ate hastily and then, sated, surged back into the cars.

Railroad dining cars were carefully designed to match the gracious ambience and efficient service that could be found in first-class hotels. Even so, serving — or eating — a meal on a swaying train required a good deal of grace and balance.

First-Class Fare

Thanks to George Pullman, everything from soup to nuts — and usually several varieties of each — was there for the asking while riding the rails.

For the price of a dollar, travelers ordering from the menu of a railroad dining car in the late 1800's could enjoy a large, varied, and leisurely meal. A passenger might begin with oysters followed by salmon, then a bit of roast quail, and perhaps a ragout of mutton, all appropriately sauced. There would be an extensive choice of pastries, French cheeses, and wines. Champagne was available at any meal — even breakfast. And all was served by attentive white-jacketed waiters in a setting fit for the finest hotel.

Several companies built elegant dining cars for the various railroads, but the man credited with inventing luxury travel was George Pullman. Known for his innovative "sleepers," Pullman in 1868 unveiled his first "diner," which he grandly named the *Delmonico* after one of New York City's finest restaurants. At $20,000 it cost nearly twice as much as a steam locomotive — but it set a standard of service that endured well into the 20th century.

The typical diner was 60 to 70 feet long and 10 feet wide. Its pantry and tiny kitchen (some had working areas as small as eight square feet) were miracles of efficiency. Tucked in every nook and cranny were meticulously organized stashes of crockery, glassware, linen, silverware, and ample supplies of food and beverages.

Even as late as the 1940's these diminutive food factories were powered by coal stoves. Perishables were stowed in an ice chest under the floor. Armed with hundreds of pans and implements, the staff of six — usually two cooks and four waiters — could turn out as many as 250 meals in a day. Special events demanded special offerings: at Christmas in 1890 one rail line offered a 12-course holiday meal featuring 45 different dishes.

The wood-paneled dining area, which accommodated up to 48 at a sitting, was often lavishly appointed with chandeliers, carpets, and picture windows. Fresh flowers brightened each linen-draped table. Passengers relaxed in upholstered chairs, gazed out at the ever-changing view, and dined their way across America in style.

The real Harvey Girls (top) were not as glamorous as the movie stars, including Judy Garland (above), who portrayed them in a 1944 film. They were, however, efficient, well educated, well mannered, and a most welcome sight to hungry, harried passengers and railroadmen.

Fine Dining at the Depot

"She was winsome, she was neat." So said one delighted customer of the comely, capable waitresses who came to be known as the Harvey Girls.

Englishman Fred Harvey had worked in restaurants and on railcars for 26 years when in 1876 he came up with an unheard-of plan. At a time when railroad lunchrooms were notoriously grim, he suggested opening a clean, high-quality dining room at the Topeka depot of the Atchison, Topeka, and Santa Fe line. Eager to try anything that might attract passengers, the fledgling railroad's managers readily agreed to Harvey's plan.

His civilized dining room and fine food were an instant success. "They make you take off your hat and put on a coat," one startled customer explained, ". . . but the grub is strictly A-No. 1." Soon opening more restaurants at other depots along the line, Harvey kept both local residents and rail travelers coming back time and again — and not just for the mouth-watering fare. Harvey's establishments offered an even greater attraction for lonesome men of the West: waitresses.

Harvey had advertised in newspapers around the country for attractive, intelligent "young women of good character," and was inundated with responses. Carefully interviewed, rigorously trained, and strictly chaperoned, the competent, crisply uniformed Harvey Girls were an immediate hit. Though their contracts prohibited marriage for at least a year, an estimated 5,000 of them wed ranchers and Santa Fe railroadmen.

Harvey's empire eventually grew to 47 depot restaurants, 30 dining cars, 15 hotels, and a ferry that crisscrossed San Francisco Bay. But his most important legacy may have been the introduction of "civilization's advance guard" in the perfectly groomed forms of the Harvey Girls.

Extravagance à la Carte

Prodigality was the order of the day during the gaudy Gilded Age. Treating food as more than mere sustenance, the new-made millionaires of the late 1800's spent fortunes on dazzling dinners, banquets, breakfasts, and balls, each one more elaborate than the last.

The meals were sumptuous 10- to 14-course affairs that featured everything from oysters to ice cream. But the food was superfluous, for the real point was the brash display of cash.

Amusements at these parties might include music by two or three orchestras, a Broadway play with its original cast, or an entire dance troupe. Party favors, such as real pearls among the oysters or cigarettes wrapped in hundred-dollar bills, were exquisite — and expensive.

Live animals, perhaps on loan from local zoos, sometimes formed the centerpiece for an event. In 1873 guests at the Swan Banquet sat down at a table "eighteen feet wide and as long as the hall," with a huge artificial lake at its center. Surrounded with flowers and foliage and crowned with a gilded cage crafted by Tiffany's, the lake show-

cased several stately swans. There was an unscheduled sideshow when two males erupted into a honking, splashing melee — the banquet, it seems, coincided with the birds' mating season. And in 1903 at C. K. G. Billings's Horseback Dinner, 36 steeds, shod in rubber, were brought to a fourth-floor dining hall. Guests sat tall in saddles with tables attached and used rubber tubes to sip champagne from their saddlebags.

Such flamboyance was in sharp contrast to the poverty in urban slums, and public censure drove more than one magnate into self-imposed exile in Europe. By the dawn of the Jazz Age, extravagant feasting had fallen from fashion.

Gilded Age nabobs flaunted their wealth in rounds of fabulous feasting. Whether an elegant dinner in the dining room of one of New York City's finest hotels (below) or an informal costume party at home (inset), the courses were multiple, the settings magnificent, and the guests the crême de la crême of the new elite.

Brady's Bountiful Board

Around the turn of the century, an era notable for big spenders and big eaters, one man — Diamond Jim Brady — came to exemplify both. Famed for his exuberant appetite, he was a familiar figure at restaurants. The owner of one favorite eatery even dubbed Brady "the best twenty-five customers we have."

Often accompanied by actress Lillian Russell, who was herself a world-class eater, Brady could devour three or four servings of everything on a 14-course menu. He chomped chocolates by the pound and washed it all down with orange juice or soda — he never touched liquor — by the gallon.

The secret of Diamond Jim Brady's prodigious feats of feasting was revealed in 1912 when he underwent surgery: doctors found his stomach was six times the normal size.

Duncan Hines, Dinner Detective

"As a boy the only thing I was really interested in was eating," claimed Duncan Hines. But he was 58 before he could devote himself full-time to his consuming passion.

From 1905 until 1938, when he quit his job as a traveling salesman, Hines spent much of his life on the road. A methodical man with a discriminating palate, he compiled a list of "superior eating places" that he had found in his travels. When friends began to beleaguer him with requests for restaurant recommendations, Hines thought he could put an end to the pestering by distributing his list in lieu of Christmas cards. But the ploy only redoubled demand for his coveted catalog. So in 1936 he bound his list in red paper, titled it *Adventures in Good Eating,* and offered it for sale.

Within two years hungry nomads had snapped up so many copies that Hines retired and took to the road as America's unofficial dinner detective. He traveled incognito — his books deliberately sported a decades-old photo — and always paid for everything he sampled. A champion of simply prepared fresh food, Hines extolled his chosen eateries in equally simple prose. "Service is plain," read one report, "but, oh, such pie!"

Hines's reputation for quality and integrity led to many invitations for endorsements. In 1949 he gave his nod of approval to a line of prepared foods that included the cake mixes which have made his name a household word.

From Dog Wagons to Roadside Diners

America's romance with diners began more than 100 years ago. Once actually mobile, lunch wagons remain popular with people on the move.

The granddads of diners were horse-drawn lunch wagons that could be wheeled up anywhere that promised a brisk noontime trade. At first, food was simply passed out through a window. Then in the 1880's Sam Jones, of Worcester, Massachusetts, got the idea of installing a counter and seating inside his wagon. The idea caught on, and Jones was joined by a friend who worked the evening hours, selling hot dogs to "night owls," thus earning the eateries their nicknames, "dog wagons" and "owl cars."

If the food was simple, the coffee was hot and respectability reigned — so much so, in fact, that the Women's Temperance League bought a few owl cars of its own to tempt tipplers out of bars and "on the wagon" with the promise of good, cheap meals. The wagons' honor sagged, however, when electric trolleys were introduced at century's end and a glut of decrepit old horse-drawn tram cars were converted to use as lunch wagons. Set on permanent sites, many of them soon became such seedy dives that no lady dared enter.

Businessman Patrick Tierney set out to change that image in 1905. Since railroad dining cars then were among America's classiest restaurants, Tierney borrowed their romance and called his cars "diners." Offering such models as the "Comet" and the "Philadelphia Flyer," he hauled each one ready-made to the buyer's property. They were sleek and fine, had newfangled indoor plumbing, and booths, or "seating for ladies." By the time he died in 1917, Tierney had rescued the lunch-car trade.

And as diners became more luxurious, their popularity grew. In 1937 they drew more than a million customers daily, and by 1948, 13 companies were turning out 250 ready-made diners a year, each one customized for its owner, each one unique.

In 1915, when the Iroquois Lunch served customers, diners were modeled after railroad dining cars. Factory built, they were delivered to their sites complete with counters, stools, dishes, and decoration.

A Sticky Problem, a Sweet Solution

Somewhat off his usual route, this driver dashed to a Long Island airfield in 1932 to satisfy a cross-country flier's need for a little Good Humor.

It was a January night in 1920, and Harry Burt had a problem: the Ohio ice-cream parlor owner's version of the newly popular chocolate-coated ice cream was too messy to hold. But Burt's resourceful son came up with a solution. Looking over a display of the shop's own brand of lollipops — Good Humor Suckers — he suggested putting the treats on sticks. It worked like a charm, and so Good Humor bars were born.

The story, of course, did not end there. Burt had other novel ideas for his product. Even before he was granted a patent for his ice-cream-on-a-stick, he had a fleet of sparkling white trucks and white-suited Good Humor men selling ice cream bars on local streets. From the start each truck's arrival in a neighborhood was announced by the cheerful jingling of bells. Children quickly learned to come running at the sound.

In 1926 the company was sold and franchised nationally. But business really began to boom in 1929 when the Chicago franchise refused to pay gangsters for "protection," and eight trucks were blown up. The event received so much news coverage that sales went through the roof.

Since then, the company's trucks have become a symbol of summer, and pure affection has provided the publicity. Drivers have appeared in countless cartoons, on at least one magazine cover, in over 100 movies, and were even the subject of a film — *The Good Humor Man*.

NATIVE TONGUE

A FEAST FOR THE EARS

Rapid-fire, wisecracking, and endlessly inventive, lunch-counter lingo is as American as apple pie (itself a dish often ordered with the cry "Eve with a lid on"). As early as 1852, a Detroit newspaper marveled at the mystery of waiters calling to the kitchen with requests for such fare as "fried bedpost, mashed tambourine and roasted stirrups." Sadly no record remains of what those culinary delights were. Later in the 19th century, prominent churchman Henry Ward Beecher was fond of requesting the particularly apt "Adam and Eve on a raft" — or two poached eggs on toast.

Often employed more for showmanship than ease of ordering, lunch-counter lingo blended everything from geography to current events. A "Dionne surprise," named for the famous Canadian quintuplets, was a sundae made with five small scoops of vanilla ice cream. "Irish turkey" was corned beef and cabbage, and "Coney Island chicken" a hot dog on a bun.

For the strong of heart, "hemorrhage" meant ketchup, a must with "gentleman will take a chance," short-order slang for the dish that has come to symbolize lunch-counter meals: a plate of hash.

Though they looked like mobile restaurants, White Tower's cleverly designed vehicles were simply delivery trucks that took hamburger buns and patties to each shop while providing advertising on the road.

Short Orders and Tall Towers

When Thomas Saxe and his father sat down to design a hamburger-and-coffee fast-food eatery, they searched for a concept and a name that would capture the workingman's imagination. At last they had it, and in late 1926 the first White Tower restaurant opened on a busy street corner in Milwaukee.

Vaguely medieval and shiny white, the one-story building with tower was a beacon of culinary cleanliness and dependability, where ordinary folks could always get wholesome food at a reasonable price. The idea was an immediate success, and by 1935 the Saxes had a chain of more than 130 tidy hamburger shops that stretched from Minneapolis to Boston.

Most of the early White Towers were tiny, a single room with a counter and a mere five or six stools. But almost every item on the limited menu cost just five cents, food was cooked to order before the customers' eyes, and service was unfailingly fast and friendly. Never mind that the hamburgers weighed only an ounce, the buns were just two inches across, and the "plates" were paper napkins; in the Depression years everyone was a potential customer. Working people also appreciated the fact that White Towers were open around the clock; to make the point, shops in the early years had no locks on their doors.

As times changed, the Saxes adapted their winning formula to keep pace with the times. New White Tower buildings were often a little larger, some had booths and stools with backs, and the basic menu was expanded. But management continued to like "quick nickels better than slow quarters," and they kept customers coming back with the promise of good, plain food at low prices.

By 1945, when New York artist Reginald Marsh sketched his *White Tower Hamburger*, the restaurant chain and its ever-present slogan "Buy a bagful" were familiar to urban Americans from virtually every walk of life.

Realistic even to the "ice cream" mounded in the open "cartons," this 1930's Berlin, Connecticut, roadside stop no doubt set many a traveler's mouth a-watering.

Putting the Show on the Road

Call it ingenuity, call it tacky commercialism, call it pure whimsy — the notion of constructing buildings in shapes that represent the food and services sold within is a genuine American phenomenon. Born in the early decades of the automobile age, the idea behind this kind of audacious architecture-as-advertising was to get travelers to slow down, look twice, and pull off the road to buy.

The symbolism of many designs left no room for confusion: a huge orange-painted sphere for an orangeade stand, a gigantic cup and saucer for a coffee shop, a towering milk bottle for dairy products. The meaning of other emblems was less direct, as in the canine-shaped café selling hot dogs, or the igloo featuring cold drinks. And some were downright mysterious, as, for example, an eatery in the shape of a gargantuan screech owl. Drive-by customers presumably braked out of sheer curiosity — "Look, dear, let's stop at that giant owl" — only to discover they had arrived at an ice cream stand emblazoned with the slogan "I scream."

Officially labeled with the stuffy tag "programmatic architecture," these wacky roadside attractions peaked in popularity between 1928 and 1934, the early years of the Great Depression. Not surprisingly, they reached their exuberant best in southern California, where showmanship dominated the refreshment business as it did most other sectors of life. For a while, at least, the region offered few building rules or codes that might stifle eccentricity.

For the most part the designer-builders were amateurs looking for sure-fire ways to launch their own mom-and-pop businesses. Giant corncobs, walk-in lunchpails, two-story ice cream cones, homey teapots, capacious chili bowls, and rib joints in the shape of porkers were some of the hog-wild results, but relatively few of these emblematic edifices still stand. Rarely built for posterity, many simply crumbled with age or were torn down to make room for urban expansion in the 1940's and '50's. Those that do remain are increasingly treated as folk art: worth saving, or even emulating.

The Hoot Hoot I Scream stand, built in 1925, was among the most famous of the 70-odd programmatic buildings that once enlivened Los Angeles and environs.

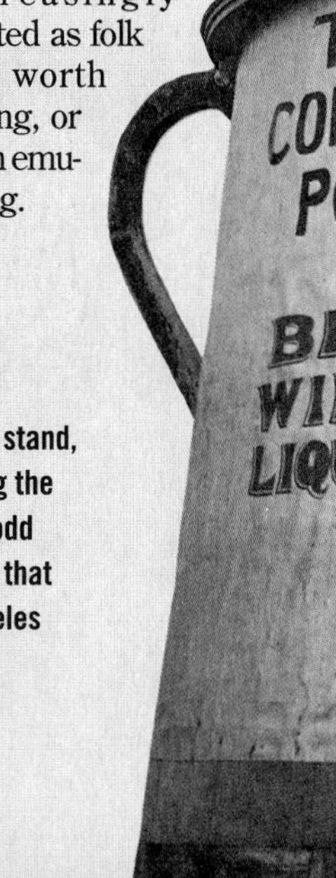

Located on a busy street corner in the heart of Bedford, Pennsylvania, this eatery was as much a draw for locals as it was for people passing through.

There is no telling what bulldogs had to do with ice cream and tamales. But then, with double-dip cones selling for only five cents, visitors at the Dog Café in Los Angeles in 1928 probably did not really care.

With a name like Van De Kamp, what could a man do in 1921 but build his Los Angeles bakery (above) in the form of a Dutch windmill and dress up his sales help to match? All that customers at Hollywood's 1946 Tail o' the Pup (right) had to do to get served was step up and call in their order through a hole in the hot dog roll. Sitting inside A. Mason's Los Angeles Airplane Café (below) was the closest that most people had come to flying in 1927. Planes, in fact, were among the more popular themes.

TIPPLERS AND TEETOTALERS

Please Don't Drink the Water

When running for his first political office in 1758, young Col. George Washington courted 391 potential voters by passing out a total of 160 gallons of rum, rum punch, wine, and beer. Though he won the election, he worried that he might have "spent with too sparing a hand."

Washington, in fact, was simply following a tradition of tippling that came to the New World aboard the *Mayflower*. As one shipboard diarist had noted, the colonists' northern landing was due, in part, to "our victuals being much spent, especially our beere." And although New England Puritans punished habitual drunkards with fines, the stocks, and a scarlet "D" emblazoned on their clothing, they thought nothing of downing spirits mixed with water at every meal. For adults and children alike, it was the preferred alternative to chancy water supplies.

Other high-potency options included imported whiskey, wine, brandy, and gin, domestic applejack by the barrelful, and a variety of home brews improvised from grains and other ingredients. As homespun versifiers cheerily proclaimed, "Oh we can make liquor to sweeten our lips/Of pumpkins, of parsnips, of walnut-tree chips."

Rum, however, exceeded all other drinks in popularity. One dissenter dismissed it as a "hot hellish and terrible liquor," and many referred to it with such colorful names as "Kill-devil," "Stink-e-buss," and "Rattle-Skull." Yet rum was consumed in great quantities at virtually all social gatherings, from church dedications to patriotic celebrations and funerals. By the turn of the 18th century, enough Yankee rum was being sold in the colonies to provide every man, woman, and child with an intoxicating 3¾ gallons per year.

LEGEND AND LORE

Foremost among the supersots in America's past was Revolutionary War hero Ethan Allen. He drank so much, some said, that it was booze, not blood, that coursed through his veins. Once, for example, Allen and a friend, on a long trek, lay down in the woods for a nap. Awakened by a rattling sound, the friend found a rattlesnake coiled around Allen and taking a bite. The friend tore it off, but the snake didn't go far. It slithered off tipsily, then collapsed — dead drunk.

A Tavern in the Town

America's first taverns appeared as soon as colonials began traveling from town to town. Located along turnpikes, at crossroads, at fords or falls in rivers, and at landings along the seashore, they quickly became the social hubs of the surrounding communities.

Here were places where the talkative and well-traveled could exchange news, receive mail, and strike deals. Locals might drop in to attend circuit court, sign up for the militia, read posted proclamations, or hear an informal "seminary of sedition" taught by some political agitator.

Licensed tavern owners frequently became people of considerable influence. Not only was there little in the way of gossip or political activity that escaped them, but their wide acquaintanceships and high visibility got them elected to second jobs as magistrates, church wardens, sheriffs, and legislators. Women found tavern-keeping a respectable occupation, though they usually took charge of a husband's business only when widowed. Recognizing the social importance of taverns, colonial governments passed laws that encouraged their establishment.

Room at the inn

Taverns provided "entertainment" — meals and accommodations — that ran the gamut from

In Their Own Words

I am sure the Americans can fix nothing without a drink. If you meet, you drink; if you part, you drink; if you make acquaintance, you drink; if you close a bargain, you drink; they quarrel in their drink, and they make it up with a drink. . . . If successful in elections, they drink and rejoice; if not, they drink and swear; they begin to drink early in the morning, they leave off late at night; they commence it early in life, and they continue it, until they soon drop into the grave. To use their expression, the way they drink, is "quite a caution." As for water, what the man said, when asked to belong to the Temperance Society, appears to be the general opinion: "It's very good for navigation."

—Frederick Marryat, 1839

rough-and-tumble roadside shanties to such genteel establishments as Philadelphia's City Tavern and Fraunces Tavern in New York City. But nowhere did they cater to the traveler's sense of privacy. A guest staying for the night could find himself sharing a bed with fleas, bedbugs, and a stranger or two. Drinking or dining alone was not tolerated either, as innkeepers quizzed newcomers unmercifully. Ben Franklin learned to deflect the inquisition by reciting a set speech upon entering a new premises. After giving his name, place of birth, profession, destination, and length of stay, he concluded with "And I have no news. Now what can you give me for dinner?"

In life, and as depicted by John Lewis Krimmel, the village tavern was a lively crossroads where travelers and locals exchanged news (left). Tavern signs often announced the owner's sentiments as well as his occupation. A. Hawley (above) proclaimed his loyalty to the new Union by depicting a lion — a symbol of England — in chains.

A tent, a few jugs of raw whiskey, and maybe a board balanced on a couple of barrels were all that was needed to start a thriving saloon in Colorado's lumber and mining camps.

The Wild West Saloon

Like its eastern cousin, the tavern, the 19th-century Western saloon served the community as more than a watering hole and gossip mill. Along with those friendly functions, it might double as post office, billiard parlor, music hall, hotel, and sometime pulpit for politicians and preachers. The saloon also served as an informal place of employment. A bootblack might ply his trade at the brass rail that ran along the bottom of the bar. Professional gamblers offered a variety of chancy diversions. And "hostesses" of uncertain virtue often enlivened proceedings in the more liberal establishments. The house usually took a cut of these earnings in exchange for the use of its facilities, and it protected customers by watching for swindlers.

A town's first saloon might be a crude affair tossed together from rough planks, but as the town prospered, the grogshops grew fancier to keep pace with changing times. Customers came to expect a fairly standard layout. Swinging doors — never locked or barred — hung at the entryway like flags of welcome. Beyond might be an anteroom where newspapers and tobacco were sold, and then came the saloon proper.

Music from a wind-up box or sometimes a piano or fiddle and the whirr-click of a roulette wheel competed with the babel of voices from the crowd gathered in the main room. At tables along one wall, often beneath lush paintings of nudes, the weary nursed their drinks, cards flashed in gamblers' hands, and business deals were struck. Opposite the tables was the saloon keeper's pride — an ornately paneled, polished bar. Expanses of gilt mirrors, kerosene-fueled chandeliers, and a generous assortment of brass spittoons completed the decor of these havens from the hubbub of life outside.

John Gough's One-Man Temperance Show

Widespread concern over the evils of Demon Rum in the 19th century kept scores of not-so-gentle temperance zealots on the lecture circuit. Few, however, were the equal of John Gough, the most theatrical advocate of abstinence ever to mount a stage.

Women were even more involved than men in the 19th-century crusade against drink. In this lithograph of the period, women of the temperance movement were depicted as warriors on horseback as they strove to rid the world of Demon Rum.

Born in England in 1817, Gough arrived in New York City at the tender age of 14 ready to seek his fortune. He found and lost a number of menial jobs, suffered almost unrelieved hardship, and took to drink for escape. With some talent as a ventriloquist, singer, and comic, he joined an acting company; his first role, ironically, was in a lampoon subtitled "The Temperance Hoax." When the troupe went bankrupt, Gough degenerated from binger to confirmed drunkard—a situation that only worsened after his wife's untimely death.

At last, rescued by the kindness of a stranger, he was persuaded to take the pledge of abstinence. Attending a meeting of reformed alcoholics, he stood to tell his story, making such a spellbinding confession that listeners begged for a repeat performance. In fact, a regular demand developed for Gough's testimony, and with each performance his theatrical powers improved. Realizing that his true calling had been revealed, Gough decided to take up temperance speaking full-time. In his first year he traveled 6,840 miles, gave nearly 400 speeches, won 2,218 converts, and received $1,059 for his efforts, a handsome sum in those days.

With a stage presence that was positively vaudevillian, he glared and growled, trembled and shrieked, then rolled his eyes and fell to the ground, frightening listeners with his horror stories. "Crawl from the slimy ooze, ye drowned drunkards," he would rail. Marveling at his facility at impersonating now the drunkard, then the hypocrite, and finally the saint, one observer told of his "restless, eager hands . . . always busy, flinging the hair forward in one character, back in another, or standing it straight up in a third; crushing the drink fiend, pointing to the angel in human nature. . . ." Gough usually left the stage dripping with perspiration.

The fact that he backslid during his 40-year crusade, going on several well-publicized benders, only added to his appeal. Shortly before Gough died at age 68, he was publicly attacked in the press for gaining great wealth from the misfortunes of others. He gladly reminded critics that temperance did in fact promise worldly, as well as heavenly, rewards to those who denounced the Devil Drink. His own success, he said, was living proof that this was so.

On the Trail With Izzy and Moe

The 1920's earned their reputation as the Lawless Decade when enforced Prohibition effectively destroyed public respect for civil law. Two of the most celebrated — if not exactly the most popular — participants in this ill-conceived effort were Izzy Einstein and Moe Smith, a team of New York Prohibition agents whose daring raids on clandestine speakeasies and slippery bootleggers became the stuff of legend.

Izzy and Moe were improbable-looking "hoochhounds." Izzy, an ex–postal clerk, was five feet five inches tall, almost as wide, and a self-proclaimed master of disguise. Moe, a former cigar salesman, was his lieutenant and straight man. Their job, like that of 1,500 other federal agents, was to discover, destroy, padlock, and otherwise disrupt the activities of all those in violation of the law. This was a tall order, for in New York City alone, tens of thousands of establishments were serving illegal liquor.

A day with the "Dry Twins," as Izzy and Moe became known, "would make a chameleon blush for lack of variations," wrote a *New York Times* reporter in 1922. Up with the dawn, the pair might flush out a rumrunner before breakfast, hit a couple of workingmen's lunch counters at noon, sur-

Izzy donned a beard and one of his many rubber noses, and Moe dressed up as a woman (above) in preparation for a speakeasy raid. The public, however, continually found ways to sneak booze by the feds, including the lady at the left with a flask tucked in her garter.

prise a "pharmacy" (where illegal spirits could be purchased as medicine) during the afternoon, and finish up with a raid on a speakeasy by night.

At each location Izzy dressed for the part: he penetrated a sports bar in football uniform, a saloon as a pickle salesman, and a Harlem club in blackface. Decked out in musician's mufti, he appeared one evening in an uptown nightclub and gave a credible performance on the trombone before uttering his standard opening line, "Dere's sad news," and shutting down the joint. The tireless duo even joined "wets" in a protest march afterward, following the crowd to the nearest watering hole for another raid.

Izzy and Moe racked up 4,392 arrests and confiscated an estimated 5 million bottles of bootleg booze before being summarily fired in 1925, perhaps for attracting too much publicity. But the fact was, no agents, however clever, could forcibly cork Americans' drinking habits. Prohibition actually saw alcohol consumption rise among some segments of society, and it cultivated a new class of criminal who found a billion-dollar opportunity in bootleg liquor. By 1929 even many temperance advocates were ready to agree with the "wets" that Prohibition was a social and legal disaster. In 1933 "the noble experiment" was repealed.

That Spirited Mix

By most accounts the cocktail is a peculiarly American invention, though just when the first mixed drink was poured and how it got its name will probably never be known. There is no shortage of theories, however, and one of the liveliest has George Washington's hat as the inspiration. As the story goes, his officers gathered one evening to celebrate a victory against the British. When supplies of spirits ran short, they mixed up what remained, and after several rounds of toasting their commander-in-chief, all 13 colonies, and each other, someone proposed a toast to Washington's feather-decorated tricorn. "Let's drink to the cock's tail," shouted the bibulous patriot. And they did.

However the mixed drink really began, its intoxicating powers were well enough known by 1806 to prompt one newspaper satirist to advise politicians to serve a round as a prelude to every speech. Anyone who swallowed a cocktail, he reasoned, was "ready to swallow anything else." The cocktail as a prelude to dinner, however, is a much more recent development. It is generally traced to the 1920's and Prohibition, when drinking in public was a criminal offense. The private living room became — by default — the only safe place to take a glass of cheer, and mixed drinks were a far better choice than the raw spirits brewed in bathtub and basement.

Cocktail parties as hospitable entertainments in their own right are essentially a post–World War I creation. As one tart observer put it, they were made to order for people who "want to meet their neighbors, but not very much."

WHAT·IS·IT

In the 1880's the Vinous Rubber Grape Company sold an assortment of spirit-filled "grapes." With flavors ranging from muscatel to gin, they were advertised as ideal for opera goers and sleighing parties. Imbibers were told to burst the grapes in the mouth "in a similar manner as fruit, ejecting the rubber skin after having swallowed the contents."

In the 1950's the ultimate in sophisticated gatherings was the cocktail party. John Koch's painting by that name depicts his own New York apartment with himself as bartender.

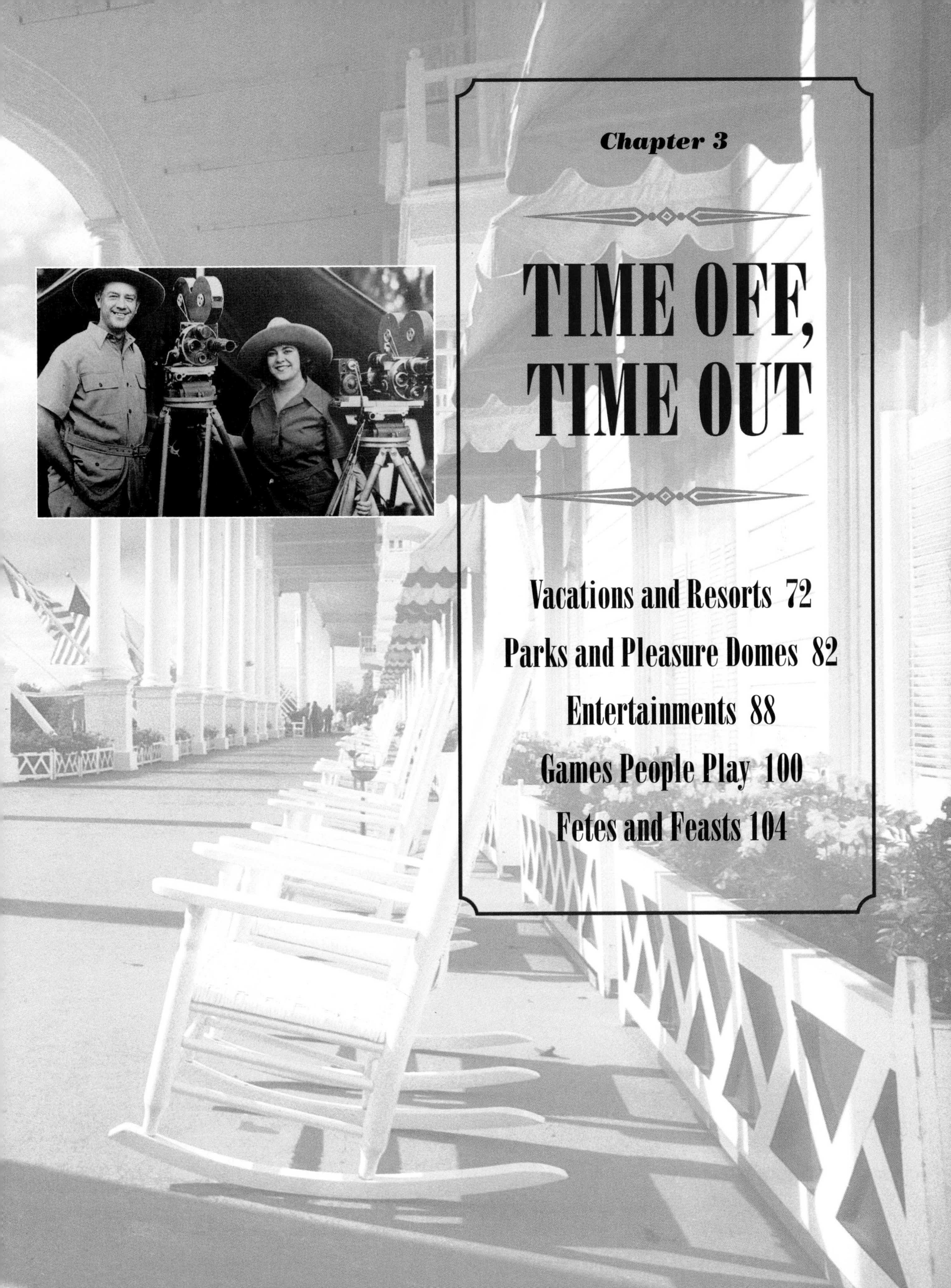

Chapter 3

TIME OFF, TIME OUT

VACATIONS AND RESORTS

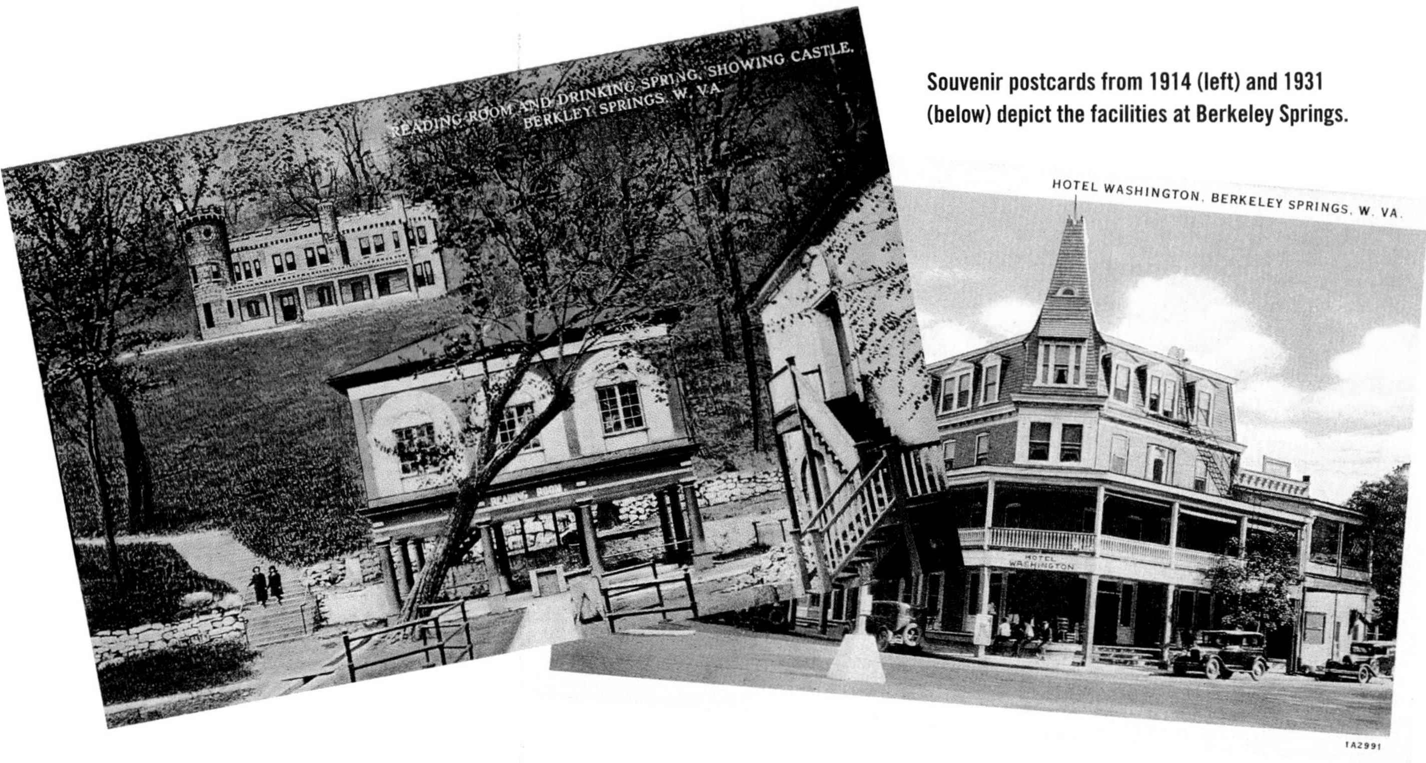

Souvenir postcards from 1914 (left) and 1931 (below) depict the facilities at Berkeley Springs.

Taking the Waters

In March 1748, during a surveying expedition through what would later become northeastern West Virginia, 16-year-old George Washington took a side trip to bathe in "Ye fam'd Warm Springs" at Berkeley Springs. The Appalachian Mountain site already was widely known at that date, and the installation of improved roads in the mid-18th century would serve to further spur the spa's popularity. Washington himself returned several times, with a variety of friends and relatives in tow for the "cure."

But in going to the spa to partake of the sweet-tasting, 74° mineral waters, the colonists were merely following an ancient tradition. The Tuscaroras, Delawares, and Catawbas had long regarded the springs as sacred healing waters. Warring tribes were even known to camp amicably side by side at the springs.

Bustling springs

The settlement that arose around the springs was incorporated as a town in 1776. When a public sale of land was held the following year,certain lots were reserved so that "these healing waters might be forever free to the publick, for the welfare of suffering humanity." The remaining lots were snapped up by the Virginia gentry — including Washington, whose hope for a home at the springs was never fulfilled.

In 1784 the town fathers declared that the ragtag assortment of bath houses and shacks along the main street were unworthy and unsightly, and gave all owners four months to tear them down. A frenzy of improvements was begun and three years later the spruced-up spa was calling itself one of the finest resorts in America. Within the 11-street grid that formed the town were public baths for "visitors and sick people," gambling houses, racetracks, and taverns, along with a playhouse, a tearoom, and elegant hotels. Now, not only health seekers but fun seekers, both hale and unwholesome, came in droves. Troupes of actors and confidence men, prostitutes and preachers, mothers in search of good matches for their daughters, and bachelors ready for any sort of impromptu amusement, all came to test the waters.

As time went on, the rollicking holiday spirit that prevailed at Berkeley Springs became the town's main attraction, and any pretense of improving health was largely forgotten. Then in 1844 a major fire roared through, destroying half of the town. New ordinances discouraging licentiousness were passed, and the once-lively resort, which in its heyday had been condemned by a Methodist bishop as a "seat of sin," quietly reverted to its original, more sedate incarnation as a peaceful medicinal spa.

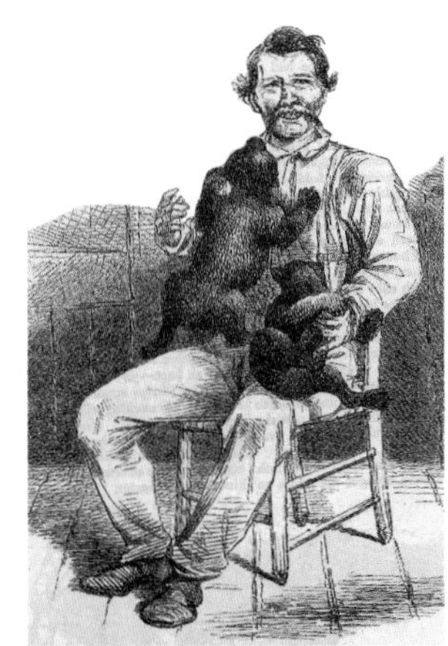

Porte Crayon, an illustrator for *Harper's Monthly Magazine,* immortalized Henry Herbel, a Berkeley Springs basketmaker. After a fight with a she-bear in which his face was clawed, Herbel killed the bear, adopted her days-old cubs, and raised them as pets.

Thomas Jefferson's Perfect Hideaway

As carefully planned and beautifully proportioned as the pattern in a Persian carpet, Jefferson's country haven was a perfect realization of his artistic ideals.

Monticello, Thomas Jefferson's gracious estate in Albemarle County, Virginia, frequently overflowed with as many as 50 guests at a time. One servant complained that it "took all hands" to care for the visitors and "the whole farm to feed them." The former president and his family were besieged by uninvited guests as well. Gawkers flocked to stare at the spectacle of the great man at home; one even broke a window to get a better view. So it is no wonder that Jefferson, who treasured privacy and a contemplative life, created Poplar Forest, a personal sanctuary on a plantation near Lynchburg, Virginia, that he inherited from his father-in-law in 1773.

As his thoughts turned to retirement during his second term in office, they led naturally to Poplar Forest. During the British raid of Charlottesville in 1781, Jefferson had taken refuge at the plantation, whiling away the time by writing *Notes on the State of Virginia.* In 1806 he took a break from his executive duties to help the masons lay the foundation for a new octagonal house he had designed. But the house — reportedly the first eight-sided home in America —was only the hub of a much larger scheme.

Taken together as a single plan, the house and its grounds comprised a series of concentric circles and octagons that culminated in a cubical room at the center of the house. At the farthest boundary a circular drive enclosed the grounds. Inside this circle an octagonal fence defined the lawn. The lawn, in turn, was divided into quarters by an approach road, a terrace green, and a double row of trees that extended east and west from the sides of the house. Inside the house a series of octagonal rooms surrounded the skylighted central dining room — which was furnished with an octagonal table.

Poplar Forest took some 19 years to complete, about half as long as was spent in creating Monticello. But that, too, was part of its master's plan. As he once said, "Architecture is my delight, and putting up and pulling down one of my favorite amusements." Here, with the occasional exception of his beloved grandchildren, no visitors were welcome. Indeed, few even knew of the existence of Jefferson's retreat, and the countryfolk around, sensing the "Squire's" need for solitude, respectfully left him alone.

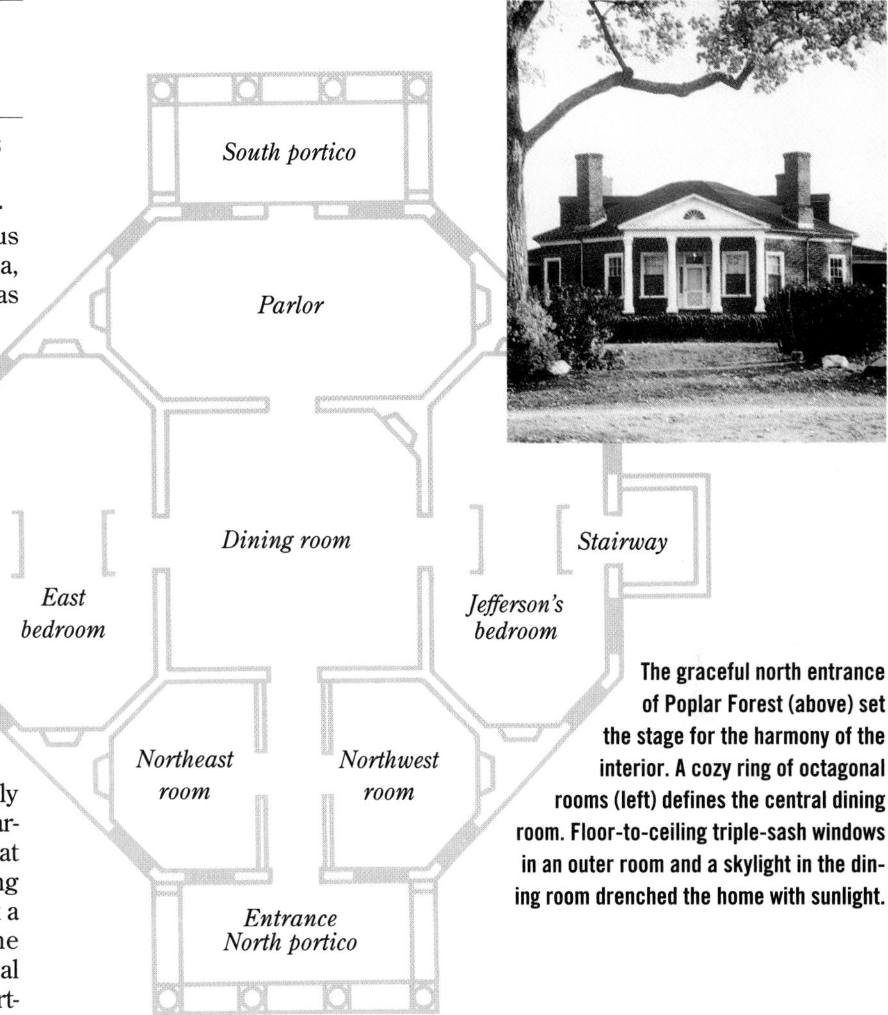

The graceful north entrance of Poplar Forest (above) set the stage for the harmony of the interior. A cozy ring of octagonal rooms (left) defines the central dining room. Floor-to-ceiling triple-sash windows in an outer room and a skylight in the dining room drenched the home with sunlight.

Executive Sanctuary

Seeking relief from the heat of summers in Washington, D.C., President Franklin D. Roosevelt in 1942 decided to build a retreat on a mountaintop in nearby Maryland. He called this aerie Shangri-La, but President Eisenhower later changed its name to "Camp David" to honor his grandson — and the name stuck.

A mere 70 miles from Washington, the site is high enough to offer welcome coolness and its relative isolation affords a refreshing break from the hurly-burly of public life. Scattered about the 200 wooded acres are 10 guest cottages, a dining hall, and Aspen Lodge, the First Family's home away from home. A swimming pool, tennis courts, and a pitch-and-putt golf green provide diversions.

Despite its coziness Camp David is also a stronghold that protects its illustrious guests. Ten chief executives and a variety of world leaders — including Winston Churchill, Nikita Krushchev, Anwar el-Sadat, and Menachem Begin — have worked and rested in its peaceful atmosphere.

When photographed in 1892, the Hotel Kaaterskill could accommodate 1,200 guests. Though built purely out of spite, its brochure was able to boast, "There is no hotel . . . where taste and wealth have more liberally contributed to secure to their guests the highest attainable degree of comfort and luxury."

The Two-Million-Dollar Dinner

The failure of a popular resort hotel to keep its menu flexible led to disgruntlement, defection, and the birth of a grand new rival hostelry.

Tourists leafing through their *Baedeker's* guide in the late 19th century found a glowing description of New York's celebrated Hotel Kaaterskill: "the most fashionable resort in the Catskills," it declared, ". . . commanding a view little, if at all, inferior to that from the Mountain House." Not mentioned was the fact that the imposing Kaaterskill and the smaller, older Catskill Mountain House were bitter rivals perched on the very same mountain.

The Hotel Kaaterskill had, in fact, been built as the result of a culinary clash between the Mountain House's proprietor, Charles Beach, and one of his best customers, wealthy Philadelphia patent lawyer George Harding. Trouble began in July 1880 when Harding arrived for his annual summer stay with his ailing wife and daughter. Sitting down to dinner, Harding asked the waiter to bring his daughter some fried chicken since she could not eat red meat. But the Mountain House ran an old-fashioned dining room: guests ate what they were served. There would be no chicken. Accustomed to having his way, Harding demanded to see his friend Beach, who was just as unyielding as the waiter. If Harding did not like the dining-room policies at the Mountain House, he was summarily told, he could build his own hotel.

Those were fighting words indeed, and with them the fried-chicken war was under way. Purchasing a fine site about a mile away, and 245 feet higher than the Mountain House, Harding put an architect to work immediately. Within three months a grand plan for "the largest mountain hotel in the world" had taken shape. New-fangled electric lighting, steam heat, an elevator, and modern plumbing (including some rooms with private baths) were featured in the elaborate scheme.

Construction began even before snow flew, and with the opening scheduled for June 1881, hundreds of workers were hired in the spring to complete the building, plant gardens and promenades, and construct a new carriage road up the mountain. On opening day Harding chartered a Hudson River steamer to bring some 200 newspaper reporters to the glittering ceremonies. The new hotel was pronounced a fabulous success.

For the rest of his life Harding would be known as "The Man Who Spent Two Million for a Chicken Dinner," though the actual cost was closer to $250,000. And while his hotel lost money more years than not, he seems never to have regretted his dramatic gesture. In fact, he retired from law to manage the Kaaterskill in person. As for the Mountain House, it began to lose business the moment the Kaaterskill opened, and by the 1890's was no longer a serious competitor for the genteel trade.

Guests and the Garden at Appledore

Although located on a rocky island 10 miles off the coast, Celia Thaxter's garden and her family's hotel attracted the cream of 19th-century New England.

From the very first season that Thomas Laighton opened his hotel on Appledore Island off the coast of New Hampshire in 1848, it was a popular resort. Built "for invalids, if they had to come, for poets, if they could and would," it attracted not only poets but the brightest lights of New England's artistic and literary circles. Nathaniel Hawthorne and John Greenleaf Whittier were among the hotel's earliest guests. Mark Twain, Ralph Waldo Emerson, and Childe Hassam were but three of the other writers and painters who gathered there later on.

Appledore House could sleep 500 guests and serve 900 at dinner. But it was not just its comforts and breezy porches, or the fact that it was the East Coast's first major off-shore hotel, or even the island's craggy charm that drew so large and creative a clientele. Among the other attractions were Laighton's daughter Celia Thaxter and the free-ranging and riotously colored garden that she planted each year. Without her, Whittier said, the island would be, "a mere pile of rocks, I imagine, dead as the moon's old volcanic mountains. Thee have given them an atmosphere."

Celia had grown up on a nearby island where her father had served as lighthouse keeper, and was only five years old when she planted her first garden, managing to coax a few flowers to bloom in the inhospitably rocky soil. By the time she was a young woman, her garden overflowed with poppies, peonies, foxgloves — more than 50 kinds of blooms. But the atmosphere that she created was more than just the garden.

When she married her tutor, Harvard-educated Levi Thaxter, at the age of 16 in 1851, Celia left her island home to live with him near Boston. Although she had rarely seen the mainland during her youth, she fit in quickly with his circle of literary friends. Charles Dickens met and admired her. Henry Wadsworth Longfellow and Oliver Wendell Holmes both encouraged her to develop her own talents as a poet and essayist: it was advice that she followed.

Early in their marriage the Thaxters lived on Appledore each summer, but after Levi nearly drowned during a stormy boat crossing, he swore to stay away from the sea. Celia, who could imagine separation from him but not from her family or garden, continued to return each year by herself, content, as she said, "to read Dante and peel squash." The Thaxters' artistic friends apparently felt the same way, for they followed Celia to Appledore. Her flower-filled rooms became a favorite salon and her garden their summer sanctuary.

American impressionist Childe Hassam and his wife were among Celia Thaxter's most devoted friends, and Appledore's most frequent visitors. Celia's garden inspired Hassam to produce some of his finest work, including illustrations for her book *An Island Garden.* His oil "Poppies" (above) shows the island's shore. "In the Garden" (left) is a portrait of Celia.

Gideon Beginnings

If Boscobel, Wisconsin's, Central Hotel had not been filled with a convention of rowdy lumbermen one September night in 1898, the manager might never have asked two complete strangers to share a room. The two, John Nicholson and Samuel Hill, traveling salesmen in need of a good night's sleep, agreed.

Before turning in that evening, Nicholson, an evangelical Christian, begged his roommate's forbearance as he kept the lamp lit and read a bit of "God's Word." Hill in turn requested that Nicholson read aloud since he, too, was "a Christian man."

Within a year the newly found friends formed a society that they named after the Old Testament leader, Gideon. Their mission, ultimately, was to place Bibles in hotel rooms: the first 25 were delivered to the Superior Hotel in Iron Mountain, Montana, in 1908, where they were enthusiastically received.

Today, some 32 million King James version Bibles are regular fixtures in hotel rooms throughout the world, placed and replaced by thousands of dedicated Gideon evangelists each year.

A Touch of Paris in the Rockies

Louis Dupuy had an unusual philosophy for an innkeeper: he would not allow anyone he did not like to stay at his Georgetown, Colorado, hotel. "This house is my own," he insisted, "and if I want guests I invite them."

Such selectivity resulted in more than one case of ruffled feelings, for during the mining boom of the 1880's, when Georgetown advertised itself as the "Silver Queen" of the Rockies, Dupuy's Hotel de Paris was the most famous hostelry in the state. Travelers — among them, millionaire railroad magnate Jay Gould — stopped in town specifically for the pleasure of sampling the hotel's food. Where else could Gould and his companions sit down to an eight-course dinner that included oysters (hauled across the mountains from the West Coast), pheasant casserole, venison cutlet, and sweetbreads, all washed down with imported French wines that were stored in huge casks in the hotel's basement?

Dupuy, who prepared all meals himself, was so knowledgeable on the subject of food that James E. Russell, an educator largely responsible for introducing home economics courses into school curricula, credited his idea to dinner with Dupuy.

Born Adolphus Gerard in Alençon, France, the young man came to America seeking adventure. (Dupuy changed his name after deserting the American army.) An accident shortly after his arrival in Georgetown left him unable to seek his fortune in the silver mines, so he decided instead to recreate an elegant European hotel. The Hotel de Paris boasted ornate rococo decor, French sculpture, Belgian crystal, and Limoges china. Perhaps more important than ambience to guests lucky enough to spend the night there, however, were the hotel's greatest luxuries: central steam heat and hot and cold running water.

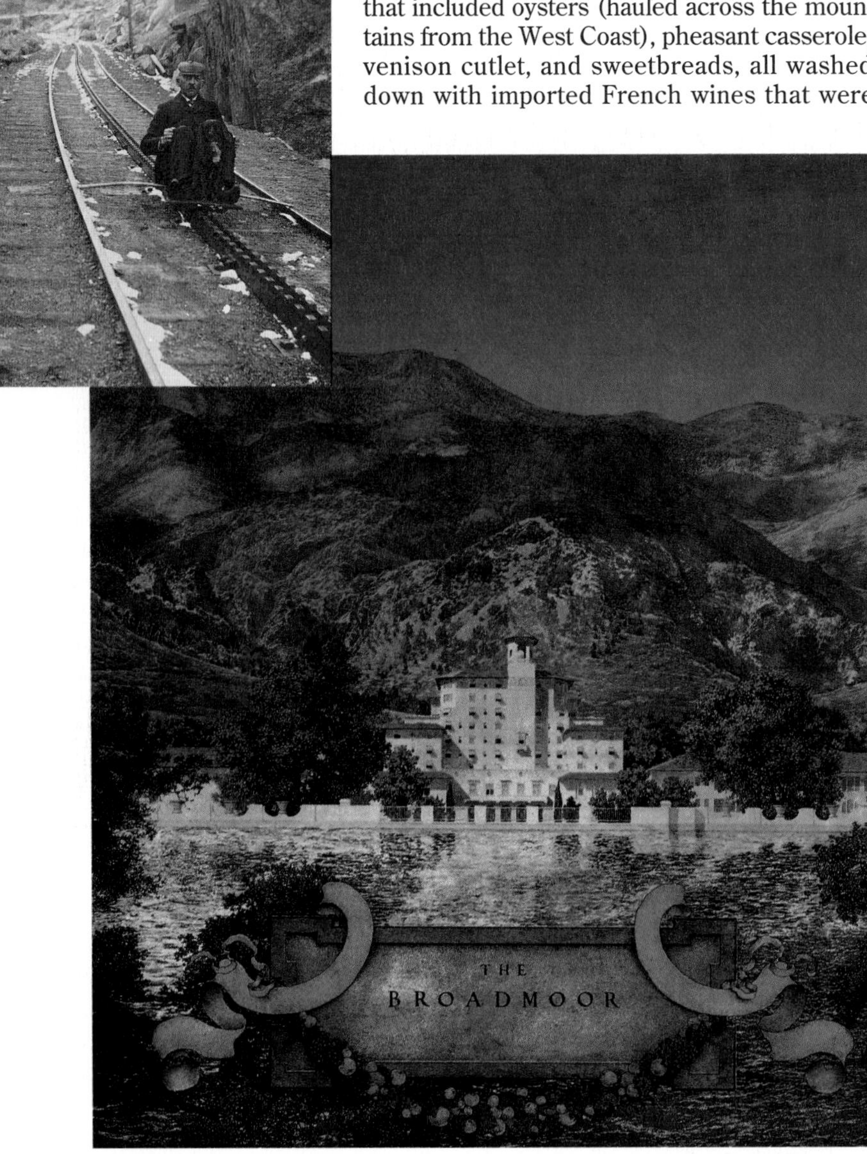

Illustrator Maxfield Parrish painted the Broadmoor in its magnificent setting (above). A steam locomotive carried tourists to the top of nearby Pikes Peak, but when the train was not in use, men sometimes devised their own means of locomotion (inset).

Rooms With a View

Explorer Zebulon Pike doubted that anyone would ever scale the mountain he discovered but was unable to climb in 1806. "No human being could have ascended to its pinnacle," he contended. By the 1890's, however, tourists by the trainload were arriving at the top of Pikes Peak, thanks to the efforts of Wisconsin industrialist Zalmon Gilbert Simmons. One spine-rattling trek to the summit on donkeyback had been enough to convince Simmons (the founder of a mattress company) to finance construction of a cog railway so that tourists could get to the top "in the greatest comfort that technology could provide."

The fact, however, that tourists were there at all, hoping to reach the peak, was not Simmons's doing. Their arrival in the area resulted from the labors of yet another man — General William Jackson Palmer, builder of the Denver to Santa Fe rail line. Palmer wanted to make a home for his bride, Queen Mellen, an eastern-bred beauty who was reluctant to live in a rough-hewn western railroad town. When Palmer first saw Pikes Peak rising from the Colorado Front Range, he was convinced he had found a spot that could make even his Queen happy: "I am sure there will be a famous resort here soon," he promised her in a letter in 1869. From the time that he founded his Fountain Colony — soon to be renamed Colorado Springs — Palmer did all he could to make that prediction come true. First he tried selling building lots, and when that proved less than successful, he took advantage of America's post–Civil War travel urge by encouraging hotel construction.

From its earliest years, Colorado Springs attracted a curious collection of American tourists and European adventurers. Few were more colorful than a young German count, James Pourtales, who built a casino on the shore of an artificial lake and christened the complex Broadmoor. Pourtales's casino went bankrupt and burned in 1897, and the property was ultimately acquired by millionaire Spencer Penrose, who rebuilt the Broadmoor on a lavish scale. From its opening in 1918, the hotel became a favorite stopover for high society. "Fifteen socialites . . . are to be quartered at the Broadmoor for the winter and have shipped their polo ponies," one newspaper reported in 1921. Life at Pikes Peak obviously had changed irrevocably from the days when Zebulon Pike stared up at the summit and Palmer first imagined its potential.

Cowboy Comforts

If the winter of 1886 had been a little less severe on the North Dakota Badlands, the Eaton brothers might have stuck to herding cattle. But with fierce storms killing off their livestock, they decided to rely on another line of business: dude ranching. Since the early 1880's, Howard Eaton and his brothers had offered free hospitality to a growing number of Easterners—nicknamed "dudes." Among their guests was young Theodore Roosevelt, whose visit was inspired by Howard's glowing description of the Badlands in a New York newspaper. Roosevelt's enthusiasm for the open range encouraged trips by other affluent Easterners, among them writer Owen Wister, who later immortalized the rugged western life-style in his novel *The Virginian*.

When the Eatons realized they were providing some 2,200 free meals a year to enthusiastic guests, Howard decided on a $10 a week charge for staying at the ranch. Visitors certainly got their money's worth: riding, fishing, hunting, and horseback camping trips to Yellowstone National Park. Cooks, maids, and bath tents with hot water were included on these outings, sparing the dudes some of the common discomforts of roughing it.

By the time the Eatons moved from North Dakota to Wyoming in 1904, similar ranches had been established in Colorado and Montana. Over the decades their visitors have ranged from city dwellers to celebrities such as Buffalo Bill, Amelia Earhart, and Will Rogers. None, however, could match the devotion of the dudes who followed the Eatons to their new location. Since accommodations were not ready that first season, no visitors were expected. But 70 showed up anyway. Not only did they help with the chores; they also paid room and board for the honor of lending a hand.

The dudes at Howard Eaton's campsite in Yellowstone National Park (top) included both men and women. Eaton's tenderfoot Easterners (above) experience the rigors of fording a stream.

By the Sea, by the Sea

An elegantly garbed throng paraded along Atlantic City's famous boardwalk on Easter Sunday in about 1910 (above, right). Five years later a more exuberant group delighted the boardwalk crowd with a spontaneous tango on the strand (above).

In 1854 a stretch of eight-mile-long Absecon Island off the New Jersey coast came into its own as the quintessential American seaside resort. Incorporated as Atlantic City, this mecca of merriment leapt to life with five brand-new hotels, a railway spur from Philadelphia, and a couple of fine new turnpikes connecting it with other large cities. By the 1880's the resort boasted a phalanx of multistoried hotels along the shore — the elegant Chalfonte and Haddon House among them — and a maze of streets whose names would later become famous in the game of Monopoly.

Each summer throngs of people donned their fashionable flannel bathing suits and headed for the beach. The suits, which might contain as much as 10 yards of fabric, were better suited to strolling than bathing, however, for when wet, the wool's weight could sink all but the strongest swimmer. Still, there was plenty of fun in seeing and being seen, especially after the hotel owners installed a handsome, if narrow, wooden boardwalk atop the dunes. Though popular, the boardwalk was not without its dangers. As one wag observed, "Nearly every day somebody falls off. . . ." He added, "In nearly every instance the parties have been flirting." Over the years the 'walk was replaced and enlarged until in 1896 it reached its present dimensions of 40 to 60 feet wide and 4 miles long.

Piers, pickles, and performers

Atlantic City's first amusement piers were thrust out to sea during the 1880's and 1890's. Howard's Pier was first in 1882; Applegate's arose in '84. Then in 1899 Heinz's Iron Pier pushed off from Massachusetts Avenue. The pickle man's pier offered free restrooms, concert-lectures, and a sun parlor that featured chairs for the weary, displays of heroic paintings, busts of Socrates and Shakespeare, a mummy, two elephant tusks — and an array of Heinz products for tasting. Anyone who visited the pier was given a free pickle-shaped lapel pin and the opportunity to purchase a sampler of the "Choicest 24 of the 57 Varieties."

The pleasure piers were host to hundreds of "hanky-panks," as the midway-type games were known, and myriad other diversions from flagpole sitters and escape artists to dance marathons and operas in English. In its hectic heyday so many stars twinkled along this shore that thousands flocked to the piers where they performed and the Steel Pier became known as the "Showplace of the Nation." Sarah Bernhardt performed *Camille,* in French, to a sellout crowd. Popular bands — from John Philip Sousa's to Glenn Miller's — delighted the holiday hordes. Nelson Eddy, Frank Sinatra, and Bob Hope played the piers in the 1930's. Sally Rand, who arrived in a farm truck after her plane made a forced landing in a field, fan-danced one Fourth of July.

One entrepreneur lived the dream of many vacationers. Capt. John Lake Young, who built the grandiose Million Dollar Pier, also built himself a three-story house on his pier. There, at "No. 1 Atlantic Ocean," he could fish from his bedroom window and keep a proprietary eye on the milling throngs who visited Atlantic City's happy havens of sun and fun.

Where'd She Go, Miss America?

On September 11, 1937, Bette Cooper, New Jersey's own "Miss Bertrand Island," was named Miss America in the Atlantic City pageant. Seventeen-year-old Bette had captivated the judges with her rendition of "When the Poppies Bloom Again" in the then-optional talent contest, swept the evening gown competition, and bested 48 other beauties in bathing suits. The prizes she was to receive included a mink coat, a Hollywood screen test, and a $200 per day vaudeville contract. But America would see precious little of its new queen, for the blond schoolgirl vanished into the night.

When Cooper failed to appear at her first press conference, the pageant promoters suspected foul play and rumors flew thick and fast. The state police put out an all-points bulletin for the capture of her kidnappers. Newspapers published a picture of the runners-up standing beside an empty throne. Even Walter Winchell got into the act and announced on his radio program that Cooper had eloped with Lou Off, her official pageant escort.

The mystery was finally solved when Cooper's father made a rueful confession. In fact, Bette *had* run off with Lou, but not for a midnight marriage. At the family's behest Off and some friends had spirited Cooper out of her hotel, hidden her on Off's boat (which was anchored about 200 feet from the Steel Pier, where she had won the competition), and then taken her home. As Mr. Cooper explained, "Bette is not the type of girl to appear in vaudeville. She isn't robust enough for the professional grind." Indeed, the young beauty had entered the competition as a joke, never imagining she'd win, and had battled a fierce cold throughout the week-long proceedings.

Embarrassed by this flouting of their bounty, pageant officials created a host of rules to prevent a recurrence. The even more embarrassed Cooper clan, for their part, was forever silent about "the incident."

Miss America of 1937 was a 17-year-old schoolgirl from Hackettstown, N. J., who had entered the competition on a dare. Surprised and somewhat embarrassed to have actually won, Bette Cooper disappeared the next day and never claimed her crown.

The Isle of Smiles

When asked why he spent so much money on Catalina Island, William Wrigley, Jr., simply answered, "Because I'm happy and because I want others to be happy." And his forthright blend of good clean fun at reasonable prices made people very happy indeed: for decades his "Isle With a Smile" has drawn thousands of visitors annually.

Wrigley had made a fortune selling chewing gum and had even bought his own baseball team — the Chicago Cubs. By 1919 he was ripe for a new challenge, and so when offered a chance to buy undeveloped Santa Catalina Island, less than 30 miles off the coast of Southern California, the Chicago businessman snapped it up, sight unseen, for a reported $3 million. Two weeks after his purchase, he sailed into a fog-enshrouded Avalon Bay. When the curtain of fog lifted, he was dazzled by the sparkling bay and the craggy peaks of the 22-mile-long island — and inspired with a Utopian vision. He promised a Los Angeles reporter "to leave no stone unturned to make it a refuge from worry and work for the rich and poor."

Wrigley was as good as his word. With the fishing village of Avalon as a focal point, his improvements over the next decade included new roads, waterworks, a bird sanctuary, a golf course, riding and hiking trails, hotels, craft centers, and acres of inexpensive "bungalettes." Five steamer ships plied the channel, ferrying people to and from the mainland. A fleet of glass-bottomed boats allowed pleasure seekers to view the magical underwater realm that surrounded the island. But Catalina's crown jewel was the octagonal Casino ballroom at the water's edge. There, in one of the largest dance halls ever built, countless Americans enjoyed their first live encounter with such luminaries of the Big Band era as Kay Kyser, Jimmy Dorsey, Benny Goodman, and Harry James. No admission was charged — the dancers were considered guests of the Wrigleys.

More than 400 movies were shot against Catalina's beguiling land and seascapes, and the presence of movie stars enhanced the scene for other tourists. Wrigley's Chicago Cubs took preseason training on Catalina, and from time to time, sports contests were staged, the most notable being a 1927 swim marathon that drew 102 contestants.

William Wrigley died in 1932, but Catalina's attractions endure. Though its luster may be a little dimmed by time and changing fashion, each year thousands of merrymakers head for the place that inspired Al Jolson to exclaim, "And so I think I'll travel on to Avalon."

Tin-Can Tourists

This camper was cleverly designed to accommodate sleeping on the road. The fold-up double bed was well protected against the elements, and the convertible car roof made it easy to change clothes.

"They drive tin cans and they eat outa tin cans and they leave a trail of tin cans behind 'em. They're tin-can tourists." So joked Floridians in the early decades of this century when they spotted the new breed of middle-class travelers who came south each winter to find a temporary place in the sun.

The first generation of motorized campers were a far cry from today's recreational vehicles. Some were just ordinary sedans, loaded down with tents, stoves, blankets, and as much housekeeping paraphernalia as could be strapped to the roof and running boards. Others were one-of-a-kind campers, home-built or customized on an automobile chassis. And campsites in those early years were equally casual — a sandy beach, a schoolyard, a clearing by the side of the road.

As for the "tin-can tourist" epithet, most motor campers wore it with pride. In 1920 a few stalwarts even organized a TCT club, complete with a chief executive (the Royal Can Opener), a secret password (nit nac), and two social get-togethers a year. Within 10 years some 100,000 motorized free spirits had joined. Honor-bound to help fellow TCT's in trouble, they signified membership by driving with an empty soup can hanging from the radiator cap.

The rigors of travel in these homemade "RV's" left many tourists wishing for greater comfort. The answer came in the late 1920's when Detroit businessman Arthur Sherman introduced a humble sort of two-wheeled camp trailer that could be hitched to the family car. While a few elegantly appointed "land yachts" were already in use by the rich, Sherman's compact six- by nine-foot box on wheels — complete with bunk beds and cooking facilities — could be mass-produced at a price that ordinary people could afford.

Known as the Sherman Covered Wagon, the prototype was introduced at the 1930 Detroit Auto Show, and its inventor came home with a fistful of orders. But scarcely had Sherman launched his new business when the bottom fell out of the American economy, taking any enthusiasm for house trailers with it. Suddenly, the notion of being "on the road," of living at casual campsites, no longer seemed a happy adventure. Too many unemployed Americans were already doing just that out of painful necessity.

A converted truck (above) made an ideal camper with plenty of room for storage both inside and underneath. The ingenious gent (below) carved his 8,000-pound camper from a spruce log. *Motor Camper and Tourist* (right) was one of several magazines published in the 1920's and 1930's that was written especially for "tin canners."

Some "tin cans" were rather elegant. Actress Ida Lupino (above) posed in the doorway of her 1936 Halsco Land Yacht. The creation made in Ohio in the 1920's (right) was outfitted with stained-glass windows, paneled sides, and tasseled shades. The interior photograph (far right) makes it clear that campers could offer all the comforts of home. R. E. Jeffery's compactly designed motor home (below) was built on the chassis of a 1905 Pierce Arrow.

PARKS AND PLEASURE DOMES

Golden Age of Terror

Charles Lindbergh called it a "greater thrill than flying a plane at top speed"; a shakier patron admitted he'd rather be beaten with a chain. Both were describing their ride on the Cyclone, Coney Island's heart-stopping roller coaster. Built of wood in 1927 at the Brooklyn, New York, amusement park, it was one of some 1,500 coasters in operation in the 1920's and is one of the few old-timers still in use today.

The birthplace of all those American roller coasters was the Pennsylvania coal country. It was there in the early 1870's that a group of enterprising businessmen converted a coal-hauling mining train to one that would carry passengers on a slow but scenic descent of Pisgah Mountain.

Eleven years later, La Marcus A. Thompson became known as the "Father of Gravity" when he installed a primitive "switchback railway" at Coney Island. (Gravity pulled the railway down one slope, then assistants pushed it to the top of the next.) It moved at only six miles per hour, yet its nickel fares mounted up to $700 a day — riches enough to inspire a host of imitators and improvers.

Among the greatest of these were Harry Traver and Frank Church. Traver's coaster at Crystal Beach on Lake Erie caused a near riot among the opening-day crowd of 75,000. (One man insisted on riding it 67 times.) Another Traver coaster at New Jersey's Palisades Park inspired the observation that "before you can remember what comes after 'Thy kingdom come,' [it] shoots you to the stars again." Many connoisseurs agree, however, that the fiercest ride of all was the Bobs coaster that Frank Church designed for Chicago's Riverview Park in 1924. As testimony to its bone-rattling thrills, the operator managed to amass a collection of some 7,000 unmatched earrings, all of them collected from beneath the wooden structure.

Thrill seekers rode sideways on one of Coney Island's early roller coasters (top). By the 1920's coasters incorporated blood-chilling drops of 80 feet or more (left). Most of the classics were torn down by the 1960's.

Painted Ponies

Stopping in Dayton, Ohio, on their way west in 1831, a group of Seneca Indians met with a surly reception but managed to entertain themselves anyway: they spotted a traveling carnival nearby and spent several days whirling around on the backs of "flying horses." Their "steeds" were part of a portable merry-go-round, one of several such contraptions — driven by real horses or by manpower — that were periodically taken on tour around the countryside in the 19th century.

An off-season handicraft of farmers and wheelwrights, such rides were crude and slow. When Gustav Dentzel, a 20-year-old German cabinetmaker, settled in Philadelphia in 1860, however, more elaborate creations began to appear. An expert carver, whose family were experienced carousel makers, Dentzel at first built relatively simple affairs, with swings for the riders to sit on. But he soon set to work on more ambitious models, using his carving skills to produce realistically spirited horses. By 1867, when he hung out a sign reading "G. A. Dentzel, Steam and Horsepower Caroussell Builder," his enticing animals "galloped" around platforms magically driven by the new steam engines. Band organs — automated instruments that featured self-playing glockenspiels, drums, and cymbals — became standard features, and every city park and county fair wanted to have one of the fanciful new devices.

Dentzel employed teams of skilled artisans — mostly German and Italian immigrants — to carve and paint his colorful menageries. From the late 1800's until the1930's, demand was such that centers in New York, Kansas, and Pennsylvania competed in producing the thousands of carousels that still delight young and old.

With the advent of electricity, carousel animals could gallop three abreast, as on this 1915 example (left).

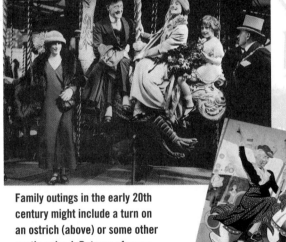

Family outings in the early 20th century might include a turn on an ostrich (above) or some other exotic animal. Patrons of many carousels (right) could try to grab a brass ring that entitled them to a free ride.

CATCH THE BRASS RING
FOR A FREE RIDE

This c. 1910 jumper was originally carved as a horse but was later painted as a zebra.

Wheels of Progress

The planners of the Chicago World's Columbian Exposition of 1893 were determined that their World's Fair would in every way outshine the Paris Exposition of 1889. And so they challenged America's civil engineers: design something even more sensational than that fair's Eiffel Tower. George Ferris responded by reinventing the wheel.

A 33-year-old bridge builder, Ferris understood the potential of structural steel. He proposed using it to build a double wheel 250 feet in diameter, which he would then suspend from a pair of towers 140 feet high. Demonstrating true genius in coordinating the project, he contracted with nine different mills to manufacture parts of the wheel. They all arrived in a five-train convoy just five months later, and assembly was completed in a matter of 10 weeks.

The axle — 45 feet long and 32 inches in diameter — was the largest shaft of nickel steel yet forged. A 1,000-horsepower steam engine turned the 1,070-ton wheel, which, at a height of 26 stories, stood four stories taller than Chicago's Capitol Building — then the tallest building in the world. The wheel's 36 elegantly veneered wooden cars each provided plush seating for 40 passengers, and the standard trip of two revolutions took 20 minutes to complete. Even though the fare was set at an exorbitant 50 cents per passenger, the Ferris wheel proved to be a premier exposition attraction, and by the fair's closing day it had grossed more than $725,000.

To build his massive wheel, Ferris raised some $700,000 from private investors. Far too large to be moved economically, the wheel was dismantled after a decade and sold for scrap.

The First Frogman

Dublin-born adventurer Paul Boyton made quite a splash in 1874 when he plunged from a ship into the gale-tossed Atlantic Ocean and calmly paddled 30 miles to the Irish coast. The secret of his success was a watertight rubber suit fitted with strategically located inflatable pockets that allowed him to bob comfortably on his back. With the aid of a double-ended paddle, he propelled himself, feet first, like a human kayak.

His stunt was intended to publicize the suit, and although it never caught on, Boyton did. Eager for fame and new challenges, he paddled across the English Channel and floated down several of the world's major rivers.

Spangled with medals for his exploits, but ever restless for adventure, Boyton next tried his hand at show business. Riding his wave of fame, he installed an "aquatic circus" at Coney Island in 1895. Considered the first self-contained amusement park, Boyton's Sea Lion Park featured 40 juggling sea lions, water races, and the Shoot-the-Chutes, a water slide toboggan ride that he invented. Boyton made a fortune by building duplicate chutes across the nation — and amassed enough money to spend his final years studying rare birds.

Cyclone by the Sea

Coney Island was often imitated in the many amusement parks that sprang up in American cities in the last decades of the 19th century. But it is unlikely that the flamboyant exuberance of New York City's fantasia of fun was ever equaled.

Riverview Park in Chicago, for example, might have had a finer roller coaster. But Coney Island had one of the first — the Oriental Scenic Railway — and some of the most daring. The dizzying Loop-the-Loop, a roller coaster that spun adventurous riders through a 360-degree somersault, debuted at Coney Island in 1901, and the death-defying Cyclone appeared in 1928. And Philadelphia's Woodside Park might have the prettiest carousel, but Coney Island had more — at one time it offered an array of over 20.

Time and tide

The five-mile stretch of dunes on this small island off the southern tip of Brooklyn began attracting summer visitors in the 1840's. Walt Whitman, for one, was known to walk the beach declaiming Shakespeare to the gulls, and P. T. Barnum brought Jenny Lind, the Swedish Nightingale, to its shores. During the 1860's a collection of hotels, bathhouses, and amusements sprouted along the strand; by the 1870's New York's upper crust had made Coney Island's south-facing beach its summer playground.

Lights flashed on in 1876, and the world of boxing found its capital in the 10,000-seat Coney Island Athletic Club. Six years later, visitors could spend the night in a whimsical elephant-shaped hotel — they entered via a staircase in one leg — or find champagne on tap at the elegant Brighton Beach Hotel. By 1886 Coney Island's foremost entrepreneur, George Cornelius Tilyou, wrote of the "English dukes and earls, French viscomtes, German barons, senators and even presidents and vice-presidents, railroad kings, merchant princes, society queens" who assembled every summer. "If Paris is France," he boasted, "then Coney Island, between June and September, is the world."

The more the merrier

Inspired by Paul Boyton's Sea Lion Park, Tilyou in 1897 founded Coney Island's most famous and longest-lived amusement, Steeplechase Park. Its centerpiece, the

For decades, this slick character's piano-key grin invited would-be jockeys to Steeplechase Park.

steeplechase ride, simulated the horse racing that was the island's most popular spectator sport. Other attractions, such as the Barrel of Love and the Human Roulette Wheel, were designed to ruffle a lady's skirt, expose a glimpse of ankle, and then, perhaps, tumble her into a young man's arms.

The Steeplechase blend of lighthearted fun and wholesome flirtation proved irresistible, and competitors moved in to cash in on the excitement. Luna Park opened in 1903 and Dreamland the following year. The amusements at these parks were designed to educate and amaze. Here, workaday New Yorkers could stroll through the streets of Cairo, visit an Eskimo village, plunge 20,000 Leagues Under the Sea, or witness the Fall of Pompeii. One popular attraction at the parks was a rescue from a simulated burning building.

But fire proved Coney Island's nemesis, for the flimsy buildings burned like tinder. Steeplechase Park was gutted by fire in 1907, Dreamland in 1911, and Luna Park in 1949. Steeplechase's Tilyou alone chose to rebuild. Ever the showman, in the interim he fenced off the smoldering ashes and posted a sign: "Admission to the Burning Ruins — 10 cents."

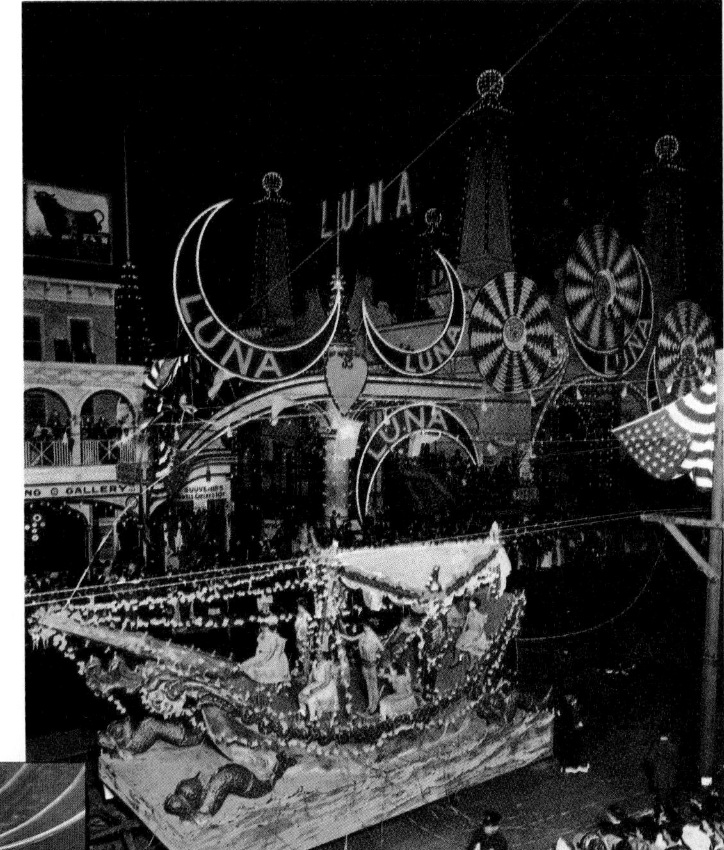

Nonstop fun was always on tap at turn-of-the-century Coney Island. Exotic floats paraded past a fanciful gate to Luna Park (top). Two adventurous ladies came in for a breathless and disheveled landing after an exhilarating swoop down Luna Park's Helter Skelter slide (above). Imposing by day, Dreamland's elaborate tower (right) was a star in the glittering nighttime skyline. One awed visitor likened Coney Island at night to "a fantastic city all of fire. . . . Fabulous beyond conceiving, ineffably beautiful."

Carnivals on Ice

Finer than a "dream castle of jasper or beryl or chrysoprase," a glittering medieval palace composed of 20,000 blocks of Mississippi River ice was the focal point of St. Paul, Minnesota's, first winter carnival. Conceived by a band of citizens as a way to counter the city's dour reputation as "another Siberia"and to inject some fun into the long, dark winter, the 1886 festival drew some 150,000 visitors. Throughout the carnival all sorts of amusements were available: dog sled races, ice skating, snowshoeing, curling, tobogganing, and elk-drawn sleigh rides. No sooner had this carnival ended than plans were being laid for bigger and better ones to come.

The next year's festivities began with the official unveiling of an array of ice sculptures set on ice pedestals brilliantly illuminated with electric light and affording a "spectacle worth a long journey to witness." On the second day an emissary from the north inspected the palace the city had erected and accepted it in behalf of the Ice King Borealis. The next day the Ice King Borealis — accompanied by Queen Aurora, ensconced in a moose-drawn crystal chariot attended by six white bears strutting on their hind legs and the colorfully uniformed members of some 100 local and visiting organizations — swept into the city and took possession of his glittering palace.

The following night everyone returned for what would become the highlight of the festival — a mock battle in which heroic legions of Borealis, King of Ice, protected their fragile castle from the encroaching forces of Vulcanus, King of Fire. The attackers sent Roman candles "screaming overhead to burst in gorgeous cataracts of sparks over the crest of the castle." Undaunted, the castle's keepers answered blast for blast until the battlements were "aflame with whirling wheels of scarlet and gold" and the forces of fire were subdued.

Other cities have borrowed on the theme and erected their own ice palaces, but St. Paul still holds the record for the largest one ever built — a frozen fantasy over16 stories tall, that starred in the 1992 carnival. The St. Paul palaces were also the first to include a functioning restaurant (1896), a working elevator (1937), and a branch of the U. S. Post Office (1940).

Not surprisingly, true love found an early home in the glistening castles. In 1888 a couple were married in the ice palace with some 6,000 carnival-goers in joyous attendance.

In a chariot drawn by fanciful chargers, King Borealis swept into St. Paul's 1888 Winter Carnival (above). The first ice palace, built in 1886, was 180 feet long, 154 feet wide, and featured a central tower 106 feet tall. The next year blanket squads gathered in front of the new palace and added to the festivities by giving the willing a heavenward bounce (right).

Treasure Island

When the gates opened on San Francisco's Golden Gate International Exposition on February 18, 1939, visitors found themselves in the midst of an exotic, and eclectic, fantasyland — a series of pavilions inspired by Mayan, Malayan, and Cambodian architecture. The fair, featuring a "Pacific Basin" motif, was as far away philosophically as it was geographically from the 1939 New York World's Fair, which had taken"The World of Tomorrow" as its theme.

The exposition's planners had investigated a number of sites for their extravaganza and rejected them all for being "too far . . . too fragile . . . or too ugly." Instead, they decided to build their own fairground on Yerba Buena Shoals, a 735-acre navigational hazard in San Francisco Bay, near the soon-to-be-completed Golden Gate Bridge. Beginning in March 1936 and working nearly round the clock for 18 months, the U.S. Army Corps of Engineers dumped rock and landfill atop the shoal until they had transformed it into a brand-new island, one mile long and two-thirds of a mile wide. With pride and optimism the exposition president, Leland Cutler, planted a flag on the new land that came to be known as "Treasure Island."

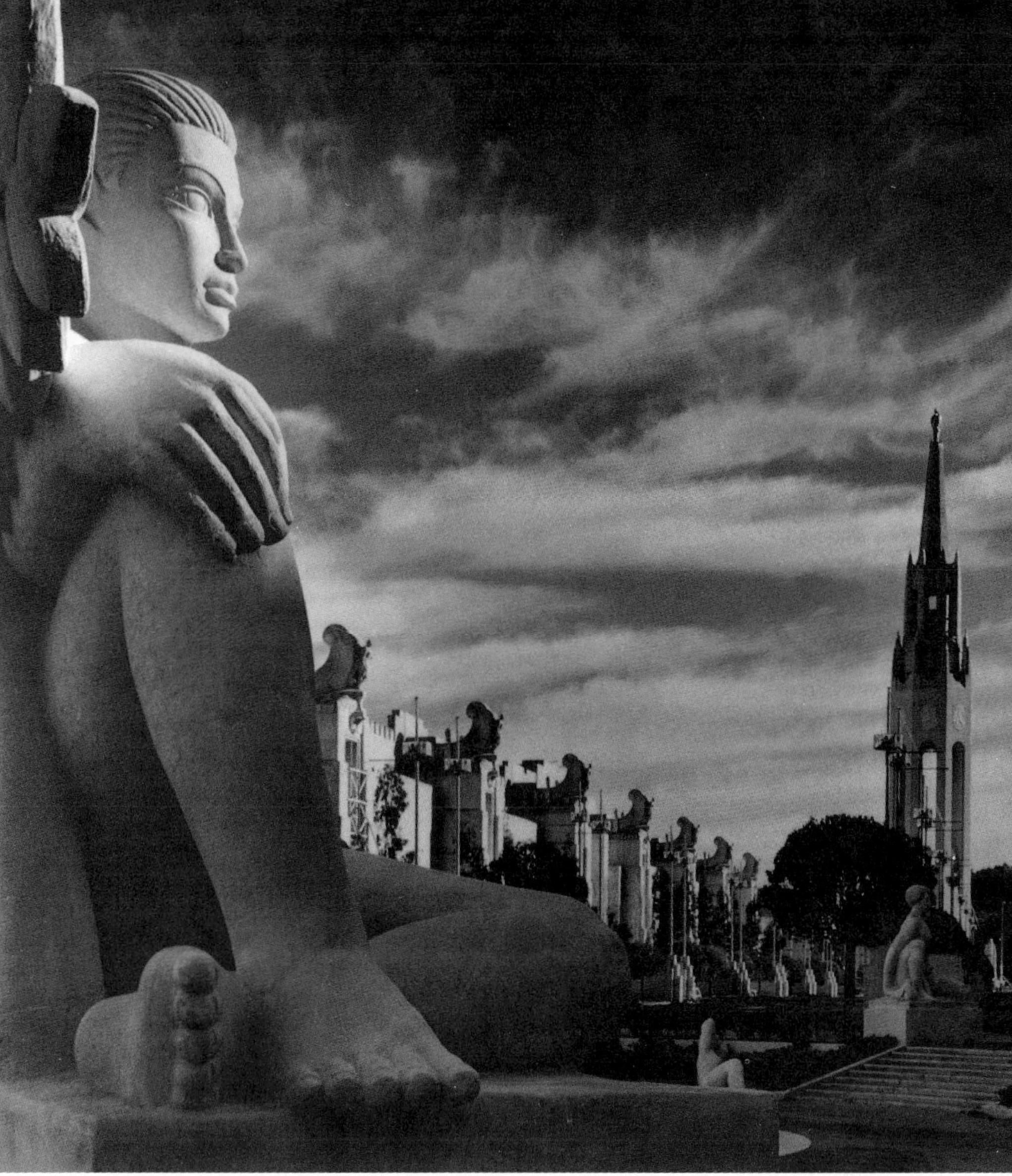

Art and architecture at the 1939 "Pageant of the Pacific" featured heroic statues, elaborate landscaping, and towering exhibit halls. At night the glow from some 10,000 colored floodlights created a shimmering fairyland bathed in rainbow hues.

Inside the Magic City

Two elephant-topped pyramids flanked the entrance to the fairgrounds, and inside the gates, visitors encountered Pacifica, an 80-foot tall, bright white statue of a woman with her arms raised in benevolent greeting. Behind her was a bright orange and blue "prayer curtain" made up of chimes that tinkled when stirred by breezes. Fair-goers wandered merrily along the Gayway's "40 acres of fun" and strolled among the Court of Flowers, the Court of the Moon, and the Court of the Seven Seas. At the Palace of Fine and Decorative Arts they could view some of the world's finest art, including Botticelli's "Birth of Venus" (affectionately known as "Venus on the Half Shell"). Other attractions included live kangaroos from faraway Australia and the "$900 crate" that aviator Wrong-Way Corrigan had flown to Ireland.

For those seeking simpler pleasures, there were Ferris wheels and dance bands, concerts in the Hall of Honor spotlighting Eddie Duchin and Count Basie, and Bing Crosby crooning in the Temple Compound. The Ziegfeld Follies and the Folies-Bergère added a touch of spice to the entertainment roster, but the adults-only admission policy at Sally Rand's Nude Ranch was the despair of many a teenage boy. For family fare a popular attraction was the Cavalcade of the Golden West, a pageant in which some 300 costumed participants struck dramatic poses intended as reenactments of great moments in history while nine narrators described the events.

Despite financial losses due to shrinking attendance, the exposition extended its run through a second season in 1940. By then, however, the specter of war had begun to cast its shadow, further dampening enthusiasm for the fair. A year later, bombs shattered the peace at Pearl Harbor, and memories of the dazzling show were all that remained of the pan-Pacific peace and unity the fair had sought to symbolize.

ENTERTAINMENTS

Billed as "The King of American Clowns," Dan Rice often dressed as Uncle Sam. His political jokes angered some but delighted many others.

A Star-Spangled Performer

He began his show business career in 1841 as half owner of a performing pig — and died penniless in 1900. But for many of the 60 years in between, Dan Rice was America's best-loved and best-paid clown.

Born Daniel McLaren in New York City in 1823, the future star ran away from home at an early age and, after trying a succession of jobs, discovered his talent for showmanship. Adopting his mother's maiden name, Rice performed a circus act with his pig, Lord Byron, until the animal died. Hooked on circus life by then, Rice stayed on, first as a strongman who caught cannonballs on the back of his neck, then as a clown who delighted audiences with his repartee.

Controversial as well as humorous, Rice developed political commentary as part of his act, and so became a favorite of both Jefferson Davis and Abraham Lincoln. Outfitting himself as Uncle Sam in a stars-and-stripes costume complete with stovepipe hat and goatee, he even went so far as to develop presidential ambitions of his own. It was a gauge of his immense popularity that when Rice declared his candidacy in 1868, more than one newspaper took him seriously.

By then Rice's wages had risen from an initial $15 per month to the princely sum of $1,000 per week. A tireless entrepreneur, he formed a succession of shows, touring in a private steamboat up and down the Mississippi and Ohio rivers with a troupe of trained horses, educated pigs, a trick mule, and a tightrope-walking elephant. These ventures brought him several fortunes; his net profit for the 1869 season alone was $125,000. But Rice was incapable of hanging on to money — what he didn't lose to bank failure and his battle with the bottle, he mostly gave away.

Although Rice died in obscurity, his legacy lives on — the result of a performance he gave when his boat pulled up in McGregor, Iowa, one day in 1870. Setting up his show on the shore, he entranced a party of five young brothers named Ringling, an event that undoubtedly influenced the beginning of their own circus career.

Barnum's Biggest Box-Office Draw

What would those Americans buy next? the English thundered. Shakespeare's grave? The Tower of London? But in fact all that P. T. Barnum wanted was their beloved elephant, Jumbo.

The British for years had gloried in the fact that the largest animal in captivity, an 11½-foot-tall, 6½-ton African elephant, resided in their own London Zoological Gardens. Thousands of children, including the royal princes and princesses, had ridden on the gentle giant's back. But by 1881 the zoo's management was worried that Jumbo might become unmanageable as he matured. So when Barnum offered to buy the beast for £2,000, the zoo quickly agreed.

Announcement of the sale raised a storm of protest — the Prince of Wales publicly condemned the deal and the Fellows of the Royal Zoological Society sought an injunction to prevent Jumbo's removal. Americans, however, reacted to the news with a patriotic pride that Barnum was quick to exploit. When an English newspaper asked what he would take to cancel the sale, Barnum piously replied that for 40 years he had always provided his countrymen with the best of exhibitions, and he could not change that now. Barnum also made much of his discovery that Jumbo's keeper, Matthew Scott, had staged a series of incidents in which the elephant appeared to refuse to leave the zoo.

Nevertheless, as Londoners mourned their loss by dressing in Jumbo boots, hats, ties, canes — even Jumbo underwear — Barnum's crew loaded the elephant onto a transatlantic steamer. When it docked in New York on April 9, 1882, an impromptu parade of spectators accompanied Jumbo to his new quarters at Madison Square Garden. Within two weeks, entrance fees had repaid Barnum his entire investment of $30,000.

Some 20 million Americans paid to see Jumbo over the next three years as he toured the country in his own "palace" railroad car. His name was used to advertise everything from tooth powder to thread, and it was Jumbo who amiably ambled across Brooklyn Bridge to test its strength before the span was opened to the public in 1883. Barnum had announced that his elephant's name would drive adjectives such as "mammoth" out of common use — and so it did.

Not even Jumbo, however, could survive a collision with a freight train, and so he died one night in September 1885 in St. Thomas, Ontario. But Barnum was prepared even for the animal's death. He had made arrangements to mount Jumbo's skin and skeleton. In this state Jumbo continued to tour, accompanied by troupes of mourning elephants that had been taught to wipe their eyes with black-bordered bed sheets.

Photographed with his trainer (above), Jumbo was touted in publicity material (left) as "the Largest & Heaviest Elephant ever seen by mortal man either wild or in captivity." Barnum's circus poster exaggerated Jumbo's height by only a small margin.

Known on both sides of the Atlantic, pioneering playwright-actress Anna Cora Mowatt is portrayed here in her role as Beatrice in Shakespeare's *Much Ado About Nothing.*

A Home-Grown Lily Blooms on Stage

Fearing scorn and social ostracism, a small, auburn-haired woman stood trembling as she read poetry on a Boston stage in 1841. She had reason for concern: in her day it was believed that only women of easy virtue or poor breeding trod the boards. And Anna Cora Mowatt's blood was as blue as her eyes.

Known as Lily by her family and friends, Mowatt had summoned the courage to defy convention only after her husband's investments had left the couple nearly penniless. While many in the upper-crust audience had shown up out of sympathy, they nevertheless left exhilarated, and Mowatt's readings became a box-office hit.

Newly encouraged, Mowatt turned next to writing and sold stories and articles to the country's most popular magazines. Then in 1845 she once again risked her reputation, braving disapproval as the author of a play. Far from shocking or disappointing audiences, however, *Fashion*, a comedy of manners in which Mowatt pricked the egos of the newly rich, succeeded in winning widespread praise. Even the then little-known drama critic Edgar Allan Poe called her work "in many respects . . . superior to any American play."

Emboldened by this new success (not to mention the improvement in family finances), Lily daringly accepted an invitation to play the lead in *The Lady of Lyons*, a popular drama, and finding life before the footlights to her liking, went on to win acclaim as an actress. Mowatt's show business career was brief — though she gained fame in England as well as America, she took curtain calls for only eight years. But by proving that she possessed both pedigree and talent, she played her finest role in making theater respectable.

The Rip-Roaring Role of a Lifetime

Performing the role of Rip Van Winkle for nearly 40 years, Joseph Jefferson embodied the fictional character for generations of Americans.

"Rip Van Winkle was not a sudden success," Joseph Jefferson conceded in his autobiography. Indeed, by the time he became intrigued with Washington Irving's classic tale in 1859, the story of a man who woke from a 20-year nap into a new world had been staged in at least seven different versions, with leading men that included both Jefferson's father and his half brother.

The son, grandson, and great-grandson of actors, Jefferson spent his life on stage, performing for the first time at age four in a minstrel act. In 1837, when he was eight years old, his family moved west, and in the nomadic life that followed, he performed in barns and log cabins. In the 1840's he even traveled south of the border, where he spent time entertaining American troops during the Mexican War.

Finally returning to the East, Jefferson made a name for himself as a gifted comedian in the New York theaters. Then, while vacationing with his family, he had the chance to do some reading and became fascinated with Rip Van Winkle. "Was not this the very character I wanted?" the actor wrote. "An American story by an American author was surely just the theme suited to an American actor." But he had to wait six years before he had a chance to try the role.

Artist George Waters commemorated Joseph Jefferson's role as Rip Van Winkle in an 1871 oil painting.

It was in London in 1865, after a four-year tour of Australia, that Jefferson was able to persuade Dion Boucicault, a fashionable playwright, to create a new version of the story for him. Opening night at London's Adelphi Theatre was a smash success — Jefferson seemed actually to have become Washington Irving's old scamp. After a run of 170 performances, he returned to New York and received an even warmer reception. From 1866 until 1904, he toured the country and repeatedly performed the role.

Like his stage character, Jefferson witnessed many changes. Having begun his career on the frontier, he lived long enough to portray Rip Van Winkle before a movie camera in an 1896 silent film of the tale.

America's Romance With a Nightingale

An engraved portrait of Jenny Lind (above) presents a somewhat idealized image of the singer, whose form also graces a candlestick (far right). Lind's popularity during her two years in America was so great that products as unlikely as cigars (right) and chewing gum were named in her honor, as were a sewing machine, a sofa, a dahlia, a sausage, and a muskmelon.

It was an unlikely partnership. P. T. Barnum had made a fortune foisting many bogus marvels on a gullible public. But Jenny Lind was the real thing — one of the great sopranos of all time, with a reputation as pure as her voice. In an era when prima donnas often doubled as courtesans, Swedish-born Lind devoted her free time to charities. Still, she drove a hard bargain.

Trained for the operatic stage in Stockholm and Paris, "the Swedish Nightingale," as Lind was known, was one of the most famous singers in Europe in 1850 when Barnum asked her to tour America. The 30-year-old star responded by demanding a fee of $1,000 per performance, a 61-piece orchestra, a staff of servants and assistants, and a carriage in each city she visited. When Barnum agreed, she had her banker check his credit, and then insisted on $187,500 in advance. The deal almost broke Barnum, who mortgaged everything he owned and still fell $5,000 short. A clergyman who had heard of Lind's good works finally made up the difference with his life savings.

Few other Americans had heard of the Swedish star, but Barnum soon changed that. He circulated Lind's photograph with a biography that stressed her benefit performances for hospitals and orphanages. Then, just before she sailed for America, he sponsored two "farewell" concerts in England and paid a critic to send American newspapers rave reviews of her performances. As a result, some 40,000 curiosity seekers mobbed the dock at Lind's arrival; 50 people were trampled, and the harbor police were kept busy fishing sightseers out of the water. Barnum himself drove Lind to her hotel, and on the way music lovers tossed 200 bouquets through the windows of her carriage.

The toast of every town

Reporters were surprised to find that the much-heralded Nightingale was far from dainty, but they had to admit that her singing justified all the ballyhoo. At one rehearsal the orchestra forgot to play, so enchanting was Lind's voice, and she brought the house down with her Scandinavian folk songs on opening night in New York.

Barnum often made a practice of auctioning off the first ticket in cities that Lind played, and admirers paid hundreds of dollars for the privilege of buying them. In Boston a coachman who had assisted her from a carriage charged fans five dollars apiece to kiss his hand, and her performance of "Home, Sweet Home" in Washington helped make that song an American favorite.

When Lind insisted on renegotiating her contract, demanding half the profit, Barnum could only agree. Over a nine-month period she performed 93 times in cities from Boston to Havana and New Orleans, always to packed houses. Then, after Barnum had earned more than $700,000 on his investment, Lind decided to manage the rest of the tour herself — a task that proved far more difficult than she imagined.

But it was Lind's marriage to her accompanist, Otto Goldschmidt, in 1852 that proved her undoing, since her fans could not accept this affront to their romantic fantasies. The singer returned to Europe, having inspired Americans with a lasting enthusiasm for fine music. Of all who heard her, only Barnum remained unmoved: the great showman, alas, was tone deaf.

Gilmore's Galas

Bigger is better" was Patrick Gilmore's credo. And Americans of the Gilded Age agreed. With their enthusiastic support the Irish-born bandmaster staged the greatest musical extravaganzas America had ever seen.

Falling in love with a military band in his home town as a boy, Gilmore studied music and, in 1846, at age 21, followed the band to Canada. Traveling southward, he was made bandmaster of Massachusetts' 24th regiment during the Civil War and was then placed in charge of Louisiana's Union military bands. His big break came in 1864 when Louisiana's newly elected governor asked Gilmore to stage his inaugural concert.

Drawing on his genius as a drillmaster, Gilmore coordinated a chorus of some 5,000 flag-waving children with an orchestra of 500. Never one to shrink from pyrotechnics, he punctuated a performance of "Hail Columbia" with shots from a battery of 36 cannons and the simultaneous clanging of New Orleans' church bells.

Gilmore's reward was a silver cup filled with gold coins, and such fame that he was able to find backers for a far more ambitious "monster band concert," as he aptly tagged his shows. In 1869 Gilmore staged a five-day National Peace Jubilee in Boston. In a "coliseum" specially constructed from 2½ million board-feet of lumber, he brought together a 1,000-piece orchestra, a chorus of 10,000, the largest organ ever built, and a bass drum 25 feet in circumference. The audience's reaction verged on hysteria, especially when 100 city firemen in full uniform marched in with blacksmith's hammers to beat time for Verdi's "Anvil Chorus."

Meticulous organization was Gilmore's secret: he used electricity to fire the big guns, and speaking tubes to communicate with lieutenants posted throughout the chorus. But his efforts could not control the 20,000 singers and 2,000-piece orchestra he brought to Boston for an 18-day World Peace Jubilee in 1872: twice the chorus fell into confusion in midsong. Still, Johann Strauss's performance of "The Blue Danube" was a wild success, and the competition of French, British, German, and American military bands stirred enormous excitement.

After a Chicago Jubilee, in 1873, Gilmore claimed he had said good-bye to his grandiose galas, but he never quite gave them up. As late as the 1890's, his annual concerts for New York's Manhattan Beach resort were performed complete with fireworks.

Shown in full regalia (right), Patrick Gilmore never lost his love for the sound of a military band. A composer as well as a showman, he and his band for many years performed an annual concert at New York's Manhattan Beach. At their 1885 performance, memorialized in the lithograph below, his band provided the music for a spectacle titled *The Last Days of Pompeii.* Despite all the fanfare, however, Gilmore is best known for his composition "When Johnny Comes Marching Home," which he wrote under a pseudonym.

DESCRIPTIVE MUSIC
"THE LAST DAYS OF POMPEII."
TO BE PRODUCED IN FIREWORKS, SEASON OF 1885, UNDER THE DIRECTION OF JAMES PAIN, of London,
MANHATTAN BEACH.
GILMORE'S BAND

The Man Who Set America Marching

Born and raised in the nation's capital, John Philip Sousa produced toe-tapping marches as a rousing — and purely American — musical form.

In 1867, 13-year-old John Philip Sousa was offered a job with a circus band. But his father had other ideas. Before the boy could run off, he stepped in and enlisted young Sousa as an apprentice in the United States Marine Band. Even then the lad was a seasoned musician. In seven years of private study, he had mastered musical theory, voice, violin, piano, flute, and an assortment of horns.

After a seven-year hitch, Sousa left the corps to play in theater orchestras, an experience that proved invaluable since, as he later maintained, "the man who does not exercise showmanship is dead." Indeed, by age 26, when Sousa was invited back, this time to lead the U.S. Marine Band, his conducting style was termed hypnotic. Standing gracefully erect, he guided the musicians with precise, dancelike motions of his head, hands, and fingers.

By changing the band's instrumentation and emphasizing musicianship, Sousa transformed it from a military convenience into one of the finest ensembles in the land, equally at ease with popular songs, theater tunes, and classical pieces. The marches he added to the repertoire — including original compositions such as "Semper Fidelis" — earned him the title of the March King, and his "Washington Post March" turned the sprightly two-step into an international dance craze.

Sousa left the marines again in 1892 to form his own band, a group of 70 musicians that toured worldwide, logging 1.5 million miles over the next four decades as it played to audiences totaling 50 million. When his band arrived in a town, schools closed and people gathered from miles around to hear programs remarkable for their variety. While Sousa loved marches best — he composed more than 100, and no concert was complete without "The Stars and Stripes Forever" — he regularly featured well-known singers and violinists as well.

His goal, he said, was to entertain, not to educate. But Sousa took his band to many cities that had never heard anything even approaching the sound of a symphony orchestra. He played music from Wagner's *Parsifal* 10 years before the work was introduced at the Metropolitan Opera, and though he disdained "canned music" (a term he coined), he was one of the first American musicians of note to make recordings.

Attributing his success to hard work rather than his evident talent, he claimed that "the first you'll hear of Sousa's retirement is when you'll hear 'Sousa dead.'" And in fact it was just after rehearsing a local band's performance of "The Stars and Stripes Forever" in Reading, Pennsylvania, in 1932 that the March King died of a heart attack at the age of 77.

John Philip Sousa was still in his 20's when he was named leader of the U.S. Marine Band (above). Although he toured America and Europe for 40 years with his own band, Sousa was linked with marches even in his old age (below). "The Stars and Stripes Forever," which he scored in 1897 (bottom), remains an all-time favorite.

The Captain and Mrs. French

One night in 1878, during the wettest summer in Ohio history — when the rain-soaked circus tent collapsed and all but one of his wagons bogged down in mud — Augustus Byron French decided he'd had enough. If he had to float his show, he reasoned, he might as well put it on a boat. Converting an 85-foot barge into a showboat, by November the self-styled "captain" was drifting downriver.

Actually, entrepreneurs had been putting shows afloat since the 1830's, and showboats plied the Atlantic Coast as well as the rivers of the Midwest and South. But none of the other impresarios had French's insight: he realized that his audience lay on the frontier, in remote settlements without any other entertainment. Nor did French's rivals have a partner like his wife, Callie. She could walk a tightrope, play the dulcimer — or steer the boat. (She was the first woman ever granted a river pilot's license.)

In this setting rocks and sandbars posed far greater threats than bad reviews. When the current carried his unpowered boat to a town, French would tie up, then send his gaily garbed performers ashore to drum up business. The shows were always wholesome family entertainment: a mix of magic tricks, comic songs, acrobatics, a "comedy farce," and a stump speech. Once, when an all-male audience boarded, obviously in search of something risqué, French indignantly sent the men home, telling them to return with their wives. They did.

With the help of steam tugs, floating theaters like French's *New Sensation* brought drama to West Virginia miners, Wisconsin homesteaders, and Louisiana Cajuns. In 1910, 22 showboats plied the Mississippi alone; but within a generation, nearly all were gone, as automobiles and movies diverted their audiences to big-city theaters.

When French's showboat came within hearing range, the townsfolk, eager for entertainment, heeded the captain's call to "listen for the toot of the calliope and make a break for the river."

Ziegfeld's Follies

At age 15 Florenz Ziegfeld ran away with Buffalo Bill's Wild West Show. Though his father, the president of a Chicago music school, caught up with him in the next town, the boy's career choice had been made. By 22 he was promoting his own show, a troupe of dancing ducks, and two years later, in the winter of 1893, he set out on a nationwide tour as the manager of a strongman. His genius as a publicist — he once matched his client in a hand-to-paw contest with a lion — brought Ziegfeld a profit of $250,000, which he gambled away within a few weeks of his arrival in New York.

The road to Broadway

Befriended by Diamond Jim Brady (who helped him pay his gambling debts), Ziegfeld was ready to take New York by storm. He began by promoting the French actress, Anna Held. A public kissing contest and the rumors, spread by Ziegfeld, that she bathed in milk soon made her the talk of the town — and made the impresario a rich man once again. International fame came in 1907 with the first of the musical revues — the "Ziegfeld Follies" — that he would stage annually for 27 years.

Feminine beauty was an obsession with the showman; he pursued it tirelessly through two stormy marriages and several affairs. In the Follies he turned his appreciation into an art form. Each of his chorines, he insisted, should be dressed as well as the wealthiest woman in the audience. He chose all their clothes himself and examined each costume as soon as it arrived, turning it inside out to make sure the lining was silky and fine so that his actresses would feel feminine and move gracefully. He kept a list of the most beautiful women he knew, and courted them tirelessly to keep them in his shows and out of the shows of his competitors.

Curiously, many of Ziegfeld's beauties didn't impress by the light of day. But he knew what really shone under spotlights. A blazing redhead might be introduced among a knot of platinum blondes. If a woman's face was plain, he'd adjust the lights to emphasize her perfect figure. His sense of style was unerring, if outrageous. The 1927 Follies boasted a segment with 19 gorgeous women playing 19 white pianos; to publicize another event, he had his "Follies Girls" play saxophones by moonlight as they danced in the surf at New York's Rockaway Beach. The 1915 Follies, which opened with an underwater scene, was designed entirely in shades of blue.

Wildly extravagant, Ziegfeld would at the last minute cut a scene that had cost him $25,000 to stage. He kept five Rolls-Royces, each with its own chauffeur, and for his daughter's playhouse he built a model of Mount Vernon. Yet he let a composer's royalties go unpaid and was constantly involved in litigation. And preferring to communicate by telegraph, he often sent telegrams to the performers at rehearsals rather than calling to them across the footlights.

The Stock Market Crash of 1929 wiped out Ziegfeld's personal fortune, and by that time Hollywood had stolen many of his staging techniques and most of his stars. Yet Ziegfeld remained unimpressed by California; if he wanted, he observed during one visit, he could have a copy built on Broadway within a week. Before "more stars than there are in heaven" twinkled on studio lots, Fanny Brice, Sophie Tucker, Eddie Cantor, and Will Rogers, among others, shone brightly on the Ziegfeld stage.

Although most famous for their displays of feminine beauty, the Ziegfeld Follies also launched the careers of some funny men. W. C. Fields, Will Rogers, Eddie Cantor, and Harry Keely appeared in the 1915 Follies (facing page). In *The Century Girl* four young charmers beamed from the scoop of a quarter moon (above).

A born showman, Flo Ziegfeld was guided by a pure sense of form and an unerring instinct for making his performers look good. Using a hoop for a halo, a Ziegfeld girl posed at the New Amsterdam Theatre (above). Exquisitely outfitted in gossamer garb, a butterfly chorus (left) fluttered through the 1920 production of *Sally*.

As much at home on the range as in the big-city parlor, the banjo brought solace to many a lonely frontiersman, as depicted by Thomas Eakins in his painting "Cowboy Singing."

Strummin' on the Old Banjo

Few sounds are so intimately linked with America's folk music as the distinctive *plink* of the banjo. Yet this seemingly all-American instrument — the choice of everyone from cowboys and mountain men to rocking-chair troubadours — is in fact of African origin.

The forerunner of today's banjo, known as the banjere, bandja, or bandshaw, was brought to this country by slaves as early as the 17th century. The instruments originally were made from long-necked gourds, with skins stretched taut over their hollowed bowls, and four gut strings for plucking and strumming.

The modern banjo, which first appeared around 1830, is thought to have been the creation of Joel Walker Sweeney, a young fiddle-playing farmer from Virginia. According to tradition, Sweeney, who grew up to the sounds of music made by the black field hands on his grandmother's farm, one day decided to make a banjere for himself, only better. Attaching a wooden neck to the rim of a circular cheesebox, and adding screw-brackets to adjust the skin tension, he was able to produce a brighter, plinkety-plunk sound. The improvement soon was copied by black musicians and then by white minstrel show performers.

As banjos grew in popularity, several styles appeared. Cowboy banjos were typically plain, sturdy, homemade affairs, while Victorian parlor banjos were factory-made and featured all sorts of fine detailing, from mother-of-pearl inlay to fancy engraving. Somewhat smaller and higher pitched than earlier examples, the new commercial banjos were the delight of genteel society. The *Boston Daily Evening Voice* noted in 1866 that "many of the ladies of the bon ton, infatuated with [banjo] music, have become expert in its management. Indeed it is not uncommon to find the banjo occupying a conspicuous corner in a Fifth Avenue parlor." Many clubs and college groups formed their own banjo bands, and much popular music was transposed and published for the banjo-playing public.

The instrument entered yet another phase of evolution in the Roaring Twenties, when the four-string tenor or pick-played banjos became identified with the music of the Jazz Age. And today the irrepressible banjo is popular again, this time as the heart and soul of the "Bluegrass" revival.

Tin Pan Alley's One-Fisted Fighter

Songwriter Harry Macgregor Woods had a knack for achieving legendary status in just about everything he did. Born in 1896, he was known to his family and friends as a gifted piano player. "You would think he had 20 fingers," his sister recalled — an observation that was all the more remarkable since Woods was born with only one hand. Completely undaunted, he conquered the keyboard by playing the melody with his right hand, and using his left wrist to work the harmony — mainly on the black keys.

Many of the songs Wood played were his own compositions. Reaching the high point of his career in the 1920's and 1930's — the golden era of Tin Pan Alley — he wrote the music, and occasionally the lyrics as well, for some 700 songs. With hits that included such enduring favorites as "Side by Side" and "I'm Looking Over a Four Leaf Clover," Woods's name became linked with a style that was happy, upbeat, and invariably wholesome.

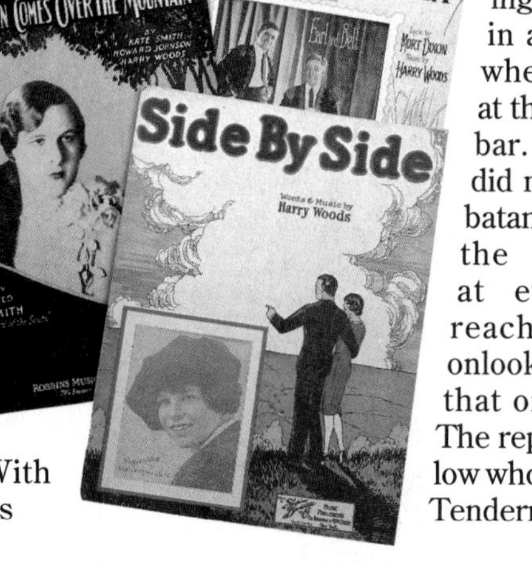

But the songwriter himself had a darker side. Claiming to have a fighter's edge since he had fewer knuckles to break, Woods earned a reputation as a barroom brawler that was as legendary as any other aspect of his life. On one occasion he was having drinks with a pal in a Manhattan café when a fight erupted at the other end of the bar. Although Woods did not know the combatants, he leaped into the fray, swinging at everyone within reach. Amazed, one onlooker asked, "Who's that one-handed guy?" The reply: "That's the fellow who wrote 'Try a Little Tenderness.' "

The Music Goes Round and Round

The Wurlitzers gained fame first for musical instruments and then for adding thrill to silent movies. But their crowning success was the jukebox.

Landing on American shores in 1853, young Rudolph Wurlitzer made a solemn vow: no matter how hard his new life, he would set aside a quarter of his earnings and someday start a business of his own. And despite the meagerest of wages, within three years he did manage to save $700. Looking around for business opportunities, Wurlitzer noticed that, though very popular in America, musical instruments were also very expensive. He was sure that he could beat the competition — and he did. Importing instruments from his native Germany and selling them at wholesale prices, Wurlitzer soon dominated the field. But his wisest decision was to move from instruments to music machines.

Five cents a song

In 1892, soon after the advent of electrical power, Wurlitzer produced the world's first coin-operated electric organ. He followed up, in quick succession, with a self-playing harp and a "pianino," an electric piano-mandolin. In 1899 the Wurlitzer Company topped itself with the Tonophone, a coin-operated player piano that offered listeners a choice of 10 music rolls for just a nickel a song. Hotels, saloons, and restaurants that were unable to afford live musicians bought thousands of them, prompting bandleader John Philip Sousa to predict the death of amateur musicianship and a deterioration in American musical taste.

In 1912 Wurlitzer turned the company over to his three sons, who produced a new sensation — The Mighty Wurlitzer, the glamorous pipe organ that filled silent-movie palaces with sound. The company's continuing success seemed assured until the Depression devastated the music business. But then, in 1934, while desperately searching for a new product that would revive the firm, one of the sons, Farny Wurlitzer, made the deal of a lifetime. Contracting with fellow musical entrepreneur Homer Capehart, he bought the license to the "Simplex," an automatic record changer. He also hired Capehart — who would become a company vice president and general sales manager — and Wurlitzer plunged wholeheartedly into the new jukebox business.

Lights! Music! Action!

Almost overnight, a rather small industry with few competitors was transformed into big business, with Wurlitzer setting new standards in design and technology. Most notably, Wurlitzer and Capehart turned jukeboxes into sound and light shows. Scrapping the dignified wood-veneer models of old, they introduced Art Deco combinations of chrome, translucent plastics, mirrored glass, and bubbling fluorescent lights, changing the models yearly to keep customers coming back. In 1936, in large part due to Capehart's marketing wizardry, Wurlitzer sold more than 44,000 jukeboxes. And America, with its irreversibly altered musical taste, was dancing happily to the strains of hits by Benny Goodman and Bing Crosby.

With its elaborate peacock motif and lights that changed color, the Wurlitzer 850 (above), introduced in 1941, was deservedly described as "super deluxe." During the 1940's everyone danced to the jukebox's beat (right).

TIME TABLE

REEL TIME

1894 *The first motion picture is Thomas Edison's* Record of a Sneeze.

1896 *John Rice and May Irwin thrill audiences with an on-screen kiss.*

1896 *Vitascope Hall, America's first movie theater, opens in New Orleans.*

1898 *The story of Cinderella, the subject of more than 50 films, is shot for the first time.*

1909 Les Misérables, *a four-reeler from Vitagraph, is America's first feature film.*

1910 *D. W. Griffith shoots* In Old California *on location in Hollywood.*

1911 *An abandoned roadhouse in Hollywood is converted to a film studio.*

1912 *Lillian Russell stars in* La Tosca *— America's first film shot in natural color.*

1914 *Charlie Chaplin's Tramp costume is made from borrowed clothing, including Fatty Arbuckle's pants.*

The Fox Theater in St. Louis, Missouri, epitomizes the grandeur of the great movie palaces.

Palaces for the People

In the heady days following World War I the movies in many ways were king. So why not build palaces to show them in? Purists might complain about Buddhas in the balconies of the lavish theaters that cropped up in cities all across America. But the public loved them — and the more ornate they were, the better.

Audiences at Houston's Majestic sat in an Italian garden surrounded by stuffed peacocks. In Baraboo, Wisconsin, the latest films were viewed in a miniature European-style opera house. And after the discovery of King Tut's tomb in 1922, theaters were suddenly awash with scarabs, sphinxes, and hieroglyphics. Even powder rooms were deluxe: the Ambassador in St. Louis featured a replica of Madame Pompadour's salon at Fontainebleau.

But perhaps the grandest of them all was the "sumptuous and stupendous" Roxy Theater, which opened in New York City in 1927. The brainchild of hash-slinger-turned-impresario Samuel L. "Roxy" Rothafel, it was billed as the Cathedral of the Motion Picture and outdid all others with its glorious excess. In the vast rotunda that served as a lobby, twelve marble pillars soared five stories to a magnificent bronze dome illuminated by a sparkling, 20-foot crystal chandelier. The floor was covered with the world's largest oval rug, more than two tons of paisley with a border representing loops of film. A battalion of ushers — "unrivaled in sweetness" — escorted patrons to the 6,214 red-plush seats, each emblazoned with the letter *R*.

But all good things come to an end, and the legendary Roxy succumbed to the wrecker's ball in 1960. The few palaces that remain are monuments to an exuberant age of innocent splendor.

The Fairest of Them All

"The world fades away when Mr. Disney begins weaving his spell, and enchantment takes hold," wrote one critic when *Snow White and the Seven Dwarfs* opened for the Christmas season in 1937. But the question for more than three years had been whether the spell was being cast or being broken as Walt Disney coaxed and coached and drove his colleagues with his daring vision of a full-length animated feature based on a fairy tale — the story of a girl who took refuge with forest gnomes after being condemned to death by her jealous stepmother.

The project was disparaged by Hollywood insiders as "Disney's Folly," and even Roy Disney, Walt's brother and business partner, pleaded, "Why can't we just stay with Mickey Mouse?" But Disney held fast to his vision, and once he was committed, no detail was too minor, no task too time consuming, no obstacle insurmountable.

A total of 149 singers auditioned for the role of Snow White — Disney listened to their voices while sitting behind a screen so that their appearances would not be a distraction — before he selected Adriana Caselotti's sweet silvery soprano. Music, in fact, played a major role in the film. Disney wanted "a new way to use music — weave it into the story so somebody doesn't just burst into

Reel Life Adventures

Simba! Captured by Cannibals! Congorilla! The titles fairly sing of steamy jungles, exotic wildlife, and danger. And for audiences in the 1920's and 1930's, tickets to these films by Martin and Osa Johnson — pioneers of the documentary — were in effect passports to adventure.

They were an unlikely pair: he had knocked around Europe as a teen and cruised the South Seas with Jack London, where he shot his first film. She possessed spirit and spunk, but had never journeyed more than 30 miles from her hometown of Chanute, Kansas. They had been married only six months when Martin suddenly announced a plan to travel around the world. "Well — all right, dear," Osa replied gamely. And off they went.

The pair first hit the vaudeville trail, where a series of lectures and showings of the South Seas film brought in enough cash to finance the trip. Sailing among the Solomon Islands and the New Hebrides, their efforts to film the Malekula cannibals almost ended with Osa "in the pot." They escaped and the film made their fortune.

In their 27 years together, the two thrilled moviegoers with the unknown — the first aerial view of Kilimanjaro, the daily life of pygmies in the Ituri Forest — and left for future generations a poignant record of worlds now gone forever.

Among their happiest years were the four spent at Lake Paradise in Kenya, filming Africa's rapidly vanishing wildlife. A crack shot and expert fisher, Osa was also a regular on best-dressed lists. When in Europe, she shopped for Paris gowns, and even in their African camps in the evening she slipped into royal blue satin pajamas with lipstick-red buttons. In the thatched-roof house that Martin built, they took their meals "with wildflowers for table decorations and the roar of lions for dinner music."

In 1928 the couple returned to New York and for six months endured real terrors — telephones, weekend parties, traffic jams. That Christmas, they both chose the gift each knew the other wanted most — a ticket back to Africa.

In 1928 filmmakers Martin and Osa Johnson posed among Ituri Forest pygmies in the Belgian Congo (now Zaire).

song." Sound effects were subtly blended with the soundtrack to link scenes together, and a long search for a yodeler equal to Disney's exacting standards was finally discovered in Jim MacDonald, the sound effects designer. Chemists whipped up 1,500 colors of paint from which the final shades were selected — including actual rouge, which studio colorists skillfully dabbed by hand onto thousands of the film's quarter-million celluloid sheets to bring a realistic blush to Snow White's cheeks.

But the greatest care was lavished on the creation of the vibrant, distinctly individual "seven little men." Disney came up with a list of 50 possible names — Blabby, Shifty, and Snoopy were among those rejected — before settling on Doc, Dopey, Sleepy, Sneezy, Happy, Grumpy, and Bashful for the miniature miners. Dopey was the shortest and the last to be named. He was envisioned as a chatterbox until genius flashed: the seventh dwarf would not speak at all. When one animator suggested he also have a humorous "hitch" step, entire sequences were redrawn.

The budget skyrocketed as work proceeded, and Disney needed an additional $250,000 to complete the film. In an attempt to wring another loan out of the Bank of America, he showed an unfinished print to a loan officer, heroically acting out the missing parts. The laconic banker said not a word until Disney walked the man to his car and at last was told, "That thing is going to make you a hatful of money."

It did that, and more. Once cast, the spell endured. *Snow White and the Seven Dwarfs* has been seen in some 60 countries. A week after the opening, Disney and his magical dwarfs made the cover of *Time.* And in 1938 they were honored with a special Academy Award: one full-size Oscar and seven little statuettes.

1915 *The Knickerbocker Theatre in New York offers a double feature.*

1916 *Mary Pickford's new contract makes her the world's highest-paid woman.*

1917 *Technicolor brightens* The Gulf Between.

1925 The Big Parade, *the most profitable silent film, and* Ben-Hur, *the most expensive, open.*

1927 *Al Jolson ad-libs the first talkie:* The Jazz Singer.

1928 *Mickey Mouse sails onto the screen in* Steamboat Willie.

1929 Wings, *starring Gary Cooper, is cited as Best Production at the inaugural Academy Awards ceremony.*

1933 *A drive-in theater opens in Camden, N.J.*

1933 *For her performance in* Morning Glory, *Katharine Hepburn receives the first of her 12 Academy Award nominations and wins the first of her 3 Oscars.*

1934 *Shirley Temple wins a special Oscar for her "outstanding contribution to screen entertainment."*

1940 *Stereo sound enhances two Warner Brothers' films:* Santa Fe Trail *and* Four Wives.

1942 *Greer Garson delivers a one-hour thank-you speech for her Best Actress award as Mrs. Miniver.*

GAMES PEOPLE PLAY

Still actively involved in his own game in 1925, James Naismith coaches his son in the fine art of sinking a shot.

The Perfect Solution

A winter sport to fill the gap between football and baseball seasons: that was what his students needed. James Naismith, an instructor at the YMCA Training School in Springfield, Massachusetts, first tried indoor soccer. But when it resulted in a broken leg and several broken windows, he gave lacrosse a try. It proved no better. Then, in the winter of 1891, he hung a peach basket from the balcony at each end of his gym and typed up a set of 13 rules for a game he had invented. Dividing his 18 students into teams, he tossed up a soccer ball for two players to tip at the center of the gym, and the first-ever game of basketball was under way.

Naismith's new sport was an instant hit. One student even stole the original set of rules, later explaining: "I knew this game would be a big success and I took them as a souvenir." Basketball spread first to other YMCA's, then to colleges. Before the rules were firmly established, games sometimes featured as many as 50 players on each side, and spectators used everything from baseball bats to umbrellas to interfere with the action. Games as a result took place inside net cages, earning players a nickname — cagers — that persisted long after the nets were gone.

Exporting the National Pastime

Albert Spalding loved baseball — and apparently thought everyone else should too. A round-the-world exhibition tour, he was convinced, would be just the thing to persuade the rest of the world to join in the great American pastime (and in the process, expand the market for the bats and balls produced by his sporting goods company).

Under Spalding's sponsorship, two teams — the Chicago White Stockings and the all-star All America squad — left Chicago on October 22, 1888, played their way across the country, then left for Honolulu. But in Hawaii their only game was canceled, and by the time the teams reached Australia, one homesick slugger was already whining "Chicago for me." The exhibitions in Rome and Paris received decidedly lukewarm receptions. And when the teams played in London, one spectator complained of "too much base and not enough ball."

After five months on tour across five continents, the players did make one significant impression. Following a game played in the shadow of the great pyramid of Cheops outside Cairo, a reporter noted that "every player took a shy at the right eye of the Sphinx with the ball, but only left fielder Jack Fogarty succeeded in giving the colossus a black eye."

Nearing the end of their world tour, Spalding's exhibition baseball teams posed on the grounds of the Villa Borghese in Rome, where they played a game before a crowd of 3,500.

In 1920, when Duke Kahanamoku was 30, he set a new Olympic record for the 100-meter race: 1 minute, 1.4 seconds.

Sink or Swim

Duke Kahanamoku had little choice about learning to swim. "My father and an uncle threw me into the water from an outrigger canoe and I had to swim or else," he once explained. "That's the way the old Hawaiians did it." But Kahanamoku did more than just keep his head above water. He revolutionized swimming by using the now-familiar flutter kick instead of the scissor kick with his overarm crawl.

With his new style Kahanamoku broke world records for the 50- and 100-yard freestyles in 1911, but his times were so spectacular that the Amateur Athletic Union refused to believe them. At age 22, young Duke put an end to everyone's doubts when he won the gold medal for the 100-meter race at the 1912 Olympics in Stockholm. It was the first of three gold medals and one silver that he would win in four Olympic games. His record would not be broken until 1924, when Johnny Weissmuller took the gold.

Kahanamoku's bronzed good looks earned him a brief stint in Hollywood, but more memorable than his films was the surfboard he brought with him. Known as the father of modern surfing, he is credited with introducing the traditional Hawaiian sport to the rest of the world.

Sports' Other Babe

Born in 1914, Mildred Ella Didrikson was the sixth of seven children, so her family nicknamed her Baby — until the day she hit five home runs in a baseball game. With that, and with a nod to the New York Yankee's Sultan of Swat, Baby was instantly shortened to Babe.

A phenomenal all-around athlete, Babe placed first in eight events at the 1931 Amateur Athletic Union track meet and, the following year, won gold medals in the javelin throw and the 80-yard high hurdles at the Los Angeles Olympics. She missed a third gold in the high jump when judges disqualified her winning leap because of her then-unconventional western roll style. She could throw a football 50 yards and once pegged a baseball over 300 feet from the outfield to home plate. In exhibition games she took to the pitcher's mound and served up strikes to the likes of Joe DiMaggio and Jimmy Foxx.

Babe's explanation for her athletic prowess was simple enough: " I can run and I can jump and I can toss things and when they fire a gun or tell me to get busy, I just say to myself, 'Well, kid, here's where you've got to win another.' And I usually do."

Following her Olympic triumphs, Babe took up yet another sport — golf — and set yet another record with 17 straight victories on the links. She met her husband, wrestler George Zaharias, when she was paired with him at a tournament.

A spectator, watching one of Babe's spectacular drives, commented, "She must be Superman's sister," but Babe had another explanation for the secret of her success on the fairway. "I simply loosen my girdle," she once quipped, "and let the ball have it."

Until her untimely death from cancer in 1956, Babe Didrikson Zaharias excelled in virtually every sport she tried — and she tried most of them. Sportswriter Paul Gallico, in fact, once asked her if there was anything she did not play. "Sure," Babe shot back. "Dolls."

Stereoscope picture subjects ranged from gently humorous to borderline bawdy — and beyond. When placed in a viewer (above), the two images merged, creating a turn-of-the-century version of 3-D viewing.

The First Picture Show

Is it not like magic, the way everything stands out in space?" rhapsodized one delighted customer. The "magic" was the invention of the stereoscope, a device used for viewing paired photographs taken with a special stereoscopic camera. Mounted on a rigid card, the photographs, when viewed through the contraption's binocular lenses, were merged into a single, breathtaking three-dimensional image.

A mad fad for stereoscopes swept the country in the late 1800's. In the days before radio, television, and motion pictures, stereoscopic emporia sprang up in cities everywhere and did a brisk business in pictures, viewers, and related paraphernalia. The public swamped the shops with requests for the latest from their favorite photographers. And stereographers systematically churned out millions of the dual images to keep pace with the demand.

While entertainment was their chief attraction, not all stereographs were intended to provoke chuckles. Educational offerings included slides on bicycling and a Holy Land series endorsed by Pope Pius X. And one set of images changed the American map. In 1872, stereographs of the Yellowstone area of Wyoming, Montana, and Idaho helped convince a reluctant Congress to create the world's first national park.

A Puzzling Passion

It was Christmas week, 1913, and Arthur Wynne, a puzzle editor at the *New York World,* was doodling around, trying to come up with something new for the holiday edition. Eventually he hit on an interlocking word puzzle set in a diamond-shaped grid, which he called "Word-Cross" and ran in the paper on December 21.

Although Wynne intended his game as a one-time event, puzzle fans clamored for more and the little grids — renamed "Cross-Word" — became a regular Sunday feature in the *World.* Readers soon began submitting samples in all manner of designs, which Wynne gratefully published — often without testing them for accuracy.

When Margaret Petherbridge Farrar succeeded Wynne as puzzle editor in 1920, she chose the puzzles more for form than for content. But she soon discovered that "the crossword addict is a savage correspondent." Frustrated puzzlers, confounded by misspellings and mismatched clues in the published games, deluged her with sarcasm and complaints. After trying a puzzle herself, Farrar grasped the problem and vowed to "edit the puzzles to perfection."

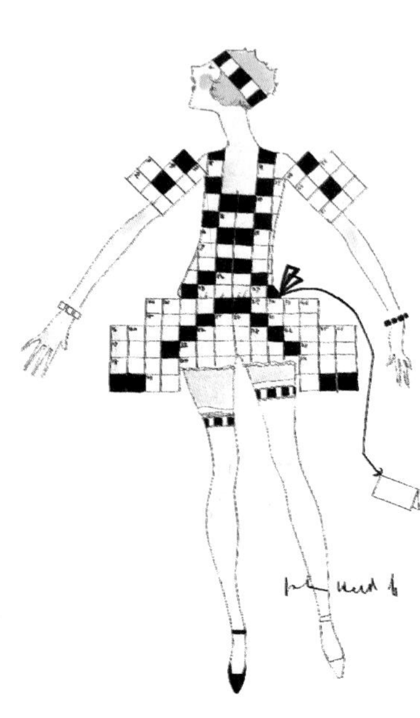

With Farrar at the helm, the *World*'s crossword puzzles got better and better. In 1924 neophyte book publishers Richard Simon and Max Schuster asked her to compile a collection of the games, which they issued, complete with a sharpened Venus Company pencil, as their first publishing venture.

Simon and Schuster's book proved an instant bestseller. In its first year it went into three editions, sold more than 400,000 copies, and caused a nationwide craze for crosswords. Sales of dictionaries and thesauruses soared. One publisher even attached an abridged dictionary to a wrist band so that it could be worn as a bracelet.

Clubs were formed, tournaments held, and courses added to college curricula. Crosswords became a daily feature in the *World.* Excessive puzzling even became a legal issue. A Chicago woman won a court judgment against her husband on the grounds that she was a "cross-word widow." And a patron at a New York restaurant — a man who refused to leave after dinner in order to complete a puzzle — was given a 10-day jail sentence for lexigraphic loitering. "More time to do my puzzles," crowed the happy convict.

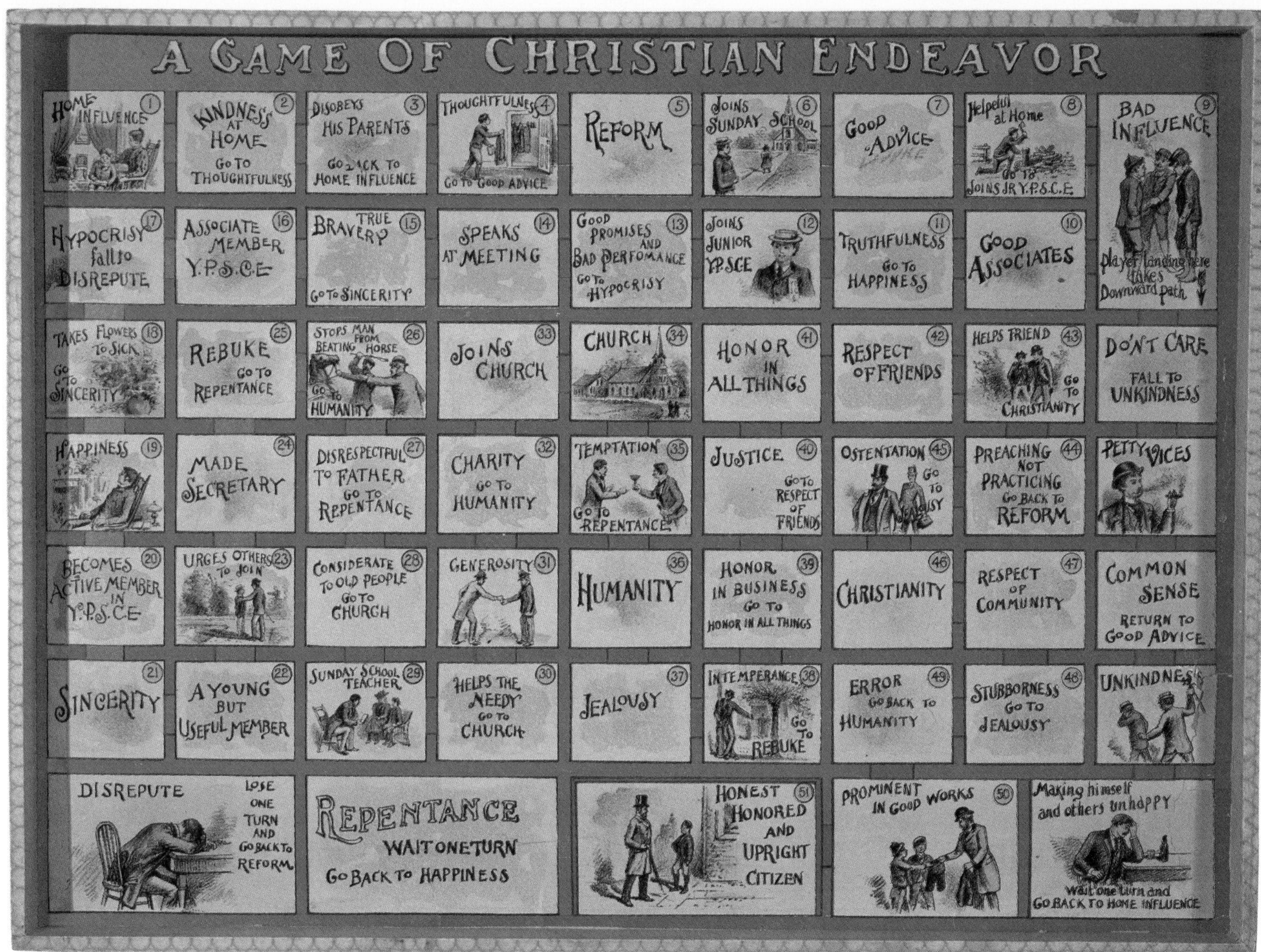

In 1896 Parker Brothers published A Game of Christian Endeavor, which celebrated "the good results sure to follow an upright life." But founder George S. Parker considered the high tone of such games "preachy" and created instead a series of card and board games based on the players' desire for fun and challenge.

Winning Games

A board game titled Office Boy, published in 1889, schooled players in "the haps and mishaps in the career of a businessman. . . . If he is careless, inattentive, or dishonest, his progress is retarded . . . if capable, ambitious, and earnest, his promotion to Head of the Firm is assured." It was one of the 100 or so games invented by George S. Parker, and to a remarkable degree it was his own story.

In 1883, at the age of 16, the "capable, ambitious, and earnest" young man from Salem, Massachusetts, created a lively card game based on financial speculation and called it Banking. Unable to find a publisher, Parker spent his savings — $50 earned by picking currants — to produce and sell 500 sets himself. Encouraged by the tidy profit that he netted, Parker published two more games and soon had a thriving business that employed not only himself but his two older brothers as well. By the early 1900's Parker Brothers had a sizable catalog offering handsome, mass-produced card games, board games, and jigsaw puzzles.

George's genius for games was virtually unerring. The company produced a table tennis game that became popular in England. A player improved the game with a celluloid ball, Parker bought the American distribution rights in 1902, and Ping-Pong became all the rage in America. With the help of his wife, George created Rook, a big hit in the teens. Parker Brothers also had exclusive licensing for Mah-Jongg, a craze of the twenties. But the brothers almost walked away from the game that became the company's ace-in-the-hole during the Depression years and the one for which it is perhaps best known. Offered the rights to Monopoly in 1934, the brothers thought it had "52 fundamental errors" and turned it down. Wanamaker's in Philadelphia picked it up, and it sold very well during the 1934 Christmas season. Realizing its error, Parker Brothers bought worldwide rights to the game in time for the following Christmas — and Monopoly was a runaway success.

Oddly enough, Parker's own favorite game never caught on. Originally titled Chivalry, its name was later changed to Camelot, but to no avail: the public never warmed to this combination of chess and checkers with its "ivoroid" knights and men. George played the game with his grandson Randolph. But the inveterate gamesman couldn't bear defeat even in play. As Ranny's skill increased, he was able to match or beat his grandfather. If it became evident he was going to lose, Ranny reported, Parker would hook his cufflinks (surreptitiously, he thought) under the board and upset the pieces. In play as in life, George Parker would then calmly rearrange the game to suit his advantage.

FETES AND FEASTS

LEGEND —AND— LORE

Good luck for a year? That's what you get in the South if you eat a dish of black-eyed peas and hog jowls on New Year's Day. The peas — or other food that swells as it cooks — ensure prosperity; add collard greens to the meal and you are guaranteed to gain greenbacks.

The Pennsylvania Dutch rely on a feast of sauerkraut to keep well through the year, while in New York State, people of German descent get off to a good start by downing herring at midnight on New Year's Eve. For Latin Americans, the lucky food is grapes — 12 at midnight ensure a fruitful year.

Japanese-Americans agree with Southerners that there is nothing luckier than black-eyed peas — unless maybe it's lobster, which they count on for health and happiness. But drop that crustacean or damage its feeler and you'd better get another — it's important that the meal be as symmetrical as possible on New Year's Day.

Strutting Their Stuff

Every New Year's Day they dance down Broad Street — 25,000 Philadelphians in ostrich plumes, sequins, and satin capes dozens of feet long. Though spectators who jam the sidewalks call it the mummers' parade, participants are apt to call themselves "shooters." With this they recall the origin of their parade: the exuberant custom of 17th-century Swedish colonists who roamed the street discharging firearms to shoot out the old year and bring in the new.

To this celebration English neighbors added mummers plays — farces performed in mask at one house after another in return for food and drink. The Irish added a love of holy-day pageants, and in the 19th century an African-American ditty — "Oh, Dem Golden Slippers" — became the parade's theme song and is played by every band in the procession. One of the most important elements in the day's events, the song provides the perfect rhythm for the Mummer's Strut — the marchers' characteristic dance.

Banned between 1808 and 1859 as a "common nuisance," mumming evolved into great public displays of fancy dress after the Civil War. Clubs with names like the "Early Risers," "Energetic Hoboes," "Red Onions," and "Mixed Pickles" were formed to create the costumes and comic skits.

While all members of mumming families were welcome to share in preparations for the parade, until 1976 custom dictated that only the males — from infants to the aged — could march. But that didn't stop women from trying. After making six costumes for participants, one woman decided to wear one herself: fooling both marchers and judges with her disguise, she took home the day's first prize.

The parading clubs known officially as the Philadelphia New Year's Shooters and Mummers Association are unique to that city. Noteworthy costumes earlier this century included the Lobster Club king clown (top) and the captain's cape (above).

Washington Crosses the Rio Grande

It might shock George Washington to see himself crossing not the Delaware but the Rio Grande, shouting commands to his men in Spanish all the while. Yet that is what citizens of Laredo, Texas, see each year as they celebrate Washington's birthday in their own special way.

The fiesta began in 1898, when a local "tribe" of the Improved Order of Red Men — a fraternal lodge — decided to promote Americanism in what was then a very Mexican town. The first year saw a two-day celebration featuring a mock skirmish in which "Red Men" seized the keys to the city. That was followed by a reenactment of the Boston Tea Party on a mock-up of a British merchant ship, plus a spectacular fireworks display.

The majority of the participants were of Mexican descent, and their enthusiastic involvement in subsequent celebrations gave the festivities a uniquely Hispanic flair. Mexican military bands crossed the border to play "The Star-Spangled Banner," and a Noche Mexicana, or Mexican Night, became a feature of the birthday fete. Across the river in Nuevo Laredo, relatives and friends joined with bullfights and folk dancing.

Today's celebrant may enjoy a jalapeño-eating contest, a carnival, and a Colonial ball at which George and Martha appear in 18th-century dress. Indian skirmishes have ceased, but each year an "Indian princess" is chosen "to foster interest in the customs and legends of the Indian cultures."

Pilgrims, Bandits, and Fantasticals

When families sit down to Thanksgiving dinner each year, they owe at least a little thanks to Sarah Josepha Hale. Fervent in her belief that a day should be set aside to express gratitude for the year's blessings, she almost singlehandedly created the holiday in the mid-19th century.

As the editor of *Godey's Lady's Book*, Hale controlled the country's most widely distributed periodical, and from 1846 on she used it to battle for her cause. Every November she published "traditional" recipes for Thanksgiving dishes, accompanying them with editorials demanding official recognition. Each summer she also wrote letters to the governors of every state. Finally, in 1863 Abraham Lincoln gave in and issued the proclamation that made the holiday an annual event.

Participants in the first Thanksgiving in 1621 would scarcely have recognized Hale's notions of traditional fare. Swans were as likely to have graced their tables as wild turkeys. Pilgrims thought potatoes inedible; apples and sweet potatoes were unknown in New England; and since there was no sugar, cranberries were not made into a jellied sauce.

But then, Americans have always tended to celebrate Thanksgiving in their own way. Butch Cassidy and the Sundance Kid imported oysters and Roquefort cheese to Utah for their Thanksgiving feast. In Norwich, Connecticut, young men used to celebrate by lighting bonfires on hilltops. Until World War II, New Yorkers were awakened by the horn blasts of "fantasticals," companies of working-class masqueraders who paraded under names such as the "Ham Guard Warriors" or the "Gilhooley Musketeers." Then they'd retire to the parks to picnic, and later to gala balls, where they danced until dawn.

Bygone Thanksgiving celebrants have included masqueraders in New York City (above left). At Plimoth Plantation (above) costumed interpreters reenact the first Thanksgiving, when 90 Indians dined with the 50 surviving Pilgrims. The Indians provided five deer for the feast: the Pilgrims cooked up codfish, sea bass, and wild fowl.

By the early 20th century large and elaborately decorated evergreens were common to most American parlors at holiday time (right). Westerners with no local balsams, however, might settle for a tumbleweed tree instead (below).

Other families, as in the posed photo below, made do with what they had.

Oh Christmas Tree!

The evergreen tree was not always a beloved symbol of Christmas in America. For years its appearance at holiday time was a source of heated debate.

Henry Schwan might have thought he was giving his congregation a gift when he set up a Christmas tree in his Cleveland, Ohio, church in 1851. But the gesture met with outrage instead. Newly emigrated from Germany, the Reverend Mr. Schwan did not realize that dragging a tree into the holiday would be regarded as sheer paganism. For while Christmas trees were by then part of the festivities in some households, Schwan's was the first tree ever to appear in an American church. Even as late as 1883 *The New York Times* was railing against "the German Christmas tree," calling it "a rootless and lifeless corpse — never worthy of the day."

It was, in fact, Germans who brought the custom of trimming trees to America, beginning in Pennsylvania in the 18th century. By 1747 the Moravians, a religious sect, were decorating their holiday tables with pyramids of greens. And by 1825 the Christmas season in Philadelphia was not complete without a walk about town to view the elaborately decorated trees.

Although still far from common in the early decades of the 1800's, the tradition of decorating trees began to spread as German settlers moved west. Not every community, however, offered a choice of evergreens. A sassafras sapling decorated with candles, hickory nuts, and hawthorn berries brightened one family's Christmas in St. Clair County, Illinois, in 1833. In frontier Kansas, dried sunflowers served as makeshift "trees," and on the high plains of Colorado, families made do with cottonwoods.

While some people would rather have decorated a tumbleweed than have no tree at all, general acceptance was slow. Articles that appeared in *Godey's Lady's Book* and other magazines helped to popularize the custom. And at Christmastime in 1850 the *Charleston Courier* proudly reported that the ladies of the city decorated a special tree to greet the arrival of soprano Jenny Lind.

By the turn of the century, the demand for Christmas trees was such that the state of Maine alone was harvesting some 1.5 million balsam firs every year. All those trees were collected from the wild — a fact that prompted President Theodore Roosevelt to urge a ban on Christmas trees. He ended his boycott only after discovering that his own sons had snuck a tree into the White House, and the head of the Forest Service, in the boys' defense, persuaded him that thinning the forest could be not only safe but beneficial. In any event the day of the collected tree was ending, for in 1901 a New Jersey farmer discovered that the ever-growing demand for Christmas trees made them a highly profitable seasonal crop.

The Man Who Loved Santa Claus

It was the political cartoons he published in *Harper's Weekly* that made Thomas Nast famous. His biting satires are credited with bringing about the defeat of New York City's infamous Boss Tweed, and it was Nast who made the donkey and the elephant political symbols. Yet the artist's most lasting influence on the American scene occurred in another sphere altogether: he is the man who designed Santa Claus.

Saint Nicholas had arrived in America with the Dutch colonists of New Amsterdam. But their Saint "Nick" was seen as a bishop, proud and tall, dressed in clerical robes and carrying a birch staff. Nast, in contrast, visualized Santa Claus as the character had been described in his own Bavarian boyhood — a rosy-cheeked, rotund figure of cheer in a fur suit.

Depicting the chubby elf of his imagination came easily to Nast. Having emigrated to New York at the age of 6 in 1846, he was enrolled in art school by the time he was 13, and just two years later had already begun his career as a newspaper illustrator. Nast's assignments included many major stories of the day, and by December of 1863 he needed a break. Designing the cover for the New Year's edition of *Harper's Weekly,* he drew a scene of a Union Army camp, but it focused on a fanciful Santa Claus, clad in stars and stripes, handing out toys to bemused soldiers.

Every Christmas for the next 23 years, Nast took a similar holiday from more serious subjects. In the process he not only gave form to the figure that Americans accept as the "real" Santa Claus, but also fixed Santa's activities in the minds of future generations. Toy-making in the North Pole workshop, the book in which Santa records children as naughty or nice, and the reindeer-drawn sleigh filled with toys were all memorably depicted by Nast. Even Santa's red suit is a Nast legacy. He decided that red would be more striking than any other hue when he illustrated one of the first colored children's books in 1866.

By 1881 Nast's depiction of Santa for *Harper's Weekly* (right) closely resembled the character we know today. An earlier version that he drew for an 1866 children's book (below) pictured Santa in a more elfin form.

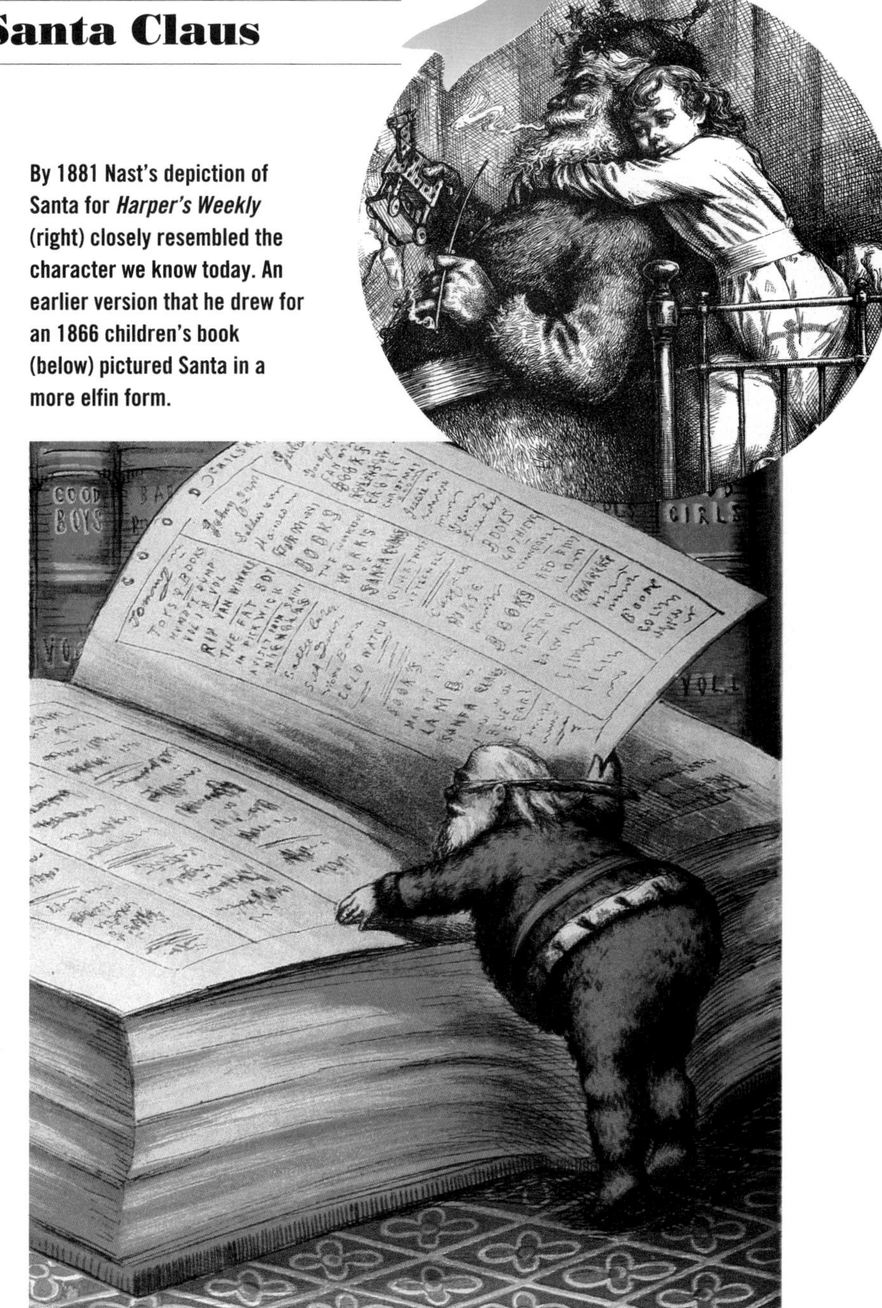

Chapter 4

FADS AND FASHIONS

THE LATEST RAGE

The Kindest of Cuts

To judge from the number of examples that survive, George Washington's profile was copied in silhouette by nearly everyone who had access to a pair of scissors in the late 1700's. Newly popular in that era, silhouette cutting was the ideal art for an energetic young democracy. Quick and cheap (Silhouette was the name of a parsimonious French minister of finance), the cutouts were both the snapshots of their day and the poor man's portrait. A person could have his likeness cut in the morning and hang it on the wall in the afternoon. Or whole families might sit individually for a cutter, and then be reunited against a watercolor or lithograph background.

Any amateur could give the art a try, but there were noted experts, including the American artist William Henry Brown. Talented enough to snip freehand — without so much as a sketch to go by — Brown attracted customers by advertising his skill at cutting portraits from memory. Tirelessly prolific and extremely clever, in 1831 he immortalized the steam locomotive *DeWitt Clinton* in lacy profile and, a few years later, cut silhouettes of the entire 65-member St. Louis Fire Engine Company to produce a 20-foot-long group portrait. Brown's chief rival was Frenchman Auguste Edouart, who toured the United States from 1839 to 1849. Edouart is known to have cut some 10,000 elegant likenesses, including the country's leading political and literary figures.

Competing with such freehand geniuses were hundreds of machine cutters who backlit their subjects against a screen and cut from tracings. Some specialized in the "hollow-cut," in which the inner profile is discarded and the outline preserved. But by midcentury such refinements no longer mattered: the daguerreotype had arrived. However delightful, the silhouette was no match for the true-to-life image of the modern age.

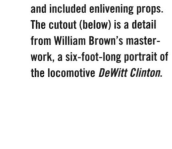

Auguste Edouart silhouetted himself at work (above). His portraits were often full-length and included enlivening props. The cutout (below) is a detail from William Brown's masterwork, a six-foot-long portrait of the locomotive *DeWitt Clinton*.

The Next Best Thing to Being There

As wraparound travelogues, panoramic paintings enabled 19th-century viewers to see the world and experience history in living color.

For many Americans in the 19th century, the world consisted of whatever they could see from wherever they happened to be standing. Books were scarce, museums were still a rarity, and travel was expensive. For a mere 25 cents, however, even the most unworldly could gaze on the exotic sites in Constantinople or tour the holy city of Jerusalem.

The means to this miracle was the panorama, a kind of travelogue picture first dreamed up by Irishman Robert Barker in the 1780's. Displayed in specially designed rotundas, panoramas were an immediate hit with the public and, by the early 1800's, were being exhibited in American cities as well. The circular showplaces were necessary since panoramas, assembled from painted panels, recreated a wraparound view in stunning detail. When a viewer stood surrounded by a landscape — which might be 50 feet high, and 400 feet in circumference — the experience was almost as exciting as being there.

Much to the delight of country dwellers, inventive Americans soon came up with yet another kind of panorama. Painted on canvases hundreds or even thousands of feet long, these were rolled on spindles like enormous scrolls, and hauled from town to town. If need be they could even be exhibited in open fields. Viewers watched spellbound as the canvases were unrolled to reveal

the drama of a whaling voyage or an ancient battle — only a short distance from home.

Panorama painting attracted artists of every caliber, but John Banvard beat all for sheer audacity. Thousands who would never have the opportunity to see the mighty Mississippi in person flocked to view his crude but faithful portrayal of some 1,200 miles of the river's shoreline. Watching with glazed eyes as Memphis rolled by and then New Orleans, who cared if Banvard had painted three miles of canvas, as he insisted, or only one, as critics claimed? Whatever its length, the painting took Banvard three years to complete from the time he first put brush to canvas in 1841. But over its lifetime it netted the artist some $200,000 in two-bit receipts.

The 1,275-foot *Whaling Voyage Around the World*, painted in the 1840's, is one of the few scroll-type panoramas to have survived. This segment shows the fleet's home port, New Bedford, Massachusetts.

When a Penny Really Did Buy Happiness

"A penny saved is a penny earned" was a common admonition to 19th-century children. But even then, the greatest spur to juvenile thrift was not virtue but joy — in the guise of mechanical banks.

Made of brightly painted cast iron and fitted with spring-action mechanisms, these worthy amusements were enjoyed as home-sized penny arcades from the 1870's through the 1920's. For while their elders soberly deposited dollars in savings institutions during those decades, children could make a little magic happen each time they put away a coin. Insert a penny and an eagle fed its young, a soldier fired his musket, or in one of the many crude ethnic caricatures patented by bank designers, Paddy the Irishman stuck out his tongue to catch a penny tossed up by a pig. The unseating of black mule riders was another favorite theme, as were trick horses, Punch and Judy, and William Tell. But one of the most popular of all designs was a bank called Tammany. It parodied the notorious "Boss Tweed" greedily stuffing pennies into his pocket.

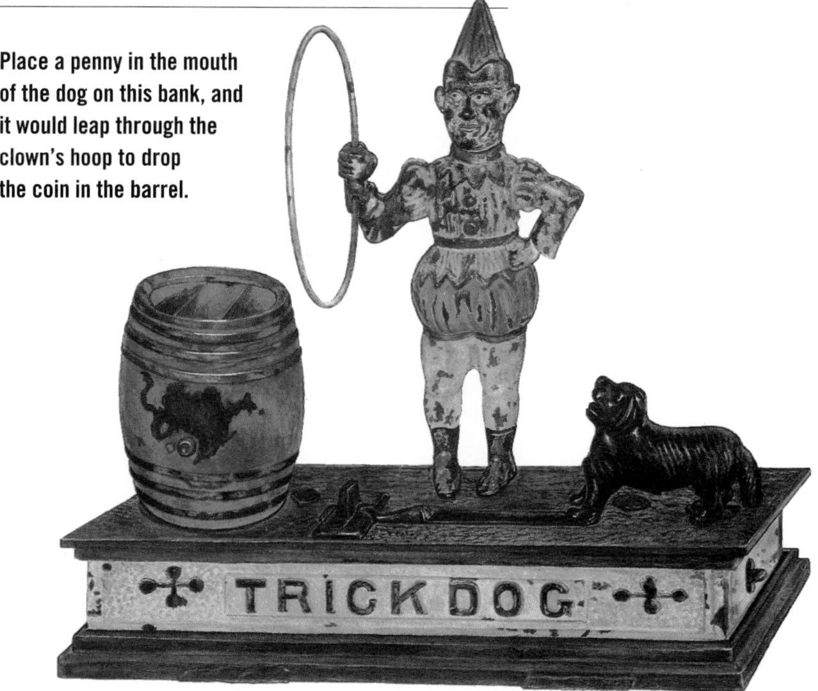

Place a penny in the mouth of the dog on this bank, and it would leap through the clown's hoop to drop the coin in the barrel.

The Bumpy Road to Self-Knowledge

The best of men have large heads and noble brows; the basest kinds, narrow heads and beetling brows. Such was the sort of news with which Johann Spurzheim, a German physician, enthralled Americans when he arrived in this country in 1832, promising the perfection of mankind through phrenology.

A newly developed "science," phrenology was based on the theory that the brain had between 35 and 45 sectors, each the seat of a separate mental faculty. The baser instincts such as alimentiveness (appetite), combativeness, and destructiveness were said to be relegated to the lower reaches of the brain. Propensities like conscientiousness ranged at midlevel, and such moral traits as benevolence and philoprogenitiveness (parental love) occupied the brain's highest realms. Since, according to the theory, the strength or weakness of each trait could be observed in the topography of the skull, a skilled practitioner had only to map and measure the bumps and valleys to know a person's true self. Better still, a good phrenologist could stimulate desirable qualities and correct weaknesses with something akin to scalp massage.

Phrenology had its debunkers as well as its devotees. An illustration in the *Illuminated Magazine* (above) satirized bump manipulation, while charts like the one at the right mapped out the brain for believers. Since anyone who wanted to could call himself a phrenologist, and the "science" had no basis in fact, the debunkers ultimately won out.

Spurzheim's prescription for self-knowledge was seized upon by legions of imitators and throngs of true believers, who spawned a burgeoning business in phrenological paraphernalia. For a few dollars any would-be practitioner could buy a complete set of equipment, including a demonstration head "inscribed with mystic numbers." Also available were lithograph "maps" of the skull, special tape measures and calipers, and hats and lotions that, when applied, influenced the development of particular brain bumps.

The most successful "bumpologist," and perhaps the most sincere, was Orson S. Fowler, who began preaching the cause in 1835 and continued until his death more than five decades later. In addition to offering private "palpations," or readings, at offices in several cities, he and family associates ran a phrenology school and a museum where visitors could examine skulls of the famous and infamous.

If sent "a good daguerreotype, three quarter pose preferred," Fowler would perform mail-order analyses. He also published a widely read journal that dispensed advice on everything from drunkenness to child rearing. Believers had their own way of communicating through classified ads. One woman, for instance, advertised her marriageability by listing her phrenological measurements: "nervous, 4; domestic propensities large, 6; . . . intellect large to very large, 6 to 7."

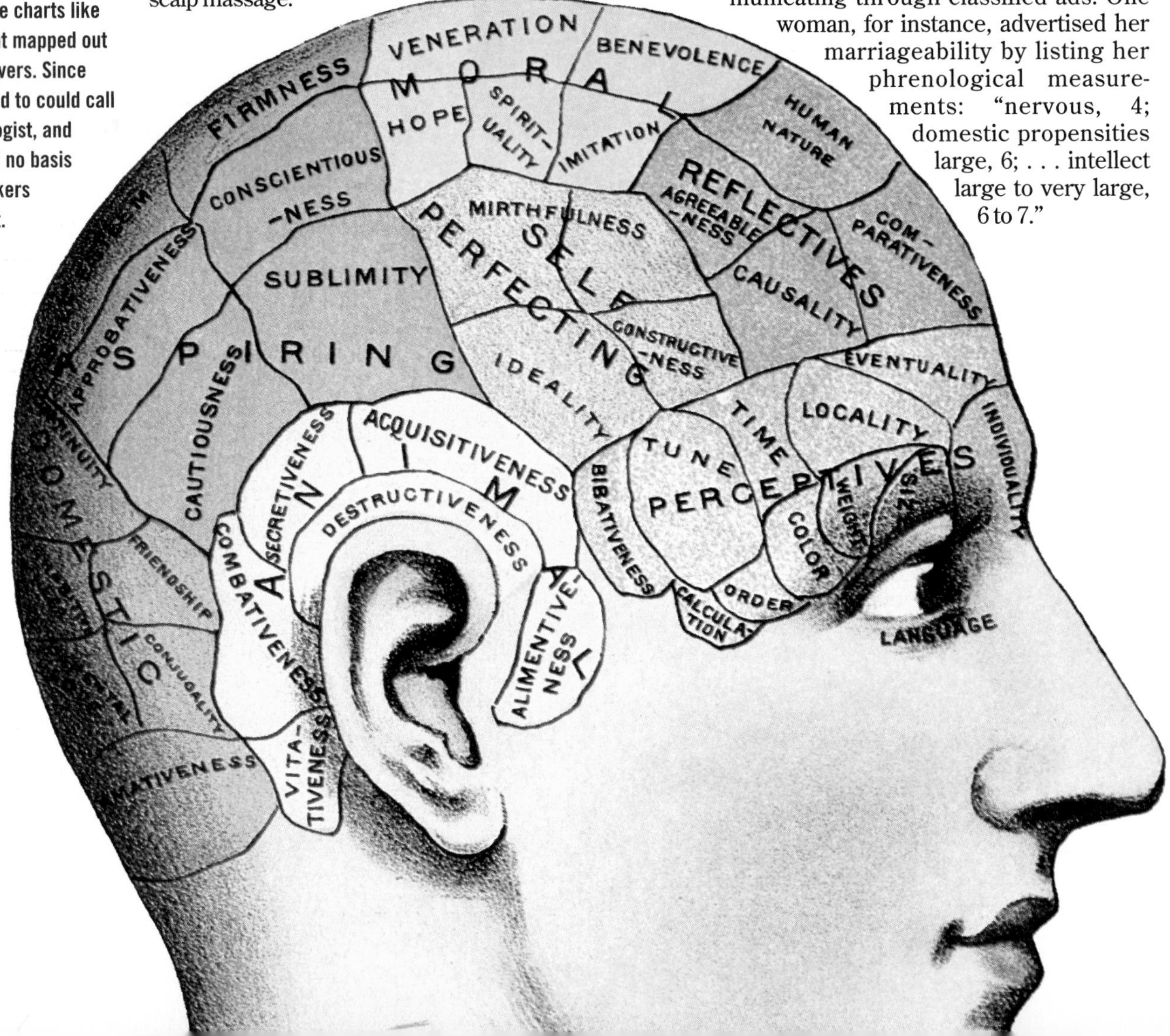

Plunging Into Health

When 19th-century Americans learned that water is good for what ails you, they dove in, swallowed the advice, and tried to wash their troubles away.

"Wash and be Healed!" proclaimed the *Water Cure Journal and Herald of Reforms*. Imported from Austria in the 1840's, hydropathy — as the water cure was formally known — treated spiritual aches and physical pains with all manner of rinses, douses, and douches. Within the decade it assumed the rank of reputable therapy, with some 200 centers, called hydros, operating around the country.

Attracting everyone from the dyspeptic to the consumptive, the cure's extravagant medical claims were based on the belief that water could wash away disease. And in an age when medicine and personal hygiene were rudimentary at best, hydropathy did enjoy a degree of success, if only for its capacity to cleanse and relax the body.

A variety of wet remedies were prescribed, depending on the ailment. But regimens typically had patients rising before dawn to drink huge quantities of water, sweat out impurities in layers of blankets, sit swaddled in wet sheets, and attend lectures on "natural" health and human physiology. At the heart of all the rigmarole was a soaking succession of sponge baths, head baths, nasal baths, sitz baths, elbow and leg baths, vapor baths, rain baths, and shocking, shivering plunge baths.

Middle-class women were the hydropath's main customers. Rigorous as the water cure was, after all, the orderly routines, outdoor exercise, sensible diet, comfortable clothing, and the welcome companionship enjoyed at hydros had their attractions. Writer-activist Harriet Beecher Stowe once withdrew to a hydropathic center for nearly a year. Her sister Catharine Beecher stayed at 13 of them, emerging each time refreshed, energized, and ready to resume her own work of reforming American attitudes toward hygiene.

An illustrated book detailing the techniques of hydropathy showed a gentle rinsing bath (left). A lampoon of the "cure" (above) portrayed a head bath as a far less soothing affair.

The Mysterious Rochester Rappings

Two children and a mischievous prank were all it took in 1848 to set off a countrywide craze for spiritualism — a craze that would last for 50 years. It all started when the Fox family moved into an old, reputedly haunted house near Hydesville, New York. Apparently planning to tease their superstitious mother, 14-year-old Maggie and 11-year-old Kate, with the help of an apple tied to a string, began making strange sounds in the night. The girls then alarmed their parents by pretending to talk to a spirit — Mr. Splitfoot — who responded with mysterious rappings.

When neighbors were brought in to listen and pronounced the spirit responses genuine, the craze was under way. Their older sister Leah, with whom the girls went to live in Rochester, sharpened Kate and Maggie's act, first spreading the word that Mr. Splitfoot was the ghost of a murdered man, then working out a system of signals — based on knee cracking and toe tapping — that enabled them to "communicate" with netherworld spirits. Much of the sisters' credibility came from their knack for making their joints crack without any perceptible movement.

As interest in the "Rochester Rappings" soared, the sisters played far and wide to standing-room-only audiences. Although Leah would pocket much of the earnings, the girls were able to make $100 or more a night in exchange for "communicating" with long-lost loved ones. With profits so easy to come by, the Foxes soon were joined by a host of imitators willing to prey on grieving parents and spouses both in America and in England. Mary Todd Lincoln and Queen Victoria were among those who fell under the spell of spiritmongers.

The sisters eventually tired of the carnival atmosphere surrounding their trade. In 1888 — with Kate's approval — Maggie made a public confession of fraud, denouncing spiritualism as hypocrisy and a social evil. But in true melodramatic fashion it came too late. Dissolute and broke, both were dead within five years. Leah, too, passed on, having made a small fortune on her sisters' "talent."

A trio of tricksters, the seemingly somber, sedate Fox sisters launched a nationwide craze for spiritualism.

Early designs for cycles included a variety of adult-size "trikes," but the gents at the right were probably among the few who ever got to ride a seven-wheeler. Bicycles like the one below, introduced in 1876, were difficult for the average rider to master. The equal-size wheels of the "safety" bicycle provided a welcome improvement.

A Cycle of Changes at Century's End

"The discovery and progressive improvement of the bicycle," declared the *New York Tribune* in 1895, "is of more importance to mankind than all the victories and defeats of Napoleon." An exaggeration perhaps — but certainly improvements in the bicycle meant more fun for all mankind. For while iron-wheeled models — bumpy, bone-shaking devices — had been around for decades, it was the "safety bicycle," introduced in 1889, that really put America on the road.

Bike mania bites the nation

With its inflatable rubber tires, cushioned seat, chain drive, and balanced frame, the "safety" was a bicycle that anyone could ride without risking life and limb. And nearly everyone did. In 1890 the cyclists in America numbered a mere 100,000 or so; within the next six years the ranks of wheelmen soared to 4 million.

Throughout the Gay Nineties, the cycling craze inspired clothing designs, songs, stories, and even advice on bicycle etiquette. Biking was also the subject of sermons and medical advisories, most of them directed at the pastime's potentially pernicious influence on morals and health. But at the same time, America's new passion was at least partially responsible for the first widespread demand for better roads.

Cycling in the 1890's was typically an organized activity. The upper crust tended toward bicycle teas and mounted cotillions in formal dress. One group, the Michaux Cycle Club, prided itself on its members' skill at "dancing" a two-wheeled Virginia reel. But even ordinary folk favored competitive clubs, races, and parades. One such affair, billed as "the greatest parade of modern times," took place on New York City's Riverside Drive in 1896. Several thousand cyclers — the majority in costumes designed especially for the event — performed close-order bicycle routines as they rode. At the end of the parade, a new Columbia bicycle was awarded to the rider whose patented one-piece "crash suit" was pronounced "so unique that it could not fail to attract the attention of the judges."

Divided skirts and dainty ankles

If bicycles were not quite so comfortable for the "fragile sex," that did not stop women from riding. Those who dared wore "bifurcated garments" — divided skirts and bloomers. The less daring chose bikes equipped with folding screens that hid a lady's exposed ankles and feet.

Temperance leader Frances Willard, at age 53, was one of those who took up cycling, at least in part to encourage men to forsake saloons and turn to healthful exercise. Willard struggled with her bicycle, Gladys, for three months before she was able to solo. But when that happy day finally arrived, she announced, "I had made myself master of the most remarkable, ingenious, and inspiring motor ever yet devised upon this planet. Moral: Go thou and do likewise!"

Gay Blades and Easy Gliders

Recalling his youth in New York City around the turn of the century, Harpo Marx once remarked that his family's only piece of athletic equipment was a single ice skate with a broken strap. "I spent many hours on the frozen pond in Central Park, skating gimpily around the edge on my one left-foot skate," he reported. He was far from the first city dweller to dream of gliding effortlessly on the perfect pair of ice skates. Throughout the second half of the 19th century, in fact, skating was all the rage.

Interest in the sport began to develop in 1848 when E. W. Bushnell, a Philadelphia mechanic, devised the first sturdy all-metal, hardened-steel skates — a distinct improvement over earlier wrought-iron and wood designs. By 1850 Philadelphians had founded the first social club for the "improvement, pleasure, companionship, and safety of skaters." And they certainly were serious about safety: in the winter of 1869 alone, club members rescued 259 skaters on the Schuylkill River.

But it was a young New Yorker, Jackson Haines, who transformed skating into a free-flowing, graceful sport. A ballet master and an actor by training, Haines developed a flamboyant style of skating that thrilled audiences but at first proved too difficult for others to imitate. And so, soon after being crowned United States Champion in 1863, Haines left to make his fortune in Europe. Setting up a skating school in Vienna, the self-styled "American Skating King" taught a generation of skaters the "Haines International Style." It was left to another New Yorker, Irving Brokaw, to bring Haines's style back home in 1908 and popularize it in America.

Meanwhile, with or without national mentors, Americans were skating whenever and wherever they had the chance. Though strictly a seasonal affair, skating was surely a favorite activity during the weeks and months that the ice lasted. During a month-long period of particularly fine ice in the mid-1860's, for instance, over 200,000 skaters turned out with their blades in New York's Central Park. And on a single February day in 1862, an estimated 12,000 skaters skimmed over the surface of Prospect Park Lake at a skating carnival in nearby Brooklyn.

By about 1876 the machinery needed to produce ice artificially was finally developed, and indoor rinks began to appear. With skating no longer confined to winter months and natural ponds, the sport became more popular than ever. Rinks provided the means both for indoor amateur recreation and for professional skating spectacles. The first such grand performance before a paying audience took place in 1879 at a gathering in New York's Madison Square Garden. As an arena full of delighted spectators looked on, hundreds of masked skaters glided in unison to the glorious strains of music provided by Gilmore's Serenade Band.

Jackson Haines (above) brought musicality and showmanship to skating, with an International Style that is still in use today. In the 1860's (right) hoops may have been the only thing that kept women from tripping over their own skirts as they skated.

Rolling Into Rinkomania

Before a Massachusetts man, James Plimpton, devised a steerable roller skate in 1863, only the most daring braved the sport. Three years later, when Plimpton opened the first roller rink, all America donned wheels and a new craze was born. While skaters thronged to the rinks in the next decades, however, they were warned of dire consequences: "bigamous marriages and other social transgressions," said The New York Times, *could be traced to the skating floor.*

Dubbed the Old Pedestrian in newspaper stories, "Payse" Weston made a career of walking. Crowds gathered to watch him compete at an indoor track at age 35 (below), and at age 85 (right) he was still going strong. A participant in long-distance races on both sides of the Atlantic, he also gave speeches on behalf of temperance and the benefits of pedestrianism. Admirers around the country formed Weston Walking Clubs.

Stepping Out With the Old Pedestrian

When, at the age of 69, Edward Payson Weston announced his intention of walking more than 4,000 miles from New York City to San Francisco, *The New York Times* was openly skeptical. "Those who know and like the old man best are a good deal worried about the outcome," the newspaper noted. Weston, however, had confounded skeptics many times before. On a bet 48 years earlier, he had walked from Boston, Massachusetts, to Washington, D.C., in 10 days to attend Lincoln's inauguration in 1861. Six years later he walked from Portland, Maine, to Chicago, Illinois, covering the 1,326 miles in 26 days.

Always fashionably turned out in tight breeches, gloves, and silk hat, Weston became such a celebrity that Europeans were eager to see him perform. Some didn't believe that a man they regarded as "a nervy little beggar of a Yankee" could beat the continent's best hikers. But at London's Agricultural Hall, Weston walked successive laps totaling 550 miles in 142 hours. A journalist described the "tremendous applause of the multitude" who watched as Weston "reeled off the laps as though he were walking for the fun of the thing." His victory won him $2,500 and the prized Astley Belt, which designated the world's best long-distance walker.

Age did not dim Weston's abilities. At 68 he repeated the journey from Portland to Chicago that he had made as a young man — and beat his previous time by 29 hours. And despite *The New York Times'* forebodings, Weston's cross-country walk was a complete triumph. He not only hiked from New York to San Francisco, but turned around and walked back: a round trip accomplished in a record 181 days.

The Bunion Derby's Cross-Country Limp

As C. C. Pyle saw it, he had a scheme worthy of his nickname — Cash and Carry. The promoter planned to capitalize on the public's marathon madness with a 3,400-mile, coast-to-coast foot race. Even though he offered generous prizes — starting with $25,000 for first place — Pyle counted on turning a profit. In addition to sponsorship by shoe and foot-care companies, he planned to collect thousands of dollars for the publicity he would bring to towns along Route 66. "It's the easiest thing I've ever seen," he gloated.

Instead of the thousands of runners he expected, however, only 200 or so started from Los Angeles on March 4, 1928. By the end of the day, dozens had quit and by early April, only 91 marathoners were left. Frank Johnson of Granite City, Illinois, who completed 900 miles, was not among them. "His left ankle was swollen to twice its normal size," his wife reported. "His lips were cracked so badly they bled when he tried to eat." Two Californians eased their feet by hitching rides — but were disqualified when officials found out. Only 55 runners remained in the battered band that finally arrived in New York City. "Some ran on their toes to save their heels," said one reporter, and "some on their heels to save their toes."

A scant 4,000 people assembled in Madison Square Garden's 18,000 seats to see Oklahoma's Andrew Payne take first place for his run of 573 hours, 4 minutes, and 34 seconds. By then the race was known as the Bunion Derby, and the promoter as "Corn and Callous" Pyle. But he had little sympathy for the athletes. "Their feet were sore sometimes," Pyle explained, "but my arms were sore all the time, from digging down in my pocket and shelling out cash."

Revenge of the 97-Pound Weakling

Nobody who ever read a comic book in the 1940's or 1950's will forget the Charles Atlas advertisements. Along with the hulking figure of Atlas clad only in his leopard-print loincloth, the ads featured the famous "97-pound weakling" getting sand kicked in his face. Atlas sometimes claimed that he had suffered just such an insult — an act that inspired him to become a bodybuilder. At other times he explained that his desire to develop his muscles was born when, as a boy, he saw a statue of Hercules. (He changed his name after seeing a statue of Atlas.)

Born Angelo Siciliano in southern Italy, Atlas came to America with his parents at the age of 11. Hard work at the YMCA sculpted his physique into such enviable shape that he won first place in a 1922 contest that proclaimed him "The World's Most Perfectly Developed Man." When he won again the following year, the promoter called off the competitions in disgust, complaining, "What's the use of holding them? Atlas will win every time."

A national figure as a result of his victories, Atlas capitalized on his popularity by developing a 13-part muscle-building course that promised every 97-pound weakling a chance to become "hero of the beach." At its peak the mail-order course annually attracted some 70,000 students, who could study Atlas's principles of "dynamic tension" in any one of seven languages. In addition to providing specific muscle-building exercises, Atlas's course dispensed advice on nutrition and life-style, a reflection of his own basic credo: "Live clean, think clean, and don't go to burlesque shows."

Ads like this one (below) made Charles Atlas a familiar figure to generations of comic book readers. Showing off on the beach in 1937 (above), Atlas was his own best advertisement. As a young man his physique so intrigued sculptors that he became a model, posing for the statue of Alexander Hamilton that stands in front of the U.S. Treasury Building in the nation's capitol, and as the figure of Washington in Washington Square in New York City.

BALL OFF RUG
IS OUT OF BOUNDS
REPLACE IT WHERE
IT WENT OFF!
PENALTY • 1 STROKE

Rinky-Dink Links

It was cheap. It was fun. It was a game anyone could play. It was miniature golf, the craze that helped America get through the Great Depression.

Perhaps it was just another example of America's unquenchable appetite for novelty, but when the public first got a taste of miniature golf in the 1920's, they greeted it with gusto. Although minigolf courses had been built as early as 1916, it was in 1927 that the relatively unknown pastime exploded into a national passion. The epicenter for the action was Garnet and Frieda Carter's mountaintop Fairyland Inn near Chattanooga, Tennessee.

Fairyland was already a duffer's paradise with its own professional course when, to keep the golf widows amused, Frieda designed an 18-hole minilinks for the inn's front lawn. If artistically tame by today's standards, her "Tom Thumb" course was challenging, with ramps, bridges, and other traps to finesse. In no time at all it was the hotel's chief drawing card.

From mountaintop to vacant lot

Mr. Carter, who knew a good thing when he saw it, patented his wife's design.The only problem to be solved before the couple could sell their new game was the playing surface, since it quickly became apparent that ordinary grass would not stand up to constant foot traffic. When they discovered a fellow who had already devised an artificial turf made of crushed and dyed cottonseed hulls for his backyard putting green, the Carters bought rights to the material and sold some 3,000 Tom Thumb courses for about $4,500 each.

During miniature golf's heyday New York City and Los Angeles alone had 1,000 courses. Fay Wray (right) was one of the many stars who teed off in Hollywood. In Manhattan, links were even located right in midtown (below). By the 1950's minigolf still had its fans but was no longer a mania.

Meanwhile, hundreds of imitators had gotten in on the act. By 1930 an estimated 40,000 minigolf greens had sprung up on vacant lots, motel grounds, apartment house rooftops, and in department store salons all across the country. As the novelty of the original designs wore thin, courses were built around such themes as the wild West, Japanese gardens, Spanish missions, and even an Eskimo village featuring blue turf, ice floes, and snowbanks. Players could also subscribe to a fan magazine and buy special miniature golf clothing, how-to books, and the sheet music for a newly composed minigolf song.

Though Americans of every age and social level were attracted to miniature golf, women were a special target. Their sex was said to have been equipped by nature to play well, given their "hereditary gift of wielding a broom day in and day out." But whether male or female, people found that playing helped to keep their spirits up during the Depression: on the average balmy evening in 1930, some 4 million Americans putted balls through little windmills and pagodas. By the following year, however, the public had begun to tire of the glut of minigreens and was moving on to new amusements.

Part of minigolf's appeal stemmed from the fact that it could be played almost anywhere. Whatever the weather, fans in Chicago putted at a fancy indoor course (left). Or families might set up a "Happy Hazard" set in their own backyard (below).

Virtually from the start, miniature golf has prompted imaginative architecture. The giant golf bag (left) dwarfed customers in Jersey City, New Jersey, in 1930. The Russian-style fantasy (below) is part of a course in Ventura, California.

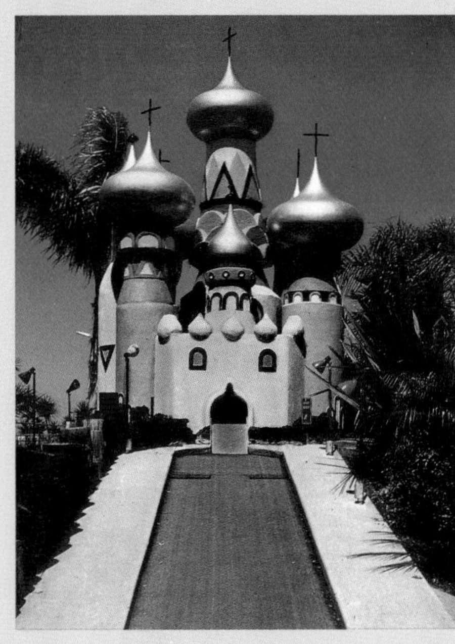

A Master of Motion and Manners

The "babies," aged three to five, were brought around by their mothers or nannies at 2:30 in the afternoon, twice a week. Older children met separately, in a class that lasted two hours; out-of-town pupils came on Saturday mornings. And no one came at all unless preceded by three letters of introduction.

The place was the Dodworth Dancing Academy, founded in New York City in the early 1840's by Allen Dodworth and for 80-some years a temple of social grace and moral propriety. "The dancing school," wrote Dodworth, "is not a place of amusement." And surely none of the thousands of society children and adults who passed through Dodworth's could have mistaken it for such as they strove to master "the five positions" and "the six elements," "six radical motions" and "the Grecian Bend." It was more like going to church.

A British-born musical prodigy who performed professionally as both a violinist and a trombonist, Dodworth introduced Americans to the idea that dancing was not some vulgar pastime, but a ritual of aesthetic and moral grace. "The rules talked about at other times should here be put into practice, until morality in little things becomes habitual," he declared. "When this habit is established in connection with the lesser duties of life, we need have but little fear for the greater."

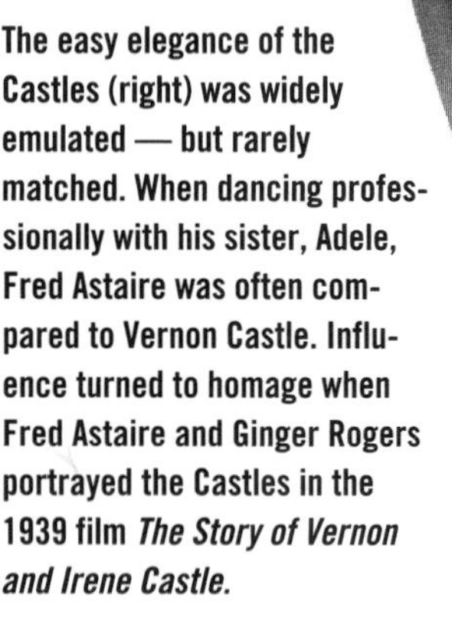

The easy elegance of the Castles (right) was widely emulated — but rarely matched. When dancing professionally with his sister, Adele, Fred Astaire was often compared to Vernon Castle. Influence turned to homage when Fred Astaire and Ginger Rogers portrayed the Castles in the 1939 film *The Story of Vernon and Irene Castle.*

Vernon and Irene

He was tall, British born, and memorably thin — "a soda straw with legs" one critic called him — and she was a coltish young American with a whimsical sense of fashion. Together they were the talk of the town and the toast of two continents. Breezily elegant, they were the pair who brought social dancing into the jazz age — and in the midst of a fevered debate over the morality of such risqué dances as the tango, made sensual dancing as respectable as a ladies' afternoon tea.

They were the Castles — Vernon and Irene — and for a few short years before World War I, this Anglo-American couple enjoyed a status somewhat akin to royalty, their every move catalogued by the press, their every sartorial choice a fashion imperative for the masses to obey. When Irene bobbed her hair and wrapped herself in a headache band of seed pearls, it rated a banner headline and created a stampede to the beauty shops. Vernon sported a wristwatch, and the timepiece's status soared from effete to essential.

Though neither had been trained as a dancer, it didn't matter a bit: what they had in abundance was style, and when they twirled and dipped, trotted and spun, ever so gracefully and ever so tastefully across acres of polished wood, all who saw them were inspired to do the same.

Vernon by common consensus was the better dancer. He was also a tireless interpreter of new dance steps, including the one-step and the turkey trot, and of course, he created the signature Castle Walk — a spritely skipping dance step dreamed up one night at a friend's birthday party. But it was Irene, the doctor's daughter from New Rochelle, New York, who made the partnership look so glorious, the dancing so effortless. Wearing one of the dazzlingly simple gowns she first had sewn up for her in Paris — "I could never compete with the . . . million-dollar necklaces sparkling in the subdued light of the Cafe de Paris" — she followed her husband's lead with the confidence of a joyous bride. "Vernon did invent the steps, often on the spur of the moment," she wrote, but she kept enchantingly afloat "by keeping my eyes firmly fixed on the stud button of his dress shirt."

And so they "breezed along happily" with Vernon instructing pupils eager to master the Castle Walk, until 1916 when he returned to England to join the Royal Flying Corps. As daring as an aviator as he was dashing as a dancer, Castle flew more than 200 missions and was awarded the Croix de Guerre for downing two German planes. But in 1918, while training American pilots in Texas, he was killed in a midair collision with a cadet. He was 30. His widow was 24.

Almost as famous for the smile he flashed as for the dances he sometimes literally dreamed up, Bill "Bojangles" Robinson was the master hoofer of his time. The meaning of his nickname has been lost to legend: some claim "bojangles" is Tennessee slang for "happy-go-lucky," others that it means "squabbler." What is beyond dispute is that it was an affectionate gift bestowed by an admiring friend in 1913.

Mister Bojangles — Dance!

To hear Bill "Bojangles" Robinson tell it, his genius was a simple matter of following instructions. "I hear the music, and something comes into my head, which I just send down to my feet. And that's all there is to it." Whatever his inspiration, his feet were hot, his manner cool, and his moves beyond fathoming to even the most astute and talented of his would-be peers.

As precociously independent as he was gifted, Robinson first danced for nickels and dimes at age six in the beer gardens of Richmond, Virginia. He joined the vaudeville and nightclub circuit at 28. Dapper, serene, and ever-smiling, as Robinson rose to stardom, he dazzled his exclusively black audiences with such showstoppers as the widely copied "stair tap," inspired, he later said, by a dream. "I was being made a lord by the King of England," he explained, "and he was standing at the head of a flight of stairs. I danced up the stairs to the throne, got my badge and danced right down again."

Though a star of the first magnitude who earned up to $3,500 a week, Robinson, like other black performers, played for years to strictly segregated houses. It was not until he was 50 that the man who coined the word "copacetic" and could dance nonstop for an hour or more without repeating a step, finally debuted for a white audience on Broadway, in *Blackbirds of 1928*. A few years later he began work on a string of movie musicals, many with a dimpled, curly-haired seven-year-old named Shirley Temple — his favorite actress and perhaps the only star equal to "the satrap of tap."

WHAT · IS · IT

In some ways this 1921 "Figure for Ballroom Dancing Practice" was the ideal partner — tireless, uncomplaining, and with no toes to tread upon. The stalwart figure had articulated elbows, a band at the waist to support the partner's hand, and a freely spinning spherical caster. Thus partnered, a shy young man could master graceful dips and intricate turns in private before venturing out to dazzle in public .

Ain't She Sweet?

While poking fun at the rouge-kneed cuties and flask-toting sheiks of the 1920's, John Held drew an enduring, endearing portrait of the era.

With his comic caricatures of madcap flappers and their raffish young men, artist John Held, more than any other, captured the devil-may-care insouciance of the Roaring Twenties. His most famous creation was Margy, the original boop-boop-a-doop girl. The embodiment of the impetuous spirit of the decade, she stood shakily on spindly legs and achingly high-heeled shoes, with her long, black cigarette holder raised at an angle to match her perpetually upturned nose. To squire Margy around town, Held created another cartoon classic, Joe College. A mindless young man in a raccoon coat by day, at night he turned into a sophisticated gadabout, complete with dinner jacket and hair slicked back to shiny perfection.

Held's drawings so perfectly mirrored the foibles of the era that no one is really sure whether he captured existing fashion in pen and ink or if the fashionable were following his cues. His true genius lay in his ability to infuse his art with both humor and biting commentary.

But he was an observer rather than a participant in the antics he portrayed. A transplanted Westerner, Held worked from his horse farm in Connecticut, enjoying a life-style that his cartoons made possible — Margy alone earned him $2,500 a week, and his drawings appeared regularly in *Life, Judge, Collier's,* and *The New Yorker.* But success did not soften his work ethic. A sculptor, writer, and tap dancer, Held became even more closely linked with the image of the era when he illustrated Anita Loos's *Gentlemen Prefer Blondes* and F. Scott Fitzgerald's *Tales of the Jazz Age.*

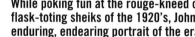

Most of John Held's cartoon characters were college kids, whom he depicted enjoying all the new fads and freedoms of the era, from kicking up their heels at frat-house parties to gadding about in roadsters. Held never attended college himself, but in the 1940's he was artist-in-residence at Harvard and the University of Georgia.

NATIVE TONGUE

WORDSMITHS OF THE TWENTIES

English got a shot in the arm in the 1920's, thanks to the slang-slinging sheiks and shebas (young men and women with "sex appeal" — itself a new term) who gave us such terms as heebie-jeebies, Freudian slip, *and* the cat's pajamas. Screwy *and* lousy *were their inventions, too.*

The Prohibition-bashers of the 1920's — who got into speakeasies with a whispered "Joe sent me" — played a part as well, bringing American sassiness to new heights with baloney, horsefeathers, *and* all wet. *Other Jazz Age expressions indicating impatience with authority include* big cheese, pushover, flat tire *(bore), and* sob sister *(woman reporter tending to sentimentality). Informality was in the air, as evidenced by* kiddo, beaut, *and* scram.

When people were sober (not spifflicated, ossified, or just stinko with hooch, or giggle water), they popularized the likes of swell, keen, swanky, spiffy, *and* hotsy-totsy, *to indicate wholehearted approval.*

About male-female relationships, however, they

maintained ironic distance. Among the terms for women were dumbbell *and* dumb Dora; *for men,* drugstore cowboy, lounge lizard, jellybean, *and* jazzbo.

Necking and petting were fine up to a point, and even beyond ("I don't particularly care to be kissed by some of the fellows I know," said one girl, "but I'd let them do it anytime rather than think I wouldn't dare"). But some drew the line: jalopies were known as "struggle buggies."

Blind dates were worth the gamble. People fell for a line, developed a crush, or got stuck on someone. As Walter Winchell once put it, they might even end up middle-aisling it. If all went phfft, well, there were other distractions. The jazz clubs were hopping, the music was swell, and the band-leaders egged on their men, "Get hot! Get hot!"

It's Lonely at the Top

Alvin "Shipwreck" Kelly set a world record: for 49 long days in 1930 he sat atop a flagpole in Atlantic City. The rationale for his aerial antics was simple enough. "I just went up for a breath of fresh air," he once explained. And other flagpole sitters had an equally simple explanation for their exploits. They were just imitating Kelly, who had started the fad with a 13-hour stint on a Los Angeles flagpole in 1924.

None, however, was a match for Kelly. LeRoy Haines, for instance, set the record for Denver, but he stayed aloft for a mere 12 days. Bennie Fox lasted 18 days in Chicago — until he decided to sneak down one night to avoid a bill collector sleeping at the bottom. When the Los Angeles City Council outlawed pole sitting, Bobby Mack returned to earth on her 21st day. Not all cities were so strict. After 15-year-old Avon Foreman of Baltimore spent 10 days on a flagpole, the mayor rejoiced that "the old pioneer spirit of early America is being kept alive by the youth of today." Not surprisingly, Foreman's stunt opened a whole new field for faddists: juvenile flagpole sitting.

The first and most famous flagpole artist, Shipwreck Kelly, did his sitting the old-fashioned way. Long-endurance sitters later put up large platforms with tents to sit in.

Dancing Fools

Charles Gonder's story was a sad one. He literally danced himself to death. Collapsing in the 1,147th hour of a dance marathon in November 1932, he died shortly after. Yet even such unpleasantness could not dampen the craze for endurance dancing. One couple won a Chicago marathon with a record-setting 5,148 hours and 28 minutes. Frank Miller and his partner, on the other hand, triumphed after a mere 1,473 hours — no record, perhaps, but impressive enough for a 56-year-old grandfather.

The rules were simple: you danced until you dropped. Most marathons allowed an hourly break, and weary dancers napped on foot as their partners propelled them around the floor. Hallucinating from fatigue, participants scratched and punched their partners, prompting the ASPCA to have one promoter arrested. "We're interested in humans as well as animals," they explained. A doctor examining dancers at another marathon said he was not concerned about their physical condition. "They'll be all right," he noted, "if they escape insanity."

Marathoners were allowed to sleep as they danced, but only the soles of their shoes were permitted to touch the floor.

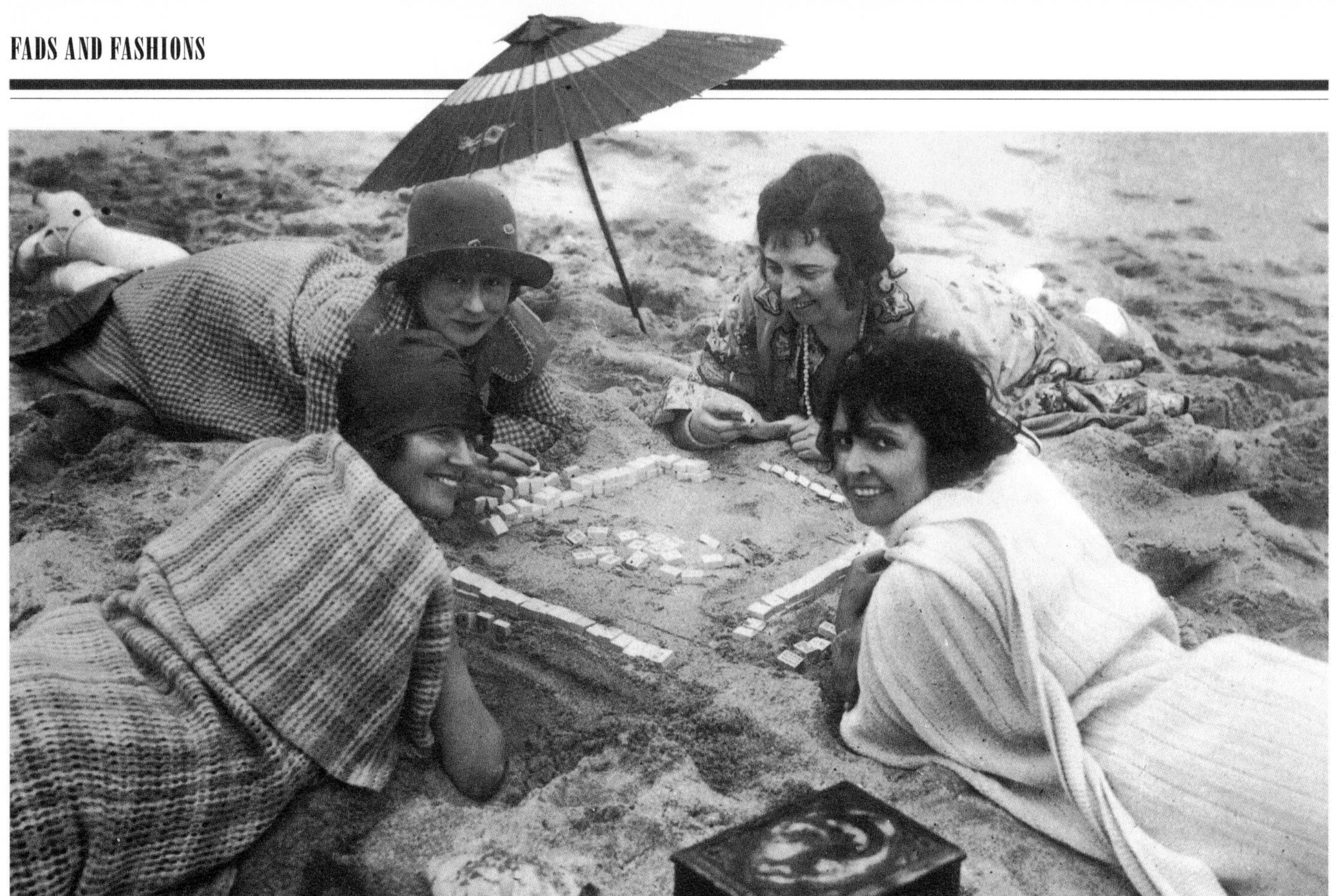

Avid players of mah-jongg created an Asian ambience whenever — or wherever — they played. Women especially took to the game. An ancient Chinese pastime played with dice and a form of dominoes, it has elaborate rules and calls for complex strategies. (The name means sparrow of 100 intelligences.)

Ga-Ga for Mah-Jongg

The year was 1922, America was ready for a party, and mah-jongg provided the perfect excuse. All across the country foursomes gathered to cast the dice and collect the tiles, assembling hands that were announced with cries of *"Pung"* and *"Chow"* in the quest to triumph with a *woo* — four matching tiles and a pair.

Joseph C. Babcock, an American businessman, had fallen under the game's spell while living in Shanghai. And it was no wonder: *The New York Times* later explained the fascination of the elaborate Chinese game by noting that it combined the psychology of poker with the variety of bridge and the science of chess.

Babcock found a ready market for the mah-jongg sets he began shipping home in 1920 — despite the fact that a complete outfit of 144 hand-carved tiles might cost as much as $500. Swept up in the craze, enthusiasts costumed themselves in silk robes and embroidered slippers when they played; the wealthy decorated game rooms in Chinese style; and hotels installed mah-jongg parlors to cater to the gaming passion of their guests.

In 1923, 1.5 million mah-jongg sets were sold. China ran short of the cattle shinbones that were used for making tiles, so shiploads were dispatched from the Chicago stockyards, along with efficiency experts to help set up assembly lines. But by 1925 the fad had faded as the fickle public embraced a new passion: the crossword puzzle.

Ping-Pong-itis

It was called wick-wack, click-clack, whiff-whaff, and even flim-flam, but it was all Ping-Pong, and it was the rage that swept the United States in the early 1900's. Middle-class Britons had developed the game as an indoor variation of the aristocratic lawn tennis, but their version, played on dining tables with cork or rubber balls, was crude and slow. It was the introduction of celluloid balls that gave Ping-Pong a real bounce and soon had the whole country afflicted with Ping-Pong-itis.

Doctors saw a lot of what they diagnosed as Ping-Pong ankle, and marathon matches led to an outbreak of wrist tendinitis. Newspapers got in on the craze and competed in publishing Ping-Pong-inspired poetry. Stockbrokers installed tables in their offices, where the bets sometimes ran to $500 per game.

Ping-Pong's novelty soon wore off. Still, the game is credited with having a lasting impact on women's dress, as female players discarded their corsets and adopted looser clothing and shorter skirts. Though Ping-Pong never regained its initial popularity, it rebounded briefly in the 1970's, this time as the popular video game Pong.

Bingo!

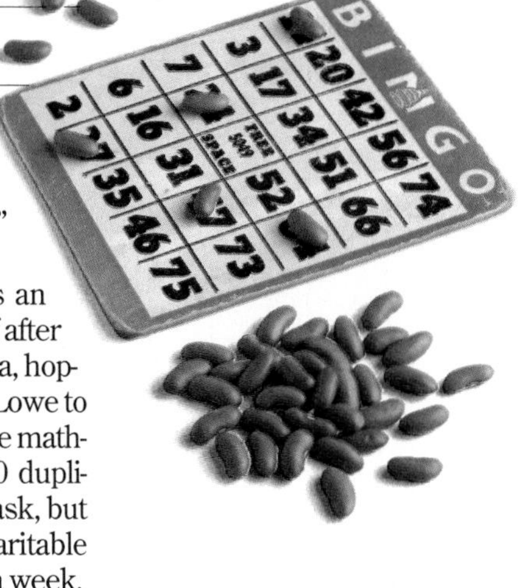

The Polish-born son of an orthodox rabbi, Edwin Lowe was the man who introduced America to a game that has become indelibly associated with church socials. Along the way he also paid for hospital clinics, uniforms for high school bands, and trucks for volunteer fire departments. And he did this all by popularizing bingo.

Simple versions of the game had been around for centuries under such names as lotto, tombola, and housey-housey; it was called beano when Lowe first encountered it in December 1929 at a carnival outside Atlanta. Lowe noticed that all the action there centered around a horseshoe-shaped table where an eager crowd was paying a nickel apiece to set beans on numbered cards in hopes of winning Kewpie dolls.

Lowe made up 12 cards and tried out an improved version of the game with friends back home in Brooklyn, New York. They were so taken with it that he couldn't get them to stop playing; they kept calling out numbers themselves after he quit. One friend also renamed the game. In her shriek of victory, she accidentally transformed "beano" into the magic word: "Bingo!"

Lowe's game, now with 24 cards, was an immediate success, but sales really took off after a parish priest in Wilkes-Barre, Pennsylvania, hoping to revive his bankrupt church, begged Lowe to expand the game for even more players. The mathematician that Lowe hired to create 6,000 duplicate-free cards almost went mad over the task, but by the mid-1930's churches and other charitable organizations were hosting 10,000 games a week.

As a form of gambling, bingo was illegal in most states, yet local police departments rarely chose to prosecute. Ironically, the game's success made it impossible for Lowe to enforce his trademark, for a judge decided that bingo had passed from private ownership into a kind of Americana.

Cuddly Kewpies

A carnival without Kewpie dolls might seem unthinkable, but prior to 1912 that was the situation. Artist Rose O'Neill had drawn her first Kewpies for the December 1909 issue of the *Ladies' Home Journal.* The wide-eyed, top-knotted, blue-winged sprites derived, she said, from the Cupids she drew to accompany love stories (Kewpie was her diminutive for Cupid). Although modeled after Cupid, "there is a difference," O'Neill once explained. "Cupid gets himself in trouble. The Kewpies get themselves out, always searching out ways to make the world better and funnier."

The beguiling babes proved so irresistible that they soon were popping up in Jell-O advertisements, on postcards, cradles, and clothing, and as valentines and Christmas ornaments. From all across the land mothers wrote to O'Neill, reporting that they were training their babies' hair in imitation of "Kewpie curls."

When fans began clamoring for "a Kewpie we could hold," O'Neill created a book of "Kewpie Kutout" paper dolls. Courted by doll manufacturers, in 1912 she contracted with a company called Borgfeldt and hired Joseph Kallus, a 17-year-old art student, to give her drawings physical form. Kewpies fairly flew out of Borgfeldt's plant in Germany; by mid-1913 it took 21 factories to keep up with the demand.

O'Neill's canny marketing of her cheerful cherubs earned her more than a million dollars before the Depression brought the fad to an end. But of this fortune, O'Neill kept relatively little for herself; lavish in her generosity, she gave money to impoverished artists almost as fast as she earned it.

The Kewpies (left) starred in four books of their own, sometimes sharing the spotlight with an irrepressible lad known as Active Artie. Kewpie dolls (above) quickly captivated the nation. O'Neill also designed a black Kewpie with white wings.

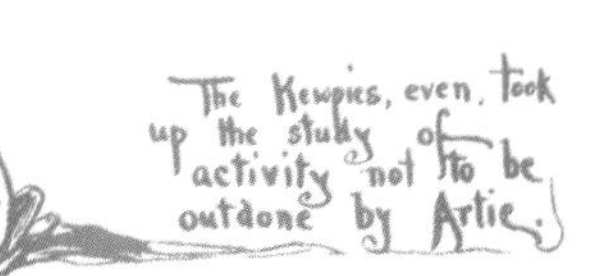

The Kewpies, even, took up the study of activity not to be outdone by Artie.

WELL-DRESSED AMERICANS

Corsets and Crinolines

Some critics claimed that tightly laced corsets cracked the ribs, weakened the lungs, and constricted internal organs; others warned that they made muscles atrophy, impeded circulation, and disrupted digestion. Reformers of all stripes railed against the contraptions, claiming that "tight lacing . . . kindles impure desires." But in spite of the occasional swoon brought on by constricted breathing, a slender waist was too enticing a goal to be wished away by crackpot health reformers.

The wasp-waist fad began in the 1820's. At its height in midcentury, up-to-the-minute women donned their corsets and had themselves cinched down as tightly as possible. Petticoats and bustles enlarged the hips, ruffles enhanced the bosom, and by the time a woman was done dressing, the final effect was one of a waist so wispy that it could easily be encircled by a beau's hands. The fictional Scarlett O'Hara's demand for lacing tight enough to produce a 17-inch waist was only a reflection of fashion reality.

Hoopla for hoops

By the 1850's skirts had become so voluminous that crinolines, the specially stiffened petticoats used to support them, were no longer adequate and were replaced by hoops and by lightweight metal cages, called cage crinolines. These underpinnings were not only lighter and cooler but also safer, for crinolines had an alarming tendency to catch fire and immolate their unfortunate wearers.

Hoops, however, created problems of their own. They had a tendency to tip up, providing titillating flashes of feminine legs. As one wag explained, "Tilting hoops are excellent. . . . We like the sex and want to see as much of them as possible."

By the 1870's the circular skirt and wasp-waist silhouette had given way to an oval with a flat front and an exaggerated posterior achieved by a rigid bustle and, often, a ruffled train. It was the athleticism of the Gibson Girl in the 1890's that finally turned the tide toward a more natural look.

W.B.
ERECT FORM
CORSETS
THIS IS THE
Latest
ERECT FORM
WEINGARTEN BROS.

The S-shaped silhouette, popular in the Edwardian era, was gained with the aid of a "rather long" corset.

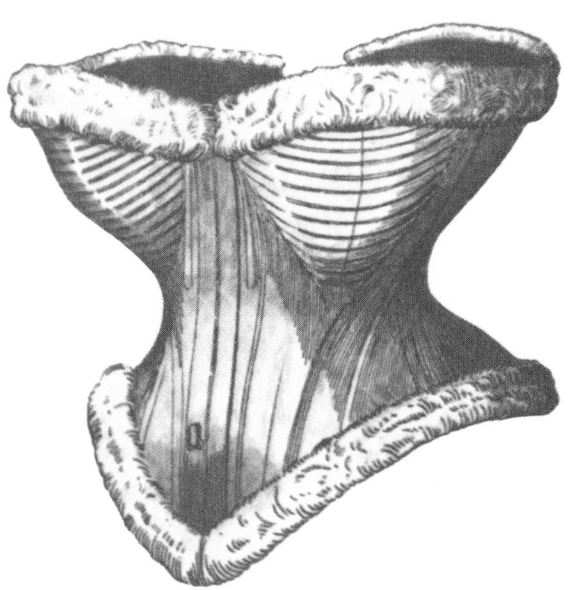

Corsets often laced up the back, making them all but impossible to don without help (above). Fur trim softened a corset's edges (left). A bustle (right) was an essential foundation garment for 1870's fashions.

The Lady in Pants

Army surgeon, prisoner of war, and Civil War veteran, Dr. Mary Walker was occasionally arrested simply for appearing in public. The problem? Her clothes. Since her costume of choice consisted of trousers, shirt, bow tie, and frock coat, law officers charged her with impersonating a man. Walker, for her part, couldn't understand the confusion. She always left her hair in curls, she explained, so that "everybody would know that I was a woman."

Considered an inspiring crusader by some and an overbearing eccentric by many, Mary Edwards Walker cared little for the opinions of others. Even as a child she sought recognition for her intelligence and refused to conform to the demure role usually assigned to girls. Following in the footsteps of her father, who was a physician, she attended Syracuse Medical College in New York and earned her doctor's certificate in 1855.

During the Civil War she campaigned rigorously to have her services accepted and in 1864 was finally commissioned as an assistant surgeon with the rank of major. Disdaining the long, cumbersome dresses of the period as wholly impractical for her work, during the war Walker wore the same uniform as the male officers: regulation trousers, overcoat, and a round felt cap decorated with gold cord.

At the end of the war she was awarded a Congressional Medal of Honor for her medical efforts, the first woman to be so honored. Although it was later revoked, as were hundreds of others, Walker continued to wear the medal on her coat at all times.

Throughout her life, though, the most attention she received was for her clothes. She created her own outfits of bloomers and frock coats and refused to bend to anyone's criticism — even shocking her family and fiancé with this attire on her wedding day. Whenever she heard of accidents caused by women's fashions, she railed against the female dress code to anyone within hearing distance and to the many people who read the constant barrage of letters that she fired off to newspaper editors. After the war she was an officer of the National Dress Reform Association.

Walker's forthright, eccentric manner made her the frequent butt of jokes, including a comedian's quip that she was a "self-made man." But nothing could make her change her mind: after her death in 1919, the lady who was married in trousers was buried in her infamous black frock coat.

When dress reform activist Dr. Mary Walker suited up, she always wore her Congressional Medal of Honor, awarded for her medical services during the Civil War.

When Buxom Was Beautiful

"A well-developed bust, a tapering waist, and large hips are the combination of points recognized as a good figure," declared one 1873 commentator. Contemporary beauty manuals also claimed that "extreme thinness is a much more cruel enemy to beauty than extreme stoutness." Striving to emulate such stately late-19th-century beauties as Lillian Russell and Jennie Jerome Churchill, fashionable women sought to create curves.

Acknowledged as the reigning beauty of her time, Lillian Russell tipped the scales at an opulent 186 pounds. Her glorious hourglass figure was maintained by unabashed eating fests with her pal Diamond Jim Brady (himself a prodigious example of the generously proportioned 19th-century male).

But what nature might deny in the way of queenly curves, nurture might provide — or artifice achieve. Unfashionably emaciated women read popular beauty books that trumpeted, "Plumpness: How to Acquire It." Edwardian style aided the unample with high-crowned hats and high-heeled boots that added desired height to one's stature. Rigid corseting narrowed the waist, which emphasized the chest and hips; corset covers lined with ruffled lace enhanced a small bust.

This majestic figure was challenged in the 1890's by the Gibson Girl and finally deposed by the flapper in the 1920's. That lean, lanky, boyish look would continue to shape the 20th-century ideal of feminine beauty.

LUXURA
NO LADY IN THE LAND WOULD LINGER WITHOUT "LUXURA" WHOSE THOUGHTS LIE IN THE DIRECTION OF BEAUTY AS REPRESENTED BY A
BEAUTIFULLY-ROUNDED AND SYMMETRICAL BOSOM
Before Treatment
After Using Two Weeks.
After Using Four Weeks.
After Using Two Months
THE ACTUAL RESULTS OF THE ORIGINAL, SAFE AND ONLY GENUINE SCIENTIFIC REMEDY FOR THE DEVELOPMENT OR RESTORATION OF THE FEMALE BUST, NECK AND FORM.
LUXURA
LENDS A GRACEFUL ROTUNDITY TO THE LEAN-CHESTED;
LOANS A CHARM AND LOVELINESS TO THE FADED CHEEK;
REMOVES DISFIGURING WRINKLES;
DEVELOPFS ALL PARTS OF THE FEMALE FORM;
NEVER FAILS, AND IS PERFECTLY HARMLESS.
Every Woman should carefully read the following pages.

The curvaceous actress-singer Lillian Russell (left) amply embodied the Edwardians' ideal feminine form. A woman who was less abundantly endowed by nature could purchase (discreetly through the mail) a variety of potions to enhance her charms (above).

The Dolls That Traveled in Style

Before there were magazines to inform women of the latest modes, milliners and dressmakers kept clients up to date with the help of fashion babies.

They were little ambassadors of taste and refinement — fashion dolls sent across the Atlantic from Europe to America from those in the know to those who hoped to be. Thought to have originated in France, the idea was borrowed by English dressmakers, who, by the early 1700's, were shipping similar dolls to the colonies. For nearly a century, until the birth of illustrated fashion magazines, these exquisitely dressed, perfectly coiffed, and completely accessorized 24-inch mannequins, known as "fashion babies," were the provincial woman's link to elegance.

"To be seen at Mrs. Hannah Teatts," read a typical ad for a well-known seamstress in a 1733 Boston weekly, ". . . a Baby drest after the Newest Fashion of Mantues [dresses] and Night Gowns & everything belonging to a dress. . . . Any Ladies that desire to see it may either come or send, she will be ready to wait on 'em. . . ."

And come they did, to study the cut and drape of a gown, the trim of a sleeve, the tilt of a hat worn just so in miniature. Wealthy matrons would order a new gown on the spot. Less well-heeled women might try their hand at recreating the style at home. But either course called for careful calculation, since what appeared resplendent on a doll was not always equally splendid on a woman.

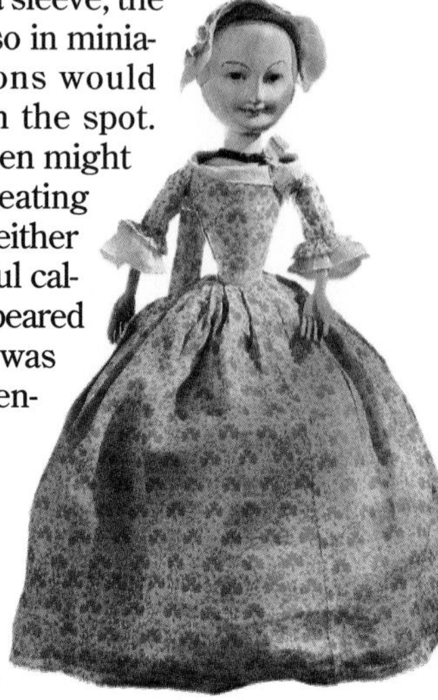

Complete to her choker and beribboned cap, this English doll is dressed in the style of the late 1700's.

At their offices on Broadway in New York City, the Buttericks printed more than just patterns. Publications included their *Quarterly*, begun in 1867, and the *Delineator*, started in 1873, which pictured enticing fashions that could be made at home by using Butterick patterns.

Patterns of Fashion

A bit of a tinkerer as well as a tailor, Ebenezer Butterick began to experiment in 1859 when his wife suggested that making clothing would be much simpler with reusable patterns. Working first with heavy brown paper (he would later switch to tissue paper), he sketched and measured, trimmed and folded, in search of a shortcut to drawing a fresh chalk pattern for each new garment. What he came up with was the archetype of the modern graded pattern — a paper template in graduated sizes that could be mass-produced, sold for pennies, and used again and again.

The Buttericks were not the first to consider the problem. A Madame Demorest, the proprietor of a dress shop in New York, published designs for her fashions in 1862, and popular magazines regularly included detailed sketches of the latest styles from Europe. But such offerings were suitable only for skilled dressmakers. Butterick's patterns were meant for everyone: with his invention he struck a blow for democracy in fashion.

His initial designs, for children's dresses and a man's shirt, appeared in June 1863. Demand was so brisk that Butterick family members who had been folding patterns in their home in Massachusetts had first to move next door and then to a nearby factory. Within a year sales potential looked so promising that the couple moved their entire operation to New York.

TIME TABLE

GREAT MOMENTS IN FASHION

1700's *Men are wearing wigs, a trend that continues until the 1790's.*

1700's *The cocked hat, later called the tricorn, is introduced.*

1720's *The hoop skirt appears, becomes widely popular by midcentury, and disappears by the 1770's.*

1720's *Men and women powder their hair for formal occasions and continue to do so until the 1790's.*

1800's *Filmy empire dresses are a radical new style. Underneath them women wear their first drawers.*

1800's *Full-length men's trousers begin to replace breeches and stockings. Worn with trousers are the new jackets with tails, and tall beaver hats.*

1840's *Fly fronts appear on men's pants.*

1840's *The first rubber galoshes are worn.*

1850's *The hoop skirt returns — this time known as the cage crinoline.*

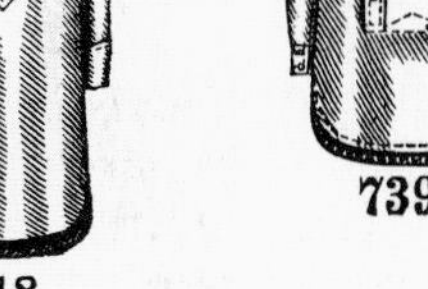

With Butterick patterns, clothing could be made at home for all members of a family. These men's shirt patterns date from the early 1880's.

What really sent the family fortunes soaring, however, was Butterick's design for a "Garibaldi suit." Capitalizing on a wave of adulation for the heroic exploits of the Italian patriot, Giuseppe Garibaldi, Butterick quickly translated the dashing uniform worn by Garibaldi and his followers into a child's-size pattern. It was an item that virtually every little boy in America had to have. And the only way most parents could provide it was through the purchase of a Butterick pattern. When Butterick introduced his line of women's patterns in 1866, his success with the sons stood him in good stead with the mothers — surely a first in the annals of fashion.

Couture Comes Out of Confinement

In 1906, when one of her customers asked for a "pretty and practical" dress for entertaining while pregnant, Lena Himmelstein Bryant responded with characteristic pragmatism. The young woman had learned to live by her wits six years earlier when, at age 20, she was widowed and left with a baby to care for on her own. Hocking her one pair of good earrings (a gift from her husband), Bryant had bought a sewing machine and begun turning out tea gowns and undergarments for women in her New York neighborhood.

Now, at her client's request, the Lithuanian-born seamstress considered the problem of designing clothes for a steadily expanding figure. Her solution was to join a flattering bodice to an accordion-pleated skirt with an elasticized waistband. The customer was delighted, and a new specialty — maternity clothing — was launched. Orders poured in from women all over New York who wanted to look as stylish through their "confinements" as they did at other times. It was not long before Bryant was obliged to open a proper bank account, but when she nervously scrawled her signature, the bank clerk interpreted it as "Lane" rather than "Lena." Too shy to request a correction, she decided to keep the new name.

A few years later, Bryant married a Lithuanian engineer, Albert Malsin, who became her business partner. Convinced that there was a market for maternity street wear as well as "at home" dresses, Malsin persuaded his wife to design some simple styles to be worn in public. Though America was still in the grip of Victorian prudishness — at first no newspaper would carry ads for Bryant's new line — the clothing was an immediate underground hit.

Word of mouth brought hundreds of eager, if discreetly veiled, customers to her side-street shop, plus thousands of mail orders specifying "plain-wrapper shipment." In 1911 the *New York Herald* conceded the obvious and ran an ad. "Doctors, nurses and psychologists agree," it claimed, "that at this time a woman should think and live as normally as possible." The floodgates had burst.

By 1917 Lane Bryant had sold a million dollars' worth of maternity clothes. Soon after, the company turned its attention to the creation of flattering fashions for larger women. And just as Bryant's designs helped retire the idea of confinement, so they helped end the tyranny of the "perfect 36."

Lane Bryant put pregnant women back in circulation with designs for clothes like this 1912-style maternity topcoat.

1850's *White becomes a customary color for bridal wear.*

1860's *The bustle appears and keeps growing until its demise about 1890.*

1860's *America's ready-to-wear industry is born.*

1870's *The mechanized shoe industry gears up.*

1880's *Divided skirts are introduced for bicycling.*

1880's *The tuxedo is first worn (at Tuxedo Park, New York).*

1890's *Women's fashion enters a new age with tailored suits, shirtwaist blouses, and Gibson Girl hairstyles.*

1900's *With the arrival of automobiles, the duster, auto veil and goggles are introduced.*

1910's *New Jersey and Louisiana outlaw protruding hat pins.*

1910's *The pullover sweater makes its debut.*

1920's *A new invention — the bra — becomes popular.*

1920's *Irene Castle sets the style for bobbed hair and headache bands.*

1930's *Zippers replace button flies on men's trousers.*

1930's *Cowboy shirts go mainstream.*

1930's *Men's bathing suits lose their tops.*

1940's *Women wear the first nylons with their new platform-soled shoes.*

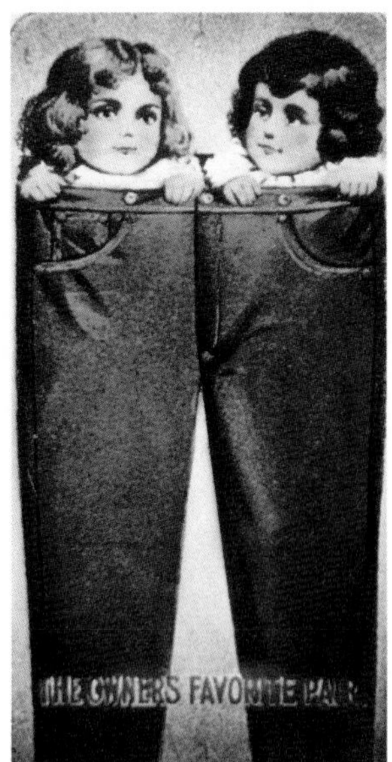

In early advertising (above and right) Levi Strauss's jeans were usually, though not always, identified with cowboys. No matter whom they were made for, however, the denim fabric, deep blue color, and riveted pockets remained the same from one generation to the next.

The Pants That Won the West

First made for California gold miners in the 1850's, Levi Strauss's blue jeans became the standard attire of the old West, then traveled around the world.

Loeb Strauss, the son of a Bavarian salesman, was 18 years old when, in 1847, he left Germany to join his brothers in the dry-goods trade in New York. Within a year — by which time he was known as Levi instead of Loeb — the young man was carrying on the family business in the backwoods of Kentucky, peddling from a wagon. And by the early 1850's he was sailing around Cape Horn on a clipper ship to join his sister and her husband in gold-rich California.

A new use for canvas

Strauss arrived in San Francisco with a supply of canvas, which he assumed the miners would buy for tents and wagon covers. But he soon discovered that the thing the prospectors really needed was durable pants: nothing then available could hold up to hard use in the mines. He had a tailor use his canvas to stitch up a stock of trousers, and Strauss once again set off in a wagon to peddle his wares — and his diligence paid off. "Those pants of Levi's" were an immediate success.

When Strauss wrote his brothers in New York to send more material, they shipped him a tough brownish French cotton called *serge de Nîmes* — a name that San Franciscans soon shortened to denim. And although Strauss called his new product "waist overalls," once again it was a foreign name that stuck. *Gênes,* the French word for Genoa, referred to a denimlike fabric made in that city. But in America, *Gênes* cloth became simply jeans. By the 1860's Strauss was able to buy a similar product woven in New Hampshire.

A riveting scheme

A shrewd salesman, Strauss realized that his drab-colored pants would sell better if he dyed them a distinctive indigo blue. Likewise, in 1872 he was quick to accept the suggestion of a Nevada tailor, Jacob Davis, who had taken to reinforcing the trousers that he made from fabric supplied by Strauss. Responding to miners who complained that the pockets burst their seams when they were stuffed with rocks and tools, Davis had rivets applied by a harness maker. Initially meant as a joke, they were such a success with the miners that Davis and Strauss took out a patent for rivet-reinforced trousers.

With that the pattern was set. Levi's remained the pants of western outdoorsmen, the indispensable cowboy garb until Easterners — including women — discovered jeans at dude ranches in the 1930's and brought them home.

all over the west they wear
LEVI STRAUSS & CO'S
COPPER RIVETED
Overalls.

Since 1865 the Stetson has been the cowboy's best friend. This one was worn by Enrico Caruso in the opera *The Girl of the Golden West.*

Boss of the Plains

"Ya can stomp a John B. plumb to death," runs one bit of old-time cowboy wisdom, "but danged if ya can make 'em unravel." And indeed, the durability of John B. Stetson's products was one reason his name became synonymous with *hat* throughout the American West. But even more important was the design. Before the New Jersey native set up business in 1865, all headwear styles came from Europe. He was the first to make hats specifically to suit the needs of the plainsman.

Stetson knew the West at first hand. As a young man with lung problems and a grim prognosis, he had left the family hat business and traveled to Missouri in search of a healthier climate. Joining a party of prospectors, he ventured as far west as Pikes Peak, where he found no gold but did regain his health. Along the way he also made himself a hat. It was high crowned to keep his head cool, and wide brimmed to shield his eyes from glare. His partners laughed, but a freight driver thought enough of it to pay Stetson a five-dollar gold piece for the hat.

Returning east, Stetson established a one-room factory in Philadelphia where he earned a modest living making hats for sale to local stores. His real success came when he recreated the hat he had made in Colorado. Calling it "The Boss of the Plains," he sent samples to western clothing dealers — and the orders poured in. By 1906, the year of his death, Stetson had 3,500 employees and was turning out 2 million hats a year.

Made of top-quality felt, Stetson's hats were designed to keep the sun, wind, rain, and dust from a horseman's head, to shade his neck, and even to water his horse. Stetsons rode into Little Big Horn with Custer and on hunts with Buffalo Bill. Annie Oakley wore a "John B.," as did Calamity Jane. In those days you could tell a cowman's range by the way he wore his Stetson: Southwesterners, for example, affected a high (cooler) crown with four creases, while riders from the windy Northwest favored a lower, flat crown. However it was worn, the hat changed the look of the West as the single piece of equipment no cowpuncher was ever without. In time, in fact, the cowboy hat was called a Stetson, whether or not it was a "genuwine" John B.

The Champion of Chilly Ears

Sensitive ears were serious business to Chester Greenwood. Because his own turned blue within a few minutes of exposure to the winter weather of Farmington, Maine, the 15-year-old could not enjoy the ice skates he had been given for his birthday in 1873. Not one to be put off, Greenwood simply invented a solution. Bending some baling wire into a pair of loops and covering them with beaver fur and velvet, he not only discovered a cure for cold ears but also came up with a million-dollar idea.

When neighbors and fellow skaters expressed interest in his newfangled ear mufflers, Greenwood put his mother and grandmother to work covering wire with fur to fill the orders. By 1877 Greenwood held a patent on his invention and began manufacturing his "Champion Ear Protectors" in quantity. This improved model boasted a one-size-fits-all adjustable frame of spring steel, and hinged ear covers that made it easy to fold them for pocket storage. What had begun as a cottage industry soon moved into a factory in downtown Farmington. By the early 1880's Greenwood was selling 30,000 pairs a year. By the 1930's his volume was closer to 400,000, and Farmington was known as the "ear muff capital of the world."

Greenwood's ingenuity did not stop with ear muffs. He invented the 15 machines used for making and assembling the various "ear protector" parts at his factory. And over the years, he devised more than 100 other products, including a self-priming sparkplug, the spring-steel rake, shock absorbers for airplanes, a washing machine, and — yes — a better mousetrap. When he wasn't selling bicycles or heating systems, Greenwood might be found operating his tourist steamboat on nearby Lake Clearwater; he also organized the first successful telephone system in his home county.

It is for his first venture, however, that Farmington sponsors a Chester Greenwood Day each year in December. Residents assemble for a parade complete with its own flag — red ear muffs on a snowy white ground — and events such as an ear muff fashion show and, of course, a coldest ear contest.

A dapper Chester Greenwood, complete with his Champion Ear Protectors, was photographed around 1885. Each year on Chester Greenwood Day his achievements are commemorated with the poem "Necessity is the Mother of Invention, or Chester Had Colder Ears Than Most of His Peers."

The Gibson Girl (above) was easily recognized by her patrician profile and magnificent crown of hair. The Gibson Man (below) had trouble keeping his mind on other things when she was near.

Charles Dana Gibson's All-American Girl

She was tall and as graceful as a gazelle, with a long neck balanced on broad shoulders and a mass of upswept wavy hair. She played tennis and golf, rode horses and bikes, and looked as coolly elegant in her shirtwaists as she did in evening dress. She was America's ideal — the wholly imaginary but thoroughly convincing Gibson Girl.

When the first of his "girls" appeared in one of Charles Dana Gibson's illustrations in the early 1890's, America was still something of a social backwater. The country's newly rich were prone to proving their worth by marrying their daughters off to titled Europeans, no matter how fusty or gout ridden. Gibson disapproved. And in his lampoons of such behavior, he created an image of American womanhood where none had existed before. In her sweeping skirts and towering pompadour, the Gibson Girl — who appeared week after week in the humor magazine *Life,* among other publications — was an enticingly noble creature.

Slightly aloof, she was a goddess forever being wooed by unworthy suitors. Not even the square-jawed, clean-shaven Gibson Man quite measured up. But while she was definitely upper crust, she was not a snob. In short, she was a paragon. Men idolized her and women looked to her to learn how to dress, walk, sit, and dine. "You can always tell when a girl is taking the Gibson Cure," wrote one observer, "by the way she fixes her hair."

In fact, the whole country seemed to be taking the Gibson Cure. People filled their parlors and bedrooms with franchised likenesses of the girl — framed as lithographs, engraved on wood, printed on chinaware, embossed on spoons, and repeated on wallpaper. So great was her popularity between the 1890's and World War I that Gibson earned as much as $65,000 a year, and women on two continents claimed to have been his original model.

During those prewar decades the Gibson Girl made a lot of people feel pride in being American, for hers was a style that few could resist. "Parents in the United States are no better than elsewhere," wrote one European visitor, "but their daughters! Divinely tall, brows like Juno . . . throats that Aphrodite might envy."

A LITTLE INCIDENT

Fashion Tips From the Stars

There was a time — right up through the 1920's in fact — when many Americans, especially the rich, looked to Paris for fashion cues. Then along came Hollywood with its new style of native-born glamour that even ordinary folks could imitate. In response to this urge to look like the stars, favorite films were often followed up by the appearance of such items as Shirley Temple dress patterns. And department stores — quick to take advantage of the trend — opened "cinema shops" featuring the latest styles from the silver screen.

Even Paris took note. After watching Mae West strut through *She Done Him Wrong* in 1933, designer Elsa Schiaparelli sat down to add some hourglass curves to the designs on her drawing board. Costume dramas had a similar effect: after *Little Women* and *The Barretts of Wimpole Street* in 1933 and 1934, Parisian streets were filled with poke bonnets and parasols, ruffled capes and trailing ribbons.

But for the average American woman, the designers of choice were home-grown talents — the unknowns whose overnight knock-offs for Macy's or Sears, Roebuck could put her into a sharp-shouldered dress just like the one Joan Crawford wore in *Letty Lynton* or the tailored slacks that were a Dietrich trademark. Among the most imitated of all was the floating, hoop-skirted confection that Scarlett O'Hara wore to the barbecue in *Gone With the Wind.* Copies were run up in every price range and in every conceivable color and fabric, though most were sensibly hoopless and it is likely that only a very few were ever worn to a barbecue.

Women were not the only ones dressing (or undressing) like the stars. When Clark Gable took off his shirt to reveal a bare chest in *It Happened One Night,* sales of T-shirts plummeted. It took Marlon Brando in *A Streetcar Named Desire* to bring the undershirt back.

If not exactly a slave to fashion, Marlon Brando (top) still set a style copied by many. The sale of Shirley Temple dolls, clothes, and other products earned the child star (above) more than her films.

A Fourth of July celebrant in 1913 appeared in the scaled-down, nattily nautical attire popularized almost 70 years before by the young prince of Wales, whose dashing outfit had inspired a fashion that circled the globe and made every mother's son a prince.

The Suit That Suited

Until blue jeans came along, perhaps no other item of clothing had ever appealed to so many as the classic sailor suit. The unisex, classless passion for mock navy gear was launched in 1846, inspired by a popular portrait of the five-year-old prince of Wales clad in a miniature naval uniform. Impeccably tailored, the prince's suit was a scaled-down interpretation of what his mother's sailors were wearing that summer: crisp, white bell-bottom trousers, white shirt with a large triangular collar squared at the back, knotted blue neckerchief, and flat, wide-brimmed white hat.

It was a style that wore well — and traveled fast. Parents quickly found that the look could be copied in whole or in part, in blue or in white, and still produce the desired snappy effect. Soon little boys in both Europe and America were being outfitted in spiffy sailor suits.

Girls, too, got in on the craze, agreeing that the sailor suit did indeed suit to a tee. With a pleated skirt instead of bell-bottom trousers, the jaunty outfit became the basis for school and camp uniforms for generations of young girls on both sides of the Atlantic — and hundreds of miles inland.

The only world left to conquer was that of adult fashion, and women cheerfully succumbed to the allure of white and blue in the 1920's and again in the 1940's. Far from the sea, the sailor suit had acquired a life of its own as a sartorial synonym for taste and verve.

Mama's Toys

The interlude of fashion harmony that boys and their mothers enjoyed by virtue of their mutual admiration for the manly sailor suit was abruptly interrupted in November 1885 by the appearance of a magazine story called *Little Lord Fauntleroy.*

The story was by the Anglo-American author Frances Hodgson Burnett, and the main character, a small American boy who inherits a British title, was modeled on her son, Vivian. As stories and boyish heroes go, the little lord, called Cedric, was no lambchop of a "Mama's boy," but a spirited, well-mannered fellow who was good at sports. But the tale's illustrator, Reginald Birch, cloaked Cedric in a fanciful outfit that owed much to Gainsborough's painting "The Blue Boy" and

The young lad (right) might well be wondering if bare skin on the bearskin would be more dignified than his fantastic get-up, inspired by the fanciful garb of the young hero of *Little Lord Fauntleroy* (above).

to the romantic costumes that the author had sewn for her own sons: a black velvet suit with close-fitting knickers, a white lace collar, and a bright red sash. A plumed Cavalier's hat capped the hero's golden, shoulder-length curls. It was a get-up just right for a dandy, and to the horror of their own flesh and blood, that's just what millions of mothers thought it was — dandy.

Before they knew what had hit them, boys up and down the East Coast were buttoned into velvet leggings, had sashes tied around their waists, lace fluffed beneath their chins, and curling irons threatening their ears. Although it was a short-lived epidemic, for years afterward the accounts of its innocent victims convey the stigma and the sting.

"The other boys were inclined to giggle," went one recollection of a Lord Fauntleroy suit, so "after protesting in vain . . . I decided to make it unwearable by flinging myself down in the gutter on the way to the dancing class." Having succeeded in "cutting the breeches" and his knees, the defiant six-year-old tore loose his Vandyke collar and escaped the baiting that awaited him. "Not only did I avoid the dancing class," he wrote. "I also avoided being photographed in that infernal get-up."

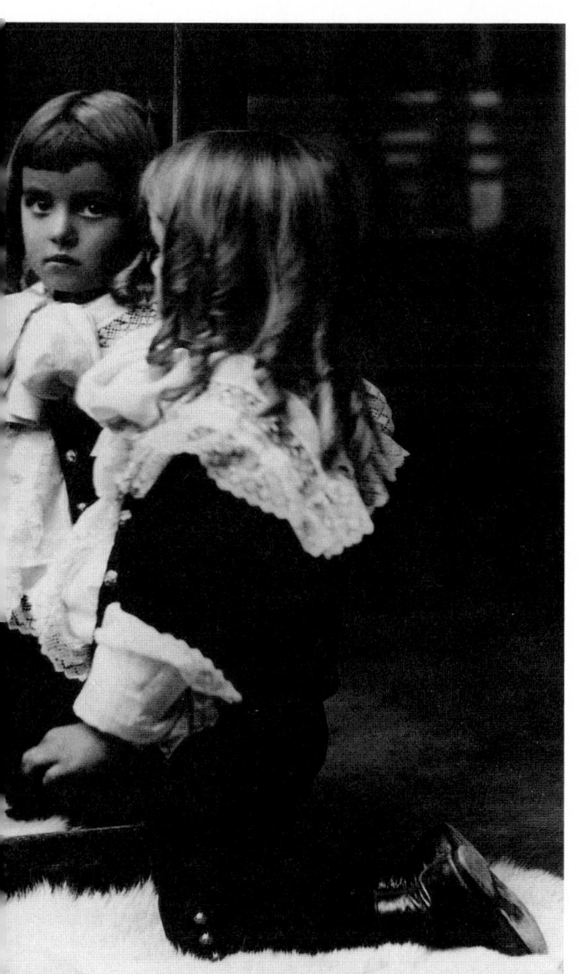

An ingenious prankster when he first appeared in a comic strip in 1902 (above), Buster Brown soon settled down to work as the trademark for the Brown Shoe Company of Missouri (below). Actors hired to portray Buster Brown in promotion campaigns toured the country, handing out prizes to children who could show them the label of the winking boy and his pop-eyed dog in their well-kept shoes.

If the Shoe Fits

Almost everyone remembers the shoes — simple one-strap Mary Janes and slip-on oxfords that were "priced according to size" — and the endearing rascal with the toothy dog who starred in the ads that sold the shoes.

"I'm Buster Brown," said the little boy in the Lord Fauntleroy suit and modest hat. "I live in a shoe." "Woof! Woof!" added his beribboned pet. "That's my dog, Tige; he lives there, too."

It didn't make much sense, but it didn't have to. By the time the Buster Brown ads began their famous run on a children's television program in the 1950's, the character had become a fixture of American culture — and commerce. Appearing first in the comics section of the *New York Herald* in 1902, then on a radio show, Buster was the brainchild of R. F. Outcault and was based on the cartoonist's precocious 10-year-old son. Like his real-life counterpart, Buster had a little sister named Mary Jane. And he had that grinning, clipped-eared scamp of a dog.

For the Brown Shoe Company of St. Louis, it was a comic strip seemingly made to order. The hero with the page-boy hairdo was quickly enlisted as a trademark for the company's line of children's shoes, and an ad campaign was kicked off in 1904 at the St. Louis World's Fair — where Outcault had cleverly set up a booth of his own and was offering Buster's face to peddlers of everything from chewing gum and horseshoes to waffle irons and bourbon.

Unruffled by the competition for its new icon, the shoe company hired several midgets to do promotional tours, costumed in Buster's Dutch-boy wig and cap. Accompanied by a series of faithful bulldogs, one peripatetic impersonator eventually appeared in every county in the nation.

Saturday Night Specials

Preachers might have praised cleanliness as next to godliness, but as far as our ancestors were concerned, baths were something to avoid. Well into the 19th century doctors stigmatized bathtubs as carriers of disease, pronouncing them especially unhealthy when filled with warm water. A rinse at the backyard pump sufficed for most country folk, while in the city a scrub with a sponge and towel (no soap) was considered more than ample.

The sponge bath, in fact, was highly recommended. It "can do little harm and almost always some good," advised the *Gentleman's Book of Etiquette*, adding "the part of the body that should first be attacked is the stomach." Other authorities meanwhile had begun to campaign for greater personal hygiene. "One may always know a gentleman by the state of his hands and nails," commented one Philadelphia pundit.

Soon after the Civil War, as attitudes continued to change, bathtubs of sheet copper, iron, and zinc began to appear in a bewildering variety of types. There were half baths, sitz baths, hip baths, foot baths, and for the modest, tubs equipped with covers that made them look like sofas when not in use.

Still, a lack of taps made the Saturday night bath a chore. Water had to be heated on the stove, then carried to the tub. Even the introduction of hot water boilers in the 1870's was a mixed blessing since the early models were prone to exploding. And getting water into the tub was less of a problem than getting it out. For years people lived in fear that "deadly sewer gas" would enter the house through drains. Consequently, as late as the 1880's in American cities (where plumbing was more up to date than the rest of the country), only one in six families had a bathtub.

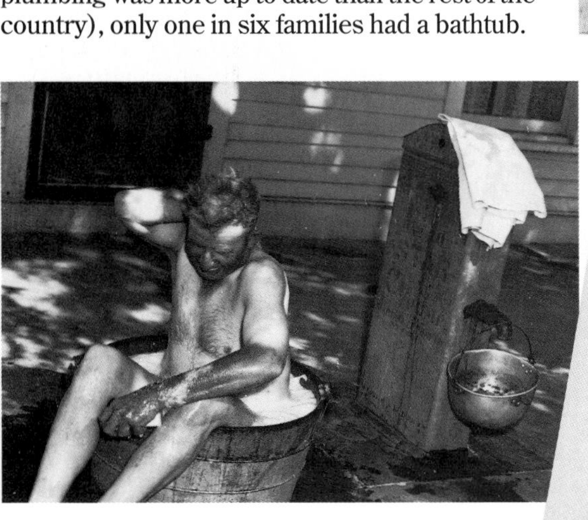

No one is safe!

Banker, baker or society woman—no matter who we are—*every one of us may offend unknowingly.*

Frank facts... about body odor!

By the turn of the century, bathing beauties (above) could soak in style in the most up-to-date houses and finest hotels. For a long time, however, other Americans would still be scrubbing up the old-fashioned way (far left). Advertisements calling attention to body odor in the 1920's (left) show how far attitudes toward bathing had changed since the 19th century.

Fashion Takes It on the Chin

There was hardly a whisker among America's founding fathers. A Philadelphia woman even wrote of her shock one day in the late 1700's when she saw not only an elephant in the street but two men with beards. In those days well-heeled gents who lived in town were likely to visit a barber once or twice a week to have their faces shaved. While there, they could also have a tooth pulled or be bled to relieve an ailment, since barbers doubled as surgeons. More often, however, men got their shaves and haircuts at home. And while no less a personage than Benjamin Franklin boasted that he shaved his own face and even sharpened his own razor, it was usually a man's wife or servant who did the honors.

Although men were cutting off their pigtails and wearing short hairstyles by the turn of the 19th century, facial hair remained a rarity. As late as 1830, one Massachusetts man was actually persecuted for wearing a beard. Within a generation, however, American men were thoroughly bewhiskered, and beards had become badges of professions. A rectangular beard, for instance, marked the engineer or scientist, while a bushy (but well-trimmed) version signaled a naval officer; the artist shaped his into a pointed Vandyke, and clergymen favored lush side whiskers called "Dundrearies."

America's fascination with beards lasted only about 25 years: by 1880, attention had turned to mustaches of every conceivable type. Since shaving with a straight razor required considerable skill, this change in fashion sparked the heyday of the barbershop as male club. Regulars kept a personal shaving mug at their local shop. And they stopped by to talk politics, catch up with friends, and read the police gazette while having their mustaches trimmed and their chins scraped clean — all for a mere six cents.

Tressing Up With the Sutherland Sisters

In an era when luxuriant locks were considered the ultimate feminine attraction, seven sisters made a career of simply letting their hair down.

"A woman's crowning glory," said the seven Sutherland sisters, "is her hair." And in the case of these 19th-century New York farm girls, it was their fortune as well. They had started out with little else: growing up in a log cabin, the sisters dressed in clothing made of grain sacks and spent their childhood herding turkeys. One thing they did have, however, was remarkable hair. Sarah, the oldest, had glossy black tresses fully three feet long — and hers were the shortest. Victoria, the next in the septet, had a seven-foot mane. Together the sisters boasted a combined hair length of nearly 37 feet.

All the girls had modest musical talents and they learned to sing in harmony (one sister sang bass). Performing together, they enjoyed some success on the vaudeville circuit, but it soon became clear that audiences were more interested in their flowing hair than their floating harmonies. By 1884 when the sisters toured with the Barnum and Bailey Circus, they climaxed their act by simply standing under a spotlight, unpinning their hair, and letting it cascade down their backs.

The oohs and aahs that greeted the act prompted the sisters to produce Seven Sutherland Sisters' Hair Grower, which — when backed by the sisters' personal appearances — sold by the barrel. By 1892 they had added a Sutherland Sisters scalp cleaner, comb, and eight shades of "hair colorators" to their line of goods and employed some 28,000 dealers nationwide.

With the profits they built a 14-room mansion near the old homestead, dressed their 17 cats in silver collars, and their dogs in seasonal changes of clothing. Undeniably eccentric, the sisters spent money faster than they earned it. Worse still, however, was the fashion for bobbed hair: catching on in the early 20th century, it brought their livelihood to a sudden halt.

Billed as the Seven Wonders of the World, the Sutherland sisters took their hair on the road and made a fortune. Profits from their appearances and products were estimated to have been in the millions.

The
FIRST
"Library-on-Wheels"
in the
CITY'S SERVICE
1922-1932
BOOKS-FOR-ALL

Chapter 5

EDUCATING AMERICA

SCHOOL DAYS

Defeating "Ye Ould Deluder Satan"

Public education was a new idea in the New World, and our Puritan forebears turned it to the good use of guarding souls as well as improving minds.

Members of the General Court of Massachusetts had two goals in mind when, in 1647, they passed a law that created the first publicly supported schools in America. Their dual aims were to foil the efforts of "ye ould deluder Satan, to keepe men from the knowledge of ye Scriptures," and to ensure that "learning . . . not be buried in ye grave of our fathers."

The law required every settlement of more than 50 families to appoint a teacher to provide instruction in the Puritan version of the three R's: reading, writing, and religion. Towns with more than 100 families had to set up a "grammer schoole," where emphasis was put on the education of boys of "hopeful promise," who studied Latin, Greek, and literature in preparation for college. Girls, on the other hand, were rarely allowed above the primary level for fear that they might lose their wits if exposed to too much reading and thinking.

If a town lacked a schoolhouse, classes could be held in the meetinghouse. Teachers were paid a meager stipend, supplied with produce, and if not residents of the town, were "boarded around" with townsfolk. Families were also expected to provide wood for the school's stove — a task that was often neglected until a child came home and complained of shivering through the day in the wintriest corner of the drafty room.

The daily routine was tied to the sun's cycle. During most of the year the day began at 7:00 A.M. and ended sometime between 5:00 and 9:00 P.M. with a two-hour break. In the winter months the schedule ran from 8:00 A.M. to 4:00 P.M.

Primitive and simple though the system was, children who spent even two or three years in these schools did learn enough to become familiar with the laws of the land — and to keep the "ould deluder" at bay.

Schooling, Southern Style

A PERSON well recommended for teaching Reading, Writing and Arithmetick, may hear of handfome Encouragement, in a Private Family on applying to the Printer.

Schools were few and far between in the South during the 18th century. As evidenced by this 1762 advertisement, capable tutors could expect to meet with "handsome Encouragement" from plantation families.

In 1752 planter Theophilos Field placed a notice in the *Virginia Gazette,* soliciting the services of a qualified tutor. His needs were simple: "Any single man, capable of teaching Greek, Latin, and the Mathematicks. . . ."

Field's was one of many similar advertisements that appeared in southern newspapers throughout the 18th century, for the gentry considered ignorance a disgrace. An uneducated member of the family was scorned as "Scandalous, . . . and a shame to his relations."

But if education was important, it was also a problem. There were some "old-field schools"— community schools built on worn-out land — but they were relatively rare, and difficult for most children to get to. Since plantations were vast, families were isolated, and the burden of schooling fell directly on the parents.

Those who could afford it sent their sons to England for a proper education. Others found tutors who would live on the plantation and teach all of the children. The assignment could be challenging. When Philip Fithian accepted a position at Nomini Hall, a 70,000-acre Virginia estate, in 1773, he had only eight pupils. The children, however, ranged in age from 7 to 18 or older, and in experience from those just learning their letters to some who could read Latin.

Fithian was a graduate of Princeton, but American tutors were the exception. More often they were Scots or Englishmen who came to this country as indentured servants, pledging four years of service in exchange for ocean passage and the chance for a new life. Whether or not they were actually trained as teachers, those who had at least a smattering of Latin, literature, and "the Mathematicks" made use of those skills when they got here.

While many indentured servants were treated as social inferiors, some, like John Harrower, who arrived in Virginia in 1774, were welcomed as gentlemen and had their own school buildings to work in. Harrower's was "a neate little House 20 foot Long and 12 foot wide" that doubled as his home. "I sleep in it by myself," he wrote his wife back in Scotland, and "have a verry fine feather bed under me."

Despite his indenture, Harrower, like many other tutors in the South, was allowed to accept children from neighboring plantations as pupils. It was his one means of earning a bit of extra money to send home and help hasten the day when he and his family would be reunited.

Many an American woman turned her home into a dame school, where children were taught to read, if not to behave. Probably few such classrooms were as spacious and well equipped as this early 19th-century parlor.

School Days at the Dame School

From the earliest colonial days into the 19th century, any respectable woman who needed a bit of an income could earn it by opening a dame school. Essentially day-care centers located in a woman's own home, dame schools could be found in most large towns.

Corralled into the dame's kitchen or parlor, young children received the rudiments of education. Classes were apt to be haphazard, and teachers stern disciplinarians. Unruly children were often punished by a rap on the head with a thimble. Kindlier dames might provide a pillow in a corner where hard-working toddlers could rest their weary heads. What children actually got out of the school depended solely on the teacher's abilities, and some teachers had little more training than their wards.

However much she knew, the dame's job was to teach children their ABCs. Those not lucky enough to have primers to work with might draw letters in sand or teach the alphabet directly from the Bible. Lucy Larcom, who attended "Aunt Hannah's" school in 1830, later wrote: "I learned my letters in a few days, standing at Aunt Hannah's knee while she pointed them out . . . with a pin, skipping over the 'a b abs' into words of one or two syllables, thence taking a flying leap into the New Testament."

Between reading and perhaps singing songs with the dame as she spun flax or baked bread, many children also learned to sew by working samplers. It was a skill that girls would use for the rest of their lives.

Surrounded by a houseful of lively children, a dame did not earn much for her efforts. A typical salary, if paid by the parents, was a few cents a week per child. If paid by the town, there might be an arrangement such as one 18th-century teacher had for "£12 and diet, with use of a horse to visit her friends twice a year."

While some of her pupils would be lucky enough to go on to a private academy, most of them never received any further formal education once they left her kitchen. For pennies a day, the dame, for nearly two centuries, helped keep literacy alive.

Brush-arbor schools like the one these Texas children attended in 1887 often served as classrooms on the southern plains until proper schools could be built.

Not Just the Little Red Schoolhouse

Throughout our history, school buildings came in as wide a variety of styles as there were minds and materials to create them.

Short on resources but long on resourcefulness, parents in Scotts Bluff, Nebraska, constructed their first school from bales of straw. For two years in the late 1800's, pupils recited lessons inside this grassy shelter while cattle on the outside nibbled it to oblivion. Temporary structures such as this were replaced or improved upon when the community prospered. The evolution of many a Kansas school was typical: they often began as simple dugouts, were replaced by sod shacks, and then by frame or stone structures.

Deciding where to build the school often sparked a lively debate. It needed to be within walking distance for most of the children, yet far enough from farms so that pranksters would not trample crops or harass animals. It should be built on land not suitable for cultivation and, if possible, be located near a road. Simple log or frame schools that lacked fixed foundations were sometimes set on skids and shifted about the countryside in response to changes in the population.

The traditional schoolhouse means many things. For some students it was a humble log cabin. This one is notable for its vertical, or "stockade," construction style and the size and number of its windows.

The schools were built from whatever materials were plentiful. Wood and stone were common in the East, sod was used on the prairies, and adobe in the Southwest. The prevalence of red brick schools in the Midwest has probably added to the myth of the "little red schoolhouse." But, in fact, most schools were painted white. Octagonal schools—the brainchild of a phrenologist and amateur architect—were easy to heat and so were popular for a time in the Middle Atlantic states.

Traditionally, a one-room school was furnished with crude backless benches that were, over time, incised by idle whittlers with "all sorts of images, some of which would make heathens blush." There were no individual desks. Instead, a slanted shelf ran along three walls and served as a writing surface; a flat shelf below it held personal items. The windows were glazed with paper greased with lard for translucence and waterproofing. This fragile glazing was often broken, and in winter the openings were likely to be stuffed with hats to help keep out the cold.

Amenities were added as budgets permitted. Yards were fenced, more to keep wandering livestock out than to keep the children in. To ensure propriety, schools sometimes had separate entrances for boys and girls—an extravagant nicety in cases when the school itself was a single room. A more pressing matter was that of privies: some schools had none; others had only one. In the early 1900's, school superintendents urged that there "be separate toilets for the sexes . . . far enough apart to avoid moral contagion."

Standardization of buildings and facilities increased dramatically in the 20th century. Playgrounds were built and flagpoles sprang up. Additional rooms and second, or even third, stories were added. What one scholar observed about the one-room schoolhouse was no less true for these later structures; from here a pupil's world widened "outward from the common room . . . in an adventure of growing and learning."

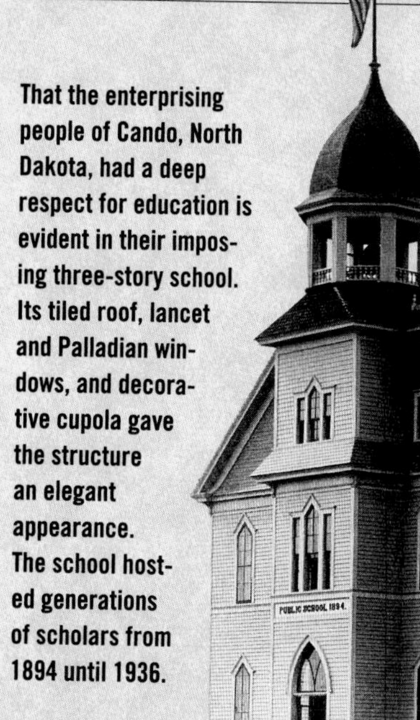

That the enterprising people of Cando, North Dakota, had a deep respect for education is evident in their imposing three-story school. Its tiled roof, lancet and Palladian windows, and decorative cupola gave the structure an elegant appearance. The school hosted generations of scholars from 1894 until 1936.

Sod schools were afflicted with eccentricities. Insects and other animals often resided in the ceiling, rain turned the floor to mud, and each spring the roof sprouted a festive crown of wildflowers.

Frontier teachers made creative use of catalogs as readers and for decorations: tinted plates from ladies' fashion magazines brightened the walls of many a school.

In Colonial America boys — and occasionally girls — were formally apprenticed to master craftsmen and left their homes to learn a trade. But by the early 20th century, schools had incorporated vocational training into their curricula and offered classes in such practical fields as home economics (above) and woodworking (right).

In *The Legend of Sleepy Hollow,* Ichabod Crane "urged some tardy loiterer along the flowery path of knowledge" with a birch switch. And many educators believed that "corporal punishment should be used to save the school, just as bullets are used to save nations." Others, however, encouraged pupils with awards such as the card shown below.

Lickin' and Larnin'

Spare the rod and spoil the child" was, for generations, the authoritarian's credo — and from Colonial times until the early 20th century, America's schoolchildren definitely were not spoiled. As one homespun philosopher explained: "Lickin' and larnin' goes together. No lickin', no larnin'."

Occasionally both the zeal and the need for discipline escalated out of control. At least one pupil died of injuries inflicted by his teacher, and a Massachusetts schoolmistress was stoned to death by angry pupils. In the war between order and anarchy teachers wielded an array of weapons that ranged from the hickory stick to physical confinement and public humiliation.

Teachers strove to fit the punishment to the crime. A malefactor might be made to wear a dunce cap or a sign — such as "Pert-Miss-Prat-a-Pace"— proclaiming her transgression. The restless were perched on one-legged stools. Whisperers were silenced by being forced to clench a stick between their teeth. Or offenders might be yoked together — a particular indignity for a boy who was linked to a girl.

One teacher punished latecomers by sending a troop of classmates out with a bell and lantern to escort them to school. But the practice eventually backfired: one day the teacher himself was late, and the class gleefully made him the star of a noisy parade through town.

Although the discipline was stern and sometimes brutal, most pupils did receive a sound education. And in the 1830's reformers began to transform the schoolhouse from a jailhouse for the unruly into a true haven for learning.

A Woman of Conviction

It began innocently enough. In 1832 Prudence Crandall, headmistress of a Connecticut girls' school, let her maid sit in on classes. Then the maid's friend, Sarah Harris, asked if she too could attend classes. Crandall was willing, but her pupils' families objected: their children were white and the new girl was black.

A delegation of parents threatened: "If you do not send her away, we will withdraw our daughters and your school will sink."

But the Quaker schoolmarm would not be moved. "Then let it sink," she told them.

The pupils were withdrawn, and the school did close for a time. When Crandall defiantly reopened her school in 1833, it was as an academy for "young Ladies and little Misses of color."

A campaign of harassment began almost immediately. In May 1833 Crandall's adversaries forced the enactment of a law forbidding the establishment of schools for nonresident blacks. Crandall was imprisoned and eventually convicted for violating the law.

The state Supreme Court ultimately overturned her conviction, but by then Crandall had accepted the futility of her efforts and moved to another state. When she died, she was eulogized as "Great, because she had deep convictions of right, and greater because neither death, life, angels, principalities . . . nor any other creature could keep her from following her convictions."

Snakes, Skunks, and Schoolmarms

Recalling how she decided between two teaching posts on the frontier, one Oklahoma Territory schoolmarm said she picked the one "where I thought there would be the most excitement. There was."

The mid-1800's found many eastern women in need of respectable employment, wanting to do some good in the world, and restless for change. Teaching answered their practical needs, and the romance of the West beckoned to them just as it did to young men.

But the realities of frontier life both in and out of the classroom sorely tested their idealism. Indians were alternately threatening and conciliatory. Mischievous children played pranks to try the teacher's mettle — including the planting of live rattlesnakes in classrooms. Wild animals, in fact, were omnipresent. Skunks (wryly called "hydrophobia cats" in one memoir) shambled about, coyotes howled and prowled, cattle stampeded. The transplanted teachers learned to ride horses and shoot guns. Referring to an encounter at the spring where she got her water, one intrepid soul reported that "I became weary competing with wildlife and shot a mountain lion one frosty morning."

Often, too, the newcomer was besieged by suitors. Though their contracts usually forbade marriage, many a teacher nevertheless accepted a proposal and settled permanently in her new homeland. Her sphere of influence then shifted from classroom to community, and the torch of learning passed to an unmarried local woman — or to a new schoolteacher from back East.

Nebraska's Fearless Maid

"Forth into the blinding storm, She led them bravely out"— and so became a national symbol of the selfless dedication of the schoolteacher.

On January 12, 1888, exactly two months before the famous Blizzard of 1888 blasted the East Coast, another storm hit the northern plains. Driven by 45-mile-an-hour winds, dense clouds exploded over Nebraska and South Dakota, dumping swirls of snow that quickly obliterated even the nearest landmarks.

Because so many children were marooned in schoolhouses, the media soon dubbed this blizzard the Schoolchildren's Storm. Especially well-known was the story of Minnie Freeman, who was trapped with her class in a little sod schoolhouse in Mira Valley, Nebraska. When the storm blew in the school's windows and tore off the roof, Freeman decided to make a run for safety. She tied her charges to one another, mountaineer-style, and led them into the howling whiteout, heading for a house about a mile away.

The entire band survived its ordeal, and Minnie Freeman was celebrated across the nation as the plucky heroine of the Schoolchildren's Storm. Grade-schoolers as far away as Boston wrote essays in her honor, and in the wake of newspaper accounts of her exploit, she received some 80 proposals of marriage.

Freeman was modest about her heroism, and in fact she did no more than many other teachers who were also trapped by the blizzard. But Minnie Freeman alone was hailed far and wide as the children's champion against the storm.

The song "Thirteen Were Saved" was inspired by Minnie Freeman's own account of leading her pupils to safety.

The Kids' Guards of Silver Street

For one of America's best-loved children's book authors, teaching a classroom of kindergartners was an experience she never forgot.

Graduation was over," Kate Douglas Wiggin recalled in her autobiography. "I had my diploma; and if it did not describe me as the source of prodigious power and learning, it did mean that I had a profession." Americans know Wiggin as the author of *Rebecca of Sunnybrook Farm* and other children's books, but she began her working career as a teacher. Diploma in hand in 1878, she was 22 when she opened the first free kindergarten west of the Rockies.

The site where she gathered her 40 tots was a San Francisco slum. With youthful zeal she transformed two sunny rooms above an old tinsmith's shop on Silver Street into a delightful little world for children, much to the amazement of her neighbors. "You'd ought to go upstairs and see the *inside* of it!" one of them proclaimed. "There's a canary bird, there's fishes swimmin' in a glass bowl... there's a pianner, and more'n a million pictures."

Kate Douglas Wiggin was one of three students to attend California's first kindergarten-teacher's training course. She opened her own school the next year.

No one knew exactly what this newfangled kindergarten was. And misunderstanding the unfamiliar word (German for "children's garden"), Silver Street's residents referred to Wiggin and her helpers as "the kids' guards." The name stuck. "I had many Waterloos in my term of generalship," she wrote, "and many a time I was a feeble enough officer of the Kids' Guards." But if Wiggin was an inexperienced general that first year, she was an enthusiastic follower of Friedrich Froebel, who had started the first kindergarten in Germany in 1837.

Froebel believed that very young children could be encouraged to learn through creative activity. He designed educational toys that allowed four- and five-year-olds to play at such things as stringing beads, folding and cutting paper, and building with blocks. His kindergarten curriculum included songs and circle games. And radical for the time, Froebel suggested that classrooms be pleasant environments with child-sized furniture and lots of attractive things to look at and learn from.

By the late 1850's, experimental kindergartens had been organized in the United States. Slowly, interest in the idea spread. "If I had been made of tinder and a lighted match had been applied to me, I could not have taken fire more easily," Wiggin wrote of her own reaction when she learned about the kindergarten movement.

She energetically led her Silver Street brood through indoor and outdoor games, guided their hands through simple sewing and weaving exercises, and played the piano for marching and songs. Her initial enthusiasm for kindergartens never wore thin. Some 50 years after the opening of her little school, she fondly recalled: "I often close my eyes to call up the picture [of it], and almost every child falls into his old seat and answers to his right name."

She had endless memories to savor. There was a letter, for instance, from a Mrs. Beer written in fear that her active son (aptly nicknamed Wriggly) would wear out his only pair of boots before Christmas. "Yung lady," she pleaded, "can you learn him settin' down?"

And then there was the curious case of Hansanella Dorflinger. "Hansanella sounds like one word, but they were twins," Wiggin wrote, adding that they "breathed together, smiled and wept together, rose and sat down together, and wiped their noses together.... Never were such 'twinneous' twins as Hansanella," she commented. "It was ridiculous to waste two names on them, for there was not between them personality enough for one child."

That perception proved true some five weeks later when Wiggin learned that the twins were actually August and Anna Olsen. Sent to the kindergarten in place of the real Hans and Ella, who had long since moved out of town, the inseparable replacement pair had, meanwhile, never once objected to their newly assigned name.

Not all the children were so docile. "They were naughty and willful sometimes, but oh!" Wiggin wrote, "I can remember moments in that room at Silver Street when one might almost hear the beat of angels' wings."

The kindergarten at the 1876 Centennial Exhibition (left) introduced the use of building toys. Ever since, such playthings have sparked the interests of children, including Frank Lloyd Wright and his son, John, the inventor of Lincoln Logs (below).

The Wright Way to Play

When Mrs. Anna Wright, mother of the architect Frank Lloyd Wright, attended Philadelphia's Centennial Exhibition in 1876, one display in particular—a demonstration kindergarten—captured her imagination. She was especially impressed with the building blocks and other new types of toys that had been designed for classroom use, permitting children to learn as they played.

As soon as she returned home, Anna Wright ordered a set of kindergarten toys for her young son. Many years later, Frank Lloyd Wright attributed his early interest in architecture to the blocks his mother gave him.

Wright's own son, John Lloyd Wright, became an architect, too, and had a hobby of designing building-block toys. He was a long way from home in 1917, working on plans for his father's Imperial Hotel in Tokyo, when the idea for a new toy came to him. It took him only 10 minutes to sketch out the prototype, which he named Lincoln Logs.

Like the original kindergarten toys, the logs are simple to use and allow endless creativity, And who can say how many budding architects they have inspired.

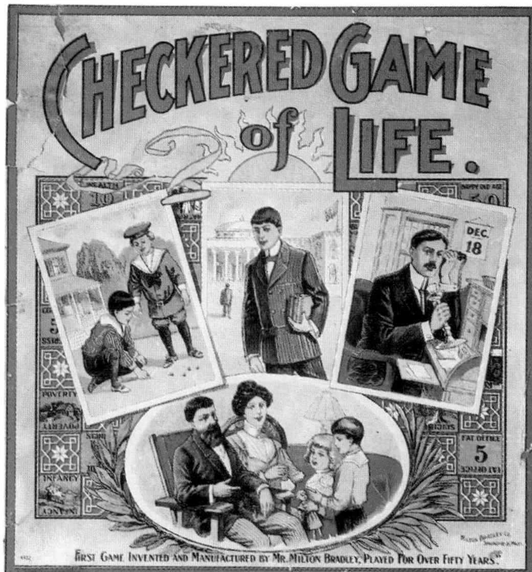

Even Milton Bradley's first board game, published in 1860, suggested his later interest in educational toys.

Toys for Teaching

As a young man anxious to establish his career in the 1860's, Milton Bradley hit on a winning plan: manufacturing board games. The decision was a sound one—before long his products were being enjoyed in countless American parlors. But Bradley, meanwhile, had begun to develop new interests as well.

An early devotee of the kindergarten movement, he realized that such schooling did not stand a chance of catching on unless the proper playthings and teaching equipment were available. By the 1870's—though kindergartens were still rarities—Bradley decided to invest in the production of educational toys for this mere handful of customers. Within a generation, however, there were over 3,000 kindergartens in America, and Bradley was supplying these early 20th-century classes with everything from crayons to child-size tables and chairs.

Crossing the street with a police officer was a genuine highlight in the day of these New York City schoolchildren. Even in 1899, the role of crossing guard was one of the more pleasant jobs in law enforcement.

Getting to School

No one ever said that getting an education would be easy, but for children in the past, studying was only half the battle. First, they had to get to school.

In sparsely populated areas, where an entire township might be served by a single school, a two- or three-mile trek twice a day was taken for granted by many children. With lunch buckets in hand, they picked their way across mountain trails, muddy roads, or snow-covered prairies for the chance to learn ciphering and spelling. Even George Washington, who grew up on a farm in Virginia, hiked seven miles to and from school each day until he was 12 years old. After that, he routinely rowed across the Rappahannock River to reach his new teacher in Fredericksburg.

Rural families sometimes got around the problem of the daily commute by boarding their children in town during the week. Others, with a pony or two to spare from the farm, might provide their youngsters with a speedy (though often hungry) form of transportation.

Commuter classes

As towns and cities became more crowded in the late 1800's, communities organized a variety of public means for getting their children to school.

The town of Quincy, Massachusetts, is thought to have been the first to provide a school wagon — the forerunner of the bus. It began making its rounds in 1869. Many school districts soon adopted the practice, including one in Maryland that refurbished a second hand circus wagon for the job. Horse-drawn sleighs full of tiny scholars were not uncommon sights during northern winters. And in the South, boats were used to pick up children along the bayous and transport them to class.

Bustling cities had a special need to help children cross streets and negotiate busy intersections. By the late 19th century, policemen were providing that service in many communities. With the shortage of men during World War II, however, the job of crossing guard more often fell to women, who continue to fulfill that role to this day.

Relatively few schools were lucky enough to have their own buses in 1920, when these children lined up for a ride in Fresno, California. Within 20 years, however, scenes like this were common, and the official school-bus color was the familiar bright yellow.

The Big Yellow Bus

Visible even in rain and fog, consistent from one state to another, the brightness of "school-bus yellow" has helped to make those vehicles the safest form of transportation in America.

National standards for school buses were adopted in 1939, following an exhaustive two-year study by Prof. Frank W. Cyr. Traveling throughout the country, Cyr found children being transported to schools in everything from wheat wagons to patriotic red, white, and blue buses.

Getting the national standards adopted was surprisingly easy, for everyone had a common goal—the children's safety.

If sitting in school is not always much fun, coming and going can be. In Lancaster, Pennsylvania, a utilitarian sled serves as the perfect winter transport for a group of Amish children. While the girls ride snugly inside the sled, the mule team provides enough "horse power" for the tag-along boys.

In horse-drawn school wagons — such as the circa 1915 example below — the driver typically sat inside with the children. The driver's position, however, did not necessarily keep schoolboy tussles from erupting en route, any more than it does today.

This lonely little one-room schoolhouse in Greeley County, Kansas, was a long way from just about everything at the turn of the century. Most of the pupils — as well as their teacher — no doubt began and ended their days with a foot-weary trek to and from school. Only a few were lucky enough to come and go by donkey.

READIN' AND WRITIN'

Tools Made to Lead a Child to Read: Early American Schoolbooks

Whether children learned their ABC's at home or in school during the Colonial era, their main tools for study were the same: primers. These little books—treasured possessions, used for generations by the families who owned them — at first were brought to this country from England. By 1690, however, *The New England Primer* was being published in Boston: 3 million copies would be printed in the next 150 years. And it was only the first of many American primers.

All contained a hefty dose of prayers and pieties along with basic reading material. The religious emphasis was important, for the primer was considered nearly as effective as the Bible in molding children (who were labeled "young vipers" by Puritan minister Jonathan Edwards) into sober and responsible citizens.

To ensure that the process worked, dour lessons were couched in verse that, if not fun to read, at least made memorization easier. The alphabet was inevitably accompanied by tiny woodcuts illustrating the often grisly rhyming jingles. "The Idle Fool / is whipt at School," children were reminded at the letter *F*. And lest they begin to enjoy themselves, the letter *Y* might admonish: "While youth do chear / Death may be near." The illustration, of course, showed a skeleton arriving at a party.

A bit of fun was often interjected in 19th-century schoolbooks. In one, children followed the fortunes of an apple pie while learning their letters (left). *Marmaduke Multiply's Merry Method of Making Minor Mathematicians* (below) offered the entire multiplication table in verse, along with charming illustrations.

27
Four times 6 are 24.
I think I've seen your face before.

28
Four times 7 are 28.
Come with me and see me Skate.

Rhymin'

Specialized books for advanced pupils were less common than primers, but grammars, readers, and spellers also delivered lessons in rhyme and in moralizing anecdotes. "Boys need dinner; girls knead dough," children chanted in one lesson on homonyms. Rev. Cotton Mather, famous for his fire-and-brimstone style, was in the habit of writing a versified lesson on goodness for his son to learn by heart every day. The collection was published in 1706 as *Good Lessons for Children; or Instructions provided for a little Son to learn at School, When learning to read.*

Mather's was not the only schoolbook with an unwieldy name. The first grammar used in Boston's public schools was barely big enough to accommodate its title: *The Young Lady's Accidence, or a Short and Easy Introduction to English Grammar, design'd principally for the use of Young Learners, more especially for those of the Fair Sex, though Proper for Either.*

And 'rithmetic

By the end of the 18th century, the number of "young learners" was increasing, and so was their work load. In 1789, for instance, a law was passed in Massachusetts requiring elementary schools to teach not just reading and writing, but decent behavior and arithmetic as well.

Since anyone who could cipher was considered extremely learned, textbook writers did their best to polish those skills. Their efforts ranged from the practical to the bizarre. One author recalled the story of the biblical King Adonibezek, who cut off the thumbs and great toes of "3 score and 10 kings" and made them scramble for their meat under his table. "How many thumbs and toes," queried the author, "did Adonibezek cut off?"

When books such as the *Schoolmaster's Assistant* were published in the early 1800's, such lessons were often made far more amusing through rhyming arithmetic. "If to my age there added be / One-half, one-third, and three times three / Six score and ten the sum will be / What is my age, pray shew it me?" (The answer is 66.) Clearly a lot had changed by then: such a text was written for young children, not young vipers.

Almanacs: Indispensable, All-Purpose Readers

If not always reliable for long-range weather forecasts, old-time almanacs were nonetheless depended on for many other purposes.

Anyone with an earache in 1768 would have welcomed a copy of the *Pennsylvania Town and Country-man's Almanack,* for it offered a number of sure-fire cures. "Rub the Ear hard for a Quarter of an Hour: Or, put in a roasted Fig, as hot as may be: Or, drop in Juice of Goose-Grease" were three of its suggestions.

First published in this country in 1639 (65 years before the first newspaper), almanacs were originally calendar-books with notes on weather, tides, and phases of the moon. Within a century, however, their usefulness had expanded dramatically. Adults relied on almanacs as virtual encyclopedias containing remedies for everything from warts to worms, recipes, household hints, advice on livestock, snippets of news, poetry, proverbs, and the occasional bawdy tale. And for children schooled at home, the almanac often served as primer, history book, and literary guide all in one.

In many Colonial households, in fact, the only books to be found were the Bible and an almanac. The Bible took care of the hereafter, it was said, while the almanac took care of the here. Demand created stiff competition among dozens of publishers, some with large circulations. Benjamin Franklin's *Poor Richard's Almanack* reached about 10,000 readers each year.

Inexpensive and readily available, they were indispensable books. Through them farmers and frontiersmen could follow politics, be inspired by an essay, and remain in touch with the civilized world. Almanacs were rarely thrown away at the end of the year. Instead, they were saved to be read and reread. The folk remedies, tales, and wit, such as Poor Richard's famous maxims — "God heals, the doctor takes the fee" — were memorized and passed along as native-born wisdom long after the almanacs had completely worn out.

Frank Leslie's
Illustrated
Almanac
for 1873
The Major & Knapp Eng. Mfg. & Lith. Co. 56 Park Place N.Y.

Often a family's only reading matter other than the Bible, 18th-century almanacs were filled with recipes and remedies as well as weather forecasts and planting advice. Almanacs were so popular, in fact, that the formula remained unchanged well into the 1800's.

In Their Own Words

"Although America is perhaps in our days the civilized country in which literature is least attended to, a large number of persons are nevertheless to be found there who take an interest in the productions of the mind. . . . There is hardly a pioneer's hut which does not contain a few odd volumes of Shakspere. I remember that I read the feudal play of Henry V for the first time in a log house."

— Alexis de Tocqueville, 1835

Benjamin Banneker, Almanac Author

Benjamin Banneker was a late bloomer. The only son of a freed slave, he spent most of his life working the family farm in Maryland. It was not until 1788, when he was 57 years old, that he became fascinated with astronomy.

Borrowing books and equipment from his neighbor George Ellicott — himself an enthusiastic amateur astronomer — Banneker learned to chart planetary changes at a table in his cabin. It did not take him long to master the complex mathematics: by 1790 he had completed calculations for a 1791 almanac.

As a black man, Banneker was unable to find a publisher at that time, but his remarkable skills did not go unnoticed. Just as he set to work on the next year's planetary chart, he was invited to join a special team chosen to survey the newly established District of Columbia. Hired by Maj. Andrew Ellicott (his neighbor's cousin) and equipped with the most sophisticated astronomical and surveying instruments, Banneker spent every night for three months taking readings that would establish the boundaries of the new nation's capital. It was work that few men of his day could have accomplished.

Banneker returned to Maryland in time to complete his 1792 almanac. This time, with the aid of an abolitionist society, he found a printer. From 1792 through 1797, in fact, Banneker's almanacs — noted for their accuracy — were published in 29 separate editions.

A variety of precision instruments were required for the Washington, D.C., survey, including the compass and equal-altitude telescope above. Banneker used this telescope to mark off the straight boundaries of the city plan.

An Eclectic Education

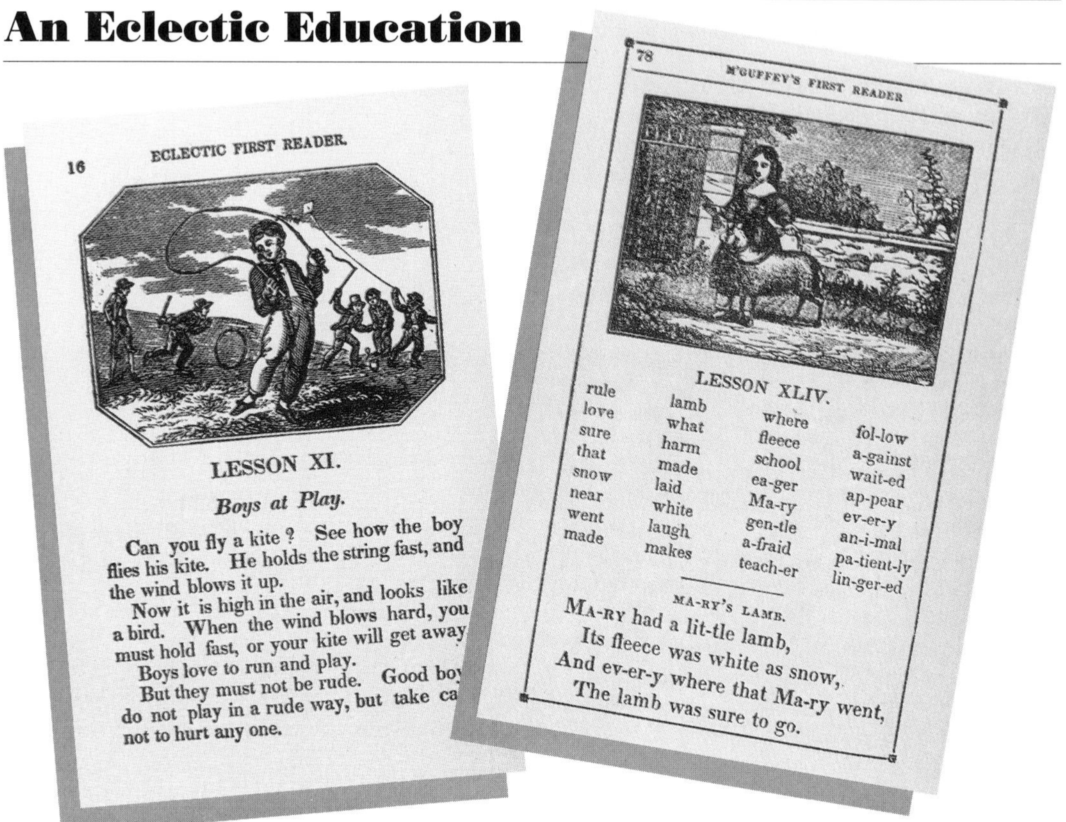

16 ECLECTIC FIRST READER.

LESSON XI.

Boys at Play.

Can you fly a kite? See how the boy flies his kite. He holds the string fast, and the wind blows it up.

Now it is high in the air, and looks like a bird. When the wind blows hard, you must hold fast, or your kite will get away.

Boys love to run and play.

But they must not be rude. Good bo[ys] do not play in a rude way, but take ca[re] not to hurt any one.

78 M'GUFFEY'S FIRST READER

LESSON XLIV.

rule	lamb	where	fol-low
love	what	fleece	a-gainst
sure	harm	school	wait-ed
that	made	ea-ger	ap-pear
snow	laid	Ma-ry	ev-er-y
near	white	gen-tle	an-i-mal
went	laugh	a-fraid	pa-tient-ly
made	makes	teach-er	lin-ger-ed

MA-RY'S LAMB.

MA-RY had a lit-tle lamb,
Its fleece was white as snow,
And ev-er-y where that Ma-ry went,
The lamb was sure to go.

William Holmes McGuffey made his *Eclectic Readers* interesting to children by interspersing pictures and little stories in among lessons on spelling and grammar. His books did much to popularize such verses as "Mary had a little lamb" and "Twinkle twinkle little star."

From the mid-19th century to the early 20th, millions of children arrived at school every day and opened copies of *McGuffey's Eclectic Readers.* Pupils might read aloud from stories with such titles as "True Manliness" and "Perseverance." Or the teacher might read them a tale like "Henry the Bootblack," which begins, "Henry was a kind, good boy. His father was dead, and his mother was very poor."

The man responsible for giving the books their high moral tone was a strait-laced Midwesterner named William Holmes McGuffey. A schoolteacher who went on to become a Presbyterian minister and a professor of moral philosophy, McGuffey was 33 when he agreed to compile two readers for the Ohio public schools. Three years later, in 1836, the books were published, and they succeeded beyond anyone's imagination. The original two volumes grew to seven—one of America's first textbook series—and between the 1830's and the 1920's, 122 million copies were sold.

Reading by the books

From the time they started school, children progressed gradually from the basics of an *Eclectic Primer,* to the *Sixth Eclectic Reader,* the equivalent of a high school text today. Each one was made up mainly of pieces drawn from other sources. McGuffey did not actually compile all the books; his younger brother, Alexander, assembled the final two and probably assisted on the earlier ones. In subsequent editions editors rewrote material to keep up with the times.

But it was, of course, McGuffey himself who established the original style of the readers, a style that seemed to satisfy both students and teachers. Lessons in spelling and grammar were thorough, but not so tough as to intimidate children. The little moral tales were preceded by new words for memorization, but never too many at any one time. And great emphasis was placed on proper pronunciation. One of McGuffey's goals was the eradication of all traces of careless frontier speech, and he was quite specific about it: "Ju-bi-lee, not ju-b'lee," he warned. "Ed-u-cate, not ed-di-cate."

Perhaps more important, at a time when schools had few books on individual subjects, the readers truly were eclectic: they contained a mix of geography, history, poetry, and literature. For many children, McGuffey provided the only exposure they would ever have to writers such as Shakespeare or Hawthorne.

Late in life, Alexander McGuffey suggested that the readers might have made millionaires of 10 people. William Holmes McGuffey, however, was not one of them. Content to leave to his publishers the burden of revising and selling the books, he never asked to alter the terms of his original contract, and his royalties for the entire series totaled only $1,000. But the books that bore McGuffey's name helped shape the minds of generations of American children.

Learning to Read With Dick and Jane

Long after other classroom experiences are forgotten, generations of Americans have no problem recalling their first primers. "Look," a book might begin, "See Jane. See Jane run. Run, Jane, run!"

Though a bit thin on plot, the adventures of Dick, Jane, Baby Sally, Mother, Father, Spot, and Puff nevertheless had a wide-ranging impact: through them, millions of children learned to read. During their years of use in public schools — from 1931 to the early 1970's — Dick and Jane primers regularly outnumbered all the competition combined. The successful formula was a slow-paced introduction to reading, with as few as 17 different words to a book, and no more than 1 new word per page.

For many years a majority of schoolchildren identified with the stories and illustrations. By the 1960's, however, the images of Dick and Jane's neighborhood with its white picket fences and lack of ethnic mix were no longer representative of American society, and by the end of the decade, Dick and Jane were out of print. But they have yet to fade from memory.

Look, Jane.
Look, look.
See Dick.
12
See, see.
Oh, see.
See Dick.
13

The Dick and Jane books taught children to read by repeating simple — usually one-syllable — words throughout the book. The pictures carefully illustrated each phrase of the text. When a child finished a Dick and Jane book, he knew what all the words meant as well as how to read them.

WHAT·IS·IT?

Because inconsistencies in English pronunciation make it a difficult language to master, Americans throughout the 19th century attempted to devise alphabets that guaranteed phonetic spelling. None of them caught on. This cryptic-looking example, the Deseret Alphabet, was invented about 1850 by Brigham Young for the Mormons in the Utah Territory. The translation reads in part: "Let us go to school. We will be late for school if we do not make haste."

When America Was Spellbound

For families who lived in country towns or on lonely farms in the 19th century, any event that brought neighbors together was welcomed as entertainment. One of the most popular diversions — guaranteed to draw whole communities for an evening at the local school — was the spelldown, or spelling bee, a uniquely American pastime.

It was Noah Webster's book, *The American Spelling Book* — known as the blue-back speller — that made the bees so immensely popular. First published in 1783, 60 million copies eventually were sold. With this one book Webster did wonders, creating a uniform American system of spelling and pronunciation that was accepted as the educational standard.

Since Webster grouped words in order of difficulty, students could be ranked according to the pages they had mastered. Proof of mastery came when they were called on to step forward and outspell their classmates (a child had to sit down if he missed a word). When students were organized into teams, spelling bees could be as competitive as any sport, far too thrilling to remain simply schoolroom activities. Proud parents wanted to be there to watch and cheer as only one child emerged triumphant — the local spelling champion.

Noah Webster took a lot of ribbing when this portrait appeared in his book. Some said he looked like a porcupine. Others insisted that the picture frightened children.

This dutiful student of penmanship is a devotee of the Spencerian method. With back erect and feet placed just so, he will copy and copy his lessons until he can swiftly and gracefully form the elaborately embellished letters that were the hallmark of fine writing.

In Search of the Perfect Script

Thanks to some no-nonsense 19th-century innovations, handwriting changed from an exercise in flowing flourishes into a crisp businesslike craft.

When James Guild, a Vermont plowboy in the early 1800's, heard that penmanship was being taught in a nearby town, he set aside his plow and immediately signed up for school. Learning to write in a fine hand, after all, was not an opportunity to be taken lightly. It offered Guild and many like him a chance to leave their hard labor behind forever.

Handwriting was taught in this country long before Guild's time, but it was America's first penmanship book — written by John Jenkins in 1791 — that sparked a widespread interest in the skill. Jenkins stressed that anyone could learn to write by mastering a mere six pen strokes. Students practiced the strokes individually, then combined them into letters and flourishes.

Jenkins soon had dozens of imitators, with self-styled penmen traveling from town to town to teach their newly learned skills. Many got by, however, more on nerve than knowledge. After only 30 hours of instruction, James Guild, for one, conducted his first class in Middlebury, Vermont, then went on to teach courses at two academies in New York. "Now was the time I studied my own ignorance," Guild confessed in his diary. "I thought that if I did not say but little and be careful how I spoke, they would not mistrust that I was nothing but a plowboy."

Two mighty penmen

With such a diverse lot of instructors, Americans practiced all sorts of writing styles. Toward the middle of the 19th century and near its end, though, two masters of penmanship made significant changes in the way letters were formed. These changes caused a

Penmanship exercises were more than just the repetition of letters. To become familiar with the idiosyncrasies of their tools, calligraphers drew figures that utilized the variety of line thicknesses possible with a flat-nibbed pen. S. W. Phillips advertised his skills as an instructor by creating an elegant swan out of pen strokes and flourishes.

revolution in how handwriting was taught.

Platt Roger Spencer's first penmanship book was published in 1848, and his "Spencerian" system of writing soon became the most popular in the country. Spencer emphasized speed and uniformity, and he suggested that students work to the rhythm of a metronome. His script was simpler than earlier styles — even the fanciest capital letters could be formed without lifting pen from paper — and therefore faster to draw. Uniformity was guaranteed by following Spencer's explicit rules for sitting properly. "The body to be erect," he explained, "and the left foot advanced until the heel is opposite the hollow of the right foot, and distant from it two or three inches."

By the end of the century, the Spencerian method gave way to yet another approach. Having devised a writing style that was much more efficient for business use, Austin Palmer published *Palmer's Guide to Muscular Movement Writing* in 1888. The Palmer method was speedier than Spencer's: its letters were further simplified, some capital letters were no longer written separately, and entire words could be completed before the pen was lifted to cross a *t* or dot an *i*.

After the turn of the century, Palmer's method was being taught almost everywhere. America at last had a uniform standard of penmanship. And if it lacked the elegance of earlier styles, it was at least easier to teach, easier to learn, and above all, much easier to read.

Rituals and Recipes for Writers

Prior to the invention of the steel pen in 1819, letter writing in America involved far more than careful penmanship. First, a pen had to be crafted from a goose quill. If a writer did not raise his own geese, he could buy quills at the market in bundles of 50. To prepare the point, he cut off the tip, cleaned out the inside of the shaft, and scraped away its outer surface. The new tip was hardened in an alum or nitric-acid solution; then the point was shaped with a sharp pen knife — a feat that required considerable skill.

Properly prepared, a quill was good for about four lines of script between dips in the inkwell. Before any dipping could be done, however, the ink had to be made either by mixing store-bought powdered varieties with water or by using one of many home recipes. One formula required soaking logwood chips, nutgalls, pomegranate peels, and green vitriol in water for eight or nine days. A weak but inexpensive ink could be made from lampblack, glue, and water. Brandy or wine was often added to keep the ink from freezing. If ink "once doth freeze," warned one authority, "it will be good for nothing."

Next, the writer had to fill his shakers of pounce and sand. Pounce — powdered resin or pumice — was used to coat thin writing papers, in order to keep ink from bleeding through. Sand was dusted on the paper to blot up excess ink. (Blotting paper was not introduced until the middle of the 19th century.)

Then the writer could get settled at his desk. With pen prepared, concoctions mixed, and implements arrayed for use, he could finally sit down and start to write that letter.

A 19th-century lass who wished to keep her diary with her so that, like Gwendolyn in Oscar Wilde's *The Importance of Being Ernest*, she would "have something sensational to read in the train," might also take along some writing equipment to keep her journal current. Travelers' writing sets included ink bottles like this one. Its double covers prevented evaporation and protected against leakage.

Refining the Rubout

Writing in longhand has always been an inexact art. Almost any page of handwritten text is likely to contain its share of slipups, cross-outs, and other errors that need to be corrected. Bread crumbs were among the earliest materials used for fixing such mistakes, since they can be helpful in removing pencil marks. Stationers also sold special "Knives for Eracing" that were used to literally scratch out misspelled words.

By the 1770's, scientists had discovered that a gummy substance tapped from certain South American trees was a definite improvement over crumbs. The gum became so identified with rubbing out mistakes that it was dubbed "rubber." Despite the product's popularity, it was not until 1858 that an American, Hyman L. Lipman, thought of attaching erasers to the ends of pencils—a bit of ingenuity that earned him a fortune.

THE COLLEGE YEARS

TIME TABLE

LANDMARKS IN LEARNING

1636 *Harvard College is founded.*

1765 *School of medicine is started at the College of Philadelphia (later University of Pennsylvania).*

1776 *Phi Beta Kappa established at the College of William and Mary, would become the first intercollegiate fraternity and, later, an honor society.*

1802 *The United States Military Academy is founded at West Point.*

1821 *Alumni Association is organized at Williams College.*

1833 *Oberlin College opens as a coeducational institution.*

1836 *Charter is granted for Georgia Female College (later Wesleyan College), the first degree-granting college for women.*

1840 *Baltimore College of Dental Surgery, the first dental school in the world, is founded.*

1848 *Boston Female Medical School is established to train women physicians.*

The Six-and-a-Quarter-Cent School

The American West of the 1840's was a place and time known for memorable characters, not the least of whom was Tabitha Moffatt Brown. Small, wiry, and a widow of 30 years, Brown was 66 when she traveled by wagon train from Missouri to Oregon in 1846. From the outset she had thought of starting a school in the new territory, but she would face more obstacles than she ever imagined.

The journey itself was a nine-month ordeal. The worst of it came when the party was robbed by their guide and left to fend for themselves in the wilderness for the last 600 miles of their trek. Brown arrived in Salem, Oregon, with little more than the clothes on her back, and no option but to spend the winter keeping house for the local minister.

Still penniless in the spring, Brown was anxious to begin working toward her goal. The opportunity arose when she found a picayune — a coin worth six and a quarter cents — in the fingertip of her glove. With it she bought three needles, then traded an old dress for buckskins, and made gloves to sell to settlers. The enterprise earned her $30 and a new start.

Traveling to West Tualatin Plain, Oregon, she was befriended by a missionary couple, who observed that many orphaned children were arriving off the Oregon Trail. Brown spoke up about her desire to open a school, and the couple offered to help. In 1847 the school was opened to both orphans and the children of local families. Two years later a charter established the school as Tualatin Academy, and in 1854 the charter was altered to provide for a companion institution, Pacific University.

Tabitha Brown's original academy building still stands at the heart of the university. It remains one of the oldest buildings west of the Rocky Mountains to be used continuously for educational purposes.

Maria Mitchell—Astronomer Extraordinaire

Clouds were moving in fast over Nantucket Island off the Massachusetts coast on October 1, 1847, when Maria Mitchell made an amazing discovery. Scanning the night sky with a telescope from her rooftop observatory, the 29-year-old Mitchell spotted an unknown comet. The discovery won her a gold medal from the king of Denmark, instant renown in scientific circles, and in 1848, election to the American Academy of Arts and Sciences. She was the first woman to be so honored.

In 1865 Matthew Vassar invited her to become the first professor of astronomy at his newly opened college for women. And though teaching claimed much of her time, Mitchell continued her research. While tracking another comet one night in 1881, she found her view was obscured by an apple tree. Putting science ahead of sentiment, she had the tree trimmed limb by limb until nothing was left of it — and withstood the banter of students who greeted her the next morning with the nickname George Washington.

Honors came to Mitchell throughout her life. But her most profound influence may have been the prestige she lent to Vassar College and the model she provided for her students. As one of them commented: "Time and money would have been well spent had there been no return but that of two years . . . with Maria Mitchell."

Maria Mitchell enjoyed a distinguished career as a professor of astronomy for much of her adult life. Shown here at the age of 60, Mitchell posed with her students on the lawn at Vassar College.

A University Built With a Tycoon's Tears

Unable to see their own son complete his education, Jane and Leland Stanford provided the children of California with a first-class university.

"Wah-hoo! Wah-hoo!" bellowed some 400 students. "L-S-J-U! STAN-ford!" The date was October 1, 1891—opening day for the Leland Stanford Junior University. Yet the joy was bittersweet for the aging couple who stood before the cheering crowd. The pair, railroad tycoon Leland Stanford and his wife, Jane, had founded the university in memory of their only child.

Leland Jr. was born to the couple in 1868 (after 18 childless years of marriage) and grew to be a precocious youngster. At 11 he built his own miniature railroad. At 15 he spoke fluent French. The boy was on a tour of Europe with his doting parents when he caught typhoid fever and died. He was just two months short of his 16th birthday.

By the time they returned home, the Stanfords had turned their devastation into decision: since they could no longer do anything for their own child, they would do something for others in his name. Meeting with the president of Harvard, they asked what it would cost to establish a similar institution; $5 million or $6 million, they were told. After a stunned silence, Stanford turned to his wife and said: "Well, Jane, we could manage that, couldn't we?"

The couple turned formidable energies to their new task. Leland, former governor of California, and president of the Central Pacific Railroad, was the man who drove in the golden spike marking the completion of the nation's first transcontinental railroad. He was now a U.S. senator. Jane, for her part, had long brought a formal elegance to her role as a wealthy politician's wife. She also, as it turned out, had an iron determination.

Only two years after the opening of Stanford, the senator died, and probate froze the flow of money from his estate. Jane's advisers suggested she shut down the university. "Stop the circus!" one business associate demanded. But the fledgling university and its students were the widow's only "children," and she refused to give up.

She found a judge who set her allowance from the estate at $10,000 a month—and then declared the university's professors to be Jane's servants so that she could pay their salaries from her personal funds. The next year, when a claim by the federal government tied up the estate again, Jane appealed directly to President Grover Cleveland for intervention. Finally, in 1896, the Supreme Court ruled in her favor.

The crisis past, Jane resumed an ambitious plan to finish a campus that many would call the most beautiful in the nation. The university today is a living monument to a beloved child—and to the loving parents who lost him.

In May 1887, Jane and Leland Stanford presided at the dedication of the university founded in memory of their son. Leland was presented with a silver trowel with which he smoothed the mortar as the cornerstone was laid.

1851 *Adelphian Society (later Alpha Delta Pi sorority) founded at Wesleyan College in Georgia.*

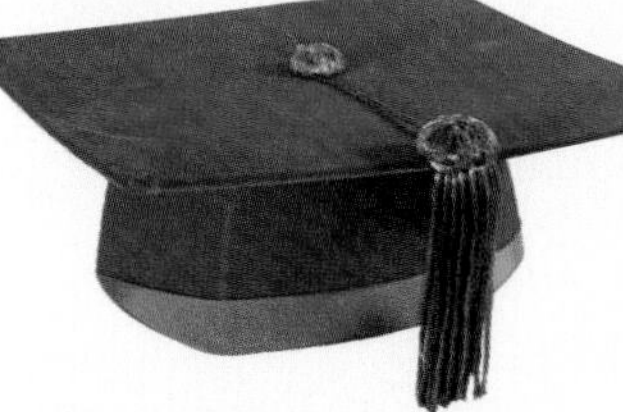

1857 *Ashmun Institute in Pennsylvania (later Lincoln University) opens as a college for black males.*

1859 *Baseball game between Amherst and Williams colleges marks beginning of intercollegiate field sports.*

1859 *Alumnae association founded at Wesleyan College.*

1862 *Passage of Morrill Act leads to creation of land-grant colleges for the study of agriculture and mechanical arts.*

1887 *The School of Library Economy is begun at Columbia College.*

1896 *Student union is constructed at the University of Pennsylvania.*

1900 *College Entrance Exam Board is founded.*

1902 *First Rose Bowl football game pits University of Michigan against Stanford.*

1912 *School of Journalism is created at University of Missouri at Columbia.*

1944 *President Franklin Roosevelt signs the Servicemen's Readjustment Act (known as the GI Bill of Rights).*

From Stanford 's earliest years, students have participated in a wide range of sports, from women's basketball to tennis and crew. Here, the 1915 crew warms up for an intercollegiate race.

William Furness (class of 1820) ensured that Harvard's 1819 food fight would never be forgotten when he created a series of drawings of the fracas. The talented Mr. Furness—who went on to become a theologian—also commemorated the "bread and butter riot" by writing a mock-heroic poem.

Reading, Writing, and Rioting on Ye Olde College Campus

Nathan threw a piece of bread. / And hit Abijah on the head." So begins a poem recalling a famous food fight in the Harvard dining hall in 1819. But it was not the first time rioting had erupted at the staid New England school. In 1766 the rallying cry had been "Behold, our butter stinketh!" and in 1807 the discovery of maggots lurking in the lunch set off what has become known as the Rotten Cabbage Rebellion.

Riots and rampages, in fact, were commonplace on early-19th-century campuses. The students were sometimes as young as 14. Food and facilities were dismal. And daily routines were inhumanly rigorous and regimented. So it was no wonder that the students' pent-up energy exploded into rioting—sometimes with deadly results. In 1840 a faculty member at the University of Virginia was shot by a student; at Yale in 1843 a tutor was stabbed to death as he tried to restrain a rampaging student.

At other colleges buildings were routinely stoned, windows smashed, bells rung in the dead of night, and teachers burned in effigy. In at least one instance the militia was called in, but the vandalism persisted until the resignation of a cranky pedant who had complained that his students were "as laborious as oxen, but as stupid as asses."

Much of the mischief was mere high jinks. Princetonians once managed to perch the president's horse and buggy on a dormitory roof. Sixteen-year-old James Fenimore Cooper roped a donkey into a professor's chair at Yale and was promptly expelled for his effort. And at one Georgia college a wily professor always carried an umbrella to protect himself from the buckets of water that students habitually heaved from their windows.

Campus reforms after the Civil War made college life less restrictive, and the adoption of physical education gave students a harmless outlet for their energy. And despite their rebelliousness, upon graduation most students proved the truth of one tutor's fond remark that "wild colts often make good horses."

Unhappy cadet Edgar Allan Poe frequented Havens's tavern and called its owner the "sole congenial soul in the entire God-forsaken place."

Havens's Haven

For 50 years, from 1824 until 1874, Benny Havens's tavern was a welcome escape for the cadets at West Point. Isolated on a bluff above the Hudson River, hemmed in by regulations, and bored by a bland and repetitious diet, the young men craved relief. Risking demerits and even court-martial, many of them regularly hightailed the two miles to Highland Falls in order to feast on buckwheat cakes, oysters, and plump turkey. But the main draw was the drink, especially Benny's flip, a potent concoction of sugar, spices, eggs, and ale.

Because the tavern was officially off-limits, the cadets posted a lookout. As a further precaution, they drank with their eyes averted so that they could honestly swear that they had "not seen" anyone drinking.

Havens was sensitive to the cadets' often meager financial means and cheerfully accepted West Point blankets and other stolen goods in exchange for food and drink. In 1838 a grateful patron honored both the saloon and the academy with a celebratory song. Succeeding classes added verses to the ditty until they numbered in the dozens.

Although Benny and his wife were barred from the grounds of West Point, in the minds of the cadets, the haven at Highland Falls was inextricably linked with the military institution that supplied so much of its business.

Down on the Farm at Vassar College

They were tough. They were tanned. They could milk cows and pitch hay with the best of them. They were the stalwart women of Vassar College during World War I.

Across the nation, the call had gone out for manpower to replace the young men who had gone to war. At Vassar, then a women's college, staff was short on the farm that supplied produce during the school year. Would students volunteer? an official asked.

Thirty-three stepped forward at once, and 12 were chosen "largely on a basis of good health," as one put it. For eight weeks in the summer of 1917, the women hoed, weeded, and harvested 36 acres of crops; tended chickens, pigs, and horses; mended fences; and raked hay.

The program worked so well that 200 students took part the next year. At summer's end, each could patriotically declare she had indeed "pitched in" for the nation's war effort.

Vassar's farmerettes bloomed as they planted, completing their tasks with an enthusiasm that confounded the expectation that the physical labor would be a hardship.

Campus Capers, Campus Cut-ups

When cars were banned from the campus in 1927, Princeton wits took to their skates in protest. Colleges, it seems, have always had their share of wise guys. While stuffing telephone booths and swallowing goldfish were the rage in the 20th century, pranks in the past included removing bedroom windows on wintry nights, stealing church bells from the chapel, and bowling red-hot cannonballs down dormitory halls.

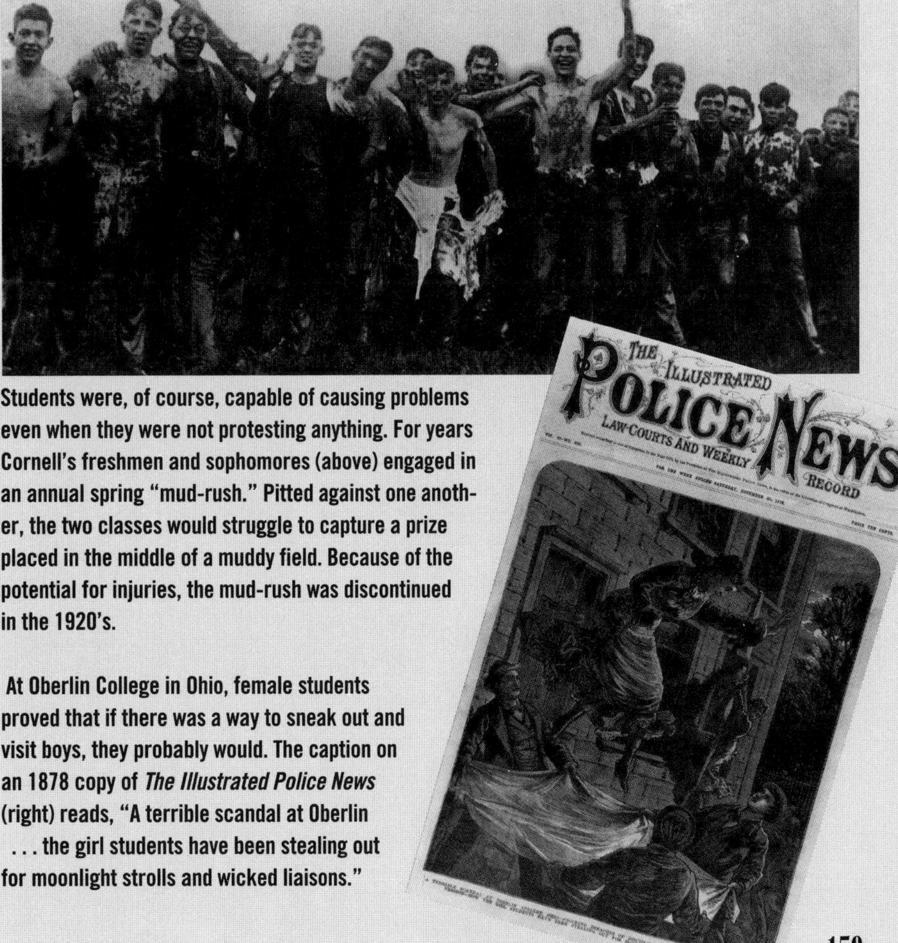

Students were, of course, capable of causing problems even when they were not protesting anything. For years Cornell's freshmen and sophomores (above) engaged in an annual spring "mud-rush." Pitted against one another, the two classes would struggle to capture a prize placed in the middle of a muddy field. Because of the potential for injuries, the mud-rush was discontinued in the 1920's.

At Oberlin College in Ohio, female students proved that if there was a way to sneak out and visit boys, they probably would. The caption on an 1878 copy of *The Illustrated Police News* (right) reads, "A terrible scandal at Oberlin . . . the girl students have been stealing out for moonlight strolls and wicked liaisons."

OUTSIDE THE CLASSROOM

Lyceum audiences enjoyed enthusiastic speakers, but cartoonists sometimes poked fun at their zeal. This 1841 pen-and-ink drawing shows meteorologist James Pollard Espy holding forth on the weather.

Lyceums Were for Learning

Arrayed in bright Arabian garb complete with glinting scimitar at his side, Bayard Taylor captivated 19th-century audiences with his true-life tales of adventure. A poet, explorer, and globe-trotting reporter who was known as America's Marco Polo, the darkly handsome Taylor was one of the most popular lecturers on the burgeoning lyceum circuit.

The lyceum movement (named for the place in ancient Athens where Aristotle taught) began in 1826 when Josiah Holbrook organized the "Association of Adults for Mutual Education" in Millbury, Massachusetts. Although the original lectures were intended to teach workingmen practical science, the idea caught on and quickly spread across the nation, with almost any subject fair game for the speaker. Eager crowds thronged to evening lectures devoted to such illuminating topics as "Missionary Life in Godless Burma," "Instinct," and "The Legal Rights of Women."

The educational aims of lyceums made them acceptable spots for young men and women to meet socially. Sometimes even the speaker himself engendered a little romance. One lecturer inspired a Massachusetts lass to gush: "It is like hearing sweet music to listen to him, besides feasting one's eyes on his beauty."

Speakers found travel on the lyceum circuit a lucrative enterprise. Fees ranged from the $5 plus oats for his horse first paid to Ralph Waldo Emerson to the $100,000 that Henry Morton Stanley earned for 100 lectures on his African expeditions. While such discourses were usually presented in a rented hall or church basement, the town of Salem, Massachusetts, built an elaborately decorated 700-seat auditorium to showcase its offerings.

Enthusiasm for the movement began to fade by the end of the Civil War, when the battle-weary public hungered more for entertainment than enlightenment. Humorists such as Mark Twain and Artemus Ward, and musical ensembles were suddenly in demand. Crowds that had once packed lecture halls flocked instead to a lighter-style lyceum. But in time these too fell out of fashion, and lyceums passed from the scene.

From Model T's to Model Americans

In the days when most Americans who drove an automobile drove a Model T, patriots raved over the Ford English School. Created by Henry Ford for immigrant factory workers, his school—and others like it—was a short course in the American Way.

The first words a Ford student learned were "I am a good American," a statement the teachers themselves took to heart. Instructors worked with missionary zeal, teaching not only reading, writing, and 'rithmetic but such worthy customs as "courtesy in public places." Students learned table manners seated at big school tables set with cups and plates, and toothbrushing was demonstrated on dolls. But Ford teachers reached far beyond the classroom. "Advisers" could, and did, conduct "investigations" to ensure that American standards prevailed in students' homes.

The climax of the course came at the graduation exercises when the students lined up in ethnic dress and climbed into a huge tub-shaped "melting pot." Moments later, each student emerged from the pot wearing a Ford-issued suit and straw hat, clutching a Ford-signed diploma—and waving an American flag.

Immigrant students at Henry Ford's Highland Park, Michigan, school (above) kept their eyes on a doll while learning how to take care of their teeth. Members of the class of 1916 emerge from the melting pot (right) at graduation exercises.

The inspirational program and idyllic setting at Chautauqua drew crowds every summer. A columned outdoor auditorium (above) held hundreds who gathered to hear lecturers on subjects from temperance to Bible history. A triple-decker pier building (far left) handled the hordes of visitors who arrived by steamboat. Al Sweet (left) conducted the pristinely uniformed White Hussars, one of many singing groups that entertained Chautauquans.

Before Chautauqua changed from summer camp to full-fledged resort, church groups had to operate from tents. The campers above are shown at their headquarters in 1882.

Culture on Chautauqua's Shore

In the rainy summer of 1874, a group of dedicated Sunday school teachers pitched four tents on the shore of Lake Chautauqua in New York. They had congregated for two weeks of organized study, but something remarkable happened. Despite the surplus of mud and mosquitoes, interested people came from far and wide to join the hymn singing and listen to the lectures. The first night some 2,000 visitors arrived, and by eight days into the session their numbers had grown to nearly 15,000.

The organizers of that first Chautauqua gathering quickly grasped that they had tapped a vein of phenomenal energy, and began expanding their camp the very next summer. Tents were replaced with chalet-style cottages, guest houses were built, and the curriculum was enriched with lakeshore concerts and a variety of lectures and entertainments. Following a promotional visit by President Ulysses S. Grant, interest in Chautauqua's programs grew so quickly that a newspaper was started to publish the busy daily schedule.

Chatauqua's organizers had recognized America's desire for refinement in an industrial age. Religion remained central to the camp's programs, but visitors could also quench their cultural thirst by listening to noted speakers and writers and learning about "radical" ideas in science and social reform. For recreation there were plenty of pageants, parades, and other sober social activities.

Inspiration in a resortlike setting proved irresistible. By 1876 the program had lengthened to eight weeks, and three new Chautauquas had sprung up—in Iowa, Michigan, and on an island in the St. Lawrence River. (Eventually there would be 30 imitation Chautauquas around the country.) In 1878 the New York site boasted an amphitheater and a "Hall of Philosophy," and soon after there were ice cream stands, a huge hotel, and double-decker steamboats landing at a triple-decker pier. At its zenith the site covered a mile and a half of shoreline and 700 acres.

But physical expansion was the least of it. As the years rolled by, Chautauqua established home-study courses that brought the exhilaration of learning to rural Americans who had never seen the inside of a university. The Chautauqua Literary and Scientific Circle signed up 8,000 members on its first try; it started 10,000 local reading groups that would count more than 300,000 members. The programs were so popular, in fact, that in the summer of 1924, the circuits, home courses, and lectures drew a combined audience of 35 million—nearly a third of the nation.

Bankrupted by the Depression, Chautauqua just managed to survive. Its summer program continues to this day, keeping alive the memory of its far-reaching educational ideals.

The Story Behind the Stacks at Our National Library

The Library of Congress survived a war, several fires, and numerous temporary and permanent moves, to become the world's largest library.

In 1800, when the national government moved to Washington, D.C., Congress, lacking a library, appropriated $5,000 to establish one. Orders were sent to London, and the first shipment of books — 740 volumes of history, law, and philosophy — soon arrived packed in 11 trunks.

Thus began what is today the largest library in the world, a collection that fills 535 miles of shelves in three enormous buildings. Among its treasures are rare texts: the oldest surviving book printed in America; the smallest book ever printed anywhere (it is the size of an ant); a scientific treatise by Copernicus; Oriental scrolls; and medieval illuminated manuscripts. The most valuable gem is a 1455 Gutenberg Bible, the first book printed with movable type.

And books are by no means the only treasures. (Out of 100 million items in the library, only about one-fourth are books.) Maps alone, some 4 million of them, fill two acres of cabinets. There are 9 million photographs providing a visual record of the wild West, the Civil War, and such important events as the Wright Brothers' first flight. America's technological history is documented by artifacts and papers that belonged to Robert Fulton, Thomas Edison, Alexander Graham Bell, and other inventors. And there are more newsreels, government papers, and sheet music stored here than anywhere else on earth.

The collections do not simply sit in archives; they can be studied and enjoyed by every citizen. But this was not always so. At first, the library was for the sole use of Congress. During Thomas Jefferson's presidency privileges were extended to the executive office, and by the 1850's the public was welcomed in. A self-confessed bibliophile, Jefferson played a key role in establishing the library's diversity.

When the British burned the Capitol during the War of 1812, Jefferson offered to sell the government his personal library of 6,487 volumes — what he called "the choicest collection of books in the United States." Many congressmen jumped at the chance; others were not so sure. The collection, after all, contained subjects in foreign languages and "books of entertainment" (novels), which were not considered "suited to the deliberations of the members as statesmen." Jefferson's offer was finally accepted, and although most of his books were destroyed in a second fire in 1851, the library had by then changed irrevocably from specialized to general interests.

Those doubting members of Congress would be surprised today to learn that their library contains books in 470 languages. It not only houses books of entertainment but, since 1870, has received two copies of each novel, short story, musical composition, and every other copyrighted work produced in this country. With its mailroom processing some 31,000 items every day, the library continually expands, offering the nation "the choicest collection of books" and a great deal more.

America's First Think Tank

At 21 feet high, with a 58-foot diameter, Chicago's refurbished water tank, shown here at its opening in 1873, proved a practical — and fireproof — public library.

Chicago was a young and vibrant city when British author Thomas Hughes visited in 1870. "This place," he wrote, "is the wonder of the Wonderful West." Just a year later, however, in October 1871, Chicago was destroyed by fire.

People throughout the world aided the rebuilding efforts. In England, Hughes helped organize a drive raising contributions "toward the formation of a free library" in Chicago.

The city quickly refurbished one of its few surviving structures — a massive iron water tank — and opened its doors in January 1873 as Chicago's first free public library. Among the original books on its shelves were volumes donated by Queen Victoria, Charles Darwin, Robert Browning, and a host of other notables. Their generosity in fact, provided the library with some 8,000 volumes, every one of them inscribed "as a mark of English sympathy."

Father Andy's Largess

When Col. James Anderson, a prominent citizen of Allegheny, Pennsylvania, made his personal library available to working boys in the 1850's, the one who borrowed the most books was young Andrew Carnegie.

Throughout his life learning would remain important to Carnegie, who never forgot Anderson's gesture. And when he retired from business in 1901—devoting himself full-time to philanthropy—Carnegie's favorite project was building public libraries.

Town councils could apply to him for a grant that, if approved, provided the money for a library building. (It was up to the towns to stock the shelves.) There was no shortage of applicants. At the time of his death in 1919, Father Andy, as he came to be known, had spent $60,364,808 building 2,509 libraries in English-speaking countries around the world.

The richest man in the world when he sold his steel company for $480 million in 1901, Andrew Carnegie was the frequent subject of editorial cartoons. After turning to philanthropy, he was often depicted at work on his hobby of building libraries.

Birth of the Bookmobile

In the early years of this century, Mary Titcomb, like librarians around the country, was doing her best to make books available to readers in rural communities. In 1904 she hired a horse and wagon (and pressed the janitor into service as a driver) to make book deliveries to drop-off points in remote corners of Washington County, Maryland.

The idea met with great success. "No better method was ever devised for reaching the country dweller," Titcomb claimed. "The book goes to the man. . . . The wagon is the thing."

Not quite satisfied, in 1907 Titcomb improved on her "method" by designing a special wagon with bookshelves on the outside and storage cases within. An actual rolling library that could travel directly from farm to farm, it was America's first bookmobile.

Other libraries quickly began to copy the idea, first with customized wagons, later with motorized trucks and buses. In the 1920's it was not uncommon for bus-driving librarians—who for the most part were young women—to require more than a day to complete their routes. "I have known the joys of the best hotels and the sorrows of the worst," wrote one intrepid driver in 1926. "Sleeping on a haystack in a barn was not the most appalling."

Still, there were places that bookmobiles could not go. To meet the needs of such communities in the 1930's, brigades of "packhorse librarians" carried books in saddlebags to mountain families in Kentucky. And in Mississippi, tenant farmers were often reached by library workers who made their rounds in bayou boats, paddling all the way.

Mary Titcomb described her custom-designed library wagon as a "cross between a grocer's delivery wagon and the tin-peddlar's cart." The original horse-drawn wagon made it possible for many rural families to read books on a regular basis for the first time in their lives. In 1912, wagons began to be replaced by automobiles, like Titcomb's updated design (left), which could reach more people per day. Books, she believed, were for everyone.

Marvels and Mastodons

Although art works lined the walls, natural wonders were what drew excitement-seeking crowds to Federal America's most fascinating museum.

In 1786 Charles Willson Peale, one of the country's foremost artists, opened a museum in his home in Philadelphia. "A school of useful knowledge," as he called it, the museum was meant "to amuse and . . . to instruct the adult as well as the youth of each sex and age."

Peale's portraits of famous Americans lined the walls, but it was his Wonderful Works of Nature that drew the crowds. A new science in the late 18th century, natural history had captured the public's imagination, and Peale threw himself into the subject with creative zeal.

He offered lectures, sculpted life-size waxworks depicting the races of man, and filled display cases with properly classified rocks and minerals. After teaching himself taxidermy, Peale set about collecting examples of every North American mammal, fish, insect, and bird that could be found. The birds in particular—eventually some 1,600 of them—were so enthralling that visitors could scarcely keep their hands off, despite written warnings that the feathers were dusted with arsenic. Eventually, Peale moved the birds to glass-faced cases that he painted to simulate naturalistic settings—the forerunners of today's museum dioramas.

Fellow citizens with an interest in science soon began making contributions: Benjamin Franklin donated the remains of his Angora cat, which were not displayed; Washington gave the museum two Chinese pheasants, which were. Jefferson made a gift of specimens collected during the Lewis and Clark expedition. Peale, in fact, was sent everything from vipers and iguanas to lava from Vesuvius, and a five-legged cow. The cow was kept tethered outside the museum since Peale wanted only subjects of educational value inside.

The collections, meanwhile, had outgrown their original quarters and ultimately were moved to

Charles Willson Peale painted this self-portrait in 1822, when he was 81 years old. Always the consummate showman, he depicted himself lifting a drapery for a tantalizing peek at displays of birds and portraits of illustrious Americans at his own extraordinary museum.

In its first decade the Peale museum was housed at the family home. Rubens Peale recalled it—complete with laundry—when he painted this picture (above) about 1860.

Independence Hall. Peale petitioned Congress for financial aid, fully expecting to have his things accepted as the foundation for a national museum. His hopes were never realized — and he remained continually on the verge of financial crisis — but he did receive help of a kind from his family.

Of Peale's 11 children who lived to maturity, 10 were named after famous artists and scientists, and several became involved in the family museum business. Among them Raphaelle, a still-life painter, also became an expert taxidermist; Rembrandt was a well-known portraitist and exhibited part of his father's collection in Europe; Rubens specialized in museum management; Franklin invented mechanical exhibits and also helped manage the museum with another brother, Titian, who painted watercolors of plants and animals.

The sons participated in their father's greatest triumph when, in 1801, he unearthed some massive bones from a bog in New York State. After more than a month of digging — and three months of assembly — they had nearly complete skeletons of two mastodons, or what Peale called Carnivorous Elephants of the North. Nothing could have caused greater excitement. One of the skeletons was displayed in Philadelphia and drew enormous crowds. The other went on tour and was eventually exhibited at a second Peale museum in Baltimore.

Charles Willson Peale retired in 1810, though not quietly. Turning to farming and inventing, he built — at age 78 — a velocipede that "goes down hill like the very devil." His museum survived him by only 27 years. When it closed in 1854, however, much of the contents passed into the hands of America's next great showman, P. T. Barnum.

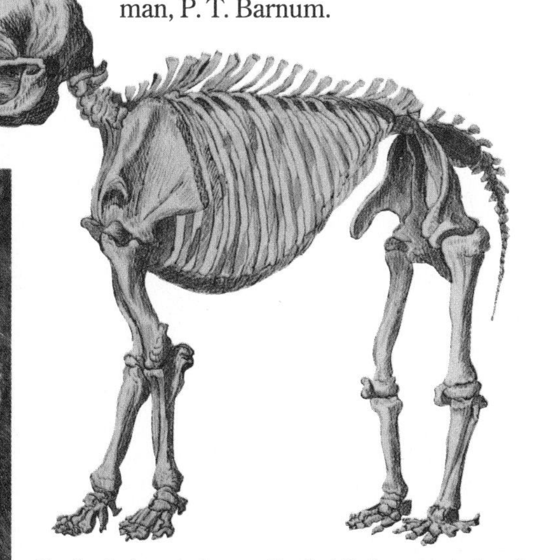

The Peales' mastodon was the first that anyone in America had seen and was of national interest. A painting by Charles Willson Peale (detail at left) depicts his family unearthing the "carnivorous elephant's" bones. Rembrandt Peale sketched the assembled skeleton (above).

A Museum Run Amok

With the advent of steamboat travel on the Ohio River in 1811, Cincinnati burgeoned into the economic capital of the Midwest. Proud of their town, many citizens dreamed of making it a cultural capital as well. They went a long way toward achieving that goal when they established, among other things, the Western Museum, which, for a time, was one of the best-known tourist attractions in the United States.

The Western Museum's animated Infernal Regions was also known as Dorfeuille's Hell, Dante's Inferno, and simply, the Regions. Citizens of Cincinnati considered it one of the wonders of the world.

The museum opened in 1820 as an educational institution, but within three years its founders discovered that displays of fossils and archeological artifacts were not enough to keep visitors coming back. Short of funds, they gave the museum to its new curator, Joseph Dorfeuille.

Dorfeuille was a master showman. Under his guidance — and with the indispensable aid of his "sublime mechanic," artist Hiram Powers — emphasis shifted from science to sensationalism.

Waxworks depicting everyone from Sleeping Beauty to George Washington were placed between displays of insects and minerals. A chamber of horrors was established, a stuffed mermaid installed, a collection of two-headed animals acquired — even a ventriloquist and a balancing act were hired briefly to dazzle viewers.

Fire and ice in the attic

But Dorfeuille had even more dramatic plans for drawing a crowd. Since Powers had a remarkable talent for sculpting and animating wax figures, he was put to work transforming the top floor of the museum into a display dubbed the "Infernal Regions." Open only at night, the Regions presented a frightening vision of hell. (Powers, disguised as the "Evil One" with a lobster claw over his nose, was sometimes there to personally frighten viewers.) Amid scenery depicting lakes of fire and mountains of ice, there were dwarfs that grew into giants, imps with flaming eyes, devils that tormented lost souls, and reptiles that devoured beautiful women. The waxworks emitted shrieks, clanks, and groans as they moved, and delivered electric jolts to anyone who dared to touch them.

The wizardry, however, depended on Powers's skills. When he left Ohio in 1834 to pursue a serious career as a sculptor, the mechanical efficiency of the exhibits declined, and debts began to mount. Dorfeuille sold the museum in 1839 and moved to New York, taking his infernal waxworks with him. Within a year, perhaps meeting its fitting end, the Regions was destroyed by fire.

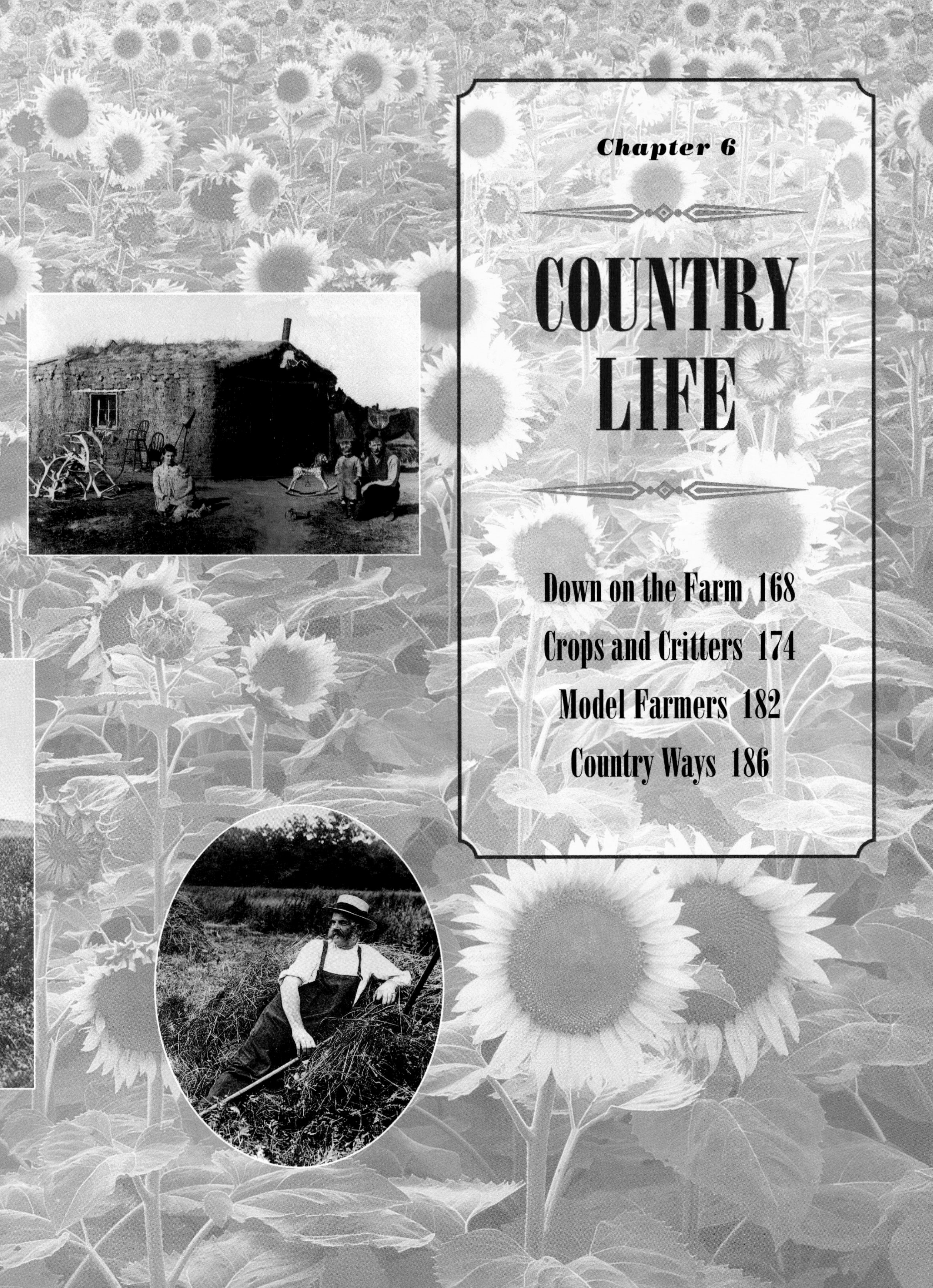

Chapter 6

COUNTRY LIFE

DOWN ON THE FARM

Country Chronicle

"All of this Pictures Containing in this Book. Search and Examin them. the are true Sketches I myself being there upon the places and Spot and put down what happened." So wrote Lewis Miller, a carpenter by trade, composer and bassoon player by avocation, and town gossip at heart. Miller was born in York County, Pennsylvania, in 1796, the year that George Washington gave his farewell address. By the end of his life some 86 years later, the nation had almost tripled in size, fought a Civil War, been threaded with railroad and telegraph lines, and celebrated its first centennial. And throughout his life Loui, as he was called, kept an informal visual diary of the many events, large and small, that he had witnessed.

Miller drew on whatever was at hand — lined or unlined paper, bound notebooks or scraps, even a railroad freight bill — eventually filling six books, or "Chronics," with more than 2,000 watercolor sketches teeming with activity and laced with earthy humor. His scenes charm the eye, warm the heart, and delight the imagination, for Miller was genuinely, affectionately intrigued by his neighbors. "What ideas in such people," he exclaimed in one of the captions that always accompanied his art.

On his crowded pages the good citizens of York plow fields, chase sheep, dance jigs, and build fences; some butcher hogs or tumble out of trees, while others brew "cherry bounce" or go for winter sleigh rides. The unexpected enlivens daily routine: a bull breaks the window of a pomade shop ("o what smack it made flying about the pavement in number"); a lawyer tries to keep rats from eating his books by feeding them cake; a man trims his wife's toenails with a hand saw. The perplexing also found its way onto his pages: "Rev. Daniel Dunn, he Deposite A Box, full of Brickbat and a few paper's in the York Bank what his Object was in so doing, not one that know it."

Miller also had a keen eye for detail, such as the bottles of brightly colored elixirs in an early-19th-century doctor's office or the brick ovens, cooking utensils, and list of "victuals" prepared at the estimable "York Hotels." His sketches thus are a treasure trove for historians, offering a richly detailed chronicle of life in rural America.

A lifelong bachelor, Miller lived out his final years with a niece in Virginia. After his death in 1882, a contemporary fondly recalled that "though a lover of the sublime, he had a keen and lively sense of the ridiculous."

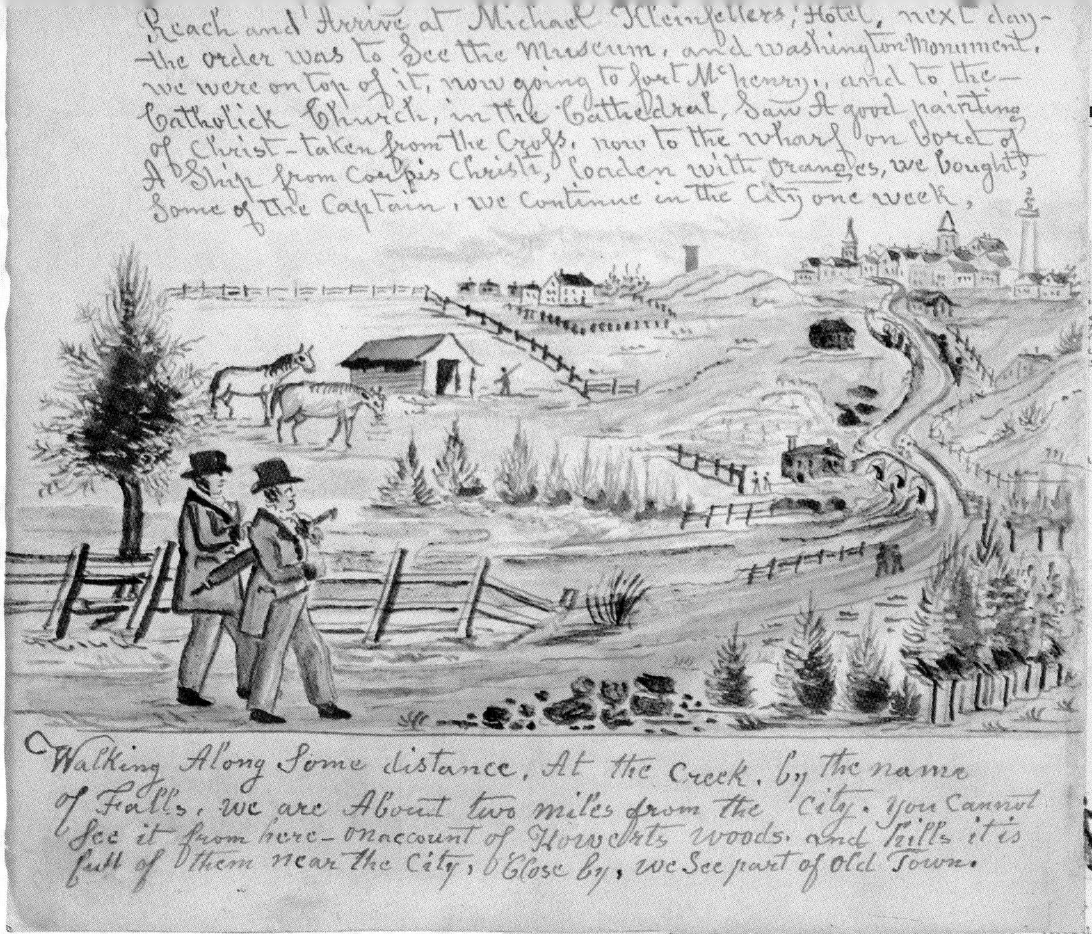

Reach and Arrive at Michael Kleinfelters, Hotel, next day-the order was to See the Museum, and washington Monument, we were on top of it, now going to fort Mc henry, and to the-Catholick Church, in the Cathedral, Saw A good painting of Christ-taken from the Crofs, now to the wharf on bord of A Ship from Corpis Christi, loaden with Oranges, we bought, Some of the Captain, we Continue in the City one week,

Walking Along Some distance, At the Creek, by the name of Falls, we are About two miles from the City. You Cannot See it from here-onaccount of Howerts woods, and hills it is full of them near the City, Close by, we See part of Old Town.

Children of Michael Eurich. and his daughter Elisa.

John König. or hannes. and the Execution. by Law for his goods. a cow is all out. ha da muss die law mir eine geben.

Nicholas Huber, old mr. Ferdinand.
Peter wilt. Jacob Rupp. Lourence Shultz.
1812.
Mrs Cath Weiser frying a Sausage, & A Hound Came and Stole it out the pan. for his Breakfast.
Woman Guard Your Kitchen.
the dog devoured with much greedinefs, while mrs. weiser was out for a Dish & fork to Serve it on the table, teach a dog and put him in a way to fulfill its demands, and you make him a moral Agent.
We Boys Puting up A Swing, on A large white oak tree, In the Woods of Peter Streber, formerly Susan Spangler Plantation, one mile from town, To leab and Skip by Swinging, William Streber, Lewis Miller, John Rouse, Daniel Baumgardner, Jacob Stroman, Henry Craver, Samuel weiser. In the Year-1812.

Ernst Willig, Confectioner.
Mrs. Kelly Her Amusement was painting-Such as we See, the Servant old fillis holding them for her, desired her to hold fast their wings
old Weaver's wagonmaker Shop in South George Street. build in 1751. and torndown by George Stine in 1850. Stood 99. years

Sodbusting Homes on the Range

Settlers on the Great Plains were offered 160 acres if they remained on the land for five years — but life on the treeless plains was far from easy.

Free land! That was the irresistible incentive offered by the Homestead Act of 1862. And thousands of families responded by traveling west to stake a claim on the treeless plains. Once there, their first priority was to build some sort of shelter. With conventional building materials, such as stones and lumber, scarce in Kansas, Nebraska, and the Dakotas, many homesteaders literally burrowed into the nearest hillside or ravine and called the dugout home until an aboveground house could be built.

Although insulated from cold and wind, these dens were unavoidably dark, dank, and crowded. So it was little wonder that pioneer families built larger, more permanent structures as soon as they could. Typically they constructed their new homes of sod, "without mortar, square, plumb, or greenbacks," as one pioneer boasted. Cut into one-by-two-foot rectangles with a spade, or lifted in continuous strips with a plow, the so-called "Nebraska marble" was the one resource in seemingly endless supply. Once harvested — a 12-by-14-foot house required about an acre of sod — the blocks were stacked to form walls and laid over precious wooden rafters to make grassy, sometimes flower-strewn, roofing.

According to a tract written for prospective homesteaders, a man could complete a one-story house, "roof and all," in just 10 days. Additionally, readers were informed, sod homes were both warmer in winter and cooler in summer than any house made of lumber. They also had the advantage of being nearly impervious to prairie fires.

Photographed around 1890, this Custer County, Nebraska, sod house, complete with pitched roof and neatly framed windows, was large enough to have a couple of rooms.

Not mentioned were the less appealing features of the "soddie." Houses rarely had interior walls, for instance, but were curtained into rooms with quilts or carpets draped over ropes. Ceilings shed dirt into food and bedding, and dripped for days after heavy rains — prairie wives would recall cooking with one hand while holding an umbrella with the other. The thick walls that made sod houses airtight also made them retain the pungent odors of buffalo-chip fuel and human occupation. And snakes and mice had no regard for the territorial rights of long-suffering families. But in true pioneer spirit "sodbusters" rarely complained. Many, in fact, took a certain grim pride in their ability to endure.

A Contagious Case of Cabin Fever

The log cabin as home to America's true heroes is an appealing myth — a myth that was concocted during the presidential campaign of 1840. Whig candidate William Henry Harrison, bent on exploiting the economic woes of Martin van Buren's term as president, styled himself a man of the people. Capitalizing on his reputation as a heroic general in Indian territory — with the nickname Tippecanoe — Harrison campaigned as a frontiersman.

"Give him a barrel of hard cider and settle a pension of $2,000 a year on him," snorted the Democrats in press attacks, "and he will sit the remainder of his days in a log cabin. . . ." But their ridicule backfired. The Whigs were delighted with the image and so were the voting masses. Log-cabin badges and songs soon appeared, and hard cider flowed at most every rally. Towns throughout the country staged parades that featured horse-drawn floats bearing real log cabins with real smoke coming from their chimneys.

In truth, Harrison's only connection with cabins was as the wealthy landlord of 2,000 acres of tenant farms. But his claim of humble beginnings was enough to win the public's loyalty — and to induce later would-be presidents to use the same ploy. As it happened, only Millard Fillmore, James Buchanan, Abraham Lincoln, James Garfield, and Ulysses Grant actually knew log-cabin living firsthand. But that did not stop other candidates from pretending.

Born on a fine estate in Virginia, William Henry Harrison nevertheless managed to campaign as the "log cabin candidate" while labeling his opponent "an epicure."

An Outhouse by Any Other Name

There's a lot of fine points to puttin' up a first-class privy that the average man don't think about. It's no job for an amachoor, take my word on it." These sage words of advice come to us from Lem Putt, the title character in a little book called *The Specialist,* written in 1929 by vaudeville comedian Charles "Chic" Sale. An outgrowth of Sale's own specialty of telling tales about a rural carpenter and his philosophy of privy-building, the 28-page booklet turned out to be one of publishing's great success stories. Within a few years *The Specialist* sold well over a million copies, and its contents were told and retold by countless Americans, most of whom were just a generation away from using a privy themselves.

Everyone could chuckle over Lem Putt's opinions on such things as locating an outhouse under an apple tree: "There ain't no sound in nature so disconcertin' as the sound of apples droppin' on the roof." Or why special attention had to be paid to digging the waste hole: "It's a mighty sight better to have a little privy over a big hole than a big privy over a little hole." Or why sturdy construction is the best policy: "You've got to figger on . . . that Odd Fellows picnic in the fall."

But the writer's success turned out to have its downside too. Much to his chagrin, Sale discovered that, over time, his name had become more closely linked with his subject than he liked. He was not amused to hear that people were no longer visiting the outhouse or privy, but the "Chic Sale" — however affectionately they meant it. The term even went global after Sale's death. During World War II American GI's decorated the doors of thousands of latrines and ships' heads around the world with the rustic moniker — a reassuring reminder of home.

Chic Sale played the part of "the specialist" Lem Putt (above) in his vaudeville act. Variously dubbed donnicker, biffy, Mrs. Jones, and Johnnie, privies have been built in both one and two-story designs (above left) and have been the subject of countless jokes (left).

People Who Lived in Grass Houses

When homesteaders arrived in the Sandhill country of northwestern Nebraska in 1904, they faced a knotty problem. Not only were there few trees or stones to build with, but the soil in the hills would not hold together when sliced into slabs of sod. With no alternatives the settlers turned to the only abundant material at hand and built their houses of hay.

Mechanized balers were widely used in Nebraska at the turn of the century. Operating out in the fields, the machines made quick work of pressing and wire-tying sweet-smelling dried hay into uniform blocks up to four feet long and two feet wide. Hauling the bales to his homesite, a farmer would then enlist his neighbors' help in stacking them in bricklike courses and staking them with wood or iron rods for stability. With enough help, all four walls might be completed in a single day. Finishing touches such as plastered and stuccoed walls inside and out, shingle roofs, window and door frames, and concrete or wood flooring could all be added at a later time.

Baled-hay structures served as homes for thousands of families, as well as for churches and schools. On the one hand, they were well insulated and soundproof — so much so that some owners claimed they could go through a tornado without hearing a thing. On the other hand, fires were always a danger, and fleas found the hay walls very hospitable. Hungry cattle also were known to hanker after them, nibbling daintily around the edges of buildings not encased in stucco, and devouring entire structures when they were abandoned.

LEGEND —AND— LORE

It gets mighty cold out on the Great Plains, which is hardly surprising since farmers claim there's only one spindly cedar to block winds that whistle down from the Arctic. Many a tale stops in midsentence as the words freeze and fall to the ground. Flames also freeze solid inside lanterns and fires stiffen in the fireplace until the spring thaw. Then the frozen words come back to life, babbling merrily on their own, and the flames dance once again on the hearth.

In the Round

Round barns, some said, were invented to "keep the devil from hiding in the corners." But in fact it was practicality, not religious scruples or aesthetic whimsy, that gave rise to the distinctive cylindrical structures. In the late 1800's scientific principles were being applied to agriculture just as earnestly as they were to other aspects of life, and farmers were being urged to experiment with the efficient use of space, such as central silos and unobstructed hay mows — features that could be successfully combined in round barns.

Building in the round, however, required accurate plans and a skilled carpenter to properly execute the intricacies of the newfangled construction technique. One of the best — and busiest — builders was Horace Greeley Duncan, who mastered round-barn carpentry in his native Indiana, then a hotbed of agricultural innovation. An enthusiastic poker player, Duncan persuaded the local "gentleman farmers" to take a gamble on the new barns. Between 1895 and 1916 he designed and built at least 16 fine examples of these structures throughout the Midwest.

Most of his clients were wealthy professionals who could afford the extra time and expense for the latest thing — and could absorb the loss if the promised but unproven economies were not realized. Their patronage allowed Duncan to work out the glitches in round-barn construction, and in 1905 he patented his design for a self-supporting roof. Round barns never swept the nation, but some still dot the Midwest, monuments to the restless entrepreneurial drive for improvement that characterizes American industry.

Round barns appeared as far east as Shelburne, Vermont (above). Barns such as the Ohio specimen (below), built by Horace Greeley Duncan, required intricate framing.

A Point Well Taken

"Light as air. Stronger than whiskey. Cheaper than dirt," chanted John Warne Gates as he stood beside the corral he had erected in a plaza in San Antonio. It was 1876 and Gates had come to Texas to try to sell farmers and cattlemen a new type of fencing — fencing made from wire. But those in his audience who were not skeptical were downright certain that the nearly invisible fencing would never contain a snorting, stamping, 1,000-pound bull bent on breaking free. A lively crowd had gathered at a safe distance to witness what they expected would be more debacle than demonstration.

Many kinds of fencing had been tried on the western plains, where wood and stone — traditional fencing materials in the South and the East — were in short supply. Enter the patient genius of Joseph F. Glidden, an Illinois farmer who adapted a coffee grinder to shape little barbs, which he then fixed in a cable made by twisting two strands of wire together. Glidden perfected his fencing in 1873, but sales were slow as an old mule until Gates took on the task of selling the wire to Texans.

The young man, who would later be known as "Bet-a-Million" Gates because of his willingness to bet on almost anything, made San Antonio his first stop. By day he chatted with the farmers; by night he gambled and gabbed with the cattlemen.

When neither side bit, he knew he'd have to prove his point. After finagling a permit to build his corral in the middle of one of the city's old plazas, Gates began touting his product. He had borrowed a small herd of lively longhorns, and at the appointed hour they were driven at a run into the corral.

The animals took one look at the flimsy wires and made a break for freedom. Painfully pricked by the "devil's rope," they retreated in shock, which quickly turned to fury. Again they charged and again they were repulsed. The wire held.

The audience waited, but the fence had won. The steers, having learned that pain dwelled in the barbs, milled in confusion in the center of the corral. Barbed wire sales took off like a shot: within a year they soared from less than three million pounds to over twelve million. "Bet-a-Million" Gates had won his first big gamble.

The fence that won the West was perfected in Illinois. Of the 394 patents granted for barbed wire, 176 went to Illinois applicants. Joseph Glidden made a fortune from the spiky fencing.

By the Bushel and Barrowful

Plowed with furrows that ran unbroken for miles and then planted and harvested by armies of workers, huge tracts of land in the West were opened to cultivation in the late 1870's. Many of these so-called bonanza farms lay in the Red River Valley between Minnesota and the Dakota Territory, where a typical spread might be five times the size of New York City's Manhattan Island. Crews working in one part of the farm might labor all season without setting eyes on those in another.

Much of the land was bought from the Northern Pacific Railroad after it went bust in the Panic of 1873. Having just completed a link connecting the Red River Valley to the Great Lakes and the densely populated East, it sold off vast tracts of right-of-way at bargain prices.

To show what riches could be wrung from the Dakota soil, the company brought in Oliver Dalrymple, a Minnesota farm manager. His first wheat harvest yielded 23 bushels per acre — and the boom was on.

Big investors spearheaded the land rush and began farming on a grand scale. Using steel-bladed plows, self-binding harvesters, and steam-powered threshing machines, the bonanzas were so successful that settlers of more modest means — but equally big dreams — soon followed. Land claims peaked in the mid-1880's, and by 1915 North Dakota was all sold off.

Starting to work on a fine spring day, a Red River Valley harrowing crew, using the most up-to-date equipment, stretched nearly to the horizon.

CROPS AND CRITTERS

Renowned as tireless workers, Morgan horses are equally well known as racers. Sulky drivers harnessed them singly or paired them up as teams for fast-paced races around the track.

Morgan's Good Sport

He was not particularly imposing, as horses go — just an undersize bay colt palmed off on Justin Morgan, a music teacher from Randolph, Vermont, in partial payment for a debt. Morgan brought the horse home in the summer of 1795 and named it Figure, but as a sickly man and a widower with four small children, he was always in need of cash. And so before long he hired Figure out to Robert Evans, a local farmer, for $15 a year.

When Evans put the horse to work, he may have wondered if the little animal would be up to the job of clearing logs and boulders from his woodlot. He need not have worried. Figure was up to it, and then some: a day in the fields proved to be just a warm-up for the horse, who could go on to win handily in an evening race in town.

That horse of Justin Morgan's, as Figure came to be known, soon gained a reputation for strength far beyond his size. Evans bought the horse after Morgan died, and neighboring mares were brought to the bay for breeding. Then an even more remarkable trait became apparent. Spring after spring every last one of the colts sired by "that horse of Justin Morgan's" turned out to be his spitting image. No matter the mare, the result was a "Morgan" — compact, powerful, with a broad chest and chiseled, graceful head.

Whatever its origins may have been — no one knows for sure — the Morgan horse is a powerful original, a "mutant" or "sport" as they say in horsey circles. Small, tough, and a fine short-distance racer, the Morgan is among the sturdiest, most equable, and versatile of horses — one of the first true American breeds. And it is the breed still favored for any work requiring gentleness and stamina.

The Indispensable Pig

Easy to raise and cheap to feed, the much-maligned pig has saved the day for many a farmer, returning — dollar for dollar — more than any other animal.

Ever since ancestors of the modern-day pig arrived here from Europe centuries ago, hogs have been a mainstay for many an American farmer, especially on the frontier. And a more accommodating, cost-effective animal would in fact have been hard to find. The pig requires no special grazing lands, thrives in most climates, breeds quickly, and is willing to eat whatever it is fed — or even to forage on its own. With only four or five animals, a farmer could produce enough meat to feed his family through the winter and provide a supply of cured pork,

They have one fault, they won't lay eggs

soap, and lard as well. Even then he might be able to turn a profit by selling one product or another to a neighbor who was too shortsighted to raise pigs of his own.

Sinewy, mean-looking animals that weighed 150 pounds at most when they were introduced here, domesticated pigs did not change discernibly for some time. But by the late 1700's Colonial farmers had developed improved methods of feeding. Corn, they discovered, was one of the things that pigs loved best to eat. And with corn as feed, 300-pound hogs — with a high fat-to-lean ratio — soon became the norm.

It was the heavily mortgaged Midwestern pioneers in the mid-19th century who benefited most from this "hog-and-hominy" approach to farming. With an inexpensive brood sow and a good supply of corn, a family could earn enough hard cash to work its way out of financial difficulties. Since a whopping 80 percent of the pig's weight — "everything but the oink" — is convertible into edible, salable material, the corn-fed hog was a lifesaver, earning itself the distinctive title of the "mortgage lifter."

A healthy litter of pigs was well worth a little pampering. The brood (above left) was kept warm in a country kitchen. The Arkansas razorback hog (above) is said to have been so small that it could roost like a chicken.

Feather Farms

BRINGING IN THE EGGS. CAWSTON OSTRICH FARM, SOUTH PASADENA, CALIFORNIA

A worker brings in the eggs at Edwin Cawston's ostrich ranch in South Pasadena. Each egg can weigh three pounds or more, has a yolk equal to those of 28 chicken eggs, and can take an hour and a half to be hard-boiled.

If ever a bird seemed likely to lay a golden egg for hardworking farmers, it was the ostrich. Toward the end of the 19th century, it seemed as if every woman of fashion had fallen under the spell of its plumage. Ostrich feathers not only adorned stylish hats from Paris to St. Louis but also were gathered into fans and trailed across shoulders in the form of boas and stoles. Although they commanded prices as high as $10 to $15 apiece, the elegant feathers appeared to have an unlimited market potential.

The birds originally were hunted in the wild on the South African veld, but by the late 1800's they were being raised on farms there with astounding success. Assuming the dry climate of southern California and Arizona would serve just as well, a handful of Americans decided to compete with the African breeders. Given the ostrich's incubation period of just 42 days and its lifespan of 80 years, the investment seemed a sure bet.

By the end of the century, a half-dozen ranches had been set up and special handlers trained to harvest the "crop" every few months. Led one by one into narrow, four-foot-high plucking boxes and hooded to avoid panic, the 300-pound birds were swiftly relieved of their plumage.

Within 10 years there were over 6,000 ostriches in the United States, but changing fashions soon put an end to the market. By 1920 the ostrich population had plummeted to about 230, and the big birds were earning farmers more for the rides they gave to the occasional tourist than for any contribution to fashion.

The Indigo Instigator

I love the vegitable world extreamly," admitted young Eliza Lucas — and it was a good thing for the colony of South Carolina that she did. Though only 16 in 1739, she already was managing 5,100 acres for her father, who had sailed off to Britain's West Indian colonies to help defend them against the Spanish. Since the war with Spain had closed the market for rice, South Carolina's agricultural mainstay, Eliza needed to develop a new crop. So she began experimenting with cotton, ginger, alfalfa, and cassava. But it was the indigo seeds her father sent her that furnished a solution.

While Lucas realized that the dyes extracted from indigo could find a ready market in the British textile industry, the difficulty of raising and processing the plant proved considerable. Lucas's first planting was destroyed by a freeze, and the second and third years' crops were sabotaged by her foremen, two Frenchmen who wanted to keep the indigo market for their country's colony of Montserrat. Lucas fired the saboteurs, and the 1744 harvest turned out to be all she could have hoped for. Indeed, it supplied part of her dowry when she married Charles Pinckney that same year.

The couple shared their seeds and know-how with neighbors, and the British government paid a bounty on the finished product. As a result planters realized a 100 percent profit on their investments within just three or four years. Lucas went on to experiment with flax, hemp, and silk production, but indigo remained her great success. When she died in 1793, George Washington served as a pallbearer. His presence honored her contributions, professional and personal (both her sons had distinguished themselves in the Revolution), to her new country. Her cultivation of indigo, and her generosity in sharing her success with others, had provided the southern colony with a secure financial base for the fight for independence.

In Their Own Words

Many waggon-loads of enormous water-melons were brought to market every day, and I was sure to see groups of men, women, and children, seated on the pavement round the spot where they were sold, sucking in prodigious quantities of this watery fruit. Their manner of devouring them is extremely unpleasant; the huge fruit is cut into half-a-dozen sections, of about a foot long, and then, dripping as it is with water, applied to the mouth, from either side of which pour copious streams of the fluid, while, ever and anon, a mouthful of the hard black seeds are shot out in all directions, to the great annoyance of all within reach. When I first tasted this fruit, I thought it very vile stuff indeed; but before the end of the season we all learned to like it. When taken with claret and sugar, it makes delicious wine and water. — *Frances Trollope, 1832*

Seeds of Success

For countless American countryfolk, the inception of free rural mail delivery during the 1870's meant a release from near total isolation. For Washington Atlee Burpee, it meant a golden opportunity.

The son of a Philadelphia doctor, Burpee had been studying medicine himself but found he could not stand the sight of human suffering, and so dropped out after a year at medical school. He then returned to a business he had been pursuing since his days in elementary school — breeding poultry. In 1876 he began selling purebred chickens, geese, ducks, and turkeys by mail, and soon added pedigreed dogs, hogs, cattle, and sheep to his stock. As a courtesy Burpee also offered seeds in the catalog so that his customers could grow their own feeds. Much to his surprise, the seeds outsold any of the livestock.

Ever a pragmatist, Burpee began aggressively pursuing the seed business, traveling throughout the United States and Europe in search of new and superior vegetables, fruits, and flowers. Eventually he was testing 7,000 seed samples a year at Fordhook, his Pennsylvania farm, where he produced an impressive list of new varieties, including such horticultural standbys as iceberg lettuce, Bush lima beans, and Golden Bantam sweet corn. Burpee also was a pioneer in recognizing the home garden as the coming market. He devoted relatively little attention to farm crops such as oats, realizing that there was far more profit in 25-cent packets of tomato seeds.

W. Atlee Burpee's greatest genius, however, was in merchandising. The catalog he sent out free to customers (thanks largely to the new rural free delivery system) was a work of art. And his genial prose made it favorite reading material in many American homes. He recommended Spanish peanuts as being "excellent for fattening hogs and children," and to an advertisement for pyrethrum powder Burpee attached a thrilling cloak-and-dagger tale of this natural pesticide's discovery in Central Asia.

He sponsored contests with cash prizes for the best produce and the best new company slogan ("Burpee Seeds Grow" won a prize in 1890), and Burpee offered a free sewing machine to anyone who could sell 300 special, 25-cent introductory packets of mixed vegetable seeds. When admiring customers named their sons after him, Burpee sometimes made a point of dropping by with a silver mug for the new little W. Atlee.

By 1915 Burpee was operating the largest mail-order seed business in the world and shipping out 5,000 to 6,000 orders every day. He bought a half-million pounds of paper that year for the printing of his million catalogs. From an original pamphlet of 48 pages, the publication

had grown into a compendium of testimonial letters and gardening tips that filled 200 pages.

A tireless innovator in business affairs, Burpee in 1891 was the first seedsman to run illustrations engraved from photographs in his catalog. Yet in his personal life he was profoundly conservative, shunning electric lights, telephones, and automobiles. What's more, it was only after the old man died in 1915 that his son, David Burpee, was finally able to dispose of the last of those prize poultry.

W. Atlee Burpee's seed catalogs were as attractive as they were informative. The colorful engravings that adorned the covers enticed customers with the promise of equal bounty from their home gardens. He wrote his own copy, freely indulging his engaging sense of humor, and offered tips to help ensure his customers' gardening success.

The now-famous fruit industry of the Pacific Northwest is a legacy of Henderson Luelling, an intrepid traveler with a missionary zeal for orchards who is sometimes known as the Northwest's own Johnny Appleseed.

Henderson Luelling, Pioneer Plantsman

Even Indians wouldn't attack Henderson Luelling. Anyone crossing the Great Plains with a wagon full of live fruit trees, they apparently assumed, must be under the protection of the Great Spirit. By the time Luelling made his westward trek in the mid-19th century, he had already moved twice: from North Carolina to Indiana, and from Indiana to Iowa. Starting a fruit tree nursery in Iowa, he stayed put long enough to see it prosper. But stirred by accounts he had read of the Lewis and Clark expedition, he was determined to get to Oregon.

In the spring of 1847, Luelling loaded two boxes on a wagon, filled them with soil, and planted them with 700 grafted saplings of fruit and nut trees. Then, with several other wagonloads of household goods, and accompanied by his wife and eight children, he headed for the Northwest.

Daily stops to water the trees made it impossible for the Luellings to keep up with any of the westward-bound wagon trains, but their faith in their mission kept them going. In all, nearly 500 trees survived the seven-month trip and were planted near Portland. Within just four years Luelling and a partner — another former Iowan named William Meek — increased their stock of trees to 18,000 and sold them readily for $1.00 to $1.50 each. Luelling and Meek also planted an orchard, and people came from far and wide to see their first crop of apples.

The fruits were much in demand and sold for fancy prices — in 1853 Luelling's apples fetched $2.00 a pound in San Francisco. That may have been what convinced him to move to Oakland, California, where he started yet another nursery. This time he met with even greater success. But adventure still beckoned, and Luelling squandered his fortune on an unsuccessful move to Honduras. He returned to California and began clearing land and planting once again, but his luck had at last run out: Luelling never recovered his fortune. He did, however, leave great wealth to others, for his trees are considered the basis of the now-vast orchards of the Pacific Northwest.

Florida's Finest

What's in a name? An extra dollar on the price of every box of oranges if the name stenciled on its side happened to be Douglas Dummett or Indian River. Born in 1806, Dummett was the son of a Barbados sugar planter who resettled his family in Florida and established a new plantation. Young Dummett adapted quickly to the change, becoming famous as a hunter and Indian fighter.

By 1830 he had begun to set up his own business on Merritt Island near Cape Canaveral. This was Seminole territory, and the long lagoon that separated the island from the mainland was known as Indian River. Merritt Island itself was covered with wild sour-orange trees, onto which Dummett grafted the buds of sweet oranges.

Creating a grove of some 1,700 trees, he soon gained a reputation for high-quality fruit in the northern markets, where his Indian River oranges arrived packed with Spanish moss in handcrafted boxes.

Their wild roots seem to have given Dummett's trees a special vigor and an ability to withstand cold, although they also benefited from their warm, coastal location. These were factors that served Dummett well, since his was the only grove in Florida to survive the terrible freeze of February 1835. Ultimately it was cuttings from his trees that revived the state's orange industry.

Dummett continued to operate his grove until his death in 1873. Even today a few trees from his original grafting remain to give visitors a taste of the fruit that was prized as pick of the crop for about 150 years. The local oranges have given the region such a famous name that, until the federal government intervened, growers all over Florida were labeling their fruit "Indian River" in hopes of luring choosy shoppers.

An article about Florida's booming citrus industry in *Frank Leslie's Illustrated Newspaper* in 1883 showed a worker sizing oranges by an old-fashioned method.

A Novel Idea That Bore Fruit

New England–born abolitionist though she was, Harriet Beecher Stowe nevertheless made another home — and part of her livelihood — in the South. At age 57 in 1868, some 16 years after her novel *Uncle Tom's Cabin* swept the nation, Stowe and her husband bought an orange grove in Mandarin, Florida.

The little town on the St. John's River was named for the delicious oranges it produced, and for 17 years Stowe was its best-known grower. Part of her success in establishing neighborly relations with the locals may have been the fame and increased tourist revenue that she brought to the town during the winter months. But Stowe also was no slouch when it came to managing her 30-acre grove — a job she performed on her own since her husband preferred to spend his days reading on the veranda. And when it came to shipping her fruit, the novelist's name proved an effective marketing tool. Her fans up North eagerly sought out the boxes marked "Oranges from Harriet Beecher Stowe."

"He Sowed; Others Reaped"

So reads the inscription on the gravestone of Ephraim Bull, the man who developed the Concord grape. Though it is America's most popular variety, Bull himself realized a profit of only $3,200 from his creation. A maker of goldleaf in Concord, Massachusetts, who gardened in his spare time, Bull had been seeking a grape that would ripen early in New England. Starting with seed from a wild fox grape, he spent 11 years producing the Concord. When he exhibited the thin-skinned, sweetly aromatic black fruit at the Massachusetts Horticultural Society's fall show in 1853, it was an immediate success — so much so, in fact, that the following spring Bull sold his entire stock of vines at the handsome price of $5.00 apiece.

Soon commercial nurseries were producing Concord vines in bulk — and paying no royalties to the breeder. As his grape grew to be the foundation of juice, jelly, and wine industries, Bull became increasingly embittered with commercial enterprise. Though he continued to breed new grapes for another 40 years — developing several new varieties — he never again shared the results.

Part of the Conestoga wagon's distinctive look came from its five-foot-high rear wheels. Considerably larger than the front wheels, they helped provide the traction needed to get through on rough, rutted roads.

Big Wheels on Route to Market

Among the unusual sights that caught the eye of one visitor to Pennsylvania in 1784 was the vast number of heavily laden wagons lumbering toward Philadelphia from the state's Conestoga Valley. The inquisitive traveler counted 700 of these "Conestoga wagons" carrying goods to market. Some 20 years later another observer claimed that at least 1,000 of them made their way to the city on every market day.

Designed by enterprising German farmers and wheelwrights of the Conestoga Valley, these wagons — with their big blue bodies, red wheels, and white linen hoods — were a colorful sight. And in their day they were considered the closest thing to perfection on the road. The bodies were boat shaped, built with the ends higher than the middle to keep cargo from slipping out on hills. Enormous iron-rimmed wheels — some 6 to 10 inches wide — offered the best available traction for muddy, deeply rutted roads or even for fording rushing rivers. Pulled by a team of four to six sturdy horses, a Conestoga could carry as many as six tons of goods.

Railroads began to replace wagons in the 1830's, by which time Conestogas had served farmers well for nearly 100 years. A reminder of their usage remains in circulation, however: long, thin, cheap cigars like those favored by the wagon drivers are still called "stogies."

A Better Cheddar

Neighbors were puzzled when Jesse Williams rented out his acreage near Rome, New York, for a season in the 1840's and, instead of tending his own dairy farm, kept himself busy touring the countryside to learn all he could about cheesemaking. Most farmers at the time thought of cheesemaking as a practical way to use up surplus milk before it spoiled. Williams, however, had calculated that an acre of pastureland was far more profitable when the end product was not milk but cheese — especially his own cheese.

Williams produced cheddar of such uncommonly high quality that he could consistently sell it at a premium price. And the question of pricing, ultimately, was what changed Williams's business from a home operation into America's first professional cheese factory. When his son went into the dairy business, Williams wanted the young man to produce cheese that commanded the same price as his own. But the son demurred since he could not match his father's skill.

In the spring of 1851, Williams solved the problem by combining milk from the two farms and producing a uniform cheddar at his own cheese works. Before long he was buying milk from other farmers as well, and in that first year of factory production, he turned out over 70,000 pounds of cheese. Wholesalers from as far away as the Midwest purchased his product, inspiring other farmers to set up similar operations. By the early 1860's New York cheddar was being enjoyed not only in America but in far-off Europe too.

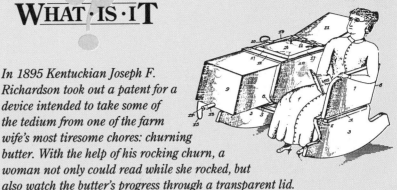

WHAT · IS · IT

In 1895 Kentuckian Joseph F. Richardson took out a patent for a device intended to take some of the tedium from one of the farm wife's most tiresome chores: churning butter. With the help of his rocking churn, a woman not only could read while she rocked, but also watch the butter's progress through a transparent lid.

Unsung Heros of the Old West

The cattle drives of the western range have been immortalized in folklore and legend, and the cowboys who led the herds are celebrated in story and song. Yet the exploits of the cowboys' counterparts, America's sheepherders, remain largely unknown — despite the fact that they, too, were men of daring and determination.

One of the loneliest and toughest jobs ever shouldered by workers in America's West was that of the drovers who took sheep to distant markets. Adequate food and water were always a concern. Here, a shepherd and his dogs tend a flock on the Utah desert.

Perils and predators

Hardworking shepherds oversaw the movement of as many as 7,500 sheep at a time from the West Coast to the feedlots in Kansas and Nebraska, where the animals were fattened for market. It was not an easy trek. The sheep had to scale passes over the Rocky Mountains, make their way across barren deserts, and ford streams, all the while avoiding such natural predators as eagles, wolves, and coyotes. Unlike cattle, sheep would not drink in marshes, scorning everything but still, clear water. As a result the animals were in constant peril of dying from thirst. A shepherd on one drive told of his water-starved flock burying their heads in each other's bodies until "they piled hot and close and perished on their feet."

The 2,500-mile march

On a drive through Arizona, the herders kept the huge flocks from wandering off at night by penning the animals in temporary corrals made of long sheets of muslin held up by wooden stakes. Even after the sheep were corralled, however, the shepherds often rode ahead on the trail in search of potential trouble spots on the next day's march. The vigilant flockmaster had to keep watch for hazards such as locoweed, which, if eaten, would damage a sheep's nervous system, and the cholla cactus, whose sharp spines caused painful body sores on the animals.

From 1870 until 1900, flockmasters trailed some 15 million head of sheep for distances of up to 2,500 miles. Although most of the long-distance herding ended with the onset of the 20th century, there were occasional sheep treks for at least another 50 years.

MODEL FARMERS

TIME TABLE

SEEDS OF CHANGE

1609 *Indians teach colonists to grow corn at Jamestown.*

1619 *The first slaves are brought to America.*

1719 *Settlers in Londonderry, New Hampshire, are the first English colonists to cultivate the potato.*

1742 *Sugar cane is grown in Louisiana, and indigo is planted in South Carolina.*

1770 *England imports 150,000 barrels of rice from Carolina and Georgia.*

1784 *England begins importing American cotton.*

1790 *Over 90 percent of America's work force is engaged in agriculture.*

1793 *Eli Whitney's cotton gin revolutionizes the cotton industry.*

1798 *John Chapman begins his career as Johnny Appleseed in the Ohio Valley.*

George Washington's Stubborn New Breed

In 1785 — after serving his country during the Revolutionary War and before his service as its first president — George Washington was spending time at his beloved Mount Vernon. It was perhaps the place where he found his greatest satisfaction, for as one visitor that year commented, "Washington's greatest pride was to be thought the first farmer in America."

The owner of 8,000 acres in the Tidewater region of Virginia, Washington was a tireless experimenter, ever seeking better ways of raising crops and livestock. He had come up with several designs for plows, as well as one for a drill that automatically placed seed in the furrow. And he was one of the first large-scale Virginia farmers to convert his fields to wheat production, declaring tobacco to be a money-losing, soil-sapping crop.

Among animals his foremost interest was the mule, the infertile offspring of a male donkey — or jack — and a female horse. European mules were excellent draft animals, hardier and cheaper to keep than horses, but American mules were a puny lot. What our farmers needed, Washington concluded was "an excellent race of mules . . . a race of extraordinary goodness."

At that time the finest jacks in the world were raised in Spain, but their export was prohibited by law. When the king of Spain learned of Washington's quest, however, he decided to make an exception and, in 1785, sent the first of two prize jacks. But when it came time to breed, the animal showed little interest in Washington's mares. Writing to his friend Lafayette in France, Washington noted wryly that the king of Spain "cannot be less moved by female allurements. . . . Or when prompted, can proceed with more deliberation and majestic solemnity to the work of procreation." The problem was solved when Washington discovered that the jack had to be stimulated by a female donkey before he would mate.

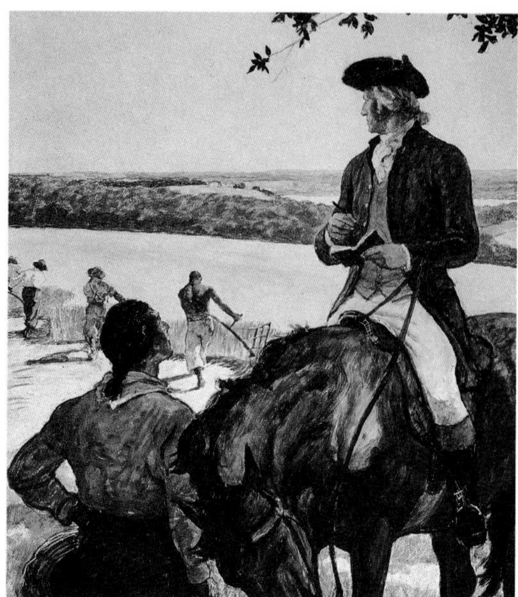

In the 1940's, illustrator N. C. Wyeth memorialized George Washington's role as progressive farmer. Dedicated to the problems of crop and livestock production, Washington kept close accounts and corresponded weekly with his overseers even while he served in office.

The other Spanish jack arrived, and Lafayette sent three more animals from the island of Malta. While the Spanish jacks produced powerful farm animals, the Maltese strain was somewhat smaller and was easily ridden with a saddle. Washington was delighted, for between the two he felt he had found the perfect mule. Breeding his jacks throughout the South, his efforts vastly improved the lot of the American farmer.

Apostle of the Good Earth

"The farmer who takes over a desolate farm, ruined by some evil and ignorant predecessor, and turns it into a Paradise of beauty and abundance is one of the greatest of artists." So wrote novelist Louis Bromfield as he described his own 18-year crusade to transform his Ohio farm into a modern-day paradise.

Born in Ohio in 1896, Bromfield was a descendant of four generations of farmers and grew up with a profound love of the land. He had every intention of following in his ancestors' footsteps, but after studying writing in college and penning several successful novels, his career took him far from Ohio, to Paris and Bombay.

His years abroad, however, did nothing to diminish his reverence for the farm. Living in France with his young family as World War II approached, he was convinced that "the nearest thing to security that unstable man could still have was the land." He shipped his family home to Ohio, bought three adjoining run-down farms, and combined them into a single farm that he named Malabar, recalling time he had spent on the Malabar Coast of India.

With nearly 1,000 acres to work, Bromfield made his farm a kind of social experiment where shareholders were invited to engage in cooperative farming and live off the land. In reviving Malabar, he hoped to show others how to restore depleted land to productivity. He wrote extensively about his theories and published four books on them, including *Malabar Farm* and *Out of the Earth,* that won him a wide audience.

What troubled him most were conservative, old-fashioned farmers who, in adhering to outmoded methods, posed "a menace to the survival of our civilization." He argued instead for strict adherence to the latest methods of crop rotation and soil conservation.

Attracted by Bromfield's reputation as an ecological guru, thousands of visitors flocked to Malabar Farm. Yet for all his good intentions Bromfield never succeeded in making the farm the economically independent unit he envisioned. His ideas, however, were sufficiently respected that after his death in 1956, the farm continued as the Bromfield Ecological Center and is now owned by the state of Ohio.

The Grandest Farm in the Land

When they married in the 1880's, Eliza "Lila" Vanderbilt and Dr. William Seward Webb set about buying up 3,800 acres of Vermont farmland on a scenic point of land that extended into Lake Champlain. Not content with developing just another rural estate for their personal enjoyment, the couple had every intention of working the property, which they called Shelburne Farms.

New Yorkers with no knowledge of farming, the Webbs nevertheless had a noble vision. They intended to expose their neighbors to state-of-the-art agricultural methods and help make Vermont a center of modern farming. Since Lila anticipated a substantial inheritance from her father, railroad magnate William Henry Vanderbilt, the couple could afford to plan such ventures.

Dr. Webb's focus at Shelburne was horses, which in the 1890's were still the principal means of transport. Indiscriminate breeding, he believed, had led to degeneration of the carriage horse. To set things right, Webb had architect Robert H. Robertson design a breeding barn that could stable up to 300 animals. The central exercise ring in the building measured 375 feet long by 85 feet wide, which made it the largest unsupported interior space in the nation. The couple also built what they called the farm barn, a cavernous five-story structure that had a central area half again as long as a football field and a loft that could store 1,500 tons of hay.

Sadly, Webb's breeding venture was doomed from the start. Vermonters were skeptical of farming advice from a city fellow, and in any case, the new horseless carriage soon rendered the carriage horse all but obsolete. So the Webbs turned their efforts to agriculture and grew much of the produce served in the New York Central Railroad's dining cars.

At its peak Shelburne Farms employed 500 people, many of whom lived on and ate off the land. Undeniably grandiose, it was at the same time among the finest modern farms in America.

Shelburne Farms was nothing if not grand. The breeding barn was one of three enormous barns on the property. The grounds were designed in part by Frederick Law Olmsted, who also created New York City's Central Park.

1817 *Henry Clay imports the country's first Hereford cattle.*

1834 *Cyrus McCormick patents the grain reaper.*

1837 *John Deere's steel plow opens the Great Plains to sodbusting farmers.*

1842 *America's first grain elevator is built in Buffalo, New York.*

1862 *The Homestead Act grants western acreage to farming families.*

1864 *Russian settlers introduce durum wheat in the Dakotas.*

1867 *The Patrons of Husbandry — later to be known as the National Grange — is organized.*

1880 *For the first time less than half of the American work force is engaged in farming.*

1892 *Gasoline tractors are introduced.*

1905 *Researchers devise the first practical milking machine.*

1916 *Techniques are developed for growing modern hybrid seed corn.*

1922 *The first electric incubator for eggs is patented.*

1935 *The one-man combine is invented.*

1950 *Only 11 percent of America's work force is employed in agriculture.*

The Farmer's Friend

Under the inspired management of Orange Judd, *American Agriculturist* was as attractive as it was forthright and informative.

Orange Judd came to his publishing career in the best Horatio Alger style. The fourth of 11 children born to hardscrabble farmers near Niagara Falls, New York, Judd was raised to "work hard, to farm well, and to understand the farmer's interests." He worked his way through Wesleyan College in Connecticut, went on to study agricultural science at Yale, and then met A. B. Allen, the publisher of *American Agriculturist,* who recognized Judd's potential and hired him as an editor in 1853.

Judd set about his new tasks with the diligence, discipline, and determination that characterized all his endeavors. He not only improved the magazine's articles with information on scientific farming, but also pitched in with general office work, wrapping and addressing every issue for the original 812 subscribers. By 1856 the young man had saved up $226 and bought out the owners.

For the magazine's credo Judd adopted a quotation from George Washington: "Agriculture is the most healthful, the most useful, and the most noble employment of man." And of woman, he might have added, for in addition to practical advice on crops, livestock, and equipment, *American Agriculturist* offered tips on ways to speed the chores of farm wives and brighten the often hard lives of their families. Under Judd's clear-eyed, plainspoken stewardship, the struggling periodical became America's foremost farming monthly, with a circulation that soon topped 100,000.

American Agriculturist did more than publish good advice. An avowed enemy of fraud, Judd was one of the first editors to screen advertisements for false claims. He regularly alerted readers to charlatans in a column that — with typical forthrightness — he headlined "Sundry Humbugs." He also created a crop reporting system that is still used internationally, and provided funds for the first agricultural experiment station, at Wesleyan College. Judd is credited as well with creating America's sorghum industry. Impressed with sorghum as a valuable crop, he imported seed from Europe and gave it away to more than 20,000 readers. But the self-described "thoroughly practical farmer" was also a bit of a romantic at heart. As part of his crusade to enhance the farmer's life, Judd distributed 3 million packets of flower seeds to his subscribers.

The Seed and Soil Specials

Giving new meaning to the term "rolling stock," railroad companies helped colleges woo farmers with the very latest in scientific agriculture.

Though farm technology was advancing with each year, educators at the turn of the 20th century found it almost impossible to reach rank-and-file farmers who had little, if any, faith in "book farming." Their unlikely ally in spreading the word about up-to-date agriculture turned out to be the railroad industry, which was eager to help farmers increase yields and so increase rail shipments. Working together, the two came up with an innovative solution: taking the college to the countryside to demonstrate the benefits of the new technology. The schools created an assortment of road shows targeted to specific audiences; the railroads provided the transportation and publicized the shows.

The first of the teaching trains began rolling in 1904; within two years they had appeared in 21 states, and by 1911, the peak year, 62 different tours were in operation, carrying 740 lecturers over 35,705 miles to almost a million people. The Arkansas hog-raising country was treated to visits from the "Squealer Special"; the "Boll Weevil Special" threaded through the Cotton Belt. A typical traveling unit might rival a gypsy caravan with its collection of lowing or cackling livestock, catalogs of goods, and lively personnel.

The locomotive lecturers were carefully chosen for their agricultural knowledge and oratorical skill — they sometimes had mere 30-minute stopovers in which to make their points. In towns where the trains stayed overnight, the classroom cars filled quickly, often to overflowing. Demonstrations proved even more powerful than words. A champion milk-producing Holstein that toured Missouri in the spring of 1911 inspired the rhyme: "No halo rests upon the brow / Of this exalted, queenly cow, / Yet thronging thousands vie to see / This bovine type of royalty."

The "colleges on wheels" were a brilliant solution to a short-term need. Enthusiasm for them began to fade in the teens, but in their heyday the trains successfully demonstrated the results that could be achieved through scientific agriculture. Thanks to the pioneering effort of the schools and railroads, farmers demanded even more information, and cooperative extension and county agent services sprang up to provide it. As one observer noted, the disappearance of the teaching train "in reality marked its final success."

On the Air

One self-proclaimed "Hill-Billie out in the sticks" swore that radio was "a blessing direct from God" — and he was not alone in that sentiment. Living far from urban centers and having only rudimentary sources of information, farmers were too often handicapped by ignorance of the latest developments in their industry. Then, on December 15, 1920, the Department of Agriculture, using a powerful navy transmitter in Arlington, Virginia, began daily broadcasts of market prices for grain and hay, livestock, produce, and dairy products.

The results were electrifying, for the broadcasts gave farmers the information they needed to conduct their business efficiently in a volatile economic environment. It helped them avoid situations like that in the often-told tale of a rancher who sent his sheep to market only to discover that the price they fetched was less than the cost of the shipping. Pressed to send money to cover the shortfall, he hotly retorted that he hadn't any money, only more sheep.

Weather reports saved farm families labor and materials by helping them schedule their work. In 1923 Secretary of Agriculture Henry C. Wallace could claim that radio weather warnings had saved $10 million for Illinois farmers and $4 million of Arkansas livestock.

Radio's effect on the multimillion-dollar farm industry was so profound that in 1921 its regulation passed from the navy — which at one point declared commercial broadcasting a "frivolous use of the nation's atmosphere" — to the Department of Commerce. Farmers expressed their enthusiasm by purchasing radios: between 1920 and 1926 ownership rose from 100,000 or so to more than half a million sets. To meet the spiraling demand, a number of commercial and university stations began airing market information, crop and weather forecasts, and other farm advisories in their own regions.

But radio's benefits were more than just economic. As Senator Arthur Capper of Kansas commented in 1932: "To the farmer, radio . . . is the sunrise devotional service, the first edition of his morning newspaper . . . the stock and grain market. . . . To the farmer's wife, radio is the cooking school . . . community club, and evening at the theater. To the farmer's children, it is the comic strip, the home teacher, a ringside seat at big-league sports, the school of the air, and the white lights of Broadway."

Radios were such invaluable companions and advisers that farmers even took them along into the fields. The combination of broadcast information and entertainment brightened the day for this New Jersey family in 1923.

Legend and Lore

Residents of the Great Plains, it seems, had imaginations as fertile as their soil. According to one proud booster, all you had to do was "Tickle the land with a hoe and the crop laughs to the harvest."

Here farmers claimed they had to set ripening melons on sleds; otherwise, the rapidly growing vines would drag the fruit across the fields, scraping and scarring it in the process. Pigs and cows were sheltered inside pumpkins of gargantuan proportions so that they could feast happily on the endlessly renewing pulp. And chickens, it was said, were so productive it took only eight eggs to make a full dozen.

The tale was also told of a boy who climbed a cornstalk and was stranded there because the corn grew up faster than he could climb down. In vain his father chopped at the stalk — but it shot up so quickly he couldn't hit the same spot twice. The only thing that saved the lad was the fact that, in the end, the corn was growing so fast that it pulled itself out by the roots.

COUNTRY WAYS

By the late 1800's some 1,200 agricultural societies all across the country were participating in state and county fairs. At the Danbury, Connecticut, fair in 1910 (above), one man paused to examine a giant squash. A daredevil provided ballooning displays (above right) in Otsego County, New York, early in this century. Currier and Ives caught the excitement of harness racing at a fairground in the 1890's (right).

A Fair to Remember

Banker, merchant, student of languages, and all-around showman, Elkanah Watson retired in his late 40's to pursue a new passion: scientific agriculture. Stocking his Pittsfield, Massachusetts, farm with little-known breeds of cattle, sheep, and swine, he soon decided to share the fruits of his experiments with interested neighbors. "In the Fall of 1807," Watson later recalled, "I was induced to notify an exhibition under the great elm tree in the public square." All that he exhibited that first time out were two Spanish merino sheep, but local response was so enthusiastic that in 1810 Watson sponsored a community cattle show. Then, a year later, he founded the Berkshire Agricultural Society to ensure that the show would be an annual event.

Unlike earlier fairs — which were primarily markets — Watson's focused on exhibits of improved seeds and demonstrations of new machinery, as well as on prize livestock. Understanding that an educational show had to be fun if it was to attract a crowd, he also included entertainment. There was a farmers' and mechanics' parade complete with brass band, and competitions (with cash prizes) that showcased everything from plowing to pickle-making and penmanship. When he discovered that many of the farm women were too shy to claim the rewards for their baked goods and handcrafts, Watson had his wife send out invitations, which courtesy obliged the women to accept.

Horse races provided excitement and much-needed income at the fairs, while oratory by local notables ensured a degree of intellectual uplift. For farmers' sons and daughters, however, the high point of each year's fair came at the end, with the "grand pastoral ball."

Watson soon lost interest in his farm , selling it in 1816 to move to Albany, New York. But even after his return to the city, he continued to promote farming societies and fairs, and within a few decades his idea caught on across the country. Rural families loved the break from their hard-working routines. More important, in an era before agricultural colleges, state and county fairs played an invaluable role in bringing new tools and techniques to farmers.

Merino Mania

Few animals were in such demand in the early 1800's as merino sheep, a Spanish breed prized for the quality and abundance of its fleece. Since Spain forbade their sale to foreigners, any American who got hold of contraband sheep was quick to breed them.

What began as a businesslike interest burgeoned into a national mania in 1807: an embargo on British textiles made everyone eager to get into wool production, and prices for merinos soared as high as $1,000 each. In 1810 the Spanish king was unseated just long enough to lose some 20,000 sheep to export, causing a dip in the value of American merinos. But the madness persisted until 1815, when the effect of the influx of Spanish sheep was finally felt, leaving American farmers with flocks of sorely devalued sheep.

Sioux City's corn palaces became increasingly fanciful with each passing year. The 1890 palace was built in Islamic style, with the colors furnished entirely by the grains and grasses themselves. The dome, for instance was made of red, calico, white, yellow, and blue corn.

The Capital of Corn

The drought of 1887 decimated harvests all over the Midwest except, miraculously, around Sioux City, Iowa. Rain had kept the fields green there and brought in a bumper crop of corn. To celebrate, a band of volunteers took 300,000 feet of lumber and 20,000 bushels of corn and built something such as the folks of Sioux City had never seen before — a many-spired Moorish palace decorated entirely with nature's bounty.

With amazing ingenuity workers covered the building's exterior with rosettes and tilelike patterns fashioned from ears of corn of many colors, combined with oats, wheat, and other grains. The roof was thatched with green cornstalks, panels depicting agricultural scenes crowned every doorway, and the whole structure was guarded by a figure of a corn god, Mondamin — made, of course, entirely from corn.

Inside, beneath the central dome, women pieced together a mosaic harvest scene dominated by the goddess Ceres. Kernels covered the furnishings, and sheaves of grain were fashioned into cornices and balconies. For souvenirs they crafted ties and artificial flowers from corn husks.

Six days of Indian dances, fireworks, and parades drew 140,000 visitors, including President Cleveland, who reportedly pronounced the palace "the first new thing" he had seen on his American tour. This success persuaded the city fathers to repeat the festival, and every autumn for the next four years saw a bigger, more elaborate corn palace. The publicity fueled a real estate boom, and for a time Sioux City hoped it might become the second metropolis of the Midwest. But a flood in 1892, followed by a depression in 1893, put an end to palace building in Iowa.

Women did most of the work at quilting bees, but the men often joined in when it came time for refreshments and talk. As an unknown folk artist made clear in this painting, young and old alike could have fun at a bee.

When Many Hands Made Light Work

Since long distances and long hours made neighborly visits few on the farm, community bees — both for work and for pleasure — were welcome affairs.

Rugged individualism may have been a hallmark of old-time country folk, but neighborly cooperation was also an essential for getting many jobs done. Because some tasks entailed more muscle than a family could muster, "bees" were organized and the community worked together whenever the need arose.

All sorts of chores from wood-cutting to sheep-shearing could prompt a bee, but neighbors met as much for the fun as they did for doing the work. Liquor and horseplay were generally part of the action when men gathered for tasks such as rolling felled trees off newly cleared fields. Women's bees ran more to tea and gossip — and there was apt to be plenty to catch up on.

The gatherings also offered the rare chance to enjoy a bit of mixed company. Corn huskings, for instance, were enlivened by group singing and playful competition. The host might hide a whiskey jug under the corn to serve as a reward for a job well done, and the boy who found a red ear could claim a kiss from the girl of his choice.

Barn raisings, the most impressive of all bees in terms of the task accomplished, also might double as occasions for romance. It was the host's job to have all the timbers prepared in advance so that they could be assembled swiftly. Then on the appointed day neighbors arrived for the bee, the men with their tools and the women with pots and provisions.

As the women exchanged news and cooked, the men put together sections of the frame and lifted them into place with poles and ropes. With many skilled hands at work, a day often saw completion of the basic structure. Then, when darkness finally fell, the whole party assembled to feast and, later, to dance by the light of pine-knot torches. And understanding elders looked the other way as their sons and daughters lingered in the dark for the rarest of all country get-togethers — the chance for a young couple to be alone.

An important fringe benefit of participation in bees was getting paid in kind when you needed help. As these Vermonters knew, trying to raise a barn unassisted would be next to impossible.

Swing Your Partner

At the same time that English settlers were introducing more serious customs in America, they also found time for dancing. Traditional country dances in which participants formed two lines, faced their partners, and performed their bows, turns, and promenades were popular with colonists everywhere. George Washington, for one, was known to cut quite a figure on the dance floor. (He was especially partial to a dance later called the Virginia reel.) Any tavern big enough to have a dance hall lured in customers by hiring fiddlers who were familiar with the latest tunes.

Both farm folk and town folk enjoyed the same dances. The only difference was that as city folk became increasingly concerned with elegance of style and the perfecting of particular steps, young men and women in the country maintained an older tradition by just kicking up their heels and having a grand time. But even country traditions changed in time. After France came to America's aid during the Revolution, French dancing became all the rage. The steps were similar to the English steps, but the French dances — *quadrilles* and the less formal *cotillions* — were performed in squares.

While rural New Englanders were among the few who continued to do the old-fashioned line dances, settlers traveling west took square dancing with them. It did not remain the same for long, however. For one thing, new American songs with titles like "The Arkansas Traveler" and "Turkey in the Straw" began to dominate. More importantly, the dancers no longer memorized movements to particular songs: the fiddler was in command, calling out the steps at random. And if the steps retained their French names — *allemande*, *chassez*, and *dos-à-dos* — the commands themselves sounded thoroughly American: "Swing in the center, then break that pair. Lady goes on and gent stays there."

In his *I Got a Gal on Sourwood Mountain* artist Thomas Hart Benton captured the breathless pleasure of swing dancing accompanied by a fiddle.

Missouri Meerschaums

Furniture was what Henry Tibbe usually made in his Washington, Missouri, workshop. But when a friend asked him to turn a bag of corncobs into pipes on his lathe one day in 1869, he was happy to oblige. The idea was not new: Indians had taught settlers how to whittle pipes from corncobs long before. But Tibbe mechanized the process — and discovered that at two for a nickel, pipes sold faster than his furniture did.

Searching for ways to improve his design and make the pipe's bowl a little smoother, Tibbe tried coating it with plaster of paris. Then, sanding the bowl and giving it a coat of shellac, he found that it looked a lot like a costly, imported meerschaum clay pipe. And according to devotees of the corncob pipe — who have included generals Pershing and MacArthur, authors Mark Twain and Carl Sandburg, and even Popeye and Herbert Hoover — these native-grown pipes smoke just as smoothly as the fancy imports.

In the early decades of this century, Tibbe's successors in Missouri were shipping out more than 28 million pipes a year. Even today, Tibbe's factory is still in business, and the town of Washington is renowned as the place where corncob pipes are made. No one knows just why this one small center in Missouri produces the very best corn for pipes. Scientists, however, have long since perfected a special hybrid for the job and call it pipe corn number 14.

NATIVE TONGUE

TALKIN' TURKEY

Our roots go back to the land and, often enough, so does our language. Imagine, for instance, what a country cousin might write home when visiting the city. . . .

Dear Zeke,

Land sakes! I've got to give you the dirt on poor cousin Slicker. I took the bull by the horns and came down to the city to see him. Well! He's all cooped up in two lousy rooms but thinks they're the cream of the crop. Rent's dirt cheap, he says, and he likes sitting on his stoop before he hits the hay. (Real porches are scarce as hen's teeth here, and the sidewalk's a pigsty.)

Well, Zeke, he thinks his job is the pick of the litter. He went on and on about it, really shoveled it on. But he just works for the city, cleaning up after all the horses. Some peaches-and-cream job! Horsefeathers! Hogwash!

Bein' that I've known him since he was knee high to a grasshopper, I tried to talk sense to him. "Slicker," sez I, "farm this job out and come home or you won't ever amount to a hill of beans." (I do get corny sometimes.) But at least somebody talked turkey to that cotton-pickin' fool. I always say, when you do something, you gotta do it whole hog.

Your cousin,
Jethro

Seeing Was Believing

In the early 1900's Americans knew that describing the "one that got away" was one thing — but showing off its picture was something else again.

"Dear Friend . . . I have decided to remain in Kansas" began the message on a 1908 picture postcard. "Cornstalks are so big," it continued, "they're cutting them up into railroad ties." As proof of this assertion, the photo on the card showed a farmer taking aim at a helicopter-size grasshopper hovering with a six-foot-long ear of corn in its clutches.

The card was one of thousands of larger-than-life postcards that small-town photographers produced early in the century. If local crops or livestock could be photographed, they figured, they were fair game for exaggeration through technical trickery. The subject might be fruit crates filled with single strawberries, a family living in a watermelon, or bullfrogs ridden like broncos. Embellished with an appropriate caption, the cards were visual equivalents of the kind of story that begins with lines like "You think these pigs are big? Shucks, I saw some the other day that make these guys look like field mice."

Not surprisingly, most of the cards originated in the Midwest and the West, where tall tales like those of Paul Bunyan and Pecos Bill were an age-old tradition and storytelling was considered a form of entertainment. Pioneers on the plains had faced such relentless hardship that poking fun at themselves became a means of survival. Their weather was meaner, their blights more brutal, and their fields more fertile than anything known elsewhere. "I'd plant a dollar but for the danger of getting a crop of eagles," scrawled one postcard writer from Kansas.

By the early 1900's photography had become relatively simple, and even small towns were apt to have a studio of sorts. If portrait business was slow, a photographer with a sense of humor could fall back on tradition. By piecing together parts from several pictures, then photographing the whole and printing it on special postcard paper, he created a new tall tale. Best of all, there was the chance that the city slicker back East who received the card just might believe it.

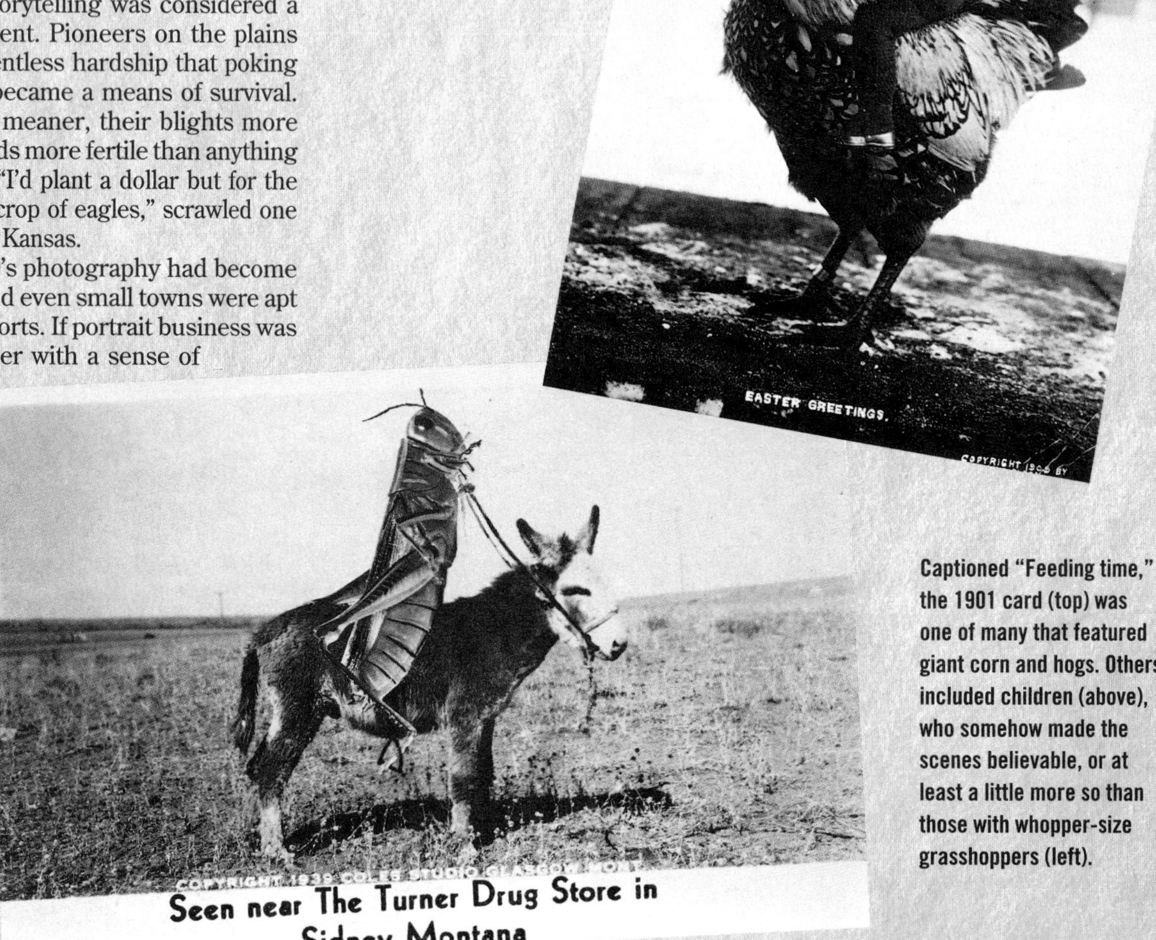

Seen near The Turner Drug Store in
Sidney Montana

Captioned "Feeding time," the 1901 card (top) was one of many that featured giant corn and hogs. Others included children (above), who somehow made the scenes believable, or at least a little more so than those with whopper-size grasshoppers (left).

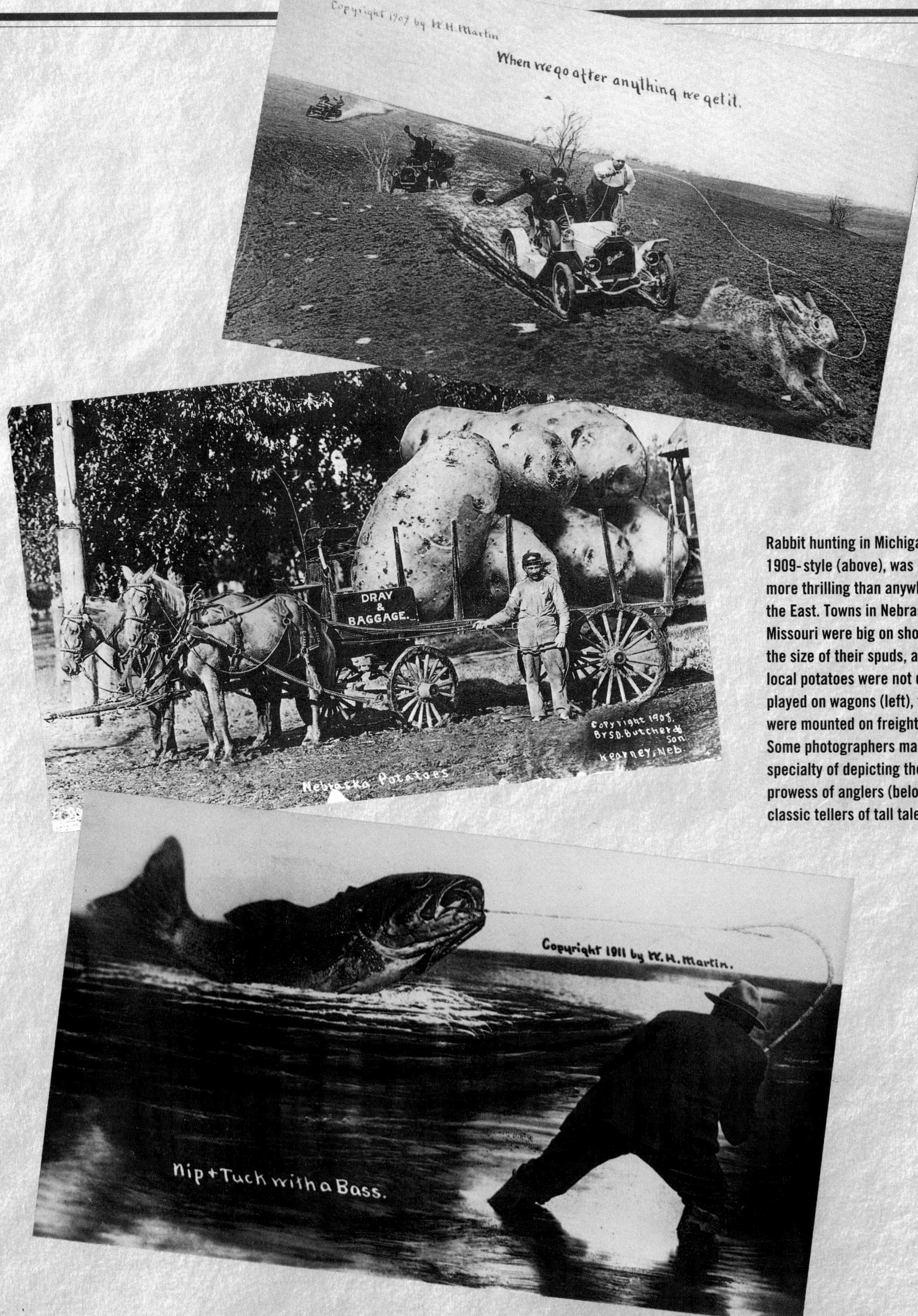
Copyright 1909 by W.H. Martin
When we go after anything we get it.
DRAY & BAGGAGE.
Copyright 1908. By S.D. Butcher & Son. Kearney, Neb.
Nebraska Potatoes
Copyright 1911 by W.H. Martin.
Nip + Tuck with a Bass.

Rabbit hunting in Michigan, 1909-style (above), was clearly more thrilling than anywhere in the East. Towns in Nebraska and Missouri were big on showing off the size of their spuds, and if the local potatoes were not displayed on wagons (left), they were mounted on freight cars. Some photographers made a specialty of depicting the prowess of anglers (below), the classic tellers of tall tales.

In 1902 artist E. L. Henry recalled a scene from his youth in New York — a visit by a country peddler whose cart was brimming with brooms and almost every other necessity for keeping house.

Back-Door Traders

Accused of spreading "raging diseases" and reviled as "tricky and contemptible . . . knaves," peddlers were widely scorned by city dwellers in the 19th century. But in frontier America, where general stores were few and the most basic necessities hard to come by, a peddler with his treasures was always welcome. Never mind if his wares were overpriced or travel worn: to the isolated farm family he was a source of news and gossip as well as goods.

Most of the early peddlers hailed from New England, particularly Connecticut, where many of their products — from tinware to clocks — were manufactured. In the first three decades of the 1800's, at least half the men in Hartford are thought to have tried peddling. It was, after all, a job that required no apprenticeship and little investment. When European immigrants began pouring into the country at midcentury, many turned to peddling for similar reasons.

Often traveling on foot with a 60-pound pack slung over each shoulder, these strong-legged merchants penetrated the most distant settlements to sell everything from sewing goods and spices to tobacco and tools. "I have seen them on the peninsula of Cape Cod and in the neighborhood of Lake Erie," wrote one observer in 1821. "They make their way to Detroit . . . and, if I mistake not, to New Orleans and St. Louis." Since their customers were apt to have little or no cash on hand, peddlers were usually willing to take grain, pelts, or "what-have-you" in hard-driven exchange, with the hope of cashing in big later.

By 1860 the ranks of peddlers had swollen to some 17,000. Most by then were traveling in horse-drawn wagons, which meant they could carry larger goods such as kettles, furniture, and bolts of fabric. Still known for their quick wit and the occasional shady deal, peddlers had, in fact, emerged as a species of folk hero. One English commentator marveled that when a customer was cheated, Americans, as often as not, blamed the victim for being gullible. The peddler, meanwhile, was permitted to escape "with the fruits of his imposition" and the excuse that "it was only a Yankee peddler trick."

Lords of the Open Road

Once peddlers proved it was possible to sell their wares in remote parts of the country, countless specialty vendors joined them. Throughout most of the 19th century, in fact, a veritable tide of itinerant workers traveled America's dusty and rutted roads.

Some, like circuit-riding preachers and judges, were men of considerable standing. They followed set routes and schedules that were dictated by the churches and courts they represented. For all their rank, however, they enjoyed little privilege. One preacher recalled how he "plunged through swamps, swam swollen streams, lay out at night, wet, weary and hungry" during 50 years of service. Much the same was true of early Supreme Court justices, who rode 1,000 miles or more each spring and fall, taking their "horseback opinions" to outlying districts.

Other itinerants wandered unheralded and at random, stopping wherever they found a receptive household. These men tended to be craftsmen or artisans who, perhaps for lack of experience or because of hard times, could not make a go of their trade at home. Some worked with the customer's own materials. When the candlemaker appeared with his molds, for instance, the housewife would bring out the tallow and beeswax she had saved throughout the year. And it was the farmer's responsibility to supply the cobbler with the leather for his family's shoes. Other artisans, too — such as tinkers, clock repairmen, carpenters, and even rat-catchers — needed only their own tools.

The occasional doctors, dentists, and lawyers who took to the road were called — with some generosity — the professionals. What they lacked in skill was often made up for in color. One celebrated Connecticut "doctor" in the late 18th century, Sylvanus Fancher, not only specialized in promoting the new smallpox vaccine, but invented a device for inoculation. It was for his traveling costume, however, that Fancher was best known. He wore "velvet small clothes," recalled a contemporary, "a parti-coloured waistcoat from which dangled a half dozen watch-chains and trinkets . . . and a faded blue cloak — all of these surmounted by a slouched hat overhanging green goggles."

One-Stop Shopping, Country Style

As communities grew and the demand for goods increased, general stores with well-stocked shelves sprang up in small-town America. By 1840 (when there still were only 26 states), Americans were shopping in more than 55,000 stores, most of them general stores.

Although each was unique in character, all had one thing in common: a near monopoly in their community. Prices as a result were high and the selections of individual items were limited. But the range of goods that the shopkeepers kept in stock was indeed general. Whether you needed clothing, hardware, medicines, farm tools, notions, kerosene, or even a new set of dishes, you probably could find it at the general store.

All manner of perishable foods also were stocked. Store owner J. W. Renoud, for instance, announced in an advertisement in 1859, "I've fine Codfish, Mackerel & Starch / Tobacco, choicest brand. / And Ginger, Pepper, Chocolate, / As good as in the land." Food was typically doled out by weight from barrels, sacks, and boxes, with little regard for cleanliness or purity. Open containers of coffee, lard, salt fish, molasses, grains, pickles, crackers, and peppermints all contributed to the store's pungent aroma.

A substantial part of the annual sales at general stores was made on credit, particularly just before harvest. This was especially true in the post–Civil War South, where merchants offered credit to farmers in exchange for liens against their crops. Translated into coupons redeemable only for merchandise from the general store, these loans often entailed exorbitant interest rates.

Despite sometimes testy relations between shopkeeper and customers, a town's general store was its social center as well. One New Englander remembered the store in his hometown as an all-male clubhouse at day's end. Dubbing it a "Yankee House of Commons," he described it as a wondrous place in which otherwise taciturn men expressed themselves freely. Their favorite mode, when no women were present, was a ribald story told in "the raciest speech God or Satan ever put in the mouth of man."

One of the classic images of bygone America is that of small-town idlers chewing the fat at the general store. For country dwellers the store was an ideal place to catch up with news of the world as well as local gossip.

So Long, General Store

Mounting complaints about high prices and limited choices at rural stores eventually led to a whole new concept in retailing: shopping by mail. Introduced in 1872, the first mass-marketing catalog was produced by Chicago-based Montgomery, Ward and Company. The firm began with $2,400 in capital and a one-page flyer listing 163 items that was mailed to members of the National Grange, America's largest farm organization.

Store owners ridiculed the idea of mail-order merchandise, but shoppers loved it. Tens of thousands of farmers opted for the convenience, improved selection, better prices, and the company's pledge: "satisfaction guaranteed, or your money back." With success Ward's catalog grew, becoming a voluminous "wish book."

It was not long before other mail-order houses appeared, most notably Sears, Roebuck and Company, which opened for business in 1893 and surpassed Montgomery Ward in catalog pages and sales in seven years. Then, with the institution of rural free mail delivery in 1896 and parcel post in 1913, there ceased to be good reason for making major purchases locally, and many a general store faded into history.

Old Sawbones

From the colonial era until the early 20th century, rural medicine was a rough-and-ready practice that all too often left unanswered the question as to who was the unluckier one — the patient or the doctor. Country physicians became inured to exhausting treks over rough roads (or no roads at all) in order to reach their patients. "A fatiguing journey is not a good preliminary to trying an operation, but we were a tough lot and could and did good work when we were dead on our feet," recalled one veteran of the horse-and-buggy era. The surgery in question was usually done on the kitchen table, sometimes with such primitive instruments as knives or small saws. Until ether and laughing gas became more widely available in the mid-19th century, the operation was likely to be performed with nothing more than a good stiff shot of whiskey to serve as painkiller.

Country doctors often spent more time traveling to and from the sick than they did in actually attending them. Rural roads were rudimentary and transportation slow, making the wait for the doctor a lengthy vigil.

Physicians' fees varied widely. Some charged $1 for sitting through the night with a dying patient; others asked $5 for delivering a child and $25 for treating cholera. Travel costs of $1 a mile might be requested, but when payment came — if it came — it was more likely to be in the form of farm produce or services than cash.

Until the end of the 19th century, medical training was lax, licensing requirements were nonexistent, and "anybody who chose could practice," wrote Dr. Samuel C. Waters of Middletown, Indiana. Dr. Waters, like some of his colleagues, had taken "three five-month courses of medical college"; other would-be doctors simply took to making calls with a practicing physician. Despite a lack of training and an array of medicines that ranged from ineffectual to lethal, the country doctor had a precious gift to offer his patients, many of whom were beyond cure in any case. As one veteran medic recalled, "It was this silent faithfulness of the old doctor in the hour of grief that endeared him to the families that he served."

The doctors' exertions to tend their patients, combined with constant exposure to disease and minimal hygiene, often led to their own untimely deaths. But many found deep satisfaction in doing what good they could. Shortly before his death at age 71, one old-timer declared, "Just so long as I can work some and play some I want to stay the Country Doctor."

Good for What Ails You

Starting with the inevitable greeting of "Alagazam," medicine shows mesmerized audiences with a colorful blend of entertainment and bogus cures.

"You are dying, every man, woman, and child," chanted T. P. Kelley, a well-known medicine show barker. Then he demanded of the assembled crowd, "Is there some way you can delay . . . the final moment?" And sure enough, there was — the patent medicine Kelley was holding in his hand.

Like many patent medicine entrepreneurs, Kelley pitched his wares in the carnival atmosphere of the 19th-century medicine show. These traveling extravaganzas featured circus performers, brass bands, magicians, and animal acts, but the real stars of the show were the vials of patent medicine that promised cures for everything from indigestion and impotence to typhoid and tuberculosis. Although some of the bigger shows

played in cities, the most enthusiastic crowds were found in rural America, where, as one performer explained, "this was the only kind of entertainment the yokels ever got to see."

Some shows were put on by individuals, but the largest were sponsored by such patent medicine manufacturers as the Kickapoo Indian Medicine Company. Its line of best-sellers included Kickapoo Cough Syrup, Kickapoo Indian Oil, Kickapoo Worm Expeller, and most famous of all, Kickapoo Sagwa, which the company claimed was made from "the secret recipes of native American medicine men." Rival pitchmen, however, insisted that Sagwa was nothing more than a mix of aloe, herbs, and stale beer.

In truth, despite the glitter of the entertainment and the pitchmen's high-intensity spiels, the success of patent medicines may well have owed much to their high alcohol content. Some, like Lydia Pinkham's Vegetable Compound, contained nearly 18 percent spirits; another, Hostetter's Bitters, packed a walloping 44 percent. Federal regulations, starting with the Pure Food and Drug Act of 1906, forced the medicine men to abandon their claims of miracle cures, and the shows began to die out after World War I. Still, a few of the gaudy galas lingered on until the middle of the 20th century.

The Hoosier Huckster

Multitalented James Whitcomb Riley spent part of his youth painting signs, playing his guitar, and charming crowds on the medicine show circuit.

Hoosier poet James Whitcomb Riley's renowned understanding of his native Indiana, it is said, grew out of his youthful experiences touring the state as a medicine show performer. After leaving school at age 16, Riley was earning his keep by giving performances as a bogus "sightless artist" when Doc McCrillis, proprietor of Doc McCrillis's Standard Remedy Show, happened upon his act.

Impressed by the young man's show business acumen, the "doctor" granted Riley's request to join his troupe. On their summer travels Riley developed his minstrel act, and eventually joined an even larger show underwritten by Townsend's Magic Oil. Billed as the "Hoosier Wizard," Riley amused the crowds with everything from banjo routines to cartooning.

The work, if not the company, was just fine. "I am having a first rate time," Riley wrote to a friend. But he conceded that huckstering for a medicine show did not enhance his image. "I shall never forget how ashamed I was in Fortville to have a cousin of mine see me beating the bass drum with that show," he confessed. His embarrassment, however, did not prevent him from penning such ditties as "Why let pain your pleasure spoil / For want of Townsend's Magic Oil."

Hamlin invoked the legendary strength of the elephant to promote its Wizard Oil, an alleged cure-all. Manufacturers of patent medicines routinely claimed miraculous powers for their products, but their pain-relieving effect was often transitory since it derived primarily from the high alcohol content of the "medicines."

In a bid to capitalize on the Native Americans' reputation as healers, patent medicine makers used tribal names for their products (above) and staged native-inspired performances to promote their products (left).

Chapter 7

CITY LIFE

CITIES ON THE RISE

Before drawing up his plan for Washington, D.C. (above right), Pierre L'Enfant thoroughly explored the land set aside for the new Federal City. He chose Jenkins Hill for the Capitol building (shown above c. 1840), noting that it "stands as a pedestal waiting for a monument."

A Capitol Idea

In 1789 Pierre Charles L'Enfant applied to President Washington for the job of chief architect of America's new seat of government. Washington, who called L'Enfant "better qualified than anyone who has come within my knowledge," readily appointed the young French military engineer, and L'Enfant began exploring the land that had been obtained for the capital — 10 square miles of swamps and forests at the confluence of the Potomac and Anacostia Rivers.

L'Enfant came up with a design that was stunning. Rejecting a rectangular street plan proposed by Thomas Jefferson as "but a mean continance of some cool imagination," he used two striking points with views of the Potomac for the "Congress House," and the "President's House." A memorial to Washington, later the Washington Monument, was a third point in the central plan. The executive and legislative buildings were hubs for long, broad avenues and malls that radiated in all directions.

Despite his genius L'Enfant's career was short-lived. He refused to cooperate with the District commissioners, claiming that he answered only to the president. Needed revenue from the sale of lots in the new city failed to materialize when L'Enfant refused to distribute his map in time for the auction. The final blow came when the imperious architect ordered the destruction of a house foundation laid in the path of one of his grand boulevards. Less than 12 months after his arrival, L'Enfant was dismissed.

Others were given the task of completing the plan, and for several decades unregulated growth obscured the original vision. L'Enfant stalked the corrupted streets and campaigned for the purity of his plan until his death in 1825. Vindication came posthumously in 1901, when restoration of the original design was undertaken. Eight years later, in homage to L'Enfant's brilliance, his remains were disinterred and reburied on a hillside in Arlington National Cemetery overlooking the final realization of his master plan.

City of Spindles

The brand-new cotton mills at Lowell, Massachusetts, were welcomed by most of the women who worked there. As one delighted employee declared, "For the first time in this country woman's labor had a monetary value. . . . And thus a long upward step in our material civilization was taken." This bold, egalitarian stroke had come about when a group of Boston capitalists got together in the 1820's to build the first planned factory city in America. Determined to create something better than the "dark Satanic mills" and slumtowns of the English Midlands, they built Lowell.

Located at Pawtucket Falls on the Merrimack River, Lowell's mills lined the river for a mile and were interconnected by some 15½ miles of canals. For their work force the mill owners turned to a previously untapped labor pool — young women of the rural middle class.

Although farm families tended to keep their unmarried daughters at home in order to protect their reputations, the mill owners did what they could to allay parental concern. Inspired by the ideals of Francis Cabot Lowell, who combined mill activities in a single complex and for whom the town was named, they constructed scores of comfortable boardinghouses where the "female operatives" would reside and spend their few leisure hours, supervised by "matrons of tried character." The city's streets were tidy and well lighted, and there was a park for recreation.

Factory conditions also were surprisingly pleasant. The women worked in sunlit brick mills amid what one cheerfully described as "the buzzing and hissing and whizzing of pulleys, and rollers and spindles." Work days, though long — 5:00 a.m. until 7:30 p.m. — were no worse than those the women had known on the farm. When not on the job, they formed "improvement clubs," took piano lessons, read books, and created the first magazine ever written exclusively by women: *The Lowell Offering.*

By the 1840's, however, the "Lowell Experiment" began to tarnish. A new generation of managers rescinded many enlightened labor policies, and the workers responded with "turnouts" — a genteel version of the strike. As conditions worsened, more-compliant immigrants replaced the spirited daughters of independent New Englanders, and by the 1860's, labor-management relations in Lowell were as bad as those found anywhere in Europe.

Though the Middlesex Mills at Lowell, Massachusetts, may seem forbiddingly utilitarian today, in 1848 they were the height of enlightened industrial architecture. A particular boon to the mill workers was the abundance of windows, which flooded the interiors with natural light.

A Dream in the Desert

If Hollywood's original developers had had their way, America's motion picture capital would still be the quietly prosperous town of lemon groves and midwestern teetotallers envisioned by Harvey Henderson Wilcox, a well-to-do Kansas prohibitionist.

Prompted by completion of the Southern Pacific Railroad link that connected southern California directly with the Midwest, Wilcox went to Los Angeles in 1883 to go into the real estate business. He guessed correctly that a land boom was in the making, and though prices in the valley had already risen to $150 an acre, the Kansas developer felt sure that he could still turn a quick profit. He acquired a 120-acre ranch seven miles west of Los Angeles in the bountiful farmlands of the Cahuenga Valley, then subdivided it into a tidy rectangular grid of 6-acre tracts and broad, tree-lined streets. Daeida Wilcox, Harvey's wife, changed the property's name from the prosaic "Cahuenga Valley–Wilcox Ranch" to "Hollywood" — a fancy name, suggestive of an English manor, that she had picked up in conversation with a stranger back East. Wilcox went her one better, planting a collection of English holly to live up to the new name.

The plants withered, but the place prospered. By 1901 Wilcox had succeeded in drawing enough like-minded buyers to bring the settlement's population to over 500. In keeping with his original philosophy, that year Hollywood was declared dry by design and residential in purpose. No dwelling could cost less than $3,000, assuring a community of fine homes.

Artist's haven

Until the arrival of the movie companies, Hollywood's best-known citizen was Paul de Longpré, a French watercolorist known for his floral still-lifes. De Longpré, who built a Moorish mansion and lavish gardens on a parcel of land traded for three paintings, attracted hundreds of tourists to Hollywood. Many of them decided to stay.

But the ban on alcohol was Hollywood's undoing. In 1911, when a motion picture crew came in search of a place to spend the winter, they found the city's only public roadhouse abandoned due to lack of trade. The rambling structure was just what the film company was looking for. They moved in lock, stock, and camera, and in a short time they changed forever the face of sleepy, small-town Hollywood.

Two years before the first movie company discovered Hollywood, the town fathers promoted its many advantages in hopes of attracting prosperous settlers.

The Venice of America

Abbott Kinney's Venice, California, featured buildings inspired by those in the Italian original. Kinney's Venice also had its own St. Mark's Square and St. Mark's Hotel (below), and visitors could see the sights aboard authentic gondolas (below right).

A lifetime of poor health sent Abbott Kinney, a wealthy New Jersey businessman, on a round-the-world quest for a favorable climate. He finally found what he was looking for in southern California and, after acquiring a large tract of land near Santa Monica, announced a startling plan. He would create a city of culture, complete with canals, on the Pacific coast — in a word, a New-World Venice.

Confounding skeptics, Kinney completed his grand vision and officially opened the town on July 4, 1905. Some 40,000 visitors strolled down avenues lined with Italian-style buildings, and walked along the banks of broad canals. They could also glide across the water in gondolas propelled by genuine Venetian gondoliers.

Though property sales were brisk, Kinney's dream of the resort as a haven for writers, artists, and thinkers never materialized. Realizing that visitors were far more interested in honky-tonk entertainment than in cultural uplift, Kinney gave them an amusement park with a giant roller coaster, camel rides, and a midway featuring the world's smallest woman.

As lighthearted as it may have been, Venice was not without problems: there were storms, fires, political turmoil, and snags such as the silt that continually clogged the canals. Still, the city's popularity remained undiminished until Kinney's death in 1920. But then it began to erode: by 1929 the filling in of the canals was begun, and before many years the "fantasy by the sea" was visited only in people's memories.

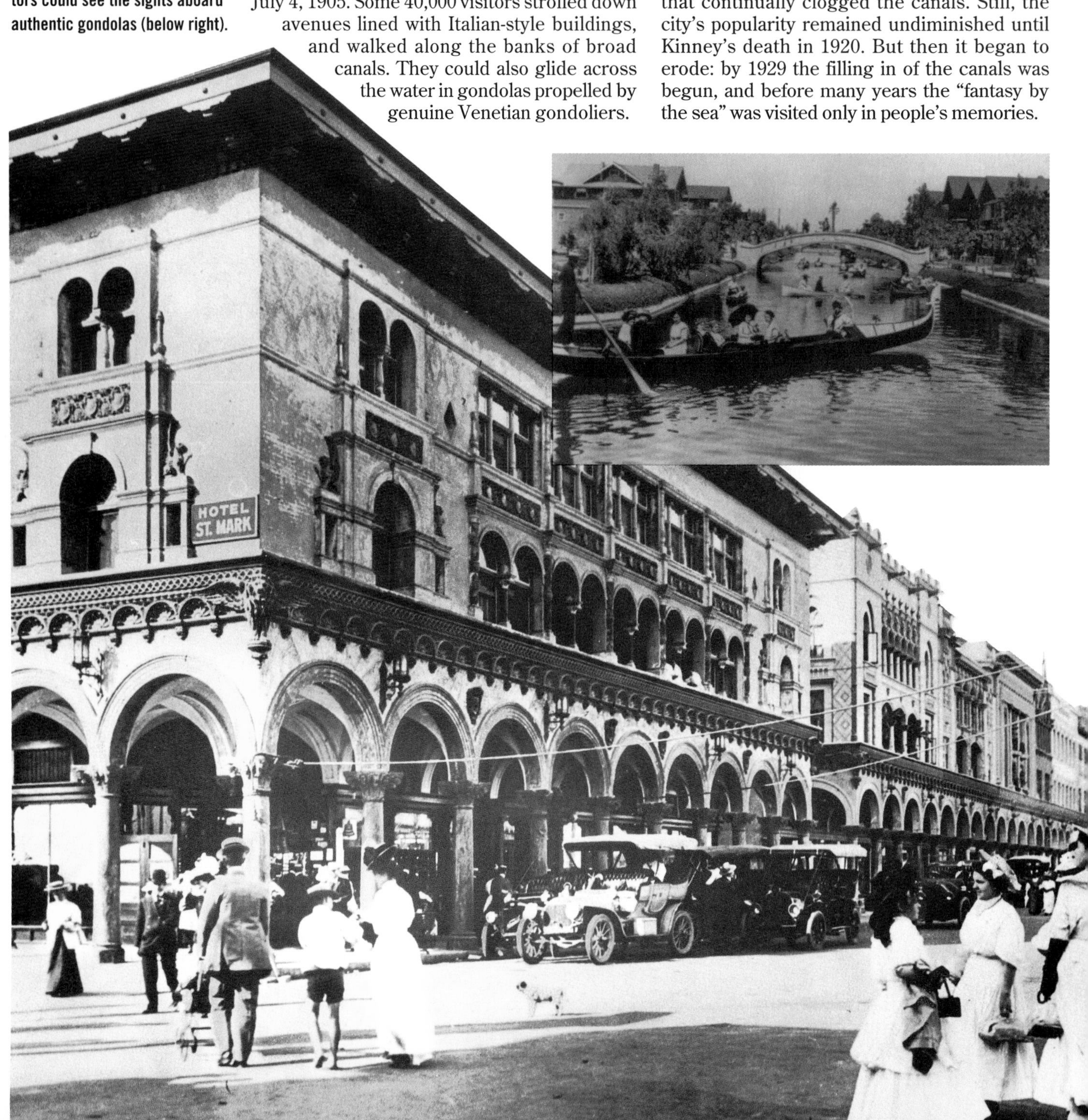

Name That Town

Chances are that Massachusetts residents no longer eat more baked beans than anyone else in the country. But for all that, Boston will be forever Beantown — and proud of it. Similarly, Cincinnati will never cease to be Porkopolis, and Cordova, Alaska, will remain the Razor Clam Capital of the World no matter what they may produce in the future.

Americans have long been fond of nicknaming their towns, a habit that shows no sign of dying out. Not all names, of course, have to do with food. Some are borne like banners advertising a town's chief industry. Danbury, Connecticut, thus became Hat City, and Huntsville, Alabama, was dubbed Rocket City. Cement City (Allentown, Pennsylvania) and Snapshot City (Rochester, New York) still rely on their namesake industries.

Other descriptive names are meant to promote tourism or tout the town's desirability as a place to live. Tillamook, Oregon, for instance, takes pride in its title as the unofficial Land of Cheese, Trees, and Ocean Breeze, while Flagstaff, Arizona, unhurriedly refers to itself as the City in the Center of the Most Amazing and Beautiful Country in the World.

Still other names fit into the find-something-interesting-to-say-about-it category: Coeur D'Alene, Idaho, for example, is the Only Town in the U.S. with an Apostrophe in Its Name. Perhaps the most tenacious place is Tombstone, Arizona — The Town Too Tough to Die.

Paper Towns and Airy Visions

Accost a farmer in these parts," wrote one 19th-century traveler in the Midwest, and "before he returns your civilities he draws from his pocket a lithographic city, and asks you to take a few building lots at one-half their value." And in fact the promotion of new towns was a popular sideline with many a farmer, because so long as there were vast tracts of empty land and investors ready to be gulled, there was money to be made. All one needed was title to some land, a survey map, and an illustration of the "town," or what one sadder-but-wiser buyer described as a "chromatic triumph of lithographed mendacity." Savvy entrepreneurs also advertised in Eastern newspapers, as few checked the accuracy of the claims.

Typical of the "paper towns" was Sumner, Kansas, where lots along the wide Missouri River were offered for sale by speculator J. P. Wheeler in 1857. In Wheeler's handsome brochure, Sumner already boasted steamboat docks, factories, churches, many fine residences, and several schools; in reality it was a dusty collection of shacks. From a population that briefly topped 2,000, Sumner sank back within a decade to 25 as most of its disappointed citizens moved on.

Not all paper towns failed to materialize, however. With hordes of settlers moving west, many were willing to accept whatever they found, turning dreams into brick-and-steel realities.

King Gillette's Metropolis

King Camp Gillette was a 39-year-old who sold bottle stoppers for a living when, in 1894, he published his socialist manifesto, *The Human Drift*. Capitalist competition, he proclaimed, not only fostered greed but also wasted human effort and was the root cause of society's ills. What was needed instead was a massive corporation made up of all the world's industries and owned by the people. Incredible benefits would result, he declared, when cooperation replaced competition, drastically reducing the need for labor. Except for a five-year stint of government service, every individual would be free to pursue personal dreams throughout his life.

An illustration of Gillette's Metropolis appeared in his 1894 book, *The Human Drift*. He envisioned a city with some 30,000 such buildings laid out in regular patterns in a parklike setting. "Compare it," he said, "with our cities of filth, crime, and misery." But Gillette's Metropolis was never to be.

Old-style cities would also become obsolete as megacities took their place. Gillette's urban ideal was his "Metropolis," designed to house upward of 60 million people in row upon row of glass-domed apartment towers. "A majestic work of art," he called it, "from sixty to seventy-five miles in length . . . a never-ending city of beauty and cleanliness."

Gillette's proposal received little notice and might have been forgotten altogether if he had not risen to sudden fame as a captain of industry. In 1901 he began manufacturing a product of his own invention: the disposable razor blade. With money no longer an obstacle, Gillette was able to devote all his energies to promoting his pet theory. But despite several more books and a barrage of publicity, he could not sell the idea. Socialists, it seemed, found the image of a multimillionaire preaching against the sins of "accumulated wealth" just a bit too much to accept.

As depicted by Maurice Prendergast, New York's Central Park (above) was a place enjoyed by New Yorkers of all classes. Dedicated to the integrity of their artistic vision, Frederick Law Olmsted and Calvert Vaux personally designed the lampposts (below) and fountains (right) that graced the landscapes in many of their projects.

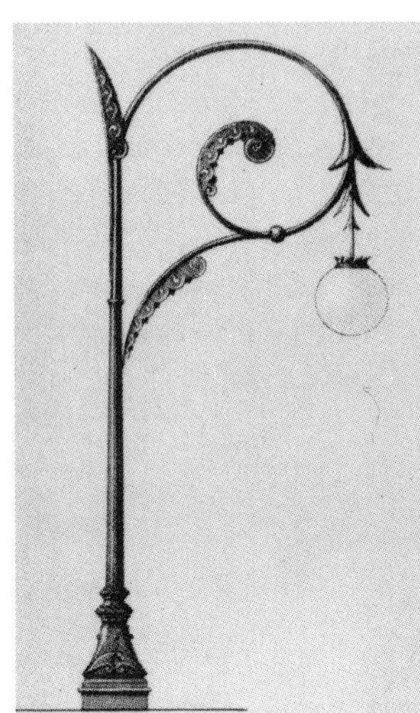

Open Spaces for City Folk

For most people, designing the nation's first great public park would be the high point of a career. But for Frederick Law Olmsted, that was just the beginning. In 1857 he and a partner, Calvert Vaux, submitted the winning plan for New York City's Central Park. By then, at age 35, Olmsted was well-known as a reporter and had studied scientific farming. But it was as a landscape architect that he would make his mark on American life.

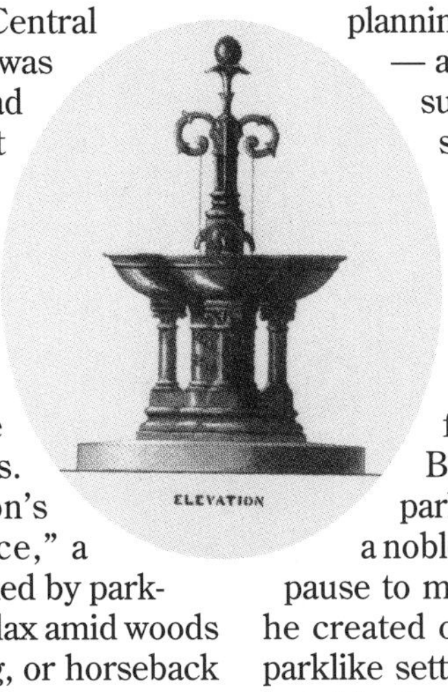

Olmsted's success with Central Park won him commissions from Montreal to San Francisco, and between 1857 and 1895 he designed 17 major urban parks. Among the greatest was Boston's seven-mile "Emerald Necklace," a series of landscaped havens, linked by parkways, where Bostonians could relax amid woods and fields and go boating, hiking, or horseback riding without leaving the city.

Before Olmsted's day cemeteries were the only open spaces available to the average city dweller. But he believed that people — particularly working people — needed a relief from urban distractions. He also recognized that "greenswards" would breathe fresh air into congested cities. And his parks were as urbane as they were rustic. Olmsted strove to make them integral to city planning in a way that would bring order to — and humanize — urban sprawl. His sunken roadways, for instance, preserve a peaceful atmosphere for pedestrians without inconveniencing commercial traffic.

Though Olmsted worked on many different kinds of commissions, he always tried to include some sort of parkland. His campus for the University of California at Berkeley incorporated a tree-lined parkway. For Capitol Hill he fashioned a noble landscape where legislators could pause to meditate. Riverside, the community he created outside Chicago, was nestled in a parklike setting. And when Olmsted served as president of the Yosemite Commission, he applied his genius for urban planning to the wilderness, helping to preserve for future generations an unspoiled landscape as a national park.

Philadelphia's Fairest

When Grace Kelly married Prince Rainier of Monaco in 1956, Philadelphians joked that her father's domain was larger than Rainier's. And it was, for John Kelly, Sr., was commissioner of the city's Fairmount Park, a place more than 10 times the size of Monaco.

The park began in the early 1800's as a five-acre tract for a reservoir on the banks of the Schuylkill River. The city added more and more land until, by 1867, its primary tract of 4,077 acres made Fairmount the world's largest fully landscaped city park.

But Fairmount's size is no more remarkable than its design, the work of Hermann Schwarzmann, a former Bavarian army officer. In 1868 this 22-year-old genius arrived in Philadelphia and — with no previous experience — went to work as an engineer for the then brand-new Park Commission. Within two years Schwarzmann had trained himself as an architect and was providing plans for an art gallery and dining salon in the park, as well as a master landscape plan. His design won out over all others submitted.

One of Schwarzmann's triumphs was the creation of the Philadelphia Zoological Garden, the nation's first, in the park. He also prepared a 285-acre site for Philadelphia's 1876 Centennial Exhibition. But perhaps his greatest success was in the joy he gave to people. "Is it possible you have never seen Fairmount Park?" wrote journalist Lafcadio Hearn to a friend in 1889. ". . . It is the most beautiful place in the whole civilized world."

The Parthenon in the Park

Because it boasts so many colleges, Nashville, Tennessee, has long been called the Athens of the South. Since 1897, though, there has been another reason: standing proudly in one of the city's parks is a full-sized replica of the Parthenon, the temple that Athenians built 23 centuries earlier.

The occasion for erecting such a monument was the centennial of Tennessee's statehood. Due to delays in construction, the celebration took place nearly a year late, but that mattered not at all to 1.8 million visitors. The city had transformed a 200-acre state fairground into an independent community with an array of exotic architecture. The city of Memphis, Tennessee, for instance, built a pyramid in honor of the ancient Egyptian capital of Memphis. Mexico erected an Aztec hall. Venice sent gondolas and gondoliers to ply an artificial lake. But it was the Parthenon that attracted the biggest crowds.

The builders had taken great pains to create an exact reproduction, securing a floor plan from the British Museum and drawings from the king of Greece. Construction was complicated by the fact that the original had been designed to sit atop a hill. Its columns bulged at the center, leaned inward, and were set at differing intervals, all so that they would give the appearance of perfect regularity when seen from below. It took a local architect months of study to duplicate all these tricks in his wood and plaster version.

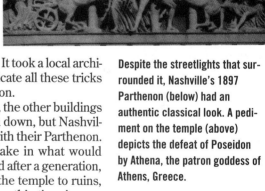

After six months of hoopla, the other buildings on the fairgrounds were torn down, but Nashvilleans could not bear to part with their Parthenon. It stayed, overlooking the lake in what would become Centennial Park. And after a generation, when weather had reduced the temple to ruins, the city built yet another one, this time in concrete. The job took 10 years — one year more than it had taken the Greeks to erect the original.

Despite the streetlights that surrounded it, Nashville's 1897 Parthenon (below) had an authentic classical look. A pediment on the temple (above) depicts the defeat of Poseidon by Athena, the patron goddess of Athens, Greece.

A Shady Business

Among its many credits Philadelphia can claim to be the capital of street trees. As early as 1700, city fathers decreed that every householder must plant one or more trees so that the town would be shaded from summer sun "and thereby be rendered more healthy." New York followed suit eight years later, as did Boston in 1711. By 1807 even the frontier city of Detroit was lining its boulevards with trees, and Natchez, known for its chinaberry trees, began subsidizing a town nursery in the early 1800's.

Experiments with growing "city" trees that were hardy and easily maintained also centered in Philadelphia, under the leadership of architect William Hamilton. He introduced the Lombardy poplar, a European favorite, and the gingko, which remains a popular street tree today. In 1784 Hamilton also imported a Chinese tree, the ailanthus, which is disease resistant and fast growing. It seemed at first to be the ideal city tree, but its ability to sprout from every crack, and its habit of losing limbs in the wind have made it the number one urban weed tree.

Not every Philadelphian was in favor of planting trees. Benjamin Franklin feared they would hamper the work of his own invention, the fire department, and refused to sell his new fire insurance to any whose houses were fronted by trees.

Cultivated Pleasures

Renowned as a center for scientific research, Henry Shaw's garden is — and always has been — a refreshing oasis of calm for the visiting public.

Scientists around the world know it as the Missouri Botanical Garden, but the people of St. Louis still call it Shaw's Garden in remembrance of its founder. All 79 of its landscaped acres were wild prairie when Henry Shaw first saw them in 1820. The 19-year-old Englishman had stepped off a steamboat just the year before with a shipment of cutlery from his native Sheffield and $3,000 borrowed from an uncle. Living in his one-room shop, he found a ready market for hardware among the pioneers who used St. Louis as a staging point for their plunge into the wilderness. By the time he was 40, Shaw had amassed a fortune of some $250,000 and decided that was enough. He retired, built a house in town and another overlooking the prairie, and set out to tour Europe.

On his travels Shaw rediscovered his childhood interest in gardens, finding particular inspiration in his visits to London's Royal Botanic Gardens at Kew. When he returned home, he was determined to make something similar in St. Louis.

Formerly prairieland outside of St. Louis, Shaw's Garden is now surrounded by the city. In the early 1900's this woman played her violin while perched on a pad of the garden's famous Victoria water lilies.

From the start Shaw's focus was as much on science as it was on beauty. One of his first purchases was a collection of 62,000 plant specimens offered for sale by a German botanist. While planning a special museum to house the collection, Shaw built greenhouses, a rose garden, a series of formal gardens, bordered paths, and landscaped vistas. When it opened to the public in 1859, Shaw's was the only botanical garden in the United States.

Over the next 30 years Shaw continually added to the garden's collections, establishing as well a school of botany at St. Louis's Washington University. At his death in 1889, he left almost all of his estate (by then worth millions) to endow the garden. He also guaranteed $200 a year to the Episcopal diocese, provided that the bishop agreed to preach an annual sermon on one of Shaw's favorite subjects — "the wisdom and goodness of God as shown in the growth of flowers, fruits, and other products of the vegetable kingdom."

Though Dr. Harry Wegeforth was a tireless promoter of his San Diego Zoo, he generally shunned publicity for himself. He did, however, manage to doff his hat for a photographer (below) while riding Queenie, the zoo's first elephant. In the 1920's the zoo's python Diabolo (left) would not eat unless it was picked up and force-fed — a popular event with the zoo-going public.

Dr. Harry's Zoo

Harry Wegeforth had always wanted his own zoo, and as a young man in 1916, he finally got his chance. He served that year as a staff physician at San Diego's Panama-California International Exposition, and as the show came to a close, he discovered that many exhibitors packing up to leave the Balboa Park fairground had caged animals they wanted to dispose of. Wegeforth offered to take the animals in.

From that point on — and always on a shoestring — much of "Dr. Harry's" time was devoted to wheedling and cajoling support for his zoo. To feed his charges he scrounged fish at the docks and spoiled vegetables at local markets. When the city government refused to give him space in Balboa Park, he enlisted an army of influential allies by offering free elephant rides to the children of San Diego. (He got space for his zoo in 1921.) And when was he ready to expand his collection, he traveled worldwide, trading species he had in abundance, such as California sea lions, for the surplus stock of foreign zoos.

From the beginning Dr. Harry gave Americans something they had never seen before: a zoo with few visible barriers. Instead of cages there were grottos for lions, mesas for zebras, and enormous flying houses for birds. San Diego's mild climate made it possible to plant each area with some of the grasses and trees the animals were used to, so that the flora was nearly as exotic as the fauna. With an almost visionary sense of how a zoo should be put together, Wegeforth chose the sites, designed the settings, selected the plants, and even planted the seeds himself.

As Dr. Harry neared the end of his life in 1941, his zoo was called the finest in the world. And when asked why he had devoted a lifetime to it, his answer was simple: "I like animals."

UPTOWN, DOWNTOWN

Like the lavish drinking halls of Milwaukee, the German Winter Garden in New York City featured elegant surroundings, first-class entertainment, good food, and generous supplies of lager. Fritz Meyer painted the garden's fashionable clientele in the 1850's.

Roll Out the Barrel

When it came to having a good time, America's German immigrants certainly were in the know. In cities with large German populations, like Cincinnati and Milwaukee, they enjoyed countless nights of family fun, lively dancing, and hearty meals in beer gardens that sparked memories of home.

Many of these rollicking establishments were sponsored by breweries, including one of the most famous, Milwaukee's Schlitz Palm Garden. Opened at the end of the 19th century, it was a spacious, elegant hall with stained-glass windows, hand-carved archways, palm trees, and banks of electric lights. It set a high standard of entertainment and featured its own orchestra, first-class visiting performers (including classical concerts and a touring band led by John Philip Sousa), nickel sandwiches bursting with meat — and Schlitz beer by the barrelful.

Despite the aura of elegance, some old-time Americans disapproved of public drinking. "The German idea of such a place," sniffed a jaded observer, "is one vast saloon, where they can meet, dance, smoke and drink the frisky lager."

Nevertheless, the Palm Garden and competitors run by the Pabst and Miller breweries prospered until anti-German feeling provoked by World War I combined with Prohibition to put an end to the glory days of the immense beer gardens. By 1919 the doors were closed forever on the Palm Garden, where genial patrons downed their brimming steins of ice-cold beer.

On the Avenue

Though highways and byways are often named for people, Colonial leader William Penn strongly disapproved of the practice. Scorning such "man-worship," he designated Philadelphia's north–south streets by number and named the east–west routes for trees and fruits. Some of the names have since been changed, but locals and visitors still can keep their bearings by chanting "Market, Arch, Race, and Vine / Chestnut, Walnut, Spruce, and Pine."

A sense of order prevails in Washington, D.C., where major avenues are named for states and many of the streets are named alphabetically, from A Street to Z Street. The next tier features two-syllable words in alphabetical order, such as Adams and Dubois; still farther out come three-syllable names: Avery, Decatur, and the like.

Patriots and presidents have been honored in cities from coast to coast, but others turned to local history for inspiration; downtown Albuquerque boasts Copper, Gold, Silver, and Lead streets. Other names simply acknowledge what once was there. New York's Wall Street did have a wall, though its name may have sprung from the anchorage — *waal* in Dutch — that stood at one end. And Hartsdale, New York, in a flush of romanticism, named streets for poets, from Keats and Shelley to Whittier and Poe.

Read All About It

They had pluck, determination, and sharp wits — but often that was all the newsboys had. In the last decades of the 19th century, many of these adolescent entrepreneurs, commonly known as newsies, were homeless waifs who not only worked the streets but also lived on them. Some who were lucky enough to live in New York City, however, could get a warm meal and a night's sleep in the Newsboy's Lodging House. This facility, established around 1854, provided for those whom author Horatio Alger, Jr., described as the "vagrant children who are now numbered by thousands in New York and other cities."

Alger was well acquainted with the brass-lunged youngsters who hawked papers in the streets, for he spent countless hours at their lodging house collecting the hard-luck tales that formed the basis for his rags-to-riches novels. Though they hardly ever made the kinds of fortunes Alger wrote about, the newboys did improve their own lot in 1899 by staging a city-wide strike against two of New York's leading dailies, Hearst's *Journal* and Pulitzer's *World.* Newsies, who bought each day's supply with their own money, refused to sell either paper until the publishers agreed to refund the cost of unsold copies.

By the early decades of the 20th century, newsboys in the streets accounted for as much as half the circulation of many major dailies. *Editor and Publisher,* a trade publication, advised newspaper owners to cater to the pint-size businessmen: "Treat them well, that is, entertain them, give them help when they need it, and invite them to Thanksgiving and Christmas dinners and they will show their gratitude by selling your papers in preference of all others."

By then the newsboys were no longer homeless waifs, but the children of determined working-class and immigrant families. Among them were many young men who would one day be in the headlines themselves: Louis Armstrong, Irving Berlin, Jack Dempsey, and Supreme Court justices William O. Douglas and Earl Warren are just a few of those who once worked as newsies.

Canny newsboys (above) were a common sight on turn-of-the-century city streets. In the painting below, newsies of an earlier era are getting their daily stock of papers.

NATIVE TONGUE

CITY LINGO

As a nation of immigrants, we have a wonderfully rich language incorporating terms from around the world. Native Americans introduced the newcomers to such local specialties as moose, skunk, *and* raccoon; hickory, squash, *and* persimmon. *Our Spanish forebears gave us a bonanza of words, from* tornado *and* poncho *to* mustang *and* mesa. *Thanks to the Germans we can attend kindergarten and shop at the deli for burgers and wursts. The French gave us* shanty *(probably from* chantier, *for logging camp),* chantey *(from* chanter, *to sing),* depot, *and* sashay. Shenanigans, shebang, *and* smithereens *hint of the riches the Irish brought over.* Kowtow, chow, *and* gung-ho *have their roots in China, while* Yankee, hunky-dory, boss, stoop, *and* spook *are among the words that descended from the Dutch. A particularly generous bequest came from our Jewish ancestors, including* mensch, nosh, yenta, *and a whole family of "sch" words, such as* schlock, schtick, *and* schmooze, *to say nothing of the nuance apparent in such commonplace phrases as "I'm telling you" and "I should live so long."*

A Moving Day in May

Pandemonium reigned each year on the first of May as New Yorkers moved *en masse*. Carters fleeced their customers, tenants were sometimes stranded, and fights and fires were common. As one participant ruefully observed: "It is not an amusement, except to landlords."

The whole of New York's population, noted an astonished Frances Trollope, seemed to be on the move, as if "flying from the plague." What she was witnessing, though, was not some great exodus. It was just the city's annual May 1 moving day. From earliest Colonial times it had been the custom for any tenant moving from one set of lodgings to another to do so on that date.

The system, which allowed the city to update its directory in an orderly way, caused little disturbance as long as New York was a town of a few thousands. But the 19th century brought fortune-seekers and immigrants by the hundreds of thousands. The population boom caused unregulated rents to skyrocket, and forced many to move annually in a quest for affordable housing. By the 1830's one out of three New Yorkers changed address every May Day.

The result was 24 hours of chaos. Carters doubled — or even quadrupled — their fees, then careered through the streets with complete disregard for the dogs, goats, pigs, and pedestrians that wandered in their way. There were accidents on every corner, and smashed furniture littered the cobblestones. Boys set fire to heaps of abandoned straw mattresses. Those who couldn't find an apartment spent the night in City Hall Park — and if they weren't gone the next morning, the police took them to jail.

Amazingly, what the *New York Evening Post* branded "an abominable custom" in 1840 persisted until the end of the century. Only then did New York's urban nomads finally settle down.

Millionaires' Row

Strolling down Cleveland's Euclid Avenue in its Gilded Age heyday, a visitor could hardly have failed to be impressed by this celebrated "Millionaires' Row." A ribbon of sandstone pavement some 60 feet wide and 4 miles long, the boulevard was lined on either side by a double row of American elms that formed a leafy bower. And there, behind the ornate cast-iron fences and set off by lush lawns up to 300 feet deep, were the mansions — some 250 opulent Gothic, Italianate, Romanesque, and Victorian manor houses. It was no wonder that European visitors compared the street favorably with the Champs-Élysées in Paris.

The homes, erected in the post–Civil War decades, belonged to the nouveaux riches who had founded such companies as Standard Oil, Western Union, and General Electric. And they had no compunctions about flaunting their wealth. The Johnson residence, for instance, had an indoor skating rink, and the Squire house boasted its own gymnasium. Charles Brush installed a pipe organ in his home that soared all the way from the ground floor to the third-floor ballroom. But the most breathtaking conceit undoubtedly was the ebony-paneled guest room that Sylvester Everett reserved exclusively for the use of visiting presidents.

Euclid Avenue had gained the favor of its wealthy residents because of its proximity to their offices — it runs right through the heart of Cleveland's downtown area. That, however, was also the avenue's undoing, since spreading commercialization eventually drove most of the householders to the suburbs. Some, such as John D. Rockefeller, Charles Brush, and telegraph pioneer Jeptha Wade, refused to leave. But to prevent the conversion of their beloved homes to commercial purposes, they left instructions in their wills to have the buildings razed at their deaths. By 1920 developers had taken the rest, so that today just three of the mansions remain intact.

An artist captured the opulence of Cleveland's Euclid Avenue c. 1880 (top). Passing beneath an imposing arch at the Everett mansion (above), a team of carriage horses seems dwarfed by the massive structure.

One Way to Pay

Save your tears for a rainy day. We are giving a party where you can play" might be the message on the printed card you found in your mailbox or were handed in a barbershop in New York City's Harlem. And there listed below would be the address for that Saturday's rent party.

A quiet, prosperous neighborhood, Harlem had been home to white judges, politicians, and businessmen throughout the 19th century. Then in 1900 word of a new subway line sparked a building boom. So many apartments were constructed in the next few years that the owners could not find tenants for them all — until an African-American real estate agent, Philip Payton, Jr., offered to fill them with people of his race.

Young, working-class men and women responded eagerly. For the first time black New Yorkers had a chance to move into handsome buildings on well-maintained streets. They paid a premium, since landlords charged black tenants more than they charged white ones — and rent parties, which had been a southern tradition, enjoyed a renaissance as a means of paying the monthly bill.

By charging guests a dime or a quarter for an evening of "Music too tight. Refreshments just right," a householder could raise the money due the landlord. There were poker and dice in the back room, pig's feet, cornbread, and bathtub gin, and a home defense officer to maintain order. One happy veteran of these events noted that "the rent party was the place to go to pick up on all the latest jokes, jive, and uptown news."

Thousands of wealthy white tourists regularly drove up to Harlem to visit famous night spots like the Cotton Club, but for just a few cents those in the know jammed into railroad flats and shimmied to some of the finest jazz in the world. Piano players developed characteristic styles on the rent party circuit, and a musician hadn't made it until he bested rivals at a chitterling strut — a loose competition featuring speed and improvisation. Keyboard maestros and future jazz legends such as Eubie Blake, Fats Waller, and Duke Ellington are among the many who got their starts at rent parties.

Sometimes neighbors would call the police to quiet down a lively gathering. But this often ended with the officers caught up in the infectious good spirits and "having a ball for themselves."

The General Store Grows Up

When department stores were first established in the mid-19th century, shopping became at the same time both grander and more democratic. Gone was the need to trek through muddy side streets and rundown waterfront districts in search of merchandise. Instead, shoppers could make a single trip "downtown" and stroll along the tidy sidewalks surrounding stores the size of city blocks. They might indulge in the new pastime of window shopping — the tempting displays behind plate-glass windows were lit at night with gas lamps. Or better yet, they could step inside, where everything from handkerchiefs and housewares to Parisian fashions were for sale under a single roof.

By 1897 Marshall Field's department store had a fleet of "glass window wagons" that delivered merchandise to customers' homes. The store maintained a barn for the horses that delivered goods throughout the city.

The looks and policies of the newfangled department stores were set by men like Chicago's Marshall Field, who began his career as a $400-a-year sales clerk in 1856 and, with partners, opened his first store nine years later. Continually outdoing each other in offering customers luxurious surroundings and services, these men were an entirely new breed of merchandisers.

Field would lose several emporiums to fire in the 19th century, but when he rebuilt, each of his marble palaces (as they were called) was finer than the last. When shoppers walked in, there could be no question in their minds that they had arrived somewhere special. Rich or poor, they were greeted by doormen — perhaps even by name. There was a tea room to lunch in, floorwalkers to answer questions, and hundreds of sales clerks. Each customer received equally courteous service. "Testify no impatience if a servant-girl, making a six penny purchase, is served before you," an etiquette book advised potential shoppers. "The rule of 'first come, first served' is rigidly observed."

Every woman was a "lady" at Field's. And whenever she went into the store, she knew that the gloss, the courtesy, and the beautiful goods were there as much for her as for anyone else. For many women department stores afforded their first exposure to fine furniture and clothing. They could examine the merchandise, learn about style, compare prices, and ask questions in comfort, without being made to feel that the item in question was perhaps beyond their means.

Such policies kept customers coming back, and Field did even more to ensure that they did. He instituted a revolutionary return policy, allowing shoppers to change their minds; promised the lowest prices in town; and insisted on honest advertising. Most important, he taught his sales help his motto: "Give the lady what she wants."

A Palace Rises in the West

Seven stories high and a quarter-mile around, the Palace Hotel dumbfounded many with its size, but dazzled with its fine food and accommodations.

If ever there were lodgings made for millionaires, they were to be found at San Francisco's Palace Hotel. First opened in 1875, the Palace was a place where banqueting silver barons ordered from sterling-silver menus, senators cut deals with gold-rush tycoons, and socialites rubbed elbows with royalty. America's first truly grand hotel — with some two-and-a-half acres of salons and suites — it stood as irrefutable proof that California's boomtown had arrived.

The Palace was built around a magnificent central court. Hotel guests needed only to peer over the balconies to find out which star or dignitary was arriving.

The gold and white landmark was the creation of William C. Ralston, a onetime Mississippi River boatman who had made a fortune by founding the Bank of California. Setting out to build a hotel that would rival the best in Europe, Ralston succeeded at a cost of $5 million. His Palace boasted electricity, telephones, five elevators, and 900 gold-plated cuspidors. All seven floors overlooked an imposing grand court that was planted with palms and topped with a translucent glass dome. And each of the hotel's 800 guest rooms had its own fireplace, closet, and private toilet.

Satirists at *Harper's Weekly* might chuckle over the headwaiter's uniform of "a purple velvet suit, powdered wig, silk hose, and pumps," but San Franciscans were proud of their Palace. And it lived up to Ralston's every ambition. Emperor Dom Pedro II of Brazil and David Kalakaua, the last king of Hawaii, were guests. In 1879 Ulysses S. Grant entered the grand court in a chariot pulled by six white horses and was welcomed by a choir of 500 voices singing from a balcony. English beauty Lillie Langtry checked in with 32 trunks, and actress Sarah Bernhardt arrived with a pet tiger cub in tow.

The Palace survived the San Francisco earthquake of 1906 (opera great Enrico Caruso was a guest at the time), but not even the hotel's 675,000-gallon private reservoir could save it from the fire that followed. Like the city itself, however, the Palace outlived its troubles. It was soon rebuilt, this time at a cost of $10 million. And in 1909, when William Ralston's son turned the golden key that opened the new Palace, he opened a new era in San Francisco's history.

Shopping Under Glass

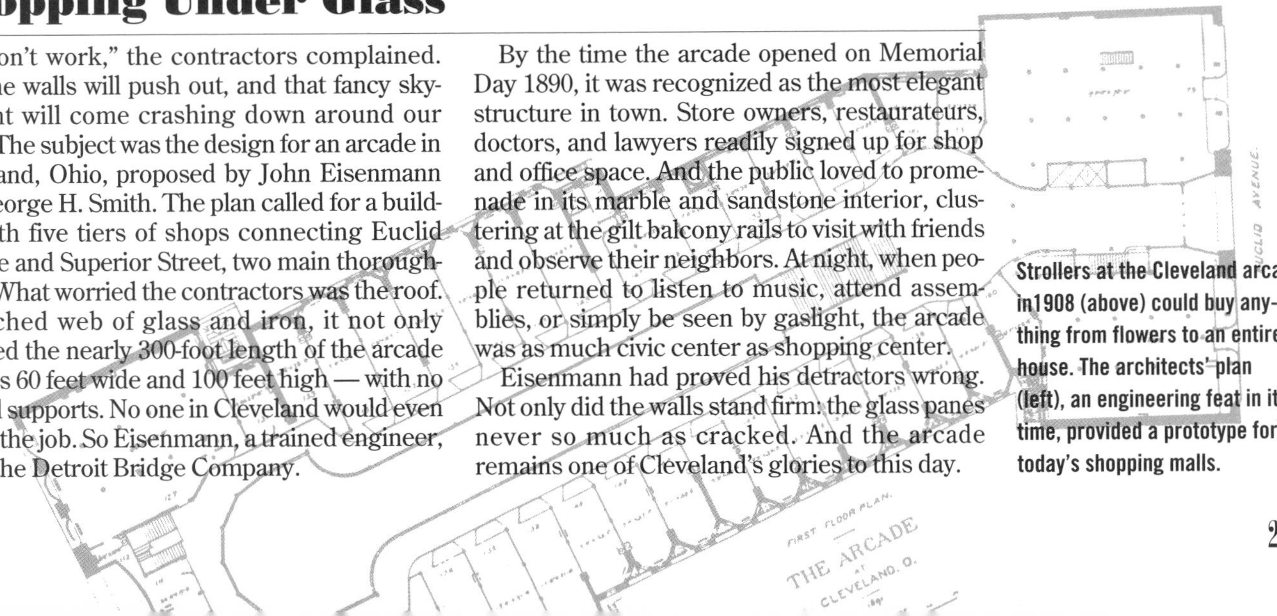

"It won't work," the contractors complained. "The walls will push out, and that fancy skylight will come crashing down around our ears." The subject was the design for an arcade in Cleveland, Ohio, proposed by John Eisenmann and George H. Smith. The plan called for a building with five tiers of shops connecting Euclid Avenue and Superior Street, two main thoroughfares. What worried the contractors was the roof. An arched web of glass and iron, it not only spanned the nearly 300-foot length of the arcade but was 60 feet wide and 100 feet high — with no central supports. No one in Cleveland would even bid on the job. So Eisenmann, a trained engineer, hired the Detroit Bridge Company.

By the time the arcade opened on Memorial Day 1890, it was recognized as the most elegant structure in town. Store owners, restaurateurs, doctors, and lawyers readily signed up for shop and office space. And the public loved to promenade in its marble and sandstone interior, clustering at the gilt balcony rails to visit with friends and observe their neighbors. At night, when people returned to listen to music, attend assemblies, or simply be seen by gaslight, the arcade was as much civic center as shopping center.

Eisenmann had proved his detractors wrong. Not only did the walls stand firm: the glass panes never so much as cracked. And the arcade remains one of Cleveland's glories to this day.

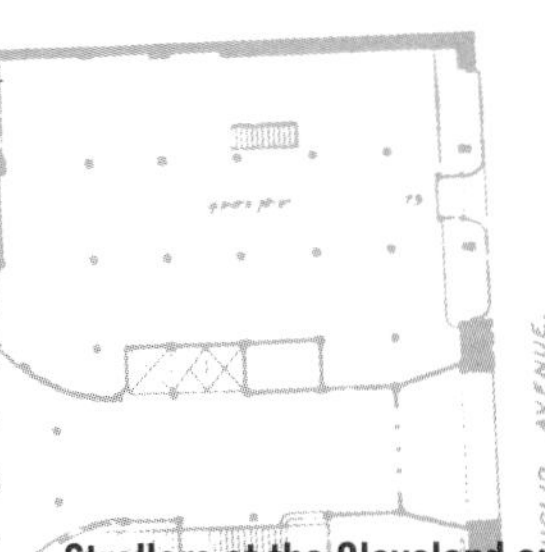

Strollers at the Cleveland arcade in1908 (above) could buy anything from flowers to an entire house. The architects' plan (left), an engineering feat in its time, provided a prototype for today's shopping malls.

Skyscraper on the Plains

While looking for an architect to design the new headquarters for his pipeline company in Bartlesville, Oklahoma, in 1952, Harold Price was advised to meet with Frank Lloyd Wright. He did just that and found that the famed architect was delighted by his request for help. It offered Wright the perfect opportunity to dust off plans he had drawn in the early 1920's for a skyscraper that had never been erected. "I am going to give you a design that I have been trying to get built for 28 years," he told his newfound client.

Wright's design called for a dramatic, 22-story building, with a facade decorated in sheets of weathered green copper. The plans, Price admitted, were a bit more grandiose than what he had in mind. "I wanted a two-story office building and a place to park 10 trucks," he explained to Wright, then added, "Why don't we compromise . . . and build a tower of 19 floors?" And that is exactly what he got.

The Price Tower, which was begun in 1953 and completed four years later, is the only skyscraper that was ever actually built from Wright's earlier high-rise plans. The architect professed to care not at all that it was not silhouetted on the skyline of New York City, where, he complained, urban "congestion" diminished the dramatic effect of individual buildings. "Trees in the forest have no chance to develop their own individuality," he insisted. This, in contrast, was a tree that had escaped the forest. Its completion, Wright boasted, demonstrated that the skyscraper had at last "come into its own on the rolling plains of Oklahoma."

Even during his lifetime Frank Lloyd Wright (above) was better known for the houses he designed than for his plans for larger structures. The Price Tower (left) is his only skyscraper design that ever was actually built.

Riding the Staircase

If Jesse Reno believed that the path of progress led upward, he surely put the theory to a test in 1892 when he patented a moving staircase. His device in fact was little more than a conveyor belt that carried people upward at such a steep angle they had to lean forward and hang on to the handrails to keep from falling off. Despite the obvious discomfort Reno (the Nevada city is named for his father) sold a few of his contraptions — including one to the operator of a Coney Island amusement stand who apparently wanted to offer his patrons a thrilling new ride.

Use of the moving staircase became less difficult when Charles D. Seeberger, who coined the name escalator, developed the now-familiar step model. Despite Seeberger's improvements, escalators failed to catch on with the public until one of his models was exhibited in France at the 1900 Paris Exposition. Throngs of visitors paid a penny each to ride the new device, and after the exhibition Gimbel's department store in Philadelphia bought and installed a Seeberger escalator. It remained in use until 1939. True to the rivalry that became a retailing legend, Macy's outdid Gimbel's a year later when they installed four banks of escalators and so became the first department store in which customers could ride the stairs all the way up to the lofty heights of the store's fifth floor.

Escalators aroused little interest until Gimbel's department store installed one in 1901. Then, all their competitors had to have their own flights of moving stairs. Bostonians rode this one at the R. H. White store in 1903.

Nearer My God to Thee

When the Methodist minister Christian F. Reisner told his congregation in 1922 that he had selected a site in upper Manhattan for his new church, he had made up his mind to rebuild on a grandiose scale. Already well-known for his flamboyant preaching style, Reisner proposed erecting a skyscraper cathedral topped by a huge, revolving cross that would shoot beacons of red and yellow light across the famous New York skyline.

At 44 stories tall, Reisner announced, his "Broadway Temple" would be "a magnificent advertisement of God's business." But since the design also included a 2,000-seat sanctuary, a swimming pool, a bowling alley, a gymnasium, and 500 dormitory rooms, it was bound to be costly as well.

To raise funds, Reisner packed his pews by featuring vaudeville acts, movie stars, and newsreels at Sunday services, and appealed to the likes of John D. Rockefeller, Jr., and J. C. Penney. He had collected more than a third of his $4 million goal when the 1929 stock market crash put an end to his plans. Though his great skyscraper never materialized, a far more modest church — just three stories high — was finally built on the site in 1952.

Promotional literature for the temple featured its soaring facade and illuminated cross.

Hugh Ferriss: Urban Visionary

As far as Hugh Ferriss was concerned, architecture went straight to the heart of the American life-style. "Our way of living," he declared, "is shown, in large measure, by the kind of buildings we build." And Ferriss was very specific about what kind of buildings they should be. He wanted to replace the jumbles of skyscrapers that had been erected in the 1920's with a coordinated design for cities.

The leading architectural artist of his day, Ferriss never got to build the city of his dreams. But he did allow others to have a look at it in 1929 when he published his ideas in *The Metropolis of Tomorrow*. His urban vision was one of mammoth, widely spaced skyscrapers, each the size of several city blocks, with the spaces between them filled by lower buildings topped with gardens. Each skyscraper was devoted to a single theme — art, science, business — and on the roofs were airports and "sky golf courses." Such amenities, Ferriss claimed, would alleviate the city dwellers' weekend rush to rural hideaways. "Instead of going up to the country," he pronounced, "the people will go 'up' for country air."

Born in 1889, Hugh Ferriss helped to shape the streamlined design of modern urban architecture. He was known primarily for his visionary drawings, both of his own ideas and those of other designers. This drawing illustrates architect Raymond Hood's 1929 concept of a suspension bridge that doubles as an apartment complex.

BLIGHTS AND BLEMISHES

Five Points, the lower Manhattan neighborhood depicted in this 1829 painting, was a noisy, smelly, roistering hotbed of lawlessness. The occasional top-hatted swell who wandered in did well to mask his sensitive nose with a handkerchief.

Murderous Corners

New Yorkers of a century ago would have wondered to see a courthouse near the intersection of Baxter, Park, and Worth streets; the address then was hardly a home of law and order. On the contrary, the area, known as Five Points, was America's worst slum, a neighborhood so rough that the police feared to enter it.

Begun as a poor man's haven where the impoverished went to dance and drink, Five Points by the 1820's had become a dumping ground for the city's poorest immigrants, who huddled together, several families to a room, in wretched tenements. These hovels, with names like "Gates of Hell" and "Brickbat Mansion," were every bit as terrible as their names suggested; the worst of them, "Old Brewery," housed more than 1,000 people in its 95 rooms and averaged a murder a night for 15 years.

Since poverty makes a fertile breeding ground for crime, Five Points became the home of the City's fiercest gangs — the "Dead Rabbits" and "Plug Uglies" among them. Turf wars turned the streets into battlegrounds, and if the police tried to intervene, the hoodlums disappeared into tunnels that connected the tenements. When the Five Pointers united against the gangs of the Bowery, as many as 1,200 toughs might sally out together — in 1857 two regiments of army troops helped the police drive them back to their dens.

Reformers turned to Five Points in the 1830's, but progress came slowly. In the early 1850's the Old Brewery was torn down, the gangs were routed, and the notorious neighborhood began its evolution into a respectable civic district.

In Their Own Words

Let us go on again, and plunge into the Five Points. . . . Where dogs would howl to lie men and women and boys slink off to sleep, forcing the dislodged rats to move away in quest of better lodgings. . . . All that is loathsome, drooping and decayed is here.

— Charles Dickens, 1842

A Scourge of Mosquitoes

In the summer of 1878 Memphis, Tennessee, seemed poised to become the premier city of the Mississippi Valley. The population had doubled in the previous decade, and many of the immigrants were well-educated Germans, who gave the city a cosmopolitan flavor.

True, it was a filthy place. Yards and streets lay full of garbage, and sewage ran in open ditches to collect in a large bayou in town. Not surprisingly, the city had been plagued in the past by

The yellow fever epidemic made gravedigging a constant chore.

cholera and dysentery, diseases related to contaminated food and water. However, low-lying Memphis had a special problem: its swamps were a perfect breeding ground for the mosquito whose bite brought on the chills and vomiting of the dreaded tropical scourge yellow fever.

The epidemic began on August 13 when a woman who lived by the river died, her skin a telltale lemony hue. Within two days 65 cases of yellow fever were reported. No one knew then that the infection was caused by the mosquitoes, so no effective measures could be taken.

The well-to-do simply fled — 25,000 in the first 14 days. Parents abandoned children in the panic. Neighboring towns turned the refugees away at gunpoint, fearing they might bring the illness with them, so that 1,300 had to camp out in tents.

Back in Memphis, 75 percent of those who remained fell ill, and 5,150 people died. Hundreds of doctors and nurses rushed in from as far away as Texas and New York. (Thirty-three of the doctors also fell victim to the disease.) Other cities donated funds and a badly needed trainload of coffins. Finally, in October, a frost curbed the mosquitoes and ended the plague.

Few of the wealthy refugees chose to return. Memphis had lost its chance at municipal greatness. But the epidemic did make it a leader of another sort: over the next few years it installed 152 miles of sewers and instituted a garbage collection service. Once a byword for filth, Memphis became a model of municipal sanitation.

A New Lease on the Low Life

Alderman Sidney Story wasn't seeking immortality in 1897 when he recommended that the New Orleans City Council establish the country's first legal red-light district. Concerned over the rapid spread of prostitution throughout the seaport city, Story believed that the flesh trade could best be confined to a 38- to 40-block area. Needless to say, he was mortified when, upon adoption of his recommendation, the press promptly dubbed the district "Storyville."

Most of the 2,000 prostitutes who registered for business there worked in spartan cubicles, but it was the 35 sporting houses that sprang up along Basin Street that made Storyville famous. The most opulent of these was Mahogany Hall, Lulu White's establishment. Called the "Diamond Queen," Lulu was spangled with the sparklers from her hands to her head — each finger sported a ring, bracelets glittered on both arms, and a necklace and tiara completed the ensemble. The furnishings for her parlor cost some $30,000. Also well-known was the palace run by "Countess" Willie V. Piazza, who was fluent in French, Spanish, Dutch, and Basque as well as English. Her monocle and two-foot-long cigarette holder of ivory, gold, and diamonds were a bit overdone, but her taste in gowns made her the fashion setter for respectable society. Typical of Willie's unerring judgment was the fact that she hired Jelly Roll Morton to play piano in her establishment.

Indeed, Storyville was a nursery of jazz. Besides Morton, Emile Lacoume (one of the very first jazzmen), Louis Armstrong, and King Oliver played on Basin Street. When the secretary of the navy closed Storyville in 1917 (ostensibly to protect the sailors at New Orleans' naval base), the prostitutes left the district where they and the early jazzmen had flourished.

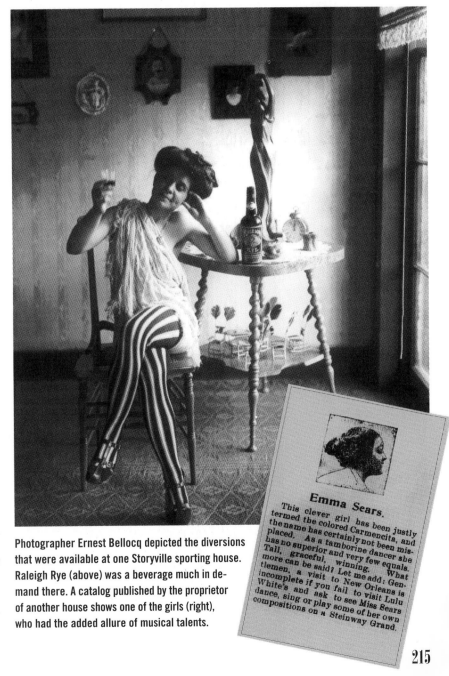

Photographer Ernest Bellocq depicted the diversions that were available at one Storyville sporting house. Raleigh Rye (above) was a beverage much in demand there. A catalog published by the proprietor of another house shows one of the girls (right), who had the added allure of musical talents.

Emma Sears.

This clever girl has been justly termed the colored Carmencita, and the name has certainly not been misplaced. As a tamborine dancer she has no superior and very few equals. Tall, graceful, winning. What more can be said? Let me add: Gentlemen, a visit to New Orleans is incomplete if you fail to visit Lulu White's and ask to see Miss Sears dance, sing or play some of her own compositions on a Steinway Grand.

SERVICING THE CITY

"It's My Fire"

Few sounds in Colonial America were as frightening as the cry of "Fire!" So when Philadelphia organized the country's first volunteer fire department in 1736 in order to fight the blazes in a systematic way, other cities were quick to follow suit. Companies of volunteers that ran bucket brigades now also had hand-pumped fire engines and hose wagons, which were set up in neighborhoods throughout the cities. Membership was considered an honor, with the most prominent citizens leading the way.

By the late 19th century fire departments in most cities were equipped with horse-drawn steam engines that could race quickly through the streets.

Much admired by the public, each company competed to be the finest, fastest, most gallant team of heroes in town. Further fueling the rivalry were offers of cash awards from insurance companies to the brigade whose stream of water touched a fire first. In time, just getting to a fire and monopolizing the nearest fireplug before the other companies arrived became as important as putting out the fire. "The competition to be first is so ardent . . . ," a British observer noted in the 1850's, that "if one of themselves fall, the rest drag on the engine regardless of his fate and occasionally break his legs or arms with the wheels." If two companies arrived at a fire at the same time, he added, "a desperate and bloody battle will rage for a considerable time while the flames are making an unchecked progress."

The volunteer companies by then were staffed less by leading citizens than by young toughs whose rowdiness often was matched only by their inefficiency. Although steam-driven engines that could pump water twice as fast as hand pumpers were available as early as 1829, for instance, volunteer companies refused to use them. Anything mechanical was considered insulting to the volunteers' physical strength. They also shunned horse-drawn wagons, preferring those that they could pull themselves. New York, Pittsburgh, Philadelphia, and many other cities suffered severe fires because of such practices, but few politicians dared to defy the firefighting companies.

The situation finally began to change in 1853 when, fed up with unnecessary fire losses, city officials in Cincinnati organized the nation's first salaried fire department and commissioned a steam fire engine — a 22,000-pound monster that could not be pulled by hand. Even then, the local volunteer companies tried to interfere with the city firefighters, but irate citizens made it clear that such highjinks would no longer be tolerated. Other cities soon established professional fire departments, leaving America's earlier proud tradition of volunteer companies to be maintained by smaller communities around the country.

Nathaniel Currier (of Currier and Ives) was a volunteer fireman, and produced several prints in the 1850's depicting fire fighters (right). The New York firemen (above) were among the volunteers who were inclined to have a fight before fighting the fire.

Firemen's Friends

Dog lovers have long marveled at the Dalmatian's talent for running with horses. "Even puppies," wrote one expert in 1911, "will soon find their way up behind the horses' heels where one would think it impossible that the horses would not strike them on the head with their hoof every step they take."

It was this characteristic that made the Dalmatian a favorite choice as coach dog and stable companion for carriage horses in America. Though no one knows precisely when they were first brought to this country from Europe, it is certain that George Washington bought a male Dalmatian in 1787 to breed with Martha's female. "A Coach dog has been purchased," Washington wrote to a nephew, "and sent for the convenience and benefit of Madame Moose: her amorous fits should theretofore be attended to."

The Dalmatian's speed, endurance, and ease around horses also led to its frequent selection as mascot for fire companies in the 19th century. Racing along under horse-drawn engines and running ahead to clear intersections with a warning bark, the black-and-white dog became a familiar emblem of a proud municipal service.

When fire-fighting equipment was motorized in the early 1900's, the horses were retired, but many of the Dalmatians stayed on. To this day they can sometimes be seen sitting up front in the cabs as fire engines race to fires.

Portland's Fiery Fourth

The heavens gathered blackness," wrote John Neal, "and a hurricane of fire swept over the city, carrying cinders and blazing fragments of wood far into the country." Neal was a novelist, but when he penned these words, he was recalling an actual scene: the fire that reduced his office and the heart of Portland, Maine, to a smoldering ruin on July 4, 1866.

In the 19th century all too many American cities experienced similar devastation when accidental blazes raged out of control. The fire that changed the face of Portland probably started when a celebratory firecracker landed in a barrel of sawdust. Flames quickly gathered force, leaped to an adjacent boat shop, then to a nearby sugar refinery, and on to a foundry. From there the fire fanned out in all directions.

Answering an all-out alarm, Portland's volunteer fire brigades, ill-trained to begin with, had difficulty getting organized since most had been engaged in Independence Day festivities. High winds, the lack of a central water supply, and a water shortage — the result of a recent drought — further hampered progress. Before pumpers were ready and working, "an incessant shower of fiery rain" was falling, igniting not only wooden roofs and houses, but supposedly fireproof buildings of stone and brick as well.

The towns of Saco, Biddeford, and Lewiston, Maine, responded to distress signals and sent assistance. But the fiery whirlwind burned on for 15 hours, ending only after playing itself out on the sandy hills of east Portland.

When the smoke cleared, the tragic scale of the city's loss became apparent. One-third of Portland — 320 acres — lay in ashes. Some 1,500 buildings, including the new city hall, the library, a museum, and scores of banks, churches, and businesses, were destroyed. Although, miraculously, only 2 people died, some 13,000 were left homeless.

As the terrible toll was broadcast in newspaper headlines nationwide, relief funds began pouring in from as far away as Cuba. The federal government sent 1,500 army tents and $50,000. New York City donated more than $100,000, Boston $25,000, and Canada sent quantities of lumber.

An unseasonable spell of good weather facilitated reconstruction through the winter, and month by month a new city began to rise on the old. Wider streets were laid out, building codes emphasizing fire-resistant materials were enacted, and an up-to-date water supply system was installed. Distinctly Victorian in style and modern in concept, the new Portland aimed to ensure that such devastation could never happen again.

On the night of July 4, 1866, as Portland burned, an amateur artist, George Frederic Morse, moved his family to safety on a hill outside the city. Then he set up his easel and, in the course of the night, completed seven paintings of the conflagration. This one is a view of Portland's Congress Street.

LEGEND —AND— LORE

Of all the legends told of cities, few are more persistent than those of alligators prowling in the sewers of New York City. But one tale, at least, may have been fact, not fiction.

"ALLIGATOR FOUND IN UPTOWN SEWER" trumpeted The New York Times *on February 10, 1935. Three youths, it seems, were shoveling the last of a slushy snowfall into an open manhole when one saw something moving in the Stygian gloom. Kneeling for a better look, he called to his companions, "Honest, it's an alligator." And so it was. Getting a rope from a nearby merchant, the boys returned to the scene, lassoed the reptile, and hauled it to the street. The hapless beast turned on its rescuers, and they had to kill the seven-foot-long monster. Neighbors suggested that the creature had fallen off a steamer from Florida that passed on the nearby river. But as the paper said, "Whence it came is a mystery."*

Road Hogs

Pigs scavenging trash were tolerated in the streets and squares of many cities. Painter Henry Mosler put a porker front and center in this view of a Cincinnati market.

"If I determined upon a walk up Main-street, the chances were five hundred to one against my reaching the shady side without brushing by a snout fresh dripping," wrote the Englishwoman Frances Trollope in 1832. She was complaining not of stray dogs or nuzzling horses, but of Cincinnati's rooting hordes of free-roaming pigs.

People put up with the porkers because of the garbage that clogged the streets in early America: kitchen slops, viscera discarded from butchered animals, mounds of fly-flecked horse manure. In some cities dogs and goats were loosed to scavenge on the mess; Charleston, South Carolina, made the singular choice of encouraging vultures. Of the maintenance menagerie, however, none rivaled the effectiveness or ubiquity of pigs — thousands of determined, snuffling, snorting trash-disposal units on the hoof.

Swine and hoses

Hog heaven it wasn't, since the pigs produced a fair amount of waste themselves, and the stench, wheezed Oscar Wilde, "made granite eyes weep." There were accounts, too, of overturned carriages, knockdowns, maimings — even deaths. In Manhattan one desperate mother rescued her child from a hungry hog that had dragged its prey across the street and was about to dine.

Early efforts to restrict the pigs failed partly because the four-footed street sweepers were more effective than the human variety, and because of pressure from the poor, who supplemented their meager diet with fresh (albeit tainted) ham or sold the pigs to slaughterhouses.

In the wake of cholera scares and epidemics in several cities at midcentury, municipal boards of health began to gain ascendancy over private interests, political corruption, and perennial custom. Public outcry finally drove authorities to provide water and work crews for public sanitation and create ordinances requiring the containment of scavenging livestock. By the 1860's the pig patrol was out of business.

Clean Sweeps

It was on an afternoon in May 1896 that they first marched down Fifth Avenue, some 2,700 strong: column upon column of street cleaners, accompanied by 10 brass bands and equipped with brooms, carts, and a new pride in their jobs. Most of the workers were smartly attired in suits of sparkling white, with a matching helmet on each uplifted head. And there on horseback at the head of the parade, personally leading the procession, was Col. George E. Waring, Jr., New York City's recently appointed street-cleaning commissioner.

Reactions to the spectacle were mixed. "Clothing the street cleaners of New York in the garb of white winged angels," read one angry letter to the mayor, ". . . should be resented as a gross impertinence." But Waring simply shrugged off the criticism, secure in the knowledge that his theatrics produced results. As dedicated as he was flamboyant, Waring nevertheless sometimes got the specifics wrong — he never wavered, for instance, in his conviction that disease was spread by "sewer gas" rather than by viruses. But the sanitation showman was a genuine pioneer in environmental reform who pointed the way to modern refuse management.

Born on the Fourth of July, 1833, Waring began his career in public service as a drainage engineer in New York's Central Park in 1857. (He was a friend of the park's designer, Frederick Law Olmsted.) When the Civil War broke out, he organized a cavalry battalion and eventually rose to the rank of colonel. After the war his passion for sanitation led to a job supervising the construction of a sewer system in Memphis, Tennessee, following the city's yellow fever epidemic of 1878. Built as a means of controlling the disease, its successful completion brought Waring international fame and numerous assignments, from Washington, D.C., to Paris, and from Havana to The Hague.

In 1895 Waring was appointed head of the Department of Street Cleaning in New York City, where, he reported, the thoroughfares were an appalling mess. "Rubbish of all kinds, garbage and ashes lay neglected . . . and in the hot weather the city stank with the emanations of putrefying organic matter . . . black rottenness was seen and smelled on every hand." Parked trucks and wagons — home to thieves and highwaymen and used by both sexes for "the vilest purposes" — compounded the congestion.

Before he could start on the streets, however, Waring had to tidy up the sanitation department itself, long a pawn of political graft. Claiming that "the most complete and lasting happiness of which we are capable comes from a sense of duty done," the former military man introduced a routine that created a proud and enthusiastic corps. Each sweeper appeared for inspection at a morning roll call and could be dismissed for such infractions as entering a saloon, using foul language, or straying from his post. In all, 1,450 workers patrolled some 433 miles of streets, some of which were swept five times a day. As for the controversial white uniforms (purchased by the wearer for $1.25), they proved a stroke of genius: Waring's "White Wings" quickly earned the public's gratitude and were celebrated in a popular song and a Broadway play.

When the political machine regained control three years later, the colonel was swept out of office. A short time later, the man who believed that "there is no surer index of the degree of civilization of a community than the manner in which it treats its organic wastes" died of yellow fever, contracted, ironically, while on a trip to Cuba to spread his gospel of cleanliness.

Over the years the battle for clean streets was waged by (counterclockwise from left) horse-drawn wagons, battalions of able-bodied broom bearers, and automotive sweepers. Members of New York City's broom corps (above) got their nickname — "White Wings" — from their pristine uniforms.

Philadelphia's Liquid Asset

While traveling in America in 1840, Charles Dickens found much to complain about. One thing that *did* impress him, however, was Philadelphia's Fairmount Water Works. That city, he noted, "is most bountifully provided with fresh water, which is showered and jerked about, and turned on, and poured off everywhere." And, he added with satisfaction, "the Water Works . . . are no less ornamental than useful, being tastefully laid out as a public garden."

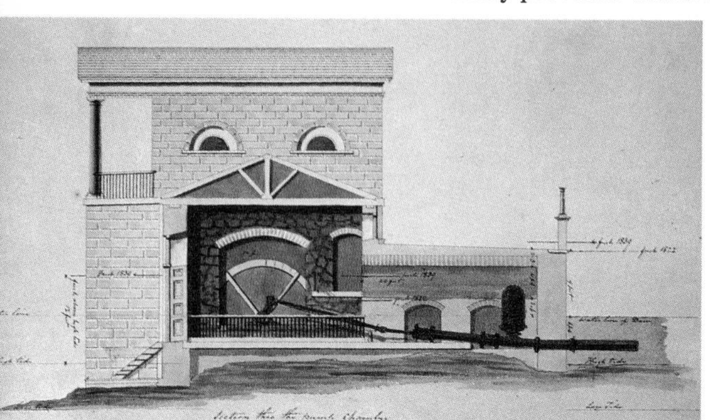

George Lehman's watercolor (below) depicted the Fairmount Water Works on its site below the reservoir in 1842. The cutaway above shows one of the water-driven pumps.

Indeed, many another writer sang their praises; artists recorded the water works' every angle on paper, canvas, and porcelain; and Europeans, when visiting this country, made a point of inspecting the sensational new water-supply system. Begun in 1812 and built in stages until 1871, the Fairmount Water Works were regarded as a mechanical wonder in an age when many people looked upon industrialism as a menace. Humming along ceaselessly, by 1844 a series of pumps — all powered by the fast-moving Schuylkill River — lifted the city's 53-million-gallon daily ration of water to a reservoir atop a hill known as Faire Mount.

Just as important, the water works were beautiful, perfectly matching the era's taste for romantic landscapes. The mill house, designed by Frederick Graff, superintendent of the works, looks like a gigantic Greek temple. Nearly 240 feet long, it is handsomely sited along the rocky east bank of the river. Entrances to the building were embellished with sculptures — created by William Rush, a leading artist of the day — celebrating the majesty of waterpower. And on the grounds promenades were punctuated with fountains, statues, and gazebos, inviting strollers to enjoy what man and nature had designed.

During the 19th century, efforts to protect water quality led to the purchase of 4,000 additional acres of riverfront property. But urban growth by then was outstripping the water works' pumping capacity, and the river was polluted. Decommissioned in 1911, Fairmount was eventually declared a national historic landmark and stands today as a reminder of the potential for harmony between public works and public pleasure.

The expense and disruption of resurfacing streets often caused city officials to postpone improvements for as long as possible. It was 1939 before these workers pulled up the stones on New York City's Beekman Street to make way for modern paving.

Surface Changes

To this day a story persists in Abilene about the man who got off his horse and promptly sank up to the brim of his hat. But Abilene was not alone in coping with streets that were masses of mud in winter and deep in dust in summer. Cities throughout the country in the 19th century were plagued by wretched, poorly maintained streets.

Efforts to remedy the situation began soon after the Civil War, but for the next 50 years progress on paving was remarkably slow. For one thing, many city dwellers objected. Since neighborhood streets served as playgrounds for children, and marketplaces where housewives bought produce from vendors' carts, there was little incentive to invite more traffic.

The paving materials themselves also presented problems. Gravel was cheap and quiet under hoof but difficult to maintain. Cobblestones and bricks were noisy and trapped garbage and manure. Wood blocks soaked in creosote wore out too fast and oozed oil and filth in the summer. In 1890 the *Detroit Journal* referred to that city's wood-block streets as "150 miles of rotten, rutted, lumpy, dilapidated paving." The best material was asphalt, which was tried as early as the 1870's. The tarlike substance is smooth, durable, and easy to clean, but it was also expensive and so for a long time was little used.

By the 1890's, however, a variety of groups were clamoring for change — teamsters, who could not drive their wagons on bad streets; health reformers, who were alarmed by the filth; and bicyclists, who demanded smooth surfaces. At the same time, American engineers invented cheaper ways to produce asphalt, and work on city streets began in earnest, paving the way for the automobile that arrived with the new century.

Chicago's Other Underworld

Without a major waterway towns in the 19th century had little chance of growing into cities, though water-bound sites were not always the easiest to build on. Chicago, for instance, benefited from its location on Lake Michigan. The land on which the city was founded, however, was actually a marsh. And so during the first half of the 1800's, Chicago's residents put up with constant floods and built raised wooden sidewalks to get around on streets that were almost invariably engulfed in mud.

Then beginning in the 1850's, Chicagoans set to work on a more permanent solution by literally giving the city a lift. Jacking up existing structures, they built new foundations underneath, constructed drainage channels, and brought in acres of landfill. By the time the job was finished several decades later, Chicago stood more than 12 feet higher than it had before.

But the city prospered so with its improvements and grew so quickly that by 1900 traffic jams made downtown streets as impassable as mud once had. Searching for a solution to its problems, the city hired the Chicago Tunnel Company to build a network of 60 miles of tunnels some 40 feet below the busiest section of town. At that depth workers could actually carve the tunnels through clay by hand. Then they lined them with concrete and laid the tracks for a narrow-gauge railway.

Most of Chicago's underground tunnels were only about seven-and-a-half feet high, with the city's telephone cables routed along the tops of the tunnels. Here, two men inspect a section of the track in 1912.

Every major skyscraper, department store, and public building had a subbasement connection to the tunnels, with the result that the little trains — with some 3,000 freight cars — could make all deliveries and remove all garbage. As soon as the tunnels were opened, they eliminated about 5,000 horse-drawn delivery wagons from the streets every day. The system proved remarkably efficient until modern transportation made surface travel cheaper and quicker. The tunnels were abandoned in the 1950's, but they remain in place today some 40 feet below the streets — unique relics of the lakeside city's past.

Whoa Down!

"There is something confused in this Broadway which makes one feel a little bewildered.... When crossing it I think merely of getting to the other side alive." This sentiment, expressed by a 19th-century visitor to New York, was doubtless shared by many a hapless pedestrian in early urban America. Ruled by "some frantic demon of haste," horse-drawn carriages and carts raced pell-mell down crowded streets, crashing into one another and rolling over anything — or anyone — that had the misfortune to be in their way.

As early as 1652, city fathers were passing ordinances intended to curb the "exceeding fast and hard riding of horses." Hefty fines — from a few shillings to "two pounds Flemish" to assuming full financial responsibility for any damages done — were imposed for infractions. But the laws and penalties had little effect.

Heedless horsemen speedily proceeding on their way made crossing the street a treacherous venture for pedestrians.

As cities grew and populations soared, traffic became even worse. New York City dispatched a detail of extra-tall police to oversee matters, but getting across its urban intersections still required a blend of heroism and foolhardiness. As one trenchant observer said, "It takes more skill to cross Broadway . . . than to cross the Atlantic in a clamboat."

When automobiles entered the fray in 1900, the compounded chaos cried out for radical reform. In other cities the police perched on platforms to regulate traffic. Manually operated semaphore signals became popular. But it was not until the 1920's, when traffic lights became commonplace at intersections, that pedestrians were finally relieved of the "thousand misgivings" that traditionally accompanied the simple act of getting to the other side.

Stop and Go

In 1898, when William Phelps Eno inherited a million dollars from his father, he decided that the time had come to devote himself not to pleasures but to public service. The vehicle for his civic-mindedness was a wholehearted attack on the chaotic traffic that was choking New York and other cities.

Following several years of intensive study, Eno published a manifesto, *Rules for Driving,* a comprehensive plan for managing "equestrians and everything on wheels or runners, except street cars and baby carriages." Eno's *Rules* outlined procedures for passing, turning, crossing, and stopping, and proposed standardized speed limits. Eminently practical, the program was adopted as law in New York City in 1903. The following year state legislators indicated their approval by mandating the first statewide uniform speed laws: 10 miles per hour in populous cities, 15 in villages, and 20 in open country.

Eno's innovative and thoroughgoing traffic solutions also won support internationally. One of his best ideas — taming traffic at multiple-street intersections by means of one-way rotaries —worked so well at New York's Columbus Circle that in 1907 the French adopted it for traffic around the Arc de Triomphe in Paris.

WHAT · IS · IT?

In the congested streets of 19th-century America, a runaway horse was an unconscionable danger. One simple solution was proposed by the inventor of the device shown here. A strong tug on a rope directed through a series of pulleys would brake the spooked steed through the magic of levitation.

The corner of Fifth Avenue and 42nd Street in New York was already one of the world's busiest intersections in the 1920's. The city made order of potential chaos by installing traffic lights controlled by officers in tall cagelike structures.

Eno's one blindspot in an otherwise brilliant career was the traffic light: he considered it inferior to direct supervision by a white-gloved, whistle-blowing traffic cop. Others, however, were eager for the innovation.

Potts's stoplight

The American Traffic Signal Company led the way when it installed the country's first electric stoplight at an intersection in Cleveland, Ohio, in August 1914. The red and green lamps winked from atop a 15-foot pole in response to commands from a policeman at the controls in a weatherproof booth below. A buzzer also sounded — two long buzzes sped traffic along the main street, while one short buzz signaled movement on the cross street. It was the right idea, but not nearly strong enough a solution.

The real challenge of traffic management was synchronization. Several inventors looked to the system of signals used at railroad crossings for inspiration, and William Potts emerged as the knight of the stoplight. A member of the Detroit police force who had the fine title of superintendent of signals, Potts is credited with inventing a series of 15 tricolored-light towers coordinated by automatic timers that were installed along a thoroughfare in Detroit, Michigan, in 1921.

Night Lights

Much ingenuity has been directed toward making the nighttime bright. The first settlers relied on their own lanterns when they ventured out after dark. In the mid-18th century Benjamin Franklin devised a whale oil lamp for use in street lighting. Gas lamps were the latest thing when the 19th century dawned — and they persisted into the 20th century in some cities. Electricity altered the night's complexion with arc lamps and neon.

Origin of the Snitching Post

On July 16, 1935, residents of Oklahoma City woke up to something entirely new in municipal services — the world's first coin-operated parking meters. Although there already were time limits on parking in the business district, compliance was voluntary — and there were few volunteers. Downtown streets were routinely packed with automobiles that parked for hours, if not days, at a stretch.

Looking for a way to improve the situation, Carl C. Magee, a sometime newspaper editor and member of the chamber of commerce, envisioned the sturdy coin-operated timer on a post that is, with minor alterations, still the standard. A team of engineers at Oklahoma State University's College of Engineering made the prototype; a small section of the city's downtown was chosen as proving ground; and 175 meters were installed at 22-foot intervals along several streets.

Motorists, who had received considerable advance notice of the metering plan, gave the newfangled devices mixed reviews. A few protesters even took the issue to court, arguing that the meters violated their inalienable right to "free use" of the streets. But the judges were unmoved and the "snitching posts" stayed.

Newspapers everywhere kept close watch on the great parking meter experiment, for other cities also were in serious need of parking relief. Four months after Oklahoma City showed the way, Dallas installed meters, and as Texas went, so went the nation.

The Secret Subway of Alfred Beach

"A Fashionable Reception Held in the Bowels of the Earth!" proclaimed a headline in the New York Herald in February 1870. Reading on, astonished Knickerbockers learned that Alfred Ely Beach, publisher, patent lawyer, and inventor, had thrown a lavish party on the 26th in a tunnel beneath the intersection of Broadway and Warren Street.

The event unveiled a theretofore secret project, for Beach's tunnel housed a pneumatically driven underground railway complete with an elegantly appointed waiting room. Partygoers who were not riding the nearly noiseless subway along its 312 feet of track were admiring the waiting room's frescoes, lounging on its luxurious settees, or listening to music from the grand piano, while others watched water splashing in the fountain or the flashes of gold as fish darted about in the aquarium.

Beach designed special equipment for digging his tunnel. His hydraulic tunneling bore later burrowed beneath New York's Hudson River and the Thames in England.

Fearing opposition from the notorious Boss Tweed — a master grafter who held all New York in his corrupt grip — Beach had taken meticulous precautions to keep his excavation secret. Having obtained a permit to build an underground "pneumatic dispatch" system for letters and small parcels, he then selected a site in an area of lower Manhattan that tended to be deserted at night. After making a deal with a local merchant to use his store's cellar as a base of operations, the inventor went to work in February 1868, assisted by his 21-year-old son, Fred, and a team of workmen bearing picks, shovels, wheelbarrows, and a hydraulic boring device of Beach's own design.

As furtive as grave robbers and as determined as bulldogs, the excavators gnawed away at the earth for 58 nights until they had created a tunnel nine feet in diameter that ran for one full block beneath Broadway. The displaced rock, dirt, and other debris from their diggings were packed into hundreds of sacks and spirited away in wagons equipped with special mufflers on their wheels. Sections of track and parts of the passenger car were then slipped in through the store's basement. Finally, Beach installed the great engine of his railway system — the "Roots Patent Force Blast Blower," a steam-driven, 100-horsepower wind machine that was to blow his passenger car to the end of the line and draw it back again at speeds of up to 10 miles an hour.

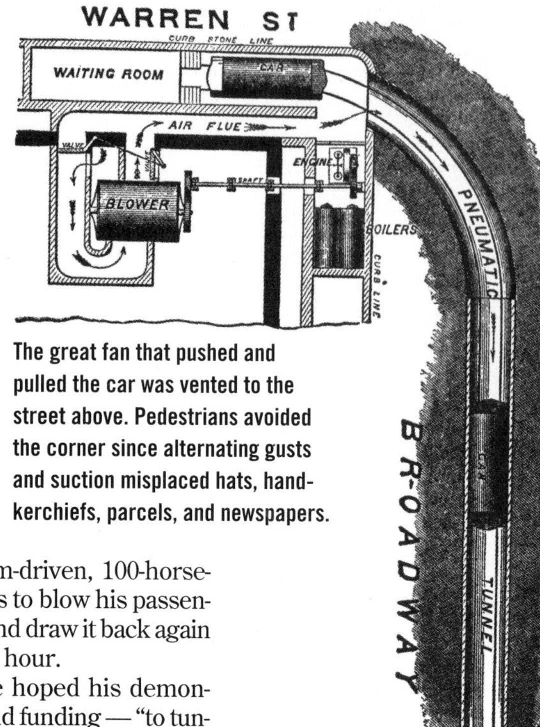

The great fan that pushed and pulled the car was vented to the street above. Pedestrians avoided the corner since alternating gusts and suction misplaced hats, handkerchiefs, parcels, and newspapers.

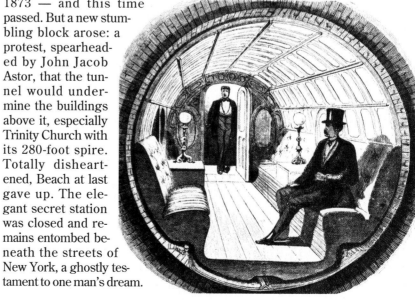

Beach announced that he hoped his demonstration would win favor — and funding — "to tunnel Broadway through its whole length" and so begin a public transportation system that would carry passengers swiftly and comfortably to stops throughout the city. But while the inventor lobbied to gain the state legislature's support for construction, Tweed had his puppet governor veto Beach's project and approve one of his own — an elevated railway. Public outcry forced a review of the proposal but to no avail. Beach's transit bill lost in the legislature by just one vote.

When Boss Tweed was finally jailed for his many swindles, the air-blown railway came up for review again in 1873 — and this time passed. But a new stumbling block arose: a protest, spearheaded by John Jacob Astor, that the tunnel would undermine the buildings above it, especially Trinity Church with its 280-foot spire. Totally disheartened, Beach at last gave up. The elegant secret station was closed and remains entombed beneath the streets of New York, a ghostly testament to one man's dream.

The pneumatic subway, furnished with upholstered seats and glass-globed lamps, was as gracious as it was graceful.

A Streetcar Named Tranquillity

"Gems of symmetry, finish, and convenience" was one writer's bubbling assessment of the electric streetcars introduced at Richmond, Virginia, in February 1888. The reporter's enthusiasm over this wondrous new public transportation system was widely shared. Within three months of opening, the Union Passenger Railway had 40 cars shuttling as many as 12,000 riders a day over 12 miles of track. Much to the delight of all those riders, the new trolleys were clean, quiet, speedy — and so inexpensive to operate that the fare was one-half that of the horse-drawn cars they were replacing.

The genius behind this burgeoning network was Frank Julian Sprague, a graduate of the U.S. Naval Academy with a passion for electrical engineering. Sprague left the navy to pursue his own interests in 1883, and the next year opened a business in New York City.

Scarcely had he hung out his shingle when a group of Richmond promoters approached him with an invitation to develop an urban rail system. Signing what he would later call "a foolish contract" to deliver "a power-plant, a complete system of current supply, and an equipment of forty cars, each with two motors" in just 90 days, the 29-year-old inventor set to work at a feverish pace.

With payment dependent on completing the task to the satisfaction of his employers, Sprague found that the challenge was even greater than he had imagined. Not only did the track routes include many sharp curves, but Richmond's hills were far steeper than expected, which placed extra strain on the electric motors.

Test run after test run revealed new kinks to conquer, but each setback spurred Sprague to greater ingenuity. Within the three-month time limit he perfected a workable design that combined a central power station with a web of current-bearing overhead wires. Each car drew power from the main supply through a connector that "trolled" along the overhead wire — and remained attached even when the car went around curves and over bumps.

In the summer of 1888, visiting executives from a Boston transit company challenged Sprague to operate a large number of the cars simultaneously. Undaunted, he pumped up the boilers that powered the steam generators, set 22 cars on a single run, and hauled the Bostonians from their hotel to watch the trolleys chugging reliably into the night. Completely convinced, the New Englanders returned home and converted their own cars to electricity.

By 1895 over 800 similar transit systems were operating in the United States, not only linking central cities to the fast-growing suburbs, but also linking city to city and state to state. In 1904 one honeymoon couple rambled from Delaware to Maine by interurban trolley, and by 1915 a sojourner could traverse more than 1,000 miles of track from Freeport, Illinois, to Ithaca, New York.

All hands, whether hired or simply riding, helped out when a trolley jumped the tracks. This common occurrence was sketched by Jay Hambridge for *The Century Magazine.*

The brilliant glow of the trolleys' incandescent lights was a welcome sight to throngs returning home after a night on the town in Richmond, Viriginia. The fleet of little four-wheeled cars made its debut in 1888.

Chapter 8

THE WILD WEST

EXPLORERS AND SETTLERS

Maverick Trader of the Upper Missouri

Fur trader Manuel Lisa was set on making money — but ended up making enemies instead. Detractors claimed his own men so despised him that Lisa did not dare to turn his back on them. According to one of the trappers who worked for his Missouri Fur Company, "Rascality sat on every feature of his dark-complexioned Mexican face." Yet Lisa — who was actually born in New Orleans and was of Spanish extraction — had supporters, too. One described him as "a man of bold and daring character, with an energy and spirit of enterprise like that of Cortez or Pizarro."

It seems likely that many of the complaints against Lisa stemmed from jealousy. No one could deny that from his headquarters in St. Louis, Lisa pioneered in opening the fur trade along the upper Missouri River. Nor could most people keep up with him. "I put into my operations great activity," Lisa once explained. "I go a great distance while some are considering whether they will start today or tomorrow." And go a great distance he did: beginning with his first trapping expedition at age 35 in 1807, he traveled a total of some 26,000 miles up and down the Missouri.

Lisa's organizational skills were as impressive as his energy. Instead of trading with Indians for his furs, he hired and paid his own trappers, who brought their pelts to his outpost on the Bighorn River. He also used his considerable skills as a negotiator to persuade the Indians to allow his men entrance into their territories, taking an Indian bride (while married to another woman) to finalize the agreement.

Lisa's standing among the local tribes remained so high that in 1814 he received an appointment as government subagent for the region. He was, in fact, so successful in his dealings with the tribes that to the day of his death in 1820, no other trader had acquired so much as a toehold in the Indian lands of the upper Missouri.

A 20th-century painting by artist Olaf Seltzer shows pioneering fur trader Manuel Lisa looking down at his men as they build his Fort Lisa on the bank of the Yellowstone River.

As many as 2,000 mountain men, Indians, and travelers sometimes gathered at the annual trappers' rendezvous. Alfred Miller, an artist touring with Scotsman William Drummond Stewart, painted this view of a rendezvous on the Green River. The scene commemorates the occasion when Stewart presented mountain man Jim Bridger with a suit of armor.

Rocky Mountain Revelry

William Ashley never intended to establish a wilderness tradition. All he wanted was a place where trappers working for his Rocky Mountain Fur Company could meet and exchange their furs for trade goods. He solved the problem by sending out word for the men to gather "on or before the 10th of July" in 1825, at a fork in Wyoming's Green River that he called "Randavouze Creek."

While buying pelts and selling supplies at the July gathering, Ashley realized that an annual rendezvous would enable him to turn a profit without the expense of setting up a permanent trading post. And it gave the mountain men a chance to enjoy a few days of frenzied sociability.

Each summer after that, Ashley sent a supply of trading goods from St. Louis, including the liquor that fueled the trappers' nonstop revelry. As tales of wild carousing spread, the rendezvous attracted not only trappers, traders, and Indians, but curiosity seekers as well. Among them was William Drummond Stewart, a Scottish aristocrat traveling in the Rockies, who was drawn, he said, by "the sound of mirth and wild music," and "the triumphant shout of drunkenness."

When they were not carousing, the men challenged one another to such feats of skill as shooting bullets into wooden posts while galloping by at full tilt. Or they simply passed the time gambling, using beaver pelts — which they called hairy bank notes — to bankroll the games.

The annual gatherings flourished until the late 1830's, when overtrapping by rival fur companies and a drop in demand for beaver fur triggered the demise of the trade. By then, some of the mountain men had found employment leading wagon trains of settlers through territory that had once been their solitary preserve.

The Luckiest Man in the West

Mountain man Hugh Glass routinely defied death — and won. He boasted that as a young man he had escaped from the pirate Jean Lafitte. Later, it was said, he outwitted an Indian chief who planned to burn him at the stake. And in still another exploit he survived an ambush that left him with an arrowhead buried in his back for weeks.

But the adventure that made Hugh Glass a legend among the trappers of the West was his survival of a grizzly bear attack in August 1823. "The bear caught him and hauled him to the ground tearing and lacerating his body in fearful rate," wrote fellow trapper Jim Clyman in his diary. Glass, who was far from young at the time, was so severely wounded that his companions decided to proceed without him. In leaving, they agreed to pay two of their party — young Jim Bridger and James Fitzgerald, according to most accounts — to stay behind and stand the death watch. After five days, however, with Glass in no apparent hurry to die, the pair abandoned him, later reporting that he had expired. With his personal effects (including his favorite rifle) in hand as proof, they collected their pay.

Glass, however, not only lived; he managed to walk and crawl to the safety of Fort Kiowa, some 300 miles away, surviving on berries and the remains of buffalo carcasses, and with the help of some Sioux Indians along the way.

When he regained his strength, Glass journeyed up the Missouri, intent on locating the men who had abandoned him. It was easy enough to find Bridger, whom, they say, Glass pardoned because of his youth. As for Fitzgerald, when Glass finally tracked him down in June 1824, he told him sternly: "Go false man and answer to your own conscience and to your God." But at least he had the satisfaction of getting his favorite rifle back.

Frederic Remington captured the essence of the western mountain man in this 19th-century sketch.

Maximilian and Bodmer traveled the Missouri River from St. Louis to Fort McKenzie, in present-day Montana, where the artist painted this sweeping landscape.

The Artist and the Aristocrat

The stout, middle-aged German prince and the slender, young Swiss artist were an odd-looking pair. But thanks to the travels of these two — Maximilian of Wied and Karl Bodmer — we have a priceless first-hand record of Indian life on the Great Plains.

Prince Maximilian, an experienced naturalist and ethnologist, had been fascinated by accounts of the Lewis and Clark expedition and was eager to see for himself the world of the frontier tribesmen. Choosing the talented Bodmer as his illustrator, and accompanied also by his valet, the prince sailed from Europe in 1832. By the following spring the party was in St. Louis, ready to set out on a 13-month journey through the remotest outposts of the fur trade in what is now northern Montana.

Conducting interviews through interpreters as they traveled, Maximilian wrote that the Indians not only were as civilized as whites, but as "honest, generous, and hospitable as well, and cleaner, too" — unusual observations in that day and age. The Indians, for their part, were intrigued by Bodmer, who on winter mornings had to wait for his paints to thaw. As Maximilian noted, "They said . . . after he had executed a portrait, that he could 'write' well."

The Swiss artist's work was completed just a few years before smallpox decimated the populations of the Great Plains. His detailed renderings are among the few records of tribes such as the Mandans, who were all but wiped out by the disease. Of Bodmer's nearly 400 drawings and watercolors, 81 were reproduced in Maximilian's 1843 book about the journey, and many are now on display at a Nebraska museum.

Bodmer depicted customs as well as scenery. The painting (right) shows a heap of elk antlers built up by the Blackfeet, who believed that adding to the pile would guarantee good hunting. The placement of feathers in the headdress of Wahktageli, a Yankton Sioux chief (far right), symbolized his war deeds.

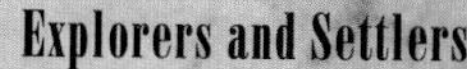

Three years after Bodmer made this sketch of a Mandan bow and decorated quiver, the tribe was all but destroyed by smallpox.

Bodmer's painting of the Mandan bison dance was engraved and sold as a print (above). On the steamboat journey up the Missouri River, hunters traveled along to procure meat for the passengers. As the encounter with grizzlies (right) reveals, the hunters' job was not always easy. Bodmer's watercolor of the return trip downriver (below) is thought to have been made from memory when he was back in Europe. The scene takes place along the Missouri in North Dakota.

A shipboard artist portrayed the *Columbia* at Robert Gray's winter quarters on Vancouver Island, where the discoverer of the Columbia River built a second ship, the *Adventure.*

Hail, *Columbia!*

Rumors of a great river in the American Northwest had persisted for decades. But it was not until May 11, 1792, when Capt. Robert Gray braved sandbars and heaving breakers at the river's mouth, that the rumors were proved true. Described as "practical, consistent, and ruthless," Gray was a trader rather than an explorer and probably picked up hints of the river's location from the natives with whom he dealt.

The doughty captain named the river for his ship, the *Columbia,* and went ashore with his fifth mate, 16-year-old John Boit, Jr. Though Boit's attention was focused mainly on the "very pretty" Indian women they encountered, the men's casual stroll was in fact of great significance. The English navigator George Vancouver arrived a few days later and claimed the area for his king. When ownership was finally sorted out some 50 years later, Gray's landing took precedence and helped secure the northwest territory for the United States.

Bitter Fruit From the Promised Land

Hall Jackson Kelley was a man obsessed. Dazzled by reports of the Lewis and Clark expedition, he dreamed in the early 1800's of the "founding of a new republic of civil and religious freedom" in Oregon. A former school teacher and surveyor, he proposed resettling some 3,000 New Englanders of "steady habits" in the Northwest, with the expectation that the U.S. government would pick up the tab.

An indifferent speaker, Kelley promoted his cause in pamphlets promising that the Indians were all friendly and the Rockies could be crossed in comfort by carriage. In 1831 he founded the "American Society for Encouraging the Settlement of the Oregon Territory" and devoted so much time to his project that he gave up most of his paying work. Yet he never attracted more than 500 emigrants and even they dropped out as

Originally a fur-trading post, Fort Vancouver was a reliable source of supply for early settlers and undoubtedly the social hub of Oregon country. It was here that Hall Jackson Kelley was nursed back to health after contracting malaria on his trek to Oregon.

Mapping the West

At a time when the Pacific Northwest was still largely unknown, a Welsh fur trader charted more than 1.5 million square miles of the region.

While plotting the Lewis and Clark expedition in 1804, Thomas Jefferson had to use a British map. In those days the only reliable map of the Pacific Northwest was one incorporating the observations of David Thompson, a Canadian fur trader and amateur astronomer. Though he lived and died in obscurity, and never profited from his work, Thompson has since been hailed as "one of the greatest practical land geographers the world has ever known."

Welsh by birth, Thompson was apprenticed to the Hudson's Bay Company at age 14 and sent to northern Manitoba. Within a year he had learned to live off the land, Indian-style, and later, with the help of a company surveyor, he became an expert mapmaker as well. When he finished his training in 1791, Thompson declined the new suit of clothes the company offered its employees and obtained instead a set of surveying instruments. In 1797 he switched his allegiance to the North West Company, a more adventurous outfit. Entrusted with searching out new trade routes, the peripatetic mapmaker traveled ceaselessly by canoe, on horseback, on foot, and by dogsled, tacking back and forth from Idaho to the Pacific coast and north into the sub-Arctic. By 1812 he had explored some one and a half million square miles.

A pious man who neither smoked, swore, nor drank — and, unusual for a fur trader, refused to sell alcohol to Indians —Thompson lived with various tribes for months at a time and eventually married a woman who was half-Cree. His devotion to astronomy earned him the Indian name Koo-Koo-Sint, He Who Watches Stars. Thompson's journals, which were as detailed as his maps, provide one of the rare accounts of tribal life before it was disrupted forever by Europeans.

federal support failed to materialize and Kelley repeatedly postponed the departure date.

In 1834 Kelley set out on his own for Oregon. Stricken with malaria, he arrived at Fort Vancouver and was treated kindly, if coolly, by the British authorities he had reviled in his writings. By 1836 he was back home, to spend the rest of his life asking Congress to reward his services. Though he failed as empire builder, he ultimately did inspire others to establish an American presence in a disputed and then-remote region.

Land of Opportunity

George Washington Bush was no ordinary homesteader. Born in the late 1700's of mixed ancestry — his mother was Irish and his father is variously reported as African, East Indian, or Native American — Bush worked as a fur trapper and a nurseryman and, despite his Quaker upbringing, fought under Andrew Jackson during the War of 1812. By 1831 he had married and settled into a prosperous life as a farmer and cattle trader in Missouri. But he nevertheless continued to suffer racial prejudice.

In the early 1840's Bush and several neighbors, hearing tales of rich land in Oregon, talked of heading west. Bush also dreamed of a better life for his five sons in the free territory of the Northwest. So in 1844 he and some friends joined a wagon train headed for Oregon, with Bush helping some of them pay their way. When the party got to the Columbia River, however, Bush found that this American territory excluded blacks — and whatever his ancestry, he was considered black. With his neighbors he continued north into British territory near Puget Sound, where he established one of the most productive farms in the Pacific Northwest and continued to dispense his, by then, legendary generosity.

So it was ironic that four years after Britain ceded the region to the United States in 1846, Bush was threatened with expulsion. But his many friends rallied and obtained legislation exempting Bush from discrimination. He died in 1863, the extremely successful and well-respected owner of a 640-acre spread known as Bush Prairie.

Don Pedro Comes to Monterey

A short-tempered Catalan soldier known as "the bear," Don Pedro Fages was indispensable to Spain during its early years in California. He arrived in 1770 as part of the "sacred expedition" that scouted sites for the first California missions. After leading an inspection tour of San Francisco Bay, he stayed on as military commander. Then, in 1772, Fages saved the fledgling settlement at Monterey from starvation: when supply ships failed to appear, he provisioned the garrison by shooting bears in a nearby canyon.

Retired temporarily to Mexico after his volatile personality angered one too many officials, Fages returned triumphantly to California as governor in 1782. No sooner was he settled than he called for his wife, Doña Eulalia, and their young son to join him. But the high-born, high-spirited Eulalia had no interest in leaving Mexico for an outpost in the wilderness. It took months of pleading to persuade her to come, and her journey up the coast took another six months.

When she finally arrived at the colonial capital in Monterey, Eulalia was so appalled by conditions and by the nakedness of the Indians that she began giving away her clothes and those of Don Pedro. She finally stopped, turning to more practical acts of charity, when her husband protested that she soon would be naked herself.

Hunting bears and leading men, Fages discovered, was far easier than marriage. Begging to go home, Eulalia tried barring Don Pedro from her room, threw fits, threatened friars, and even wrote a secret letter requesting her husband's transfer to civilization. But eventually she gave in. "Thanks to God that we are now living in union and harmony," wrote Fages. He served until 1791, then at last returned to Mexico.

A Bit of Moscow on Bodega Bay

As he neared the end of a tour of his country's northern Pacific outposts in 1805, Russian nobleman Nikolai Rezanov was anxious to return home. Even so, he stopped to visit the Russian colony at Sitka, Alaska. And there he found his countrymen literally eating crow. Famine gripped the Russian-American Fur Company's outpost, and as an official in the company, Rezanov was determined to save it.

Buying a ship that was moored in the harbor, Rezanov filled it with trade goods and headed for San Francisco to barter for supplies. There, unfortunately, he found that the Spanish commander, Don José Argüello, was not allowed to trade with Russia. He could entertain Rezanov as a guest, however, and Rezanov (who was 40) took the opportunity to woo Argüello's beautiful 15-year-old daughter, Concepción. Rezanov proposed and was accepted, but before the marriage could take place, the couple had to get permission from both the pope and the tsar.

Rezanov sailed off, promising to return within two years. But he never made it to Moscow, for he died while crossing Siberia. (Years passed before Concepción learned of his death, and she eventually entered a convent.) Though Rezanov never reached Moscow, his report to the tsar did get through. In it he recommended that Russia extend its colonies southward from Alaska into California. Not only would this open the possibility of trade with Spain, but food could be grown there for the Alaskan settlements.

In 1811 a Russian emissary bartered with the Indians for some land near Bodega Bay, and by the next year there was a settlement, which came to be known as Fort Ross. Russia maintained its little outpost in Spanish America until 1841, when it sold the land to rancher John Sutter, who was to become a central figure in the California gold rush.

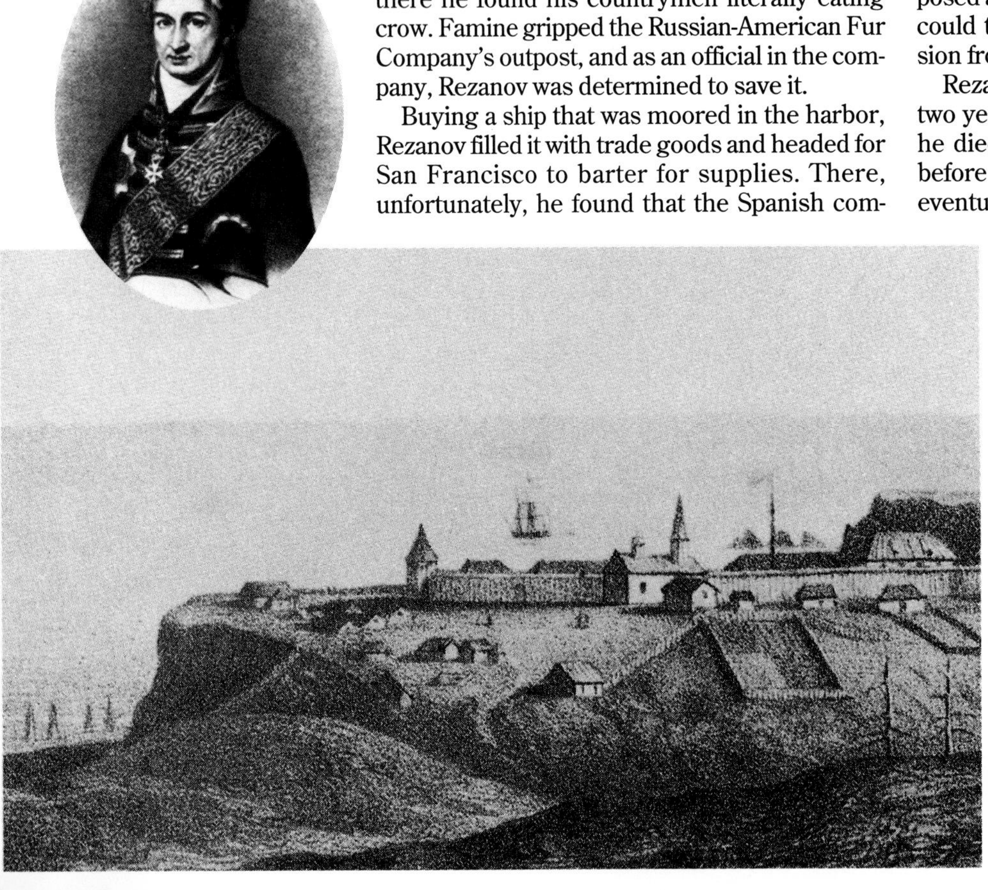

Nikolai Rezanov (above left) never lived to see his idea of a Russian settlement in California fulfilled. Pictured in 1877, Fort Ross (left) still looked much as it did when the Russians built it.

"What a Country This Might Be!"

On the Pacific Coast between the 1820's and 1840's, cowhides were known as California bank notes — and the name was no joke. Cattle ranching in those days was California's primary industry, and hides and tallow were the colony's main medium of exchange.

The basis for what came to be called the hide and tallow trade was the seemingly limitless number of cattle that roamed California's grasslands, all of them descended from a few hundred animals introduced by Spanish friars some 50 years before. *Vaqueros* rode down and slaughtered the beasts by the tens of thousands. They then skinned the animals, stripped off the best meat and tallow-bearing fat, and left the rest to the coyotes.

The market for the products was at San Diego, which had a good harbor and a climate that was ideal for drying hides. In exchange for tallow (used for candle making) and hides (for making boots and shoes), seamen on American merchant ships offered manufactured goods from furniture to fireworks — virtually "everything under the sun," wrote Richard Henry Dana in *Two Years Before the Mast,* for, he noted, "the Californians are an idle, thriftless people and can make nothing for themselves." A Harvard student who had gone to sea in 1834 after a bout with measles, Dana was Yankee to the core. He was scandalized to see Californians buying shoes made from their own cowhides, but made in a Massachusetts factory. The same hide, he noted, had been around Cape Horn twice by the time a Californian put it on his foot.

In all, the West Coast ranchers shipped out the better part of a million and a quarter hides by 1845, when indiscriminate slaughter had at last destroyed the wild herds. But it was Dana's account of his experiences, published in 1840, that ultimately had the more lasting effect on California's economy. "In the hands of an enterprising people," he wrote, "what a country this might be!" And Yankees took note.

William Hutton, a soldier stationed in California in the 1840's, sketched several scenes of the hide and tallow industry. At the *matanza*, or slaughtering ground (above), hides can be seen drying on racks in the background. The workers (left) are boiling down fat, then skimming off the tallow for making candles.

NATIVE TONGUE

THE REIGN OF SPAIN

Long before the macho American cowboy rode the western range, there was the Spanish-speaking vaquero *— and such an influential* hombre *was he that he left our language enriched by many horse- related terms.* Buckaroo, rodeo, mustang, bronco, stampede, lasso, *and* chaps *(short for* chaparejos*) all have their roots in Spanish.*

So do many place names — Rio Grande, El Paso, Santa Fe, and Yerba Buena Island, for instance, are pure Spanish, as are the names of several states. Colorado refers to the reddish color of the Little Colorado River, and Nevada — in allusion to its mountain peaks — means snowy.

Even features of the landscape itself, such as mesas and canyons, were named by the Spanish, as were some of the creatures they encountered, from burros and buffalos to mosquitoes (from mosca, *fly) and cockroaches (from* cucaracha*).*

Wouldn't the conquistadors — whose descendants gave us such colorful terms as pronto, savvy, incommunicado, *and* vamoose *— be surprised to see what they started? We also have them to thank for* haciendas, siestas, patios, *and* plazas, *to say nothing of* tequila, tortillas, tamales, *and* tacos.

Although Point's missionary outpost had little in the way of goods to offer the Indians in Montana, the novelty of sitting for a portrait (above left) was often reason enough for a visit. The scene (above) shows Blackfoot Indians setting up their tepees at an encampment.

The naïve quality of Point's art is part of its charm. In this firelit scene he depicted a council of Nez Percé chiefs arrayed in their ceremonial finery.

Wilderness Chronicler

Charged with the responsibility of keeping a journal in the wilderness, a missionary priest used his paintbrush to create a delightful record.

Nicolas Point was 42 years old when he set out with Father Pierre Jean De Smet to evangelize the Indians of the Rocky Mountains in 1841. A French-born Jesuit priest, Point had by then been in the United States for six years, patiently serving as a college administrator while waiting to be sent into the wilderness. He finally got his chance when the Flathead Indians invited the Jesuits to open a mission in western Montana, and in late April he joined De Smet for the long trek from Missouri.

Appointed official diarist for the journey, Point began a journal that, over the next several years, swelled into a rich account of the still-virgin West. His descriptions of wildlife and prairie flowers, of undulating plains crisscrossed with clear-running rivers, are among the few written records of the region's pristine beauty. Even more remarkable, however, are the luminous illustrations Point added to convey his impressions of the Flathead, Blackfeet, Nez Percé, and Coeur d'Alene tribes and their homelands.

Initially, Point noted, it was the splendor of the wilderness landscape that moved him to paint. Soon, however, he was making sketches to amuse and instruct his Indian hosts, whose love of color was equal to his own. In doing so, Point discovered that the Indians seemed to understand his religious teaching most readily through pictures. "This method of instruction had two noticeable advantages," he wrote. "While the truths entered their souls through their eyes, the great virtues were infused into their hearts."

Patron of the Arts

The adventurous second son of a Scottish noble family, William Drummond Stewart was as brave as he was impetuous. He had already served as captain in the King's Hussars and was a Waterloo veteran when, in 1833, he first visited the American West. Traveling all the way to the Rocky Mountains, he found high adventure hunting for buffalo and living the life of the mountain man.

Thoroughly enamored of the West, the intrepid Scot enjoyed the trip so much that he returned to the Rockies in 1837, this time with an artist in tow. Alfred Jacob Miller, whom Drummond had met en route in New Orleans, had been born in Baltimore but had studied painting in France and Italy. Though he worked primarily as a portrait

In this atmospheric painting Alfred Jacob Miller depicted the adventurous Scotsman William Drummond Stewart meeting with an Indian chief. The chief is firing a rifle into the air, an act that was considered a demonstration of friendship.

artist, he readily accepted his new patron's unusual commission: Stewart wanted him to make sketches of all there was to see — particularly Indian life — on a caravan from St. Louis, Missouri, to the Green River in Wyoming. It was a golden opportunity for Miller and for posterity.

Once again Stewart spent the summer playing the role of gentleman mountain man, buffalo hunting and cavorting with trappers at their annual rendezvous. Miller meanwhile worked steadily at his sketchbook, recording both the glories of the scenery and the incidents that occurred along the way.

Later, in New Orleans and during a stay in Scotland, Miller made paintings based on his drawings. He pictured Sioux Indians on the warpath, quiet moments in camp, and his buckskin-clad host (who by then was *Sir* William) leading a party of hunters across the vast western landscape. In short, he filled the Stewart castle with one of the finest pictorial records of the West and captured a way of life that was soon lost forever.

Royal High Jinks on the Plains

The cast of characters reads like a novelist's late-night fantasy: Buffalo Bill Cody, Gen. George A. Custer, and a thousand Sioux on horseback. All had gathered to entertain the latest in a long list of well-heeled foreigners who had fallen under the spell of the American West. This time the guest of honor was none other than Grand Duke Alexis Romanov, son of the Russian tsar.

It was January 1872 and the coldest winter in memory when the young duke, after a leisurely tour of the eastern states, headed west to hunt buffalo. Two months of planning had gone into the arrangements for "Camp Alexis" on the snowy Nebraskan plains, where the visitor was greeted by a cavalry band playing "Hail to the Chief." Under the direction of Gen. Philip Sheridan, the camp lacked few comforts. It was made up of some 40 tents — the duke's own was heated and had a wooden floor and carpeting. Enormous hospital tents were used as dining rooms, whose fare was prepared by chefs, from supplies hauled out from Omaha. The Sioux, led by Chief Spotted Tail and arrayed in their best feathers and beads, had come at the request of Buffalo Bill and obliged the duke by performing a war dance.

Early on the morning of January 14, after a night of memorably generous toasts, the party rode out in search of buffalo. An early thaw made the air springlike, and the clear skies and dazzling landscape could not have been more picture perfect. Cody and Custer led the way: their charge, topped with a fur turban, joined them on a superb black stallion, brandishing his revolver.

Seventeen miles from camp they encountered a buffalo herd, and Custer rode in to cut a large bull loose. It fell to Buffalo Bill, however, to make sure their guest (a notoriously bad shot) got a buffalo, and he replaced Alexis's revolver with a rifle. When the bull was just a few feet away, the young man took aim, and the bull was his. It was the duke's 22nd birthday, and the popping of champagne corks could be heard in celebration of his wilderness adventure.

Before leaving the West, Grand Duke Alexis sat for his portrait with a reclining George Custer. He also presented Buffalo Bill with a diamond-studded buffalo pin and cufflinks.

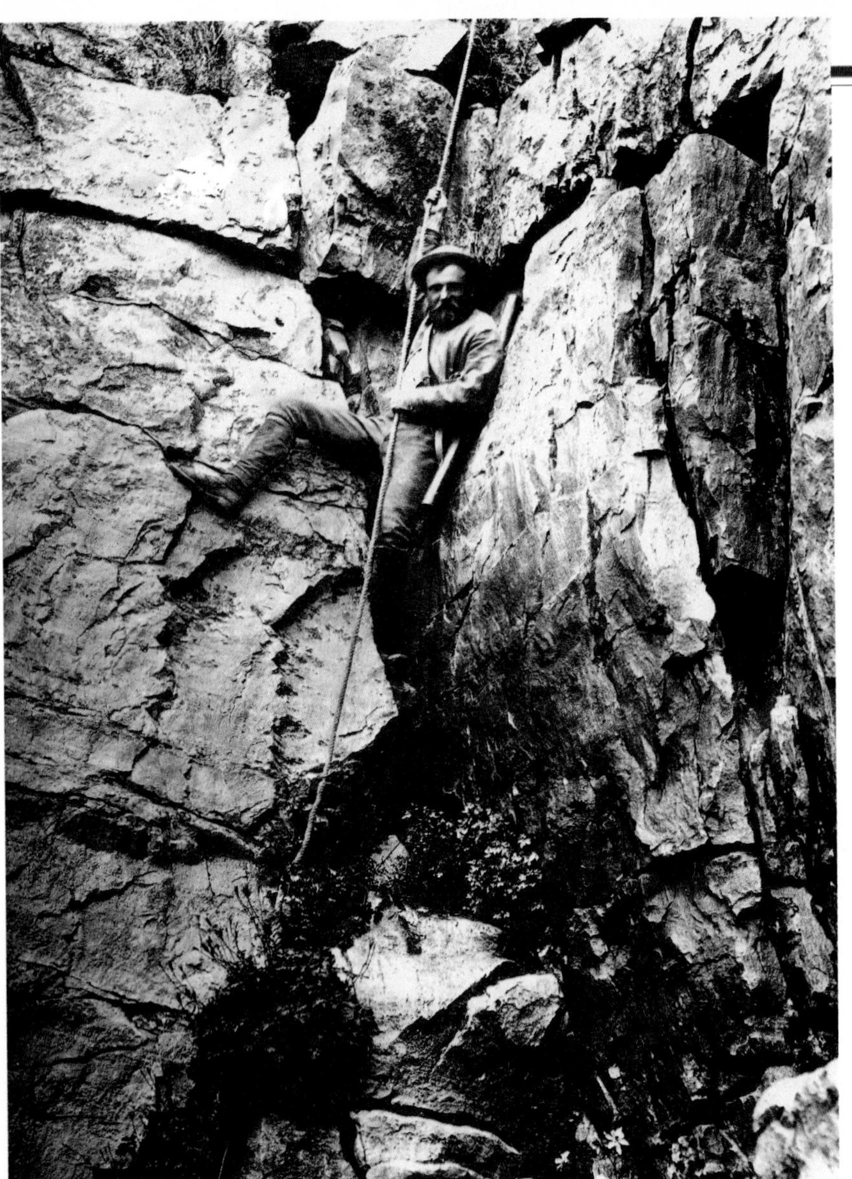

As a young man, geologist Clarence King found adventure in his fieldwork. In his later years the talented rockhound raconteur delighted his admirers with tales of scrapes, escapes, and the occasional brush with death.

Rockhound Raconteur

To his friend historian Henry Adams, Clarence King was the ideal American: vigorous, adventurous, literate — and fast out of the gate. In 1863, a year after graduating from Yale with a science degree, the Rhode Island–born youth headed west, stopped to visit the famous Comstock Lode in Nevada, then continued on foot across the Sierras.

After a chance meeting with a member of the California Geological Survey, King joined the project as an assistant geologist. Less than three years later, he won congressional approval for the exploration and mapping of a 100-mile-wide swath of territory extending from eastern Colorado to the California border — a fossil-rich strip that was also the proposed route of the transcontinental railroad.

King proved himself a masterful administrator as well as a first-rate scientist. His report on the western ranges, with its innovative contour maps and vivid prose, still stands as the definitive geological work on the area. King's reward was his appointment as the first director of the U.S. Geological Survey. After a brief tenure, however, he stepped down in order to seek his own fortune in the mines — a goal that eluded him utterly and distracted him from the exercise of his genuine gifts.

A collection of sketches that was published in 1872, *Mountaineering in the Sierra Nevada*, won King critical acclaim as a writer, and his exposure of a bold diamond-salting hoax that same year made him a national hero. But his restless nature seemed to require constant challenge and better judgment than he proved to possess. He spent the second half of his life in debt to the friends he so masterfully transfixed, an armchair raconteur living off a brilliant past.

Audubon's Last Look

John James Audubon embarked on the last of his travels through North America on the eve of his 58th birthday in 1843. He planned to journey from his New York home to the Rocky Mountains to observe wildlife for his book *Viviparous Quadrupeds of North America,* and to get a look at the western Indians immortalized by painter George Catlin. But after learning of the hardships he would likely face, he decided on a less strenuous steamer trip up the Missouri River.

In what proved to be a sort of armchair excursion, Audubon viewed the flora and fauna mostly from midstream, with specimen collecting limited to brief forays ashore. His few encounters with Indians elicited the sour judgment that their glory had been exaggerated. Audubon's journal nevertheless is rich with accounts of bird sightings and of mammal specimens purchased or received as gifts — the elk and grizzly bears, wolves and red foxes that would find their way into his final work, along with dozens of rhapsodic passages on buffalo, the artist having been completely smitten by their splendor.

Aububon painted the thirteen-lined ground squirrel on his western trip.

From games and pastimes (left) to chores such as spinning yarn (below), the intricate tapestry of pueblo life was recorded in the unique photographs taken by Charles Lummis.

Spokesman for the Southwest

Of the many outsize characters who shaped the image of the American West, few so successfully straddled eccentricity and respectability as Charles Lummis. A minister's son and Harvard dropout, Lummis began his western adventure with a 3,507-mile, 143-day hike from Ohio to California in 1884. "The longest walk for pure pleasure that is on record," Lummis called it; but there was pain in it, too — and profit.

Before leaving his newspaper job in Ohio, he had arranged for the *Los Angeles Times* to publish dispatches he would send ahead, and so was already famous when he arrived in California. Stories of his mishaps — including a broken arm he set with his canteen strap at the base of a cliff in Arizona — made him a legendary figure at 26.

But that was just the start. After a few frenzied years with the *Times,* Lummis suffered a bout of paralysis that cost him two months in bed. He then decided to visit friends in New Mexico, and there began a lifelong love affair with things Spanish and Indian.

Lummis plunged into an exploration of the surviving Hispanic and Pueblo cultures by interviewing elders, recording songs and stories, and despite his still-useless left arm, exploring the Anasazi cliff dwellings with archaeologist Adolph Bandelier and taking glass-plate photographs with a 40-pound camera. He was the first to photograph the rites of the Penitentes, a cult of self-flagellants who reenacted the Crucifixion on Good Friday. Everything western struck the displaced New Englander as superior, and he seemed perpetually in need of proving himself a fit part of it.

Slightly built but doggedly athletic, Lummis broke wild horses and teased rattlesnakes for sport, and affected a red sash as part of his everyday costume. He was, without a doubt, vain and self-promoting. Yet his zealous affection for his adopted territory was both genuine and grounded in years of serious work. He published 17 books in his lifetime, the majority of them on the Southwest — a term he popularized — and its history.

Back in Los Angeles in 1893, Lummis became an influential, if cranky, citizen who indulged in a remarkable burst of civic organizing. He founded the Sequoyah League to improve the lot of Indians, the Landmarks Club to save the early Spanish missions of California, and the Southwest Museum, devoted to promoting and preserving the indigenous culture. A booster of the most perceptive sort, the inventor of the slogan "See America first" found value in what others dismissed, and by sheer force of will guaranteed its preservation for later generations.

Ranchers and Cowhands

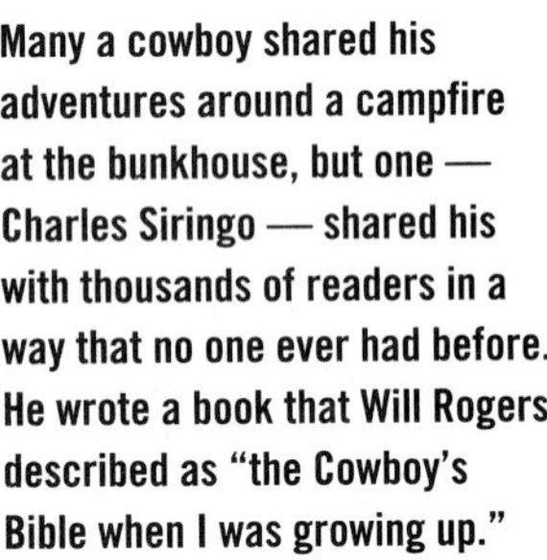

Many a cowboy shared his adventures around a campfire at the bunkhouse, but one — Charles Siringo — shared his with thousands of readers in a way that no one ever had before. He wrote a book that Will Rogers described as "the Cowboy's Bible when I was growing up."

True-Life Tales for the Armchair Cowboy

Charles Siringo may have been exaggerating when he claimed his first book sold a million copies — but perhaps not by very much. Published in 1885, *A Texas Cowboy or Fifteen Years on the Hurricane Deck of a Spanish Pony* was the first authentic autobiography written by a working cowboy. And as such, it was devoured by almost every ranch hand who could read, as well as by city folk who dreamed of living the wrangler's life.

"My excuse for writing this book is money — and lots of it," wrote Siringo, who was 30 and working as a shopkeeper in Kansas when the book appeared. But if money was the object, he also had plenty of stories to tell, having begun his career as a cowboy in Texas at the age of 11.

Known as a man who was courageous to the point of recklessness, and a keen shot with a six-shooter, Siringo had experienced exactly the kinds of adventures that fans of the West wanted to read about. Best of all his tales were true, and his gritty, wholly unsentimental style made them all the more engrossing. He had ridden the Chisholm Trail, slogged through cattle drives in the rain and in baking heat, stopped stampedes in the wee hours of the morning, roped buffalo, and slept in the grass at night with a bellyful of jackrabbit that he had caught himself.

He also introduced some memorable characters, such as his first employer, Shanghai Pierce, the self-proclaimed "Webster on cattle, by God, Sir," and Billy the Kid, whom Siringo helped track down. After hearing about the Kid's capture by Pat Garrett in 1880, Siringo reported: "Kid was the last man to come out with his hands up. He said he would have starved to death before surrendering if the rest had stayed with him."

After his stint as a shopkeeper, Siringo seems to have decided to return to the adventurous life. Following the sucess of his first book, he spent 20 years as a Pinkerton detective chasing fugitives — among them, Butch Cassidy and the Wild Bunch — and wrote five more books chronicling those exploits and more in the Wild West.

The Cowboy Look

Since a cowboy had to travel light on the trail, his clothing, by necessity, was absolutely practical. But looks were important, too. Many men were particularly fond of their broad-brimmed hats — a style developed by Easterner John B. Stetson. Affectionately referred to as war bonnet and conk cover, the cowboy hat kept rain and sun off a man's face and was used to carry water and fan campfires. A man simply did not travel without it, nor without his bandanna. Tied at the back of the neck, the bandanna could be pulled up over the nose in a dust storm; taken off, it doubled as a sling or bandage.

A cowboy might splurge a bit to buy fur or leather chaps to protect his legs from chafing on the trail. But he could spend serious money when it came to boots. The high-heeled style was practical since it kept the foot from slipping through a stirrup. Few self-respecting cowhands, however, would settle for plain-old store-bought boots, which commonly sold for about $10. Their tastes ran instead to custom-made affairs tooled with lone stars and crescent moons — boots that could easily cost an entire month's pay.

A painting by Charles Russell portrays one of the worst jobs on a cattle drive: riding at the end of the herd, where dust was fierce and the bandanna a constant necessity.

The Legend of Deadwood Dick

Nat Love led a high-ridin', rip-snortin' life — or so he said. His autobiography, *The Life and Adventures of Nat Love,* published in 1907, is full of the sort of romantic cowboy yarns where the hero — himself — always beats impossible odds. "I gloried in the danger," he wrote.

Boasting of his many bullet wounds and close calls with Indians, hailstorms, and wild animals, Love seemed never to find himself in a fix from which he could not escape. He claimed he rode 100 miles in 12 hours bareback on a horse, was adopted by an Indian tribe, survived for days without food in a snowstorm, and even galloped into a Mexican saloon on his horse, ordering drinks for both himself and his steed. Among his friends, he said, were Billy the Kid, Jesse James, and Bat Masterson — and he claimed a "handsome young Spanish girl" as his first love.

Separating fact from fiction

Love told so many tales, in fact, that it is impossible to know which, if any, are true. But he undoubtedly did come a long way from the Tennessee log cabin where he was born into slavery seven years before the start of the Civil War. At 15 he traveled to Dodge City, Kansas, got himself a $30-a-month job as a cowpuncher at the stockyards, and then worked as a cattle driver.

It was on one such trip in 1876 that his larger-than-life adventures supposedly began. Entering a Fourth of July rodeo in Deadwood, South Dakota, Love was able to rope, throw, tie, and saddle a wild horse in nine minutes, breaking all known records and earning the nickname Deadwood Dick (the name of the fictional hero in a then-popular series of Western adventures).

Like other cowboys of African descent (about a quarter of all cowboys were black), Love surely endured discrimination, but he wrote nothing about it. He clearly wanted his readers to see him as he saw himself: "mounted on my favorite horse . . . my trusty guns in my belt . . . I felt I could defy the world."

Most of what is known about Nat Love is what he claimed for himself. He wrote that in 1890 he gave up the range for the railroads. Whether he was truly a cowboy when he stood for this picture — or was simply posing as the character he created — no one knows.

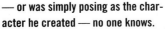

Roundup Time on the Range

Cowboys used specially trained mounts, called cutting horses, to separate individual cattle from the herd. Here, Emory Sager rides his horse Old Blue as he cuts out a steer at the Shoe Bar Ranch in Texas in the early years of the 20th century.

He might sing songs about drifting along like a tumbleweed, but in fact nobody worked harder than a cowboy, especially at roundup time. Until the late 19th century when barbed wire enabled ranchers to fence in their land, cattle grazed in mixed herds on the open range and roundups were twice-a-year chores. In the fall ranchers rounded up the herds to pick out the animals they would send to market. The big roundup, however, took place in spring before the young calves became separated from their mothers. Then, hands from all ranches in the district assembled on the range to sort out the herds and make sure that each calf got marked with its owner's brand.

The roundup might take anywhere from a few weeks to a couple of months. And if it looked like bedlam at times, activities actually were carefully orchestrated. They had to be, since a roundup could involve hundreds of square miles and as many as 300 to 400 cowboys. Each cowboy might have 10 horses or "remounts" that were managed by wranglers. The ranches also sent along their own chuck wagons and cooks. In charge of everything was the wagon boss, a roundup captain chosen by the ranch owners. His word was law as he marshaled the men in groups and sent them out to comb sections of the range.

Rising before dawn, the men in each team pulled on their boots, gulped down steak and coffee, and mounted up. Led by the wagon boss, they rode out, forming a circle perhaps 20 miles across. Then they worked their way back in, driving along any cattle that they found. Some riders searched ravines and thickets for strays and prodded them back to the herd. By afternoon there might be 1,000 cows milling in the center of the circle. Then it was time to remount and begin the process of sorting and branding. Only with sundown did the work end, and after a bowl of soup or stew, there would be hardly an hour left for playing poker.

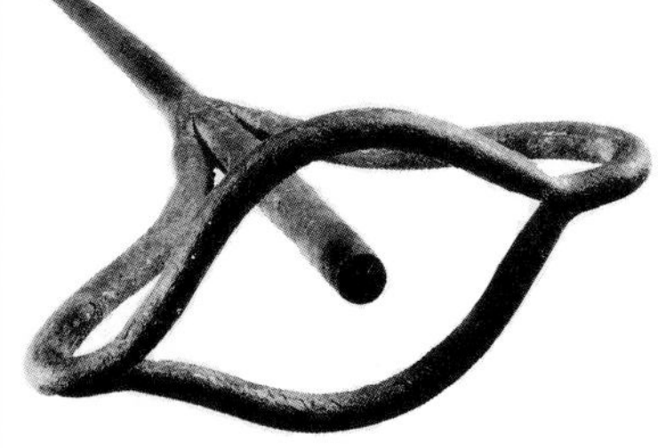

The Cattleman's Scepter

In the 1840's, Texas cattleman Sam Maverick refused to brand his herd, and ever since, all unbranded cattle have been known as mavericks. Most ranchers, however, would never have been so foolish, for — especially in the days when herds roamed freely on open range — a brand was the most reliable way to identify a cow as one's own. "A branding iron," said one old timer, "is to a rancher what a sceptre is to a king."

Hernando Cortés, the Spanish conquistador who introduced cattle to the New World in the 16th century, also introduced the branding iron — essentially an iron rod with the owner's "trademark" worked at one end. Cortés chose three Christian crosses for his brand, and cattlemen to this day have followed suit, devising symbols of their own. Designs had to be registered with the county before being burned into their ultimate destination — a calf's left haunch.

Many ranchers have had a little fun with their brands. A Mr. Money, for instance, used a dollar sign for his. Others have been rebuses — Mr. Ford's "4D," for instance, and Mr. Crosby's "+B." But cleverness aside, it has always been more important to design brands that are difficult to alter. One cattleman who used his initials, "IC," is said to have lost his cattle to a rustler who added a "U" on each cow's hip. When the true owner stole his cows back, he in turn added a "2" — I see you too.

Cattlemen have been inventive in designing their brands. The Hog-Eye iron (above) made the mark at the right. The others (from left to right) are Rocking Chair, Walking A, Lazy S, Terrapin, and Rocking K.

Making and Breaking the Perfect Pony

"There ain't no hoss that can't be rode; there ain't no man that can't be throwed," runs an old cowboy adage. Breaking in a wild horse — the first step in making the perfect cow pony — was, in truth, work that no one looked forward to on a ranch. Success in "riding out" a bronco (the word is Spanish for rough) might cure the horse of bucking, but it could also leave the rider bruised and bleeding. There are even stories of cowboys falling dead from the saddle.

So it is hardly surprising that ranch hands generally were glad to leave the job to itinerant bronco "peelers" or "busters," who hired on to break horses at a few dollars apiece. They commanded great respect, and one of the greatest — a man known throughout the Texas Panhandle — was Matthew "Bones" Hooks. Born in 1867, the son of former slaves, Hooks worked roundups even as a child, when he drove a chuck wagon. As a young man he came to be called "one of the best riders who ever sat leather," and in working the range for 25 years, he firmly established his reputation as a bronco buster.

But the most remarkable proof of his skills came in 1910 after he had retired and taken a job as a railroad porter. He was on a train near Amarillo when he overheard passengers talking about a horse no one could ride. The temptation was too much. "I can ride that horse," he promised, and agreed to do so at the Pampa depot for $25. When the train pulled in at Pampa, Hooks donned boots and Stetson, rode the horse to a standstill, and was back in his porter's uniform before the train was ready to pull out again.

In the days when ranchers got their best cow ponies from wild and semiwild stock, a bronco buster might ride as many as six or eight mounts a day, staying with each one for an hour. This might be repeated for several days before the horses got used to a rider — and the rider got his well-earned fee. Tex Crockett showed how it was done at a Wild West show in 1919.

Cattleman With a Mission

The man who could be called the father of America's cattle industry was not a cowboy but a priest. In 1678 Father Eusebio Kino, an Italian scholar and Jesuit priest, traveled from Italy to Spain to await his first missionary assignment. Two years later, he was on his way to Mexico, where he explored, drew maps, and made great progress with his missionary work. But that was not enough. In 1687, when he was about 42, Kino traveled north and, during the next 24 years, founded 24 missions in what is now northern Mexico and Arizona. At each site he established a ranch, and wishing to introduce European culture, he bred and gave away thousands of head of hardy longhorns. Then he taught the native people the Spanish routines of the roundup, branding, and butchering. Many of the finest vaqueros in the early West were Indians. A tireless horseman himself, Father Kino, like any real cowhand, preferred to sleep on the ground, with only a horse blanket for a mattress and his saddle for a pillow.

The Cattleman's Long Drive

By the 1860's America's railroads were inching westward, but they did not yet pass through Texas. If a rancher wanted to sell his cows, he had to take them, by cattle drive, to railheads in Abilene, Wichita, or one of the other cowtowns along the rails.

For some 20 years, until the mid-1880's, the long drive — which could involve hundreds of miles and months of riding — was part of every

New Mexico artist Ila McAfee portrayed the welcome break on a cattle drive when longhorns watered at a river. Lack of water caused many hardships and great losses.

Biscuits, Beef, and Son-of-a-bitch Stew

On the earliest cattle drives, each trail hand carried his own provisions in a sack. All that changed in 1866 when Texas cattleman Charles Goodnight bought a surplus army wagon with sturdy iron axles and converted it into a chuck wagon. The innovation was so practical that it was soon copied by other ranchers. Manufactured versions also became available.

"Chuck" was western slang for food, and the thing that distinguished Goodnight's wagon from all others was the chuck box — a storage cabinet with a door that folded down to make a worktable for the cook at the wagon's rear. Many chuck wagons also had water barrels strapped on, tarpaulins to cover the cooking area in rainy weather, and a sling for carrying a day's worth of "prairie coal" (dried cow chips) underneath.

At the call of "chuck away, come and get it," the trail hands gathered for meals. The menu might be a bit monotonous — coffee, biscuits, red beans ("prairie strawberries"), fried steak, and the concoction of cow innards known as "son-of-a-bitch stew" — but no one was allowed to complain about the food.

The cook — often an old cowboy referred to as Cookie — worked longer hours than the other men and was well paid to ensure that meals were always on time. Cooks had a reputation as despots, probably at least in part because of the working conditions they had to endure: they might have wet fuel one day, and frozen supplies the next. And with so many hungry men to feed, they had to enforce a strict etiquette. Woe to any cowboy who helped himself to food without permission or, worse yet, rode into camp from upwind so that dust enveloped a meal in the making. But since the men relied on Cookie to cut their hair, mend their clothes, bandage their injuries, and dose them with whiskey for snakebite, they put up with his tyranny. As one piece of old-time trail wisdom cautioned, "Only a fool argues with a skunk, a mule, or a cook."

The chuck box on the back of a wagon provided both pantry and worktable. No one was allowed to eat at Cookie's table, however. Cowboys, like these in the 1890's, ate from their laps.

cattleman's year. The average herd taken to the cow towns numbered about 2,500 head. For the rancher there was plenty of money to be made, even if he suffered losses en route, since a longhorn worth $3 or $4 in Texas could fetch $40 when it reached the eastern markets. And the hired hands who rode with the herds were paid only $25 to $40 a month.

Life on the trail was grueling: most cowboys remained on the job for only seven years or so. There were usually about six men to every 1,000 longhorns on a drive, and 15 to 20 miles was considered a good day's progress. Getting the entire herd across a river could take a whole day — and sometimes even longer. The trail hands also had to contend with heat, dust, thunderstorms, and hailstones big enough to knock a man off his horse.

But possibly the worst of the drive's challenges was the lack of sleep. Since the hands worked in shifts after dark, some never got more than five hours of rest. All through the night, two riders would circle the herd in opposite directions, singing gentle melodies as they went. As every cowboy knew, singing helped keep the cattle calm. Some even believed that the mere sound of a human voice would prevent longhorns from stampeding. On bad nights, one hand recalled, the cowboy who could "keep up the most racket" — sing the best — "was the pet of the bunch."

Capturing the drama of a stampede was one of artist Frederic Remington's toughest challenges.

Stampede!

Cowhands faced many dangers when they rode at top speed over unfamiliar ground in the dark of the night, trying to stop a herd of panicked cattle.

For cowmen on cattle drives, few hazards were more feared than stampedes. And stampedes happened all too often, for the Texas longhorn cattle of the 19th century spooked easily: in the dark of night, almost anything could set them off. Lightning storms were a common cause of stampedes, but if the cattle were especially nervous — when they were new to the trail, for instance — a sneeze, a glimpse of a haystack looming in the moonlight, or the mere snap of a twig could have the same effect. Without warning, and all in an instant, the entire herd would thunder off in panic.

The animals' loud bellowing and the vibrations from thousands of pounding hooves immediately alerted all hands back in camp that a stampede was under way. Leaping to their horses, the cowboys would try to overtake the cattle at the front and change their path, forcing the herd to turn in a wide circle. If that could be managed, the worst was over, and the animals would eventually run themselves out.

Collecting the strays after a stampede might keep a cowboy in the saddle for 24 hours without a break. Losses could be substantial, since cattle were often trampled in the panic and others were crippled from falls. Worse yet, with each stampede the cattle lost weight — the last thing a drover wanted while on the way to market.

Home on the Range

The best-known of all cowboy songs was actually the work of Brewster Higley, an Ohio doctor, and Daniel Kelley, a musician from Rhode Island. The two met after moving west to seek their fortunes on the plains of Kansas.

Higley had written the lyrics as a poem he called "Western Home," and Kelley put it to music. Their version was published in the December 1873 Smith County Pioneer. *It was virtually identical to the one sung today — except that it lacked any reference to "home on the range." The refrain, it seems, was added by trail-riding cowboys who took the tune back to Texas.*

Though crooned at campfires in the West, "Home on the Range" did not reach national fame until the 1930's, when members of the press used it to serenade Franklin Delano Roosevelt on the night he was first elected president. News had apparently gotten out that it was Roosevelt's favorite song.

Jinglebob King of the Pecos River

Cattle baron John Chisum never lost touch with the day-to-day maintenance of his herds and often worked side by side with his hired hands. A dyed-in-the-wool wrangler, he scorned beds, preferring to sleep on the floor at his ranch house.

It was said that if John Chisum thought the price was right, he would "drive a herd straight through hell and deliver to the devil himself." He had started small, with a partnership in a herd of 1,200 and a contract to sell meat to the Confederate Army. But by the 1870's no rancher cast a longer shadow than John Chisum, the Cow King of New Mexico.

Chisum had nothing to do with the famous cattle trail known as the Chisolm Trail. A rancher and cowman so skilled at his craft that he could pick a troublesome steer from a herd after circling it once, he worked a ranch that, at its peak, sprawled along 150 miles of the Pecos River and covered an area roughly half the size of New England. His herds were reputed to number between 60,000 and 100,000 head of cattle, and Chisum himself once "reckoned" he could fill an order for 40,000 steers "without trying too hard."

Popularly known as "Uncle John," the cattle king appeared so unassuming that he was once mistaken for one of his hired hands. After watching him perform some chore, a stranger asked, "Working for Old Chisum?" "Yes," he is said to have replied, "working for Old Chisum."

Maintaining thousands of animals meant unending work. At a time when the open range was studded with small ranches and free-ranging cattle that mingled indiscriminately, great efforts were made to establish proper ownership of the animals. Chisum's cattle were particularly distinctive, thanks to the "jinglebob," a deep slash on the ear that left a flap dangling and gave his spread the nickname "Jinglebob Ranch." He also branded his cattle with a bar that ran from shoulder to hip across the cow's left side. One season he and his hands branded some 18,000 calves.

Chisum's hospitality was as vast as his ranch. At his adobe "Long House," where his niece presided over two full-time cooks, the table could easily accommodate 26 visitors. Chisum surrounded the house with an oasis of cottonwoods, roses, flowering hedges — and even songbirds imported from his native Tennessee. Chisum never married. He died in 1884, leaving the memory of a man who was larger than life.

Dreamer on the Dakota Plains

Medora von Hoffman de Mores painted a watercolor of the 26-room château (below) that her husband, the marquis, had built for her. The dashing de Mores (bottom) was impetuous by nature, a trait that doomed all his enterprises to failure.

One day in 1883, a stranger alit from the Northern Pacific Railroad near the Little Missouri River and surveyed the area with an entrepreneurial eye. He was the Marquis de Mores, a 24-year-old French nobleman, who had come to the Dakota badlands with a promising idea. He planned to ship butchered beef, rather than live cattle, to eastern markets in refrigerated railroad cars, and in May of 1883 he swung into business.

Bankrolled in part by his father-in-law, a wealthy New York banker, de Mores bought 9,000 acres of land and 10,000 cattle. He built a slaughterhouse, an icehouse, cattle pens, a rail spur to connect his plant to the main line — and a 26-room château for his wife, Medora. In her honor he named this whole extravagant encampment after her. In less than a year the town had grown to 84 buildings, including 3 hotels, 3 groceries, a dry-goods store, and the office for a newspaper, the *Bad Lands Cow Boy*.

But de Mores had more castles in the air than cattle in the marketplace. During the four years that he operated his ranch, he spent more time and money improving his plant than he did slaughtering and shipping beef. And the feisty Frenchman's aristocratic manner alienated neighbors and business associates. He made no effort to cooperate with established custom and enraged ranchers by fencing off his pastures on an otherwise open range. Tension mounted until de Mores became involved in a shoot-out in which a man was killed. He was arrested for murder, tried, and acquitted, but resentment against the arrogant outsider never abated. When he opened his own shops, the rumor spread that his beef was diseased. New York merchants launched a price war that wiped out any profit he might have earned.

Finally, in 1887, the marquis's father-in-law called a halt to the enterprise. De Mores returned to Europe and pursued one ill-conceived project after another until 1896, when he was killed while on an expedition to North Africa.

Pearl of the Prairies

"Full of ginger and snap, with more energy than business sense" was the way one observer described the members of the Cheyenne Club in Wyoming. But in fact the cattle barons who belonged to the institution had business sense to spare: during its heyday club members could claim some of the highest personal incomes in the nation.

Founded in 1880, the Cheyenne Club was housed in a three-story mansion noted for its meticulously maintained wine cellars and other amenities. Strict rules prescribed gentlemanly behavior for the 200 handpicked members. There would, for instance, be no swearing, cheating at games, or "offensive" drunkenness within the club. The rules did not prevent one clubman from carrying on two games of chess and one of tennis simultaneously. (He shouted his chess moves from the lawn.) Another, however, had to resign after shooting holes in a painting of cows that he considered a "travesty on purebred stock."

Cattle — the foundation of the men's fortunes — were taken seriously, but not solemnly. Noting that the members, dressed in tuxedos, bore a striking resemblance to their white-fronted cattle, one wry fellow dubbed them "Herefords."

But the cruel winter of 1886–87 blasted the barons' fortunes by killing off their cattle. And the glory days of the so-called "pearl of the prairies" ended with those harsh winter winds.

The Great Die-Up

When the birds headed south in the autumn of 1886, even those that usually stayed the winter flew away. Despite this ill omen few plainsmen suspected how very bad the winter would be. From November 1886 through February 1887, blizzards howled continually across the plains from Montana to Texas. Already weakened by a summer-long drought, some 50 to 90 percent of the free-ranging cattle died. Ranchers ruefully called it the "great die-up." Many lost everything in those four frigid months.

When spring finally came, the days of the open range were finished forever. Those who could rallied their remaining stock and adopted cattle-sparing strategies such as limiting grazing areas and raising fodder for winter feeding.

In the devastating storms of 1886–87, cattle froze by the thousands, their gaunt bodies so piteous that one rancher recalled: "We couldn't stand it, we had to shoot them."

Lawman, scout, and legendary gunslinger, Wild Bill Hickok was portrayed by artist N. C. Wyeth in the midst of one of his favorite pastimes — gambling over a game of cards.

Gambling Gunfighter

Wild Bill Hickok might have finished his poker game at the Number 10 saloon in Deadwood, South Dakota, if he had not violated one of his basic rules: never sit with your back to the door. But Bill, an inveterate gambler, was talked into pulling up a chair in just that position and so was caught totally unawares on August 2, 1876, when "Crooked Nose" Jack McCall wandered over from the bar and pumped a bullet into the back of his head. Hickok, known as one of the fastest guns in the West, never had a chance. But then, neither had many of his own victims.

Reliable estimates put the number of men killed by Bill —always, he insisted, for good reason — at 30 to 36. But Hickok, who willingly spun tales for journalists who trekked west to interview him, boasted that he had killed over 100. His favorite story told how he singlehandedly wiped out 10 members of the McCanles gang, 6 with his gun, 4 with the Bowie knife he kept tucked in his red sash. The truth, however, was less dramatic. Wild Bill had killed only two of them — one in his hiding place behind a door and another behind a curtain — and mortally wounded a third as he tried to escape. But the reporters faithfully recorded his exaggerations, and his fictionalized deeds became the basis for widely popular dime-novel thrillers such as *Wild Bill, the Indian Slayer* and *Wild Bill's First Trail.*

Hickok served as a scout for the Union army during the Civil War and continued to do so on occasion after the war ended. In 1871 he was appointed marshal of Abilene, Kansas, a position he lost shortly thereafter, along with its $150-a-month salary, when he mistakenly shot and killed his own deputy. For the next five years Wild Bill drifted from one frontier town to the next, until he finally arrived in Deadwood with the notorious Calamity Jane, a woman who dressed, swore, and drank like a man — but reportedly carried a torch for the handsome Hickok. After his death she tearfully pronounced his body "the purtiest corpse I ever saw."

Though dapper and dandified in appearance, Wild Bill Hickok nevertheless was one of the fastest — and most accurate — shots in the West. Believing you should shoot first and ask questions later, Hickok "traded in on his ability to kill without hesitation and without regret."

Trolling for Troublemakers

Isaac Parker had a tall order to fill when he was appointed a federal judge in 1875. It was his duty to bring justice to an area of some 74,000 square miles in western Arkansas — a wild and rugged land that provided lawbreakers with countless places to hide. Almost immediately he swore in 200 deputy marshals, broke them into teams, and sent them out from Fort Smith to scour the countryside for criminals. Each team was equipped with a prison wagon — a sort of jail on wheels — warrants made out in the name of "John Doe," and authorization to pick up anyone they "suspicioned."

If a suspect tried to flee on horseback, Parker's men usually shot the horse, not the man — and for good reason. The deputies earned $2.50 for every prisoner they brought back to Fort Smith alive, but nothing for a dead man.

Once under arrest, the prisoners helped with daily chores such as collecting firewood and peeling potatoes. "If they muttered," one deputy recalled, "they didn't get so much to eat." At night they slept outdoors, shackled to a chain that was stretched between trees or fastened to the prison wagon's wheels. The wagons usually arrived back at the fort filled with a motley array of ne'er-do-wells that ranged from whiskey peddlers to murderers. The serious offenders particularly feared Parker's brand of justice, for he was known as the "Hanging Judge." In all, he handed down more than 150 death sentences — almost half of which were carried out on the gallows.

The Lady Wore Six-Guns

Myra Belle Shirley first ran afoul of the law as a teenager, when she had a brief affair with Cole Younger of the Jesse James gang. Spurned by Younger, who had fathered her daughter, Pearl, Belle then teamed up with a succession of lovers on the wrong side of the law — including Jim Reed, with whom she had a son, and a man named Blue Duck. Around 1880 she settled into a marriage with a part-Cherokee outlaw named Sam Starr, who supplied part of her famous moniker: Belle Starr.

Far from being content in a supporting role, Belle was a partner-in-crime with her love interests and, for a time, led her own gang of thieves on horse and cattle raids in the Indian Territory of Arkansas and Oklahoma. She and her cohorts were not always successful in their endeavors, however, and each of them served some time for their offenses.

Starr's nicknames — the Petticoat Terror and the Bandit Queen — derived from her fashion sense, some rudimentary education, and a decidedly imperious manner. She sported velvet gowns and plumed, wide-brimmed hats, her brace of six-shooters ever in place as a hardboiled accessory to the finery. She is said to have charmed a prison matron into giving her a light work load and to have sweet-talked some of Judge Parker's deputies into a lunch that turned out to be rattlesnake stew. Once, when her hat blew off and her current lover failed to retrieve it, Starr drew her gun and upbraided the gallant: "Now, damn your greasy hide, you pick up that hat, and let this be a lesson in how to treat a lady that you won't forget!"

The Bandit Queen was riding alone on February 3, 1889, when she was shot through the back. Suspicion fell on a neighbor and on her own son — who was angry, so the story goes, because his mother had whipped him for riding her favorite horse without her permission. But no one was ever charged with the crime.

There is a statue of Belle Starr in Bartlesville, Oklahoma. She stands with her gaze steady and her gunbelt in place — an ironic choice to symbolize the glory of the Frontier Woman.

Demurely sidesaddle on her horse, Belle Starr cut a deliberately elegant figure (left). Her daughter was responsible for the epitaph on her grave marker (below), but Belle herself once summed up her experiences by saying, "I regard myself as a woman who has seen much of life."

"Buffalo Bill's Wild West" was still a dramatic spectacle in 1908 (right). Annie Oakley (below and far right) thrilled audiences by shooting glass balls tossed in the air, and other moving targets. At one point she reportedly earned $1,000 a week — more than the president of the United States.

Bill and Annie

She called him "the kindest, simplest, most loyal man I ever knew." He, in turn, called her "the champion shot of the world." They were Buffalo Bill and Annie Oakley, and their regard for each other was genuine. Annie achieved world renown as a sharpshooter with his traveling show, "Buffalo Bill's Wild West." And the show enjoyed its greatest success, netting close to $1 million a year, when she was its star. The two worked together over the course of 17 years, touring both America and Europe.

Bill was already the stuff of legend when he first took a show on the road. Born William Frederick Cody in Scott County, Iowa, in 1846, he had enjoyed a varied career as a horse wrangler, pony-express rider, and sharp-eyed army scout — one of the best in the West. But it was when his life and adventures were sensationalized, beginning in the 1860's, in a series of dime novels by E. Z. C. Judson — alias Ned Buntline — that he gained international fame as Buffalo Bill.

When Cody began to tour with a troupe of horseback-riding cowboys and Indians in 1883, he was smart enough to realize it was Buntline's Buffalo Bill that the public wanted to see. His show featured buffalo stampedes (with live animals), stagecoach robberies, bronco riding, and roping. Although the show was billed as authentic and educational, his cowboys were always spotless, his Indians always bedecked in war bonnets and paint, and his recreations of Indian attacks always ended with Buffalo Bill saving the day.

Annie Oakley, on the other hand, was the real thing. Born Phoebe Anne Moses in 1860, she had taught herself to shoot as a child in order to hunt for food for her family. Years later, while competing in a shooting match, she met her future husband, crack shot Frank Butler, whom she beat. When the couple joined Buffalo Bill's extravaganza in 1885, Annie took the spotlight and Butler became her manager. In one of their most dazzling acts, Butler swung a glass ball at the end of a string, and Annie, with her back turned, sited the moving target in a mirror and shot it with her gun slung over her shoulder.

She was universally admired. Chief Sitting Bull (another star of the show) called her Little Sure Shot. In Berlin Crown Prince Wilhelm

Even in his later years Buffalo Bill cut a fine figure. His distinctive goatee and fringed jacket were lifelong trademarks.

insisted that she shoot a cigarette out of a holder while he held it in his teeth. In Paris the King of Senegal tried to buy her for 100,000 francs. In London, where Bill staged a command performance of his show on the grounds of Windsor Castle, Queen Victoria called her a "clever little girl."

By the time the two retired from show biz — Annie after a train accident in 1901, Buffalo Bill in 1916, shortly before he died — the West was a tame place compared to what it once had been. But for everyone who saw the show and for generations afterward, it lived on just as Buffalo Bill portrayed it. Perhaps more than anyone else, in fact, Bill, Annie, and their troupe of cowboys and Indians created the myth of the Wild West that remains with us today.

Buffalo Bill (front row, right of center) posed with his cowboy troupe on a London stage before a western backdrop.

Bulldogger Bill

The phenomenal popularity of "Buffalo Bill's Wild West" inspired dozens of imitators. In the early 20th century none were more successful than the Oklahoma-based "Miller Brothers' 101 Ranch Wild West Show." Among its most spectacular performers was Bill Pickett, a cowboy of African and Cherokee descent who invented the daredevil steer-wrestling event called bulldogging.

In an act described as "wilder than a wolf," Pickett bested steers by riding them down on his horse, Spradley. Then he would leap to the ground, grab the steer by the horns, dig in his heels, and — much as a dog baits bulls — clamp his teeth down on the animal's extremely sensitive upper lip. Theatrically throwing up his hands to show that he was only holding on with his teeth, Bill would then "fall to one side of the steer, dragging along beside him till the animal went down." (Steer wrestling at rodeos is still called bulldogging, and Pickett was enrolled in the Rodeo Hall of Fame for his contribution to the form although his original "bite-'em" style is no longer allowed.)

Bill Pickett's daring exploits inspired a 1923 motion picture titled *The Bull-Dogger.*

Beginning with his first appearance with the "Miller Brothers' 101 Ranch Wild West Show" in 1905, Pickett was billed as "the Dusky Demon of Oklahoma." He continued to tour North America and Europe — with Will Rogers and Tom Mix as his sometime assistants — until the Miller brothers went bankrupt in 1931. Wherever he went, his stunt was a showstopper and a big box-office draw. When he played in London before the royal family in 1914, for instance, King George V applauded so enthusiastically that Queen Mary had to slap his hands to remind him that such a spirited display was at that time considered inappropriate for royalty.

A Texan by birth, Pickett was a working ranch hand as well as a show-business cowboy. It was said that he had hit on his act after observing ranch dogs rounding up troublesome cattle. To Zack Miller, one of the three brothers who operated the 101 Ranch show, Pickett was always "the greatest sweat-and-dirt cowhand that ever lived — bar none."

Legend and Lore

First appearing in Century Magazine *in 1923, tall-tale character Pecos Bill was surely the biggest, meanest, toughest man that ever rode the West. Weaned on moonshine and raised by a pack of coyotes, Bill set out looking for a band of cowhands "so hard they can kick fire out of a flint rock with their bare toes." He was swinging a rattler as a lariat and riding a mountain lion when he showed up in their camp, and they made him their boss.*

Bill was the one who taught broncos how to buck and there was nothing he couldn't ride, including a tornado. Nothing, in fact, could harm old Pecos Bill — until the day he saw a city slicker decked out in a cowboy outfit and laughed himself to death.

ALL THAT GLITTERS

Golden Onions

Six years before gold was discovered at Sutter's Mill, a ranchero was searching for stray horses in the San Feliciano Canyon some 35 miles northwest of Los Angeles. Pulling some wild onions from the ground to make a meal, he noticed a telltale glitter of yellow among the roots. And so it was that Francisco López discovered gold in California and became the agent of a minor rush.

Within months of his discovery in March 1842, scores of local ranchers were scouring the canyon and collecting caches of the precious dust. One man, Abel Stearns, sent "20 oz. California weight of placer gold" to the Philadelphia mint for assay. This was the first California gold seen back East, but unlike the discovery at Sutter's Mill that triggered the gold rush of 1848–49, its arrival raised not a ripple of interest.

The locals extracted about $8,000 in gold before the deposit played out. After three years, most of the gold-seekers abandoned their dreams of El Dorado and returned to their accustomed routines as ranchers and traders.

Slippery Jim

James G. Fair unabashedly boasted that "I've always built my success on other men's failures." His contemporaries were equally frank in their observations. "Gross, greedy, grasping, mean and malignant" was the way they described the man known as Slippery Jim.

Born near Belfast, Ireland, in 1831 and raised on a farm in Illinois, Fair had joined the California gold rush at age 18. Achieving moderate wealth, he then sold his stake and moved to Virginia City, Nevada. There he teamed up with three partners and gradually built a mining empire of unrivaled wealth from the riches of the Comstock Lode — a cache of gold and silver so fabulous that it prompted one observer to exclaim that "the top had been pried off Nature's treasure-vault."

Rich beyond counting, Fair still maneuvered for more. He vetoed a raise for an employee with the excuse that "a hungry hound hunts best." He once told his wife that a particular stock was going to go "sky high." She promptly invested her own savings — some $7,000 — as did a few friends with whom she shared the information, which sent the market up. Fair took the opportunity to sell his holdings in the company. And then it collapsed, as he knew it would. Out of the profit he realized, Fair reimbursed his wife, who had, of course, lost everything. "My dear, I'm afraid you'll never be a speculator" was all the explanation that he offered.

Jim Fair died in 1894, divorced from his wife, estranged from his children, and alienated from his partners. He left behind a fortune of some $45 million — and a reputation prompting obituaries that were less than kind. The San Francisco *Examiner* summed up his life with an ancient proverb: "The Gods show their contempt for riches by those on whom they bestow them."

Zoom Down the Flume

When not standing in as a daredevil amusement, the flume (top) carried logs from mountaintop saw mills to subterranean mines. Timber was in constant demand to repair mine shafts.

"If the truth must be spoken, I was really scared almost out of reason," confessed H. J. Ramsdell after his wild ride down a V-shaped lumber flume in Virginia City, Nevada.

The flume was an express timber-delivery system that relied on water as its medium and gravity as its motive power as it ran steeply down the slopes of the Sierra Nevada. It had been erected by John Hereford to keep the Comstock Lode supplied with wood to shore up mine shafts and for fuel. Logs fared reasonably well as they flashed down the flume at extraordinary speeds. But human passengers? Such a use had never been contemplated.

All this changed one day in 1875 when Ramsdell, a correspondent for the *New York Tribune*, was touring the sawmills with mine owners James Fair and James Flood. On an impulse the two millionaires dared the reporter to jump aboard a crudely improvised boat — a "pig trough with one end knocked out" — and shoot the flume with them. Joined by two other men, the party set out in two boats. They rocketed downward, dizzily guessing their speed to be 100 miles per hour. "Every object . . . was gone before I could see clearly what it was," Ramsdell later wrote. "Mountains passed like visions and shadows."

In fact the five completed the nerve-shattering 15-mile ride in 35 minutes. With all the mischief by then shaken out of him, Flood vowed, "I would not make the trip again for the whole Consolidated Virginia mine."

In Their Own Words

The country [Nevada] is fabulously rich in gold, silver, copper, iron, quicksilver, marble, granite, chalk, plaster of Paris, (gypsum), thieves, murderers, desperadoes, ladies, children, lawyers, Christians, Indians, Chinamen, Spaniards, gamblers, sharpers, coyotes (pronounced Ki-yo-ties,) poets, preachers, and jackass rabbits.

No flowers grow here, and no green thing gladdens the eye. The birds that fly over the land carry their provisions with them.

When crushed, sage brush emits an odor which isn't exactly magnolia and equally isn't exactly polecat — but is a sort of compromise between the two.

— Mark Twain, 1861

Gold Fever

Lax claim laws, easy pickings, and gold by the fistful were lure enough for some 20,000 people who thought there was no place like Nome.

During the autumn of 1898, three Scandinavians — John Brynteson, Jafet Lindeberg, and Erik Lindblom — quietly panned about $2,000 worth of gold from Anvil Creek, a branch of the Snake River near present-day Nome, Alaska. Try though they did to keep their findings secret, word leaked out. By summer thousands of prospectors, driven by gold lust, had marched, sledded, skated, and even bicycled to the southwestern shore of the Seward Peninsula, hoping to arrive in time to stake claims of their own.

The Johnny-come-laters, however, found slim pickings, since the Scandinavians, along with about three dozen other men, had already staked claims encompassing some 7,000 acres. The irate newcomers moved to jump these claims but were forced back by the local military garrison. A temporary peace settled over Nome in July 1899 when more gold was discovered in the sand along the beach. Available to anyone with a shovel and a sifting device, the bounty of the beaches attracted thousands more, and two months of patient panning yielded a total of $1,000,000.

Thanks to its rapid growth and remote location, however, Nome was ripe for plunder. Corruption, in fact, became the law of the land in 1900 with the arrival of Alexander McKenzie and his pawn in crime, Judge Arthur H. Noyes. McKenzie's scam was breathtaking. He formed the Alaskan Gold Mining Company, had Judge Noyes declare previous claims invalid due to improper filing, and then took them into receivership in his company. The pair worked at a hectic pace: within 24 hours of their landing five claims were swept into McKenzie's sack — and their blatant brigandage persisted for a year.

Nome's citizenry naturally objected, but the nearest federal court was in San Francisco, more than half a continent away. It took months and two separate writs to arrest McKenzie and restore rightful ownership of the claims. When he was sentenced on February 11, 1901, the presiding judge declared that his "high-handed and grossly illegal proceedings . . . may be safely said to have no parallel in the jurisprudence of this country."

Fortunes could be made in Nome with the simplest of equipment (above). Some 20,000 people followed the call of gold to the Alaskan outpost and threw up a tent city on the beach (below).

TIME TABLE

SHINING MOMENTS IN MINING

1822 *Galena (the Latin for lead ore) in Illinois is the site of America's first mineral rush.*

1828 *Gold is found in the Georgia town of Dahlonega — a Cherokee word meaning precious yellow.*

1848 *The California gold rush is triggered by the discovery of gold in the stream at John Sutter's mill near Coloma.*

1854 *Five California miners turn up a 162-pound gold nugget, the world's largest.*

1858 *Gold is found in Colorado, triggering the "Pikes Peak or Bust" rush.*

1859 *America's richest silver strike occurs at Nevada's Comstock Lode.*

1863 *"My Darling Clementine" is published, immortalizing miners as '49ers.*

1863 *With the discovery of gold in Alder Gulch, some 10,000 hopefuls establish Virginia City, Montana.*

1868 *Boom towns are turning into ghost towns. Star City, Nevada, founded just seven years earlier, has only one family left.*

Going for Gold the Hard Way

While prospecting in California in 1848, wrote Henry Simpson, his partner, Charlie Holmes, suddenly called him to his side. "He was holding in his hand a piece of gold about as large and thick as my double hands outspread," reported Simpson. Better yet, old Charlie had uncovered "the richest treasure the world ever saw!"

The story, enticing but untrue, appeared in *Three Weeks in the Gold Mines,* written by Simpson as a guide to California. It was only one of many books dashed off just in time to take advantage of America's raging new epidemic, gold fever. While a few of the guides were authentic and provided helpful tips for hopefuls heading west, many more were pure humbug — cut-and-paste collections of government reports, newspaper clippings, and hearsay, with a few useless maps and inspirational songs thrown in, all tossed together by armchair travelers who had never set foot west of the Mississippi.

Gold field guidebooks could not always be trusted. Many who placed their faith in them were seriously misled.

Filling men and women with false notions about the riches to be had in the gold fields was a minor mischief done by such guides. Far more dangerous was the "advice" — often offered in several languages — on getting there. Some suggested the worst possible routes and vastly underrated the problems of a cross-country trek — "The journey is one of the most delightful and invigorating," said one. Others gave faulty information about supplies needed for the trip, thus causing many innocents severe suffering, if not actual starvation.

But people struck with gold fever did not learn their lesson easily. By the time of the 1859 rush to Colorado, the claims and advice in the guides were worse than ever. As one guide to Pikes Peak promised, "*Gold* will be found there in a solid mass."

Dame Shirley Finds New Digs

California mining camps were, for the most part, bastions of male society, where comforts were few, civilized conduct a rarity, and the language invariably salty. Into this rough-and-tumble environment in 1849 came Louise "Shirley" Clappe, a self-described "frail, home-loving little thistle." Raised in respectability in Amherst, Massachusetts, she went west with her husband, Dr. Fayette Clappe, who provided medical care to camps along the Feather River in northern California for nearly two years.

To everyone's surprise Shirley not only survived the experience but set "roots right lovingly into this barren soil." Awed by the beauty of her canyon surroundings and by the "wild and barbarous life" so foreign to her background, she described everything she saw in a series of lengthy letters that she wrote to her sister Molly. These 23 letters, much admired back East, were gathered together and published in the *California Monthly Magazine* in the mid-1850's under the pen name Dame Shirley. Ignored for decades by historians, they are now regarded as one of the finest sources of firsthand information on mining camp life as it truly was.

Virtually nothing escaped Shirley's curiosity and comment. "Did I not martyrize myself into a human mule, by descending to the bottom of a dreadful pit, . . . actuated by a virtuous desire to see with my own two eyes the process of underground mining?" she asked. Not content to be merely an observer, she tried her hand as "a *mineress,* that is, if the having washed a pan of dirt with my own hands, and procured therefrom three dollars and twenty-five cents in gold dust . . . will entitle me to the name."

But Shirley's most vivid descriptions were reserved for the community of miners, cardsharps, Indians, and vigilantes she lived among at the Rich Bar camp — a mushrooming town of some 2,500 fractious inhabitants. On August 4, 1852, Shirley reported to her sister that "in the short space of twenty-four days, we have had murders, fearful accidents, bloody deaths, a mob, whippings, a hanging, an attempt at suicide, and a fatal duel." On other occasions she also wrote in detail about a duel, a hanging, and a camp funeral. "Only think of such a shrinking, timid, frail thing, as I *used* to be," she confessed in amazement to Molly.

With their few supplies on pack animals, the Manley party made their grateful escape from Death Valley.

Death Valley Days

Most of the hopefuls who packed their wagons and headed for California during the gold rush followed the Oregon or California trails. But one group, leaving Salt Lake City just before the snow began to fly, decided to take their train of 100 wagons along the more southerly but relatively unknown Old Spanish Trail. With no reliable maps to guide them through what was called "damned dubious-looking country," disagreements inevitably arose and the wagon train splintered into small parties. By late December one band of 22 people found themselves in a desert valley, their provisions exhausted, their oxen faltering, and the treeless Panamint Range rising like a wall before them.

With the party facing almost certain death, two of the group, William Lewis Manly and John Rogers, were chosen to seek help. Traveling across mountains and desert for 270 miles, the pair finally crested a ridge and looked down to discover acres of lush grazing land. At the nearby mission of San Fernando, they were able to acquire pack animals, food, and saddle horses.

Recrossing the range and what would ever after be called Death Valley, they reached the encampment they had left 26 days before. Thinking at first that everyone was dead, Manly fired a shot in the air; with that the survivors crawled weakly from beneath the wagons to embrace the returning heroes. Days later as he led them out of the valley, Manly — who would later write an account of the experience — remarked that only a man of deepest faith could believe that God had ever smiled upon "a corner of the earth so dreary." The party reached San Fernando on March 7, 1850, the gold fields still 500 miles ahead.

Life *inside* the cabin was not what she was accustomed to either. "Last night, our company being larger than usual," Shirley explained, "one of our friends was compelled to take his tea out of a soup-plate! The same individual, not being able to find a seat, went outside and brought in an empty gin-cask." But despite the many hardships she endured, when it came time to leave, Shirley had mixed feelings about saying goodbye. "Really — everybody ought to go to the mines," she wrote, "just to see how little it takes to make people comfortable in this world."

In the gold-rush era, only about 8 percent of California's population was female. This properly dressed matron posed while bringing a basket of lunch to some miners in 1852.

1873 *To honor President U. S. Grant on a visit to Central City, Colorado, the sidewalk at the new hotel is paved with silver.*

1875 *A gold strike in South Dakota leads to establishment of the Homestake Mine — said to be the most productive underground gold mine in the Western Hemisphere.*

1877 *Silver is discovered at Tombstone, Arizona; the deposits eventually yield some $36 million.*

1877 *Leadville, Colorado, founded as a gold camp in 1860, booms again with new discoveries of silver, gold, lead, and other metals.*

1882 *Marcus Daly's Anaconda silver mine in Montana turns up rich copper deposits.*

1890 *After 12 years of fruitless efforts, "Crazy Bob" Womack finds a rich vein of gold in Poverty Gulch at Cripple Creek, Colorado.*

1890 *Leonidas Merritt and his six brothers find iron in Minnesota's Mesabi Range.*

1896 *Gold in Alaska! Some 100,000 hopefuls head for the Yukon's Klondike district.*

1906 *Federal Mint opens in Denver, producing 167 million gold and silver coins in its first year.*

1914 *A gold-lined geode —20 feet long, 15 feet wide, and 40 feet high— is unearthed at Cripple Creek, Colorado.*

1942 *The War Production Board deems gold mining nonessential and shuts down mines until the end of the war. Most never reopen.*

Roundabout Route to the West

Horace Greeley might have urged young men to "Go west" in the 19th century, but it was a New York State expressman, John Butterfield, who tried to get them there.

Butterfield began his career as a stagecoach driver in Albany in 1820, and within 30 years he controlled most of the stage lines in western New York. By the time Congress authorized funds for an Overland Mail express from Tipton, Missouri, to San Francisco in 1857, Butterfield was well positioned to make a bid for the job. In order to win the $600,000-a-year federal contract, however, Butterfield had to win the support of southern congressmen by agreeing to a route that, rather than heading due west, made a semicircular loop from Missouri through Texas and what is now southern New Mexico — an extra 1,000 miles. Many hooted at the decision, but Butterfield's enthusiasm for his ox-bow (as the route was dubbed) knew no bounds.

The gold rush brought so many settlers to California that Congress voted funds for a mail route. The Overland Mail was the first, taking a southwestern route. In this 1859 sketch the stage was passing through the Tucson area.

While spending about $1 million on the project, he supervised construction along much of the line, which included roads, ferries, bridges, and some 200 way stations. On September 16, 1858, he rode triumphantly westward with the mail on the first coach out of Missouri, as far as Fort Smith, Arkansas. And he soon was able to boast that his coaches leaving Tipton or San Francisco could indeed get the mail, as well as any passengers willing to pay $200, to the opposite destination within the scheduled 25 days.

Not everyone who rode the coaches was as thrilled with the Overland Mail as Butterfield. Customers endured 2,800 miles of what one rider described as "the worst road God ever built." Since the stage drivers did not stop at night, the constant jostling from rocky roads and mountainous hairpin turns made sleep possible only with total exhaustion. Passengers complained of the lack of toilet and bathing facilities, the rancid food, and drunken, foul-mouthed stage attendants. They also rode in fear of buffalo stampedes, which were known at times to overturn the coaches. Since tempers were easily frayed under such conditions, words often came to blows among passengers, prompting drivers to scream "Indians!" to restore order.

Despite Butterfield's enthusiasm, and the dependability of his deliveries, his ox-bow route was doomed. With the beginning of the Civil War in 1861, it was supplanted by a more-direct western route. And by the end of the decade, the railroad had become the new overland express.

Tom Bell, Stagecoach Robber

A story told about one of California's most notorious highwaymen during the gold-rush era was of the time when — during a holdup — he paused to bandage a bullet wound in his victim's leg. Then, stopping an oncoming wagon, he ordered the driver to take the injured man to the nearest doctor — but not, of course, before he had taken his wallet.

Such was the contradictory nature of Dr. Thomas J. Hodges, alias Tom Bell. A native of Tennessee, young Hodges arrived in California around 1850 after serving as a physician in the Mexican War. Discovering that he could not support himself as a doctor in the gold fields, he turned to gambling. Then, after losing everything (and adopting his alias), he had a go at grand larceny, which landed him behind bars in 1855.

In no time at all Bell escaped and soon was leading a gang of former prisoners in what was then a brand-new form of crime — stagecoach robbery. Bell was no killer, but he did terrorize the countryside. His cunning for catching travelers unawares was legendary: he kept the highways covered by working out of a series of way stations where he and his gang could hide.

It was men in his own gang, however, who led a vigilante to Bell after a fumbled robbery in 1856. His captors allowed him exactly four hours to make his peace and write his family. In a letter to his mother, Bell asked her to warn his old friends "never to enter into any gambling saloon, for that has been my ruin." But remorse had come too late. Few tears were shed moments later when Bell was hung from the limb of a sycamore.

Delivery on the Double

Courageous young men all, America's pony-express riders lived by an unwritten code of honor: mail first, horse second, self last.

"Wanted," read a newpaper advertisement in 1860. "Young, skinny, wiry fellows not over 18. Must be expert riders, willing to face death daily. Orphans preferred." And it was a fact: only the most daring needed apply for a job with the pony express. Created as a central mail route in the year before the Civil War began, it was America's first rapid-communication system. The 10-day delivery time it promised between St. Joseph, Missouri, and Sacramento, California, was 15 days faster than the Overland Mail. And the wiry little express riders (120 pounds maximum) lived up to the promise. During the first east-bound run, rider Warren Upson had to cross the Sierra Nevada alone in a blinding snowstorm, yet the mail still arrived only slightly behind schedule.

But icy mountain trails, flooded rivers, and scorching deserts were just a part of what riders had to contend with on their routes. They continually faced the threat of holdups and Indian attacks as they rode in relays night and day, changing horses every 10 to 15 miles, and riders about every 75. Reading about their exploits in journals such as *Hutchings' California Magazine,* America thrilled to the express riders' exploits.

One of the longest rides was made by William Cody (later known as Buffalo Bill), who was hired at the age of 15. On one occasion he stayed in the saddle for 21 hours and a 322-mile round-trip after discovering that his relief rider had been killed. The fastest trip on record occurred when President Lincoln's inaugural address was delivered to Sacramento in 7 days and 17 hours. Much of the success of that trip was due to the courage of rider "Pony Bob" Haslam, who carried the document 120 miles with a rag stuffed in his mouth to stop the bleeding from an Indian attack. Even the horses at times were heroic. Once when a rider was slain, his mount galloped on to the next station with the mail.

After almost 19 months, however, when 650,000 miles had been ridden, 34,753 pieces of mail delivered, and only one sack of mail lost, the pony express was awash in debt. And when the transcontinental telegraph was completed in October 1861, the brave and solitary riders were forced to ride on to far less exciting jobs.

Pony-express riders could change horses in two minutes and outride most Indians. A poster (right) touted the service in July 1861. Just four months later the pony express ended.

PONY EXPRESS!
CHANGE OF TIME! REDUCED RATES!
10 Days to San Francisco!
LETTERS
WILL BE RECEIVED AT THE
OFFICE, 84 BROADWAY,
NEW YORK,
Up to 4 P. M. every TUESDAY,
AND
Up to 2½ P. M. every SATURDAY,
Which will be forwarded to connect with the PONY EXPRESS leaving ST. JOSEPH, Missouri,
Every WEDNESDAY and SATURDAY at 11 P. M.
TELEGRAMS
Sent to Fort Kearney on the mornings of MONDAY and FRIDAY, will connect with PONY leaving St. Joseph, WEDNESDAYS and SATURDAYS.
EXPRESS CHARGES.
LETTERS weighing half ounce or under............$1 00
For every additional half ounce or fraction of an ounce 1 00
In all cases to be enclosed in 10 cent Government Stamped Envelopes,
And all Express CHARGES Pre-paid.
☞ PONY EXPRESS ENVELOPES For Sale at our Office.
WELLS, FARGO & CO., Ag'ts.
New York, July 1, 1861.

Camels in the Corral

Transporting freight to mountainous mining camps was often a problem for mine owners. For a time, however, some believed they had found the ideal solution in a pack animal that could carry twice as much as a mule could pull, was unfazed by snow, and unbothered by altitudes — the camel. First imported by the army in 1856, the sure-footed beasts of burden were adopted for mining use in Nevada, Montana, and the Pacific Northwest. But the experiment ultimately failed because sight of the exotic creature caused other animals to stampede. Mule skinners, moreover, hated the camel's foreignness and its disposition. They simply could not stand it when the response to their whippings was likely to be a potentially lethal kick or a deadly accurate splattering of spit.

The survivors of camels imported for service in the U.S. Army were still working as pack animals in 1877.

Boom-Town Culture

Opera houses — they were the ideal monuments to the quickly amassed fortunes that made them possible, oases of refinement in mining towns like Leadville, Butte, and Central City. Before the streets got paved in many a boom town, and while most of the hoped-for audience was still tracking gold dust into saloons, opera houses were popping up across the West like prairie flowers after a spring rain.

"A city is not a city until it has some grand temple dedicated to pleasure and amusement," proclaimed the Denver *Daily News* after the 1881 opening of silver tycoon Horace Tabor's Grand Opera House. Like many of its rivals, it was lavishly outfitted, with not only a painted ceiling, stained-glass skylight, and crystal chandelier, but also a huge curtain with a scene of ancient Rome and the only dressing rooms with hot running water west of Chicago. Others were far more humble. The National in Central City, Colorado, was a converted stable, and folks in Carbon, Wyoming, made do with a dirt-floored log building.

The range of "culture" offered in such establishments was equally diverse. Audiences might strain to hear Oscar Wilde's discourse on the "Ethics of Art," or thrill to a performance of *Uncle Tom's Cabin.* Curiosities such as children who played adult roles, or women who played male parts could be counted on to draw a crowd. And now and again, genuine opera — or at least Gilbert and Sullivan — was even heard.

But what transpired on stage frequently took a backseat to the socializing in the lounge. And the owners were not necessarily any more culturally inclined than their clientele. The night Horace Tabor's Denver palace opened for business, he glanced up at a portrait hanging prominently in the lobby. "Who's that?" he demanded. "Shakespeare," replied the manager. "Who?" Tabor persisted. "The greatest writer of plays who ever lived." "Well, what has he ever done for Colorado?" retorted Tabor. "Take it down and put my picture up there!"

In 1877 the Cheyenne Opera House (top) was part theater, part saloon. Actress Helen Western (right) kept miners coming back for more when she played a male role.

Madam of the Mines

In the lore of the Wild West, her two-room cottage on D Street has become a rococo mansion, and her plain English face has been transformed into that of a sultry Creole beauty. But in real life, Julia Bulette, the "Darling of the Comstock," needed no such embellishments. Born in Liverpool, England, she came to America as a young woman, settling in Louisiana. She married but, shortly after, left her husband and took up a life of easy virtue to support herself.

When she moved to Virginia City, Nevada, sometime before 1861, the town was still a morass of muddy streets, wooden shacks, raucous bars, and boardinghouses. Probably in her mid-30's by then, Julia was one of the few single women in town. Not surprisingly, her clean cottage with its oversized mahogany bed and damask curtains soon became its most popular way station.

Julia, it seems, was as generous as she was genteel, and to miners as starved for affection as they were for sex, she must have seemed a veritable angel of mercy. She rode in a Fourth of July parade, was made an honorary member of a local fire company, and helped raise money to care for wounded Union soldiers. When the boom of 1863 made Midases all around town, Julia — whose favors were said to fetch as much as $1,000 a night — prospered as well. What she didn't spend on parties for her friends or give to those in need, she spent on herself — conservative silk dresses and furs, piles of tastefully bourgeois jewelry, and plenty of frilly lingerie. But as Virginia City settled down, and wives and children became established in the population, Julia's status suffered.

One morning in 1867 she was found strangled in her bed, her jewels and furs missing. The townfolks' response showed just how deeply divided they were in their attitude toward her. On the day of her funeral, every mine in the area shut down and 16 carriages filled with the town's leading men followed the hearse to the cemetery. "True she was a woman of easy virtue," declared one gent. "Yet hundreds . . . had cause to bless her name." But while the man who was eventually hung for Julia's murder awaited his trial, Virginia City wives treated him like a hero, bringing cakes and wine to him in jail.

Poised and proper, Julia Bulette posed for her portrait with her honorary fireman's hat on display at her side.

Fast-Dealing Lady of the Wild West

Boom-town poker pro Alice Ivers claimed to know why there were not more players like her. "Women," she declared, "have too many nerves."

Alice Ivers was 19 when she met and married Fred Duffield, a mining engineer, in 1870. The couple soon settled in Lake City, Colorado, a town where the chief entertainment was playing cards in the saloons. Out of boredom, perhaps, prim young Alice — a schoolteacher's daughter — tagged along to watch. Intrigued by what she saw, she began to study the games, paying special attention to the way players kept their "poker faces" as the stakes mounted. At home she practiced by herself at the kitchen table until one night she finally asked to join in a game of faro — and broke the bank.

When Duffield was killed in a mine accident shortly afterward, leaving Alice penniless, she lost no time in getting a job as a dealer. A natural as well as a novelty, blue-eyed Alice soon joined the high-stakes gambling circuit, drifting from game to game. Along the way she acquired a Colt .45, a taste for cigars, and a reputation for absolute imperturbability. When she won big, she celebrated big, several times blowing everything on New York shopping sprees, then returning west to start anew.

Alice was 42 and working in a Deadwood, South Dakota, saloon when a drunken miner pulled a knife on fellow gambler William Tubbs. Taking aim, Alice blasted the miner's arm. It must have been love, for she and Tubbs soon were married, adopted seven children, and took up chicken farming. After her husband's death Alice returned to the tables, finally cashing in her own chips for good in 1930 at the age of 79.

Salting the Earth

One day in February 1872 a pair of grizzled miners walked into San Francisco's Bank of California carrying a canvas sack for deposit in the bank's vault. When the cashier asked them to empty the bag so that he could write a receipt for the contents, he watched, dumbstruck, as a shower of uncut diamonds and raw gemstones danced onto the counter. The men took their receipt and left and, within minutes, the head of the bank, William Ralston, was told about the transaction. With that the mining swindle of the century was under way.

The miners, Philip Arnold and John Slack, seemed relieved to confide in the banker, who encouraged them to capitalize on their find. But Ralston, a cautious man, wanted to send a mining expert to confirm their tale. He agreed to the miners' stipulation that the man be led blindfolded to and from the mine field so that its location could be kept a secret. When the expert returned with a positive report, a sampling of the stones was sent to Tiffany and Company in New York for appraisal and was declared of "enormous value."

Next, Henry Janin, a ranking mining expert of the day, inspected the secret site, and he too declared it overflowing with gems. Finally convinced, Ralston organized a $10 million stock offering in the San Francisco and New York Mining and Commercial Company. Arnold and Slack were given $600,000 — and promptly lit out for parts unknown. Then the other shoe dropped.

Clarence King, head of the 40th Parallel Survey, and a team of geologists had studied the territory where the lode was supposed to be, and had failed to find so much as a diamond chip. With his reputation at stake, King did some sleuthing and, with a search party, discovered the field in northwestern Colorado. Dozens of rubies were indeed lying about and a few diamonds glittered among the shale — one of which prompted a team member to proclaim that the field "not only produces diamonds but cuts them also!" A close inspection of the "raw" stone revealed the unmistakable marks of a lapidary tool. The field had been salted with $35,000 worth of rough stones that Arnold and Slack had purchased in Europe and planted in Colorado. King had the proof he needed; with a single telegram he exploded the hoax.

Shattered by the news, Ralston personally reimbursed all of his investors. But he never recovered his reputation. Three years later, his bank failed, and he was found, mysteriously drowned, in San Francisco Bay.

The setting for the gambit that launched the great diamond hoax of 1872, San Francisco's Bank of California was sketched in quieter times by Walter Yeager.

Bogus Stakes and Lucky Strikes

In mineral-rich Colorado, many 19th-century fortunes were made by mining the earth — and some by mining the credulous.

William Lovell's luck was not the greatest. In the winter of 1877–78, for example, the world-weary produce merchant hauled a wagonload of chickens over Colorado's Mosquito Range to sell to miners working the newest silver finds. A snowstorm caught him by surprise, his chickens froze solid, and the newly dubbed "Chicken Bill" had to be rescued and led to safety.

Lovell's head was soon spinning with stories of fortunes being dug from the earth, and in no time at all he was pickaxing a stake of his own on the appropriately named Fryer Hill near Leadville. Right behind him were a pair of German cobblers-turned-prospectors who had been grubstaked by Leadville's mayor, Horace Tabor. Though no more inclined than Chicken Bill to work hard, the Germans got lucky and struck a spectacular vein that came to be called the Little Pittsburgh. The two men quickly sold their stake, but Tabor held on to his — selling out later for $1 million — and started buying claims on the hill.

Chicken Bill, meanwhile, was getting nowhere with his pick; so he simply stole a load of ore from the Little Pittsburgh, dropped it down his empty shaft, and asked Tabor, renowned for his affable gullibility, to have a look. Tabor took it off his hands for $900, and since that amounted to a year's wages for Lovell, Bill felt he'd had the last laugh. But Tabor sank a deeper shaft down through the false find and struck a seam that yielded him another $150,000. And so it went for years: Tabor making millions in the mines and Chicken Bill making do with near misses and salted claims — though none of Bill's later victims ever fared quite so well as the mayor of Leadville.

A con artist and four henchman stood for a portrait in the 1890's. Soapy Smith (center) was the brains of the gang that gulled miners with small-time scams like the old shell game — called thimblerig — and three-card monte.

Soft Soap and Hard Cash

He earned his nickname the easy way, by hiding $10 and $20 bills under a soap wrapper, then hawking the bars for $5 apiece — making certain, of course, that only his shills got the cakes with the big bills. That was one of Jefferson "Soapy" Smith's cleaner cons. Another was barbershop roulette, played in a storefront in Denver in the 1880's. A sign in the window offered a shave and a haircut for two bits, but once lathered up, customers discovered the price had jumped to $1. With a razor glinting at their throats, they were only too willing to pay.

Like the boom-town miners who were his prey, Smith had come west in search of gold — which he found not underground, but in the pockets of his marks. "Spare the locals" was the honor-among-thieves rule that kept him in business. When a challenger appeared in town, however, the stepped-up predation proved too much for Denver, and Smith obligingly moved on.

In 1892 he transferred operations to Creede, a silver-mining camp with a ready supply of newcomers to be fleeced. And fleece them he did, with card games, bunko schemes, and "Colonel Stone," a cement statue Smith displayed as a scientific exhibit. Handbills trumpeted: "The Missing Link! See him in the flesh (petrified)!" — and for 25 cents apiece, hundreds did.

Shameless as he was, Smith occasionally diverted some of his profits to the poor and even appeared before a Sunday school class as a self-proclaimed bad example. He next followed the gold diggers north to Alaska, where his luck ran out: a pack of Skagway vigilantes shot him dead.

WHAT · IS · IT

Many a gold miner may have wished that all he had to do was wave a magic wand to find the precious metal. This 1901 "magnetic dowsing rod" was touted as the next best thing.

NO. 3, MAGNETIC MINERAL ROD. PRICE BY EXPRESS, $18.00.

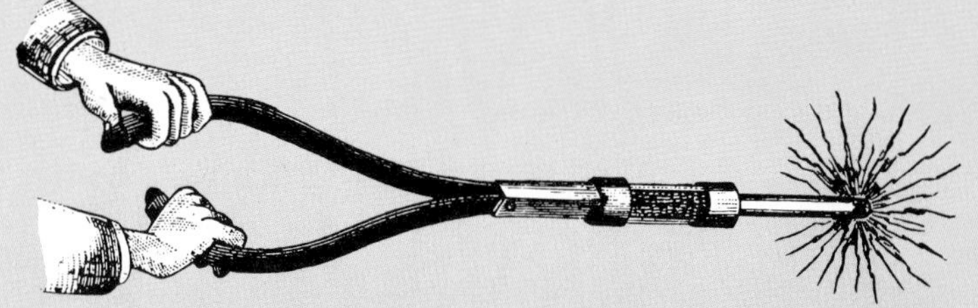

Chapter 9

BUSINESS AND INDUSTRY

INVENTIVE AMERICANS

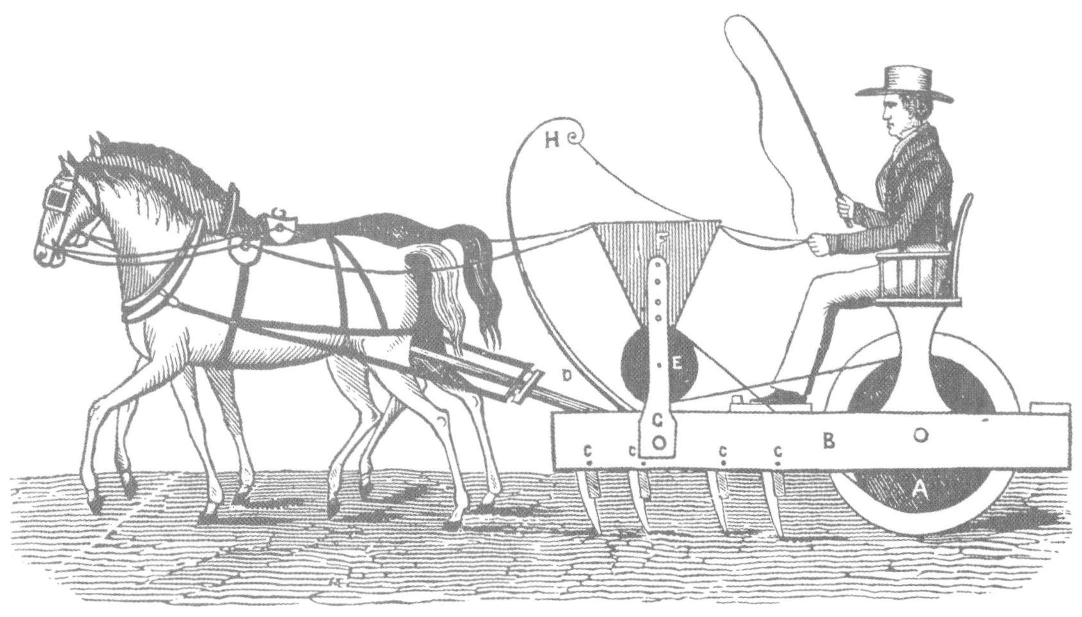

Rufus Porter (above) made his living as a painter and publisher, but he was also an inventor. A "field engine" for harrowing, sowing, and rolling in one sweep (right) was one of his more down-to-earth creations.

The Era of an Uncommon Man

Of all the creative geniuses America has ever produced, Rufus Porter was surely one of the most prolific. Among his many inventions he can claim a washing machine, a chain-stitch sewing machine, a prefabricated house, and a steam-driven automobile. He also played a fine fiddle as well as the fife, earned a fair living as a painter of signs, houses, and murals, founded magazines, and wrote books.

Porter was born in Massachusetts in 1792 — the fourth year of George Washington's first presidency — and came of age with the industrial revolution. He dropped out of school at age 12 and, impatient with the prospect of life as a shoemaker that his family was planning for him, abandoned his cobbling apprenticeship when he was 15, taking to the road as an itinerant painter and part-time musician.

From then until the end of his long life in 1884, Porter bestrode the twin crafts of art and invention. Blessed with a wide-ranging constellation of talents, including a dreamer's imagination and the problem-solving skills of a master mechanic, in 1820 he developed a camera obscura — a crude projection device that allowed him to paint portraits quickly — and soon became a one-man industry of original art for hire. That same year he worked out all the essential features of a dirigible, which he called an "aerial locomotive," and predicted that it would "succeed eventually and constitute the principal and general instrument of

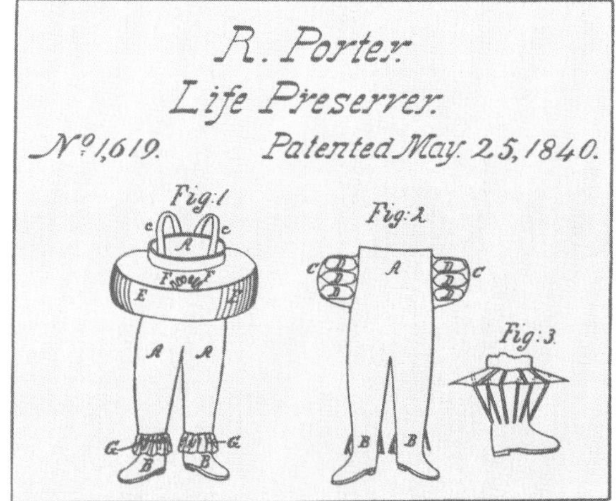

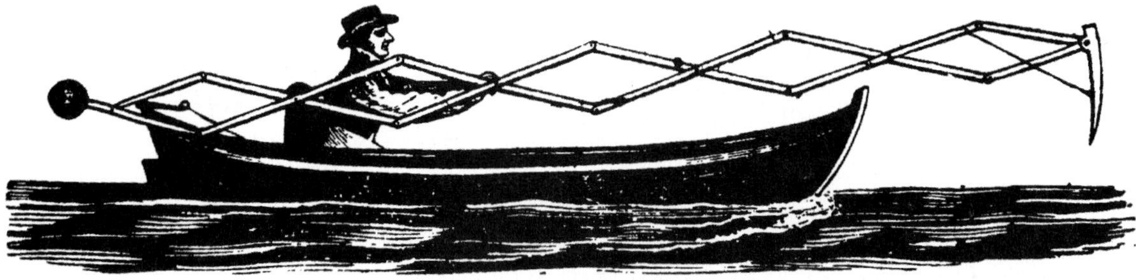

Safety at sea was ensured by Porter's personal flotation device (above). His "new method of rowing boats" (left) gave a solitary mariner a long reach over the water.

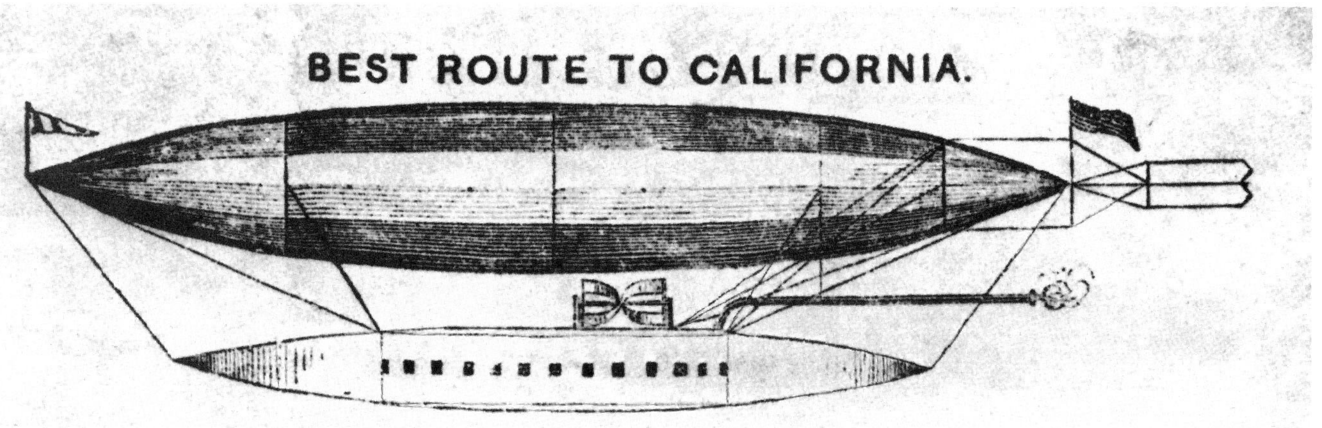

transportation of merchandise, as well as mails and passengers, throughout the world."

The one consistent flaw in Porter's genius, however, was a near-total lack of interest in marketing his inventions. Announcements of his creations often stated that "the plan . . . promises immense advantage, which the Inventor is disposed to share with any person who will aid him in introducing the invention to general use." Sometimes he sold an idea to a more enterprising soul — who then reaped the profits — but more often the idea was abandoned when new challenges seized his restless attention. This unworldliness perhaps contributed to Porter's relative obscurity.

In his spare time, this "ambitious and chimerical Yankee" was a prodigious journalist and publisher. Besides penning treatises on art theory and religion, how-to instructions for painting, and essays celebrating the dignity of the working man, he founded the *New York Mechanic* in 1840 and the *Scientific American* in 1845. Although Porter poured his energy into the magazines, even supplying *Scientific American* with editorials in simple, breezy verse, he stayed at the helm only long enough to assure their sustainable vitality, then sold them for modest returns.

Undaunted, undimmed, and indefatigable, Porter persisted in his unsung role as an American Renaissance man, blithely embodying his own cheerful admonition: "Don't stop at the corners / To drag out the day / Be active — be active / And work while you may."

Anticipating Zeppelin by almost 50 years, Porter flew a small working model of his "aerial locomotive" in 1847 (above). His ingenious scheme for moving houses was powered by a horse on a treadmill (below).

World View

Rufus Porter's landscapes were popular as paintings and as murals. Unlike his contemporaries from the realistic school, Porter urged that an artist "imagine various scenes in his mind, diverse from anything he has seen." But Porter's art, with its combination of freehand painting and stenciled elements, observes strict rules of composition that enhance the refreshing directness and simplicity of the images. This 1838 mural from a house in Massachusetts is a charming example of his talent and philosophy.

Prophet Without Profit

He had a reputation as a grump in his old age, with little good to say about his fellow man. And in fact Oliver Evans may have been entitled to a bit of bitterness. Born in 1755, he had a flair for technology in an era that was decidedly untechnological. Throughout his life, people laughed at his inventions, which included a high-pressure steam engine, a machine gun, an automobile, central heating, and a refrigerating system — some 80 designs in all.

The one that ultimately had the most enduring effect was his plan for the world's first automated factory. Evans began work on the project in 1780 when he joined his brothers at their Wilmington, Delaware, flour mill. The process of turning grain into flour, he discovered, had changed very little over the centuries. It was slow, clumsy, labor-intensive work. Evans, moreover, was shocked by "the great quantity of dirt constantly mixing with meal from the dirty feet of everyone who trampled it."

It took him five years, but by 1785 Evans had completed a mill in which water powered a system of conveyors as well as the grinding stones. Essentially, grain could be poured in at one end of the mill and come out as clean flour on the other. Three times as much grain could be processed as in the old way — and at less than half the labor cost. All the same, when he showed his technological wonder to local millers, Evans wrote, the response was, "'It will not do! it cannot do!!' — it doing perfectly well at the same time."

The inventor's annoyance increased when his contemporaries began building grain mills based on his patented design without paying his licensing fee. (Even Thomas Jefferson was an unwitting offender when his contractor copied Evans' work. He paid promptly once aware of the problem.) By 1837 — 18 years after Evans's death — at least 1,200 Evans-style mills were in operation. And automated factories of every description built since that time owe their efficiency to Oliver Evans.

Rubber Barons

Charles Goodyear was obsessed with rubber. Never mind that the gummy stuff wilted in the summer's heat and went brittle in winter's cold: Goodyear was convinced that it could be transformed into a stable, useful substance. And so, from the early 1830's until 1844, he worked ceaselessly, sacrificing his own health, the support of his family, and the succor of friends in his pursuit of the "elastic metal."

Subsisting on an income derived from the manufacture of small novelty goods, pawning anything he could — at one point he even hocked his children's schoolbooks — and cadging support from increasingly skeptical investors, Goodyear devoted himself to his experiments. At night in his kitchen, with intuition as his guide, he mixed rubber with turpentine, magnesia, and other substances. Some of the additives relieved rubber's stickiness but none bestowed reliable resilience.

In 1838 Goodyear met Nathaniel M. Hayward, who was on the brink of patenting a process for curing rubber by mixing it with sulphur and exposing it to sunshine. The two made an agreement in which Hayward's patent was assigned to Goodyear, and Goodyear continued his perfectionistic tinkering. Finally, one day in 1839, Goodyear accidentally dropped a sulphur-laced blob of rubber on a hot stove where it "charred like leather." As he later related, "Nobody but myself thought the charring worthy of notice." Inspired, Goodyear spent years at his stove, mixing, heating, cooling, testing, and retesting until, through a process a British competitor dubbed "vulcanization," he came up with rubber that was both dry and pliable.

Triumphant at last, Goodyear patented some 500 uses for rubber — curiously overlooking its potential for tires. But he continued to fall victim to his own innocence. His patents were poorly

Physician-turned-realtor-turned-capitalist, Benjamin Franklin Goodrich helped get the economy of Akron rolling when he moved his offices and manufacturing plants there in 1870.

FACTORIES OF THE B. F. GOODRICH RUBBER COMPANY, AKRON, OHIO.

protected, and he spent much of his newfound income in lawyers' fees. Dishonest business agents and poor investments absorbed the rest. When Goodyear died in 1860, his long-suffering family found themselves heir to a $200,000 debt.

A good way to get rich

Rubber finally came into its own when Benjamin Franklin Goodrich bought a New York factory that produced Goodyear rubber goods. Seeking a location that offered less competition, in 1870 Goodrich moved his company to Akron, Ohio, which was offering incentives to attract new business. Seeing in rubber the answer to leather's shortcomings as a hosing material, B. F. Goodrich got his company going with cotton-covered rubber fire hoses. Long before it began making tires, the firm's fortune was founded on small goods such as garden hoses and gaskets, belting, billiard table bumpers, and rollers for wringers.

For those who want to *know* which tires to buy
a day of demonstration is worth a year of argumentation
CLASS A
GOODRICH TIRES
CLEAN SCORE

By 1909 automobiles had created a new avenue of opportunity for the rubber companies: tires.

What·is·it

"An inventor," wrote Mark Twain, "is a poet — a true poet — and nothing in any degree less than a high order of poet." He regarded inventors so highly, in fact, that on several occasions he put his own poetic skills to the test with various inventions. The one shown here, "Mark Twain's Patent Self-Pasting Scrap Book," was patented in 1873 and had the novel feature of self-pasting pages. "Wet the page with sponge, brush, rag or tongue," he instructed, "and dab on your scraps like postage stamps." The book was a modest success — 25,000 copies were sold. Twain also received patents for an adjustable clothing strap and a history game, but neither proved profitable.

The Real McCoy

Steam helped power the industrial revolution, but steam engines all shared a common problem — overheating. Whether a train was midjourney or a factory halfway through a job, the engine had to be shut down and cooled while a man made the rounds with his oil can and lubricated all the moving points. The delays in such a system were not only inconvenient but costly. Then along came Elijah McCoy.

Born in Canada in 1844, the son of fugitive slaves, McCoy studied engineering in Scotland. On his return to America, he settled in Michigan, only to discover that engineering was closed to him because of his race. He was forced to settle for a job as railway fireman, stoking and oiling the engine.

With his training McCoy was quick to recognize the problems of steam and soon was busy devising a better system. In July 1872 he received a patent for an automatic lubricator that delivered a steady flow of oil to all friction points on an engine — thus eliminating the need to shut down. The device was widely adopted for use, but McCoy was a perfectionist. For the rest of his life, he continued to improve on his original design, eventually earning well over 50 patents.

A product so important to industry had its imitators from the start, of course. But since dependability was absolutely essential when it came to steam, customers learned to insist that their engines be equipped with "the real McCoy."

Elijah McCoy always realized that the simpler a device was in design, the more dependable it was apt to be. His 1872 engine lubricator — the principle of which is still in use — became an industry standard.

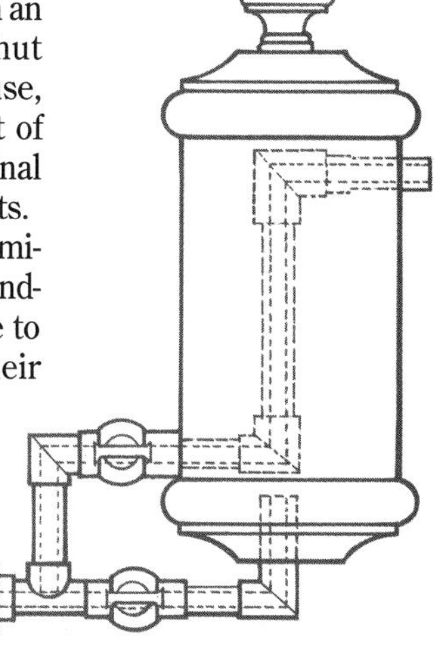

Clocking Time in Terryville

When 14-year-old Eli Terry was apprenticed to a clock maker in 1786, most Americans still lived and worked by the sun, for clocks were possessions that few could afford. Those who wanted one could expect to pay about $80 for a handcrafted timepiece with brass works and a tall wooden case — in an era when the average family's income was about $100 a year.

By the time Terry completed his training and set up a shop of his own in Plymouth, Connecticut, he had an idea for a clock that nearly everyone could afford. He would make the works out of wood rather than brass, and instead of making each clock to order, he would mass-produce interchangeable parts that he could either assemble later or sell to other clock makers.

It was a brash idea, but it succeeded, largely because in setting up his clock factory (America's first) in 1800, Terry followed the lead of his Connecticut neighbor, Eli Whitney, and used water power to drive the machinery. Before long, Terry and a few assistants were able to work on as many as 20 clocks at a time and could wholesale them at $30. When he received an order for 4,000 clock movements in 1807, Terry moved to a larger factory, spent a year modernizing it, expanded to 12 workers, and easily met his three-year deadline.

Eli Terry started out making fancy tall-case clocks (left) but ultimately specialized in inexpensive shelf clocks (above).

Revolutionizing the clock industry was enough to cause the area of Plymouth around the factory to be renamed Terryville. But Terry's greatest claim to fame was his 1814 invention of a wood-cased shelf clock that turned America into a nation of clock-watchers. Yankee peddlers could sell the Terry clock for just $15 and soon were selling similar clocks from Terry's competitors as well. By midcentury an English visitor would report that "wherever we have been . . . in cabins where there was not a chair to sit on, there was sure to be a Connecticut clock."

Seating the Multitudes

The modest little advertisement in an 1822 issue of the *Connecticut Courant* was headed simply "Chairs. L. Hitchcock." But it heralded a revolution both in the furnishing of American homes and in the lives of American workers. Before Lambert Hitchcock's day, most people had little choice when it came to furniture. If they were rich, they ordered up-to-date styles from professional cabinetmakers. If they were not, they were likely to sit at homemade tables on simple benches and chairs.

In the 1820's, stylish in seating meant "fancy chairs" with turned legs and painted decoration — creations requiring far more skill than most farmers could muster. So when Hitchcock set up his water-powered factory north of Hartford, he began mass-producing chair parts that the average man could put together at home. The success of his "kits" — particularly in the South, where there were fewer skilled cabinetmakers — was such that Hitchcock soon was able to offer his own fancy chairs for as little as $1.50 each.

Commonly made with cane or rush seats, Hitchcock's graceful designs featured yet another of his innovations. Instead of being decorated by artists meticulously painting freehand, his chairs were painted by an assembly line of workers who used up to five compatible stencils to create a variety of motifs. People without special training as craftsmen could easily learn to do the job. Hitchcock's small army of workers — men to run the saws and lathes, women and children to stencil and finish — was soon turning out 15,000 chairs a year. And the New England hamlet was transformed into a thriving factory town, called Hitchcocksville, of course.

Tiny Hitchcocksville, a true company town, was made up of workers' housing as well as the factory itself.

Colt's Castle

Most everyone in Hartford thought their native son Sam Colt was slightly crazy in the early 1850's. The young proponent of the revolver had already had one factory fail. Now, barely solvent again, he had announced plans to drain a swampy parcel of land known as South Meadows, build a two-mile dike to protect it against spring flooding by the Connecticut River, then erect a huge pistol-producing armory.

Hartford at the time was a sleepy seat of government, not an industrial hub, and it had never seen anything quite like Colt's determination. When a banker refused to sell Colt a plot of land for a fair price, the gunmaker — who was at least credit rich — bought up all the bank's stock and threatened to fire the banker. Colt got his way.

By the fall of 1856 the massive stone factory and complex of outbuildings called Colt's New Armory were complete. Set on a rise overlooking the tamed river, it more closely resembled a medieval castle town than the modern factory that it was. Behind its looming main building — 500 feet long, 60 feet deep, and four stories high — lay the smaller work buildings, watchtowers, and workers' housing. The banks of the river were planted with willow trees, which not only stopped erosion but also supplied the material for Colt's new sideline — wicker furniture.

But it was inside the armory that the real business went on. The peerless network of foundries, engine rooms, tooling machines, and conveyor belts was staffed by nearly 500 workers. And when they started turning out 150 to 200 pistols a day, there were few who any longer doubted the wisdom of Colt's $1 million investment.

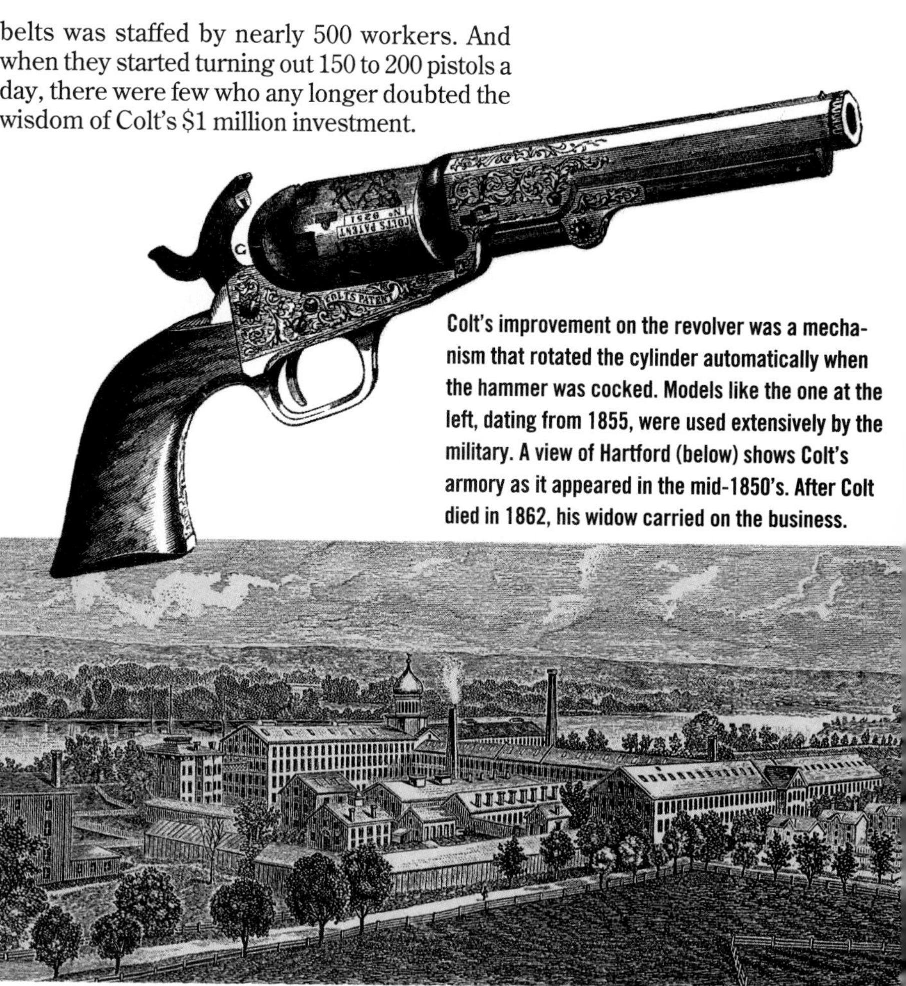

Colt's improvement on the revolver was a mechanism that rotated the cylinder automatically when the hammer was cocked. Models like the one at the left, dating from 1855, were used extensively by the military. A view of Hartford (below) shows Colt's armory as it appeared in the mid-1850's. After Colt died in 1862, his widow carried on the business.

The Colonel of Corn Mash

Neither history nor legend credits any one genius with the invention of bourbon, but there is little argument about who elevated Kentucky's "country whiskey" to a reputation for aristocratic excellence. Though Colonel Edmund Haynes Taylor, Jr., did not know much about whiskey when his bank took over a couple of financially troubled distilleries after the Civil War, his talent for management soon placed him in the forefront of the industry.

Taylor was the first to insist on — and he successfully campaigned for — a bottled-in-bond act to guarantee content. Once the act passed, all the ingredients had to be listed on labels, which prevented bottlers from adulterating true bourbon with prune juice and straight alcohol — or something even worse.

Taylor also had a flair for advertising. When he started his own company, he camouflaged his Frankfort, Kentucky, distillery as a fantasy castle, and tourists flocked for a taste of antebellum splendor (and miniature free samples). But his biggest coup was introducing the southern specialty to northern tipplers. Alert to a surplus of empty Old Taylor bottles in nearby St. Louis, the colonel, it is said, shipped three freight cars of them to New York City, where they were displayed behind the bar in all the best drinking places — and soon set off a demand for bourbon in the Big Apple.

Colonel Taylor never hesitated to emphasize his family ties to General Zachary Taylor. But it was his own face and signature that appeared on the labels for Old Taylor bourbon.

"Now I Can Do My Work"
"I am 19 years old and I have been married five months. I felt weak, sick, and rundown. Every afternoon I used to lie down. My mother advised me to take Lydia E. Pinkham's Vegetable Compound. I did and now I feel strong and full of energy. I do all my work and feel as well after a day's work as I did in the morning."—Mrs. Edith Mae Ralston, Tyre, Pennsylvania.
LYDIA E. PINKHAM'S
VEGETABLE COMPOUND
Your health means happiness for the child
LYDIA E. PINKHAM'S VEGETABLE COMPOUND
(CONTAINS 15 PER CENT ALCOHOL) THIS IS ADDED SOLELY AS A SOLVENT AND PRESERVATIVE
RECOMMENDED FOR THE TREATMENT OF NON-SURGICAL CASES OF
WEAKNESSES AND DISORDERS
FEMALE GENERATIVE ORGANS
LYDIA E. PINKHAM MEDICINE CO.
LYNN, MASS., U.S.A.
SHAKE THE BOTTLE BEFORE USING

Even in the 1930's Lydia Pinkham's Vegetable Compound was a popular cure-all for "female complaints." Although Lydia's portrait no longer smiled from the bottle's label (above), her likeness appeared as a picture on the wall in one ad (above left). The use of testimonials from satisfied customers was another common ploy in Pinkham ads.

Savior of Her Sex

Few women enjoyed as much renown in the late 19th century as Lydia Pinkham did. Her face appeared in newspapers around the country, her name in countless household medicine chests. As the originator of Lydia E. Pinkham's Vegetable Compound — a women's cure-all — she was every female's friend, a self-proclaimed savior of her sex.

Born to a family of New England Quaker reformers in 1819, Pinkham grew up with a (not-unfounded) distrust of contemporary medical practices. By the time she had children of her own, she was brewing "safe" herbal medicines for her family's ailments. One concoction of roots and seeds steeped in a solution of about 18 percent alcohol turned out to be particularly effective against back aches and "female maladies." Pinkham gave it away by the bottleful to friends and neighbors who suffered from such things as "bearing down pains" and "falling of the womb."

By 1875 Pinkham's family was in deep financial distress. Just as despair was setting in, however, two women appeared at the door asking to buy a "vegetable compound" they had heard about. Quickly coming up with a price — five dollars for six bottles — Pinkham sold her brew for the first time and saw no reason why it had to be the last.

Lydia's sons warmed to the idea and took over the marketing side of the venture, peddling bottles to pharmacies throughout the Northeast. Sales were modest at first, but by 1879 they decided to emphasize the compound's trustworthiness by placing a portrait of their mother on the label. They also launched an advertising campaign in which their mother's face smiled benignly above sensationalized copy. "Clergyman Killed by His Own Wife," read one ad. "Female Complaints the Cause."

The best marketing stroke, however, was Pinkham's own. She used her ads to advance the idea that male physicians were ill prepared to handle female afflictions, and encouraged women to write her with questions. They would be answered, she promised, by "women only." She received about 150 letters a day and employed a staff of women to answer them with confidential commonsense advice.

Pinkham died in 1883, but not before seeing sales climb to a quarter of a million dollars a year. Family members continued the business, which was expanded to include pills and a "blood purifier" and lasted into the 1960's.

Mr. Soule's Winning Gamble

Dubbed "the medicated sportsman" in the newspapers of his native upstate New York, Asa T. Soule was a teetotaling, churchgoing entrepreneur who never let ethics get in the way of business. By the time he reached age 49 in 1873, Soule had made a tidy bundle out of farming, real estate, and patent rights and was ready to try something new.

For $125,000 he became the owner of a patent medicine called Doyle's Hop Bitters, "The Invalid's Friend and Hope," and then proceeded to stun acquaintances by borrowing a huge sum to spend on advertising. But Soule's hunch proved correct. Within six years Hop Bitters (which probably owed much of its efficacy to a heavy dose of alcohol) was one of the most popular patent medicines in the country, and Soule was a millionaire.

By then well on his way to becoming a leading citizen of Rochester, New York, where his medicine was made, Soule decided to add to his prestige by buying the city a baseball team. Although baseball at the time was highly corrupt and considered by many on a par with gambling, it also drew big crowds. Soule capitalized on the game's popularity by having the players' shirts emblazoned with the name Hop Bitters instead of the name of the town, and even christened the local baseball diamond Hop Bitters Park.

When this team was to forced to disband after a bribery scandal, Soule quickly formed another — which one newspaper dubbed "The Gambler's Friend and Hope." Then he began backing sculling races, a sport that was even more vice-ridden than baseball.

While Soule's financial fortunes held steady, his association with shady games began to sully the corporation's image, and he decided to link his product to something loftier than organized sports. Meeting with the trustees of the University of Rochester, he offered to donate $100,000 if the school would change its name to Hop Bitters University. The offer was declined.

His popularity waning in New York, Soule moved to Kansas in 1883, where he invested heavily in land. He would never again manage to duplicate his earlier success — but that did not deter cowboys from stopping him on the street to touch a genuine millionaire "for luck."

Little Blue Bottles of Relief

There was nothing "gay" about the 1890's for anyone afflicted with a cold. Relief, such as it was, came in the form of unpleasant poultices that, rubbed on the chest and forehead, often caused blisters and other skin irritations. Or sufferers might lean over a stove to inhale herbal steam from a vaporizer — and perhaps be severely burned.

With his own son suffering from a bad cough, one enterprising North Carolina pharmacist, Lunsford Richardson, decided to come up with something better. Making use of a laboratory that belonged to his brother-in-law, Dr. Joshua Vick, Richardson kept up his experiments until he hit on a concoction that seemed effective — a blend of a little-known Japanese mint oii extract called menthol, mixed with camphor and eucalyptus oil in a petroleum-jelly base. The ointment that he produced not only vaporized by body heat alone, but was also safe on the skin.

Calling his formula Richardson's Croup and Pneumonia Cure Salve, he set about mixing up batches by the kettleful and packaging it in little blue jars. Local sales were so encouraging that by 1905 Richardson sold his drugstore and invested his $8,000 life savings in a laboratory, meanwhile enlisting the aid of his son, Smith, whose croup had originally inspired the product.

Hoping to develop an international clientele, Smith convinced his father that the mentholated ointment needed a catchier name. Choosing "Vick's" in honor of the brother-in-law, and "VapoRub" to distinguish their product from all other salves on the market, the Richardsons embarked on one of America's first mass mail-advertising campaigns. Word spread, sales eventually soared, and by the time of Lunsford Richardson's death in 1919, his little blue bottles of Vick's VapoRub had achieved recognition — and brought relief — on both sides of the Atlantic.

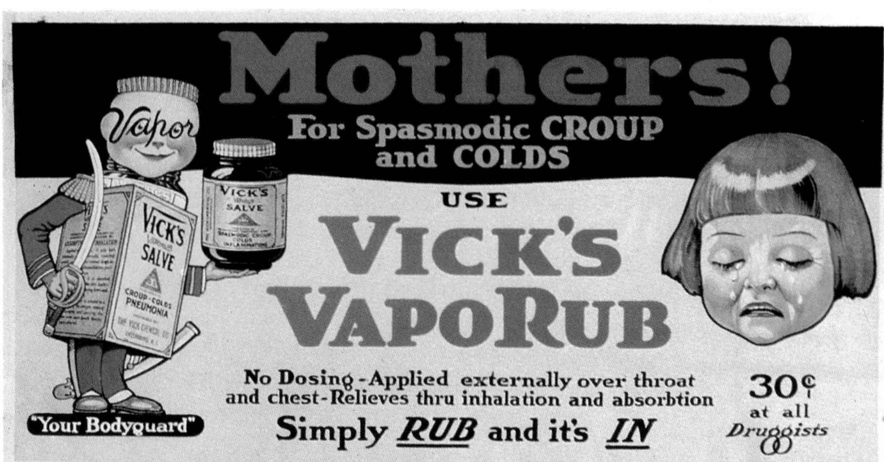

Millions of cold-congested children and adults have breathed a little easier since Vick's VapoRub was developed in 1890. The formula has remained virtually unchanged since then.

A foot clad in nothing more than an arch support or bunion pad became Dr. Scholl's trademark even though, in his early days, people complained that such pictures were indecent.

First Aid for Aching Feet

William Scholl lived by his personal credo: "Early to bed, early to rise, work like hell and advertise." The developer of some 1,000 foot-care products, he managed to make his name virtually synonymous with relief from bunions, corns, and fallen arches.

It was as a young shoe salesman in Chicago at the turn of the century that Scholl realized how uncomfortable most shoes were for his customers. Such was his skill at adjusting the fit, however, that many people sought out his services, even waiting to shop at night when he began studying medicine by day.

When young Dr. Scholl graduated in 1904, he had already perfected an arch support called the "foot-eazer" and was developing a uniquely personal sales technique. Dressed formally in a long frock coat (perhaps to appear older than his 22 years), he would walk into a shoe store, pull the skeleton of a human foot from his pocket, and toss it on the counter. By the time he had delivered a lively lecture on the anatomy of the foot — ending, of course, with a plug for his product — a sale was practically assured.

As one of the few people addressing the problem of foot comfort, Scholl did a brisk business. Establishing his own company in 1907, he opened a branch in Toronto the following year and established a factory in London by 1910. As revenues grew, Scholl continued to demonstrate his flair for promotion. In 1916, for instance, he sponsored a nationwide Cinderella Foot Contest that sent women scurrying to record their footprints on a specially designed machine at their local Dr. Scholl stores. When a panel of judges selected and showed off the most perfect print, Scholl confidently predicted, women all over the country would purchase his products in an effort to improve their own feet.

Foot care, in fact, motivated most of his activities. He authored a correspondence course and put out a monthly magazine for shoe salesmen, sponsored a series of walking contests, and on his world travels, assembled a collection of antique footware. Throughout his life Dr. Scholl continued to pioneer new products — everything from orthopedic sandals to support stockings — though he was hardly his own best customer. In all his 85 years, he developed only one corn, from a new pair of shoes bought on a trip to the Far East. Unfazed, he simply applied a patented Scholl corn remedy and was on his way.

Though stories vary as to how Robert Chesebrough came up with the name Vaseline, there is no doubt that customers have continually come up with new uses for the product he developed in the 1860's. This novelty ruler helped promote the popular household remedy.

The Jelly With a Thousand Uses

As a chemist experimenting with kerosene production in the 1850's, Robert Chesebrough was fascinated by the possibilities of petroleum. So when he read about the country's first big oil strike in Titusville, Pennsylvania, in 1859, he spent everything he had on a round-trip ticket, rushing to the site without knowing exactly what he was looking for.

Walking around the oil field, however, he started asking questions about a substance called rod wax, a jellylike residue that continually had to be cleaned off the pumping equipment. It was nothing but an annoyance, he was told — except when a worker had a cut or burn. Then, a little of the gunk rubbed on the injury seemed to ease the pain and promote healing.

Taking a keg of the wax back to his laboratory in Brooklyn, New York, Chesebrough refined it to a clear gel and tested its healing powers by cutting and even burning himself. Convinced that it worked, he named the product Vaseline and sent samples to doctors and druggists, confidently expecting the orders to roll in. When they did not, Chesebrough set out by buggy to give away free samples to housewives in New York State. The reception was so enthusiastic that within a few years Vaseline was selling in pharmacies at the brisk rate of a jar per minute.

Throughout his life Chesebrough remained Vaseline's most enthusiastic booster. Seriously ill with pleurisy in his late 50's, he instructed his nurse to slather his entire body with Vaseline — and credited it with his recovery. And until his death at 96, he attributed his longevity and good health to an unusual addition to his diet: the spoonful of Vaseline he ate every day.

A Solution That Stuck

Newly wed in 1920, Josephine Dickson was a novice in the kitchen and was forever slicing her fingers and burning her hands. Every evening her husband, Earle, would return to their New Jersey home from his job as a cotton buyer at Johnson & Johnson and devotedly patch up her hands with the best sterile gauze that money could buy.

Earle's carefully applied bandages, however, kept slipping off Josephine's fingers as she went about her work. And so, determined to design a bandage that would stay put, Earle sat down at the table, laid out a length of surgical tape, sticky side up, and placed a strip of gauze down the middle. Then, covering the whole thing with crinoline, he rolled it up tight. Whenever necessary, Josephine could now snip off a piece, pull away the crinoline, and apply a patch without need for an extra pair of hands.

When shown the new bandage, the company's president immediately recognized its potential. Within a year Johnson & Johnson was producing Band-Aids, and by 1924 they were being sold as the now-familiar individual strips. Earle, meanwhile, went on to become a vice president of the company, by which time — hopefully — Josephine had some help in the kitchen.

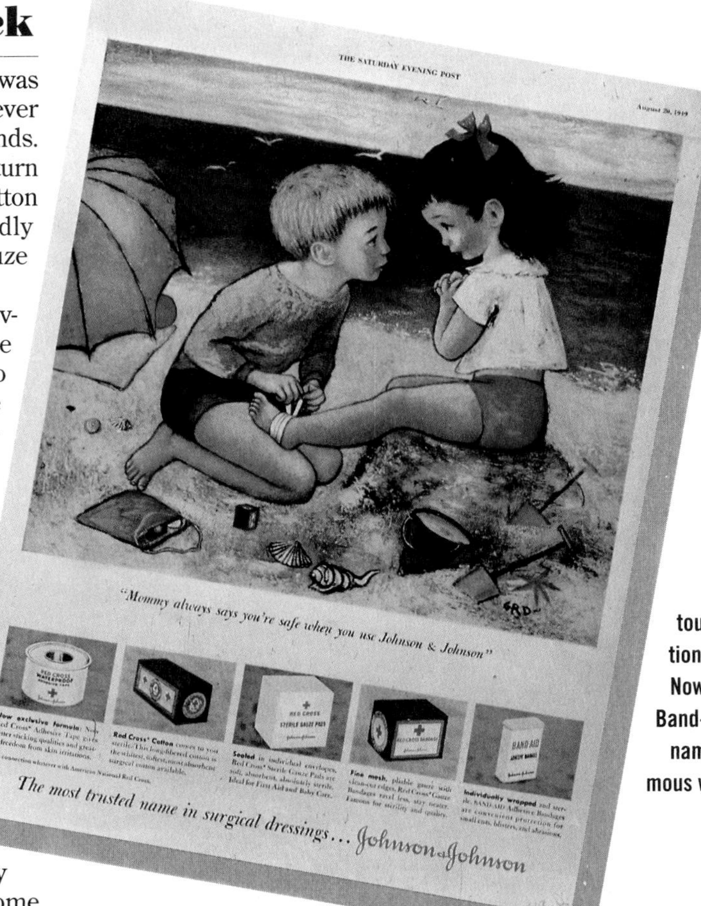

From the time that Band-Aids made their commercial debut, advertisements have touted their easy application and sterile protection. Now, more than 100 billion Band-Aids later, the product name has become synonymous with adhesive bandage.

Ads from the 1940's (above) proclaim the virtues of Dixie Cups in all their guises. In earlier times the public had shared cups and dippers (right) — and shared their germs.

Drink to Good Health

Dixie Cups owed their initial acceptance to a demand for safe drinking water but later became the thing to ask for if you wanted ice cream in a cup.

All that Hugh Moore meant to sell at first was a nice clean drink of water. For just a penny, thirsty customers could step up to one of his porcelain dispensers, fill a little paper cup with cool water, drink up, and toss the cup away. There would be no more risking one's health by drinking from a communal dipper. It was a great idea, except for the fact that no one in 1908 wanted to pay a penny for a drink of water — not even one endorsed by the Anti-Saloon League.

Germ-free drinking

Within the year Moore's business was on the brink of failure; so he tried a different approach — selling the cups instead of the water. With a $200,000 investment from a health-conscious businessman, he transformed his American Water Supply Company of New England into a paper-cup company. It was a change that mirrored the nation's mood. Moore's home state of Kansas had just become the first state to outlaw public dippers for health reasons. And when the shocking results of a study about germs found on public drinking vessels was published, the rest of the country followed suit. Suddenly, disposable cups were in demand for schools, trains, offices, and waiting rooms. Moore's hygienic little Health Kups — as he called them — were there to ride in on the tide of public concern.

Still, Moore was not quite satisfied. Health Kups sounded stodgy: he wanted a livelier name. In 1919 he found it right next door at the Dixie Doll Company, whose owner agreed to let him use the name.

During the 1920's, when commercial ice cream became all the rage, Moore was ready with the cups for handy individual servings. No matter what brand might be stamped on the label, every kid in the country, it semed, was asking for a Dixie cup.

Bossie and Me

In the early years of this century, two Vermont brothers, John and Charles Norris, decided to add something new to their product line for dairy farmers. For $150 they bought the recipe and rights to a cure-all ointment called Bag Balm from the druggist who had cooked up the formula some 15 years earlier, and began to market it.

The mix of lanolin, pine oil, and petroleum jelly was just the thing for soothing and healing Bossie's and Flossie's udders when they became chapped. Farmers swore by the stuff, with some even buying it by the 60-pound case.

But as it turns out, cows have not been the only ones enjoying the Bag Balm cure. Although it has always been labeled "For Veterinary Use Only," it has been bought by surgeons who use it for softening their hands, by sailors for treating rope burns, by skiers for healing chapped faces, and by horseback riders for soothing sore rumps.

Still owned by the Norris family, the company, which produces nearly a million cans a year, continues to receive testimonials from satisfied customers: farmers, for instance, who smear Bag Balm on fruit-tree grafts, a soldier who greased his Howitzer with it, someone else who used it for greasing bedsprings, and kayakers who brought it along when they braved the chills of Tierra del Fuego. Many of Bag Balm's fans, in fact, have never been anywhere near a cow.

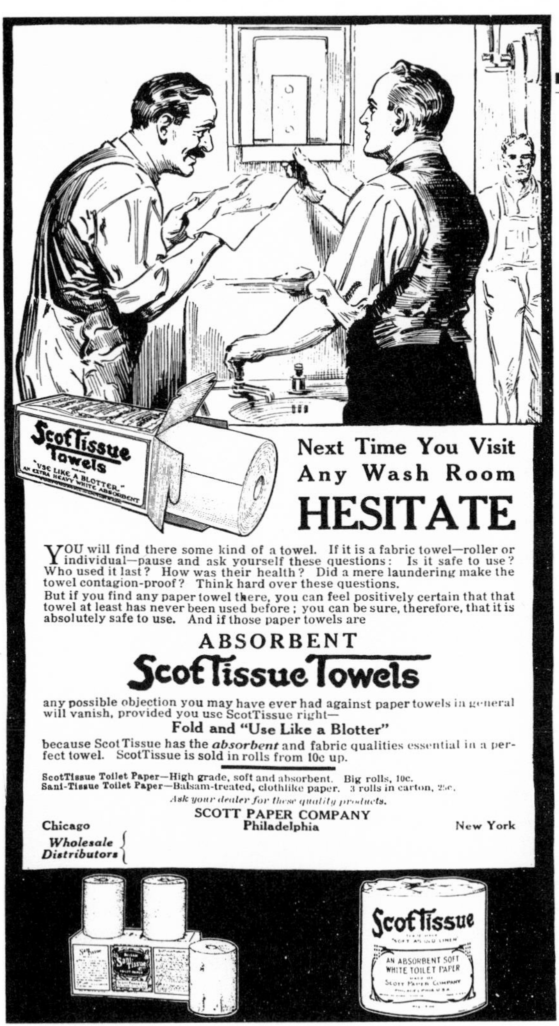

Paper on a Roll

In order to avoid unnecessary embarrassment, suggested an ad in the early 1900's, "don't ask for toilet paper — ask for ScotTissue." Few things, in fact, have been as hard to sell at the outset as toilet paper. As long as privies were the norm, few people were willing to spend money on "medicated paper," as the stuff was called, when old mail-order catalogues would do just as well. Even after indoor plumbing became commonplace, there was that mortifying moment of having to ask the grocer for a package — which was usually kept hidden under the counter.

In the 1880's two brothers, Irvin and Clarence Scott, began to change all that. Working in Philadelphia, they began putting perforated toilet tissue on rolls that were just the right size for the home bathroom, instead of selling it in flat sheets in industrial-size packages. Until the turn of the century, Scott made tissue for other merchants, at one point producing over 2,000 brands. Then, just as newspapers and magazines were beginning to accept toilet-tissue advertisements, the company began phasing out the other labels and concentrating on its own — Waldorf at first, and then ScotTissue.

Even as their reputation was being established for one product, the Scott Paper Company found a second use for paper on a roll. Following the example of a teacher who sought to stop the spread of cold germs among her pupils by cutting towels from paper, the Scotts began packaging SaniTowels for business use in 1907 and, soon after, introduced ScotTissue Towels for the home.

By 1915, when these ads appeared, it was finally considered acceptable to show a picture of a roll of toilet tissue in a magazine (left). At the same time, the public was beginning to realize that communal towels in offices, schools, and homes were unsanitary (right).

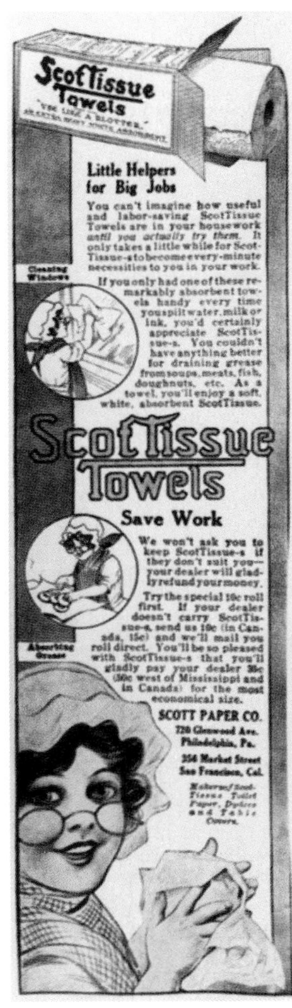

Stick 'Em Up

Invented as a means for sealing food wrappers, Scotch Tape really caught on only after its original use had become obsolete.

Whatever the chore that requires patching, masking, packaging, or mending, there seems always to be a roll of tape in a tartan wrapper that was made just for the job. Before the 1920's, however, do-it-yourselfers had to make do without mending tape.

It was then that salesmen for 3M — at that time a fledgling sandpaper manufacturer — noticed that craftsmen in the automobile plants they serviced were having a tough time making a clean job of painting the then-popular two-tone cars. Back at the factory, technician Richard Drew set to work on the problem, and by 1925 the company was able to introduce a brand-new product — masking tape — that has been used by painters ever since.

Soon afterward 3M tackled yet another sticky issue. This time it was a request from bakery suppliers who wanted to use the newly invented cellophane for wrapping their products but needed a way to seal it. Once again, it was Richard Drew who came to the rescue. After months of experimenting, in 1930 he came up with a way of sticking glue on cellophane strips and, with that, Scotch brand transparent tape was born.

Always colorfully clad in plaid, Scotch Tape's kilted mascot has for decades demonstrated the product's uses to musicians, librarians, and home owners.

The clear tape at first seemed doomed to failure since a means for heat-sealing cellophane was invented at the same time. Almost immediately, however, people started coming up with other uses for the product. During the Depression it was a boon to home owners trying to save money by doing their own household repairs. Schoolteachers, shopkeepers, office workers, and others all discovered that cellophane tape was indispensable. The list only grew when another 3M employee, John Borden, made taping even easier by designing the first Scotch Tape dispenser in 1932.

MERCHANTS AND TRADERS

Trapper John

When John Jacob Astor started work in the fur trade in New York City, it was the kind of small-scale enterprise in which an ambitious immigrant could make his mark without much capital. And in 1786, a little more than a year after he first headed up-country with a backpack full of German toys to trade for animal skins, the young man from Waldorf, Germany, opened a small shop of his own, where he bought and sold furs and musical instruments. Acting as his own agent, Astor tramped through New York State on foot and traveled by boat to Montreal and the Great Lakes in search of furs for the New York and London markets.

By 1800 "Trapper John" was worth an estimated $250,000 and, prompted by his wife, soon plunged into the booming China trade. Astor, wisely starting with what he knew best, set up a string of fur-trading posts and agents that stretched from the East to the Pacific Northwest and supplied ships based in New York. Like his competitors, he quickly learned to make the most of every voyage. En route to China, his ships were filled with furs; on their return they carried the black gold of Chinese tea. By the time he got out of the fur trade in 1834 to devote himself to the New York real estate he had bought with beaver skins, the Astor name was a synonym for wealth.

The China Trade

It was, for a few years in the late 1700's and into the early 1800's, a bit like sending down to the general store for necessities. "Please to purchase if at Calcutta two net bead draperies," went a typical request. "If at Batavia or any spice market, nutmegs and mace, or if at Canton, two Canton crape shawls of the enclosed colors at $5 per shawl."

Indeed, for the average housewife of Salem, Massachusetts, sending off to China for household goods was a simple matter of buttonholing a local ship's captain — and Salem, which had its rich trade with the British West Indies cut off after the Revolutionary War, was a city teeming with captains. Beginning in 1786, when Elias Hasket Derby's *Grand Turk* followed the trail blazed by the famed *Empress of China* to the docks at Canton, Salem became the heart of the lucrative trade with China and ports between. Derby had sent his ship out with a grab-bag cargo of local goods valued at $32,000. When it returned to Salem 18 months later, it was loaded down with silk, porcelain, and tea valued about $100,000.

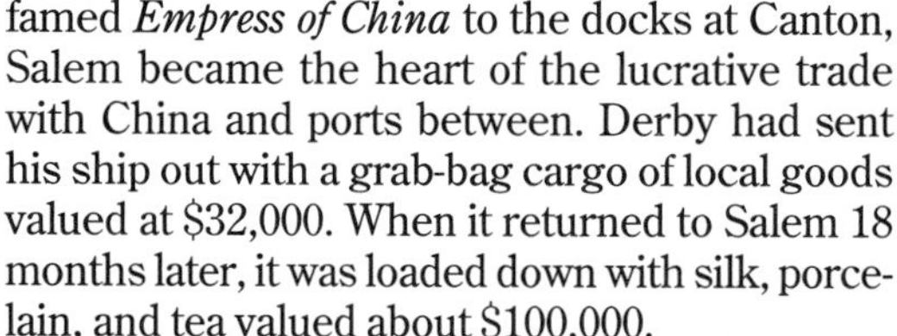

Everyone, naturally, wanted a share in this market, and those who could not afford ships of their own paid commissions to have their treasures carried around Cape Horn and across the Pacific. Large transshipments of American tobacco and French wine, ginseng and iron ore shared

From 1699 to 1842 Canton (right) was the only Chinese port open to foreign trade. There New England foodstuffs, tobacco, whale oil, and other goods were exchanged for tea, silks, porcelain, and decorative items like this painted fan (left).

Timothy Dexter embellished his Newburyport home and grounds with an astonishing array of statues of his many personal heroes.

space in outgoing holds with cartons of shoes and boxes of candles. On every return voyage the vessels brought back thousands of pieces of the "best Nankin blue and white Stone China," the porcelain that every respectable family wanted to adorn its dinner table and which every merchant wanted to mark up and sell elsewhere.

Most buyers settled for one of the stock patterns that Chinese artists created for the American market. But special orders based on sketches or famous paintings were common, as were the sort of interpretative errors inevitable in this commercial meeting of East and West: "This is to be in blue," one Chinese artist faithfully lettered onto the work at hand. "This in red."

Merchant's Mad House

Timothy Dexter may have been a bit eccentric, but there is no doubt at all that he had an uncanny knack for making money. Soon after moving to Newburyport, Massachusetts, the barely literate young leather dresser used his own modest funds plus those of the well-off widow he had married to buy supposedly worthless Continental currency. When Secretary of the Treasury Alexander Hamilton made good on the new nation's "liberty" notes in 1791, Dexter became rich overnight.

Much to the amazement of his neighbors, Dexter then is said to have made a series of improbable coups in the shipping trade — and gotten even richer. He should have lost his shirt on the warming pans that he sent to the West Indies, for example. But the pans sold, for use as strainers and dippers. The coals he foolishly shipped to Newcastle arrived in the midst of a shortage caused by labor strife and also sold for top dollar.

But for all his success as a merchant, Dexter made his real splash as a local character. A perennial sot, the self-styled "Lord Timothy Dexter" peppered the local newspaper with outrageously misspelled advisories and titled his autobiography *A Pickle for the Knowing Ones; or, Plain Truths in a Homespun Dress.* When readers complained of the lack of punctuation, Dexter threw in a page of periods, commas, and the like so that "thay may peper and solt it as they plese."

Even more fantastic was Dexter's private pantheon of heroes — Washington, Jefferson, Adam and Eve, and Venus, the Roman goddess of love — all perched atop stone columns planted on his lawn. When Dexter died in 1806 at the age of 60, his house stood as monument to the man who described himself with uncharacteristic understatement as "very luckkey in spekkelation."

Building Well Is the Best Revenge

James Lick was a youthful cabinetmaker when he asked for a young woman's hand in marriage. But her father, a wealthy mill owner, spurned the offer, claiming Lick was far too poor. Stung by the insult, Lick left his native Lebanon County, Pennsylvania, in 1825 and spent the next 22 years in South America, where he earned a tidy fortune from a variety of activities, including building pianos.

When California became part of the United States in 1847, Lick apparently decided on a change of scene. With $30,000 in hand, he moved to San Francisco just in time to witness the start of the gold rush. While others ran off to try their luck in the gold fields, however, Lick began to buy real estate, from the Santa Clara Valley to Lake Tahoe.

Shrewd speculation soon made him one of the wealthiest men in San Francisco — and possibly California's first millionaire — though it hardly showed in the way he lived. Reclusive and decidedly eccentric, Lick dressed in rags and for a time made his home in a shanty. Even after building himself a 24-room mansion, he used only one room, sleeping inside an unfinished grand piano.

Lick's personal pleasures may have been limited to the shelves he kept filled with scientific books and the time he lavished on his gardens, yet he was no miser. In 1852 he spent a quarter of a million dollars to build a three-story flour mill near San Jose, installing parquet floors, imported cedar and mahogany paneling, and the latest machinery. Californians called it Lick's Folly, but in truth it was Lick's revenge. He sent photographs of the mill back to Pennsylvania so that people could see just how fine a mill his wealth allowed him to build. Then in 1861 he constructed the extravagantly luxurious Lick House, which dazzled guests for years as San Francisco's finest hotel.

As his fortune grew, Lick became increasingly obsessed with creating a suitable monument to his wealth. He considered building a huge marble pyramid on the shore of San Francisco Bay and alternatively came up with a scheme for erecting huge statues of his parents. Ultimately, however, while providing for a variety of charities, Lick left some $700,000 toward the construction of a giant telescope that he hoped would "prominently connect his name with the history of science." And indeed it did. "As long as San Francisco and the state of California shall endure, the name of James Lick will be associated with them," reported the *Daily Evening Bulletin* at the philanthropist's death in 1876. The Lick Observatory remains an internationally famous center of astronomical research, and Lick himself is buried at its base.

Though James Lick (left) lived austerely, his hotel in San Francisco boasted a marble and mahogany dining room (above) based on a salon at Versailles. More than 30 comets have been discovered at the Lick Observatory (top), which was built on Mount Hamilton and is now part of the University of California.

Ben Hecht's Hidden Treasure

While writer Ben Hecht was not known to be much of a businessman, he certainly was rich in imagination. Nearly broke when he arrived in Miami, Florida, in 1925, Hecht was supposed to start work on a movie script but soon spotted a far more lucrative way to repair his sagging fortunes: the great Florida land boom. "The City of Miami had turned itself into a real-estate cornucopia," Hecht recalled. "A hundred thousand people were getting rich selling building lots to each other." The activity was so frenzied, he noticed, that no one found time for the usual vacation pleasures. "Nobody went swimming. Nobody sat under the palm trees. Nobody played horseshoes," he declared.

Armed with a novel scheme, Hecht approached Charles Ort, one of the area's leading real-estate dealers. The building lots on Ort's latest acquisition — the island of Key Largo — would sell faster, he suggested, if buried pirate treasure were to be discovered there. Hecht and a friend, Joseph P. McEvoy, promised to provide not only the treasure but also the publicity. For the modest sum of $5,000 a week, they said, they would ensure that newspapers around the country heard about the spectacular discovery. Ort and his partners readily agreed.

Hecht and McEvoy first tried to arrange a treasure cruise for New York socialites. When none proved interested, they struck a deal with a local beachcomber named Captain Loftus, who was to "discover" the loot. Handing Loftus a pirate map and $100, Hecht traveled to Key Largo to bury the treasure — genuine doubloons (on loan from a friend in Cuba) stashed inside two enormous Spanish vases.

Hecht's first glimpse of Key Largo was a rude awakening, for it offered little more than a small patch of beach and a dense mangrove swamp. While he privately regarded the entire island as a "snake-covered, bug-haunted jungle," Hecht nevertheless sent stories of the great discovery to newspapers around the country. Just as he predicted, reporters arrived in droves, eager to interview the captain. Much to Hecht's delight, Loftus proved to be "the greatest natural liar I had ever seen in action."

The result was a rush to dig on Key Largo, though treasure seekers were not allowed to turn over even one shovelful of dirt until they had purchased a lot. In just a week over $1 million worth of property had been sold on the island. Hecht himself wisely had bought none of it. "I was certain that the boom was due to collapse at any hour and take everything down with it," he confided. And that is just what happened early in 1926.

The wheeling-dealing Mr. Ort, who had bragged to Hecht that he was worth $90 million, ultimately was reduced to sleeping in a parking lot. Hecht, however, returned to New York with over $10,000 literally in his pocket — since he never trusted the overextended Miami banks enough to deposit so much as a penny of his own money in any of them.

Perhaps 99 out of every 100 visitors to Florida in the mid-1920's came to take advantage of the land boom. Picture postcards (right) were printed to vaunt the glories of newly cleared land, subdivisions, and apartments. Contemporary magazines like *Life* (left) were quick to find fun in the foibles of land speculation.

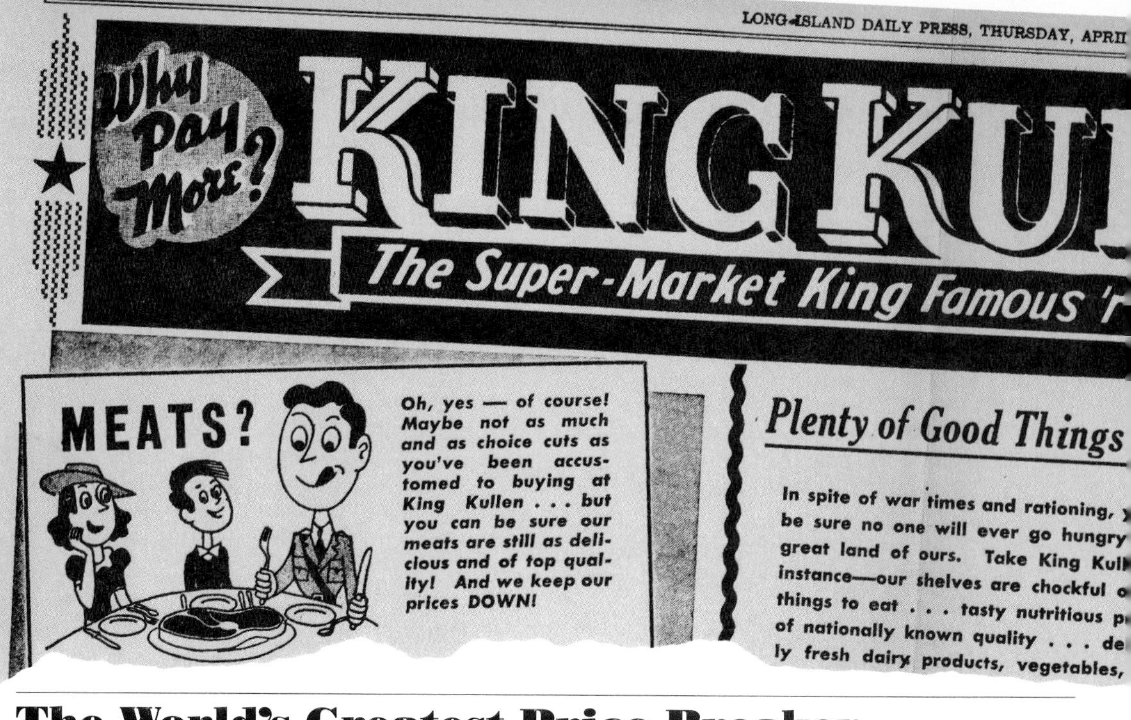

Page Thirty
LONG ISLAND DAILY PRESS, THURSDAY, APRII
Why Pay More?
KING KU
The Super-Market King Famous 'r
MEATS?
Oh, yes — of course! Maybe not as much and as choice cuts as you've been accustomed to buying at King Kullen . . . but you can be sure our meats are still as delicious and of top quality! And we keep our prices DOWN!
Plenty of Good Things
In spite of war times and rationing, be sure no one will ever go hungry great land of ours. Take King Kul instance—our shelves are chockful things to eat . . . tasty nutritious p of nationally known quality . . . de ly fresh dairy products, vegetables,

"How does he do it?" King Kullen asked in his grocery ads. Even during World War II, the supermarket king was able to offer customers meat and "plenty of good things to eat" at prices they could afford.

The World's Greatest Price Breaker

By 1929 anyone who wanted to could shop for groceries at a self-service store or one of several large chains. But that year Michael Cullen, a branch manager for the Cincinnati-based Kroger grocery stores, came up with an even better idea: cut-rate stores of "monstrous size." To keep costs down, Cullen suggested in a letter to the company's management, the stores should be located outside the high-rent districts of cities, where there would also be plenty of space for large parking lots. He wanted to sell 300 items at cost and 200 items at five percent above cost, he wrote. "Can you imagine how the public would respond to a store of this kind?"

Cullen, however, never got an answer to his query, since no one ever bothered to pass his letter along to the company's president. So he resigned, found backers of his own, moved east,

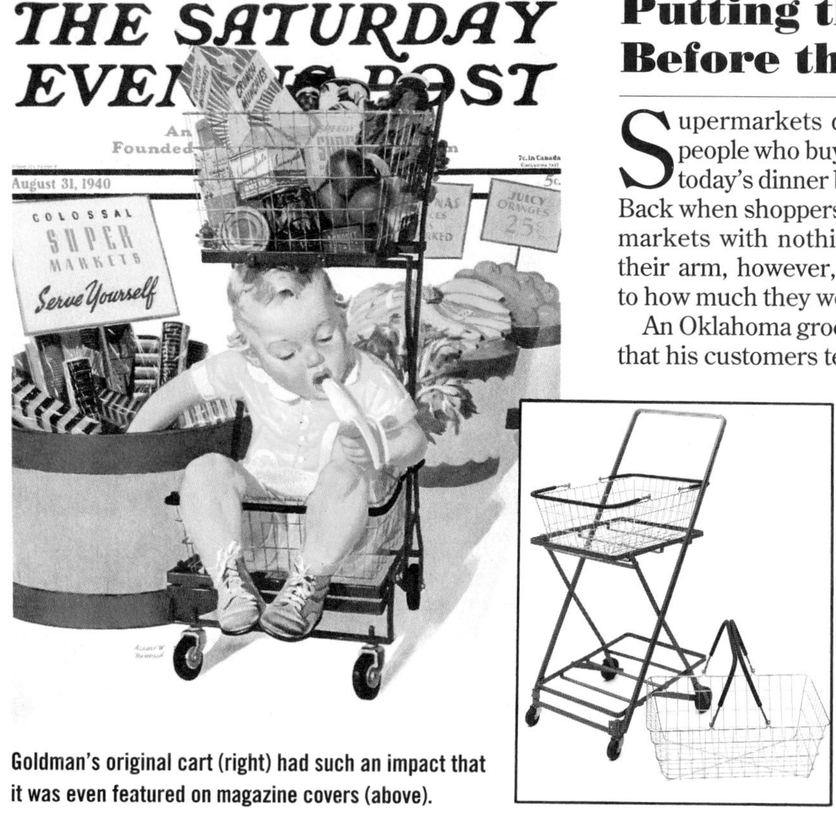

Goldman's original cart (right) had such an impact that it was even featured on magazine covers (above).

Putting the Cart Before the Shopper

Supermarkets depend on supershoppers: people who buy not only what is needed for today's dinner but for several days to come. Back when shoppers cruised the aisles of supermarkets with nothing more than a basket on their arm, however, there were practical limits to how much they were willing to purchase.

An Oklahoma grocer, Sylvan Goldman, noting that his customers tended to stop when the baskets became too heavy or too full, tried to figure out a way around the problem. Finally, late one night in 1936, inspiration struck. While staring at some folding chairs, he realized that by adding wheels and raising the seat in order to put a basket on top and another below, he could turn a chair into a cart for shopping. Customers could manage twice as much merchandise as

and in 1930 opened America's first supermarket — King Kullen — in Queens, New York. Even passersby on the highway could read the slogans next to the King Kullen name: "The World's Greatest Price Wrecker" and "How Does He Do It?" People showed up in droves to find out.

Cullen did it just as he had said he would. His stores occupied some 5,000 to 6,000 square feet and were roughly ten times bigger than large grocery stores of the day. They offered no frills and were heaped with bargains. Cartons of merchandise were stacked on the floor, canned goods were piled into pyramids. In time, Cullen began leasing floor space to vendors of cosmetics, hardware, and other items, which further reduced his overhead. But it was primarily because of volume buying that he was able to offer customers unheard-of prices.

"Chain Stores read these prices and weep," gibed Cullen in full-page newspaper advertisements. "Drop your prices, give the poor buying public a chance." What Depression-era shopper could resist? People flocked in from as far as 30 miles away to take advantage of the King's bargains. And chain-store owners were forced to take notice as well, for while the average A&P grocery store at the time grossed about $6,000 a month, King Kullen took in some $53,000.

In six short years Cullen had a sizable chain of his own — 15 supermarkets. By then he also had plenty of competitors. The first, a 50,000-square-foot Big Bear market in New Jersey, opened in 1932 and made King Kullen look puny by comparison. In its first year 16 cashiers were needed to check out nearly 250,000 customers a week. "Some day," prophesied one of the owners in 1933, "supermarkets will do nearly all of the business all over the country."

before, and the carts could be folded up out of the way when not in use.

Goldman had several dozen carts built and, hoping to attract hordes of curious shoppers, ran an ad in the local newspapers heralding his "revelation in food buying." Although people did come, few were interested enough to get behind the wheels. One woman told Goldman she was done pushing baby buggies; men remarked that they were strong enough to carry their own baskets, thank you! Undaunted, Goldman hired actors to set an example by happily pushing loaded carts through the aisles. The ploy worked and customers began shopping in a big way. Not only did Goldman's business thrive: other store owners soon were begging for carts. Taking out a patent, Goldman started manufacturing his "Cartwheels," the demand for which rose steadily with the rise of supermarkets.

Goldman, whose invention made him one of the country's wealthiest men before his death at age 86, never stopped refining his design. Stronger, sturdier "Nest Karts" came along in 1947, and airport luggage carts naturally followed. His carts now are second only to automobiles in numbers of four-wheel vehicles worldwide, and his original occupies a place of honor at the Smithsonian Institution in Washington, D.C.

S.O.S. for Grocers

The name Charles Stilwell is not likely to make most people's list of famous inventors. Yet in 1883, at the age of 38, Stilwell gave the world something genuinely useful: the brown paper grocery bag.

Cut, folded, and pasted on a machine of Stilwell's own design, the bag was known as the S.O.S., or self-opening sack, when it first appeared. Machines for making paper bags had been in use since the 1850's, and square-bottomed bags had existed from the 1860's. What made Stilwell's machine unique was the fact that it produced a sack that could be snapped open with a shake of the wrist and stand upright on its own, thus leaving the grocers' hands free to pack purchases. It was a time saver that helped revolutionize the grocery business.

Originally produced by the Union Paper Bag Machine Company of Philadelphia, the S.O.S. machine was called the Stilwell Square. While Stilwell made several improvements after receiving his initial patent, the machine has actually changed very little since his time. Today Americans continue to use his practical sack at the rate of billions of bags per year.

"Dingdong, Avon Calling!"

Peddling books door-to-door in the late 1870's, David McConnell found a sure-fire way to make himself more welcome as he traveled his rounds throughout the East. On each stop, the young pitchman gave his customers — mostly women — a small vial of perfume he had concocted in exchange for their time. Much to his surprise, on return trips he discovered that his perfume was more in demand than his books.

So in 1886 McConnell gave up bookselling, created the Little Dot Perfume Set — five home-brewed floral fragrances in little bottles — and launched a business of his own. Operating out of "a room scarcely larger than an ordinary kitchen pantry" in New York City with his wife as sole assistant, he was "bookkeeper, cashier, correspondent, shipping clerk, office boy and manufacturing chemist" for the new enterprise, which he called the California Perfume Company.

Soon however, McConnell hired Mrs. P. F. E. Albee, a former colleague in the book business, to sell his product door-to-door. When the New Hampshire widow took to the road, she sold not only the five fragrances, but also a new career option for women. Inspired by McConnell and encouraged by Albee, women responded enthusiastically to the newfound opportunity for flexible, respectable employment.

Like the oak tree that became its symbol, McConnell's company grew from a small beginning into a mighty thing. In 1928, impressed by the resemblance of the countryside surrounding Shakespeare's home in England to that around his laboratory in Suffern, New York, McConnell dubbed a new product line Avon, and in 1950 the California Perfume Company officially became Avon Products, Inc. By the time the beauty products giant reached its centennial, some 40 million women across the nation and around the world had worked as "Avon ladies."

Clad in long dress, hat, and gloves, Mrs. P. F. E. Albee set the standard for friendly respectability among Avon ladies.

Babies Are Their Business

One evening in 1927 Daniel F. Gerber grew impatient in his Fremont, Michigan, kitchen as he waited for his wife, Dorothy, to finish making supper for their seven-month-old daughter. Equally exasperated, Dorothy "dumped a whole container of peas into a strainer and bowl, placed them in Dan's lap and asked him to see how he'd like to do that three times a day, seven days a week." After trying his hand at mashing and straining, Gerber discovered that he didn't like it at all. And that set him thinking.

According to popular wisdom of the day, infants were not ready for solid food until they were a year old. Any modern mothers who thought otherwise had two options — they could buy drugstore-prepared baby food with a doctor's prescription, or they could endure the tedium of mashing and grinding their own at home. With the help of his father and the family-owned Fremont Canning Company, Gerber decided to investigate the possibility of manufacturing ready-made baby foods.

He experimented with various methods of cooking and straining vegetables and fruits, then tested the results on local babies, who gobbled them with gusto. Gerber then surveyed hundreds of mothers: would they buy prepared baby foods if the price was reasonable and the product easy to find? The response was a resounding "yes." Grocers, however, still needed to be convinced, so in 1928 young Dan Gerber launched a national advertising campaign for his newly developed line of baby foods.

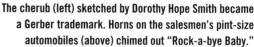

The cherub (left) sketched by Dorothy Hope Smith became a Gerber trademark. Horns on the salesmen's pint-size automobiles (above) chimed out "Rock-a-bye Baby."

Cost being a distinct concern, Gerber sought a means of attracting attention to what were to be fairly small ads. Intuitively, he felt that mothers would respond to a picture of a healthy, happy infant. A quick charcoal sketch of a baby girl by Dorothy Hope Smith, he decided, had exactly the right freshness and charm.

Those first ads also featured coupons entitling readers to six cans of baby food in exchange for a dollar and the name of their local grocer. Within the year tens of thousands of jars were shipped to mail-order customers. And the grocers, confronted with the names of so many would-be buyers, realized that Gerber was onto a good thing and began selling the product. So too did many other food companies, who jumped into the competition for this new market. Gerber's, however, remained preeminent, and in 1941 the Fremont Canning Company became the Gerber Products Company. In 1943 it stopped producing adult foods and five years later proclaimed: "Babies are our business . . . our *only* business."

Meet Cynthia

More silent than Garbo yet far more social, Cynthia was a cool blonde possessed, said Lester Gaba, her tireless escort, of "unbelievable chic." The fact that she was a store-window mannequin, crafted in plaster by Gaba himself, was beside the point. In the 1930's she was the toast of New York's café society.

Prior to Gaba's time, display dummies were crude assemblages of papier-mâché, iron, wood, and wax rigidly cast in stilted poses. As one wag summed it up, they looked "like human beings who had died and forgotten to lie down." It was Lester Gaba, a young artist from Hannibal, Missouri, who changed all that.

Gaba's father owned a clothing store, and from an early age Lester showed skill and enthusiasm for window dressing. In 1930, at the age of 23, he was ready for something bigger and moved to Chicago, where some soap sculptures that he carved for a promotional display earned him a raise, a promotion, and a hunger for new horizons. In 1932, packing "a clean shirt and one of my soap sculptures," Gaba set off for New York.

After two years of struggle, he began receiving a steady stream of assignments for his little statues, mostly for advertising illustrations. When *Advertising Arts* magazine asked him to write an article, he "rattled off a tirade" against the imported mannequins then in general use for window displays, saying they looked nothing like typical American women. Best and Company, a prominent department store, challenged him to come up with something better. And so the "Gaba Girls" were born.

Gaba's remarkably lifelike plaster figures were made in the image of real people — albeit real *famous* people such as models, movie stars, and comely socialites. Their naturalness captured the attention of shoppers, prompting one store after another to place orders with the artist for more.

The celebrated Cynthia was among the mannequins created for Saks Fifth Avenue, and her "eerie, almost human quality" caught even Gaba by surprise. He had a duplicate made, took it home, and when famed milliner Lilly Daché dropped by, she was so enchanted that she invited the mannequin to the opening of her new salon. Thus launched, Cynthia became the stuff of society columns. Louella Parsons reported her engagement to Charlie McCarthy. Tiffany, Cartier, and Harry Winston loaned her jewels — she appeared in a tableau as Lady Godiva, wearing only the Star of the East diamond. And once she led the Easter Parade on Fifth Avenue. But ultimately she proved even more fragile than fame. While in a beauty parlor, Cynthia slipped from her chair — and shattered. Far from brokenhearted, her Pygmalion later confessed: "Cynthia had become a Frankenstein to me, and I was rather relieved that she decided to — retire."

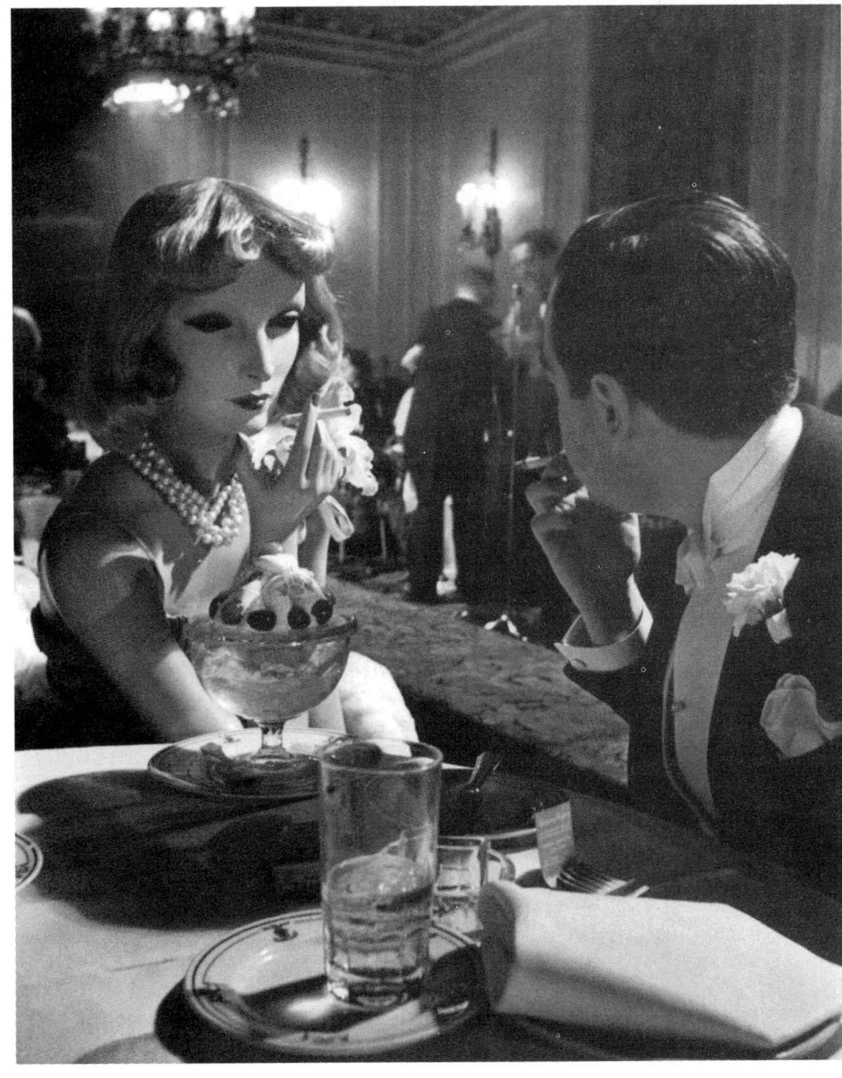

Lester Gaba's soignée dinner companion is his mannequin, Cynthia. For months after her introduction to society at a salon opening, Gaba gallantly toted the 100-pound figure wherever she was invited.

CAPTAINS OF INDUSTRY

Cheaper by the Dozen

A household with 12 children might suggest a scenario for sheer confusion, but the Gilbreth family proved that just the opposite could be true.

From the day they were married in 1904, Frank and Lillian Gilbreth worked together pioneering "motion" studies that would make the world's workplaces more efficient. As important as the couple's contribution to industry might have been, however, it was eclipsed by their fame as parents of 12 rambunctious children — an enterprise that held America spellbound. Strangers seeing the full complement of Gilbreths for the first time were likely to gasp and ask, "How do you feed all those kids?" Frank Gilbreth always had a ready answer: "They come cheaper by the dozen, you know." The line was later adopted as the title of a book and a movie (starring Clifton Webb and Myrna Loy) that immortalized the family's antics.

Efficiency by design

The Gilbreths' technique for "work simplification" improved production by eliminating unnecessary steps and strain, and ultimately affected the design and work patterns of everything from factories to surgery rooms. It also had an impact at home.

In a sense, the family's big Victorian house in Montclair, New Jersey, served as a kind of laboratory. No household task remained unexamined or unimproved for long. The children were filmed while doing simple routines such as brushing their teeth and washing dishes, and the results were studied frame by frame to discover how to perform the tasks with fewer motions. Even tonsilectomy was made more efficient when all 12 children turned out for surgery on the same day.

Similarly, Frank Gilbreth turned promptness into a rewarding game. On his return from business trips, he always whistled an "assembly call" as he strolled up the front walk, and young Gilbreths immediately came running in response. (The record muster — timed with a stopwatch — was six seconds.) Latecomers were chided, but Frank also used the assembly calls as a time to distribute gifts, with the best going to the promptest. Sundays were set aside for committee meetings. Everyone had a voice in managing family affairs, and chores were put out to competitive bids.

Frank and Lillian Gilbreth gathered with 11 of their 12 children at the home on Nantucket Island where they spent many cheerfully efficient summers.

If there was a single overriding passion that united the household, it was learning, and the learning took place at almost any time. In order to ensure that everyone knew German and French, for instance, the bathrooms were equipped with phonographs that spewed lessons while the children washed, morning and night. Dinner conversation was often punctuated by math quizzes featuring tricky double-digit mental multiplication. Summer vacations on Nantucket were enlivened with daily messages written in Morse code. Fortunately the Gilbreths had the good sense to season the lessons with humor, so that translators might be rewarded with messages like, "Bee it ever so bumble, there's no place like comb."

When Frank Gilbreth died of a heart attack at age 56, his family's efficiency stood it in good stead. Lillian was able to raise the children herself while continuing her own career. There had been method to the madness after all.

"What do you want to save all that time for?" Frank was once asked. "For work, if you love that best," he responded. "For education, for beauty, for art, for pleasure. For mumblety-peg, if that's where your heart lies."

NATIVE TONGUE

MONEY TALKS

"Money isn't everything," someone once said, "but it's way ahead of whatever is in second place." Root of all evil or no, it definitely is inescapable. We speak, for instance, of found money, pin money, easy money, hush money, and even mad money for a shopping spree.

Money has enriched our language for a long time. Some expressions, such as moneybags *and* filthy lucre, *have been around for centuries. Others refer to coins long since out of circulation. The French* picayune, *for example, was worth only pennies when it was used in America in the 18th century, and the word is still used for things of little value.* Two bits *has meant 25 cents since the 17th century when a Spanish 12½-cent piece, called a pieca, was mispronounced as "bika" or "bit," by Americans.*

Of course we Americans have coined a few expressions of our own. We have needed dough since the 1840's (do-re-mi in the 1920's), and dough was bread in the 1950's. We cared not a cent in the 1830's, but not a dime a decade later. Penny-pinching arrived with the 20th century, by which time America was looking out for wooden nickles, which, as everyone knew, were not worth a red cent.

Troubadour of the Tycoon Age

Even in an era when muckrakers were bashing monopolies, big business had its champions. Elbert Hubbard — a one-time soap salesman with a bent for bohemianism and a penchant for public relations — roused millions of workers to the cause of the employer.

By the time he was 39 in 1895, Hubbard had left soap sales behind and founded the Roycroft shop, a commune of craftsmen in East Aurora, New York. Dubbing himself Fra Elbertus, Hubbard oversaw the shop's production of furniture and books, and publicized his work ethic in his own magazines. While espousing the virtues of such things as quality over quantity, Fra Elbertus also preached on other subjects. Writing all the advertisements as well as articles for his magazine *The Philistine*, for instance, he often used ad space to praise the likes of Standard Oil or James J. Hill's railroad trust.

But nothing pleased businessmen half so much as a little essay that Hubbard wrote in 1899. "If you work for a man, in Heaven's name work for him," it began. "If he pays wages that supply you your bread and butter, work for him, speak well of him, think well of him, and stand by him." Entitled "A Message to Garcia," the essay purportedly told a tale of the Spanish-American War in which Lt. Andrew Rowan was sent into the Cuban jungle alone to find and deliver news to Gen. Calixto Garcia. According to Hubbard, Rowan acted selflessly, promptly, doing exactly as he was told "without asking any idiotic questions." Hubbard contrasted him with the "frowsy ne'er-do-wells" found all too often in the work force. Their slipshod assistance and halfhearted work, he said, made life hell for the long-suffering employer.

To Hubbard's surprise the essay was taken up as a corporate battle cry. During the early 1900's 40 million copies were printed in 20 languages. (Hubbard's son once claimed that there were 80 million copies in print by 1925.) Employers made it required reading for their workers, military officers distributed it to their troops — and every Boy Scout in America received his very own copy.

Hubbard's taste for artistic dress (above right) belied his aggressive tactics. His philosophical ramblings (right) were always packaged in aesthetic wrappings.

Digging for Diamonds in Your Own Backyard

On the lecture circuits of the late 19th century, few subjects were more popular with a public eager for self-improvement than the gospel of wealth through virtue. And no one spoke more persuasively on the subject than Russell Herman Conwell, a Philadelphia-based Baptist minister. Audiences throughout the country gathered time and again to hear him deliver his famous lecture on that theme, a lengthy, rather rambling discourse titled "Acres of Diamonds."

Thoroughly inspirational, the address began with a parable Conwell had heard while traveling in Baghdad. It was the story of Al Hafed, a guileless Persian farmer who went off in search of wealth and died disappointed, even while acres of diamonds — the Golconda mine — lay undiscovered in his own backyard.

Bringing his audiences back to their own backyards, Conwell drew a parallel. Wealth was not dependent on where you are but *what* you are, he told them. Plain, straightforward common sense and application were what it took. And, he informed each roomful of ready believers, it was nothing less than man's Christian duty to seek wealth. "Money," he declared, "is power; money has powers; and for a man to say, I do not want money, is to say, I do not wish to do any good to my fellow men."

Launching then into the rags-to-riches tales of individuals from John D. Rockefeller and John Jacob Astor to the inventor of rock maple candy, Conwell hammered home the message that success is a matter of seizing the opportunities that God presents. Great men, he assured his audiences, are everywhere, waiting to recognize their potential. "Greatness consists not in holding some office; greatness really consists in doing some great deed with little means. . . . He that can be a blessing to the community in which he lives tonight will be great anywhere."

Conwell certainly lived according to his precepts, for that one lecture proved to be his own "acre of diamonds." He made millions on it, delivering it a total of some 6,000 times. (A gala for the 5,000th performance in 1914 brought in some $9,000.) Conwell then invested the proceeds in the founding of Philadelphia's Temple University, several hospitals, and many other good works.

Reverend Russell Conwell helped inspire America's belief in the the power of the self-made man.

Woman of Iron

Present-day Lukens Steel Company traces its success back to the intelligent — if initially reluctant — leadership of a young Quaker widow.

Rebecca Lukens did not welcome her promotion in 1825. A 31-year-old mother of three with another child on the way, she would have preferred to remain a housewife. But she had promised her dying husband, who had inherited his iron-milling business from Rebecca's father, that she would carry on. In fact she had little choice, since he had borrowed heavily to move into the then-new field of producing boilerplate. (He was betting on the future of that novelty, the steam engine.) "Necessity," she wrote at the time, "is a stern taskmistress."

Fortunately, as a Quaker Lukens had received an unusually thorough education for a woman of her generation: she had even studied chemistry at the secondary-school level. She proved a natural at marketing and was far ahead of her male associates in grasping the potential of railroads when they expanded into her area of Pennsylvania. Within a decade she was shipping boilerplate as far away as New Orleans and even England. By the time she died in 1854 , she had made her mill the foremost manufacturer of boilerplate in the United States.

Lukens, moreover, achieved this without sacrificing her Quaker principles. When the Boston Navy Yard wanted to place a particularly large order, she refused, explaining that she would not contribute to the manufacture of warships.

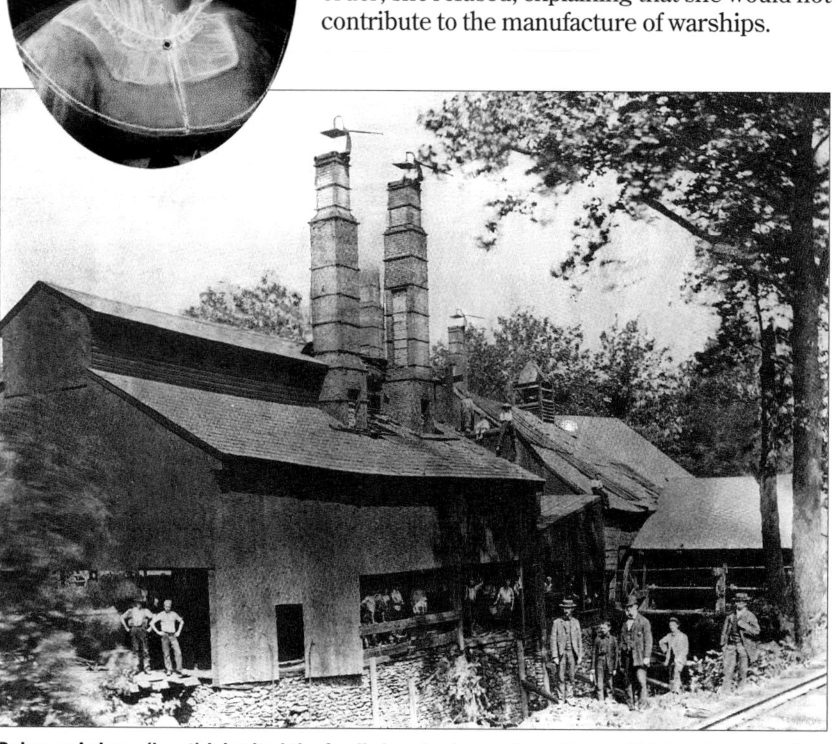

Rebecca Lukens (inset) inherited the family iron business, the original mill (above), and a pile of debt in 1825. By 1850 she had forged "a very superior mill" and a thriving business.

Seven Fortunes for Seven Sons

Meyer Guggenheim looked more like a tailor than a miner when he arrived in Leadville, Colorado, in 1881. And in fact that was how the bewhiskered Swiss immigrant had gotten his start in the United States. But he had since made money in stove polish, lye, imported lace, and railroad stocks. Now, determined that each of his seven sons should become a millionaire, Guggenheim began looking for ways to get in on the silver boom. For a few thousand dollars he picked up a couple of flooded mines, pumped them dry, and soon was clearing $2,000 a day in lead and silver.

Aside from his own shrewd eye for a deal, however, Meyer's greatest asset was the obedient, gifted, and loyal Guggenheim boys — Simon, Benjamin, William, Daniel, Solomon, Isaac, and Murry. Deciding that too much of his profit went to the smelters, Meyer set up his own plant in the late 1880's and put Simon to work there. Benjamin, who had studied mining at Columbia University, began scouting a site for a new smelting plant, which William, who had studied metallurgy at the University of Pennsylvania, would help manage.

With Isaac serving as the family treasurer and Murry in charge of sales, Meyer had time to plan

Star of Bethlehem

When Charlie Schwab went to work at a Pennsylvania steel plant in 1879, the ambitious 17-year-old started as a day laborer. But within six months, through charm, hard work, and many nights of study, he had ascended to the position of assistant chief engineer. Assembling a laboratory at home, Schwab studied metallurgy on his own time and, by means of improved quality control, streamlined production techniques, and better labor relations, managed to make great savings for the company — and for its owner, Andrew Carnegie. By the time he reached age 35, Schwab was president of Carnegie Steel, earning $1 million or more per year. And that was just the beginning.

One secret of Schwab's success was his willingness to take risks, a trait he exercised by gambling at Monte Carlo (although he strove to hide this from his strait-laced boss). Chancy business deals, such as when he persuaded Carnegie, who was considering retirement, to sell out to J. P. Morgan in 1901, were another outlet for his thrill seeking. The result of that coup, U. S. Steel, was the largest steel company in the world, with 213 mills, 41 iron mines, 57,000 acres of coal fields — and Charles M. Schwab as president.

The Guggenheim men (from left to right, Benjamin, Murry, Isaac, Meyer, Daniel, Solomon, Simon, and William) created a formidable mining empire in the Gilded Age.

the conquest of the whole smelting and mining industry. In 1890 Daniel persuaded Porfirio Díaz, the imperious president of Mexico, to allow the Guggenheims to exploit that country's cheap labor and rich ores; Solomon stayed to purchase mines and build another smelter. Meyer's beloved boys went on to build an empire that dominated mining from Alaska to Chile to the Congo, reaping rich harvests of copper, silver, lead, tin, gold, diamonds, and nitrates. As one bested business opponent once ruefully observed: "What one Guggenheim missed, another was sure to think of."

The brothers lavished their millions on mansions, priceless art collections, and philanthropic foundations — which would have pleased Meyer had he witnessed it. But the elder Guggenheim had died in 1905, after an unsuccessful operation. Staunch to the end, he had refused all anesthetic, preferring instead the consolation of a cigar and music from a gramophone to dull the pain of the surgeon's blade.

But Schwab's maverick personality chafed under the constraints of the new consortium. He quit after two years to become his own boss at a tiny rival, Bethlehem Steel. Cooler heads viewed this as professional suicide. Ever the gambler, however, Schwab devoted himself to the manufacture of structural steel. His luck held: a boom in skyscrapers, plus contracts for ships and armor plate in World War I made Bethlehem the second-largest steel company in the world.

Believing that "spending creates more wealth for everybody," Charles M. Schwab used up every bit of his prodigious fortune — and then some.

Though Schwab's personal fortune reached $200 million, his expenses outran his income. He kept 300 men busy on his Pennsylvania estate, where his chickens were housed in a replica of a French village. The despair of his accountant, Schwab insisted his bad investments were good deals since the losses reduced his taxes. He couldn't resist a hard-luck story and gave vast amounts to charities and beggars — which is about what he was at his death in 1939. When executors tallied up his estate, they found that the legendary steel magnate was $338,349 in the hole.

"Put not your trust in money, but put your money in trust."
— Oliver Wendell Holmes, 1858

"Some men worship rank, some worship heroes, some worship power, some worship God, and over these ideals they dispute — but they all worship money." *— Mark Twain, c. 1898*

"Acquaintance, n., *A person whom we know well enough to borrow from, but not well enough to lend to."* *— Ambrose Bierce, 1906*

"Gentlemen prefer bonds." *— Andrew Mellon, c. 1926*

This Registers the amount
of your Purchase.

Cash Register King

His business associates laughed when John Patterson paid $6,500 for the rights to "Ritty's Incorruptible Cashier" in December 1884 — but they had long since stopped snickering by 1911 when National Cash Register sold its millionth machine.

The Dayton-based entrepreneur was one of very few buyers of the prototype cash register that James Ritty, an Ohio bar owner, had invented to deter employee pilferage. When the ugly duckling device — it looked like a clock dial set atop an adding machine — turned Patterson's retail store from a $1,000-a-month loser into a $1,000-a-month earner, he realized it had unlimited potential. After the machine was improved with the soon-to-be-familiar pop-up numbers, cash drawer, and bell, Patterson took ownership and developed a crack sales force to market it.

John Patterson built a multimillion-dollar business on a product that, at first, no one wanted — the cash register.

A new kind of sales force

In Patterson's time the typical salesman was a jovial, cigar-smoking back-slapper — a style that definitely did not suit the aspiring cash register king. Instead, he began his sales training by treating a likely young man to a stay in a luxury New York hotel and a suit of custom clothing in order to give him a taste of what success could bring. Then the trainee was enrolled in Patterson's "Hall of Industrial Education," where salesmen-to-be acted out selling success stories, sang company songs, and memorized a sales primer written by Patterson's brother-in-law.

Once the salesman had absorbed the primer's prescribed responses to all the excuses a "P. P." (prime prospect) might use to escape buying, he hit the road to cover his own exclusive territory. Patterson insisted that a salesman should be able not only to sell one register for every 400 residents in a territory, but also to sell the same customer an "upgrade" when a new model became available.

A ringing success

Patterson was a remarkably benevolent employer. The commissions he paid were generous and consistent; the factory he built was light and clean, with swimming pools, medical clinics, a cafeteria, and attractive landscaping. When rivals criticized his largesse, he simply replied, "It pays."

But Patterson was also a heartless competitor who kept a "gloom room" filled with cash registers from companies he had ruined. By 1913, in fact, his ruthlessness had earned him a conviction for unlawful restraint of trade, and he faced a year in jail.

And then a devastating flood hit Dayton. Patterson immediately seized command and set his assembly line to work turning out rowboats and his cafeteria to baking bread for refugees. He became such a hero that, when the waters receded, an appeals court overturned his conviction. With that, the grateful citizenry turned out en masse and feted the triumphant tyrant with a gigantic victory parade.

THE NATIONAL CASH REGISTER CO.

Early cash registers imitated fine furniture: one model (top) had a mahogany case; another (center) looked like a highboy with a crown. Livestock delivered the goods when National Cash Register arrived in India (above). A register-shaped pavilion (right) was featured at the 1939 New York World's Fair.

The Pace That Launched a Thousand Ships

Where's your shipyard? asked representatives of the British Admiralty when they came to the United States in 1940 to buy some ships from Henry Kaiser. In fact, the eighth-grade dropout had never built a ship before, and the "shipyard" he showed his guests was nothing more than a barren mudflat that he thought might be a good site for a yard. The British, however, needed ships in a hurry — German U-boats were sinking theirs faster than they could be replaced — and Kaiser had a reputation for speed. He had built thousands of miles of highways, bridges, aqueducts, and pipelines and was famous for completing the mighty Hoover Dam two years ahead of schedule. So when he promised quick delivery, they decided to give him a chance.

Kaiser took on an established shipbuilder as a partner and gathered useful information at the Ford assembly line. Within 3½ months his engineers had built an enormous shipyard on the Pacific Coast (the first of seven), pushing the work ahead so fast that they completed many of the structures before the architects could finish the plans. Four months later Kaiser launched his first boat, and the British order for 30 ships was fulfilled five months before the deadline. In 1941 Kaiser went to work for his own government.

The sum of its parts

The secret of his speed was prefabrication: individual teams assembled separate components for each ship, then huge cranes brought all the parts together. Instead of riveting piece to piece as boatbuilders traditionally did, Kaiser welded the parts together — with much of this work being done by the women who made up 25 percent of his work force. To find enough workers, Kaiser advertised all over the country and brought the applicants in by special trains. In this way he hired more than 10,000 people in New York City alone. Eventually his payroll covered some 200,000 workers.

Soon Kaiser was producing a ship a day (he launched some 1,490 ships — a third of the total wartime production — by the time peace was declared). Most were clumsy "liberty ships," designed for easy construction. But whereas other firms needed two months to complete one of these freighters, Kaiser turned them out in 30 to 35 days. This astonishing schedule was further reduced when Kaiser set yard against yard in friendly but fierce competition. Working around the clock, his Oregon yard assembled a ship in the unheard-of time of 10 days; not to be outdone, the Richmond, California, yard bettered the feat by launching one in just under 5 days.

Kaiser's success made him a hero with the public, a fact he exploited in his ongoing battles with wartime red tape. When the navy rejected his plan to fit flight decks onto freighter hulls and turn them into miniature aircraft carriers, Kaiser used his connections and went directly to the president. Vindication came from Winston Churchill, who declared that the 50 "baby flat tops" Kaiser built had turned the tide of war in the Pacific.

Some of Kaiser's projects were less successful. His dream of turning out a fleet of "flying box cars" — freight airplanes that could move half a million men at once — foundered in a partnership with the enigmatic Howard Hughes. An expenditure of $20 million produced a single plywood prototype, the infamous "Spruce Goose." Now a museum, this flying boat remains the largest plane ever built. But it flew only once and then for only about one mile.

Liberty ships such as the *Hinton R. Helper* (left) were produced by Henry Kaiser's shipyards at a breathtaking rate. Kaiser's ability to turn "can't" into "can" inspired an admiring cartoonist (below). The industrialist used an 81-piece model (bottom) to show how his crews assembled ships in a matter of days.

Dirty Dan

He was coarse, illiterate, and apparently incapable of conducting an honest business transaction. Every deal he considered a potential swindle, every partner a probable mark. But for the fact that he ended up broke, the name of millionaire Dan Drew might be as familiar today as those of his robber-baron rivals.

"I got to be a millionaire afore I know'd it, hardly," Dan Drew was quoted in 1879, just before he died at age 82. Generous only in his gifts to the Methodist Church, Drew made money with ruthless zeal until he was out-swindled in 1870.

Entering the world of finance as a cattle drover in New York State, Drew put herds together on credit, then drove the cattle south. The night before arriving at the New York City market, he would feed the animals a dose of salt. Next morning, the thirsty beasts would lap up huge amounts of water and tip the scales much heavier than when they left home.

With the profits from this "watered stock," Drew jumped into the steamboat wars raging on the Hudson River in the 1840's and moved on to even wilder speculation in railroad shares. As a director of the Erie Railroad, he made a killing manipulating the stock, and then used his financial might to wreak havoc on the stock market, banks, and foreign exchange, ruining thousands.

"He holds the honest people of the world to be a pack of fools," a contemporary critic said of Drew, who was as devoted to prayer meetings as he was to robbing people. The pious speculator was praised for a $250,000 gift he made to found a Methodist seminary, but in fact he had given only his "note." When he died penniless, it proved as worthless as his word had been in life.

Wildcatter's Revenge

Her writing was more that of the moralist than the muckraker, a serene indictment offered to her readers out of a sincere belief in what was right. And when Ida Tarbell took a look at John D. Rockefeller's Standard Oil Company, she found much that needed to be made right.

Tarbell was 43 and well established on the staff of *McClure's* magazine when editor S. S. McClure let her write an investigative series on Standard Oil, the country's largest monopoly in the early 1900's. Tarbell had worked for several years as a writer in Paris and had written important features for *McClure's*. But she was also a daughter of the Pennsylvania oil fields: her father was a manufacturer of oil tanks and the friend of many independent oil producers, and she had grown up hearing the bitter stories of men whose businesses had fallen to Rockefeller.

Her report on Standard Oil's practices thus was lit by both fact and moral outrage. "Life ran swift and ruddy and joyous in these men," she wrote of the young entrepreneurs who poured into Pennsylvania after the Titusville gusher of 1859. "There was . . . nothing they did not hope and dare. But suddenly . . . a big hand reached out from nobody knew where, to steal their conquest and throttle their future."

Ida Tarbell (left) and her journalistic clout helped topple John D. Rockefeller's imperialistic Standard Oil Trust, portrayed above.

By 1879 Rockefeller's big hand controlled 90 percent of the country's oil industry, and in pitiless prose Tarbell exposed the clandestine tactics that had made this possible. She detailed the illegal railroad rebates, the strong-arming of independent producers, the systematic crushing of competition in the conversion from rail shipments to pipelines, and much more.

Tarbell had done her homework and it showed. Court records from innumerable lawsuits against Standard Oil were supplemented by interviews with former Rockefeller associates and victims to build a powerful case. By the time the series ended, 19 months after it began, all America was talking about Tarbell — except her billionaire subject. "Not one word about that misguided woman," John D. was heard to mutter. Her findings eventually fueled a federal investigation that culminated in the dissolution of the trust in 1911.

Though Tarbell was expected to continue writing exposés, she was in fact a true believer in capitalism, and she would spend nearly as many years chronicling "The Golden Rule in Industry" — as practiced by men such as Henry Ford — as she had in pinning Rockefeller to the wall.

Teddy the Trust-Buster

Greed alone cannot explain how the money men of the 19th century amassed their enormous fortunes. It took plenty of manipulation as well — trading on inside information, driving competitors out of business, dumping stocks. And it took the studied noninterference of the United States government, which reflected the national attitude of laissez-faire.

It was not until 1890 that the Sherman Anti-Trust Act was passed to defend against monopolistic restraint of trade. But the legislation remained on the shelf for over a decade while monopolies, or trusts, continued to grow in size and number, and talk of curbing their power was denounced as radical. Even Teddy Roosevelt, who had dared to suggest the need for some modest checks on business while he was governor of New York, later warned against "wrong-headed attacks" on industry. The country as a result was stunned in 1902 when Roosevelt, as president, instructed his attorney general to break up the Northern Securities Company — a railroad monopoly organized by E. H. Harriman, J. P. Morgan, and James J. Hill — using the Sherman Act as his weapon.

On the morning after the suit was announced, the stock market plunged. "Wall Street is paralyzed at the thought that a President of the United States would sink so low as to try to enforce the law," one newspaper observed. But Roosevelt, who was a champion of business, went after only the "malefactors of great wealth" and ushered in an era of reform, ultimately bringing 45 suits against illegal trusts.

NO MOLLY-CODDLING HERE

Teddy Roosevelt (right) was famous for his slogan "Speak softly but carry a big stick." It was a weapon he used tellingly against illegal trusts, whose chairmen are depicted below as "The Bosses of the Senate."

THE BOSSES OF THE SENATE.

The Penny-wise Prodigal Son

It was a perfect match: Hetty Green knew better than anyone how to make money, and her son, Ned, certainly knew how to spend it. Though worth $100 million, the "Witch of Wall Street" once stuffed Ned's clothes with newspapers rather than buy him a winter coat. And in 1882, after young Ned injured his knee while sledding, Hetty took him to a charity clinic. When the doctor recognized her and demanded payment, she left and never returned. Years later the leg, still unhealed, was amputated. In the early 1890's, when Hetty bought Ned his very own railroad down in Texas, some said it was to make up for her guilt over the lost limb. Actually, it was time to launch him in business.

"The Colonel," as Ned came to be known, cut a broad swath in Texas, traveling about the state in a palatial private railroad car named for his girlfriend, Mabel. In 1894, thanks to Ned, Dallas saw its first automobile, and to satisfy an interest in rose growing, he built 27 acres of greenhouses. Ned, however, had enough of his mother in him to turn that hobby into a money-making cut-flower business, just as he transformed his railroad from a money loser into one of the premier rail lines of the Southwest.

After his mother's death in 1916, Ned inherited half of her fortune — some $50,000,000 — and began to indulge his whims on a truly grand scale. He maintained a fleet of 25 cars, and since he handed out $20 gold pieces to every policeman he met, he didn't worry much about tickets. He built an airport for his own use at his Massachusetts estate, with a hangar where he moored a blimp. His yacht, a five-deck former passenger ship, he sawed in half in order to add 40 feet amidships and make it the longest private yacht in the world.

A good-hearted fellow, Green built his own radio station so that he could share private concerts with the public, and sent radio transmitters around the countryside so that the music would reach the most remote Massachusetts farms. His greatest gift to the state, though, was the inheritance tax paid upon his death in 1936. It was so huge that the state was able to cut its general tax rate by 30 percent that year.

Ned Green (right) inherited some $50 million from his mother, Hetty Green, the notorious "Witch of Wall Street." Unlike Hetty, Ned spent freely to amuse himself. On display at his estate in New Bedford, Massachusetts, were a fully rigged vintage whaling ship and the oldest windmill in New England (below).

James Gordon Bennett, Newsmaker

When James Gordon Bennett inherited the New York *Herald* from his father in 1872, it was already America's premier newspaper. Not satisfied, Bennett spent more than 45 years — and hundreds of thousands of dollars — making it one of the most famous in the world.

He usually got good value for his money. The $300,000 that he invested in reporting on the Spanish-American War, for example, enabled his paper to scoop all the others when the battleship *Maine* was sunk.

Much to the annoyance of his reporters, Bennett insisted that he, not they, get credit for the stories. He was enraged by the public adulation of Henry Stanley when the reporter fought his way through eastern Africa to find Dr. Livingstone. "Who thought of looking for Livingstone?" Bennett thundered. "*Who paid the bills?*" Yet he could also be public spirited. During the financial panic of 1873, he hired the staff of one of New York's fanciest restaurants to operate soup kitchens for the poor.

Nor did he lack self-confidence. A great lover of speed, Bennett in his youth helped introduce coach racing to New York. After a hard-drinking evening he often could be found tearing down country roads behind his team, roaring and screaming, stark naked in the driver's box. When he was 25 years old, Bennett and two friends each staked $30,000 on a midwinter yacht race from New York to England. Bennett, the only one of the three who actually sailed with his crew, came in the winner.

An English caricaturist captured James Gordon Bennett's nonchalant style (left). An avid sailor, the well-traveled publisher of the New York *Herald* owned a succession of yachts celebrated for their luxury (above).

Forced to resettle in Paris after a broken engagement and a duel with his fiancée's brother, Bennett sponsored international races for everything from the newfangled automobiles and airplanes to motorboats and balloons. But his yachts probably ate up more of his fortune than any other interest. Others might boast bigger boats, but few, if any, were as luxurious as Bennett's. His *Lysistrata* had a suite for the master on each of its three main decks, a Turkish bath, and an electrically ventilated dairy where Bennett kept the Alderney cow that supplied his table with milk at sea.

Queen of Palm Beach

They're very economical," Eva Stotesbury explained when questioned about her golden bathroom fixtures: "You don't have to polish them, you know."

The man who bankrolled such extravagance was Edward Stotesbury, a leading financier in Philadelphia who had led a decorous life until he decided it was time to revel in his laurels. Charmed by the vivacious widow he had met on an ocean voyage, the dapper 61-year-old proposed. Equally captivated, Eva Cromwell accepted, and on January 18, 1912, they married.

After a Palm Beach honeymoon, the new Mrs. Stotesbury threw herself into the task of teaching her husband "how to play." She lavished more than $3 million on their 147-room mansion. At the party celebrating the house's opening, four orchestras coaxed couples to the dance floor and guests roamed through rooms decorated with perfumed silk flowers and exotic Oriental carpeting. Even the basement was a wonder, housing bakeries, a barber shop, and a movie theater.

Despite their generosity Ned and especially Eva were decorously snubbed by old-line Philadelphians. But Palm Beach, where the Stotesburys had honeymooned, eagerly embraced Eva as its queen. El Mirasol, the Spanish-style mansion she built there, was staffed by 75 servants and 15 gardeners. Monkeys chattered in its zoo and lovebirds cooed in the aviary.

The Stotesburys' Palm Beach parties were lush and legendary. "Queen" Eva, crowned by an emerald-and-diamond tiara so heavy that it gave her a stiff neck, nevertheless reigned with gracious ease. At midnight Stotesbury himself would entertain their guests by beating on a small drum or warbling *The Old Family Toothbrush That Hangs on the Sink* — a favorite song.

Eva Cromwell shattered the hopes of old-line Philadelphia women when she married Edward T. Stotesbury, the city's wealthiest, most eligible bachelor.

THE COOTIE
7

Chapter 10

GOING PLACES

FROM COACHES TO CARS

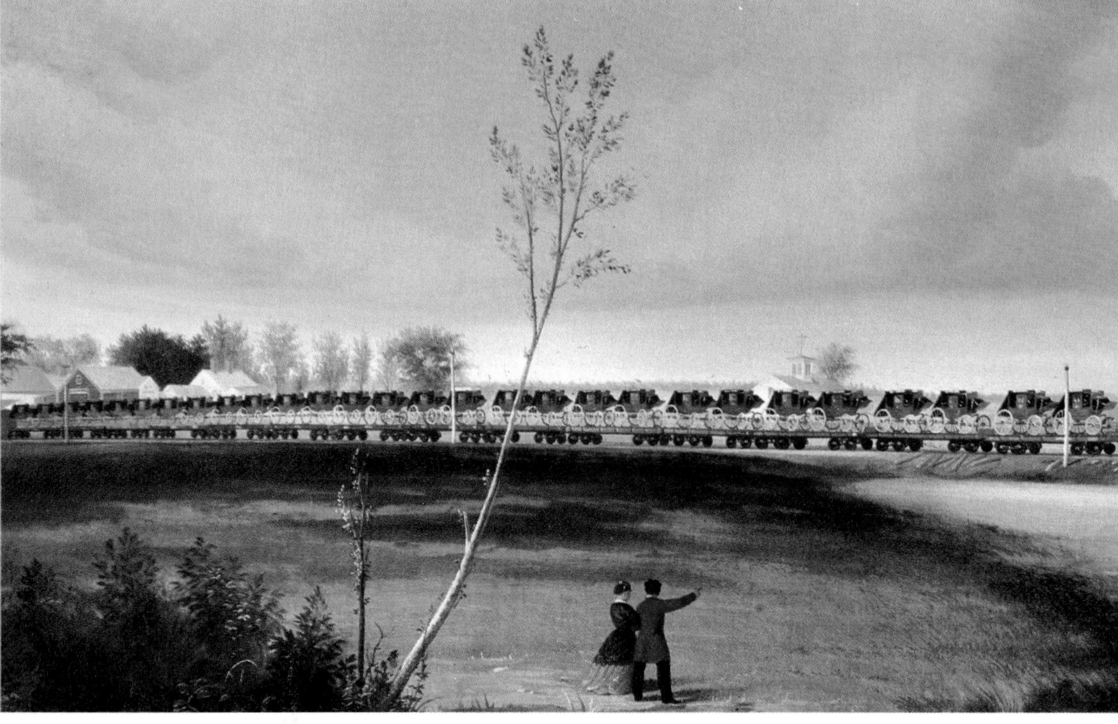

On a red-letter day in 1868, a grand total of 30 Concord coaches was shipped west by railroad to Wells, Fargo and Company. The scene was painted by John Burgum, the same man who did the decorative painting on the coaches themselves.

The Coach That Helped Win the West

Anyone who has ever seen a Western movie where a Wells, Fargo stagecoach rolls into town (or is held up while trying to) is familiar with the Concord coach. Although built in New England, the Concord was such an important part of life in the Old West that it has been called the Coach that Conquered the Prairie.

The Concord was named for the New Hampshire town where it originated and was built in the shop of coach maker J. Stephens Abbot and wheelwright Lewis Downing. In 1827, two years after setting out as partners, the pair hit on the design that would make them world famous. Abbot and Downing styled their coach after contemporary English carriages but modified the design in ways that made it uniquely American.

Riding over what in those days passed for roads was bumpy at best — so the freshman manufac-

Sleigh Bells Ring!

Hear the sledges with the bells — Silver bells! What a world of merriment their melody foretells!" With those lines poet Edgar Allan Poe summed up 19th-century America's love affair with sleighs. Indeed, sleighing remained one of the most popular winter activities right into the early 1900's.

Sleighs were an off-season specialty of carriage makers who, as the century progressed, came up with an amazing variety of designs. The Albany Cutter, the Portland Cutter, and the Boston Booby, for example, all were elegant sleighs with graceful runners. Others such as the Victoria were modeled after carriages, tiny push sleds were

Sledding in New York City could be chaotic when elegant cutters encountered enormous barges in the snow.

turers suspended the coach body well above the axles on leather straps — this gave the Concord a soothing side-to-side sway, rather than a jarring rattle over the ruts. The full-bodied coaches were crafted of oak and painted in bright colors with scrollwork trim and decorative landscapes on the doors; the interiors were comfortably upholstered with leather or plush. Abbot's and Downing's formula proved so successful that no major changes were ever needed in the coach's basic design.

Models were built to accommodate anywhere from 6 to 12 people, with plenty of space for luggage and mailbags on the coach's flat roof. Though the Concord was a passenger vehicle in all parts of the country, it was also used for transcontinental mail delivery by both Wells, Fargo and Company and Butterfield's Overland Mail Company. For western towns in the 19th century, the scheduled arrivals of those companies' coaches were eagerly awaited events that provided a welcome influx of goods and news.

The fame of the Concord coach was such that Abbot and Downing filled orders from such distant lands as Australia, South Africa, and Bolivia. It was only with the appearance of Henry Ford's Model T that another American vehicle would enjoy such a huge success.

---

designed for use on skating ponds, and enormous sledges were built to serve as buses and to take the place of wagons for hauling loads in winter. For sleighing parties there were fancy "barges" that resembled sailing ships and were pulled by as many as 14 horses. Few events were quite so exciting as turning out with the rest of the town for a promenade of sleighs on a fine winter day.

While popular, sleighs were not the easiest vehicles to control. Stopping short was impossible, sharp turns caused them to overturn, and the silent runners made collisions a very real possibility. Bells were adopted as a safety feature, and their sound soon became an inseparable part of sleighing. Poe's words aside, most were brass or bronze (silver produces a dull sound), and the country's sleigh-bell capital was East Hampton, Connecticut. Some 30 bell companies competed there, earning it the name of Jingletown.

Biggest Wagon-Maker in the World

John M. Studebaker was 20 years old when he left South Bend, Indiana, in 1853 and headed west to seek his fortune in the California gold fields. And succeed he did, though not by digging for gold. He prospered instead by making much-needed wheelbarrows for miners.

Studebaker had learned carpentry and smithing back in South Bend, where he had worked with his older brothers in their fledgling wagon-building business. Though short of money, the Studebaker brothers were honest, hardworking craftsmen. They built first-rate wagons that were handsome as well, and in 1857 added carriages to their line. Their big break came that same year when the government offered them a contract for 100 wagons if they could fill the order in six months. They accepted the job, invented the means for kiln-drying hardwood, and finished the wagons with time to spare.

Receiving word that his brothers could use his help, John returned from California in 1858 with $8,000 to invest in the business. His timing was just right. When the Civil War broke out, the brothers were awarded large government contracts to build wagons, caissons, meat and ammunition carriages, and even a beer wagon for the Union troops.

At the war's end in 1865, the firm continued to prosper. Its wagons were favorites among the vehicles of the surging westward migration, and brothers Peter and Jacob joined the family business. By 1876 the Studebaker wagons were selling from coast to coast, and the company could boast at the nation's centennial that it was the world's largest builder of wagons and carriages. By the end of the decade that translated into $1 million in sales each year, evidence that the Studebakers were indeed true to their credo: "Always give more than you promise."

The Studebaker brothers built their reputation on the quality of their wagons. Their company remained in business for over 100 years and was the only one to make a successful transition from horse-drawn wagons to streamlined automobiles.

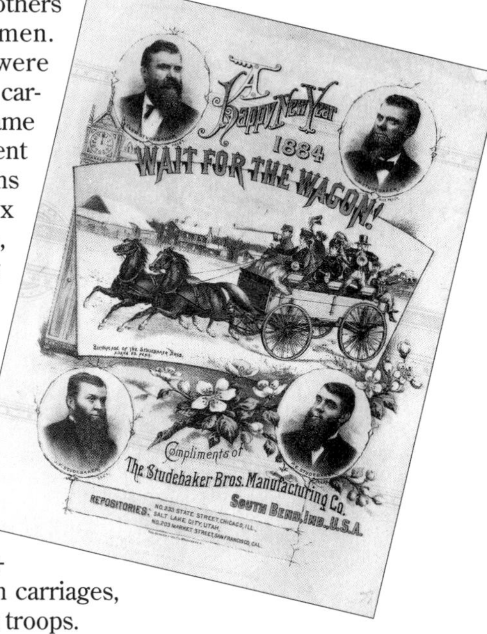

Horseless Carriages on Parade

The 1899 auto parade was a newsworthy Newport event. Press coverage of the affair helped win public acceptance of what were seen at first as mere playthings of the rich.

When the Oliver Hazard Perry Belmonts brought the first autombile to Newport, Rhode Island, in 1897, cars quickly became all the rage. With everyone enamored of the newfound playthings, Mrs. Belmont decided two years later to stage a grand auto parade and obstacle race. There would be prizes both for decorations and for driving skill, with the latter devilishly tested by a maze of pedestrian-shaped obstacles.

The extravaganza took place on September 7, 1899, and the competition for vehicle decoration was keen. But Mrs. Hermann Oelrichs' car, festooned with satin streamers, wisteria, white and pink hydrangeas, and 12 white doves, was the clear winner. Col. John Jacob Astor, a hero of the Spanish-American War, was impressive in his clematis-covered Pope-Waverly, driving it, one reporter noted, "with the same cool-headed dash that distinguished him while serving under fire." But Harry Lehr, full of champagne and mischief, piloted Mrs. Astor's auto with perverse determination, gleefully flattening every obstacle on the course.

After the race the contestants whiled the night away at a dinner dance. When the party finally disbanded, the flower-bedecked coaches, scintillating with tiny electric lights, set off into the darkness — a procession described by one enchanted viewer as "a veritable pageant of fairy chariots."

Here, There, and Back Again

"What Columbus did for sailing, Charles Glidden did for motoring," claimed one enthusiastic admirer. Glidden, who had pioneered in long-distance telephony with Alexander Graham Bell, retired in 1900 and soon set out with his wife to see the world. They traveled some 46,528 miles through 39 countries, primarily in a jaunty English-made 16-horsepower Napier automobile. Delighted by the experience, Glidden took it upon himself to persuade the public that automobiles were a safe means of travel. On his return to America, he organized the Glidden Tour, a motoring competition that championed reliability rather than speed.

On July 11, 1905, 33 contestants set out from the offices of the Automobile Club in New York City and headed north for a 12-day, 867-mile junket through New England. The American Automobile Association's rules set time limits for each leg of the journey and, to discourage speeding, points were deducted for arriving too soon as well as too late. Honor compelled motorists to report any help they received along the route.

There were a few accidents — Mrs. J. N. Cuneo's White Steamer went off a low bridge when she swerved to avoid another car. Returned to the course, she finished the day's run and was "heartily congratulated for her pluck." A Cadillac whose driver was seduced into "comparing speed" was upended, causing its passengers "several gashes . . . contusions of the body, and wrenched arm muscles."

The main trial for vehicles in this inaugural tour was an arduous eight-mile run up the slope of New Hampshire's Mt. Washington. A morning rain had left the road slick and "masses of dense clouds" made the trip "unusually perilous." Still, most of the contestants handily completed the ascent in about half an hour.

A lack of roads was no deterrent to the hardy wayfarers of the Glidden Tour. The manufacturer whose entry won the competition was presented with the Glidden Cup — a powerful sales incentive with the newly eager car-buying public.

Glidden's reliability rally was so successful that it became an annual event. Until the runs were discontinued in 1913, each one brought more-challenging destinations and a larger field of participants. Popular interest in the contest swelled, and crowds gathered even in remote locales to view the passing autos. As one witness reported, the parade "had an enchanted appearance, as the Crusaders of old in quest of the Holy Sepulcher must have looked to the feudal yokelry."

The Over-Land, Over-Sea Auto Race

On Lincoln's Birthday, 1908, a crowd of some 250,000 people thronged Times Square in New York City to witness the start of one of the more improbable feats in automotive history. Six automobiles, three of them made in France and driven by French teams, plus single entrants from Germany, Italy, and the United States, were poised to drive the 12,000 land miles from New York City to Paris.

The original route called for the participants to drive, in the dead of winter, across the United States to San Francisco, then sail to Valdez, Alaska, drive down the presumably frozen Yukon River and across the Bering Strait to Russia, and then on to Europe and the French capital.

Waiting for the race to begin, the doughty drivers idled in their open vehicles — the cars all lacked roofs and many also lacked windshields — smiling for the many photographers and cheered by the entire crowd. Finally the president of the Automobile Club rose and launched the mad adventure with a shot from a golden pistol. With that they were off, each car flying a 46-star American flag in addition to its native colors. The American team in its shiny new 60-horsepower Thomas Flyer quickly took the lead.

On the cross-country trip, the cars had to be dug out of snowdrifts and dragged from mud sloughs. Roads — where they existed — alternately froze and thawed, and the cars' radiators had to be drained every night to prevent bursting. Repairs caused delays of many days; a wolf pack dogged the travelers' tracks in Wyoming; and tires blew out regularly — especially when the Flyer took to railroad tracks and bumped along atop the ties. By the time the racers reached San Francisco, the field had narrowed to four: two French entries had abandoned the course.

The Americans were the first in and promptly sailed for Valdez, only to be recalled when the route was changed. Back in Seattle, they were met with the news that the Italian and the French teams had already left for Japan. The Yanks sailed in a few days, and on their arrival in Kyoto swiftly drove the 300 miles to Tsuruga, where they boarded a ferry for Vladivostok on May 17.

"Sharing the trail with camels and donkeys," the Flyer sped across Manchuria into Siberia, catching the now-leading German team at Lake Baikal. Alas, it was just too late to board the same ferry, so the Americans had to sail the next day.

On July 26, the Germans motored into Paris, four days ahead of the Americans. But the Yanks had a 15-day credit for their side trip to Alaska, while the Germans had a 15-day penalty for shipping their car partway across North America. When these final calculations were completed, the little Thomas Flyer took the laurels.

The Thomas Flyer's success in the 1908 race (top) proved American cars the equals of their European competitors. Cosponsored by *The New York Times* and the Paris newspaper *Le Matin*, the 1908 dash across three continents began in New York's Time Square (above) and ended at French paper's offices. Bad weather plagued the course, frequently marooning the contestants in mud or snow (left).

The Start of Something Big

Engineer Charles Kettering was known as a monkey-wrench scientist — a pliers-and-screwdriver man — because of his firm belief that trial-and-error research was more likely than mere theory to produce results. And in fact he often managed to develop the very things the "experts" deemed impossible. He held 140 patents for inventions as diverse as high-test gasoline, safety glass, and quick-drying auto paint.

But Kettering truly earned himself a place in automotive history when he invented the self-starter. Before he came along, cars were started with a hand crank — a contraption that was anything but safe. If the crank kicked back, it could cut the motorist's hand or even break an arm. The process was strenuous as well: climbing up and down to adjust the throttle and spark and to crank again and again was too much for many people, including most women.

Kettering paid no attention to the theorists who claimed an electric starter would be too heavy in a car. He had already developed a small motor that was used for electrifying cash registers (another supposedly impossible dream). In 1911 he adapted the motor for use in cars. Cadillac immediately contracted for 4,000, and by 1914 the electric starter was at least optional equipment on every car except Henry Ford's Model T.

Going on to serve as head of research at General Motors, Kettering never stopped tinkering. "The desire to know is infinitely more important than knowing how," he declared, and ensured a future for that belief by cofounding the Sloan-Kettering Institute for Cancer Research.

The Flying Teapot

It accelerated from 0 to 60 in 11 seconds, puffed steam and whistled as it went down the road, and got up to 10 miles to the gallon — of water. When first offered for sale in 1899, it was the car of the future. It was the Stanley Steamer.

The brainchild of Francis and Freelan Stanley, identical twins from Maine, the car was a marvel of simplicity. Its steam-powered engine needed no transmission or clutch and included just 13 moving parts, with the result that a Steamer almost never wore out. The fastest car of its day (racing models approached 200 miles per hour), it was also as powerful as a locomotive and could climb Mount Washington in just 27 minutes.

But there were drawbacks. It took 30 minutes to warm up the car and build up an adequate head of steam in its boiler. The boiler itself was heated by a kerosene burner that sometimes shot jets of flame from under the hood, terrifying onlookers. And the car was expensive — one 1908 model cost as much as $2,500. (Ford's Model T's that year were selling for $825 and $850.) But orders consistently rolled in to the Stanley factory.

The real obstacle to the Steamer's success, however, was the Stanleys themselves. No two cars built in their factory were alike. They refused to advertise, and screened all customers, rejecting any they deemed unworthy of their car. Payment had to be in cash since they believed installment plans were immoral, and any request for a written guarantee sent them into a rage.

Nor was the Stanley sense of humor any help. After answering many questions about the possibility of boiler explosions, for example, they took firecrackers to trade shows and set them off beneath the Steamers in order to scare the crowds. They also liked to dress in identical dark coats and derby hats, climb into matched Steamers and race around the countryside in tandem. When a driving accident killed Francis in 1918, Freelan retired and sold the company, which was out of business by the mid-1920's.

In 1897 the Stanleys (above) demonstrated an early version of their Steamer. Later models, with the steamer under the hood (left), had evolved from horseless carriages to genuine automobiles.

TIME TABLE

AUTOMOTIVE ADVANCES

1893 *Frank Duryea drives America's first successful gasoline-engine car on the streets of Springfield, Massachusetts.*

1896 *Henry Ford builds the quadricycle, his original automobile.*

1898 *Electric cars provide taxi service in New York and Philadelphia.*

1899 *Hit while helping a lady alight from a trolley, New Yorker Henry Bliss becomes the first American auto fatality.*

1899 *Olds Motor Works, the country's first auto factory, opens in Lansing, Michigan.*

1899 *To curb the problem of runaway horses, Boston bars automobiles from in its parks from 10 A.M. to 9 P.M.*

1900 *Drivers licenses — called Engineer's Certificates — are issued in New York at the National Automobile Show.*

1902 *An auto debuts on the Broadway stage, as a getaway car in the musical* Beauty and the Beast.

1903 *Motorized trucks begin their run as cargo carriers.*

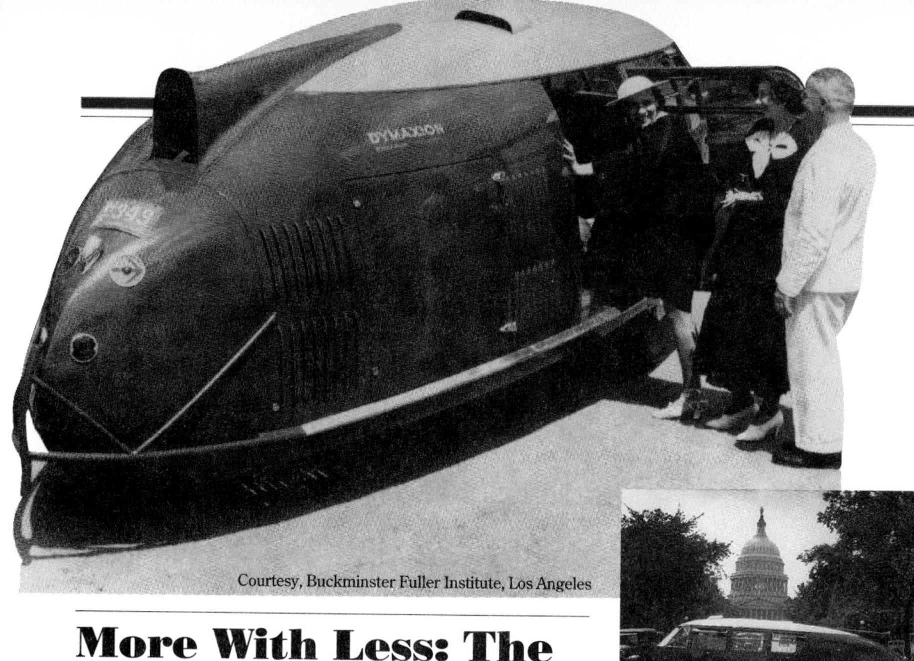

Courtesy, Buckminster Fuller Institute, Los Angeles

The lightweight Dymaxion was built of aluminum and balsa wood. The car featured rear-wheel steering, which allowed it to parallel park in the space of its own length.

More With Less: The Dymaxion Car

When Buckminster Fuller set out to design a car in 1932, his goal was the same one that later led him to invent the geodesic dome: do more with less. Thus he proceeded to create the first truly aerodynamic automobile, the bullet-shaped Dymaxion (Fuller's own word, from *dynamic* and *maximum*).

It was a car like none other. It steered like a boat, with a single rear wheel as the rudder, and had a periscope for rear vision. With room for 11 people, it was light enough to get 40 miles to the gallon and could cruise at speeds up to 120 miles an hour.

When the driver of a "Dymaxion No. 1" died in an impromptu race, the car was unfairly blamed for the accident. Still, Fuller could have sold many more. But he closed the factory instead, saying he had learned as much as he could from the car and was ready to move on.

The GI's Best Friend

Gen. George Marshall called it "America's greatest contribution to modern war." To the average GI, though, the Jeep was his Iron Pony and his Leaping Lena — the car that could go anywhere and do anything.

With the approach of World War II, the army needed a new kind of transport, something more practical than a motorcycle and more versatile than a truck. Automakers were asked for prototypes but had to produce them in just 49 days. Willys-Overland nearly lost the chance for consideration since it could not work that quickly. But the general-purpose vehicle that it ultimately delivered was too remarkable to ignore. Four-wheel drive and a powerful engine allowed it to run off road as well as on. It could climb 60-degree hills, yet was light enough that two men could set it back on its wheels if it did turn over.

The army placed an order, and some 660,000 Jeeps were manufactured before the war ended. Besides moving soldiers and supplies, they pulled antitank guns and, when mounted with machine guns, proved ideal for desert-raiding commandos. With a belt stretched around a wheel, a Jeep could power anything from a buzz saw to an olive press; race it uphill, it was said, and the water in the radiator became just warm enough for shaving.

The Jeep was no limousine. The windshield wipers had to be pushed by hand, and the ride felt a bit like falling down a flight of stairs. But drivers became very fond of the gutsy little cars. After driving through 1,300 miles of jungle to escape the Japanese, two Americans were told their feat was impossible since there were no roads where they claimed to have traveled. "Shh! Not so loud," one Yank replied. "Our Jeep hasn't found out about roads yet, and we don't want to spoil it."

Flying was about the only thing a Jeep could not do, but it surely seemed to try. According to army lore, the Jeep could turn on a dime and leave nine cents change.

1903 *Dr. H. Nelson Jackson and his chauffeur cross the roadless continent by car in 63 days.*

1905 *Buses carry passengers on New York's Fifth Avenue.*

1905 *Car buyers begin paying on the installment plan.*

1908 *Ford's Model T is introduced.*

1910 *Two hundred automobiles are shipped to ranches in Texas, replacing horses as mounts for cowboys.*

1910 *Hiram Johnson does his gubernatorial stumping by automobile in California.*

1910 *A fully equipped dashboard wows the auto world.*

1921 *Warren Harding is the first president to travel by car in an inaugural parade.*

1926 *The federal highway numbering system is introduced: even numbers for east–west routes, odd numbers for north–south.*

1928 *America's first cloverleaf interchange guides traffic in Woodbridge, New Jersey.*

1930 *Wishing to "see America backward," two men drive coast to coast and back again in reverse gear.*

1939 *An air-conditioned car goes on exhibit at the Chicago Automobile Show.*

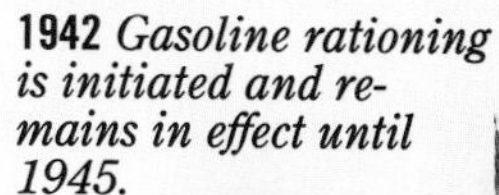

1942 *Gasoline rationing is initiated and remains in effect until 1945.*

Known as "the human comet," Barney Oldfield took on cars, trains — even a plane — as in this 1910 race with stunt pilot Lincoln Beachy.

The Dirt Track Daredevil

He started his career racing bicycles, touring the Midwest as the Champion of Ohio. Then in 1902 daredevil Barney Oldfield got his big break: a friend who was helping mechanic Henry Ford build a racing car asked for his help. Maybe it was because the car spit flames and had cylinders the size of powder kegs, or perhaps it was because it was steered with handlebars — but the other two men refused to drive it. Oldfield, in contrast, was willing to take the chance.

Although he had never driven an automobile before, Oldfield defeated the reigning champion after only a week of practice. Within a year he amazed crowds at the Indiana State Fair when he became the first auto racer to cover a mile in less than a minute.

The first race made Ford's reputation as an automobile manufacturer; the second brought Oldfield a deluge of invitations to drive. Over the next 15 years he drove a fleet of dramatically named racers: the Winton Bullet, the Peerless Green Dragon, the Big Ben, and the Golden Submarine. With his trademark cigar clamped between his teeth, he brought many of them home first.

Oldfield's secret was a complete lack of fear; he raced against freight trains for recreation, shooting his car over railroad crossings inches ahead of oncoming locomotives. Other drivers complained that he was a menace, and three spectators and a mechanic were killed in the course of his countless crashes. But it took reckless daring to bounce and skid those heavy cars around the dirt tracks of the day.

Such was Oldfield's reputation as the fastest thing on wheels that it continued long after his retirement from racing in 1918. For years, whenever a cop stopped a speeder on the highway, the question most likely to be asked was "Who do you think you are, Barney Oldfield?"

Oldfield earned his reputation at a time when most people had never been inside an automobile. Though he was a bit of a brawler, his swagger endeared him to the public.

The Indy 500 Tests Men and Machines

The race at the Indianapolis Motor Speedway may be one of the most exciting events of the year, but it is also a proving ground for auto comfort and safety.

Nearly 40 million people watch the "Indy 500" every year, whether in person or on TV. Yet spectacle was secondary as far as the race's founders were concerned. The Indianapolis businessmen who created the 2½-mile-long speedway intended it as a "great outdoor laboratory," a testing ground for automotive technology.

Over the decades, however, the track has tried human endurance as much as it has engines. In 1911 the race's first year, it took 6 hours and 42 minutes to complete the 200-lap event. And although the track was paved with brick, the drivers had to contend with such hazards as wind, dust, and flying pebbles since most of the cars lacked windshields.

Even at the 74.6 miles-per-hour winning speed of 1911, the sharp turns of the rectangular track were hard to negotiate. Wrestling the wheel in the early cars blistered many a driver's hands and even dislocated a few arms. More than one driver has observed that during a race his nerves gave out before his reflexes. The rush of adrenaline, moreover, can have strange effects. Wilbur Shaw, a three-time winner, started the

Ray Harroun made racing history in 1911 when he won the first Indianapolis 500 in his bright yellow Marmon Wasp.

The All-American Gravity Grand Prix

It began modestly enough in 1933 with three kids racing down a hill in Dayton, Ohio, in cars they had built from crates and scrap metal. A news photographer happened to see them and was so taken with the event that he talked his boss at the Dayton Daily News *into a $200 donation for an organized meet. When it was held in August that year, some 40,000 people were on hand to watch as 362 boys raced their homemade motorless cars.*

From that beginning an annual All-American Soap Box Derby took shape, attracting boys by the hundreds from all parts of the country. Before long a corporate sponsor became involved, a special track was built in nearby Akron, the rubber capital, and awards were presented by such stars as Roy Rogers, Pat Boone, and Jimmy Stewart.

Yet the race somehow remained a boy's real-life adventure story: a test of true ingenuity and grit. There was 14-year-old Gib Klecan, for instance, who coated himself and his entire rig with graphite to cut down wind resistance, and won in 1946. In 1952 little Joey Lunn from Georgia crashed his car in the first heat — but emerged from the first-aid tent in time to ride his "Ramblin' Wreck" downhill to victory.

In 1971, "boydom's greatest sports event" was opened to girls. Each year the contestants parade down Akron's main street — now with an official police escort — and in honor of their tradition, every racer is addressed as Champ.

1937 race with an open cut on his hand: when he pulled across the finish line, doctors said that a week's worth of normal healing had taken place.

Engineers considered the 500 miles in "the brickyard" equal to 50,000 on the highway, and they soon learned that the less temperamental a car, the more likely it was to win. The results of their tinkering and tuning ultimately showed up in everyday autos. Ethyl gasoline, four-wheel brakes, seat belts, hydraulic shock absorbers, high-compression engines, fuel injection, and turbochargers are among the advances that emerged from the fight for Indy prize money.

One fundamental innovation was introduced in the very first running of the Indy. Racers in those days drove with their mechanics on board to keep an eye on cars coming up from behind. Driver Ray Harroun came up with the idea of using a rearview mirror instead and installed one on his Marmon Wasp. Without the weight of an extra person, his car needed far fewer tire changes than others — pushing him past faster competitors to victory.

Today there are hundreds of auto-racing tracks in America. Yet when 33 engines rev up at the "Indy 500" each May, there is no question as to which track is number one.

The excitement of the first Indy 500 was captured both in the poster (above) and in the shot of cars roaring into a turn (left). Will Jones drove a Case (#9), as did Joe Jagersberger (#8). Louis Disbrow raced a Pope-Hartford (#5).

The Lincoln Highway was a vast improvement over typical roads of the time, but it was hardly a high-tech wonder. Photos from the 1920's show a sign in Utah and a view of the highway at Nevada's Cave Rock.

America's Main Street

In 1904, when the United States conducted its first national road survey, it did not much matter that many an American byway was an unimproved dirt road that ended in a water-filled ditch at the edge of town. Most early motorists were well-heeled adventurers who gloried in the hardships of the road and had enough time and money to overcome them.

By 1912, however, with a million car owners eager to see the country, drive to market, or simply get out of town, bumping over bad roads was no longer considered fun. It fell to Carl Graham Fisher — the man who invented carbide headlights and helped found the Indianapolis Motor Speedway — to sound the alarm that would send America hurtling into the modern age. Fisher's proposal was as simple as it was visionary: to build a highway across the continent, smoothly paved and paid for by public subscription. "Let's build it before we're too old to enjoy it," Fisher challenged an audience of automakers and suppliers in September 1912. Before the night was over, he had pledges for $300,000.

Fed by checks as small as Woodrow Wilson's $5 and as large as Goodyear Tire's $300,000 gift, the fund soon topped $4 million. Though Henry Ford would have no part of Fisher's scheme, Packard's president Henry Joy agreed to head the effort. Joy not only contributed $150,000 but also came up with a name for the organization and its road: the Lincoln Highway Association.

Popular enthusiasm for the project mounted as small towns vied for the privilege of being on the highway. By the time the final route was announced in August 1913, the association had taken in contributions from 45 states, despite the fact that the highway would cut through only 12 of them, in a clean line from New York's Times Square to Lincoln Park in San Francisco — roughly the path of today's Interstate 80.

Thousands of communities hoping for an economic windfall from the highway were disappointed by the proposed route. But the excitement generated by the Lincoln Highway Association led to far more than the construction of a single road. The promise of a national highway system had been planted in the public's mind. In 1923 the federal government took the Lincoln Highway project under its wing. From that time on, linking the states with smooth paved roads was no longer a project for visionaries, but was instead a government guarantee.

Mission Possible

The idea of building a road into the Alaskan wilderness had been campfire talk for more than 30 years — until the Japanese attack on Pearl Harbor in 1941 abruptly made it a strategic necessity. As defense against possible invasion, American troops and supplies would have to be transported deep into the Territory from below the Canadian border. The only existing route, however, was on the open sea along the vulnerable Pacific coast. So the Army Corps of Engineers was charged with the task of building a highway, 1,520 miles long and 24 feet wide, across a vast obstacle course of mountains, forests, and swamps.

The starting point was the town of Dawson Creek, British Columbia. In March 1942, surveying teams set out — on foot, by plane, by packhorse, and by dog team — marking the center of the route with streamers and flares. Following hard behind was a 20-ton tractor that crashed through the wilderness like a rogue elephant and was in turn pursued by a pick-and-shovel-wielding army — 11,000 soldiers and some 16,000 civilians hired to speed the job along.

They parlayed the impossible into a dazzling series of technical miracles. Where not so much as a trail had existed before, ditches were dug, bridges were built, and the road was graded — at a rate of eight miles a day and a cost of nearly $100,000 a mile.

Winter and summer, food and recreation were in short supply, and working conditions were brutal. "If you touched anything metal with your bare hands," recalled one soldier of winter in Alaska, "you couldn't tear your skin loose." In summer the men were plagued by heat, humidity, and huge swarms of mosquitoes, but work continued around the clock, seven days a week. Despite the difficulties some combination of wartime pride and the challenge of an impossible task took over wherever military discipline left off. Eight months after it began, the "five year job" of building the Alcan Highway was done.

Engineers devised ingenious means for building the Alcan Highway as efficiently as possible. Pontoon bridges like this one allowed supplies into a site but were easily dismantled and moved on to the next site.

Galloping Gertie Gives Way

Steelworkers completing the ribbonlike Tacoma Narrows Bridge in Washington in 1940 were the first to warn of problems. On windy days, they reported, the roadway's violent heaving was enough to give them motion sickness. Soon after the 2,800-foot bridge officially opened on July 1 that year, locals gave it a nickname — Galloping Gertie — and edgy engineers were recalculating to see if the $6,400,000 structure could be stabilized. Still, motorists came from miles around for the stomach-tossing pleasure of driving across the undulating expanse.

Confidence in Gertie's durability grew. On the morning of November 7, however, a 40-mile-per-hour wind set the span heaving up and down in waves three feet high that rose and fell some 36 times a minute. By 10:00 A.M. the bridge was twisting as it heaved, with the ends turning and pulling in opposite directions. It was as if the roadway had come alive: first one side rose into the air and then the other, until a piece of the midsection broke loose and plummeted into the sound.

Gertie continued to spew steel and concrete into the water until 11:10. And then she was gone, leaving behind only a few expensive lessons in bridge building. When Tacoma got a new span in 1948, the roadway was wider and the girders bracing it were deeper, stronger, and designed so wind could pass right through. Gertie's problems were not to be repeated.

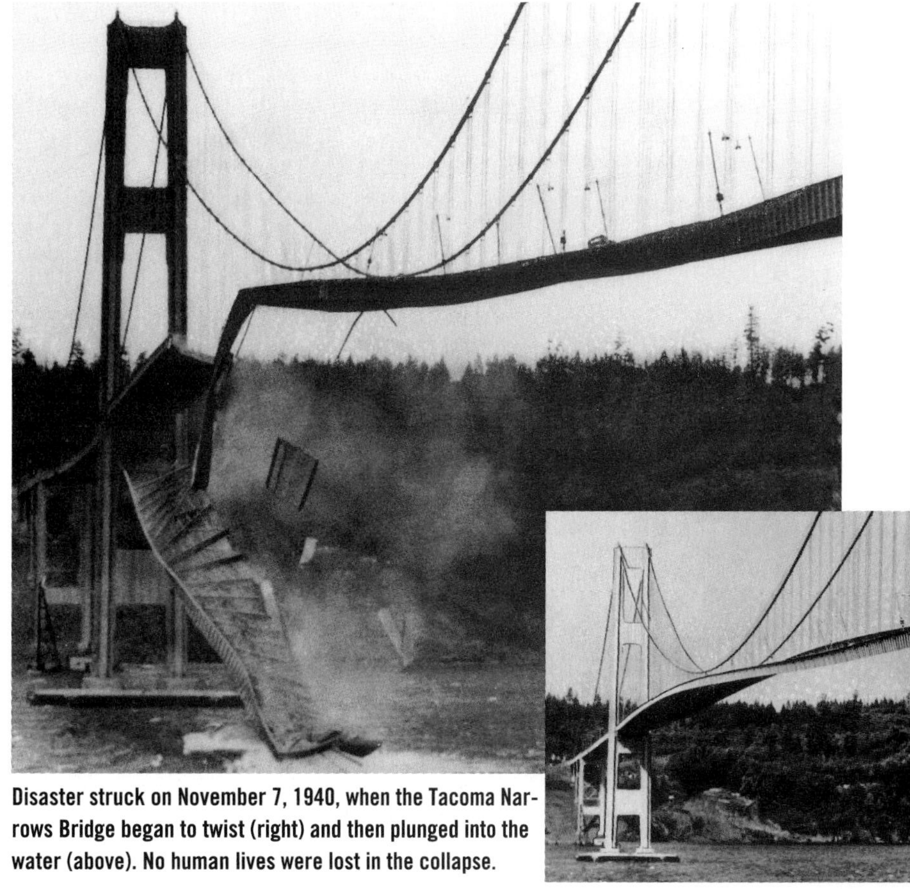

Disaster struck on November 7, 1940, when the Tacoma Narrows Bridge began to twist (right) and then plunged into the water (above). No human lives were lost in the collapse.

Show Me the Way to Go Home

Getting from here to there in the early days of auto travel was more of an art than a science. Road maps were nonexistent, most routes were unmarked, and though landmarks were of some help in finding the way, drivers had to know what to look for if they were to know where to turn.

As early as 1901, newly formed automobile associations came to the rescue by publishing travel guides. The best-known of these, the Blue Books, were issued in multiple volumes covering different parts of the country. Until about 1914 the maps in such guides were strip maps showing specific routes rather than whole regions. Instructions for following the routes were spelled out in minute detail, generally beginning with setting the odometer at zero, and noting landmarks and intersections at particular mileage readings along the way. Helpful information on road surfaces, alternative routes, and restaurants was duly noted, making it possible to plan a trip weeks in advance.

In 1907 G. S. Chapin was the first of several mapmakers to publish a new kind of book, the photo-auto guide. In these, routes were illustrated with photographs depicting landmarks and intersections. With someone along to flip the pages and act as navigator while the driver kept an eye on the road, it was hard to go wrong with a photo-auto guide. If, however, that landmark willow tree happened to have been struck by lightning, a person just might end up in Iowa instead of Nebraska.

America Finds Its Way to the Road Map

Lengthy descriptions for following routes made the early Blue Books and other travel guides cumbersome, yet it was not until the 1920's that they were fully replaced by maps. Part of the problem was the lack of consistency in road names: what was known as the Post Road in one town might well turn into Main Street a few miles east or west, and squeezing all these local names on a map was all but impossible.

The situation began to change in 1916 when the Rand-McNally Company offered a $100 prize to the employee who came up with the best new idea in mapmaking. A young draftsman, John Brink, won with his suggestion that major roads be assigned numbers that would be posted alongside the highway and, of course, would correspond to markings on Rand-McNally's maps. Brink's first effort, the Illinois "Auto Trails," appeared in 1917 and triggered a competitive frenzy of mapmaking and road marking. The myriad numbers and symbols used by rival map companies soon became just as confusing as the old street names.

A breakthrough finally came in 1920 when Wisconsin began giving its roads official numbers. The rest of the country soon followed suit, and within five years more than 75,000 miles of highways had been assigned U.S. route numbers. When the now-familiar little black shields used as U.S. route markers appeared on both roads and maps in 1927, getting there was no longer such a chancy affair.

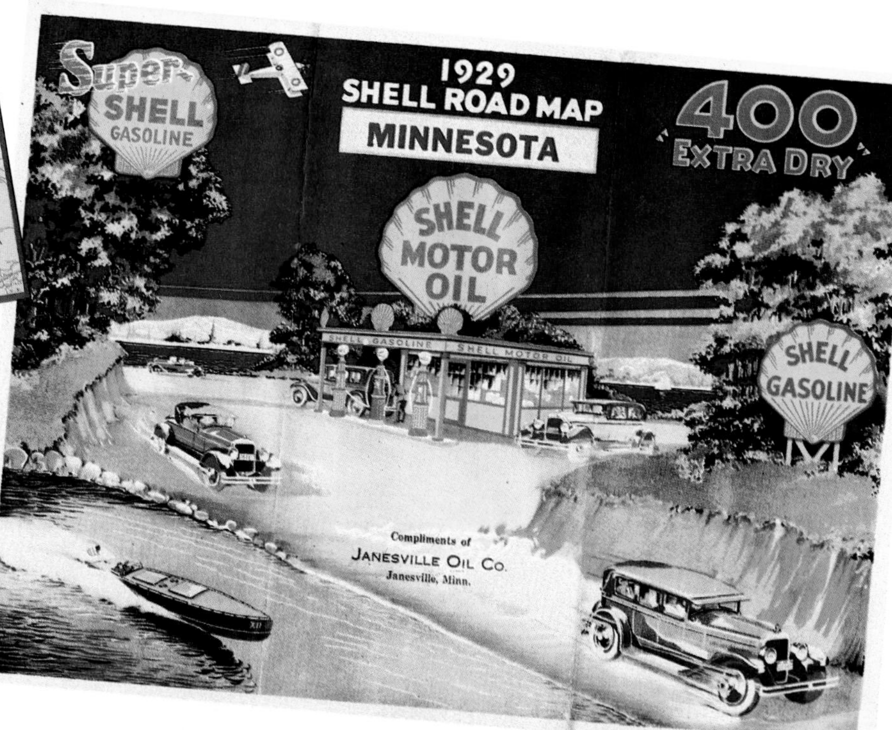

Oil companies first gave away maps (right) in the 1920's, a practice that lasted until the 1970's. Since some people have trouble reading conventional maps when driving south, Esso in 1955 came up with the idea of producing one with Florida on top (above).

Highway Pirates

Soon after filling stations first dotted the highways, oil companies realized that offering something "free" brought in a lot of extra business. Product promotions in the 1920's were more elaborate than simply giving the customer a mug for purchasing a full tank of gasoline, however. Shell Oil of California, for example, attracted thousands with elaborate treasure hunts.

When a contest was on, Shell stations from San Jose to Seattle were decked out with skulls and crossbones, attendants wore high boots and eye patches, and customers greedily collected "clew slips" that led them to a special digging field. On a designated day, hordes of spade-toting contestants waited behind a rope to be let onto the field. And there the lucky diggers turned up their treasure — not doubloons, but little plaster-of-Paris shells stuffed with certificates redeemable for merchandise at local stores.

In 1927 a Shell Oil promotion was hard to miss: Jolly Roger skulls leered from every surface, buccaneers checked your oil, and the station was topped with a giant treasure chest.

Cleaning Up Their Act

Phillips Petroleum had its Highway Hostesses — registered nurses who used white handkerchiefs to check for grime and made sure that rest rooms exuded the sanitary scent of disinfectant. And Texaco had its White Patrol, which cruised well-traveled roads in matching Chevrolet coupes to make regular inspections of station "facilities."

It was the late 1930's, a new day in hygiene had dawned on American highways, and the furiously competing oil companies were its most vigilant guarantors. The time was right. In the first 30 years of motoring, dirt roads, flat tires, and stripped gears had become part of the language. Yet there remained one travel hazard that scarcely dared speak its name — the essential stop by the side of the road known as "picking flowers."

As the Depression began to lift and the number of motorists began to soar, the big oil companies started to see the possibility of selling dignity along with a tankful of gas. It came in the guise of clean, well-stocked rest rooms at major pit stops. Hot and cold water flowed, soap was free, and the words "certified" or "guaranteed" on highway signs reassured travelers at a glance.

Such zeal was too good to last, of course. Although the facilities would remain, the much-touted hygiene was soon but a quaint memory.

To display "Registered Rest Room" shields, Texaco station owners had to sign pledges to uphold high standards of sanitation. The notices were a welcome addition to the highway scene.

WHAT·IS·IT

Why fill up at an ordinary gas station if you could pull up to a full-service temple instead? When the City Beautiful movement complained of too many urban eyesores in the late 1920's, the Atlantic Refining Company responded in classic style. Looking to ancient Greece for architectural inspiration, it turned some of its stations into the prettiest spots for a lube job on any city block.

RIDING THE RAILS

Westward the Rails

If ever there was proof that nothing worthwhile is achieved without a struggle, the Erie Railroad was it. America's first trunk line, forming a direct link between New York and the Great Lakes, the Erie was 20 years in the making.

Chartered in 1831, the line was held up at first by political struggles with canal and stagecoach companies that fought the railroad nearly every mile of the way. The Erie, moreover, was routed through exceptionally difficult terrain. Cliffs along the Delaware River were nearly vertical, and men had to be lowered in baskets to drill holes for the black-powder charges that would blast out a railbed. Near the New York–Pennsylvania border, where the route crossed the deep gorge of Starrucca Creek, they had to build a stone viaduct 1,200 feet long and 110 feet high — a structure hailed as the country's most beautiful work of masonry.

But nature was not the only source of trouble. Irish work crews brawled and rioted without end. Farmers sabotaged work in progress. Leaders of the Seneca tribe demanded a bounty of $10,000 for building rights on their land. And the Erie's financing was constantly at risk as costs crept ever upward.

When the 483-mile line at long last was completed in 1851, the railroad's management proudly staged a spectacular inaugural trip. Setting out from the easternmost terminal at Piermont, New York, on May 14 were some 300 dignitaries, including President Millard Fillmore and his cabinet, several governors and senators, a covey of business leaders, and the Erie's own board of directors. Secretary of State Daniel Webster rode on an open flatcar — with his rocking chair lashed down for safety — in order to enjoy the scenery.

And there was plenty to see all along the way. Throngs of banner-waving villagers hailed the passengers at each stop. At many they were welcomed with cannon blasts, speeches, and local bands. "Oh little Elmira!" said one speaker, "how will you bear such honors?" At Allegany a contingent of Indians greeted the train. But the grandest fete took place at the final stop in Dunkirk. With parades, fireworks, a 13-gun salute, and a gigantic feast, it was one of the parties of the century — and the work it celebrated was likened to no less a feat than the building of the pyramids.

East Beats West

James Strobridge, the hard-knuckled head of construction for the Central Pacific Railroad was incensed when one of the line's owners told him to hire Chinese laborers. He had repeatedly refused to do so since, like most Americans of his day, Strobridge regarded California's Chinese immigrants as strange little heathens who washed themselves daily "like women" and ate such "unChristian" foods as dried seaweed and mushrooms. In Strobridge's view they were, as a result, totally unfit for construction work.

But in the end he had no choice, since his white work crews kept leaving for the gold fields and by 1865 the task of building the line was woefully behind schedule. Soon after they started, the 50 Chinese workers that he hired were able to grade a longer, better railbed than the white crews. It swiftly became clear that if he wanted something done fast and done well, the Chinese were the ones to do it.

Within the year the Central Pacific not only recruited more Asians from California, but brought them from China as well. Ultimately some 10,000 Chinese laborers were pounding spikes and blasting passages through the mountains. They were, moreover, quick to find a way to do any job that was handed to them. With the aid of an Irish crew, they laid 10 miles of track in 12 hours and won a race as the line neared completion in 1869.

The line might never have been finished but for the Chinese, more than 1,200 of whom lost their lives in the effort. Yet old prejudices died hard. In the keynote speech at the completion celebration on May 11, 1869, everyone imaginable was thanked — except for the indispensable Chinese.

Chinese crews worked all day, every day, and seemed able to do almost anything. In the winter of 1866, one crew pulled three locomotives — and an entire wagon train — over the Sierra Nevada by hand.

The 180 arches of the Long Key viaduct contributed to the Key West rail line's reputation as the world's most beautiful train ride.

Henry Flagler's Keys to Success

More than once Henry Flagler was told that his "overseas railway" to the Florida Keys was impossible. "Nobody can build this road," warned a friend. "Nobody has the money nor the brains nor the grit to do it." But Flagler was confident. "It's perfectly simple," he explained. "All you have to do is build one concrete arch, and then another. . . ." And that is just what he did, creating a 156-mile-long elevated railroad from the mainland to Key West — a line that came to be known as the Eighth Wonder of the World.

Flagler was 53 — and a millionaire many times over — when he retired as a partner in Standard Oil in 1883 and headed south for his first extended visit to Florida. Once there, he seized the opportunity to invest in Florida's undeveloped east coast and plunged into creating what he predicted would become an American Riviera.

Since there were no first-class accommodations for visitors, Flagler built a string of grand hotels including the Alcazar in St. Augustine, the Breakers at Palm Beach, and the Royal Palm in Miami, all the while transforming the surrounding towns and swamps into luxury resorts. To make sure that monied folk could get there in style, he consolidated and improved a collection of rickety local rail lines, creating the Florida East Coast Railway. By the 1890's, thanks to Flagler, it was possible to board a train in New York City and travel in comfort to St. Augustine without having to change at any station along the way.

Yet his most audacious project still lay ahead. Despite the raised eyebrows of friends and advisers, Flagler sent a surveying team to Florida's tip and to the islands beyond in 1902. Actual construction of his overseas railway began two years later. What he had undertaken was a true engineering feat — the creation of a railbed on foundations sunk in water up to 30 feet deep, with the spans between islands as much as seven miles long.

The project faced other challenges as well. Scorching heat, clouds of mosquitoes, and poor working conditions led to constant labor troubles, and bringing steel and supplies to such an inaccessible site was difficult at best. But even a hurricane, which caused millions of dollars' worth of damage and killed more than 100 workers in 1906, was insufficient to discourage Flagler.

Over seven years and $20 million after work began, the line reached Key West in 1912. Flagler rode triumphantly aboard the first train down the tracks. "Now I can die happy; my dream is fulfilled," he told a cheering crowd. And within 18 months he was dead. Without his energy the line fared poorly. Then in 1935 the railbed was destroyed in a hurricane. Flager's 156 miles of concrete arches remained, however, and were later reworked to support a highway down the Keys.

The railroad's viaducts were crafted from a German cement that cured in the water. Once begun, the concrete work could not be interrupted; crews had to work night and day to complete the job at hand.

Riding in High Style

Advertisements in the 1890's emphasized the laid-back ease and comfort of train travel.

Well-wishers cheered as twin engines, draped in bright bunting and floral garlands, chugged out of a Boston depot pulling eight of George Pullman's most elegant cars. It was May 23, 1870, just a year after the rails had met at Promontory, Utah, and 129 excursionists, members of the Boston Board of Trade and their families, were aboard for America's first coast-to-coast train trip.

This was no mere pleasure jaunt: the San Francisco–bound businessmen wanted to stimulate trade with the West. Still, pleasure wasn't absent, for the Pullman cars were as fine as any first-class hotel. Carpeted floors and plush drapes muffled noise and kept the dust out. Five ice closets and a refrigerator amply supplied the dining car. Children played in one salon while adults browsed in two well-stocked libraries or gathered around one of two parlor organs to sing.

There was even a printing press on board for turning out a daily newspaper. The editor described such things as the passing terrain and shared the experiences of the journey by noting, for example, that "Indians are now seen at almost every station."

No one complained of any lack of luxuries aboard the Pullman Hotel Express. The swaying car and softly clicking wheels were the only reminders that they were on the road.

Arriving in San Francisco on May 31 after a journey of almost nine days, the merrymakers remained there for about three weeks before reboarding their rolling palace. By July 4 they were back home again in Boston, full of enthusiasm for the West. "All agree," announced the paper's farewell edition, "that the excursion has . . . done much to annihilate the idea of distance and separation, and to bind together the East and the West in indissoluble bonds."

A Run for the Coast

By 1876, transcontinental train travel had settled into a fairly routine seven-day crossing time. So the public's interest was intense when theater impresarios Henry C. Jarrett and Harry Palmer, anxious to rush an acting troupe to San Francisco for a scheduled opening date, made a startling announcement: they planned to sponsor a high-speed, nonstop train that would zip across the country in a mere 3½ days — half the usual travel time.

Jarrett and Palmer soon won the support of James Gordon Bennett, Jr., publisher of the New York *Herald,* who agreed to pay half the cost of the trip in return for exclusive rights to the story. The pair also convinced five railroad companies to clear the tracks all the way to the Pacific, thus eliminating transfer delays. Finally, to fill up their train, dubbed the Transcontinental Express, the promoters offered 16 round-trip seats at $500 each. The tickets, enshrined in gleaming silver presentation cases, were snapped up almost immediately. But even amid all this enthusiasm there were signs of trepidation: a number of passengers finalized their wills before boarding the three-car special.

A huge crowd met the "lightning train" at the Oakland wharf after its record-setting 84-hour trip from New York.

Rocketing across the country, sometimes reaching speeds of more than a mile a minute, the express soon gained a new name — the "lightning train." Crowds gathered at crossings, lit bonfires, and cheered as it sped by, and local bands serenaded the hurtling engine as it flashed past. And Jarrett and Palmer accomplished their mission. The Transcontinental Express arrived in San Francisco just under 84 hours after leaving New York. The feat was talked about for many years after — and the show went on.

Adventures in Second Class

"Civility is the main comfort that you miss," wrote Robert Louis Stevenson in a model of understatement as he rattled across America aboard an emigrant train. Twenty-eight years old, almost penniless, but deeply in love, the young writer was determined to join his future wife, who was living in California. Setting out from Scotland in the summer of 1879, he deliberately chose modes of travel that were cheap and held the promise of bohemian adventure. So when he arrived in New York after a second-class sea voyage, he bought a train ticket amid "a babel of bewildered men, women, and children," took a ferry to New Jersey in a driving rainstorm, and there boarded a train bound for California.

There were no Pullman cars on emigrant trains, no plush carpets, no sleepers. People purchased straw cushions and boards, stretched them between the hard wooden benches and snatched what rest they could. There were no dining cars either, just train vendors and wayside eateries. When an accident put the train behind schedule, "we paid for this in the flesh," Stevenson recalled, "for we had no meals all that day." Emigrant trains also gave way to express trains — "They cannot, in consequence, predict the length of the passage within a day or so."

Changing trains in Chicago, Stevenson confessed himself "dog-tired . . . hot, feverish, painfully athirst." A subsequent change brought cleaner cars — a welcome relief since the originals "in which we had been cooped up for more than ninety hours had begun to stink abominably."

Throughout the journey the trainmen were curt and the passengers "mostly lumpish fellows . . . with an extraordinary poor taste in humor." Stevenson "fell sick outright" while crossing Wyoming and was "astonished . . . to meet with little but laughter." He reached the West Coast "like a man at death's door" 13 days after leaving New York. With the end of the ordeal in sight, Stevenson wrote, "Not I only, but all the passengers . . . threw off their sense of dirt and heat and weariness, and bawled like schoolboys. . . . For this was indeed . . . 'the good country' we had been going to so long."

Comfort was catch-as-catch-can aboard the inexpensive emigrant trains. Their crowded cars shuttled new arrivals from the nation's borders and port towns to their final destinations across the continent.

Getting Time on Track

When the ball dropped in New York City at noon on Sunday, November 18, 1883, it signaled not a new year, but a new way of keeping time. Until that day the nation had run on solar time — from coast to coast each town marked noon at the moment when the sun hit its zenith in that area. Consequently there were at least 80 "time zones" in North America.

In the horse-and-carriage era such disparities were easily tolerated, but with the advent of intercity railroading, such imprecision caused chaos — and collisions. It was a problem tailor-made for the fastidious imagination of Charles F. Dowd, who in the late 1860's began tinkering with time. He ultimately concluded that the nation should be divided into four one-hour time zones, using meridians 15 degrees apart, and published his proposal in 1870.

Shortly afterward William F. Allen, editor of two railroad guides, took up the study of standardizing time for the American Railroad Association. After much investigation he recommended Dowd's plan, and railroad leaders made it official in 1883.

Across the nation time stood still while clocks caught up with the new decree. Crowds gathered in train stations, watches in hand, making a subtle yet profound shift in the way things were done. Dissenters vowed that they would continue to live on "God's time, not Vanderbilt's," but the benefits of the new system were swiftly apparent. Dowd, however, did not live to see Congress finally pass the Standard Time Act in 1918. In 1904, at age 79, he was run over by a train.

The original time-zone plan used straight meridians to delimit the regions. Later plans, based on geography and local custom, created the now-familiar bends.

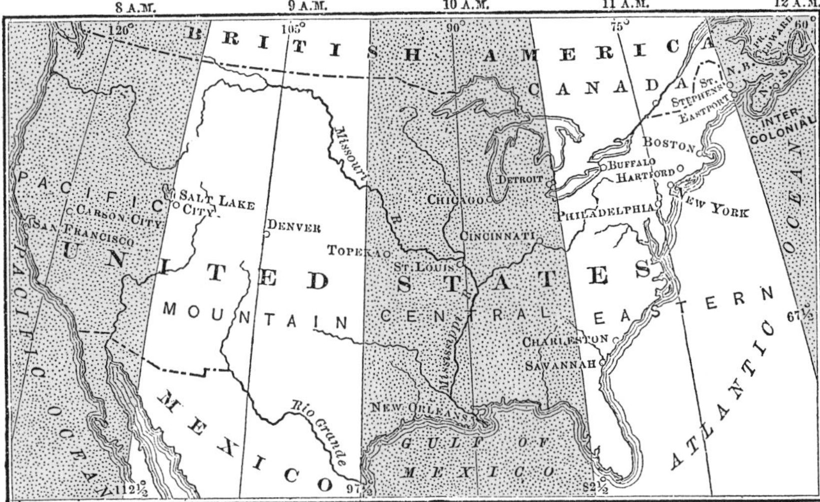

Railroad brakemen had one of the most dangerous jobs — turning the brake-wheels on the tops of moving cars. Neither in fair weather nor foul was there any room for a false move.

Life on the Rails

The first time young Henry Clay French saw a train, he watched a brakeman fall to his death between cars. He told himself then and there that, once he became a railroad man, he would never be so clumsy. And he never was. French stowed away on the very next train he saw and, at age 13, signed on as a messenger with the Hannibal & St. Joe line in Missouri.

That was in 1873, and it marked the beginning of French's 57 years on the rails. In those days railroad men were a breed apart and their way of life was many a boy's dream of true adventure. Jauntily capped and uniformed, railroad workers were unflappable in the face of continual danger. They were constantly on the move and called no place home. And they smelled of tobacco, frequenting saloons in their off hours. For French and for many others, the dream never tarnished.

Within a year the lad had learned the Morse code and advanced to the position of telegrapher. At 16 he took his first turn as a switchman, a job that entailed running between cars and fastening link-and-pin joints to couple them — while the train was moving. "Wary feet," French wrote of the job, "were needed every instant." French later said that the switchman's job was the "most dangerous," but brakeman, the job he tackled in 1876, carried its own measure of hazard. Up through the 1880's few trains had air brakes. Instead, the brakemen — usually two to a train— had to stop the train manually by running along the roof and turning brake-wheels at the ends of the cars. "We lived on the car tops," said French of the challenge, "weather did not count." But to a boy bitten by the railroad bug, riding on the roof of a speeding train in ice storms and in scorching sun meant pure excitement, for it was a job that required heroic wits, nerve, and perfect timing.

There were plenty of other thrills to experience as well. The first time French arrived by train in Dodge City, for instance, he saw Bat Masterson gun down two outlaws. On another occasion the train had to pause while French cut down a hanged horse thief from an overhanging bridge. He and the crew doused all lanterns whenever they rode into the cowtown of Hunnewell, Kansas, for the cowboys there thought it fun to shoot lanterns out of the trainmen's hands. Nature also offered challenges. French once had to shovel grasshoppers off the track where a giant, migratory swarm had made the rails so slick that the locomotive could get no traction. A prairie snowstorm was a far more serious threat: it could cause a train to plow into a herd of buffalo before the animals were seen.

For men like French, however, no other life was imaginable. Over the years he served as everything from messenger to engineer, doing stints as conductor, agent, baggageman, and fireman for 15 different rail lines. His last job was with the Union Pacific, a line he joined in 1909 and stayed with until his retirement as yardmaster in 1930.

Comrades both on the job and off, these railroad men gathered for a Thanksgiving feast at a Union Pacific roundhouse.

All Aboard! With Poppy Ayers

His career with the Erie Railroad began in 1841, and for the next 30 years Henry Ayres was the dean of conductors. The Erie could not have had a better front man to meet the traveling public: passengers loved him and called him Poppy.

A great bear of a man, Poppy made his presence felt. He was a sight to remember, particularly in winter when he came lumbering down the aisles to collect tickets, his 300-pound frame wrapped in a fur-trimmed coat, and a coonskin cap on his head.

Poppy's size could be daunting to anyone who opposed him. It was Poppy, for instance, who advanced the conductor from the role of mere ticket taker to "captain," with control over the movements of his train. The change came about because of Poppy's concern that the conductor had no way to signal the engineer in case of an emergency. So he ran a cord from his car to the locomotive and tied a stick to its end. If the stick jumped, he told the engineer, stop the train. Resenting the encroachment on his authority, the engineer cut the cord. Ayres rerigged it, and once again the engineer cut it. With that, Poppy pulled off his coat and offered to fight it out. This time the cord remained.

To his passengers Poppy was a friend in deed. On one trip in 1849 he found an old woman in tears — she had left her umbrella behind on a ferry boat. Teasingly, Poppy promised to have it sent to the train by telegraph, and tugged on his newly installed cord. Then he went back to the baggage car — where he knew full well that all forgotten luggage on the ferry had been placed — and retrieved the woman's umbrella. "Who'd ever 'a' thunk," marveled the happy passenger, "they could send umbrell's?"

Two conductors, photographed in 1864, were meeting to synchronize their watches. Thanks to men like Poppy Ayres who set the style, conductors had a no-nonsense approach to passenger safety and timely arrivals.

Courageous Kate, the Railroad Heroine

On the dark and stormy night of July 6, 1881, young Kate Shelley's heroism made her a legend in her lifetime — and her story is still being told.

It would be remembered as one of the worst storms of the century, with thunder, lightning, and gale-force winds raging through the night, and floods threatening the railroad bridges around Moingona, Iowa. Fifteen-year-old Kate Shelley, who lived with her family near the bridge across Honey Creek, lay awake listening to the storm. Then, just after midnight, she heard a tremendous crash: the bridge had given way and a locomotive had plunged into the torrent below.

Shelley knew immediately what she had to do — get to the railroad station and stop the approaching passenger express. Despite her mother's protests, she headed out into the storm. By the time she reached a nearby bridge over the flooded Des Moines River, her lamp had gone out. In pitch darkness, crawling on hands and knees, she inched across the 673-foot span, terrorized with fear. Finally she made it to the far side and ran the last half mile to the station in time for the agent to telegraph ahead and stop the train. Then she led a rescue party back to Honey Creek.

It took Shelley three months to recover from her adventure, but she was rewarded with nationwide attention, as well as a gold medal and $200 from the Iowa state legislature. Gifts from many donors helped ease the plight of her poor widowed mother, and in later years Shelley was given the the job of station agent at Moingona. The honor she prized most, though, came from the railroad men themselves: for the rest of her life they made scheduled stops at her creekside house so that she might ride free whenever she wanted.

In Their Own Words

When I meet the engine with its train of cars moving off with planetary motion . . . when I hear the iron horse make the hills echo with his snort like thunder, shaking the earth with his feet, and breathing fire and smoke from his nostrils . . . it seems as if the earth had got a race now worthy to inhabit it.

— Henry David Thoreau, 1854

Hoboes who carried their worldly goods in small bundles (above) were known as "bindle stiffs." In hobo parlance a box car (below) was a "Pullman side-door," and its roomy comfort was greatly preferred over riding a "tramp's ticket" — a grooved board balanced on the support rods that extend underneath each car.

Hobo Life

Let there be no mistake — "a hobo," as one authority explained, "is a migratory worker, a tramp is a migratory non-worker, and a bum is a stationary non-worker." Of the three, hobo was definitely the highest calling.

When railroads boomed at the end of the Civil War, they gave rise to this whole new class of riders: veterans who had trouble readjusting to civilian life. Others were attracted to the vagabond life by the lure of freedom and adventure; hard times — especially the economic crises of 1873, 1893, and even 1929 — also helped swell the ranks of the footloose fraternity.

Since the law did not protect railroad rights-of-way against trespass, increasing numbers of vagrants gravitated to the tracksides, where they camped together in "jungles" just outside the rail yards. Different races mixed there in remarkable harmony, gathering around camp fires to share a mulligan stew — a meal made from a few pennies' worth of vegetables and perhaps a stolen chicken, all cooked together in a can. Hoboes did not hesitate to snitch a shirt from a "gooseberry bush" — some innocent's clothesline — but jungle rules ensured that they shared food and blankets, and that they replaced firewood and cleaned all pots before moving on.

Though empty boxcars were the most desirable means of unticketed travel, they were checked continually by railroad detectives — known as "cinder dicks" and "bulls." And every hobo knew that, if discovered, he risked a beating or even being tossed from the moving train. So

the men sought alternatives and, as one hobo put it, learned to "ride a train the way an Indian brave could ride a horse: they could hang onto belly, back, neck or rump." The trick was to jump on the train just after it left the well-policed railroad yard. Any misstep meant a fall beneath the wheels, and accidents earned many a hobo the sardonic nickname Shorty. Deaths were so common that the land along the tracks became a potter's field.

Yet at certain seasons the migrant brotherhood was tolerated, even welcomed. Hoboes (the term may derive from *hoe boy*) supplied an essential labor pool for 19th-century agriculture. By the 1890's, when the hobo tribe was perhaps 60,000 strong, they made up one-third of the wheat-harvesting crews.

For despite the rags they wore, many among the "train barnacles" were in fact talented, educated men who prided themselves on earning their way. Among the more illustrious graduates of the rough-and-tumble school of the open road were author Jack London, actor Clark Gable, and Supreme Court Justice William O. Douglas.

Road Scholar

There have been many pretenders to the title "King of the Hoboes." But none among them was more articulate than Leon Livingston: when he retired in 1910 after 27 years on the road, he published some half-dozen memoirs under his hobo monicker, A-No. 1.

Born to a middle-class family in San Francisco, Livingston ran away from home at age 11. Since he was too young to find regular work, he took up the hobo life, "apprenticed" to a man called Frenchy. An experienced wanderer and convict-

Riding under a car between the wheels (above) or atop a car up on the roof (left) meant at best a precarious perch. But it did offer a hobo the advantage of concealment from the probing eyes of railroad authorities.

ed highwayman, Frenchy amply fulfilled the starry-eyed youth's "ideas of a hero." When the pair parted, Frenchy gave Livingston the nickname A-No. 1 and urged him always to be true to his title.

Believing that the world "owed him a living," Livingston subsisted on meals pinched from the free-lunch counters at various saloons or grudgingly doled out by "charity societies." He slept in hobo jungles or among the shrubbery in public parks and stowed away on trains in relentless — but apparently futile — pursuit of a cure for his case of "wanderlust."

Throughout his books Livingston gives repeated and strict instructions on ways to avoid contracting this ailment. His sincerity, however, is undermined by lyrical descriptions of western scenery and paeans to the hypnoptic lure of the "clickity click and clackaty clack . . . 'Song of the Rails.'" The reader comes away with little doubt that "America's most celebrated tramp" considered his life the grandest of adventures.

A-No. 1 eventually chalked his monicker on mileposts from the Klondike to the Amazon. He kept a record of his peregrinations and boasted that he had ridden the rails for 471,215 miles — and paid just $7.61 for tickets.

In time, Livingston settled down with a wife and wrote the tales of his life as a wanderer. They sold so briskly at railroad newsstands that he was able to equip himself with a mahogany bed, silk pajamas, and other such unnomadic amenities.

Hobo Signs

For men who lived by their wits, a tip or a warning was a priceless find, and hoboes shared such tidbits freely. Scrawling with chalk on fence posts, barns, and station buildings at their every stopping place, hoboes left marks that might seem like childish doodling but in fact were a code of hieroglyphs offering advice to others who came that way.

A simple cross, for instance, might indicate "angel food" — the meal a mission would provide if the hobo sat through a sermon — and a trail of arrows pointed the way. A pair of upraised hands warned of a homeowner with a gun, while a mark that looked like the teeth of a comb told of a "bone-polisher": a mean dog. If, as his train pulled into the station, a seasoned hobo saw a semicircle arching over a spot, chances were he would not climb out from under the car, for that was the sign of a vigilant town and hostile police.

A similar code had been used in the European underworld as early as the 16th century, but by World War I the police there had learned to read it. Only in the United States does it still survive — and here only among a shrinking band of aging vagrants.

AFLOAT IN AMERICA

On-Board Horsepower

In the early 19th century, ferrymen plying America's rivers put an age-old idea to work—horsepower. They brought teams of horses on board their boats to walk on treadmills or circle capstans, thereby turning the boats' paddlewheels. Blind horses were much sought after for the job, and mules were sometimes used as well.

Such arrangements were not nearly so unwieldy as they may sound. As early as 1807, a 40-ton teamboat, as the craft were called, was making its way up and down the Ohio River, powered by just six horses.

The teamboat never did have an era all its own, since it came into being at just about the same time as steamboats. Still, the vessels enjoyed nearly a quarter century of use, traveling inland waters in a variety of shapes and sizes. But steam ultimately won out, and by the mid-19th century the surviving horse-powered boats were but backwoods curiosities.

Canal Boat Travel

They were not for the faint of heart or the weak of stomach. But for those willing to endure the close company of strangers while watching the countryside slip by, canal boats were just the thing. For well over three decades, until competition from railroads made them obsolete, canal transport was unquestionably the fastest, easiest way to move freight and passengers. By 1823, before the Erie Canal was even completed, boats traveling the segment from Utica to Rochester were jammed with people willing to pay $6.25 for the privilege of making the two-day, two-night journey under the most primitive conditions.

Small barges (above) could be towed by a single mule, but to keep up a four-mile-per-hour pace, larger passenger barges (below) might require several.

The earliest canal boats were low, crude boxes designed not for comfort but to fit inside canal locks measuring 15 by 90 feet. Gradually, however, more elegant designs appeared. Indianans, for instance, got a taste of luxury in the 1840's when they traveled the Wabash and Erie on boats like the *Silver Bell*. Its cabin had imported lace curtains and a Brussels carpet, and the team of mules that pulled the boat from the towpath alongside the canal were outfitted with burnished silver harnesses.

It became feasible to go on deck: which was a great relief, notwithstanding its being a very small deck, and being rendered still smaller by the luggage, which was heaped together in the middle . . . it became a science to walk to and fro without tumbling overboard. . . . It was somewhat embarrassing at first, too, to have to duck nimbly . . . whenever the man at the helm cried "Bridge!" and sometimes, when the cry was "Low Bridge," to lie down nearly flat. But custom familiarises one to anything, and there were so many bridges that it took a very short time to get used to this.

— Charles Dickens, 1842

Whether plain or fancy, however, canal travel was dictated by the demands of space. A single central cabin served as dining hall, game room, and unventilated communal bedroom. Sleeping arrangements were simple: on many boats, benches lining the cabin converted into cots, and hammocks were slung from the ceiling. As one traveler noted, male and female alike slept fitfully in the noisy cabins, "packed like herrings in a barrel . . . bumping against the sides of the locks."

The Collins Line's transatlantic steamers, including the *Baltic* shown here, were the prototype of modern luxury liners.

Transatlantic Luxury

As proprietor of the "Dramatic Line" of sailing ships — named after Shakespeare and other theatricals — Edward Knight Collins was by the mid-1830's deeply engaged in transatlantic shipping and passenger transport. He had a knack for giving the public not only what it wanted, but what it did not even know it wanted — cabins on the upper deck, for one thing, and even soda fountains.

Collins had just launched his largest, most luxurious packet in 1838 when maritime history changed abruptly. It was then that a puffing steamship arrived in New York Harbor a mere 15 days after leaving Bristol, England. That was all Collins needed to see. Although his sailing ships continued to ply the Atlantic, he thereafter concentrated on steam, eventually winning a U.S. mail contract that subsidized construction of five enormous steamships.

In April 1850 his *Atlantic* set out from New York. Plain without, but richly decorated within, it was ship enough to bring Jenny Lind to America and to eclipse Britain's Cunard line. The *Arctic,* the *Baltic,* the *Pacific,* and the *Adriatic* soon followed, and it seemed the Collins Line could do no wrong — until late 1854, when the *Arctic* sank off Newfoundland and Collins's wife and two of his children died when their lifeboat sank. That was the first in a series of disasters, and within four years the mighty Collins Line had disappeared.

Yankee Clipper

"I never yet built a vessel that came up to my own ideal," Donald McKay once said — which may explain why each of the towering clipper ships that emerged from his East Boston boat yard was not only faster but more beautiful than the one that came before.

Nova Scotia born, McKay apprenticed in New York before settling in Massachusetts. In 1842 he completed his first commission, the 392-ton *Courier,* a packet built for the coffee trade. McKay's revolutionary design for the ship (it had a flat bottom and sharp bow) inspired much scoffing — until the *Courier*'s fleet passage to Rio and back won converts all around. The young builder soon had an order for a fleet of transatlantic packets and a shipyard of his own.

With valuable cargo such as Chinese tea on board a clipper, every day saved in transport meant money to the owners. McKay, ever obliging, provided the speed. His *Sovereign of the Seas* was the first to better 400 nautical miles in a day and was exceeded four years later by another of his designs, the *Lightning*. The discovery of gold in California called for quick passage around Cape Horn: McKay came through with the beautiful *Stag Hound* in 1850, and later the *Flying Cloud,* which sped from New York to San Francisco in less than 90 days. The record still stands.

Ever ambitious, McKay launched the *Great Republic* in October 1853. At 4,555 tons and 335 feet in length, she was the biggest wooden vessel ever built. Two months later, the proud behemoth was destroyed by fire as she waited to pick up a cargo of grain in New York Harbor. McKay, undaunted, simply rebuilt the giant ship.

Donald McKay — wearing a top hat, with his back to the photographer (above) — watched the launching of his last clipper ship, the *Glory of the Seas,* in 1869. The painting (right) depicts the same ship 10 years later in New York Harbor.

They Just Kept Rolling Along

Nicholas Roosevelt and his bride, Lydia, first traveled down the Mississippi River by flatboat in 1809. The trip — a combined honeymoon and scouting mission — was as placid and uneventful as their second journey would prove wild and adventurous. Acting as agent for Robert Fulton and Robert Livingston, Nicholas had been sent out to determine if steamboats could work the Mississippi as profitably as they did the rivers of the East.

Almost everyone he met along the way insisted it could not be done. Diligent and dutiful, the young engineer nevertheless continued to study the river's currents, sound its depths, and scout the shore for supplies — including coal deposits — then reported back to his employers that the future was theirs.

The *New Orleans,* the first steamboat on the Mississippi, survived a literal baptism by fire on its maiden voyage in 1811.

Two years later he and Lydia, who by then was pregnant, set out from Pittsburgh aboard the brand-new steamer *New Orleans,* heading for the Gulf. All along the Ohio River awestruck settlers watched as the "fire-canoe" smoked toward Louisville. There were skeptics among the watchers. "Your boat may go *down* the river," Cincinnati's mayor predicted, "but as to coming up, the very idea is an absurd one." Roosevelt answered the detractors with a round-trip excursion from Louisville to Cincinnati.

Back in Louisville, while they waited for the river to rise high enough to smooth out the treacherous Falls of the Ohio and allow the *New Orleans* to pass, Lydia gave birth. Declining offers of land travel, she continued on the voyage.

Almost as soon as the *New Orleans* cleared the roiling falls, the surrounding countryside began to heave and roll — the boat had made it to the Mississippi River just as the powerful New Madrid earthquakes began to strike. For days the travelers navigated a swirling horror of crashing trees and flooded banks, geysers that spurted mud, and channels that disappeared as they steered into them. One night they tied up to an island tree and woke to find that the island had sunk. A fire on board added to their troubles. But the river at last grew calm at Natchez, and a swift final run brought the boat safely into New Orleans on January 10, 1812. The family — and the age of steam — had arrived.

By the 1880's steamboats were common on inland waterways. Some were designed to haul freight (below), others (right) to accommodate pleasure seekers.

Up until the mid-19th century, more than half the steamboat accidents on America's rivers were caused by snags — mats of debris that ripped open the boats' hulls.

Captain Shreve Desnags the River

For early riverboat captains, one of the worst hazards of travel was the possibility of hitting snags, accumulations of debris and half-sunken trees that could tear open a boat's bottom. Most every river had its share of snags large or small, but the worst of them all was the impassable monster known as the Great Raft of the Red River, an ancient snarl of toppled trees, knotted roots, and mud in northwestern Louisiana.

Born of a long-ago flood and packed thicker each spring, the mighty logjam eventually choked sections of the river for about 150 miles, closing it to navigation and contributing to flooding. In 1828 a team of engineers estimated that clearing the Great Raft would cost $2 million to $3 million — if it could be done at all. But that was before the bulldog tenacity of Capt. Henry Miller Shreve, a seasoned Mississippi boatman, came into play.

While superintendent of Western River Improvement, Shreve persuaded the government to finance construction of an ingenious snag-boat he had designed. By ramming into trees, hoisting them aboard, then cutting them into pieces that could drift harmlessly away, his twin-hulled *Heliopolis* in 1829 broke through the Mississippi's notorious Plum Point snag in a mere 11 hours.

In 1833 Shreve was invited to take on the Great Raft itself. Coordinating a small fleet of snag-boats modeled on the *Heliopolis,* Shreve set to work at once and spent 2½ months clearing some 70 miles of river before the money allotted for the job ran out. For the next five years Shreve returned as often as funding allowed and gnawed away at the snag until the Great Raft was but a bad memory — and the bustling river town of Shreveport a dawning reality.

Walking on Water

"I've done something nobody else has ever done," announced Capt. Charles W. Oldrieve — and given the piety of the age, it's a wonder he wasn't pilloried for blasphemy. What he had done was nothing less than walk on water from Cincinnati to New Orleans in just 40 days, all for the sake of a very worldly $5,000 bet.

The adventure began on the Ohio River on January 1, 1907. Oldrieve's backer, Capt. J. W. Weatherington, and Arthur Jones, a proxy for another man who is said to have proposed the bet, led the way out of Cincinnati in a gas-powered boat. Oldrieve's wife, who contemporary accounts described as "robust," followed in a rowboat. (Mrs. O. would scull beside her husband every inch of the 1,600-mile course, calling out support and warning of dangers in the river.) Last in the procession was the champion himself, his 100-pound form balanced on the pontoonlike contraptions that kept him afloat.

Six inches wide, seven inches high, several feet long, and weighing 20 pounds apiece, Oldrieve's water booties were made of canvas stretched over lightweight frames. Flaps on the bottoms provided traction and kept the wearer from backsliding. Miraculously, they worked.

Down the Ohio the party went and on to the Mississippi, undaunted by rain, sleet, chills, and fever. Nearing New Orleans, the Oldrieves were caught in an eddy but, rescued by a passing coal ship, they pressed on. At last, on the morning of February 10, they swept triumphantly into New Orleans — with about an hour to spare.

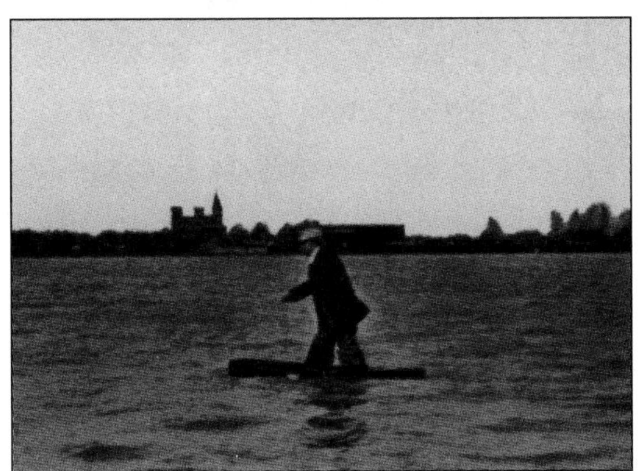

The slight figure of Capt. Charles Oldrieve was captured for posterity as he passed Arkansas City, Arkansas, on his watery pilgrimage from Cincinnati to New Orleans.

Legend and Lore

"I'm half wild horse and half cockeyed alligator and the rest o' me is crooked snags an' redhot snappin' turkle," crowed Mike Fink whenever introductions were needed. Born around 1770, the King of the Keelboatmen inspired a trail of legend as wide as the rivers he sailed on.

A crack shot who sported a red-feathered hat on his carrot-topped head, Fink carried a handcrafted .45-caliber rifle that was "slicker'n a wildcat and quicker in action." It was said that he once shot the tails off a litter of piglets in a duel with Davy Crockett — who had merely clipped the ears of an old tomcat 150 yards off.

As for Mike Fink's monumental thirst, it was said that he could down a gallon of whiskey a day. The secret of his amazing capacity? It was the result, he claimed, of the buffalo robe he once had eaten — hair and all — to provide a protective coating for his stomach.

Pathfinder of the Seas

Naval brass may not have been overly fond of Lt. Matthew Fontaine Maury, but to mariners throughout the world he would forever be a hero — the pathfinder of the seas. Maury's difficulties with his superiors were much of his own making. As a young midshipman (and a brilliant mathematician) he challenged their knowledge of navigation and later wrote a series of editorials advocating naval reform. No one liked admitting that the arrogant Young Turk was right. So when an accident in 1839 left 33-year-old Maury lame, officers had no regrets about assigning him to the obscurity of the Depot of Charts and Instruments. It was a move that would change history.

The depot's storeroom was lined with thousands of ships' logbooks in which captains, for more than 70 years, had recorded their observations of winds and currents around the globe. That gave Maury an idea. Why not collate the records to create a systematic guide to navigation? With such charts, he asserted, a young mariner would have "the experience of a thousand navigators to guide him on his voyage."

In 1847 the navy published Maury's first volume of charts for the North Atlantic and followed up later with charts for the rest of the Atlantic and for the Pacific and Indian oceans. A simple system of arrows showed current direction and speed, while "wind brushes" indicated the direction and force of seasonal winds in each location. Also included were notes about storm patterns, fog, calms, and other critical information that would help a captain determine the safest, speediest sailing course at any given time of year.

Matthew Fontaine Maury is commemorated in the capital of his home state of Virginia with a monument that links him permanently with the world's oceans.

The value of Maury's charts was demonstrated dramatically in 1851 when Josiah Cressy, captain of the clipper ship *Flying Cloud,* used them on a voyage from New York to San Francisco via Cape Horn. The trip, which usually took five months, was completed in less than three. In the 1860's Cyrus Field would use Maury's charts to determine where and when to lay down the first transatlantic telegraph cable.

Within a short time Maury was deluged with orders. Any gaps in information on the original charts were closed when he suggested that captains could trade in their logbooks for free copies of the next edition of *Wind and Currents.* More than 1,000 responded.

Maury's brash manner and his work for the Confederate Navy during the Civil War diminished his reputation during his lifetime, but not for posterity. To this day mariners everywhere are guided by Matthew Maury's charts.

Storm Warriors

When the Revenue Marine, forerunner of the Coast Guard, was created in 1790, its job was to chase down smugglers. Rescue at sea was left to local volunteer organizations. But with meager training and equipment, such groups were often a poor match for offshore emergencies.

As maritime traffic — and the number of deaths — increased in the 19th century, the public demanded that something be done. Beginning in 1848, Congress provided funds for life-saving equipment, but it was little more than a gesture. It was not until 1871 — following a year of particularly alarming casualty statistics — that Sumner

Surfmen used the breeches buoy — a lifesaver with pants attached — to transport wreck victims from sea to shore. This 19th-century rescue tool was still in use in the 1950's.

Kimball was made chief of the Revenue Marine.

With that, everything changed, for Kimball created a professional Life-Saving Service. Replacing volunteers with full-time "surfmen," he recruited only those who were strong, agile, literate, and thoroughly versed in the workings of his redesigned surfboats. Weighing up to 1,000 pounds and holding six rowers, the boats could be launched right into the waves. Many of the surfmen at first made fun of the bulky little craft, but soon discovered that they were reliable no matter how stormy the sea. Another new piece of equipment was the Lyle gun, which could be used to shoot a cable from the beach to a ship in distress. Once the line was secure, a heavy rope or life-saving gear could be sent out from shore.

Kimball's most important innovations, however, were the introduction of regular inspections of staff and equipment, and daily drills and practice sessions. The professionalism and effectiveness of the service improved immeasurably, and true-life tales of the surfmen's bravery in near-impossible situations soon were being told everywhere.

The brawny, daring surfmen became romantic heroes, celebrated in literature and song as "storm warriors" and "soldiers of the surf." In time, though, the arrival of gasoline-powered rescue boats reduced the numbers of oarsmen and rescue stations that were needed — and advances in ship technology reduced the need for rescue in the first place. In 1915 the Life-Saving Service was absorbed into the newly formed Coast Guard, and a brave tradition of service was handed on.

Ida Lewis, Keeper of the Light

For all their lonely hours of vigilance manning the beacons that keep ships safe, few lighthouse keepers have ever been widely known by name. But there was one notable 19th-century exception. Idawalley Zorada Lewis — Ida for short — gained such wide renown that even President Grant (who got his feet wet when he came to visit her) told a reporter, "To see Ida Lewis, I'd gladly get wet up to my armpits."

Lewis earned her reputation during the 50 years she spent at Lime Rock Light in Rhode Island's Narragansett Bay. The daughter of the official keeper, she began assuming some of her father's duties after he suffered a stroke in 1857. What brought her fame, however, was not the ships but the lives she saved. A strong rower and accomplished swimmer, Lewis pulled 18 people from the bay over the course of her career.

She was only 15 the first time she rowed out to the rescue, somehow managing to haul into her own boat four young men who had capsized their yawl and could not swim. On another occasion she brought three drowning shepherds safely to shore — then rowed out again and towed their sheep to safety. Although these feats were heralded locally, Lewis did not win wider recognition until 1869, when a New York reporter wrote a gripping account of her rescue of two soldiers whose sailboat foundered in a gale. The story was eagerly read all across the nation.

Tourists soon flocked to see the newly famous heroine; the city of Newport presented her with a skiff, the *Rescue;* financier Jim Fisk had a boat house built for it; and other gifts and honors flowed in. A feature on Lewis in *Harper's Weekly* pondered the knotty question of whether it was proper for a woman to do the things she did, then came down heartily in her favor, declaring only "a donkey" would consider the saving of lives "unfeminine." Suffragettes also took proud note of her competence in their journal, *Revolution.*

Ida Lewis received many proposals of marriage, and accepted one of them. But the union lasted only a few months: Lewis soon left her husband and returned to her beloved lighthouse. In 1879, seven years after her father's death, Congress belatedly recognized her service by giving her a gold medal and an official commission as lighthouse keeper. She performed her last rescue at the age of 65 and died at her post three years later in 1911.

The painting (below) records one of Ida Lewis's many headlining rescues at sea. In her later years Lewis (inset) was celebrated throughout the world for her bravery.

UP, UP, AND AWAY

Wise got as far as commissioning this transatlantic balloon but never did make the journey.

John Wise Gets Off to a Flying Start

Americans in the 1800's were enamored of the idea of air travel. For some, like balloonist John Wise, flight was more than mere fancy.

His first ascent was modest enough — a nine-mile journey from Philadelphia, Pennsylvania, to Haddonfield, New Jersey, in 1835. But the success of that short balloon flight persuaded 27-year-old John Wise to make aeronautics his career. Of the 446 ascents he ultimately made, one in 1859 was noted the world over as proof that long-distance balloon flight was possible.

Wise made a point of studying weather patterns with each of his ascents, and it was his discovery of a high-altitude air current running from west to east that prompted his first long-distance journey. By riding the wind, he was convinced, it should be possible to fly across the continent and even on to Europe. As a test he decided to make a nonstop float from St. Louis to New York City.

Commissioning a new balloon for the occasion, Wise dubbed it the *Atlantic* and inflated it with gas. Then on the evening of July 1, 1859, he lifted off from St. Louis with three companions, a cargo of roast turkey and champagne, a sack of mail, and a lifeboat. Soon the balloon was whizzing along at 50 miles per hour, and by eleven the next morning it passed Buffalo. Over Lake Ontario, however, the *Atlantic* ran into a gale that sent it slamming along the water's surface. Wise jettisoned the cargo — even the boat and the mail — in an effort to gain altitude. Though the balloon made it to shore, it crashed through the woods and finally lodged in a massive tree.

A newspaper picture of Wise's 1859 crash captured the drama but inaccurately showed his lifeboat still attached.

Wise climbed down, having covered 1,200 miles in 19 hours and 50 minutes. He never made his planned flight to Europe — a quarrel with backers aborted his one attempt. But his record for long-distance flight remained unbeaten until 1900, 21 years after Wise, at 71, disappeared on a balloon trip over Lake Michigan.

An Aerial Hoax

Astounding News" screamed the headline of the New York *Sun* — and so it would have been, had it been true. The news story in question on April 13, 1844, claimed that an Irish balloonist had crossed the Atlantic. The fact was, though, it was only a flight of imagination penned by Edgar Allan Poe.

Poe had arrived in New York City a few days before with only $4.50 in his pocket, desperate to attract the publishing world's attention. Editors at the *Sun* quickly accepted his proposal for a hoax — it was, after all, a guaranteed scoop — and Poe set to work. Using the name of a real aeronaut, he described in great detail a flight from Wales to South Carolina, accomplished in 75 hours and all by accident: Poe claimed that the balloonist's original destination was Paris.

Poe was part of the crowd that gathered outside the newspaper office on the 13th, and took great glee in watching believers fight for copies of the paper. The *Sun* enjoyed a jump in circulation — but when the truth emerged, it was Poe's reputation as a romancer that soared.

WHAT · IS · IT

The lure of flight was so irresistible to 19th-century Americans that they would try almost anything to be airborne. This contraption — a flying bedframe concocted by a Connecticut man in 1855 — was to be lifted by six rotors, four driven by compressed air and two by the pilot's feet.

The High-Flying Balloonatic

She may have been "a brave, enthusiastic and accomplished Yankee girl" as her hometown newspaper claimed. But to her neighbors in Easton, Pennsylvania, Lucretia Bradley was known as "the balloonatic" — and with good reason.

Bradley had bought an old, worn balloon from the famous aeronaut John Wise for $100 and, despite his cautions, quickly put it to use. Filling it with hydrogen, she lifted off in January 1855 and quickly shot up to an altitude of two miles. As the atmosphere thinned, the gas inside the balloon expanded faster than it could escape through the safety valve. The balloon swelled, then exploded with a sound like a cannon blast, jolting Bradley from her enraptured contemplation of the view. Fortunately, a large section of the tattered silk balloon remained caught in the rope netting and functioned like a parachute. Bradley dropped swiftly but safely back to earth, singing, she later said, "a song of praise to the Creator of such a scene of beauty and sublime grandeur" as that which surrounded her in this aerial adventure.

But her first adventure proved her last. She ordered a new balloon, causing John Wise to marvel that "woman, when really determined, seems to be more daring than man." Yet she never took the new balloon aloft. Danger could not cow her — but apparently her neighbors' ridicule did.

Lucretia landed hard but got up and walked away unscathed after her terrifying descent.

Down on the (Balloon) Farm

When Carl Myers and Mary Hawley met and married in upstate New York in 1871, they shared the same lofty aspirations. He was an ingenious designer of balloons and the gas generators for filling them. She would be his test pilot.

A crowd of 15,000 gathered to watch her maiden flight on July 4, 1880, in Little Falls, New York. She had chosen a professional name for the occasion — Carlotta, the Lady Aeronaut — and was never called Mary again. The first flight went so smoothly that Carlotta could not wait to try another. Indeed, she would make more than 60 flights in her first two years as a pilot. Nattily outfitted in blue flannel suits trimmed in gold, with gaiters and a jaunty straw hat, Carlotta made precision landings look easy. At Saratoga Springs she once made identical landings eight times in a row.

Carl, meanwhile, was busy managing Carlotta's career as well as his own. To keep up with the demand for balloons, the couple bought a 30-room mansion on five acres of land in Frankfort, New York, and named it Balloon Farm. Carl had a printing press, carpentry and machine shops, a chemistry lab, and a loft for laying out and cutting hundreds of yards of fabric. Out on the grounds, employees immersed the fabric in a syrup of boiled linseed oil and turpentine to make it airtight. Elsewhere on the farm, aerial gymnasts rehearsed their acts on a trapeze. Partially inflated balloons dotted the grounds, one writer noted, like some kind of gigantic mushroom crop.

Although Carlotta officially retired as a balloonist in 1891, Carl remained active in the air and was still pedaling about on his invention called the Sky Cycle — a tiny, foot-propelled dirigible — at the age of 68.

The "beautiful and fearless Carlotta," as Mary Myers (left) called herself, was the most popular balloonist of her day. A clever composite photograph (below), makes the Myerses' Balloon Farm look even grander than it was.

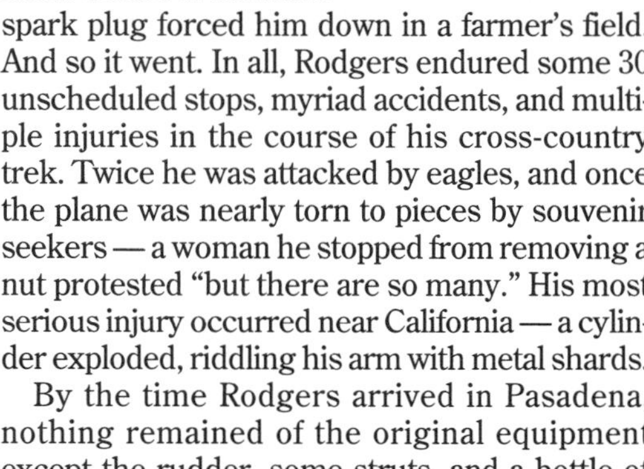

Crashing Along in the Vin Fiz

"The machine hasn't been built that can do it," said Orville Wright when he heard of the 1911 cross-country air race sponsored by William Randolph Hearst. But since the first to make it in less than 30 days would win $50,000, Wright built a Model EX biplane and entered it with Cal Rodgers, his star pupil, as pilot.

The maker of a new grape drink offered to bankroll the flight if Rodgers would name the plane after the drink — Vin Fiz. Rodgers was also to receive bonuses for every mile that he logged, as well as a private train (complete with living quarters, hangar, and car) to serve as a mobile base. The only things the pilot had to pay for were fuel and spare parts. What could he lose?

The first plane to cross the continent (below) spent more time on the ground than in the air. Its backer, however, got plenty of promotional mileage out of the trip with posters (above right) for his soft drink, Vin Fiz.

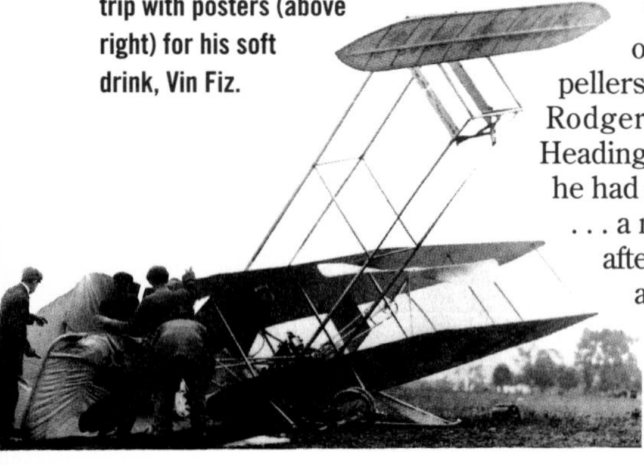

The EX was not much more than an oversized box kite with twin propellers and a 35-horsepower engine, but Rodgers was just the man to handle it. Heading out of New York on September 17, he had a good first day. "No man ever had . . . a more perfect engine," said the pilot after flying 84 miles in 105 minutes. But at takeoff the next morning, Rodgers crashed into a chicken coop and demolished the craft. His mechanics rebuilt it in 40 hours, and he was back in the air — going just 98 miles before a defective spark plug forced him down in a farmer's field. And so it went. In all, Rodgers endured some 30 unscheduled stops, myriad accidents, and multiple injuries in the course of his cross-country trek. Twice he was attacked by eagles, and once the plane was nearly torn to pieces by souvenir seekers — a woman he stopped from removing a nut protested "but there are so many." His most serious injury occurred near California — a cylinder exploded, riddling his arm with metal shards.

By the time Rodgers arrived in Pasadena, nothing remained of the original equipment except the rudder, some struts, and a bottle of Vin Fiz. Though his time in the air totaled just 3 days, 10 hours, and 4 minutes, repair sessions had extended the trip to 49 days, far exceeding the 30-day limit. Rodgers, consequently, could not claim the prize. Worse yet, repair bills had consumed all his bonuses. Still, he had proven transcontinental flight was possible. Or as he put it, "What matters is: I did it, didn't I?"

Master Birdman

Brash, arrogant, and contradictory at best, Lincoln Beachey hated his audiences as much as he loved them. "They pay to see me die," he admitted. And, indeed, he was a master of death-defying aerial daredevilry.

Although he had begun his career as a touring balloonist, Beachey realized by 1910 that airplanes were stealing the show. He made a deal with aircraft builder Glenn Curtiss to perform as an exhibition flyer and then taught himself to fly, crashing plane after plane in the process. Within six months, though, Beachey could make the aircraft of the day perform maneuvers no one had believed possible. "You can fly a kitchen table if the motor is strong enough," he declared.

Flying under bridges was a Beachey specialty. During his first summer at the controls, he swooped under the International Bridge at Niagara Falls.

Beachey could dive under telephone wires, or swoop down and lift a handkerchief off the ground with the tip of a wing. He was famous for his "death dip," cutting his engine in midair to plunge in a drop that made spectators faint. And he set a new altitude record (at 11,642 feet) by climbing for an hour and 48 minutes until he ran out of gas, then spiraling back to earth unpowered.

Lincoln Beachey's standard flying outfit was a pinstripe suit and a golf cap worn backward.

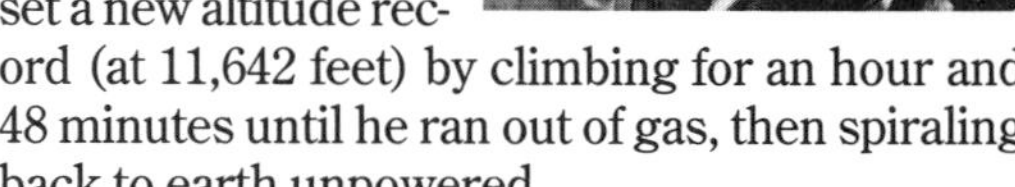

When the newspapers blamed him for the death of less-talented copycats, Beachey retired in disgust. But news that a French flyer had managed to loop-the-loop sent him back into the air. He soon was putting his custom-built Curtiss plane through triple loops, and earning $1,000 a day for performing the feat.

His luck finally ran out, however. In 1915, as a star attraction at the Panama Pacific Exposition, one last death dip tore the wings off his plane, and Beachey, at 28, drowned in San Francisco Bay.

Photographed in 1925, two members of the flying team 13 Black Cats simultaneously snatched hats from men on the ground.

Those Heart-Stopping Barnstormers

The end of World War I resulted in countless hangars full of surplus airplanes — and thousands of surplus pilots, too. But while the flyers had a hard time finding peacetime employment, they could buy a Jenny biplane, still in its crate, for as little as $300. And so the more-adventurous took to the air as barnstormers, a name borrowed from old-time troupers who were as likely to perform in barns as in theaters. For a time barnstorming was one of America's most popular entertainments.

One-man traveling air shows

Flying cross-country, a pilot might buzz a likely-looking village at low altitude to see how much excitement could be generated by the appearance of a plane. If the reaction was enthusiastic, he would find a field to land in, then charge the curious a few dollars for a ride or, better yet, thrill spectators by performing aerobatic stunts.

Then, as barnstormers found themselves competing for crowds, stunt flying grew ever more outrageous. When loop-the-loops no longer amazed, pilots took to flying upside down, staging mock dogfights, and dropping bouquets into ladies' laps. Soon airborne acrobats were climbing out of the cockpit — often without parachute or safety straps — to stand on the upper wing, perform handstands, or hang by their knees or teeth from the landing gear. One man won fame by swinging from the axle and landing in haystacks. Nor were men the only stunt flyers. Mabel Cody, Buffalo Bill's niece, was among the famous barnstormers. In her act she would leap from plane to plane in midflight or climb from speeding boats and cars onto moving aircraft.

By 1925 such high jinks had gone too far. One touring company, the 13 Black Cats, was offering to crash a plane head-on into an automobile for $250, and for $1,200 it would dive the plane into a house. Fatalities had become so routine that Congress in 1926 passed the Air Commerce Act, effectively prohibiting stunt flying.

Though the era of the barnstormers was over, their influence lived on. They had aroused the public's interest in air travel. From their ranks, moreover, came flyers who would become some of the world's most respected aviators, among them Charles Lindbergh and Jimmy Doolittle.

Poised atop a biplane's wing, barnstormer Gladys Ingle concentrates on the bull's-eye of her wing-mounted target.

PRINCESSES OF AIR FLY OVER NATION IN THRILLING DERBY

Progress of participants in the Women's Air Derby was reported regularly in newspapers (above). But if the press made "princesses" and "petticoat pilots" of the fliers, the public took them seriously and even wrote songs about a new brand of heroine — the "aviatress" (below).

Powder Puff Derby

In an era of aeronautic mania, the 1929 Women's Air Derby was a publicist's dream. The press called the entrants the "Flying Flappers," "Lady Birds," and "Sweethearts of the Air," and the grueling race they were about to undertake was dubbed the "Powder Puff Derby." But to the 20 aviators who signed up for the 2,800-mile, eight-stop run from Santa Monica to Cleveland, it was a not-to-be-missed opportunity to demonstrate that women were perfectly able to fly planes.

Two years after Charles Lindbergh's historic flight across the Atlantic, only 40 American women had the pilot's license and 100 hours' solo flying time required of race contestants. The 18 who signed up ranged from headliners such as Amelia Earhart to exhibition fliers hoping for a share of the $10,000 prize money. As a group they held a staggering number of records for endurance and speed, and they shared a bravado born of the open cockpit. In the words of German stunt pilot Thea Rasche (who with Jessie Miller of New Zealand brought the derby's roster to 20), flying "was more thrilling than love for a man — and less dangerous."

Amid a blizzard of press coverage, the contestants assembled at Santa Monica's Clover Field on the afternoon of August 18. One by one their craft lifted into the air: monoplanes, biplanes, zippy coupes, and lumbering cabin sports. Though the first and shortest leg of the course — a 60- mile hop to San Bernardino — was uneventful enough, on the second leg disaster struck. Marvel Crosson's plane nose-dived into the desert, and two fliers were forced down with sand in their tanks. Critics called for an end to the race after Crosson's body was found along with her unopened parachute. But the surviving fliers decided they had to push on. When Blanche Noyes' plane caught fire at 3,000 feet, she landed, doused the flames with sand, and took off again. Ruth Elder, in turn, made a forced landing in a field where she could see large animals looming in the distance. Considering her plane's bright red fuselage, she prayed, "Let them be cows."

On the next-to-last day, Ruth Nichols was forced out of the race after colliding with a tractor on an airfield's runway. But when 23-year-old Louise Thaden arrived in Cleveland on August 26, with a total flying time of 20 hours, 20 minutes, the point had been made. Completing the derby "was of more import than life or death," declared Thaden. It was flown "with the object of proving that women are capable of good flying, to prove that commercial aviation . . . is safe."

"Lady Lindy" Indeed

Amelia Earhart had been flying for eight years in 1928 when she was asked to be the first woman to fly the Atlantic — as a passenger. Though the flight put her in the headlines, it was not the kind of recognition she had in mind. She meant to make her own mark, and no one went at it with more determination. While George Palmer Putnam, her agent and later her husband, made sure Earhart received the lion's share of attention in every competition she entered, she honed her skills and built endurance.

By early 1932, at age 34, she was ready to take on the Atlantic: five years to the day after Charles Lindbergh's flight, she aimed her single-engine Lockheed Vega east out of Newfoundland, bound for Paris. The night was clear at first, but at 12,000 feet the Vega's altimeter went out and lightning flared. Earhart coaxed the craft above the storm, only to be sent spinning toward the sea when its wings iced over. Righting the plane within sight of the whitecaps, she heard an ominous vibration behind her and looked back to see flames shooting from the plane's cracked manifold.

Four hours into the flight, she had to make a choice: reverse course and try to land with a heavy load of fuel, or press on. On she flew, for another 11 hours, until the Irish coast materialized through the mist. Rather than push her ailing aircraft further, she touched down in a green pasture and stepped out. "I've come from America," she announced to the farmer who appeared in the field. "But who was with you?" he asked in amazement. "Who flew the plane?"

Amelia Earhart flew solo over the Atlantic in 1932 (the first woman to do so), and she did it in record time — 14 hours and 56 minutes. The press dubbed her "Lady Lindy" because of her uncanny resemblance to Lindbergh.

Tender Loving Care in the Air

All Boeing manager Steve Stimpson had in mind for the new job of flight attendant in 1930 was someone to soothe passengers and hand out lunch. Then Ellen Church showed up in the San Francisco office of Boeing Air Transport, the precursor of United Airlines. A registered nurse with a passion for flying, she got straight to the point. Why not hire nurses to take care of your passengers? she asked, and in no time at all, Stimpson did.

Enlisted as chief stewardess, Church wrote her own job description. Her nurses could weigh no more than 115 pounds or stand taller than 5 feet 4 inches. For $125 a month they were required, among other things, to offer to remove passengers' shoes and put on their slippers, swat flies before takeoff, and make sure passengers did not go out the exit when looking for the lavatory.

On May 15, 1930, Church debuted the role of stewardess on a flight from Oakland to Cheyenne. There were grumbles from the cockpit, but the passengers loved the extra attention. And by the end of the first week, Church had earned her stripes: noticing a man in severe abdominal pain in midflight, she suspected it was appendicitis and told the pilot he had to land. The pilot was furious. "Beat it!" he responded. But when Church reminded him that she, too, had a professional duty to fulfill, he grudgingly landed the plane. A doctor quickly confirmed Church's guess, and the chastened captain apologized.

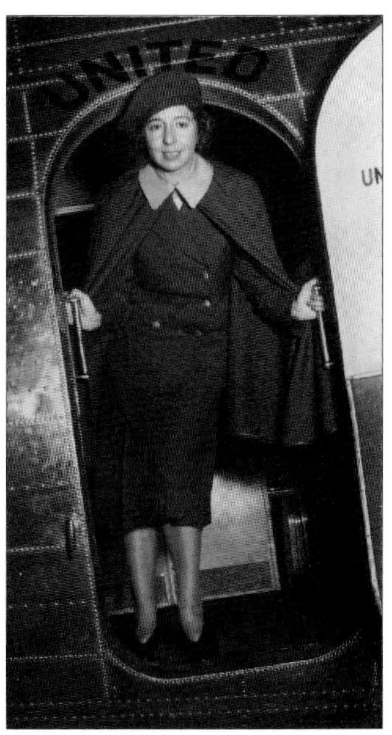

Ellen Church (above) posed in the green twill uniform and cape she designed in 1930. By 1939 United's stewardesses still wore neatly matched outfits (left), but with a more stylish look — complete with parasols.

Fastest Man of the Earth and Skies

A childhood passion for bicycle racing and a lifelong love of tinkering gave Glenn Curtiss a unique edge on the new market for motorcycles at the turn of the century. By 1903, in fact, the 25-year-old native of Hammondsport, New York, was well known both as a motorcycle racing champion and as the maker of some of the best lightweight combustion engines in the country.

Glenn Curtiss created a sensation in 1910 when he flew his *Albany Flier* down the Hudson River from Albany, New York, to New York City in less than three hours of flying time.

Curtiss's reputation attracted the interest of flying enthusiasts, who wanted engines for their dirigibles. But he might have confined his own speed records to the roadways had he not met Dr. Alexander Graham Bell. Bell, who had been caught up with flight early on, asked Curtiss in 1907 to build him an engine for a flying machine. Two years later he persuaded the younger man to join him in earnest, and by early 1908 their Aerial Experiment Association launched the *Red Wing*. A biplane with a 30-foot wingspan and a 24-horsepower Curtiss engine, the *Red Wing* flew only 300 feet before stalling. But when a later model called *June Bug* routinely flew as far as 1,000 feet without a hitch, Curtiss and Bell entered it in a one-kilometer competition sponsored by *Scientific American*.

A huge crowd gathered in Hammondsport to watch the *June Bug*'s flight on July 4, 1908. At about 7:30 P.M., Curtiss eased the boxy biplane into position, headed across the field, and lifted into the air. As the spectators watched in amazement, he flew past the finish line, banked, and circled around to land. When he stepped out of the plane, he was definitely an aviator — not a bike man — and soon would be a hero as well.

In July 1909 Curtiss took the *Scientific American* trophy a second time, for a flight of almost 25 miles. Then he headed for Europe, where he captured the prestigious Gordon Bennett Cup and won praise as "the fastest man of the earth and skies." And the next year he made headlines for long-distance flying, winning $10,000 for a 150-mile flight down the Hudson River from Albany to New York.

Not simply a showman, Curtiss made real and lasting contributions to aviation. He established the first school for pilots, invented the first practical hydroplane, and built the NC-4s, one of which was first plane to make a transatlantic flight, as well as the famous Jennys of World War I.

Doolittle Flies Blind

One of the most daring of the early pilots, James Doolittle, seen here in 1925, later won fame as a hero of World War II.

James Doolittle was already famous as a stunt pilot when he took on the challenge of flying "blind" to demonstrate the possibility of instrument-guided navigation in 1929. Up until then, aviators had been at the mercy of the weather. If there were low clouds and fog, one saying warned, no man could hope to land safely "unless God flies him in." Doolittle put it another way. Knowing how to crash, he explained, was part of a pilot's life. But that was hardly the image that aviation companies wanted to project.

In 1928 Doolittle was made director of the Guggenheim Fund's Full Flight Laboratory at Mitchell Field in New York. Working with engineers under a variety of difficult flying conditions, he spent nearly a year testing the latest devices developed especially for flight. Among them were Elmer Sperry's nonmagnetic gyrocompass, which aided pilots in making turns; a barometric altimeter; and a two-way directional radio receiver for picking up signals from a powerful new radio beacon at the airfield.

In great secrecy Doolittle practiced flying blind for several weeks, checking and rechecking his equipment for possible problems until he was certain of success. Finally, on September 24, 1929, he slipped a canvas hood over the cockpit of his *Consolidated NY-2,* fixed his eyes on his gauges, and took off. Guided only by instruments, he successfully flew a course of some 15 miles, then came in for a safe, if slightly sloppy, landing. "Fog peril overcome," heralded *The New York Times*. In the new age of flight, crashing would no longer be a commonplace in the pilot's life.

Flying Flivvers

In 1929 William Piper was a successful oil company executive with his feet planted firmly on the ground when, at age 48, he bought into a failing aircraft company in Pennsylvania. Learning to fly himself, Piper soon became convinced that everybody belonged in the air. All they needed, he believed, was the right plane.

By 1931 he saw to it that they had just that — a squat, inexpensive, maneuverable aircraft. It was the Model E-2 Cub, and Piper managed to sell 24 of them that first year, at $1,325 apiece. As the Depression lingered on, however, sales dropped the following year and again a year later. But Piper was so sure of his product that he simply dipped into his own funds to keep the business afloat. Then in 1936 he bought the company outright, introduced a new, improved Piper Cub at the bargain price of $1,270, and sold 523 of them.

What made the Cubs so affordable was Piper's assembly-line production. As the country's first mass-produced planes, the Cubs were nicknamed the Model T's of aviation and flivvers of the air, and Piper himself was dubbed the Henry Ford of aviation. By 1940 his factory employed over 1,000 workers, most of them young men and women who were willing to put up with rock-bottom wages — 44 cents an hour, or half what they could earn making cars in Detroit — in exchange for the opportunity to learn to fly.

With America about to enter World War II, Piper shrewdly gave the army a gift of 10 Cubs and was rewarded with orders for thousands more to be used as reconnaissance and supply planes. Though they were called puddle-jumpers and grasshoppers, the Cubs proved as versatile as could be and were beloved, as Piper knew they would be. "Any fool can fly a Piper," he maintained, "I planned it that way."

Piper's plane was not just easy to maneuver; it could also fly close to the ground. Here, a can of gasoline is passed up to a Cub during an endurance race.

A Bruiser of a Cruiser

Theater-goers in the 1920's and 1930's were known to gasp and applaud when the curtain went up on stage sets by Norman Bel Geddes. The designer also drew raves for his streamlined radios, furniture, and even skyscrapers. But in 1929 his flair for innovation reached a new peak when, with the help of German engineer Otto Koller, he designed *Air Liner Number 4* — a visionary vehicle that was meant to float as well as fly, and resembled a cruise ship with wings.

On paper at least, Bel Geddes's flying resort had a wingspan the length of two football fields and landed on huge pontoons. A planned staff of 150 — 1 crew member for every 3 passengers — included such niceties as a manicurist, a librarian, and seven musicians. When passengers were not in their staterooms, they could eat in a 200-seat formal dining room (or one of three private dining rooms), exercise in the gym, have their hair done, or stroll along glass-enclosed promenades.

Lift-off for the 700-ton sky giant would take 20 engines, though only 12 would be needed to maintain a cruising speed of 100 miles an hour. At that rate a trip from the Midwest to Europe could have been accomplished in a leisurely 42 hours. As cumbersome as it may now seem, *Number 4* was thought commercially feasible. But the design was drawn on the eve of the Depression — and Bel Geddes's flight of fancy never got off the ground.

Bel Geddes's multilevel design included suites on deck 7, and a promenade that was to be 17 feet wide and 450 feet long.

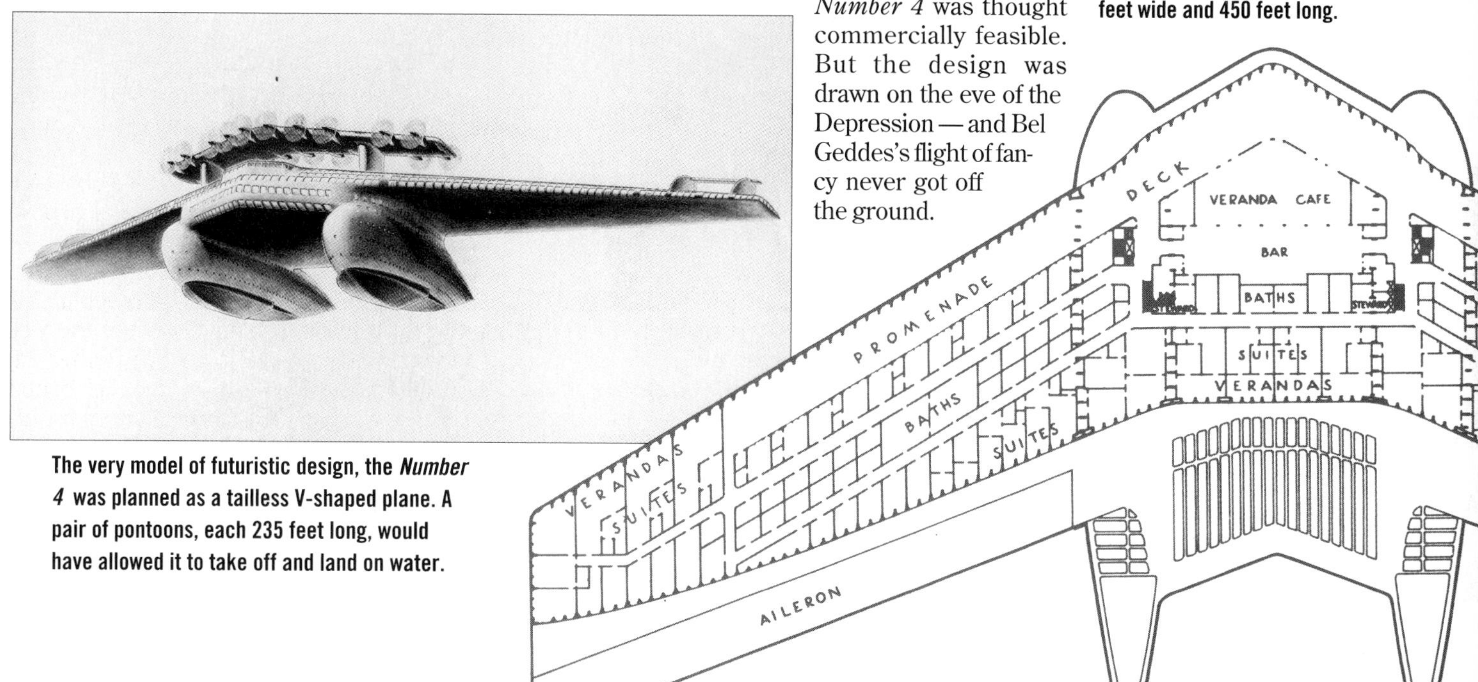

The very model of futuristic design, the *Number 4* was planned as a tailless V-shaped plane. A pair of pontoons, each 235 feet long, would have allowed it to take off and land on water.

NBC
MORT
IMPORTED
SEATS NOW AT BOX OFFICE
THE SCREEN STEPS ON A MINEFIELD!
HUGH O'BRIAN
MICKEY ROONEY
JAMES MITCHUM
"AMBUSH BAY"
RENT
VICTORIA
SIZZLES!
IN
CAT ON A HOT TIN ROOF
AND
"BUTTERFIELD 8
WHISKY
HOWARD
FORUM
American Dream

Chapter 11

KEEPING IN TOUCH

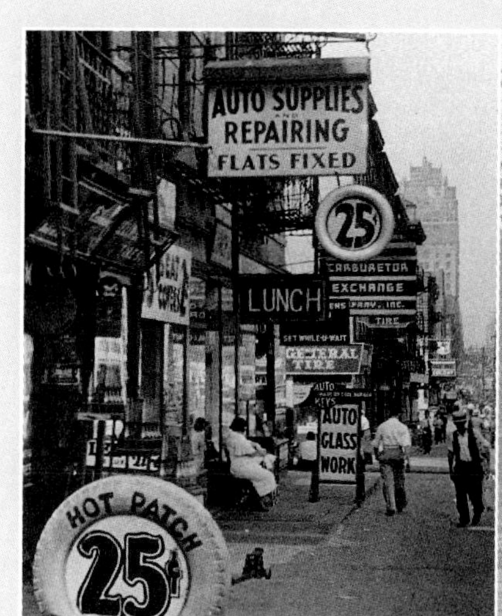

SPREADING THE NEWS

Broadcasting's First Man on the Street

The clanging of a handbell and the cry of "Oyez, oyez, oyez" ("Hear ye, hear ye, hear ye") were welcome sounds in many Colonial towns, for they signaled the arrival of the day's news. In an era when newspapers were rarities and few people owned clocks, citizens relied on the town crier to shout out both the latest news and the hour.

Making his rounds by day and by night, the crier was entrusted with notices of town meetings, weddings, and auctions. He was the one who told of delays in the departures of sailing ships and gave descriptions of lost children. In Salem it was the crier who called residents to the execution of a witch, and in Boston the crier spread the news of Paul Revere's ride.

In Massachusetts the law guaranteed criers a payment of two pence for each notice they aired. But there as elsewhere criers served as more than a news service. They also were expected to slip in reminders of civic duties — keeping livestock fenced in, for example. And the crier was de facto town watchman. As long as his bell kept ringing, people knew that all was well. But if he should sound a wooden rattle, that was all people needed to come rushing out in alarm to fight a fire, perhaps, or rally for revolution.

The role of town crier was one that colonists brought with them from England. The job called for a man of sober temperament — and a big voice.

Ringing Out the Message Loud and Clear

The peal of the town crier's handbell was but one of many jinglings, dings, and dongs that filled the air before there were such things as traffic lights, sirens, and car horns. In towns large and small all across America, bells were the medium for messages of many sorts.

Bells bedecked wagons, sleighs, and streetcars to warn of their approach. Locomotives likewise were equipped with bells — not only for cautioning those ahead to get away from the track, but also to inform ticketholders that the train was pulling in. On the farm the clang of an iron bell summoned the family to dinner. Country folk also tied bells of different tones on everything from cattle to turkeys so that they could identify their livestock by sound alone.

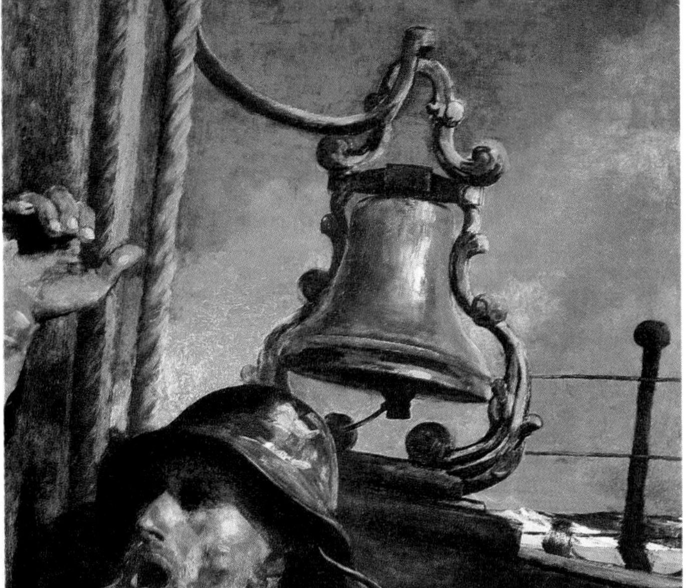

When the circus came to town, the parade might feature a wagon-mounted carillon that clanged out hymns and popular tunes, and children would come running to the bells of popcorn and ice cream vendors. Other bells on the street told of the arrival of the milkman, the cracker seller, the vegetable vendor, and the peddler with his wagonload of goods. Homes of the well-to-do were equipped with wires, bells, and pulls that were used to summon servants. And most every factory had a bell that rang at 5:00 A.M. to waken workers and again at 7:00 to call them to work.

Each town had a bell that rang to announce fires, pealing in codes that sent firefighters to the right neighborhoods. And church bells were rung not only for Sunday meeting but for births and funerals, weddings and holidays. According to one authority, the bell ringer should be able to sound the same instrument "joyously, solemnly, alarmingly or informingly" by his handling of the rope alone.

Even children and their toys (above left) contributed to the clamor of bells in the 19th century. Bells were very important aboard ships (left), particularly as signals to other ships at night, in fog, or in stormy weather.

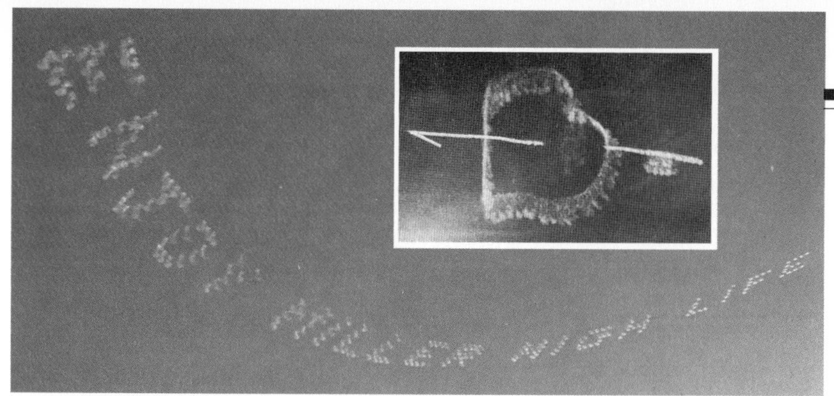

Skywriters typically spell out messages but sometimes try a bit of sky art, such as a heart for an aerial wedding.

Madison Avenue Soars to New Heights

Almost as soon as man learned to fly, advertisers took to the air. Early techniques ranged from hanging signs from surplus military blimps to shouting messages from low-flying aircraft. But it was skywriting — originally developed for military signals by Major John Savage of the Royal Air Force — that really seized the public's imagination. By the time Savage patented his invention in 1923, he had moved to New York, which would become the hub of skywriting. Right on through the 1930's, New York residents received heavenly messages almost daily.

For Savage's system, the pilot pumped a mixture of oil and liquid chemicals into a pair of oversized, red-hot exhaust pipes while flying two or three miles above the earth. This produced a stream of white smoke 40-feet thick that held together for 10 minutes or so. The real key to the technique, though, was the pilot's expertise as he traced the shapes of individual letters in the sky with his small, speedy plane. A single mile-high letter might require as many as 15 miles of flying, and a single dot could be the size of a city block. Trickier still was the fact that the messages were written backward, at least from the pilot's point of view, since he viewed them from above and the public saw them from below. Erasures were impossible and mistakes embarrassing, for they were visible to millions.

But the impact was such that skywriting became a standard feature at everything from airshows to corn-husking contests. In 1949, however, it became possible for airplanes, flying in tandem, to puff smoke from radio-controlled smoke generators. Before long, the new "sky-typists" had all but replaced precision writers in the air.

The Unbreakable Code

When marines captured the Japanese island of Iwo Jima in 1945, the operation was directed entirely in Navajo. In fact, by that point in the war, 420 Navajo marine "code talkers" were stationed in the Pacific, transmitting and translating the only code the Japanese were never able to break.

Interception of radio messages had been fairly common until Philip Johnston, a veteran of World War I, intervened in 1942. The son of missionaries, Johnston had grown up with Navajos in Arizona and was one of the few non-Indians with any proficiency in their dauntingly complex language. Using it to construct a code in which a dive bomber became a "chicken hawk," and a submarine an "iron fish," Johnston presented the idea to the marines and then trained an initial group of 30 Navajo volunteers to use it.

The complexity of Navajo — the meaning of many words changes with intonation and the sounds are very difficult to mimic — made it a perfect vehicle for a verbal code. While Navajos who had been trained as code talkers could translate messages 90 times faster than coding machines, Navajos who had not been trained or were not completely bilingual could not even begin to understand it.

The code was used from 1942 until the end of the war. It remained a secret until 1968, when the code talkers were awarded special medals.

Navajo code talkers Cpl. Henry Bahe, Jr. , and Pfc. George Kirk transmit messages from a jungle via portable radio.

NATIVE TONGUE

TALKING WORDS

Americans have words aplenty for a favorite pastime — talking. If it's dirt we're after, there's always scuttlebutt *(a 19th-century sailors' term for the shipboard water bucket and gathering spot for gossip). Or we can expect to hear it on the grapevine. Short for* grapevine telegraph, *this term has been around since 1859 when news of Nevada's Comstock Lode was passed along on a secretly strung telegraph line.*

Not all of our talking words are native products. Sauce *was a British term, but by the 1830's Americans had turned it into* sass. Spiel *comes from German,* palaver *from Portuguese,* parley *is French,* schmooze *Yiddish — and* blarney, *of course, is Irish.*

Other words, such as chitchat, bibble babble, yackety yak, *and* hem and haw, *have less to do with national origins than with simply mimicking the sounds of human speech.*

Still other words derive from our very capacity to talk and listen. We are likely to get an earful from big mouths and windbags; we talk people's heads off; and we jaw and chew the fat, though not with someone who talks back. We might ask them to shut up, or more politely, suggest they button their lips. But we'll always have the last word.

THE PRINTED WORD

Ben Franklin, Newsman

"To publish a good newspaper," wrote Benjamin Franklin after buying the *Pennsylvania Gazette* in 1729, "is not so easy an undertaking as many people imagine it to be." By then a veteran of his brother's paper, the *New England Courant,* and active in Philadelphia as the "Busy-Body" columnist of the *American Weekly Mercury,* Franklin was only 23 when he took over the *Gazette* and turned it into the most influential paper in the Colonies.

Although self-educated, he was editor, printer, writer, and a tireless innovator all in one, applying his genius to commerce, politics, and society with equal diligence and wit. For the amusement of his readers, Franklin dreamed up a comic cast of correspondents with names like Anthony Afterwit and Alice Addertongue. And he startled his public with outrageous proposals, once suggesting, for instance, that the Colonies thank England for emptying her jails onto their shores by shipping a cargo of rattlesnakes home to the mother isle.

Franklin's view of freedom of the press was no less original. "If all printers were determined not to print anything till they were sure it would offend nobody," he wrote, "there would be very little printed." Yet one of his greatest journalistic innovations appeared in the advertising section. Until his time, ads were little more than jumbles of run-on listings. Franklin carved the lists into single entries (including those for his famous stove) set off with headlines and eye-catching product symbols — a pair of spectacles, for example, called attention to an optician's notice — and by 1750 ads filled six pages of his paper.

Franklin's skill at capturing the public's attention with print was such that it made him rich. At the age of 42 he was able to retire from the *Gazette* and turn his talents to science and politics.

Ben Franklin, as editor, was not above writing — and answering — letters to himself in the pages of his paper.

WHAT·IS·IT

Thought to be America's first political cartoon, this sketch appeared in Benjamin Franklin's Pennsylvania Gazette *on May 9, 1754, and may have been designed by Franklin. It was a call for unity at the onset of the French and Indian War. "The Confidence of the French," wrote Franklin, ". . .seems well-grounded on the present disunited State of the British Colonies."*

James Gordon Bennett, Sr., began his newspaper at a desk made from boards and a barrel. By the time he retired in 1867, the paper had a daily circulation of 90,000.

Lively News From a Plucky Publisher

Good taste was not the secret of the success enjoyed by James Gordon Bennett, Sr. Nor was he inclined to curry favor with the powerful. What made him and his New York *Herald* the talk of their day was calculated sensation — well phrased, irreverent, and irresistible — placed side by side with no-holds-barred reporting. "Five hundred dollars reward," ran a typically titillating *Herald* notice, "will be given to any handsome woman, either lovely widow or simple semptress, who will set a trap for a Presbyterian parson, and catch one of them *flagrante delicto.*"

Starting his own paper at a time when more than a dozen journals were already well established, the Scottish-born Bennett gambled on New Yorkers' appetite for hard news spiked with the shocking. And he won. The first issue of the *Herald* appeared on May 6, 1835, selling for a penny (though in 15 months the price was raised to two cents and circulation was claimed to have reached 40,000). The second issue carried the first money-market coverage ever to appear in a newspaper, and it was followed soon after by stock exchange reports.

Working 16 hours a day at a makeshift desk in a Wall Street basement, Bennett at first was his own reporter, editor, and ad salesman — "one poor man in a cellar against the world." Within three months, however, he was able to hire an old police reporter to help out. When the great New York fire broke out in December 1835, the *Herald* produced the best coverage in the city, including a map of the fire zone and a sketch of the Stock Exchange in flames.

With solvency, Bennett's ambitions really took off, and the daily mix of gore and gossip soon was leavened with reports from the *Herald's* international correspondents. Still, the original spirit of the paper remained — prickly, populist, and beyond easy imitation. "It would be worth . . . a million dollars," said one rival publisher, "if the Devil would come and tell me every evening, as he does Bennett, what the people of New York would like to read about next morning."

The World According to Pulitzer

Signs lined the walls of the New York *World's* city room: ACCURACY. TERSENESS. ACCURACY. And even when the boss was away, he cabled reminders to the paper's staff. "Get the facts," read one long-distance critique. "Bank robber described as short — what is short? Four feet? Five feet? Be exact." Other admonitions spilled regularly from the lips of publisher Joseph Pulitzer, who combined high-mindedness and practicality, with the result that he not only elevated the standards of journalism, but also launched two papers, the New York *World* and the *St. Louis Post-Dispatch,* that became immensely influential.

Born in Hungary, Pulitzer emigrated to America in 1864 as a 17-year-old speaking little English. Though frail and suffering from poor eyesight, by 1878 he had served in the Union Army, done a stint as a reporter for a St. Louis German-language newspaper, and become an American citizen, a lawyer, an alumnus of the Missouri legislature, and a fierce Democrat.

That same year he decided on journalism as a career. Purchasing the bankrupt *St. Louis Dispatch* for $2,500, he merged it with the failing *St. Louis Evening Post* and doubled their circulation with a mix of reformist politics and pulp news. Then, five years later, while en route to Europe, he bought the troubled New York *World* and worked a similar miracle, appealing to workers with a pledge that the *World* would "fight all public evils" in its "battle for the people." Pulitzer also knew how to build circulation by such tricks as offering the first comics page and hiring "girl reporter" Nellie Bly.

Although the *World's* reputation sank during a foray into sensationalism in the 1890's, Pulitzer was able to restore its standards and continued to run the paper until his death in 1911.

A caricature in *Judge* magazine in 1911 pictured Joseph Pulitzer next to a "press muzzle" and proclaimed him the "Champion of Freedom of the Press."

By Pigeon Post and Pony Express

Reporters and publishers literally got their news on the fly in the 19th century. Carrier pigeons like these could wing messages from point to point at speeds approaching 75 mph.

Back in 1811 when the seven-story Exchange Coffee House in Boston was America's tallest building, its second-floor reading room was the nation's news center, too. This was thanks to the manager, Samuel Topliff, Jr., who regularly rowed out to the harbor's mouth to gather information from incoming ships, then entered it in two books he made available to his patrons.

The New York newspapers seized upon this idea, and soon sailors for competing editors were deciding who got the news with bloody brawls. James Gordon Bennett, Sr., who founded the New York *Herald* in 1835, however, beat them all by buying a swift sloop, which he sent racing out to sea. Bennett in turn was scooped by another ingenious Bostonian, Daniel Craig, who boarded ships with a cage full of carrier pigeons that allowed him to wing his news back at up to 75 mph. Loath to be bested, Bennett struck a deal with the newcomer: he bought news from Craig, paying him $500 for each hour the *Herald* got the news ahead of its New York rivals.

When war broke out with Mexico in 1846, Bennett improved on Craig by combining relays of pigeons with a pony express. These couriers were so swift that Bennett often published his reports of the battles before the War Department could release its own version.

The spread of telegraph lines in later decades put an end to pony expresses, and to most pigeon posts — but not all. As late as 1935, 76 pigeons roosted on the roof of the New York *Journal;* its editor found the birds the fastest way to send film and news back to the lab from local events.

Dr. Livingstone, I Presume?

Henry Morton Stanley (below) triumphed over a childhood so bleak it could have been concocted by Charles Dickens. His encounter with Dr. Livingstone (right) inspired his own African explorations, which led to a knighthood.

"I will tell you what you will do," explained James Gordon Bennett, Jr., publisher of the New York *Herald.* "Draw a thousand pounds now, and when you have gone through that, draw another thousand, and when that is spent, draw another thousand . . . and so on; but FIND LIVINGSTONE." Such were the instructions he gave to his young reporter Henry Morton Stanley on an autumn day in Paris. And so began one of the greatest journalistic exploits of all time.

The object of the hunt — Dr. David Livingstone — was a renowned Scottish explorer and missionary who had dropped from sight in 1869 while searching for the headwaters of the Nile. The hunter was a Welsh orphan and "workhouse brat" who ended up in the United States after running away to sea. Stanley began his career in journalism by sending letters to newspapers about his experiences in the Civil War — he had fought on both sides. He later won his position at the *Herald* by paying his own way to modern Ethiopia to join a British military expedition, then reporting its success two days before the news reached even Queen Victoria.

Stanley began his search for Livingstone in 1871. At Zanzibar he assembled an entourage of nearly 200 bearers and guards and began his

Around the World in Record Time

"What Girls Are Good For" ran a headline in the Pittsburgh *Dispatch* on January 14, 1885. And such was the condescending tone of the article below it that teenage Elizabeth Cochrane shot off a letter demanding equal pay for equal work. Apparently impressed, the editor printed her note, sent her $5, and offered her a job. Under the pen name Nellie Bly (a character in a Stephen Foster song), the high-minded girl soon was writing exposés of the exploitation of women who worked in local factories.

Circulation soared, but advertisers complained. So when Bly found herself relegated to the society pages, she promptly left for Mexico. She spent six months there, writing about official corruption until the government asked her to leave. Unbowed, she went to New York and began writing for Joseph Pulitzer's *World.* Sweatshops, bribery in the state legislature, corruption in city hospitals, "mashers" in Central Park, and marriage brokers all felt the sting of Bly's pen.

In 1889 she took a busman's holiday and beat the imaginary 80-day round-the-world travel time of the fictional Phileas Fogg. Her editor had said he'd prefer to assign that story to a man, but by threatening to go to a rival paper, Bly won his support. Off she went, riding steamships, trains, burros, sampans, and rickshaws, to arrive back in just 72 days, 6 hours, and 11 minutes. Now one of the most famous journalists in the country, Bly got her own bylined column in the *World.*

Her marriage to a Brooklyn industrialist in 1895 sidelined her career, but she came back on the beat in 1919 and wrote a column for *The New York Evening Journal* until the time of her death in 1922. Her campaign for equality had been so successful that her obituary described her not as a woman reporter, but simply as "America's best reporter."

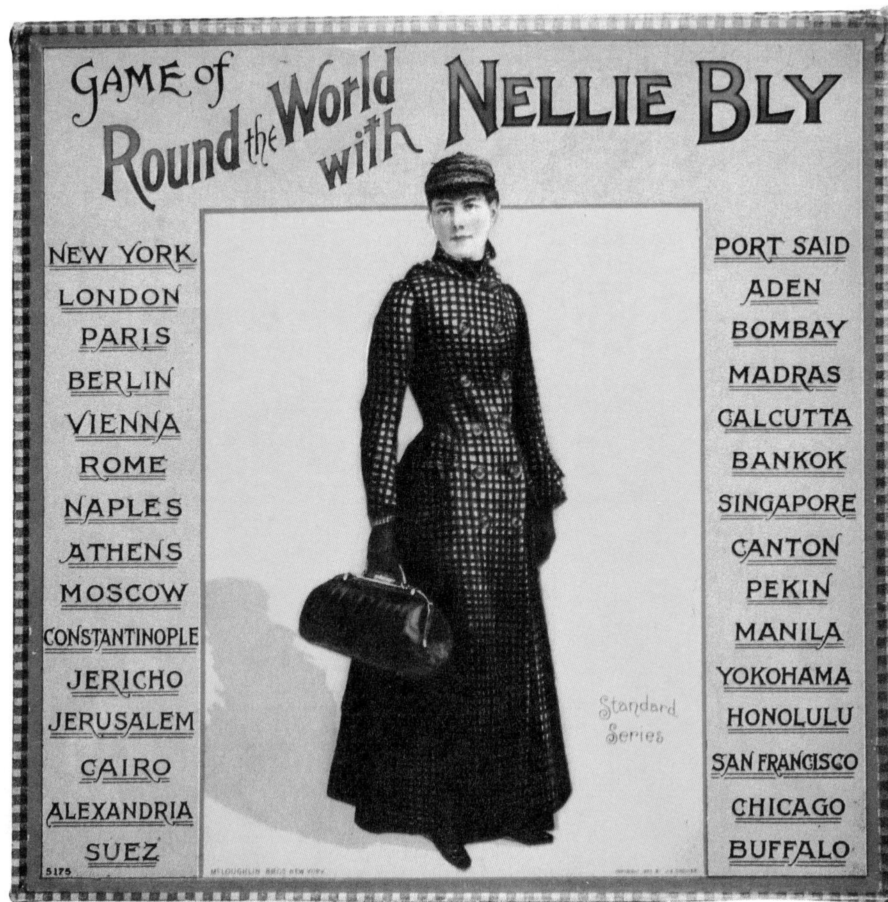

Truth proved stranger than fiction when journalist Nellie Bly handily beat the speed record Jules Verne described in his novel, *Around the World in Eighty Days.* Bly's picture appeared on the box of a commemorative board game that allowed armchair travelers to mimic her famous exploit.

march into territory that a previous British expedition failed to penetrate. Over the next eight months he coped with mass desertions, mutiny, smallpox, elephantiasis, hostile terrain, and an attack by a local tribe. But Stanley persisted, and on November 10 he found Livingstone on the shores of Lake Tanganyika. Though the misplaced missionary declined rescue, he did write a gracious letter of thanks to the *Herald.*

Britain's fury at Stanley's coup was predictable — many there refused to accept Livingstone's letter as genuine until it was authenticated by his son. But Bennett's reaction was surprising: the egotistical publisher was enraged by the adulation given to his employee. Still, in 1874 the *Herald* joined the British *Daily Telegraph* in sponsoring Stanley's search for the source of the Nile.

Sanguine about his relationship with his mercurial sponsor, Stanley on a subsequent trip to what he had dubbed the "Dark Continent" named a section of water between a "furious cataract" and a "dangerous rapid" for James Gordon Bennett, Jr.

The Wit and Wisdom of Mr. Dooley

A creation more famous than its creator, Mr. Dooley saw his witty commentary published not only in newspapers but in several books as well.

A fanatic is a man that does what he thinks th' Lord wud do if He knew th' facts iv th' case." Such was the sort of remark readers came to expect from saloon keeper Martin Dooley, the comic creation of Chicago newspaperman Finley Peter Dunne. Of Irish parentage himself, Dunne invented his thickly brogued barman-philosopher for a Chicago paper in 1893 as a means of commenting on political events of the day. The fictional Mr. Dooley could get away with saying far more than any mortal could—and no subject was sacred. On one occasion he suggested that a hero's triumphal arch be built of bricks, "so th' people will have somethin' convenient to throw at him as he passes through."

Mr. Dooley's observations, delivered to his friend Hennessy — or Hinnissy, as Dooley had it — skewered Republicans and Democrats with equal zest. Reformers were compared to "a man that expicts to thrain lobsters to fly in a year." Judges fared no better in Mr. Dooley's estimation. "Ye take a lively lawyer that's wurruked twinty hours a day suin' sthreet railroad comp'nies an' boost him ont a high coort an' he can't think out iv a hammock." As for vice presidents, the saloon keeper was skeptical indeed. "Th' vice-prisidincy . . . isn't a crime exactly. Ye can't be sint to jail f'r it, but it's kind iv a disgrace. It's like writin' anonymous letters."

Mr. Dooley's opinions at first were focused on issues of concern to Chicagoans. But with the onset of the Spanish-American War in 1898, he began to address national concerns as well and soon won fame from coast to coast. Dunne moved to New York in the early 1900's and continued his Dooley columns for another 15 years. Throughout that time his scorn for the rich and powerful was counterpoint to his empathy for the poor, particularly for the women and "chilhern" whom he considered the greatest victims of society's ills.

He Snooped to Conquer

Brash, egotistical, and a consummate gossip, Walter Winchell was the country's best-known journalist between 1930 and 1950. Some 7 million people read his syndicated column "On Broadway," which appeared in the New York *Daily Mirror*. Twenty million more tuned in to his radio program on Sundays in time to hear his famous opening, greeting "Mr. and Mrs. America — and all the ships at sea."

Born in New York City in 1897, Winchell left school for vaudeville at 13, and spent several years touring the Midwest as a second-rate hoofer. Compiling an amateur gossip sheet in his spare time, he finally found his calling in 1922 when the editor of *Vaudeville News* hired him as a writer. Winchell joined the staff of the *Evening Graphic* in 1924 and rose by stages to become a theater critic and columnist, then moved to the *Daily Mirror* in 1929.

One of Winchell's early gossip columns, "Broadway Hearsay" (right), debuted in the first issue of the *New York Evening Graphic* in September 1924. The commentator's Sunday-night radio show (top right) was a trifle tamer than his columns.

His tireless pursuit of New York gossip became legendary. With the permission of the police, he sped through New York's streets in a car equipped with a radio receiver, a flashing red light, and a siren (sometimes beating police and firefighters to the scene). Although he disliked celebrities, he kept a table at the fashionable Stork Club, where he held court in the evening and dug up the latest dirt on starlets, bubble dancers, G-men, and what he called "debutramps."

But if the gossip was hot, it was the columnist's way with words, known as Winchellese, that was his true trademark. His pithy remarks were salted with terms of his own invention. Couples did not marry, they "middle-aisled it" or got "welded." If expecting a child, they were "storked," and if the marriage failed, they might be "Reno-vated."

During the 1930's and 1940's, Winchell's renown was such that a favorable mention in one of his columns could make a book a best-seller or turn a movie into a box-office hit. His prominence also brought him into contact with the underworld: gangsters wooed him, mobs provided him with free bodyguards, and one hit man actually used Winchell as his intermediary when surrendering to the FBI.

As the years passed, however, Winchell's political commentary grew ever more strident. An ardent anti-Communist and champion of the McCarthy investigations, he devoted more and more of his column space to feuds and vendettas. Broadway, meanwhile, was losing its glitter, and by the 1960's Winchell's star had faded. As one observer noted, "You can't be the historian of something that no longer exists."

Robert Ripley's Quest for the Curious

A man with two pupils in each eye, a human unicorn, and a genuine one-armed paper-hanger — these were but a few of the astonishing discoveries that earned Robert L. Ripley the title of the Modern Marco Polo. For 30 years, to the delight of millions, his "Believe It or Not" newspaper feature offered a peek at the world's most bizarre people, objects, and events.

It was as a young sports cartoonist for the New York *Globe* in 1918 that Ripley stumbled onto his unique career. Stumped for material one day, he decided to illustrate a collection of unusual sports records — the fastest backward 100-yard dash (14 seconds), for instance, and the longest rope-jumping session (11,810 jumps). Then, musing over a headline, he tried and discarded "Champs and Chumps" before settling on the title that would make him famous.

"Believe It or Not" was an instant success. Appearing once a week and later daily in the *Globe,* it was expanded to include all sorts of curiosities that Ripley uncovered, often on his own treks to some 200 countries. BION, as the series came to be known, brought Ripley to the attention of William Randolph Hearst, who syndicated the feature in 1929. With that, Ripley's salary jumped to $100,000 a year, 10 times his previous earnings. And that was just the beginning.

In time, "Believe It or Not" was picked up by 300 newspapers worldwide and read by 80 million people in 17 languages. Ripley retained several people to scour the globe for subject matter, and used 66 employees to verify the odd facts and answer correspondence. That alone was no mean feat since Ripley received an average of 8,000 letters a day. With the passing years, books, films, vaudeville appearances, and museums called Odditoriums extended BION's reach. Beginning in 1930, Ripley also brought "Believe It or Not" to the airwaves. One particularly notable broadcast was made from the bottom of the Grand Canyon, another from the North Pole.

Ripley's stories could not always be verified, but that did not seem to matter. His feature was a success, said one associate, because it satisfied the "urge to flee . . . into the realm of the incredible."

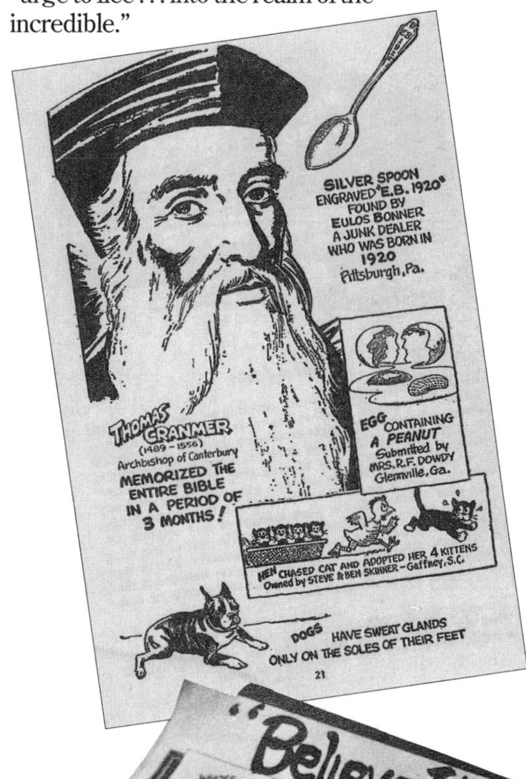

Sitting at his desk (below), Ripley produced his feature every day for 30 years. On his travels he often posed for photographs with his subjects, such as the New Guinea head hunter (above). But Ripley also picked up a few curious habits of his own: he refused to dial any telephone, kept a side-wheeler and a Chinese junk as pleasure boats, and bought expensive cars — but was afraid to drive them.

The Kid All America Took a Shine To

He appeared in 1895 in a cartoon known as "Hogan's Alley" — a funny-looking kid in a nightshirt, just one among a gang of street urchins. But the public warmed to him above all others in the crowd, dubbed him the Yellow Kid because of his shirt, and clamored for more. In no time at all the jug-eared, goofily grinning tyke became a star.

A creation of artist Richard Outcault, the character endeared himself to readers week after week in Pulitzer's New York *World.* The cartoons invariably portrayed slapstick scenes set in the back alleys and slums of New York, where the Kid, looking like a loony cherub, commented on everything by means of saucy, street-slang wisecracks written on the front of his shirt.

It did not take long for other publishers to figure out that cartoons as popular as this one sold newspapers — and lots of them. They battled one another by offering ever bigger, more colorful comics sections — and sometimes luring away the competition's talent. By 1896 Outcault was creating "Yellow Kid" comic strips for Hearst's New York *Journal,* where the character and his antics drew chortles from an even wider public.

Outcault, meanwhile, was no slouch at managing the career of his fictional star. The Yellow Kid appeared on lapel buttons, cigarette packs, games, comic books, and as toy statuettes. The artist took merchandising even farther after he dropped the Kid in 1898 and came up with a new cartoon character — Buster Brown — who made the artist wealthy through his influence on fashion.

The Yellow Kid's face was everywhere in the late 1890's. This advertisment for newsboys copied the slangy style typical of the Kid's comic strip.

Simple Problems — Silly Solutions

America's love affair with gadgetry has given rise to some remarkable inventions. None, though, can ever compare to the jury-rigged contraptions immortalized in the cartoons of Rube Goldberg, a onetime mechanical engineer. Goldberg's zany ingenuity was such that his name has long since been synonymous with any device that turns a simple job into something ridiculously complex.

Attributing his contrivances to a Professor Lucifer Gorgonzola Butts, Goldberg published the first of them — an automatic weight-reducing machine — in 1914. This improbable device employed a falling doughnut, a bomb, a bursting balloon, a hot stove, and a giant bell-shaped cage to trim excess pounds from an overweight man. Appearing in the New York *Evening Mail,* the cartoon was followed by scores of other madcap inventions for everything from turning sheet music to opening eggshells and emptying ashtrays.

Within 35 years, Goldberg created some 60 comic series. One of them, "Foolish Questions," debuted with a cartoon of a man who fell from a 50th-floor window. "Have an accident?" asked a passerby. "No thanks. I just had one," the man replied. Readers loved it so much that hundreds wrote in with foolish questions of their own.

Another Goldberg hit was a guy named Boob McNutt, the quintessential numbskull and lovable loser. Years after Goldberg retired the character, he was blamed for sabotaging the 1940 presidential bid of onetime Indiana Governor Paul V. McNutt. "People just won't take a chance on a fellow named McNutt," the also-ran lamented, "because he might turn out to be a Boob."

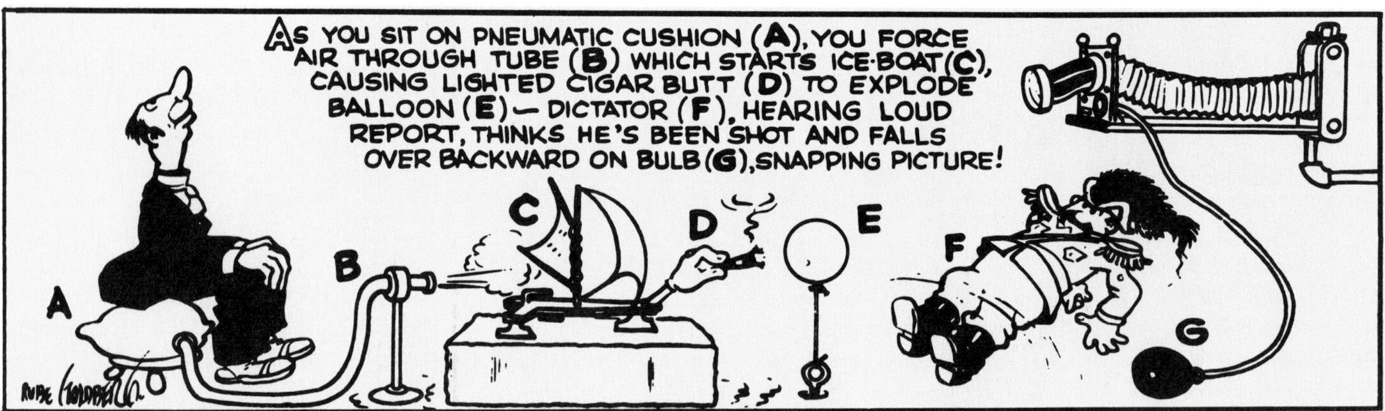

Rube Goldberg, known as the "Dean" of cartoonists, demonstrated the hard way to shoot a self-portrait with one of his typically loony inventions.

I HAVE AN ANNOUNCEMENT TO MAKE
THE HOTEL WANTS ME TO REMIND YOU THAT THE CUSTARD PIES BEING SERVED ARE FOR EATING.
CHEE I'M TIRED
FOO
COMIC CHARACTERS CONVENTION
5-3

Comic Cavalcade

A newspaper war in the 1890's spurred the growth of the comics page. The funnies, it seemed, attracted readers who loved the outlet for a quick escape and a chuckle and in turn became devoted fans (and buyers). Publishers such as Pulitzer and Hearst devoted money and space to daily strips and to Sunday supplements with the added lure of color. In 1935, at the height of comic-strip popularity, Hearst offered a special 32-page weekend section.

Readers always had— and still have — their favorites. They empathized with the homey humor of the ever-battling couple Jiggs and Maggie in "Bringing Up Father," and with the characters that appeared to age along with their fans in "Gasoline Alley." For those who fancied something with a bit more zip and zap, there were adventure-packed strips such as "Flash Gordon" and "Dick Tracy." Other strips proved harder to place. "Krazy Kat," a Hearst favorite featuring a dueling cat and mouse, did not do well on the comics page. But the publisher liked it so much that he tried it in the art and drama sections, where it won fame and the devotion of thousands, including Woodrow Wilson and poet e.e. cummings.

Most of the funnies made their point through slapstick humor, but some strips had a serious side. "Little Orphan Annie," for one, decried communism and the New Deal, and fans loved it. Editors at the Chicago *Tribune* realized that when they skipped the strip for one day and found their office flooded with complaints. A front-page apology ran the next day.

Where but on the comics page could freeloaders, hillbillies, babies, and possums all come together (above) — and to the delight of so many?

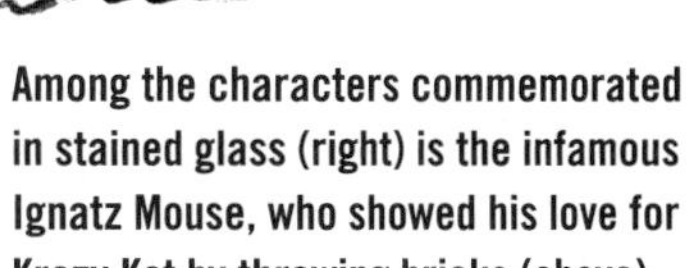

Among the characters commemorated in stained glass (right) is the infamous Ignatz Mouse, who showed his love for Krazy Kat by throwing bricks (above).

MY WIFE'S GONE TO THE COUNTRY, HOORAY, HOOOORAY
MUTT, I BROKE A PERFECTLY GOOD DATE TO COME HERE TO KEEP YOU COMPANY SO CUT OUT THE COMEDY AND GET THE CARDS.

Some of the funnies' most unforgettable faces include (from far left): Barney Google, who debuted in 1916 and was usually seen with his horse Spark Plug. Jiggs of "Bringing Up Father" was created in 1913, the perpetually spike-haired Nancy in 1940, and Felix the Cat in 1923. Betty Boop, of course, has remained ageless since she first appeared in 1931.

WHAT WAS THAT?! DID YA HEAR IT? HEAR IT NOW?
!
!
!

Mutt and Jeff (center) have been around since the 1900's, Dick Tracy (above) since 1936, and Popeye (right) appeared in 1929.

Sarah Had a Little Lamb

Though few people can recite more than the first stanza of "Mary's Lamb," the 24-line poem that begins "Mary had a little lamb," its words have been intoned by tots since it first appeared in print in 1830. The poem was the work of Sarah Josepha Hale, a 42-year-old writer and editor, who composed it as a favor to a friend intending to set the words to music.

A widow with five children, Hale would become nationally known as the editor of Godey's Lady's Book. *"Mary's Lamb," meanwhile, achieved fame of its own. It was printed on silk handkerchiefs and included in* McGuffey's First Eclectic Reader; *the first line was recorded by Thomas Edison on his brand-new invention the phonograph; and Currier and Ives published a print of Mary and her lamb.*

But while every child might have memorized "Mary's Lamb," few ever knew who wrote it. And so Hale late in life had to ward off several people who claimed they were the author, as well as at least three Marys who swore they were the model for Hale's sheep-loving lass.

Leslie had lost none of her charms when she posed for this photo at the age of 62. Throughout her career her fame as a fashion setter rivaled her renown as a publisher.

The Empress of Journalism

A unique phenomenon in her time, Miriam Leslie was at once among the most scandalous women of the Victorian era and one of the most respected.

The $1 million she left to the women's suffrage movement was nothing if not generous. But Mrs. Frank Leslie also left an even greater legacy: an indelible image of female competence and independence.

Born Miriam Folline in New Orleans in 1836, she was groomed for adventure by an erratic, ne'er-do-well father who inspired his strikingly beautiful daughter to master French, Italian, and German. Married for the first time at 17, by 21 she was divorced, had been on a stage tour with Lola Montez, and had landed husband number two: the eccentric Ephraim Squier, a railroad president and archaeologist 16 years her senior.

It was on Squier's arm, at Abraham Lincoln's inaugural ball in 1861, that publisher Frank Leslie first spotted Miriam in a low-cut satin gown. He and the Squiers soon were scandalously intertwined. Ephraim was made editor of *Frank Leslie's Illustrated Newspaper*. Miriam became the editor of his *Lady's Magazine* and, later, two other publications. Frank, meanwhile, moved into the Squiers' home.

Highly publicized his and hers divorces permitted Frank and Miriam to tie the knot in 1873. But their legitimate bliss lasted only until 1880, when Frank died and his widow discovered his empire was bankrupt. Legally changing her name to Frank Leslie to retain control, Miriam put her diamonds up for collateral, borrowed $50,000, and carried on. She halved the company's publications while making a huge financial success of the *Illustrated Newspaper* and *Frank Leslie's Popular Monthly*. Reigning for another 15 years as the Empress of Journalism, she earned up to $100,000 a year while meeting a weekly payroll of $32,000 and running New York's liveliest salon. If, until her death in 1914, people shook their heads when they spoke of her, no one could deny that she had lived life to the fullest.

Shocking Pink

It was lurid, lewd, and literally colored pink. But most of all, under the early editorship of Belfast-born Richard Kyle Fox, *The National Police Gazette* was read by thousands. It offered something for everyone, from the lively "Noose Notes" to "Crimes of the Clergy." No murder was too gruesome, no sex scandal too outrageous for the barroom and barbershop crowds who fought over each new issue. "Be interesting and be quick about it" was Fox's editorial credo, and what his poorly paid (but well-watered) writers

THE NATIONAL POLICE GAZETTE
THE LEADING ILLUSTRATED SPORTING JOURNAL IN AMERICA.
NEW YORK, SATURDAY, JULY 23, 1887.
SHE TOOK HER COCKTAIL LIKE A LITTLE MAN.

The *Gazette* was never without shock value. On this issue's cover a Mexican heiress is about to down a drink.

could not conjure up with words was driven home with illustrations that left little to the imagination.

Over time, Fox began to lard his mix of spicy vice with ever fatter morsels of theater and sporting news (the *Gazette* was the first paper with a sports page). He promoted high-stakes boxing matches as well as a long list of bit-part actresses dubbed "Favorites of the Footlights." Yet while the writing in the paper grew less boisterous and sensational during Fox's 45-year tenure, on the front page nothing would do but bared ankles, arrests, and axe murders.

FELL FROM GRACE—SHINING LIGHTS OF THE MARLBORO (MASS.) REFORM CLUB CAUGHT HEN-STEALING AND CIDER DRINKING.

LASHED HER TRADUCER.

The illustrations in the *Gazette* sometimes were the best part of the paper. Women wrestlers were favorites, but a scene like that of Miss Mary Castner "cowhiding" her cousin (left) would do in a pinch. Pictures of scoundrels caught in the act (far left) also were sure to boost circulation.

The Midas of Magazines

Cyrus Curtis knew early on what he wanted. At age 13 he had his own two-cent weekly newspaper (circulation 400) in his home town of Portland, Maine. And when he was 22 and living in Boston in 1872, he started his first magazine, the *People's Ledger*.

Even then, Curtis sensed that a publisher, if he hoped for success, had to offer something unique. In the *Ledger* that special something was a short story in every issue. Then, after moving to Philadelphia and starting the *Tribune and Farmer* in 1879, he invited his wife, Louisa, to edit the "women's page." It was an immediate hit, so popular in fact that in 1883 Curtis turned the page into a separate supplement that came to be known as *The Ladies' Home Journal*. Within a year its circulation climbed to 25,000.

Curtis was wise enough to realize that his talents lay in the business end of publishing, and he forever left the job of editing to those who did it best. By the time Louisa turned the *Journal*'s editorship over to her future son-in-law, Edward Bok, in 1889, circulation had topped 400,000. Bok added new features and attracted attention by putting a different illustration on the cover every month. Curtis, meanwhile, revolutionized the magazine industry by building up advertising, offering subscription deals, and paying the highest prices anywhere for stories by some of the world's best writers. As a result, the *Journal* in 1903 became the first American magazine to reach a circulation of 1 million.

But Curtis's success story did not stop there. In 1897, he purchased a failing magazine called the *Saturday Evening Post* for $1,000. Putting an imaginative editor, George Lorimer, in charge, he spent millions revamping it and ended up with one of the best-loved, most widely read magazines ever produced. To many it seemed that Curtis had the Midas touch — which was not much of an exaggeration. By the time of his death in 1933, he was able to give away millions of dollars to hospitals, schools, and music organizations.

The Ladies' Home Journal offered just the right mix to make its mark — advice columns such as "Heart to Heart Talks," decorating tips, needlework patterns, great fiction (including pieces by Kipling and Mark Twain), and of course, plenty of romance.

Even his friends called Ned Buntline (above) "the great rascal." The author of hundreds of dime novels (right), Buntline was also a political activist and is credited with giving the jingoistic American party its common name: the Know-Nothing party.

Ten Cents a Tale: Ned Buntline's Dime Novels

He was a bigamist, a bounty hunter, and a convict, and he earned a dishonorable discharge from the Union Army. But under the pen name Ned Buntline, Edward Z. C. Judson created a pantheon of right-minded native heroes, from "Buffalo Bill" Cody to "Wild Bill" Hickok — and in the process helped invent the dime novel.

Judson learned of buntlines — ropes used to restrain the sails on square-riggers — when he ran away to sea at age 11 and became a cabin boy. He later joined the navy, rising to the rank of midshipman before quitting to start a magazine. When it and another publication failed, Buntline decamped — leaving a debt for his partner to pay. Setting off to hunt criminals in Kentucky, he used his reward money to start a successful magazine in Nashville, Tennessee — yet abandoned it after a scandal erupted because of his involvement with another man's wife. In the fight that ensued, he shot the husband. After the dead man's cronies organized a lynching, however, Buntline's noose was cut and he lived to tell the tale.

Ned's genius blossomed on a trip west in 1869 when he met a young Indian scout named William Cody. By inventing a series of exploits and packaging them in pocket-size paperbacks that sold for just a dime, Buntline turned Cody into a national hero — and himself into America's best-paid author.

Working at lightning speed ("I once wrote a book of six hundred and ten pages in sixty-two hours," he bragged to an interviewer), Buntline cranked out more than 400 novels. His philosophy of writing was direct and to the point: "If a book does not suit me when I have finished it, I simply throw it in the fire and begin again."

Critics hated his hodgepodge of clichés, violence, and piety. But readers, especially boys, loved them. Buntline earned enough money to support his concurrent and consecutive wives in style, and to indulge a favorite sideline — delivering temperance lectures while he was drunk.

The Reluctant Wizard

"When I was young I longed to write a great novel," L. Frank Baum wrote to his sister in a copy of his first book, *Mother Goose in Prose.* And then he added, "but to please a child is a sweet and lovely thing that warms one's heart and brings its own reward."

Already in his forties when he began writing for children in 1897, Baum, the son of a well-to-do oilman, had enjoyed modest, if short-lived, successes as an actor, playwright, producer, and chicken breeder. But he had also endured spectacular failures in successive stints as traveling salesman, purveyor of dry goods, and newspaper editor. Yielding to his mother-in-law's persistent prodding, he began to write down some of the stories that he'd been telling his four sons. Whimsical and vivid, one in particular about an emerald city would determine the course of Baum's life.

Published in 1900 as *The Wonderful Wizard of Oz,* the book was a true original: the first fairy tale with an American heroine, setting, and theme. Children responded with electric enthusiasm: within two weeks the first printing of 10,000 had sold out. Baum responded by penning five more Oz stories, then tired of the task and brought the

In *The Wonderful Wizard of Oz* (opposite), Dorothy's Kansas gumption formed a perfect foil for the foibles of her cherished companions (above).

series to a halt. His fans were heartbroken, but Baum held firm until 1911, when bankruptcy forced his hand. He reluctantly took up his pen again and made eight more trips to Oz. Carefully managed by his wife, Maud, the family fortunes rebounded. The Baums built a house in California, called Ozcot, and children from across the country came to sit at the feet of the Royal Historian of Oz and listen to his tales of their favorite land.

Then in May 1919 Baum suffered a stroke and died. In *The Emerald City of Oz,* he had closed off access to his fabled metropolis with a Deadly Desert. As he lay dying, Baum regained consciousness long enough to speak his last words to Maud: "Now we can cross the Shifting Sands." The Cowardly Lion, the Tin Man, and the rest of his creations, it seemed, had got Frank Baum for keeps.

Adventure Syndicate

The Rover Boys, Nancy Drew, the Bobbsey Twins, and Tom Swift all sprang full-blown from the mind — and writing factory — of one man.

What Henry Ford did for the automobile, Edward Stratemeyer did for the adventure story. And in the guise of Tom Swift, the Hardy boys, and a long line of other characters, the prim, bespectacled writer from New Jersey won the hearts of American boys and girls.

The son of a 'Forty-Niner, Stratemeyer grew up with tales of derring-do in the California gold fields. But the reality of his life was an education that ended at eighth grade and a job clerking in his brother's tobacco shop. Then in an idle moment one day in 1888, he started scribbling a story on a piece of brown wrapping paper. A boy's magazine bought the odd manuscript, paying the author $75 — six weeks' wages as a clerk — and Stratemeyer was off on an adventure as dazzling as any he could have imagined for his readers.

For the next few years Stratemeyer made a modest living by supplying stories and serials to magazines, including a brief stint of ghostwriting as Horatio Alger after that prolific author's death. Then he struck his own mother lode with the discovery that, by toning down the violence in dime novels and binding them in hard cover, he could gain parental approval for these books, which were teenagers' favorites. Best of all, the price per volume could be increased to 50 cents. His Rover Boys series, begun in 1899, alone sold 5 million copies by the time it ran its 30-volume course.

Edward Stratemeyer's business sense was as keen as his skill at storytelling. Under a variety of pseudonyms, he and his stable of hacks turned out hundreds of books for young teens that featured the adventures of clever, resourceful, upwardly mobile adolescent heroes and their breezily cheerful families.

One series bred another, and even Stratemeyer, who could write a book a week, found himself unable to keep up with the never-ending demand. So in 1906 he organized the Stratemeyer Syndicate. Assigning a pen name to each series, he supplied plot outlines and character descriptions to various hacks who wrote the texts for one time fees of anywhere from $50 to $250. To preserve the illusion of genuine authorship, Stratemeyer swore all his writers to secrecy and scheduled his meetings so that no two of them ever chanced upon each other in his waiting room.

A librarian for the Boy Scouts of America denounced the books, but a 1926 survey found that 98 percent of the children polled cited a Stratemeyer title as their favorite book. By the time he died four years later, Stratemeyer had completed 150 books of his own and midwifed some 700 others. But his passing was never noticed by his readers, for his daughters stepped in to ensure that the syndicate's prodigious output never faltered.

JUST KIDDING!

Publicity's Prankster

A notice in the *New York Evening Post* in October 1809 was enough to disturb anyone who read it. "DISTRESSING," it began, "Left his lodgings some time since, and has not since been heard of, a small elderly gentleman, dressed in an old black coat and cocked hat, by the name of KNICKERBOCKER." Although a printed response claimed that passengers had seen such a person on the Albany coach, by mid-November the elderly gent's landlord ran a notice of his own. He had found "a very curious kind of written book" among his lodger's things, he said, which he would sell if the delinquent rent was not promptly paid.

With that, all of New York was abuzz with gossip about the missing author. And when Diedrich Knickerbocker's satirical *A History of New York* was published on December 6, it enjoyed instant celebrity. Only later did readers discover that the work's real author was 26-year-old Washington Irving, who had planted the notices as a puckish (and highly successful) publicity stunt.

As this title page of *A History of New York* suggests, the book parodied events in the years of Dutch settlement.

Man-Bats on the Moon!

An illustration of Herschel's man-bats appeared with the stories in the *Sun*. Richard Locke, the real author of the Great Moon Hoax, gained a reputation as a science-fiction writer.

From the very first issue of the New York *Sun* in 1833, readers had come to expect news of a sensational cast. Even so, they could hardly have been prepared for the "Astronomical Discoveries" reported on its pages in 1835. In a series of articles beginning on August 25, *Sun* subscribers were informed that life had been discovered on the moon.

And each new installment of the story proved more amazing than the last. In part one, readers learned that this exciting discovery came from no less an authority than the eminent British astronomer Sir John Herschel. The first day's report dwelt on his remarkable telescope, which was seven times more powerful than any before it. With it, readers were told, Herschel could examine the moon's surface as if he were looking at "terrestrial objects at the distance of one hundred yards" with the "unaided eye."

Best of all were the detailed descriptions of the things that Herschel saw. There were, for instance, at least 38 species of trees, some of which resembled earthly firs and yews, and mountains of solid amethyst. While examining a lunar shoreline through his lens, Herschel "obtained a glimpse of a strange amphibious creature of a spherical form" that rolled along the pebbly beach. In a "delightful" valley he spotted herds of bisonlike creatures whose eyes were shaded by hairy veils. Among the other oddities was a type of single-horned goat of a bluish lead color that "would be classed on earth as a monster," as well as beavers that walked upright, carried their young in their arms, and built dwellings that were heated by fire.

The most astonishing discovery, however, was saved for the fourth article on August 28. While gazing at one of the more remote regions of the moon, Herschel spied humanoid man-bats. Equally adept at flying and walking, they "averaged four feet in height, were covered, except on the face, with short and glossy copper-colored hair, and had wings composed of a thin membrane." Observing the creatures engaged in conversation, Herschel reported, "We hence inferred that they were rational beings . . . capable of producing works of art and contrivance."

By week's end, of course, all of New York was reading the *Sun* and talking about the discoveries. Clergymen sermonized, scientists pondered, and competing dailies did their best to catch up with the late-breaking news. As for the *Sun*'s publisher, Benjamin Day, and his clever new reporter — Richard Adams Locke, who had made up the whole story — they chuckled at having pulled off one of the better newspaper hoaxes of the age. Within a matter of days, the *Sun* had become the most widely read daily in the world. And as for Sir John Herschel? When he found out about the hoax, he magnanimously pronounced the whole thing most amusing.

When Newsreelers Really Made the News

An entry from the diary of a Vitagraph employee dated March 30, 1899, includes a startling bit of information: "Filmed miniature of Windsor Hotel fire with little rubber figures jumping out of windows." Vitagraph was hardly alone in such antics, for in those days awkward equipment and slow travel made news photography all but impossible. Moviemakers, as a result, recreated the news by whatever means they could and hoped no one would notice.

At the turn of the century, Thomas Edison filmed his own version of Africa's Boer War near his home in New Jersey. Similarly, cameraman Edward Amet in 1898 presented what he said was actual footage of a U.S. naval victory off Cuba. In fact the "battle" was fought in Amet's Illinois backyard with the help of a painted backdrop, model ships, and a wave maker. A naval officer later asked how he could have photographed the battle since it occurred at night. "I used moonlight film," Amet lied, "and a six-mile lens."

Disasters also invited creative filming. The Biograph Company, determined to be first with a newsreel of the 1906 San Francisco earthquake and fire, staged a tabletop version. It built a two-piece base of cardboard and clay that could be pulled apart to create a convincing earthquake chasm. On top were miniature hills covered with cardboard houses. When an assistant set the models on fire, the cameraman started rolling. Even the mayor of San Francisco believed the film was the real thing.

When the news involved prominent people, newsreelers often turned to look-alikes. Thus, when Selig Polyscope filmed Teddy Roosevelt's 1909 African hunt in its Chicago studios, it used a retired zoo lion and a toothy actor — then the company simply waited for news that Roosevelt had actually shot a lion before releasing the reel.

Just before the Biograph company's version of the San Francisco earthquake and fire was filmed in 1906, technician F. A. Dobson stood poised to put the fire out.

Lonely at the Top

In 1876 Sgt. John O'Keefe of the U.S. Signal Corps was assigned to a lonely one-man weather station on the summit of Pikes Peak. There he recorded weather conditions and telegraphed the data to towns throughout the region.

In order to amuse himself, the bored bachelor began to enhance his reports with tales of danger and derring-do. The most outrageous told of the time his wife and child were attacked by mountain rats with a "voracious appetite for raw meat." O'Keefe reported that he rescued his wife by wrapping her in zinc roofing material, and she in turn killed off some of the beasts with bolts of electricity from a storage battery. But, alas, they were too late to save their daughter. The rats had left nothing but her "peeled and mumbled skull."

O'Keefe eventually retired from his post. But not before his stories had been picked up as fact by newspapers back East, and he had become something of a folk hero.

In order to make his story convincing, O'Keefe went so far as to dig a grave and erect a marker for his fictional daughter.

ONE PICTURE IS WORTH . . .

The 1835 lithograph *Ruins of the Merchant's Exchange, N.Y.* was an early attempt to illustrate current events. Nathaniel Currier, an enterprising young printer, had the picture in circulation in record time — a mere four days after the fire.

First Impressions: Currier Before Ives

For many people, the names Currier and Ives conjure up a pastel, hand-colored image of a long-gone, idealized America: sentimental scenes of horse-drawn sleighs and skating ponds that probably are prettier and more tranquil than most of what the 19th century actually knew firsthand. But before the famous partnership took off in 1857, Currier toiled alone in his shop in lower Manhattan, creating stirring scenes of spectacle and catastrophe — and coincidentally helping launch the field of pictorial journalism.

After a long apprenticeship in lithography — a late-18th-century printing technique that involved the making of images from inked stones — 22-year-old Nathaniel Currier had started building his own business. When a fire broke out in December 1835 and destroyed much of old New Amsterdam, Currier quickly commissioned a local artist to capture the scene, and four days later the city was eagerly buying prints of his *Ruins of the Merchant's Exchange, N.Y.*

Currier turned disaster into gold again in 1840, when a Boston–New York steamer burned off the coast of Long Island. The New York *Sun* ran a special extra edition with a Currier print — *Awful Conflagration of the Steamboat* Lexington — as the lead illustration. Orders for copies poured in from around the country.

Currier's reading of popular taste, and that of James Ives, who joined the firm in 1852 and became a partner in 1857, remained perfect for another three decades. Whether their tone was shrill or sentimental, the pair continued to crank out prints that an eager public bought with zest.

Spreading the Word

Responsibility for billboard advertising can be laid at the feet — or hurled at the head — of P. T. Barnum. Before the pioneering showman's time, outdoor advertising existed on a modest scale — mainly in the form of posters and miniature boxwood cutouts of performers that were hung outside theaters. But it was the garish paintings that were displayed on Barnum's American Museum in New York to illustrate the exhibitions inside, that opened the Pandora's box. Peering down on potential patrons, a gaudily painted two-by-three-foot visage of the promoter also helped awaken giddy visions in the hearts of all who had something to sell.

Almost overnight, wood engravers began churning out huge plywood silhouettes, lithographers ran off bigger and bolder broadsheets, and a small army of dead-of-night painters dabbed pitchmen's rhymes on miles of public curb before the morning rush hour dawned. No spare surface seemed to be safe from the seller's zeal, no bare patch of nature was left unscathed. Telegraph poles were papered from top to bottom with handbills, and the banks of the Hudson River were lined with billboards that were lit by searchlights from ships that passed at night. Barns loomed before advertisers like vast empty canvases, waiting to be filled — as did the virgin stone of Nevada's canyons. Even the human body was cleverly "sandwiched" and paraded along city streets to promote mustard plasters and all manner of other goods. People wondered where it would all end.

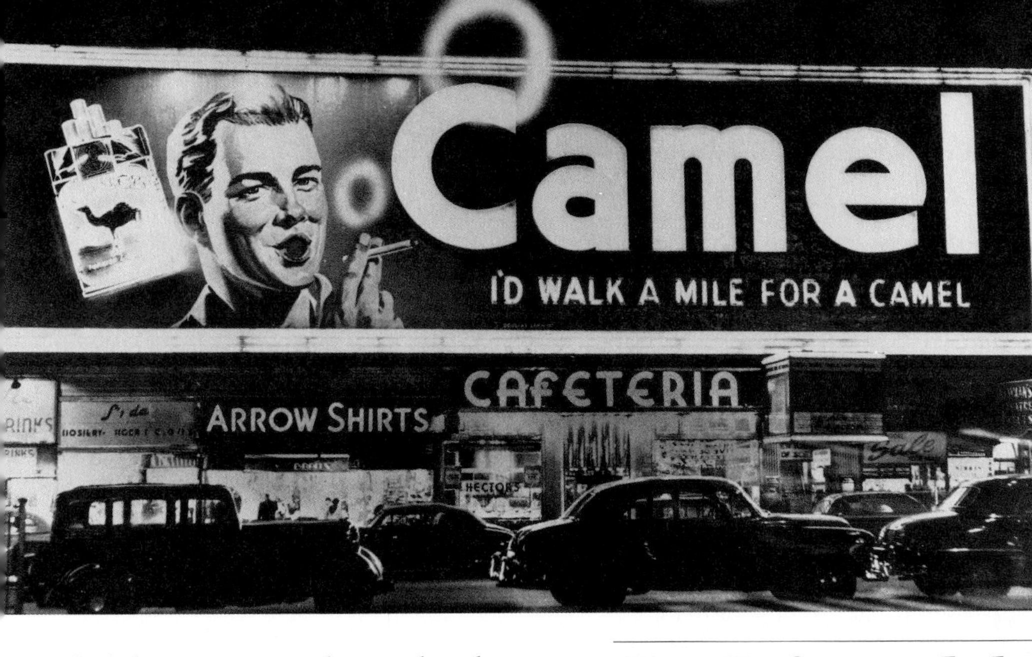

A crown jewel of commercial art, this Camel sign puffed real smoke rings over New York City's bustling Times Square.

And the answer turned out to be, almost nowhere, for with every passing decade the signs grew larger, and more numerous. By the late 1860's an estimated 275 independent billposting and board- and rock-painting firms were at work all across the continent, slathering slogans by day and by night.

But the best was yet to come. In 1891 the first electric billboard was erected — a 50-by-80-foot amusement park advertisement that featured 1,457 lamps twinkling high above Madison Square in New York City. Ever more sophisticated devices soon depicted a chariot race and popping corks overhead as Broadway was transformed into the Great White Way, and the rest of America into a year-round carnival of lights.

In 1869 sign painter J. Josephs turned the full force of his fanciful imagination on his shop in Buffalo, N.Y. (below), covering its every surface with images. Outdoor advertising in the 1930's (left) was more prosaic.

War Paint and the Christy Girl

Howard Chandler Christy's first commission as an illustrator, at the age of 10, was a portrait of a bull rendered in house paint and proudly hung over the door of the buyer's butcher shop. The $10 he earned for the job must have made a big impression on the Ohio farmboy, for Christy deferred developing his talent for landscape painting and portraiture until he'd made his mark in the lucrative field of illustration.

By the time he was 17, in 1890, Christy left home to pursue his career in New York. The illustrations he made for popular journals led to a rift with his painting teacher, who refused to speak to him for years. Undaunted by the slight, Christy jumped at the chance to work as a military artist in the Spanish-American War where he made frontline sketches of Teddy Roosevelt and his Rough Riders.

The vivid, sympathetic pictures he sent from Santiago made him one of the country's most popular military illustrators at the age of 25. Commissions for battle scenes and military portraits rained down on him, and ever the patriot, Christy later painted persuasive recruitment posters for both world wars.

Curiously, it was also a military painting that established his reputation as an authority on female beauty. To relieve the tedium of drawing yet another picture populated entirely by men, he insinuated a lovely young woman — the imagined sweetheart of a homesick soldier — into a sketch. "The Soldier's Dream" was a smash, and the Christy Girl, natural successor to the Gibson Girl, was born.

The artist's wife, Nancy Palmer Christy, was the model for some of Christy's most famous — and successful — recruitment posters. As testament to his eye for beauty, he was the sole judge at the original Miss America contest.

Seals of Approval

They were colorful, eye-catching, inexpensive to produce, and easy to distribute — a perfect advertising medium. And from the 1910's to the 1930's, poster stamps — company giveaways that might be as small as postage stamps but were as appealing as posters — served in just that role.

Small in size, big in impact

Since poster stamps followed in the wake of old-fashioned trade-cards, their miniature size was, perhaps, not so surprising in their day. But as many in the array shown here make clear, what *was* startling about them was their modern look. The printing firms that produced the stamps took great pride in their craft. One St. Paul company made sure its customers knew they were getting "Poster stamps that are real miniature posters, not gummed stickers," and said as much on its own stamp. Advertisers newly awakened to the attention-getting potential of vibrant graphic design tried to outdo each other — in high style. Maxfield Parrish, Edward Penfield, and many other leading illustrators of the day were employed as stamp designers, thus helping make the public more art conscious.

Companies stuck their stamps on business letters, packages, sales receipts — almost everything. And the general public loved the little stick-ons. Throughout the 1920's and 1930's, people assembled collections, sometimes buying the stamps in sheets and pasting them into special albums. Thousands also joined collector's clubs and subscribed to the *Poster Stamp Bulletin*. In time, virtually every kind of organization from sports associations to railroad lines, service industries, and charities advertised through stamps.

The medium stamps out in style

Ultimately, though, interest in the peewee posters faded. The popularity of radio and the growing number of national magazines in the 1930's prompted many companies to spend their advertising dollars elsewhere. It was certainly easier to describe a product in a radio spot or a magazine ad than on a tiny stamp. And the new media could guarantee that a single ad would reach thousands of homes.

EDISON
MAZDA
EDISON DAY
October 21st
35th Anniversary
P-138

1915
$3300
Peerless
C.T. SILVER CO. NEW YORK
WALTON STUDIO N.Y.

After all-there is nothing
like A GOOD BOOK!
Brubaker
CHILDREN'S BOOK WEEK
November 7th to 13th

1930
MICHIGAN
TRAVERSE
CITY
JULY
9-10-11
CHERRY FESTIVAL

INSURE BEFORE IT HAPPENS
ACCIDENT·LIABILITY·COMPENSATION
MINNEAPOLIS INSURANCE AGENCY

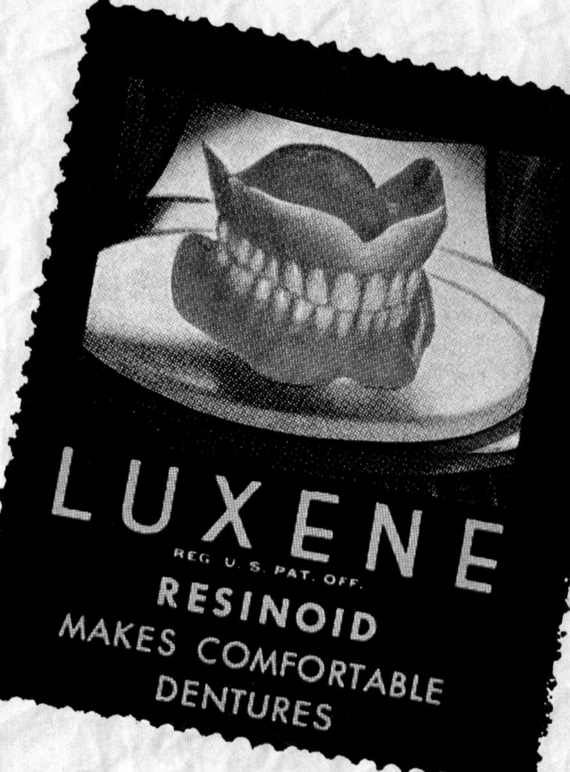
LUXENE
REG. U.S. PAT. OFF.
RESINOID
MAKES COMFORTABLE
DENTURES

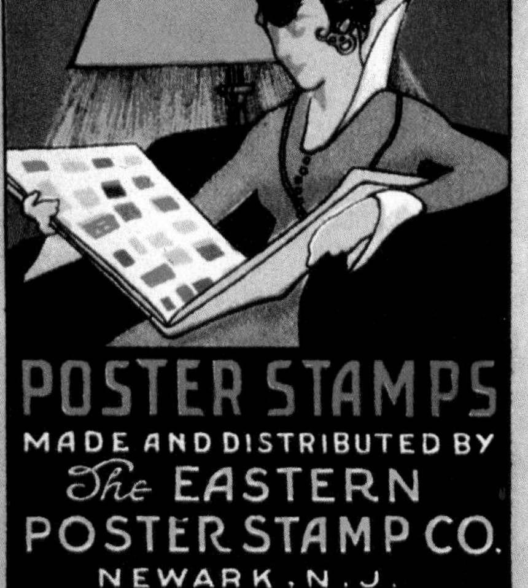
POSTER STAMPS
MADE AND DISTRIBUTED BY
The EASTERN
POSTER STAMP CO.
NEWARK, N.J.

INTERNATIONAL
PHILATELIC EXHIBITION
1936
NEW YORK
U.S.A.

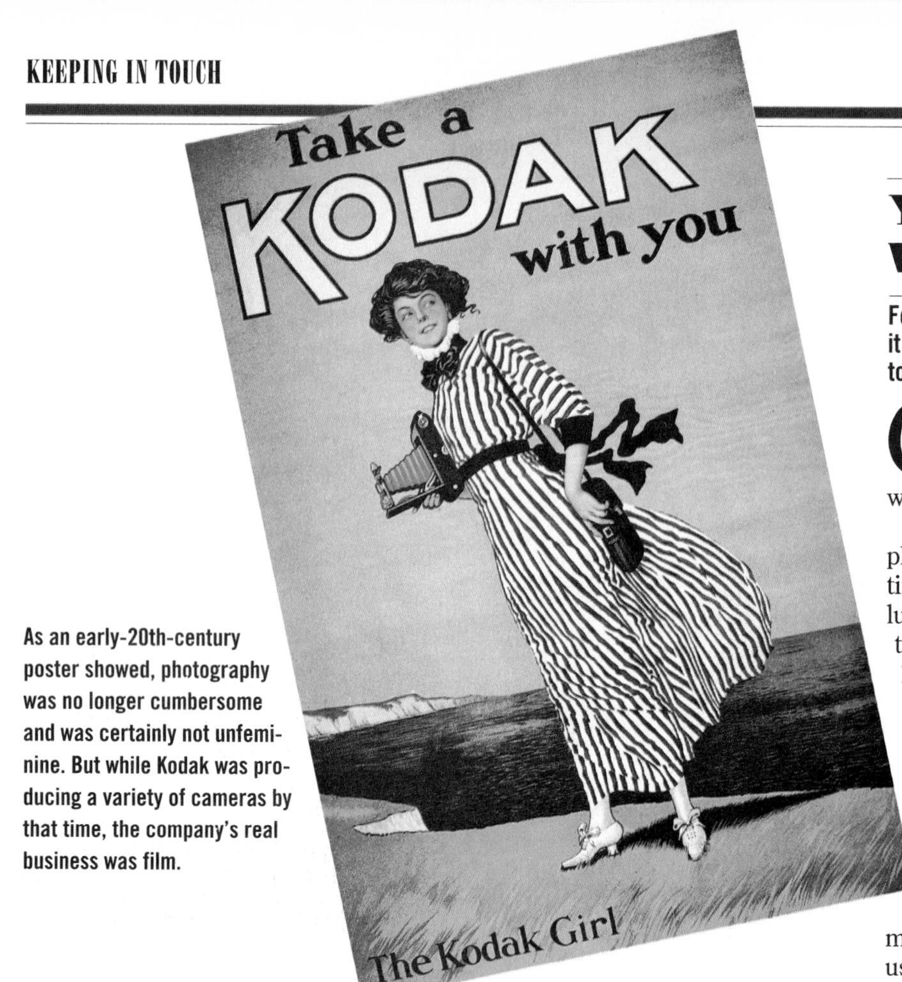

As an early-20th-century poster showed, photography was no longer cumbersome and was certainly not unfeminine. But while Kodak was producing a variety of cameras by that time, the company's real business was film.

You Press the Button, We Do the Rest

For some 40 years after photography was introduced, it remained an unwieldy art. Once George Eastman took it up, however, it got easier by the year.

George Eastman once remarked that he had never smiled until he was 40. Yet, hard-driving industrialist though he was, Eastman was the man who put the smile in the snapshot.

Before his day, the grimacing faces typical of photographs were the result of long exposure times that required the subjects to hold absolutely still for a minute or more. But from the time that Eastman first took up photography in 1877, all that began to change.

Right from the start, photography was more than a hobby for the 23-year-old native of Rochester, New York. Like other technically minded men of the era, Eastman was interested in the chemistry of photography and in finding ways to make the process quicker and easier. Night after night he experimented, cooking up batches of chemicals on his mother's stove. By 1879 he had devised a ready-to-use "dry" plate that captured much of the commercial photography market. And by 1884 he had

The Chicago and Alton Railroad Company called its prize-winning picture (above) "The Largest Photograph in the World of the Handsomest Train in the World." Looking like elves, a team of men set up George Lawrence's huge one-of-a-kind camera (left).

something even better: a flexible paper-backed film that could be wound on rollers.

To sell this new product — and encourage amateur photography — Eastman designed a small, black box camera that cost $25 and came loaded with a 100-exposure roll of the film. All the photographer had to do was pull a string to cock the shutter, turn a key to advance the film, and press the trigger. When the roll was used up, the customer simply shipped the camera back to Eastman for developing and reloading. "You press the button, we do the rest" was his motto.

The new camera was not only easier, it was quicker. With an exposure time of one twenty-fifth of a second, it made the snapshot a reality.

Eastman called his camera the Kodak, a word he invented because it could not be confused with anything else and because he considered *K* a "strong, incisive letter." Certainly sales were strong: 13,000 in the first year, with the czar of Russia among the customers.

Eastman put much of his profit back into research: one of his chemists invented the first commercially produced celluloid film, and Eastman collaborated with Thomas Edison in making motion picture film. By the 1890's his staff had perfected the chemistry for daylight-loading film, which allowed customers to load the cameras themselves. He followed up with ever cheaper, simpler cameras: the pocket Kodak in 1895 and the Brownie in 1900.

An aggressive businessman, Eastman bought up related companies, forcing competitors to close down, and controlled nearly 80 percent of the film market by the 1920's. At his death in 1932, he was able to leave more than $75 million in gifts to Rochester and to colleges around the country.

Actors parodied old-time picture-taking at the turn of the century (left). By that time amateur photography was easy. Eastman's first (22-ounce) box camera (bottom) appeared in 1888 and came with instructions (below) that showed it was as simple as one two three.

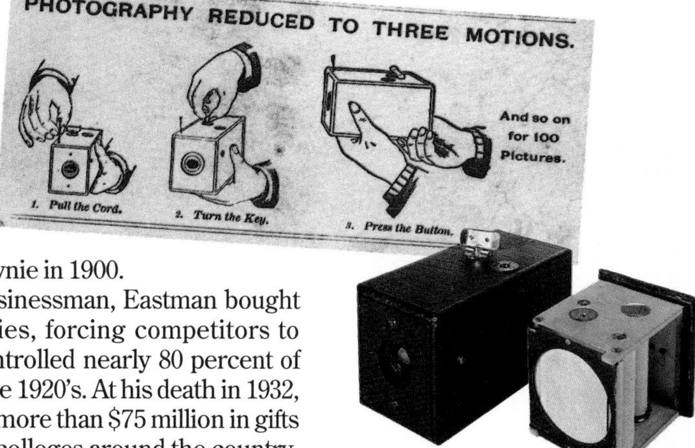

George Lawrence Gets the Big Picture

"The Hitherto Impossible in Photography Is Our Specialty," read a sign at the door to George Lawrence's studio. And that may have been what attracted the Chicago and Alton Railroad Company when it wanted to commission a photograph three times the size of any that had ever been made before.

The railroad was immensely proud of its new train — the first to have matching cars from cowcatcher to parlor car — and officials wanted to find a way to exhibit their prize at the Paris Exposition of 1900. What they needed was a photograph that would show all seven cars in detail. Accurate enlargement was not yet possible, and a composite, seamed together, simply would not do. So the only way get a 4½-by-8-foot picture was to shoot it with a mammoth camera.

Undaunted by the enormity of his assignment, Lawrence spent 2½ months building a camera so large that its bellows alone were 20 feet long. Weighing 1,400 pounds when fully loaded, the camera had to be moved around by railroad flatcar and was operated by a crew of up to 15. Ten gallons of chemicals were needed to develop each shot, but the results were flawless. Stunned judges in Paris sent a representative to Chicago to make sure the camera actually existed, and then awarded Lawrence's photo the Grand Prize of the World.

But that was not the last of Lawrence's exploits. An interest in aerial photography soon had him shooting panoramic views from balloons and rigging kites with cameras that could be operated by cable. In 1906, shortly after the San Francisco earthquake, he shot views of the ruins by kite and once again won national fame. Nothing he did, however, captured the public's imagination quite so grandly as his eight-foot photo. As for the camera itself, its usefulness ended with its original purpose: it was far too large to last.

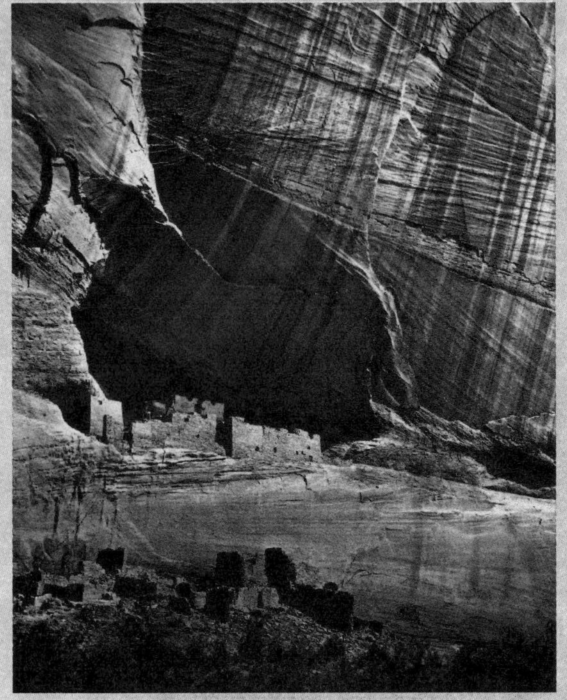

The scene (above) was one of some 3,500 that Mathew Brady and his assistants recorded during the Civil War. Timothy O'Sullivan, who worked with Brady, later traveled west and shot views like this one of Canyon de Chelly, Arizona (left).

Picture This

When pioneering news photographer Mathew Brady roamed battlefields during the Civil War, his camera's long exposure time meant that he could shoot only static subjects. But that did not detract from the poignancy of his pictures. Purchased as individual prints or as stereoscopic slides, they were the first news photographs most people had ever seen. And they told a moving story.

Brady was not the only one to recognize the power of the new medium. After the war, photographers lugged their rigs out West and sent back dramatic images — Indians, boomtowns, scenic vistas — that fired the imagination. Indeed, William H. Jackson's views of the Yellowstone area helped win its status as the world's first national park.

It was the 1880's, though, before photojournalism really came to the forefront. With the invention of half-tone printing, it became possible to reproduce photos in newspapers and magazines. This set the stage for reformers like Jacob Riis, whose turn-of-the-century pictures of New York tenements helped awaken America's social conscience. Not only did pho-

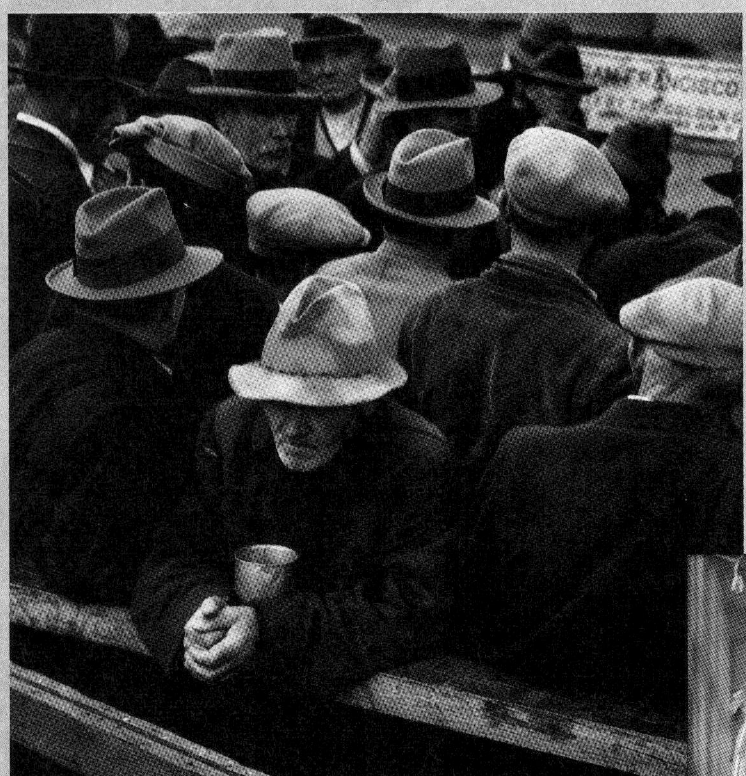

Interest in photojournalism arose around the turn of the century and grew from there. Children working at the Loudon, Tennessee, millworks (right) were photographed by Lewis Hine in 1910. Dorothea Lange recorded the despair on a San Francisco breadline (above) in 1933.

Arthur Fellig, known as Weegee, was one of New York's best-known news photographers in the 1930's and 1940's. Two women living it up at Sammy's in the Bowery (right) were caught by his camera, as was "The Critic" (below).

tographs inform, it seemed: they recorded history too. Nowhere was that better demonstrated than in the images produced by the Farm Security Administration in the 1930's and 1940's to document rural America's vanishing way of life. By the late 1930's, magazines such as *Life* and *Look* were featuring the work of photojournalists, and readers could turn page after page to discover who and what were in the news around the world.

Social reformer Jacob Riis was one of the first to reveal the darker side of life with pictures of tenements (left). Magazine photographer Margaret Bourke-White showed viewers the inside workings of industry, as above in the 1930's.

DROPPING A LINE

Mail delivered by Snowshoe Thompson carried his own distinctive marker (above). Norwegian by birth, Thompson (below) is sometimes credited with introducing the sport of skiing in the West.

The Skiing Mailman

PEOPLE LOST TO THE WORLD. UNCLE SAM NEEDS A MAIL CARRIER," said the two-line, bold-faced appeal in a winter issue of the 1856 Sacramento *Daily Places and Transcript.* The notice caught the attention of John Thompson, a burly young farmer who, as a former gold prospector, well knew what it was like to be "lost" in a Sierra mining camp. Each winter, from first snowfall to the spring thaw, not even a letter passed between the California communities on the western side of the mountains and the scattered Nevada towns along the eastern slope. The resultant isolation could be awful.

In a flash of inspiration, Thompson recalled the sport of skiing from his childhood in Norway and devised a rough pair of skis. His "Norwegian snowshoes" were 10 feet long, weighed 25 pounds, and were lashed to his boots with primitive straps. But they worked.

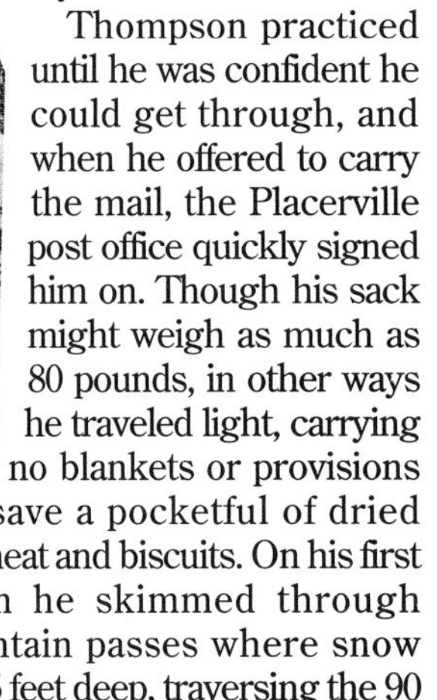

Thompson practiced until he was confident he could get through, and when he offered to carry the mail, the Placerville post office quickly signed him on. Though his sack might weigh as much as 80 pounds, in other ways he traveled light, carrying no blankets or provisions save a pocketful of dried meat and biscuits. On his first run he skimmed through mountain passes where snow drifted 25 feet deep, traversing the 90 miles to Genoa, Nevada, and back in just six days.

For the next 13 years "Snowshoe" Thompson, as he became known, was the winter lifeline for hundreds of lonely folk marooned in the mountains. On his biweekly rounds people relied on him to carry not only the usual mail but also essential medicines and ore assays. He even carried a printing press, piece by piece, through the passes. His pay was minimal. The government mail contractor reneged on his part of the bargain early on, so Thompson was left to collect a dollar from addressees for each letter delivered, if he could.

When the completion of the Central Pacific Railroad brought an end to his service in 1869, Thompson's grateful clients petitioned Congress to grant their skiing mailman a pension. But before it could act, Thompson's once boundless energy gave out and he died at home in bed, at age 49.

Jack Knight's Amazing Night Flight

Midwinter in 1921, the fledgling airmail service faced cancellation. Incoming President Warren G. Harding was looking for places to cut spending and thought it an easy target. Trains were cheaper, more reliable, and more commonly used to transport mail over long distances. Transcontinental mail service, moreover, involved relays of planes and trains to keep the mail moving from coast to coast. And planes operated safely only during the day.

To win public approval and congressional support before Harding took office in March, the Post Office Department announced a bold publicity stunt: on the morning of February 22, 1921, it would begin a round-the-clock relay airmail service between New York and San Francisco. The inaugural flights would feature two planes flying west and two heading east. If all went as planned, the planes would land every 200 to 300 miles for refueling and a change of pilots and, flying through the night, arrive safely on the other coast the following day. The nighttime fliers were to be guided by bonfires lit on the ground at strategic points along the way.

Fly-by-night hero

On the appointed morning the westbound planes ran into foul weather and were grounded in Chicago. One of the eastbound planes fared even worse, crashing at Elko, Nevada, and killing the pilot. But the fourth plane flew gamely on. At North Platte, Nebraska, veteran pilot Jack Knight took over. After a delay for repairs, he took off

In 1918 regular airmail service was begun between New York City and Washington, D.C. (left). Undaunted by injuries from a recent crash, Jack Knight (below) flew the mail by night from Nebraska to Illinois.

shortly before 11:00 P.M. Guided by the soft glimmer of the Platte River 2,200 feet below him, Knight landed comfortably in Omaha two hours later, only to find that his relay had not shown up. With the success of the whole endeavor resting in the balance, Knight decided he had to go on.

Flying now over unfamiliar territory, with nothing but a compass and a torn road map for navigation, he flew east into a snowstorm. Unable to land in Des Moines because of the snow, Knight sputtered on to Iowa City, where, with the help of a surprised night watchman, he was able to land, refuel, and take off again. The snow finally stopped, but Knight still had to cope with thick fog in the Mississippi Valley before finally touching down in Chicago — an instant hero — at 8:40 A.M.

A fresh pilot took over for the remainder of the eastbound flight, which ended uneventfully at 4:50 P.M. in New York, 33 hours and 20 minutes after the journey had begun. Congress, impressed, gave the airmail service its blessing.

The Mail Pooch

A note on his collar declared: "To all who may greet this dog, Owney is his name. He is the pet of 100,000 mail clerks in the United States. Treat him kindly and speed him on his journey, across ocean and land." Since dogs and postmen are traditionally considered adversaries, this unusual aegis for a mongrel terrier may come as a surprise. But Owney was no ordinary dog.

How he got his name is lost in the mists of memory, but how he came to be the mascot of the U.S. mails is the stuff of legend. One autumn night in 1888, the disheveled pup slipped into the post office in Albany, New York, and bedded down on a heap of canvas mail bags. Postal workers took pity on the pooch and left him alone as long as he didn't make a pest of himself. Far from being a nuisance, the dog demonstrated a remarkably even temper and soon took a proprietary interest in the mail sacks. He became a familiar sight perched atop the pouches, riding along with them to the railroad loading dock, and occasionally accompanying them to far-off destinations in New York, Denver, and beyond.

To ensure that Owney was always sent back to Albany, his new friends at the post office made him a collar bearing his name and home address. The rail postmen began attaching their own local routing tags to the roaming Rover and it wasn't long before Owney was jingling "like the bells on a junk wagon," as he jogged along. The collection eventually grew to 1,017 tags and formed an impressive record of 143,000 miles logged and countless hearts won. Even the postmaster general joined in and gave Owney a jacket that would display his medals — and distribute their weight more evenly.

Owney crisscrossed the United States several times, made at least one foray into Alaska, and in 1895 even went completely around the world. His four-month odyssey began in Tacoma, Washington, and included stops in Japan, China, the Middle East, and the Mediterranean before his arrival back in New York with nary a ripple in his poise.

Owney retired to Albany two years later, but the quiet life didn't sit well with the globe-trotting terrier. He took his last trip, to Toledo, Ohio, where he died of a mysterious gunshot wound on June 11, 1897. His postal friends had the body stuffed, and now Owney stands guard permanently at the Smithsonian Institution's National Postal Museum.

The unofficial mascot of the Post Office Department from 1888 until 1897, Owney traveled wherever the mail went — including Europe and the Far East. A unique mail category, "registered dog package," safeguarded his journeys.

Wish You Were Here

The year 1905 was a good one for getting into the postcard business, for the penny greetings had by then become a mania that was racing across the continent like some exotic strain of flu. "There is now no hamlet so remote," wrote one wit of the raging craze, that it "has not succumbed to the ravages of the microbe postale universelle."

Incubated in Germany some 20 years earlier, the postcard germ, as social commentators dubbed the fad, first appeared in America at the World's Columbian Exposition in 1893. By the turn of the century the microbe had become a ubiquitous infection — "postcarditis" was a favorite diagnosis — and few American households were immune. Every town, city, and state saw to it that its leafy green Main Street or highest peak made it onto a promotional card; every family counting itself among the middle or upper classes displayed on the parlor table an album bulging with images of the the Sphinx, the Eiffel Tower, and Niagara Falls. According to the *Post Card Dealer,* one of several journals that popped up to report on the craze, one young suitor even proposed marriage by penny postcard. Postcard "showers" enjoyed a fad with friends who deluged an honoree with as many as 200 cards.

But amid all the good fun there were also excesses, including a case of smuggling in which cards embossed with morphine and cocaine were mailed to a New York prison. And in 1912, local postmasters were permitted to confiscate some of the more risqué cards, such as those showing "feminine ankles, lovers in romantic attitudes, and pictures of animals 'portrayed without fashionable attire.' "

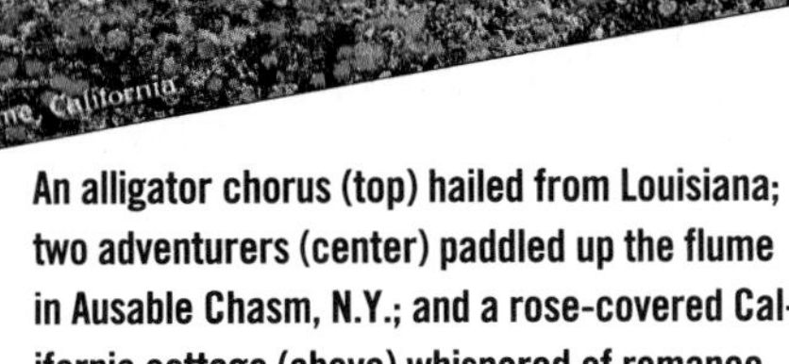

Rose Covered Home, California

An alligator chorus (top) hailed from Louisiana; two adventurers (center) paddled up the flume in Ausable Chasm, N.Y.; and a rose-covered California cottage (above) whispered of romance.

White Mountains, N.H. Mount Pleasant House

New Hampshire's Mt. Pleasant House Hotel (above) welcomed guests with flying pennants. A satire of beach tourists (right) was meant to inspire a chuckle.

I'VE MET SOME PROMINENT PEOPLE HERE

TIME TABLE

POST HASTE

1639 *A Boston tavern is chosen as the site for processing overseas mail.*

1673 *Monthly mail service between New York and Massachusetts is initiated with the first trip on the Boston Post Road.*

1775 *The Continental Congress appoints Benjamin Franklin as the first postmaster general.*

1792 *Congress makes mail theft a capital offense.*

1839 *Envelopes come into use for enclosing mail.*

1845 *The letter informing Zachary Taylor that he has won the presidential nomination lands in the dead letter office — 10 cents postage due.*

1847 *The Post Office Department issues the first stamps: a 5-cent issue depicting Benjamin Franklin and a 10-cent issue featuring George Washington.*

1858 *Albert Potts of Philadelphia invents letter collection boxes, which are installed on streets in New York and Boston.*

1870's *Gummed envelopes make their debut.*

1893 *The Post Office issues its first commemorative stamps to publicize the World's Columbian Exposition. Each of the 16 stamps depicts an incident in the life of Columbus.*

1897 *One year after Rural Free Delivery is established, Sears, Roebuck and Company says it is selling four suits and a watch every minute, and a buggy every 10.*

1911 *Earl Ovington, the first U. S. airmail pilot, flies mail from Garden City to Mineola, N.Y.*

1913 *Parcel post is inaugurated.*

1917 *An open-air post office with a roof and a pink stone floor — but no walls — opens in St. Petersburg, Florida.*

1918 *The Post Office issues a sheet of stamps with a biplane inadvertently printed upside down. A sheet bought for $24 sells six days later for $15,000.*

1920 *Post Office Department approves the use of postage meters.*

1942 *V-mail — letters on microfilm for U.S. servicemen — is introduced.*

The Parcel-Post Kid

Accounts vary as to where the 53 cents' worth of postage were affixed. Some say the stamps were pasted to a little suitcase sent along with preschooler May Pierstorff the day her parents mailed her to her grandmother. Others say they were glued to a tag attached to her coat, along with her granny's address in Lewiston, a few hours by train from the child's home in Grangeville, Idaho.

May's parents, it seems, had discovered that it was cheaper to send her care of the U.S. mail than to pay the full fare the railroad demanded for children traveling alone. After all, at 48½ pounds, May fell within the parcel post's 50-pound weight limit, and back in 1914 it was not, technically speaking, against the law to ship a child — as it would have been had they tried to send a live pig or a piece of Limburger cheese, since postal regulations barred most live animals, as well as articles that could be termed smelly. Baby chicks, however, were welcome, and that was how the Grangeville postmaster decided to classify little May.

Off she went, tagged, stamped, and by all accounts perfectly content. She was driven to the train station, handed over to the baggage clerk, and on arrival in Lewiston, was taken directly to the post office and then to her grandmother, who pronounced the whole operation "as smooth as buttermilk." None the worse for wear, May Pierstorff lived to the ripe old age of 78 and died in California, of natural causes.

Junk Mail

"Neither snow nor rain," runs the unofficial pledge, shall stay "these couriers from the swift completion of their appointed rounds." And through the history of the U.S. Post Office, these couriers on their rounds have toted a staggering volume of items — as well as a few astonishing ones. A resourceful farmer once shipped a ton and a half of hay by parcel post from Oregon to Idaho; a coconut was sent fourth class from Miami to Detroit with address and postage affixed to the hull; and sections of prefab housing have been mailed to building sites to save on trucking costs. When Harry Winston donated the Hope Diamond to the Smithsonian Institution in 1958, he kept costs down by sending the gem in a plain brown wrapper by registered first-class mail. Poisoned candy, loaded pistols, and assorted parts of the human body — in various preservatives or simply "as is" — also have been routed through the mail.

Occasionally a fuss ensued. Assorted mishaps involving the escape of theoretically benign creatures, such as ladybugs, led to bans on mailing more notoriously dangerous species such as black widow spiders and snakes of any kind. And after some cheapskate shipped an entire bank building — 80,000 bricks in all, packaged in small bundles — from Salt Lake City to Vernal, Utah, in 1916, the postmaster general put the service's collective foot down. No more buildings, he decreed. But some 9,000 tons of gold bricks were happily transported from New York to Fort Knox between January 1940 and January 1941, a job for which the Post Office collected over $1,600,000 in postage, insurance, and surcharges.

Confronted by a mixed heap of parcels and envelopes containing who knows what, a team of postal workers in 1912 systematically sorted the mail to keep it moving on its way.

BY WIRE AND AIRWAVE

Taking the Phone on the Road

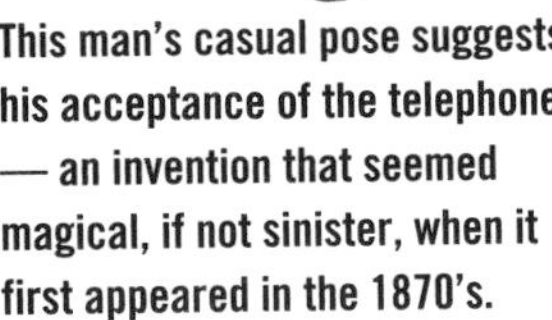

This man's casual pose suggests his acceptance of the telephone — an invention that seemed magical, if not sinister, when it first appeared in the 1870's.

Visiting the Philadelphia Centennial Exposition of 1876, Dom Pedro II, emperor of Brazil, stopped to chat with a young speech teacher he had met previously in Boston. The man, Alexander Graham Bell, was at the fair to promote a new machine of his own invention, the telephone. The affable emperor agreed to try the device and, placing the receiver to his ear, was treated to Bell's recitation of Hamlet's "To be or not to be" soliloquy. Delighted and astonished, Dom Pedro exclaimed, "It talks!"

But the public proved to be a harder sell. "It is a scientific toy . . . for professors of electricity and acoustics," one detractor proclaimed, "but it can never be a practical necessity."

Determined to prove the critics wrong — and through his success to win the blessing of his future father-in-law — Bell and his assistant, Tom Watson, embarked on a demonstration tour. Bell would sit on stage with a telephone connected to leased or loaned telegraph wires; while Watson was stationed any number of miles away. After a brief introduction and shouted greetings, Watson would then awe the audience by bursting into song; his repertoire included *Yankee Doodle, Hold the Fort,* and the sentimental favorite *Do Not Trust Him, Gentle Lady.* What he lacked in tone, Tom more than made up for in power, and his trilling, combined with the novelty of its transmission, received thunderous ovations.

But critical reaction remained mixed. A prominent scientist proclaimed the device "the greatest marvel," whereas the *Providence Evening Press* wondered if "the powers of darkness are somehow in league with it." It was Gardiner Hubbard's opinion, however, that counted most, and in 1877 he finally gave permission for Bell to marry his daughter, Mabel. The telephone and its inventor lived happily ever after.

Crowds packed the lecture hall in Salem, Massachusetts, when Alexander Graham Bell demonstrated his intriguing new invention — the telephone — early in 1877.

Smooth Operators

Eavesdropping was a temptation in the days before automatic dialing. Phone company regulations strictly forbade "monitoring" calls.

The first phone operators, in the late 1870's were teenage boys, many of them former telegraph messengers. Unfortunately, the rambunctious lads could be rude to customers and were sometimes less than diligent — phone service might be spontaneously suspended so that the crew could cheer on a fistfight.

Although working outside the home was considered not quite proper for young ladies, social convention was set aside to remedy the desperate situation. In a very short time, almost all operators were female, known as "hello girls" or "the voice with a smile."

Maintaining their equanimity was not always easy, given the rigors of the job. The young women — some employers only hired unmarried women between the ages of 17 and 20 — had to clean their working quarter (frequently a loft or dusty attic), occasionally rousting out resident mice and pigeons.

When customers called information, especially in rural areas, that's literally what they wanted: a recipe, a stock market price, the feature at the local theater. An operator might be asked to provide a wake-up call, or to listen for a baby crying near a dangling receiver while its mother visited a neighbor. Grateful subscribers showered the girls with gifts, but others were more demanding. Many customers disliked the impersonality of phone numbers and insisted their names be used; this meant the operator had to memorize which of dozens of jacks went to which home. But worst of all was the torture of the time report — every 15 seconds the poor souls on that shift intoned, "When you hear the signal, the time will be . . . ."

Saved by the Bell

Alexander Graham Bell's first coherent telephone message — "Mr. Watson, come here; I want you" — was in fact a cry for help. He had spilled battery fluid on his pants and instinctively made the first emergency phone call. And phones have been helping out in crises ever since.

In rural areas, in particular, Bell's amazing new invention became a vital lifeline. Farmers relayed news of tornadoes, storms, or impending frosts in time for others to round up livestock and protect crops. Many a tale is told of heroic operators who remained at their posts to warn about floods and coordinate rescue efforts even as the waters rose around their switchboards.

Nor were their urban colleagues any less dedicated. A New Jersey operator once received a call from a panicked druggist, who said that a customer had walked off with a bottle of acid instead of eye drops. Tracking the woman down through calls to a postmaster, relatives, and other subscribers, the operator finally located her in a New York City hotel just moments before she gave her eyes an acid bath.

A reporter covering a potential suicide once proved equally resourceful. While police debated ways to coax the man in from a hotel's 14th-floor ledge, the newsman simply placed a call to the room. Following an ingrained reflex, the would-be suicide dashed in to answer the telephone.

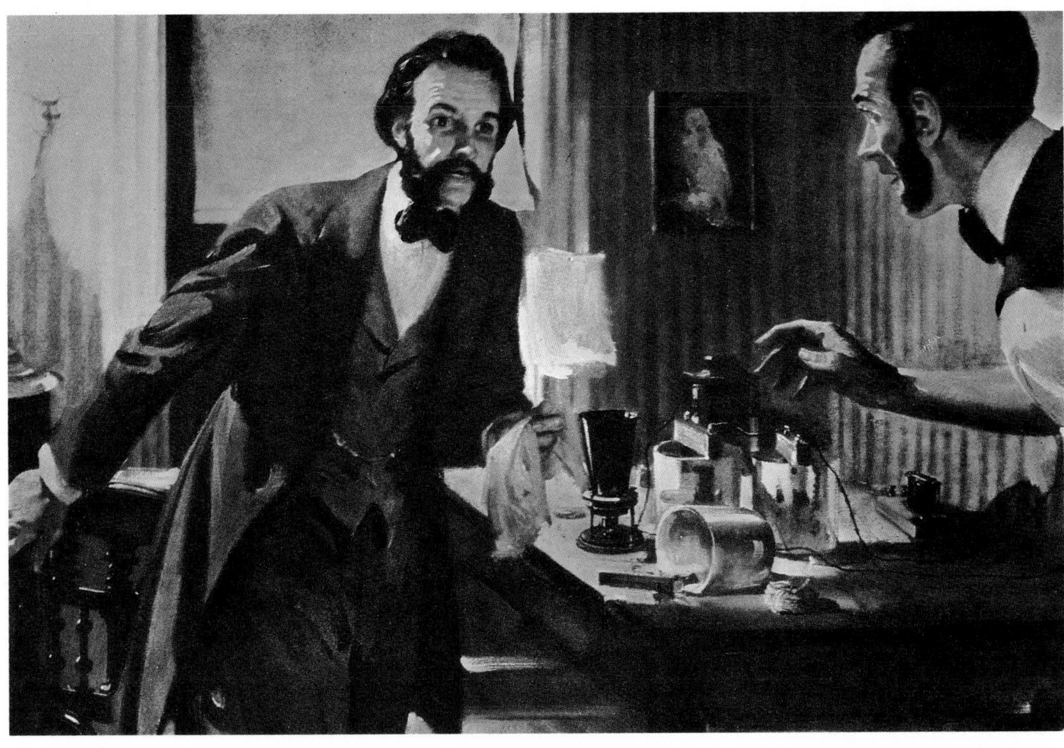

An accidental splash of acid prompted Alexander Graham Bell to make the first phone call, which his assistant, Tom Watson, answered by rushing in from a room down the hall.

Hoy Hoy, or Hello?

When Alexander Graham Bell's newfangled telephone appeared in 1876, a problem presented itself immediately. What do you say when you answer the phone? Bell was all for "Hoy! Hoy!"—the salutation he used for the rest of his life. But even as the public warmed to his invention, his greeting left most people cold. "What is wanted?" and "Are you ready to talk?" were also tried but fell flat. Then Thomas Edison came to the rescue with "hello" — a word that Bell heartily disliked, as did contemporary telephone officials, who deemed it "undignified." But the public embraced the term and its use spread rapidly. By 1880, when the first National Convention of Telephone Companies met, conventioneers sported badges that said "HELLO." Mark Twain that year published the word in his comic sketch "A Telephone Conversation." Two popular songs — "Hello, Ma Baby" in 1899 and "Hello, Central, Give Me Heaven" in 1901 — showed how completely the word had been adopted. And even AT&T had begun promoting its switchboard operators as "hello girls." Yet well into the 1940's, etiquette books were still agonizing over the propriety of the greeting.

In order to keep working in the winter, Lieutenant Mitchell devised a parka made of bed ticking and wolverine fur.

Wiring WAMCATS

It would be hard to imagine a place less hospitable for building a telegraph line than the Alaska wilderness in 1900. But that was exactly what the Army Signal Corps was commissioned to do. After an energetic start, the project (called the Washington–Alaska Military Cable and Telegraph System, or WAMCATS) slowed to a standstill. So in 1901, the army sent in 1st Lt. Billy Mitchell — a 21-year-old veteran of the Cuban and Philippine campaigns — to find out what was holding up progress.

Virtually no work was done in winter, Mitchell discovered, because of temperatures that plummeted to more than 70° below zero. But nothing was being done in the summer, either, because Alaska's swampy terrain and clouds of bloodthirsty mosquitoes made it nearly impossible to bring in supplies. With not a single passable road in the wilderness, a packhorse could carry no more than 200 pounds for 15 or 20 miles a day in summer. By contrast, the same animal might haul as much as a ton of gear over frozen snow.

The solution, the young officer suggested, "was to work through the winter getting the material out," in order to begin construction in the summer, "when we could dig holes in the ground and set the telegraph poles." Mitchell scouted the forbidding landscape by dogsled that winter, and in the spring of 1902 the first crews set out to begin digging postholes in the still-frozen earth. Swathed in mosquito netting in summer and in goggles and layers of fleece in winter, they chopped and dug their way across the country, hunting caribou and bear when supplies ran low.

From the port of Valdez (where an underwater telegraph cable linked Alaska to the States), the line ran north to Eagle City, then the rugged miles west through the mountains to the Bering Sea. Three days shy of the June 1903 deadline, Mitchell himself made the final connection. "America's last frontier," he would later quip, "had been roped and hogtied."

A leader at age 21, Mitchell went on to become an airborne hero in World War I.

Crossed Signals on an Icy Sea

No place aboard the *Titanic* seemed to be busier on April 14, 1912, than the wireless room, where two operators worked nonstop. Shipboard wireless — introduced by Marconi in 1898 — was still a glorious novelty when the "unsinkable" luxury liner made her maiden voyage, and frivolous greetings from passengers to friends were piled high in 1st Operator Jack Phillips' in basket.

All that day, Phillips had also been receiving warnings from other ships of unusually heavy ice in the North Atlantic. The news was duly relayed to the ship's officers, but by 9:40 P.M., when yet another iceberg warning came in from the *Mesaba,* Phillips was too busy to pass it on, and he cut short a similar message from the *Californian* around 11:00.

Only 40 minutes later, the *Titanic,* racing along at full speed, plowed into one of those icebergs, and by 12:15 Phillips, with operator Harold Bride, was madly tapping out distress signals. The lights of the *Californian* could be seen 10 miles away, but her wireless operator had gone off duty at 11:30 and there was no response. A full 58 miles away, the *Carpathia* picked up the frantic crackle and sped to the rescue, arriving after the *Titanic* had gone down with some 1,500 passengers. Still, she was in time to pull 705 survivors out of the icy waters. From that day on, Marconi's wireless was viewed not as a novelty, but as a necessity, and a 24-hour radio watch soon was required of every passenger ship at sea.

JUST AS THE
SHIP WENT DOWN
A SONG OF THE SEA

Throughout April 14, 1912, wireless messages from other seagoing ships alerted the *Titanic* crew of nearby icebergs, one of which would bring the great ship down.

Say It, Sing It, or Send It by Wire

For many Americans at the turn of the century, the sight of a telegraph messenger at the door meant "Reach for the smelling salts!" And neither Western Union nor its rival, Postal Telegraph, was pleased with the role of bearer of bad news. So after 1910, they were encourging good-news messages, sending them out in bright seasonal envelopes to indicate no fainting was necessary.

In the 1930's the companies offered 25-cent Fixed Text telegrams (FT's) to make message sending even easier. By giving senders dozens of prewritten sentiments to choose from in each of some 50 categories, the FT eliminated any dilemma over what to say. Need to cheer someone on? How about Pep-Gram number 1359: "We are behind you for victory. Bring home the bacon." Forgot to send a Mother's Day card again? Perhaps message 432 would do. "Please accept my love and kisses for my father's dearest Mrs."

Of course, would-be poets who wanted to compose verses of their own could do so, for only a little extra. The same option carried over to the singing telegrams — or Sing-O-Grams — that were all the rage by the late 1930's. Lovers, parents, and pets alike were treated to over-the-phone serenades by homey choruses of telegraph operators, or in-person croonings at the front door. "Be mine, forever, be mine, my Valentine!" a messenger might sing with heart-felt emotion — and high hopes of an appreciative tip.

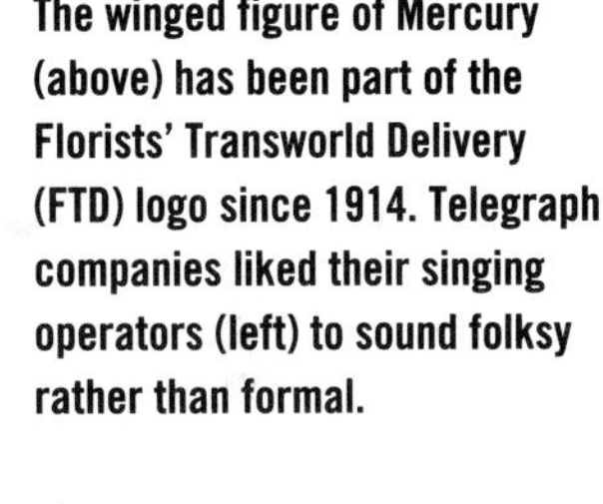

The winged figure of Mercury (above) has been part of the Florists' Transworld Delivery (FTD) logo since 1914. Telegraph companies liked their singing operators (left) to sound folksy rather than formal.

For those who believed that actions speak louder than words, another option arose in 1910: flowers by wire. From the start retailers took their promise of worldwide service seriously. The truth of their claim was perhaps never more clearly demonstrated than in the 1930's when Rear Adm. Richard Byrd had a birthday bouquet wired to his mother from "Little America" in Antarctica.

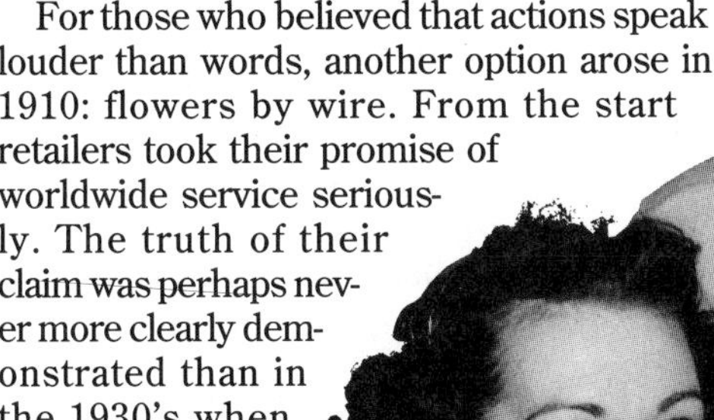

Getting the antenna high enough was a trick in the early days of radio, prompting the use of a balloon to do the job (left). Recorded music programs at KDKA soon were followed up with baseball scores, live orchestras, farm news, and specialties such as Spike Shannon's pep show (below).

The Birth of Broadcasting

It was 1919 and Frank Conrad, a gifted engineer at the Westinghouse electrical plant in Pittsburgh, was experimenting on his own. Tinkering with the radio technology he had helped develop during World War I, Conrad tried to signal a handful of other "wireless" buffs from a makeshift studio in his garage. Then, to add a little interest to his transmissions, he turned the microphone toward his Victrola. Listeners who picked up the signal could hardly believe their ears — music being sent through space!

By the summer of 1920, Conrad was broadcasting semiweekly concerts, and scores of amateur radio operators were tuning in. Most were hunched over homebuilt receivers made in part by wrapping yards of copper wire around oatmeal boxes. But Westinghouse was interested, too, and backed Conrad in an effort to reach a wider audience. On election night, November 2, they were ready to try, using a 100-watt transmitter and the call letters KDKA. This time there were thousands of listeners. "It's Pittsburgh!" they marveled as news of the election returns came through. And it was history. Before long, all of America would be tuning in to radio.

John Brinkley (below) looked like a doctor and talked like a doctor, and many believed he was. But the press lampooned him (left).

Kilowatt Quackery

Possessed of a phoney medical license and a charismatic personality, "Doctor" John R. Brinkley made a name for himself in radio when he started broadcasting over his own Milford, Kansas, station in 1923. Using the call letters KFKB ("Kansas First, Kansas Best"), Brinkley reached listeners far and wide for 13 hours a day, delivering a mix of fundamentalist religion, country music, and educational lectures.

The doctor's popularity really soared in the late 1920's when he began a daily "Medical Question Box" show, answering letters from listeners at $2 a query. Although Brinkley willingly tackled all manner of complaints on the air — and prescribed his own patent medicines as cures — the specialty that made him famous was countering "flat tires" and other sure signs of "failing manhood." His improbable solution for the problem was to implant goat sex glands in human males, a procedure that earned him the nickname Goat Gland Brinkley. The doctor performed the operation himself at a hospital he built expressly for the purpose. (Patients could pick out their own donor goats from a pen next door.) And there was no shortage of patients: by 1928 he was performing some 40 operations a week at up to $1,500 per implant.

Not surprisingly, the American Medical Association was none too fond of Brinkley, nor was the Federal Radio Commission. By 1930 the two managed to strip him of both his medical and broadcast licenses in Kansas. But that did not stop the wily doctor. Moving to Texas, he opened a new station, XER, just across the border in Mexico, where he operated a 500,000-watt transmitter — the most powerful in the world. And even after the government cracked down on XER in 1934, Brinkley managed to continue his self-promotion over a variety of stations until his death in 1941.

Radio's Oracle

Marriage problems, money woes, inferiority complexes — these were just a few of the dilemmas that radio's "Voice of Experience" addressed daily in 15-minute broadcasts. The mellifluous Voice, which remained on the air from 1928 until 1940, was that of Marion Sayle Taylor, a self-made social worker whose advice reached millions of troubled people, though they did not even know his name. (Taylor was so secretive about his identity that even his checks were signed simply "Voice of Experience.")

The Voice was a genuine beacon of hope with a host of listeners. Receiving as many as 30,000 letters a day, he read only the most dramatic on the air and was never at a loss for answers. In his spare time he recorded his stock advice in more than 100 pamphlets and 8 books (including *Stranger Than Fiction* and *Making Molehills out of Mountains*). Millions were sold, with the profits donated to charity.

Taylor came to know the darker corners of human nature. Murderers confessed their crimes, mothers were reunited with abandoned children, and thieves were enabled to return stolen goods. But perhaps the oddest case of all was that of a man who had pawned his false teeth. "I'm always admonishing you men who are out of work to grit your teeth and go after jobs," said the Voice, "but you can't very well grit 'em if you haven't got 'em. So I guess I'll have to get 'em for you." With the teeth back where they belonged, the toothless listener did as he was told and found a job.

Theater of the Mind

The family gathered in the living room, dimmed the lights, turned the dial to their favorite station, and then the magic would begin. First came the sound of a slowly creaking door, and then the disembodied human voice "welcoming you into the inner sanctum." It was radio, it was live, and in large part, it was the sound effects that made shows like *Inner Sanctum, The Green Hornet,* and *Young Dr. Malone* so convincing to audiences in the 1930's and 1940's.

Creating the illusions was a job that required perfect timing, and coordination with all the characters in the story. Sound-effects technicians could make an audience believe a horse was galloping across a prairie (by pounding halved coconut shells on a tray of sand) or that the hero was facing a raging fire (by crumpling cellophane near the microphone). Even something as simple as the sound of footsteps, however, had to be varied to suggest an angry man, a skipping child, or a woman running in high heels. But the illusions were effective. When people listened, for example, to Jack Benny "walking downstairs" to open his vault and heard a succession of keys, doors, alarm bells, clanking chains, and a quacking duck, the scenes in their imaginations probably were funnier than anything that could have been created on stage.

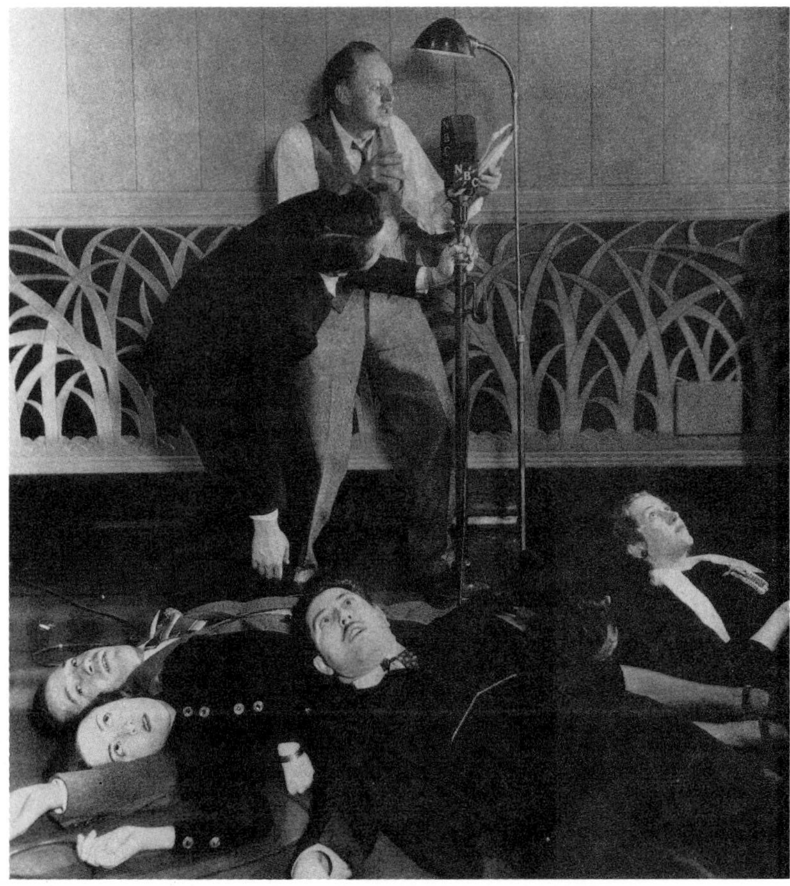

Sarah Jane Troy (above), simulating a crash through a door for WOR, was the first female sound-effects person. An actor, a sound-effects man, and groaning "victims" (below) enact a *Lights Out* drama for NBC.

Making Time on the Airwaves

Some listeners groused that it was too sensational. But that never stopped others from tuning in each week to *The March of Time.* Modeled after its sponsor, *Time* magazine, and launched in 1931, the program became the most popular news documentary in the annals of radio.

Since most radio news at the time was little more than a rehashing of highlights culled from the day's newspapers and wire services, *The March of Time* was indeed unique. With its lively reenactments of episodes in the week's news, it offered all the drama of a newsreel, giving folks in their living rooms the feeling that they were right there where history was happening.

The show was broadcast live, with the news stories recreated in the studio by teams of actors, sound-effects engineers, and musicians. Throughout its 14 years on the air, *The March of Time* attracted some of the brightest talent in the business. Orson Welles, Agnes Moorhead, and Arlene Francis were among thoses who delighted in impersonating the newsmakers of the day. Another, actor Dwight Weist, earned the title Man of a Thousand Voices since, from one moment to the next, he might be Adolf Hitler, Fiorello LaGuardia, John L. Lewis, or the man in the street.

Linking all the stories together was the program's most memorable announcer, Westbrook Van Voorhis, whose portentous tones lent an air of weighty believability. But then, listeners really did not have any trouble believing. They just had to tune in, shut their eyes, and they *were* there.

The March of Time **remained on the air until 1945, with actors such as Roy Atwell and Jack Smart reenacting the news.**

The Man Behind the Mask

Brace Beemer (above) played the Lone Ranger for 13 years. Shown in a publicity poster (right), the masked man got even with more than 2,000 bad guys during his 22 years on radio.

"Who was that masked man?" a voice was sure to ask as the sound of hoofbeats faded away. And the answer was invariable: "You don't know? That was the Lone Ranger."

On the air for 22 years (and a grand total of 2,956 live broadcasts), *The Lone Ranger* debuted in January 1933 on Detroit's WXYZ. Believing that radio could capitalize on the public's interest in Westerns, station owner George Trendle had come up with the idea and enlisted the help of free-lance writer Fran Striker to turn his outline into a story. (Trendle would later collaborate on *The Green Hornet* and *Sergeant Preston of the Yukon* as well.)

What they developed for their Depression-era audience was a shining, wholesome paragon of a hero. The ranger, whose "real" name was John Reid, spoke perfect English and never smoked or drank. Nor did he start out "lone." Reid supposedly was the only one of a group of six Texas Rangers who survived an ambush by the ruthless Butch Cavendish. Reid too would have died in the attack had he not been saved by his old Indian buddy, Tonto.

From that time on, John Reid added to his mystique (and ultimately caught up with Cavendish) by donning a mask and adopting the name Lone Ranger. Of course, he was never really alone. "As long as you live, as long as I live, I will ride with you!" Tonto had pledged when he saved the life of his faithful friend, whom he called Kemo Sabe. Riding high on their mounts, Silver and Scout, to the sounds of the *William Tell Overture* each week, they made a decidedly dashing pair.

And lots of children apparently agreed. To gauge response after the first few months, the station offered free popguns to the first 300 listeners who wrote in. They were swamped by more than 24,000 letters. Even when the program caught on nationally, it remained perfectly tailored to children's interests. For though serialized, there were no cliffhangers: each episode of *The Lone Ranger* was complete unto itself. All the better to send kids off to bed satisfied, content to fall asleep dreaming of the glamorous sign-off, "Hi-yo, Silver! Away!"

Your friend,
The Lone Ranger

Radio's Pint-Size Pundits

They were funny, unpretentious, and just like kids everywhere — except for one thing: they seemed to know the answers to everything. "Tell me what I would be carrying home if I brought an antimacassar, a dinghy, a sarong, and an apteryx," the host of radio's *Quiz Kids* asked his five young contestants the first time the program aired in June 1940. While listeners scratched their heads, the precocious kids fired back answers as easily as if they had been asked to recite their ABCs.

For a nation already addicted to radio quiz shows, the new 30-minute weekly program was a real winner. The engaging guests (sometimes as young as 4 but never more than 16 years old) were a source of endless amazement, particularly to host Joe Kelly, a genial man with a third-grade education who had all he could do to pronounce the words on the question cards. But that was part of the show's charm.

Each contestant — some 600 appeared between 1940 and the final radio show in 1953 — was awarded a $100 savings bond per show. The three who made the highest scores each week were invited to return. Thus some of the youngsters became national celebrities who were invited to the White House, made appearances with such personalities as Jack Benny, and had toys named after them.

An early favorite among the kids was seven-year-old Gerard Darrow, a whiz at natural history who not only could recognize some 300 species of birds but, reportedly, knew their songs as well. When he struck out after his ninth week, the public begged for more, and the producers brought him back for occasional encores.

Math prodigy Joel Kupperman signed on at age five in 1943 and, on the sheer strength of his answers, remained a contestant for six years.

Though few got to be stars, finding kids brainy enough to appear on the show turned out to be easier than anyone had imagined. Most of them came from average homes and went on to successful careers. One, James Watson, even grew up to win a Nobel Prize in medicine.

Quiz Kids Ruthie Duskin, Gerard Darrow, Harve Fischman, and Richard Williams dressed up (and hammed it up) at a benefit to sell war bonds.

Although *Quiz Kids* normally aired from Chicago, the youngsters sometimes made guest appearances, as here at New York's Town Hall.

Traveler's Guide to America's Past

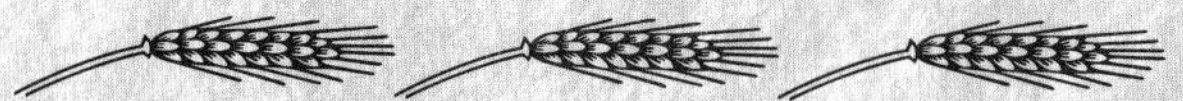

ALABAMA

GAINESWOOD
805 South Cedar St., Demopolis, Ala.
The state's most elegant antebellum mansion, built by a wealthy cotton planter, features imposing porticoes and a lavishly detailed interior that includes many original furnishings.

OLD NORTH HULL STREET HISTORIC DISTRICT
Reception center, 310 North Hull St., Montgomery, Ala.
Twenty-seven restored structures here present a unique summary of 19th-century southern life. Among them are a one-room log cabin, a dogtrot house, an 1818 tavern, a school, and a grocery store.

RUSSELL CAVE NATIONAL MONUMENT
Off Rte. 72, Bridgeport, Ala.
This huge rock shelter, first occupied some 9,000 years ago and used until about A.D. 500, is the oldest-known site of human habitation in the Southeast.

SPACE AND ROCKET CENTER
Off Alt. Rte. 72, Huntsville , Ala.
A vast collection of aerospace artifacts, including the actual *Apollo 16* spacecraft, make this one of the largest, finest space museums in the world.

TANNEHILL HISTORICAL STATE PARK
Off I-59, McCalla, Ala.
The primary attractions at this 1,500-acre woodland preserve are blast furnaces and other relics of a pre-Civil War ironworks, a precursor of Birmingham's present-day iron and steel industry. But there are also log homes, farm buildings, and an operating grist mill and a cotton gin that recall the state's pioneer era.

TUSKEGEE INSTITUTE NATIONAL HISTORIC SITE
Tuskegee Institute, Tuskegee, Ala.
The famous university was founded in 1881 by Booker T. Washington as a training school for African-Americans. Visitors can take walking tours of the campus, stopping in at Washington's home, and at the George Washington Carver Museum, which honors the genius best known for discovering 325 uses for peanuts.

ALASKA

ALASKALAND PIONEER PARK
Airport Way and Peger Rd., Fairbanks, Alaska
Among the reminders of Alaska's past at this 44-acre park are a reconstructed gold-rush town with authentic log cabins; a replica of an Indian village; and a sternwheel riverboat that once plied the Yukon.

BARANOF MUSEUM
101 Marine Way, Kodiak, Alaska
Housed in a warehouse built by a Russian fur trader in the early 1800's are relics of the region's Russian, American, and Native American inhabitants.

KLONDIKE GOLD RUSH NATIONAL HISTORICAL PARK
Visitor center, Broadway and Second Ave., Skagway, Alaska
Once the jumping-off point for the Klondike goldfields, Skagway was a turn-of-the-century boomtown. Dozens of shops, saloons, and other structures have been restored, recalling its boisterous past.

SITKA NATIONAL HISTORICAL PARK
Visitor center, 106 Metlakatla St., Sitka, Alaska
A stunning collection of totem poles punctuates a trail through this 106-acre wooded park, where native teachers demonstrate wood carving, beadwork, and other crafts. Also part of the park is nearby reconstructed Saint Michael's Cathedral, with priceless icons, and the 1842 Russian Bishop's House.

TOTEM BIGHT STATE HISTORIC PARK
North Tongass Hwy., 10 miles north of Ketchikan, Alaska
On display beside a sheltered cove is an excellent collection of totem poles, as well as a reconstructed native community house carved and painted to resemble the face of a huge bird.

ARIZONA

BISBEE
Rte. 80, 26 miles south of Tombstone, Ariz.
Built on the slopes of Mule Pass Gulch, this mining town was the state's richest city in the late 1800's. In addition to touring an underground copper mine by mine car, visitors can stop in at the Bisbee Mining and Historical Museum.

HUBBELL TRADING POST
Off Rte. 264, Ganado, Ariz.
Founded in 1878 by John Hubbell, a friend and advisor of the Navajo, this massive stone trading post demonstrates the role of the Indian trader in the Old Southwest — and still sells rugs, jewelry, and other Native American handcrafts.

JEROME
Alt. Rte. 89, 32 miles southwest of Sedona, Ariz.
Once a bawdy, bustling boomtown that yielded a billion-dollar bonanza of copper and other ores, Jerome is now a haven for artists and retirees who have restored many of its picturesque old buildings.

MISSION SAN XAVIER DEL BAC
Off I-19, nine miles south of Tucson, Ariz.
Superbly designed and richly decorated both inside and out, this mission, known as the White Dove of the Desert, was completed in 1797 and is an outstanding example of Spanish colonial architecture.

NAVAJO NATIONAL MONUMENT
Off Rte. 160, 20 miles west of Kayenta, Ariz.
Three Indian ruins here, dating from about A.D. 1250, are among the finest in the state. Perched on red sandstone cliffs, they can be seen only on ranger-guided tours but are well worth a visit.

PIPE SPRING NATIONAL MONUMENT
Off Rte. 389, 15 miles west of Fredonia, Ariz.
This fortified Mormon ranch house, built of red sandstone and completed in 1872, recalls the region's cattle-ranching past. Guides sometimes demonstrate crafts and ranching techniques.

SHARLOT HALL MUSEUM
415 West Gurley St., Prescott, Ariz.
The vintage structures here include the Territorial Governor's Mansion; the home of explorer-politician John Frémont; an ornate Victorian house; and several others. The museum's collection of period artifacts, begun by poet-historian Sharlot Hall, provides a vivid glimpse into Indian and pioneer life in the Old Southwest.

TOMBSTONE
Rte. 80, 26 miles south of Benson, Ariz.
The site of the shootout at O.K. Corral, this silver mining center prospered in the 1880's and earned a reputation as one of the wildest places in the West. Among the reminders of its rough-and-tumble past are the Bird Cage Theater, its walls peppered with bullet holes; the Crystal Palace Saloon; the courthouse; and, just outside of town, Boothill Cemetery.

ARKANSAS

BATHHOUSE ROW
Visitor center, Central and Reserve Aves., Hot Springs, Ark.
The highlight of Hot Springs National Park, these eight lavishly decorated bathhouses date from the early 1900's and recall the heyday of this famous spa.

EUREKA SPRINGS HISTORIC DISTRICT
Visitor center, Rte. 62W, Eureka Springs, Ark.
The heart of this century-old health resort, located in the Ozarks, includes several elegant old hotels and a wealth of whimsically ornate late Victorian homes.

OLD WASHINGTON HISTORIC STATE PARK
Visitor center, Rte. 4, Washington, Ark.
Once a bustling hub for settlers heading into Texas, then a sleepy backwater, Washington is among the country's best preserved early 19th-century villages. Points of interest include the blacksmith shop where, tradition says, the first of Jim Bowie's famous knives was forged.

OZARK FOLK CENTER
Rte. 382, Mountain View, Ark.
Ozark folk culture comes vividly to life with craft demonstrations and musical performances at this 50-building museum complex.

QUAPAW QUARTER HISTORIC NEIGHBORHOODS
Old State House, 300 West Markham St., Little Rock, Ark.
The historic heart of Little Rock is replete with fine old homes and other structures. Among those open to visitors is the Old State House, an elegant Greek Revival structure completed in 1836 and now a museum of Arkansas history. Nearby at the Arkansas Territorial Restoration, a cluster of five homes and outbuildings reflect the lifestyles of pre-Civil War Arkansas.

CALIFORNIA

BODIE STATE HISTORIC PARK
Off Rte. 395, south of Bridgeport, Calif.
More than 100 structures remain from the 1880's heyday of this mining ghost town, once among the wickedest in the West. Wooden and weather-beaten, the abandoned buildings testify to the hardships of the miner's life.

CABLE CAR MUSEUM
1201 Mason St., San Francisco, Calif.
Antique cable cars and vintage photos can be seen here, as well as the machinery that operates the city's cable cars.

COLUMBIA STATE HISTORIC PARK
Off Rte. 49, north of Sonora, Calif.
Much of this old mining town, once hailed as the Gem of the Southern Mines, has been restored. Visitors can take a stagecoach ride and drop in at the jail, the schoolhouse, a miner's cabin, and many other sites for an authentic sampling of life in the gold-rush era.

EL PUEBLO DE LOS ANGELES STATE HISTORIC PARK
Visitor center, 622 North Main St., Los Angeles, Calif.
Near the site where Los Angeles was founded in 1781, its early days are evoked by the 1818 Avila Adobe, the city's oldest house; the 1822 Old Plaza Church; the Mexican market on Olvera Street; and other attractions.

FORT ROSS STATE HISTORIC PARK
Rte. 1, Jenner, Calif.
This Russian outpost overlooking the sea, established in 1812 to supply settlements in Alaska, has one original building and several reproductions that recall 29 years of Russian presence on the Pacific Coast.

HEARST-SAN SIMEON STATE HISTORICAL MONUMENT
Rte. 1, San Simeon, Calif.
On his estate overlooking the Pacific, newspaper magnate William Randolph Hearst built his dream castle — a group of palatial structures furnished with his huge collection of artworks and antiques.

LA PURISIMA MISSION STATE HISTORIC PARK
Purisima and Mission Gate Rds., Lompoc, Calif.
Rebuilt from ruins, this large complex in a rural setting provides one of the state's best displays of early 19th-century mission life, with craft demonstrations and exhibits on mission industries.

MARSHALL GOLD DISCOVERY STATE HISTORIC PARK
Rte. 49, Coloma, Calif.
At the site of the discovery that triggered the California gold rush, a replica of John Sutter's sawmill and other exhibits memorialize the lives and times of James Marshall, who made the find, and the 49ers who came to exploit it.

MISSION SAN CARLOS BORROMEO
3080 Rio Rd., Carmel, Calif.
Amid lovely gardens stands one of the prettiest missions in the state. Founded in 1770 by Fra Junipero Serra, father of the California missions, its restoration began in the 1870's, prompted in part by the efforts of Robert Louis Stevenson.

MISSION SANTA BARBARA
Upper Laguna St. Santa Barbara, Calif.
This gracefully proportioned complex overlooking the Pacific is rightfully known as Queen of the Missions. The 10th of the 21 California missions and one of the best preserved, it was founded in 1786.

MONTEREY STATE HISTORIC PARK
20 Custom House Plaza, Monterey, Calif.
Seven adobe structures, most of them from the 1830's and 1840's, are relics of the era when Monterey was the capital of Mexican California. The Custom House, from about 1827, is the state's oldest public building; the Larkin House was built by the U.S. consul to Mexico, who combined New England and Spanish features to create the distinctive — and gracious — Monterey style of architecture.

OLD SACRAMENTO STATE HISTORIC PARK
Visitor center, Second and J Sts., Sacramento, Calif.
Dozens of 19th-century buildings have been restored in the city's historic hub, among them the western terminus of the Pony Express. Also here is the California State Railroad Museum, with vintage rolling stock and displays on railroading.

OLD TOWN SAN DIEGO STATE HISTORIC PARK
Visitor center, 2645 San Diego Ave., San Diego, Calif.
The park, in what was once the heart of California's oldest Spanish settlement, includes the Seeley Stable, with a display of horse-drawn vehicles; La Casa de Estudillo, an 1827 adobe residence; and the home of the city's first newspaper.

SAN FRANCISCO MARITIME NATIONAL HISTORICAL PARK
Museum, foot of Polk St.; Historic Ships, foot of Hyde St., San Francisco, Calif.
A superb summary of Pacific Coast shipping is on view at the park's National Maritime Museum, which displays a huge collection of ship models and other maritime relics; featured at nearby Hyde Street Historic Ships are several vintage vessels, including a steel-hulled square-rigger built in 1886 and a side-wheel ferry.

SOUTHWEST MUSEUM
234 Museum Dr., Los Angeles, Calif.
Founded by pioneering ethnographer Charles Fletcher Lummis, the museum features one of the country's best collections of artifacts of Native Americans, past and present.

COLORADO

BENT'S OLD FORT NATIONAL HISTORIC SITE
35110 Rte. 194 East, La Junta, Colo.
In the 1830's and 1840's, the fortified adobe trading post here on the Santa Fe Trail was a vital meeting place for trappers, traders, and Indians. Guides and furnishings in a replica of the fort offer a convincing picture of 1840's frontier life.

CENTRAL CITY
Off Rte. 119, Black Hawk, Colo.
The city that sprang up at the site of Colorado's first gold rush, dubbed the richest square mile on earth, once was so prosperous that it vied with Denver for selection as the territorial capital. Many buildings remain from that era, among them the Central City Opera House, where performances are still given each summer.

DURANGO & SILVERTON NARROW-GAUGE RAILROAD
Depot, 479 Main Ave., Durango, Colo.
The country's oldest continuously operated narrow-gauge railroad, once used for hauling ore and miners, now takes tourists on thrilling steam-powered trips through stunning mountain scenery.

GEORGETOWN
Visitor center, 620 Sixth St., Georgetown, Colo.
The Hotel de Paris, a famous old hostelry, and the elegant Hamill House, home of a mining magnate, are but 2 of some 200 Victorian structures still lining the streets of this former mining center.

LEADVILLE
Chamber of Commerce, 809 Harrison Ave., Leadville, Colo.
Once a fabulously wealthy mining hub, Leadville celebrates its hurly-burly past with such attractions as the Horace Tabor House, home of the city's first mayor; the Matchless Mine, where he made much of his fortune; the Tabor Opera House; and many fine Victorian structures.

MESA VERDE NATIONAL PARK
Off Rte. 160, east of Cortez, Colo.
Tucked into cavernous alcoves on the sides of the huge mesa are the ruins of more than 600 Indian cliff dwellings built about A.D. 1200. Cliff Palace, the largest, has more than 200 rooms and 23 kivas (ceremonial chambers).

MOLLY BROWN HOUSE
1340 Pennsylvania St., Denver, Colo.
The lavish 18-room home of the "Unsinkable Molly Brown," survivor of the *Titanic* disaster, exemplifies the high living made possible by mining wealth.

MUSEUM OF WESTERN ART
1727 Tremont Pl., Denver, Colo.
In the 1880 redbrick Navarre Building, works by Frederic Remington, Charles M. Russell, and some 50 other artists portray the American West from the 1860's to the 1940's.

CONNECTICUT

GILLETTE CASTLE STATE PARK
Off Rte. 82, Hadlyme, Conn.
This 24-room fieldstone fantasy was built by actor-playwright William Gillette, who was famous for his portrayals of Sherlock Holmes. Filled with eccentric furnishings, the mock medieval castle commands majestic views of the Connecticut River Valley.

MYSTIC SEAPORT MUSEUM
Rte. 27, Mystic, Conn.
More than 60 buildings make up this recreated 19th-century New England seafaring town. Besides climbing aboard the *Charles W. Morgan*, an authentic Yankee whaling ship, it is possible to watch a wood-carver fashioning a ship's figurehead, find out how cordage is made, and sample other activities that were essential to the age of sail.

NEW ENGLAND CAROUSEL MUSEUM
95 Riverside Ave., Bristol, Conn.
In addition to viewing a fine collection of hand-carved carousel figures, visitors can watch artisans restoring vintage pieces.

NOAH WEBSTER HOUSE
227 South Main St., West Hartford, Conn.
The birthplace of Noah Webster, compiler of the first American dictionary, and a small museum commemorate the man known as "schoolmaster to America."

NOOK FARM
Visitor center, 77 Forest St., Hartford, Conn.
Highlights of this literary enclave are Mark Twain's Victorian home and the simpler residence of Harriet Beecher Stowe, the author of *Uncle Tom's Cabin*.

OLD NEWGATE PRISON AND COPPER MINE
Newgate Rd., East Granby, Conn.
The dank depths of a copper mine here served as a prison for Tories during the Revolutionary War, and later became the country's first state prison.

PRUDENCE CRANDALL MUSEUM
Village Green, Canterbury, Conn.
Here in her Canterbury Female Seminary, schoolmarm Prudence Crandall in 1833 established New England's first, but short-lived, school for African-American girls.

SHORE LINE TROLLEY MUSEUM
17 River St., East Haven, Conn.
On display are about 100 trolleys and interurban-transit cars. Visitors can also take a three-mile trolley ride and watch restorers at work on antique cars.

WEBB-DEANE-STEVENS MUSEUM
211 Main St., Wethersfield, Conn.
This attractive residential complex includes the Joseph Webb House, visited by George Washington; the home of diplomat Silas Deane; and the home of Isaac Stevens, a tanner and saddler.

DELAWARE

HAGLEY MUSEUM
Rte. 141, Wilmington, Del.
In addition to the original E. I. du Pont gunpowder mills and the du Pont family home, exhibits here explore the development of American industry since colonial times, from grist milling and tanning to toolmaking and paper manufacture.

HISTORIC HOUSES OF ODESSA
Main and Second Sts., Odessa, Del.
Beautifully restored in this former grain-shipping port are the Brick Hotel Gallery, with an exceptional collection of furniture by John Henry Belter; the 1774 brick Georgian-style Corbit-Sharp House; and the 1769 Wilson-Warner House.

LEWES HISTORICAL COMPLEX
Third and Shipcarpenter Sts., Lewes, Del.
Located at the mouth of Delaware Bay, the complex includes a country store, a doctor's office, and a maritime museum, as well as a Coast Guard Life Saving Station and a replica of a lightship that once marked the entrance to the bay.

NEW CASTLE HISTORIC DISTRICT
Old Court House, Delaware St., New Castle, Del.
Surrounding the town green is a superb ensemble of homes and public buildings, many from the era when New Castle was Delaware's colonial capital. Information on a self-guided walking tour is available at the Old Court House, built in 1732.

WINTERTHUR MUSEUM
Rte. 52, Winterthur, Del.
Considered by many to be the country's finest collection of American furnishings and decorative arts, tens of thousands of objects are displayed here in 175 period rooms that Henry Francis du Pont reconstructed in his mansion. The adjoining Galleries at Winterthur offer interpretive exhibits on the decorative arts.

DISTRICT OF COLUMBIA

FORD'S THEATRE
511 Tenth St. NW, Washington D.C.
The playhouse where President Abraham Lincoln was assassinated on April 14, 1865 has been restored to its appearance on that fateful night.

LIBRARY OF CONGRESS
10 First St. SE, Washington, D.C.
The world's largest library, housed in three buildings, boasts an ever-growing collection of more than 90 million items, from books and sheet music to maps and microfilms. The 1897 Thomas Jefferson Building is a richly decorated extravaganza. The Art Deco John Adams Building dates from 1939 and the James Madison Memorial Building was built in 1980.

NATIONAL AIR AND SPACE MUSEUM
Independence Ave. and Seventh St. SW, Washington, D.C.
The collections here include such historic craft as the Wright brothers' *Flyer;* Charles Lindbergh's *Spirit of St. Louis*; and John Glenn's earth-orbiting *Friendship 7.* More than 20 galleries cover all aspects of flight, from ballooning to space exploration.

NATIONAL BUILDING MUSEUM
F St. between Fourth and Fifth Sts. NW, Washington, D.C.
Housed in a landmark building that is in itself worth a visit are displays on the building arts, including one on the architectural treasures of Washington, D.C.

NATIONAL MUSEUM OF AMERICAN HISTORY
Constitution Ave. and Fourteenth. St. NW, Washington, D.C.
This treasure trove of Americana traces our country's social, political, cultural, and technological development. Exhibits range from the flag that inspired the national anthem to the Inaugural gowns of First Ladies, locomotives, stamps, and Archie Bunker's easy chair.

NATIONAL PORTRAIT GALLERY
Eighth and F Sts. NW, Washington, D.C.
A sort of collective family album, the exhibits here feature paintings, drawings, statues, and photographs of men and women who have made significant contributions to the nation's development.

U.S. CAPITOL
Capitol Hill, Washington, D.C.
With its imposing dome dominating the Washington skyline, the Capitol is well known as the scene of many historic events. Less well known is the grandeur of the settings for those events — the soaring Rotunda, the Old Senate Chamber, and many more, all of them embellished with priceless paintings, statuary, and rich architectural detail. Visitors can also obtain passes to witness both houses of Congress in action.

WASHINGTON MONUMENT
The Mall at 15th St. NW, Washington, D.C.
Begun in 1848 and finally completed in 1884, the famous memorial to the first president, at 555 feet, is the world's tallest masonry structure. The observation room at the top offers unsurpassed views of the city.

WHITE HOUSE
1600 Pennsylvania Ave. NW, Washington, D.C.
The home of every president since 1800, the White House has been altered and enlarged many times and was completely renovated during the Truman administration. Guided tours take in several of the public rooms, all of which are furnished with artworks and antiques.

FLORIDA

ART DECO HISTORIC DISTRICT
From Sixth St. to Twentythird St. and Ocean Dr. to Alton Rd., Miami Beach, Fla.
Surviving in this area from the 1930's and 1940's are some 800 structures in the playful, streamlined Art Deco style — one of the largest concentrations of such buildings anywhere.

HENRY MORRISON FLAGLER MUSEUM
Cocoanut Row, Palm Beach, Fla.
The home of Henry Morrison Flagler, the railroad builder and resort developer known as the Father of Florida, is a 55-room mansion overflowing with luxury.

JOHN F. KENNEDY SPACE CENTER
Rte. 405, 39 miles east of Orlando, Fla.
At the launching pad for America's space program, visitors can see exhibits that range from actual spacecraft to a piece of moon rock. They can also take a bus tour that explains the workings of the center.

KEY WEST HISTORIC DISTRICT
Chamber of Commerce, 402 Wall St., Key West, Fla.
Located at the western tip of the Florida Keys, easygoing Key West has long had a special allure for artists and writers. Among its attractions are Ernest Hemingway's home and the Audubon House, recalling a visit by John James Audubon.

RINGLING MUSEUMS
Rte. 41, Sarasota, Fla.
The lavish waterside estate of circus showman John Ringling includes the family residence, modeled on a Venetian palace; a museum and sculpture garden filled with treasures amassed on the Ringlings' travels; a gallery of circus memorabilia; and a theater whose interior was built in 1798 for the Queen of Cyprus.

ST. AUGUSTINE HISTORIC DISTRICT
Information center, 10 Castillo Dr., St. Augustine, Fla.
Our nation's oldest city, founded by Spain in 1565, still has a charmingly Spanish atmosphere. Many Spanish-style buildings line streets off the country's oldest public square, and Castillo de San Marcos, the fortress built to protect the settlement, still stands on the city's waterfront.

THOMAS A. EDISON WINTER HOME
2350 McGregor Blvd., Fort Myers, Fla.
The home and laboratory where Thomas Edison spent 33 working winter vacations remain much as they were in his day and include the largest collection of Edison mementos anywhere.

VIZCAYA MUSEUM AND GARDENS
2351 South Miami Ave., Miami, Fla.
James Deering, a co-founder of the International Harvester Company, in 1916 completed this, his dream house — a 70-room waterfront palace set amid formal gardens and furnished with antiques and art collected on his foreign travels.

GEORGIA

CALLAWAY PLANTATION
Rte. 78, 5 miles west of Washington, Ga.
Besides barns, a blacksmith shop, and other buildings, this working farm, settled by the Callaway family around 1785, features an old log cabin, a simple home from 1790, and an 1869 brick mansion.

DAHLONEGA COURTHOUSE GOLD MUSEUM
Public Square, Dahlonega, Ga.
The 1836 brick courthouse contains exhibits on the country's first major gold rush, which occurred here following the discovery of the precious metal in 1828.

GEORGIA AGRIRAMA
I-75 at Eighth St. (Exit 20), Tifton, Ga.
At this 95-acre museum, interpreters grow crops and operate such facilities as a sawmill, a cotton gin, and a turpentine still in a re-creation of old-time farm life.

MARTIN LUTHER KING, JR. NATIONAL HISTORIC SITE
522 Auburn Ave. NE, Atlanta, Ga.
Civil rights leader Martin Luther King, Jr. is honored at his birthplace, gravesite, and the church where he preached.

NEW ECHOTA STATE HISTORIC SITE
Rte. 225, Calhoun, Ga.
At the former capital of the Cherokee Nation, reconstructions of their supreme court building, newspaper office, and other structures recall a proud heritage.

SAVANNAH HISTORIC DISTRICT
Visitor center, 301 West Broad St., Savannah, Ga.
Encompassing all of the original city plan devised by James Oglethorpe, the founder of Georgia, Savannah's historic heart is a delightful mosaic of parks and shaded streets lined by homes and other buildings embellished with the city's trademark wrought-iron grillwork.

STONE MOUNTAIN PARK
Rte. 78, Stone Mountain, Ga.
In addition to a sculpture of Confederate heroes carved into the granite monolith, the park offers a re-created antebellum plantation, a collection of antique cars, and rides on a replica of a vintage steam train.

WESTVILLE
South Mulberry St., Lumpkin, Ga.
This village is made up of buildings erected before 1850 and brought here from the surrounding area. Populated by costumed guides, they hum with activity as bricks are made, shingles are split, and cabinets are joined.

HAWAII

BERNICE PAUAHI BISHOP MUSEUM
1525 Bernice St., Honolulu, Hawaii
The museum has a huge collection of Hawaiian relics, including examples of the feather robes once worn by its kings.

IOLANI PALACE
King and Richard Sts., Honolulu, Hawaii
This opulent Victorian structure, completed in 1882 by Hawaii's last king, is the only royal palace in the United States. Used as the capitol after the overthrow of the monarchy in 1893, it is now restored to its original splendor as a royal residence.

MISSION HOUSES MUSEUM
553 South King St., Honolulu, Hawaii
Recalling the first Christian missionaries in Hawaii, this complex includes the 1821 Frame House (Hawaii's oldest), the 1831 Chamberlain House, and the 1841 Printing House.

PU'UHONUA O HONAUNAU NATIONAL HISTORICAL PARK
Rte. 160, Honaunau, Hawaii
At this ancient place of refuge for those who broke sacred laws, visitors can admire reconstructed thatched buildings, replicas of carved wooden gods, and demonstrations of native crafts.

U.S.S. ARIZONA MEMORIAL
Visitor center, Rte. 99, Honolulu, Hawaii
The memorial, spanning the sunken hull of the battleship *Arizona,* honors those who died in the surprise Japanese attack on Pearl Harbor in 1941.

IDAHO

FORT HALL REPLICA
Upper level, Ross Park, Pocatello, Idaho
Established in 1834 as a fur-trading post and later prospering as a way station for travelers heading west, the frontier fort has been meticulously re-created.

IDAHO CITY
Rte. 21, 37 miles north of Boise, Idaho
Once a gold-rush boomtown — and, briefly, the biggest city in the Northwest — this sleepy backwater retains the aura of its glory days.

NEZ PERCE NATIONAL HISTORICAL PARK
Visitor center, off Rte. 95, Spalding, Idaho
Twenty-four separate sites in the park, linked by an auto tour route, commemorate the history and heritage of the region's Nez Perce Indians.

OLD MISSION STATE PARK
Off I-90, Cataldo, Idaho
The Greek Revival Indian mission here, completed in 1853 by Jesuit missionaries and Coeur d'Alene Indians working side by side, is Idaho's oldest building.

WALLACE HISTORIC DISTRICT
Off I-90, Wallace, Idaho
At this one-time hub of a fabulously rich mining region, visitors can explore its past at the Wallace District Mining Museum and take guided tours of the Sierra Silver Mine.

ILLINOIS

BISHOP HILL STATE MEMORIAL
Off Rte. 34, Bishop Hill, Ill.
About 20 buildings remain from a utopian colony founded here in 1846. The Steeple Building houses a museum; primitive paintings by a former resident are displayed at the church.

CAHOKIA MOUNDS STATE HISTORIC SITE
Off I-55, Collinsville, Ill.
Some 60 ceremonial and burial mounds mark what was once the largest Indian city north of Mexico. Monk's Mound, covering 14 acres and 100 feet high, is North America's largest Indian earthwork.

FORT DE CHARTRES STATE HISTORIC SITE
Rte. 155, Prairie du Rocher, Ill.
Participants in 18th-century garb gather for an annual rendezvous at the ruins of the finest French fortress in the country. They demonstrate old-time crafts and perform traditional dances to salute the French influence in the heartland.

GALENA HISTORIC DISTRICT
Chamber of Commerce, 101 Bouthillier St., Galena, Ill.
Galena is Latin for "lead ore," the metal on which this river port built its fortune. Among the points of interest are Ulysses S. Grant's one-time home, a blacksmith shop, and the old newspaper office.

JOHN DEERE HISTORIC SITE
Off Rte. 2, Grand Detour, Ill.
A reconstruction of the blacksmith shop in which John Deere invented the plow that broke the plains, and his home, restored and furnished with period antiques, can be visited here.

LINCOLN HOME NATIONAL HISTORIC SITE
Eighth and Jackson Sts., Springfield, Ill.
It was in this house that Abraham Lincoln learned in 1860 that he was the Republican presidential candidate. Now restored, the home is furnished with period pieces and family possessions.

LINCOLN'S NEW SALEM STATE PARK
Rte. 97, Petersburg, Ill.
Reconstructed on their original sites are most of the homes and shops in the frontier village where young Abe Lincoln lived for several years in the 1830's.

OAK PARK HISTORIC DISTRICT
Visitor center, 158 Forest Ave., Oak Park, Ill.
From 1889 until 1909 Frank Lloyd Wright lived in Oak Park, which now contains the largest concentration of his work anywhere. Unity Temple and Wright's home and studio are open to visitors; a walking tour passes 23 other Wright buildings.

INDIANA

CIRCUS CITY FESTIVAL MUSEUM
154 North Broadway, Peru, Ind.
In a town that was once a winter haven for circus folk, posters, costumes, and other mementos recall life under the Big Top.

CONNER PRAIRIE
13400 Allisonville Rd., Noblesville, Ind.
At the 1836 Village here, complete with homes, general store, and carpenter's shop, costumed guides invite visitors to join in as they perform traditional chores.

HISTORIC NEW HARMONY
Visitor center, the Atheneum, Arthur and North Sts., New Harmony, Ind.
Two successive utopian communities flourished here. The first was founded in 1814 by George Rapp, a Lutheran separatist who in 1824 sold the town to Robert Owen, a social reformer. Sites of interest include the Atheneum, a visitor center; Dormitory Number Two, which housed craft shops and living quarters; and the Labyrinth, an elaborate hedge maze.

INDIANAPOLIS MOTOR SPEEDWAY
4790 West Sixteenth St., Indianapolis, Ind.
Built as a testing ground for automotive improvements in 1909, the track soon became the site of the Indianapolis 500 automobile race. The Hall of Fame Museum displays many cars that have won the race, as well as antique and classic autos.

JAMES WHITCOMB RILEY HOUSE
528 Lockerbie St., Indianapolis, Ind.
The home where Hoosier poet James Whitcomb Riley lived for 23 years has been preserved as it was in his day, right down to his hat and cane lying on his bed.

LEVI COFFIN HOUSE
Rte. 27, Fountain City, Ind.
Built in 1839, this brick Federal-style home was the Grand Central Station of the Underground Railroad. It is estimated that Levi Coffin and his wife here sheltered some 2,000 escaped slaves en route to Canada.

IOWA

AMANA COLONIES
Amana Colonies Travel Council, Main St., Amana, Iowa
These seven communities settled by a German religious sect in the mid-1800's retain an aura of bucolic charm. Visitors can learn of the people's traditions at several sites, including the Museum of Amana in Amana, and the Barn Museum and Communal Kitchen Museum, both in Middle Amana.

EFFIGY MOUNDS NATIONAL MONUMENT
Visitor center, Rte. 76, McGregor, Iowa
Here on a bluff overlooking the Mississippi River are nearly 200 Indian burial mounds, including 26 in the shapes of giant bears and birds. Great Bear Mound, the biggest one, is 137 feet long.

HISTORIC GENERAL DODGE HOUSE
605 Third St., Council Bluffs, Iowa
The opulent home of railroad builder-financier Grenville Mellen Dodge has been beautifully restored and decorated in the style of the 1870's and 1880's. Many of the furnishings are family pieces.

LIVING HISTORY FARMS
Hickman Rd. (Rte. 6), Des Moines, Iowa
Ongoing demonstrations and exhibits at this 600-acre complex trace the evolution of farming in Iowa. Crops are raised and livestock cared for at an Indian village; an 1850's Pioneer Farm; an 1870's country village; the 1900 Farm with horse-drawn machinery; and the thoroughly modern Farm of Today and Tomorrow.

PELLA HISTORICAL VILLAGE
Visitor center, 507 Franklin St., Pella, Iowa
Twenty buildings, among them a gristmill, a bakery, and a pottery shop, recall the Dutch heritage of this charming village.

RIVER ADVENTURE
Third St. at Ice Harbor, Dubuque, Iowa
Some 300 years of Mississippi River history come to life at this complex, which includes two paddle-wheel boats, the Woodward Riverboat Museum, the National Rivers Hall of Fame, the Dubuque Heritage Center, and a working boatyard.

VESTERHEIM
502 West Water St., Decorah, Iowa
One of the country's largest immigrant museums, Vesterheim celebrates the heritage of the Norwegians who settled here. A wealth of folk handicrafts, home furnishings, and other relics are displayed in a dozen historic buildings, including an 1877 hotel (the main exhibit area) and a sturdy stone-and-frame mill (the oldest building in town).

KANSAS

AMELIA EARHART BIRTHPLACE
223 North Terrace, Atchison, Kans.
The Gothic revival house where the pilot was born in 1897 contains period furnishings and mementos of her career.

BOOT HILL MUSEUM
Front St., Dodge City, Kans.
With a mixture of replicas and the real thing, this re-creation of Dodge City's famous Front Street recaptures the aura of the boomtown's wild and wicked 1870's heyday. Mock medicine shows and shoot-outs are often reenacted on the street, and visitors can take in performances at the Long Branch Saloon.

COUNCIL GROVE
Chamber of Commerce, 117 West Main St., Council Grove, Kans.
The last staging post for travelers heading west on the Santa Fe Trail was also the site where Indians and government agents negotiated the treaty permitting whites passage on the trail.

EISENHOWER CENTER
Rte. 15, Abilene, Kans.
At this memorial to Dwight Eisenhower, memorabilia and displays at his boyhood home and other facilities recall his roles in both political and military life.

HOLLENBERG PONY EXPRESS STATION
Off Rte. 15-E, Hanover, Kans.
This simple structure was one of the way stations where riders for the Pony Express changed horses or, at every third station, were replaced by another rider.

MARTIN AND OSA JOHNSON SAFARI MUSEUM
16 South Grant St., Chanute, Kans.
Films, photos, and memorabilia here focus on the African and South Seas travels of the pioneering wildlife photographers and authors.

NATIONAL AGRICULTURAL CENTER AND HALL OF FAME
630 North 126 St., Bonner Springs, Kans.
Three buildings here bulge with implements and artifacts of farming and country life, and the Hall of Fame honors innovators in agriculture. Vintage steam threshers and other old-time machines are sometimes put into action.

KENTUCKY

ASHLAND
Main St. and Sycamore Rd., Lexington, Ky.
The elegant home of Henry Clay, rebuilt on its original foundation and enhanced by 20 acres of landscaped grounds, is furnished with family belongings.

CUMBERLAND GAP NATIONAL HISTORIC PARK
Visitor center, Rte. 25E, Middlesboro, Ky.
This scenic mountain park preserves the pass, pioneered by Daniel Boone, through which a flood of settlers traveled west across the Appalachian Mountains.

FORT BOONESBOROUGH STATE PARK
Off Rte. 627, nine miles south of Winchester, Ky.
In a replica of the frontier fort built by Daniel Boone and a band of settlers, pioneering life is dramatized by exhibits, artifacts, and costumed craftspeople.

KENTUCKY HORSE PARK
Iron Works Pike, off I-75, Lexington, Ky.
In the heart of bluegrass country, exhibits, demonstrations, and horses galore recall the region's equine heritage. All breeds are represented at the International Museum of the Horse; also here is the American Saddle Horse Museum and a monument to the great Man O' War.

LOCUST GROVE
561 Blankenbaker Lane, Louisville, Ky.
Once the home of Revolutionary War general George Rogers Clark, this handsome 18th-century brick Georgian mansion and several outbuildings have been restored to their 1790's appearance.

McDOWELL HOUSE AND APOTHECARY SHOP
125 South Second St., Danville, Ky.
The restored home of Ephraim McDowell, a pioneering surgeon who lived and worked here in the early 1800's, has been furnished as it might have been in his day. His adjoining apothecary shop displays 19th-century medical items.

OLD FORT HARROD STATE PARK
College St., Harrodsburg, Ky.
At the first permanent white settlement west of the Allegheny Mountains, James Harrod and his fellow pioneers built a sturdy log fort. In this reproduction of the original, complete with blockhouses and stockade, artisans demonstrate woodworking and other pioneer crafts.

SHAKER VILLAGE AT PLEASANT HILL
Rte. 68, Pleasant Hill, Ky.
Some 30 buildings have been restored in this Shaker community, where costumed interpreters demonstrate the crafts and skills that sustained these pious, industrious people. Guest rooms furnished with Shaker reproductions are available in several of the buildings and the Trustees' Office houses a restaurant serving Shaker specialties.

LOUISIANA

ACADIAN VILLAGE
Off Rte. 167, Lafayette, La.
Authentic Acadian buildings — a chapel, general store, homes, and others — have been assembled here to re-create a typical 19th-century bayou settlement and celebrate Acadian culture.

LONGFELLOW-EVANGELINE STATE COMMEMORATIVE AREA
Rte. 31, St. Martinville, La.
Set amid attractive gardens, an authentic 1836 plantation dwelling and a reproduction of an Acadian cabin recall the Evangeline legend and the Acadian way of life.

RURAL LIFE MUSEUM
Essen Lane, off I-10, Baton Rouge, La.
Commemorating the day-to-day life of rural folk, the museum includes an Acadian cabin and other typical folk structures; a working plantation with all its outbuildings; and an exhibit building with a collection of everyday tools and furnishings.

ST. FRANCISVILLE
Rte. 61, 27 miles north of Baton Rouge, La.
Several choice plantation homes can be visited in the vicinity of this picturesque old town, among them Oakley, where John James Audubon completed 32 of his bird paintings; Greenwood, a multi-columned Greek Revival mansion on a still-operating plantation; and Rosedown, an elegantly furnished mansion set off by century-old gardens.

SHADOWS-ON-THE-TECHE
317 East Main St., New Iberia, La.
Built in the 1830's by a sugar planter, this stately home set among live oaks beside the Bayou Teche is representative of the lifestyle of wealthy southern planters.

VIEUX CARRE′
Visitor center, 529 St. Ann St., New Orleans, La.
Comprising some 66 blocks at the heart of old New Orleans, the Vieux Carré or French Quarter is an oasis of picturesque charm. Characterized by a unique blend of French and Spanish influences, the district contains a mix of public buildings, homes, shops, and restaurants, and is best explored at leisure and on foot.

MAINE

FORT WESTERN MUSEUM
Bowman St., Augusta, Maine
It was from this 1754 stronghold, said to be New England's oldest surviving wooden fort, that Benedict Arnold set out with his troops in 1775 on a heroic but doomed march on Quebec.

MAINE MARITIME MUSEUM
263 Washington St., Bath, Maine
In the town where some of the finest wooden ships of the 19th century were built, apprentices still craft small vessels. The bygone seafaring age also is recalled by restored shipyard buildings, boat models, and an authentic schooner.

PORTLAND HEAD LIGHT
Shore Rd., Cape Elizabeth, Maine
Authorized by George Washington and immortalized in Henry Wadsworth Longfellow's poem "The Lighthouse," this picturesque beacon has been guiding ships past dangerous rocks for over two centuries.

ROOSEVELT CAMPOBELLO INTERNATIONAL PARK
Campobello Island, New Brunswick, Canada. Accessible by bridge from Lubec, Maine
Swimming, fishing, and sailing filled the days of young Franklin D. Roosevelt, who summered here as a child and later brought his own family to this island retreat. For visitors today it seems as if the Roosevelts might appear at any moment in the 34-room home that remains much as they left it.

SHAKER VILLAGE
Rte. 26, Sabbathday Lake, Maine
Echoes of an earlier time fill the last active Shaker village. More than a dozen buildings remain, including the communal residence and the meetinghouse, where furniture and handicrafts are displayed.

WADSWORTH-LONGFELLOW HOUSE
487 Congress St., Portland, Maine
The cradle in which the poet was rocked, the desk where he composed many of his great works, and other family furnishings, mementos, and portraits still grace the boyhood home of Henry Wadsworth Longfellow.

YORK
Chamber of Commerce, I-95 and Rte. 1, York, Maine
The York of the early 1700's lives on in its historic district — in the original desks and benches of its one-room school, one of the oldest in the state; in the Old York Gaol, among the oldest remaining British public buildings in America; and in John Hancock's pre-Revolutionary warehouse.

MARYLAND

BALTIMORE AND OHIO RAILROAD MUSEUM
Pratt and Poppleton Sts., Baltimore, Md.
America's oldest depot is the gateway to its largest railroad museum, where more than 80 vintage cars and locomotives evoke the romance of the railroad era.

BARBARA FRITCHIE HOUSE
154 West Patrick St., Frederick, Md.
While others cowered when Confederate troops marched by, legend says, Barbara Fritchie boldly waved Old Glory from her door. Among the memorabilia in this replica of her home is a cane she reputedly used to chase Confederates off her porch.

CHESAPEAKE AND OHIO CANAL NATIONAL HISTORICAL PARK
Visitor center, 11710 MacArthur Blvd., Potomac, Md.
The 184-mile canal was built to link the Ohio River with the eastern seaboard, but was rendered obsolete by the railroad even before it was completed. Exhibits at the visitor center tell the story of the historic waterway, and in summer visitors can take barge trips on the canal.

CHESAPEAKE BAY MARITIME MUSEUM
Navy Point, St. Michaels, Md.
On view here is the largest existing collection of traditional bay craft, from an Indian dugout to a crab dredger and racing sloops. Among the museum's other nautical delights are a boatbuilding shop and a historic cottage-style lighthouse.

COLONIAL ANNAPOLIS HISTORIC DISTRICT
Historic Annapolis Inc., Old Treasury Bldg., State Circle, Annapolis, Md.
Prominent on the skyline of Maryland's colonial capital is the graceful dome of the statehouse, the oldest state capitol still in legislative use. Among the other fine old buildings in the district is the elegant brick residence of William Paca, a signer of the Declaration of Independence.

FORT McHENRY NATIONAL MONUMENT
East Fort Ave., Baltimore, Md.
Francis Scott Key, a Baltimore lawyer, watched as British bombs and rockets rained on this fort during the War of 1812. Inspired by the sight of the American flag still flying at dawn, Key penned the poem that would become our national anthem.

U.S.F. CONSTELLATION
Pier One, Pratt St., Baltimore, Md.
Launched in 1797 and our oldest warship still afloat, this venerable vessel saw service in the War of 1812, the Civil War, and other conflicts, and is now is a prime attraction of Baltimore's Inner Harbor.

MASSACHUSETTS

ADAMS NATIONAL HISTORIC SITE
135 Adams St., Quincy, Mass.
Though John and Abigail Adams named their fine federal home Peacefield, later generations called it simply the Old House and occupied it until the 1920's. Collections there today represent 140 years of Adams family life and range from furnishings to historic documents.

BOSTON NATIONAL HISTORICAL PARK
Visitor center, 15 State St., Boston, Mass.
The "park" comprises the many historic sites that can be visited along Boston's three-mile-long Freedom Trail. The city's Revolutionary past is recalled at such landmarks as the Old North Church (where Paul Revere hung his lanterns) and a replica of one of the ships involved in the Boston Tea Party. And those who travel to the end of the trail will reach the Bunker Hill Monument, commemorating the first major battle of the Revolutionary War.

CONCORD
Off Rte. 2, west of Boston, Mass.
This charming village was a major 19th-century literary center. Within a short distance of one another are seven historic sites, including the Orchard House where Louisa May Alcott wrote *Little Women,* and the Old Manse, which was home to both Ralph Waldo Emerson and Nathaniel Hawthorne.

FRUITLANDS MUSEUMS
102 Prospect Hill Rd., Harvard, Mass.
House museums here commemorate two former idealistic communities: a Shaker settlement begun in 1791 and the transcendental society started by Bronson Alcott in 1843.

HANCOCK SHAKER VILLAGE
Rte. 20, Pittsfield, Mass.
This charming village features 20 fine examples of Shaker architecture — including dormitories, a meeting house, and a famous round stone barn — and many rooms authentically refurbished with Shaker furniture and products. Cooking, farming, and crafts such as broom- and chair-making are demonstrated.

HISTORIC DEERFIELD
Off Rte. 5, Deerfield, Mass.
Once a lonely frontier outpost, Deerfield is now one of the best-preserved colonial towns in New England. Twelve homes are open to the public and display a magnificent selection of antique furnishings.

HOUSE OF SEVEN GABLES
54 Turner St., Salem, Mass.
This 1668 house, famous as the setting for Nathaniel Hawthorne's novel, has been restored to look as it might have in his day. Hawthorne's birthplace is among the other old Salem buildings at the site.

LONGFELLOW NATIONAL HISTORIC SITE
105 Brattle St., Cambridge, Mass.
Henry Wadsworth Longfellow wrote some of his best-loved poems — among them, *Evangeline* and *The Song of Hiawatha* — in this house. Furnished as it was in Longfellow's time, the house contains many of his papers and artifacts.

LOWELL NATIONAL HISTORICAL PARK
Visitor center, 246 Market Street, Lowell, Mass.
A variety of tours here explore the city's pioneering role as a planned industrial community. Visitors can view the area by trolley or canal barge, and walking tours demonstrate the workings of waterwheels and other equipment.

MINUTE MAN NATIONAL HISTORICAL PARK
Battle Road visitor center, Rte 2A, Lexington, Mass.
These 750 acres of parkland recall the fateful confrontation of "embattled farmers" and British troops in 1775. Highlights include a replica of the Old North Bridge and Daniel Chester French's famous Minute Man statue.

NEW BEDFORD HISTORIC DISTRICT
Information center, 70 North Second St., New Bedford, Mass.
In the mid-1800's New Bedford was a busy whaling port, and its waterfront district reflected the wealth of its citizens. Fourteen blocks there have been restored to look as they did when Herman Melville wrote of New Bedford in *Moby Dick.* The district also has a whaling museum featuring scrimshaw, marine paintings, and a half-scale replica of a whaling ship.

OLD STURBRIDGE VILLAGE
Rte. 20, Sturbridge, Mass.
Some 40 authentic 18th- and 19th-century buildings were moved here to re-create a New England village, circa 1830. Sheep graze on the green and farming and household chores are performed daily. Visitors can view the workings of water-powered grist- and sawmills and watch the village blacksmith, cobbler, potter, and tinsmith ply their trades.

PLIMOUTH PLANTATION
Rte. 3, Plymouth, Mass.
In this tiny settlement — surrounded by a stockade fence and complete with houses, garden plots, and animals — visitors can sample life as it was lived in the 1620's. Part of the fun is meeting "colonists" who actually seem to live and work here. Nearby is a replica of the Mayflower and a re-created Indian campsite.

SALEM MARITIME NATIONAL HISTORIC SITE
U.S. Custom House, Derby Street, Salem, Mass.
Salem once was among the most important seaports in America and the center of the 19th-century clipper-ship trade. Its illustrious past lives on at such sites as Derby Wharf, the old Custom House, the West India Goods Store, and the home of Elias Hasket Derby, the man often called "America's first millionaire."

SAUGUS IRON WORKS
244 Central St., Saugus, Mass.
America's first successful ironworks was founded here in the 1640's. The ironmaster's 1646 house still stands, and the works — where 17th-century forging techniques are demonstrated — include a reconstructed furnace, a blacksmith shop, and a water-powered forge.

THE WITCH HOUSE
310 ½ Essex St., Salem, Mass.
Visitors who enter Judge Jonathan Corwin's home are following in the footsteps of the men and women accused of witchcraft in 17th-century Salem. Exhibits recall the superstitious frenzy of the witch-hunting winter of 1692. Nearby at the Witch Museum, a multimedia show dramatizes the events.

MICHIGAN

FAIR LANE
4901 Evergreen Rd., Dearborn, Mich.
Henry Ford's 56-room mansion, completed in 1915, included such up-to-date amenities as a central vacuum cleaning system and its own powerhouse.

FORT MICHILIMACKINAC
Fort Michilimackinac State Park, off I-75, Mackinaw City, Mich.
Built by the French in 1715, the fort here was a major outpost in the fur trade. Visitors today can inspect the barracks, commander's residence, and other facilities in an accurate replica on the original site.

HENRY FORD MUSEUM AND GREENFIELD VILLAGE
Oakwood Blvd., Dearborn, Mich.
A monument to one man's passion for collecting, Henry Ford's museum is a cornucopia of Americana , with everything from steam engines and horse carts to kitchen appliances and decorative arts. In his adjoining Greenfield Village, relocated and reconstructed homes and workshops, including one of Thomas Edison's laboratories, recall the birth of American industry.

HISTORIC FAYETTE TOWNSITE
Fayette State Park, Garden, Mich.
Now a ghost town, Fayette was founded in 1867 to support an iron smelting industry. Some 20 original structures remain, among them the furnaces, a beehive-shaped charcoal kiln, the opera house, and the company office.

IRON COUNTY MUSEUM
Museum Lane, Rte. 424, Caspian, Mich.
Eighteen structures make up this re-created 19th-century mining and logging village. Prominent in the settlement are the engine house from the nearby Caspian mine and the home of Carrie Jacobs-Bond, who composed "I Love You Truly."

MACKINAC ISLAND
Visitor center, Fort and Huron Sts., Mackinac Island, Mich.
An oasis of calm where automobiles are banned, this island in Lake Huron has been a summer resort since the mid-1800's. Fort Mackinac, dating from 1781, and John Jacob Astor's fur warehouse recall more turbulent times when the island was a strategic Great Lakes crossroads.

MINNESOTA

THE DEPOT: SAINT LOUIS COUNTY HERITAGE AND ART CENTER
506 West Michigan St., Duluth, Minn.
In a renovated 1892 railroad depot, four floors of exhibits encompass everything from antique dolls and clothing to Indian portraits and Native American crafts. A highlight of the center is Depot Square, a re-creation of turn-of-the-century Duluth featuring 24 old-time stores.

FARMAMERICA
County Roads 2 and 17, Waseca, Minn.
Minnesota farm life from 1850 to the present is re-created here at farmsteads representing different eras.

FOREST HISTORY CENTER
2609 County Rd. 76, Grand Rapids, Minn.
The buildings here include a blacksmith shop, a bunkhouse, and an employee's store — just as would have been found at a lumber camp in 1900. The center also has woodland trails and offers special exhibits on forestry and the local Indians.

GRAND PORTAGE NATIONAL MONUMENT
Off Rte. 61. Grand Marais, Minn.
The grand portage was the "great carrying place," an overland trail that took fur trappers from Lake Superior to the Pigeon

River, gateway to the inland beaver country. The trading post built here more than 200 years ago has been reconstructed, and visitors can hike the old portage trail.

OLIVER H. KELLEY FARM
Rte. 10, Elk River, Minn.
The fields here still are worked with 19th-century equipment, just as they were in the day of Oliver Kelley, the founder of the Grange movement. In the farmhouse interpreters make molasses, churn butter, and do other chores.

PIPESTONE NATIONAL MONUMENT
Visitor center, off Rte. 75, Pipestone, Minn.
At the quarries where local Indians obtained the special red clay for their calumets, or ceremonial pipes, visitors can watch demonstrations of pipe-making and other Indian crafts.

SOUDAN UNDERGROUND MINE STATE PARK
Off Rte. 169, Soudan, Minn.
Located in the Vermilion Range, the park centers on the Soudan Iron Mine, the oldest and deepest in the state. Guided tours include a 2,400-foot descent by elevator and a train trip through the mine.

MISSISSIPPI

BEAUVOIR
West Beach Blvd. (Rte. 90), Biloxi, Miss.
This modest seaside cottage, with wide porches and tall windows designed to take advantage of cool breezes, was the home of Confederate President Jefferson Davis and his family. Also on the property is the tomb of the Unknown Soldier of the Confederate States of America.

FLOREWOOD RIVER PLANTATION
Rte. 82, Greenwood, Miss.
A Greek Revival home and some 20 outbuildings, from smokehouse to sorghum mill, make up this re-created 19th-century cotton plantation. Guides demonstrate period crafts and, in late summer, visitors can try their hand at picking cotton.

LONGWOOD
140 Lower Woodville Rd., Natchez, Miss.
From the outside, the largest octagonal house in the country seems a stunning abode. Closer inspection, however, reveals that only the basement was ever completed: with construction interrupted by the Civil War, the rest remains an empty—but imposing—shell.

NATCHEZ TRACE PARKWAY
Visitor center, Tupelo, Miss.
Boatmen carrying cargo down the Mississippi River used to sell their goods — and their boats — in Natchez before traveling home on a wilderness trail to Tennessee. The scenic parkway follows its route, with many historical and archeological sites preserved along the way.

OLD COURT HOUSE MUSEUM
Court Square, Vicksburg, Miss.
Legend has it that during the siege of Vicksburg in 1863, this Greek Revival courthouse was spared when the city's Southern defenders sent word that Northern soldiers were being held in the building. Now a museum, it displays Indian relics and Civil War mementos.

ROWAN OAK
Old Taylor Rd., Oxford, Miss
This antebellum house was the home of William Faulkner, Nobel Prize-winning delineator of life in the South. Faulkner's presence is felt most strongly in his office, where the outline of his novel, *A Fable,* is written on the walls, and his typewriter seems to await his next inspiration.

STANTON HALL
401 High St., Natchez, Miss.
Among the most elegant of the many mansions in Natchez, this lavish home was built by a cotton broker who filled it with fine marble mantels, gold-leaf mirrors, and other imported furnishings.

MISSOURI

HARRY S. TRUMAN NATIONAL HISTORIC SITE
Information center, Truman Rd. and Main St., Independence, Mo.
Harry Truman so loved this home that he used it as his Summer White House. Among the many family belongings still there are Truman's hat and coat, hanging in the front hall as if in readiness for one of the former president's famous morning walks.

JEFFERSON NATIONAL EXPANSION MEMORIAL
Off I-70, St. Louis, Mo.
Ever since the Lewis and Clark Expedition set out from St. Louis, the town has been a gateway to the West. The famous Gateway Arch, 60 stories tall and made of stainless steel, now dominates a riverfront park. Trams inside the arch carry visitors to observation windows at the top; at the base is the Museum of Westward Expansion.

MARK TWAIN BOYHOOD HOME AND MUSEUM
208 Hill St., Hannibal, Mo.
Appropriately, a whitewashed fence surrounds the garden of this house in the river town of Hannibal, immortalized by Twain in *The Adventures of Tom Sawyer.* Twain memorabilia fills the museum next door, and across the street is the home of the real-life Becky Thatcher.

STE. GENEVIEVE
Visitor center, South Third St., Ste. Genevieve, Mo.
Architectural treasures in the form of French colonial homes line the streets of this river town (Missouri's oldest), which was settled by French Canadians.

THOMAS HART BENTON HOME AND STUDIO
3616 Belleview Ave., Kansas City, Mo.
In this Victorian home lived 20th-century artist Thomas Hart Benton, who captured everyday life in the Midwest on canvas. His home and carriage house-studio hold many personal belongings.

WATKINS WOOLEN MILL STATE HISTORIC SITE
Rte. 69, six miles north of Excelsior Springs, Mo.
This sturdy brick mill was opened in 1861 — just in time to do a booming trade in blankets and cloth during the Civil War. It is the country's only 19th-century textile factory with working original machinery.

MONTANA

CHARLES M. RUSSELL MUSEUM
400 Thirteenth St., Great Falls, Mont.
Charles M. Russell arrived in Montana at age 15 in 1880 and spent the rest of his life there, working as a cowboy, living with Indians, and painting some 4,500 pictures of

the West he knew and loved. The cowboy artist's home and studio feature the most extensive collection of his art anywhere.

FORT BENTON
Off Rte 87, 40 miles north of Great Falls, Mont.
Founded in 1846 as a fur-trading post, Fort Benton later prospered as the northernmost steamboat port on the Missouri River. Part of the original fort still stands, along with many 19th-century buildings and a museum with displays on the fur trade and the steamboat era.

GRANT-KOHRS RANCH NATIONAL HISTORIC SITE
Off I-90, Deer Lodge, Mont.
Montana's past as cattle country is commemorated at the headquarters area of a ranch whose herds once grazed on a million acres. Operated as a living-history museum, the spread features the cattle baron's home, as well as bunkhouses, barns, and other outbuildings.

HELENA HISTORIC DISTRICT
Chamber of Commerce, 201 East Lyndale St., Helena, Mont.
Prospectors panning for gold first struck it rich in Helena in 1864, and the region remained rich with subsequent mineral discoveries. The city's historic district is as a result a shining example of boomtown grandeur. Its mansions and public buildings (including a magnificent cathedral) represent Victorian architecture at its eclectic best.

MUSEUM OF THE PLAINS INDIAN
Rtes. 2 and 89, Browning, Mont.
Exhibits feature the ceremonial traditions, history, and artifacts the Blackfoot, Northern Cheyenne, Sioux, Chippewa-Cree, and other Indians of the northern plains.

VIRGINIA CITY
Rte. 287, 60 miles south of Butte, Mont.
One of the most colorful towns in Montana, Virginia City knew more than its share of gold strikes, vigilantes, and lawless living. Today buildings along five streets have been restored in this truly authentic gold-rush ghost town.

WORLD MUSEUM OF MINING AND HELL ROARIN' GULCH
West Park Street, Butte, Mont.
On the site of the Orphan Girl Mine, Butte's boomtown past is brought to life at a reconstructed 19th-century mining camp and a museum focusing on the city's history as "the richest hill on earth."

NEBRASKA

BUFFALO BILL RANCH
Off Rte. 30, North Platte, Nebr.
The sharpshooter-showman built this spread with earnings from his Wild West Show. Visitors can tour William F. "Buffalo Bill" Cody's 19-room home and a barn containing memorabilia from his shows.

HOMESTEAD NATIONAL MONUMENT
Rte. 4, Beatrice, Nebr.
A Civil War veteran, thought to be one of the first applicants under the Homestead Act of 1862, staked his claim here for 160 acres of land. A log cabin similar to the one he lived in contains typical furnishings and tools, and exhibits at the visitor center recount the history of the homestead movement.

SCOTTS BLUFF NATIONAL MONUMENT
Rte. 92, Gering, Nebr.
For more than 250,000 pioneers traveling on the Oregon Trail, this promontory was both a welcome landmark and an ideal campsite on the long trek West.

STUHR MUSEUM OF THE PRAIRIE PIONEER
Rte. 34, Grand Island, Nebr.
A narrow-gauge steam railroad takes visitors to several re-created prairie settlements, including a railroad town complete with depot and dozens of 19th-century structures. Indian artifacts and mementos of pioneer life, such as clothing, tools, and furnishings, also are on view.

WILLA CATHER HISTORICAL CENTER
Historical Center, North Webster St., Red Cloud, Nebr.
Red Cloud was the hometown of the celebrated novelist, who wrote of life on the prairie. Visitors can tour Cather's childhood home and other sites associated with her writing, including the Historical Center, which displays original manuscripts and other memorabilia.

NEVADA

BOWERS MANSION
4005 Rte. 395N, Carson City, Nev.
Built in 1864 by Nevada's first millionaires — Sandy and Eilley Bowers, who struck it rich in the Comstock Lode — the mansion contains some original furnishings.

GENOA
Off Rte. 395, four miles north of Gardnerville, Nev.
Nevada's oldest permanent white settlement features a replica of the Mormon Station, a fortified trading post that provisioned travelers. Among the exhibits at the nearby Genoa Courthouse Museum is a display on Snowshoe Thompson, who won fame for delivering mail on skis.

NATIONAL AUTOMOBILE MUSEUM
10 Lake St., Reno, Nev.
Two hundred antique and classic automobiles can be seen here, as well as recreated period streetscapes.

NEVADA NORTHERN RAILWAY MUSEUM
1100 Ave. A, East Ely, Nev.
Based in the old depot, the museum exhibits the rolling stock, roundhouse, and other facilities of the Nevada Northern Railway. Excursion trains are sometimes run on the museum's 32 miles of tracks.

VIRGINIA CITY HISTORIC DISTRICT
Visitor center, C St. between Taylor and Union Sts., Virginia City, Nev.
Dubbed Queen of the Comstock Lode, this once fabulously wealthy mining metropolis has been restored to its 1870's appearance. Present-day attractions range from the Castle, one of many sumptuous miners' mansions, and Piper's Opera House, to a firemen's museum with vintage fire-fighting equipment.

NEW HAMPSHIRE

CANTERBURY SHAKER VILLAGE
Rte. 93, Canterbury, N.H.
The first building erected at this Shaker community was a meetinghouse. Raised in 1792, it still stands along with 21 other restored and furnished structures on

some 600 acres. Tours of the village include demonstrations of Shaker crafts, gardening, and harvesting.

MOUNT WASHINGTON COG RAILWAY
Off Rte 302, Mt. Washington, N.H.
New England's tallest peak was already a tourist attraction in 1869 when a cog railway began taking people to its 6,293-foot summit. The little steam locomotive still makes the climb, giving visitors superb mountaintop views.

ROBERT FROST FARM
Off Rte. 28, Derry, N.H.
Robert Frost lived here as a young man in the early 1900's. The restored farm, which served as the setting for some 43 of his poems, includes a nature trail.

SAINT-GAUDENS NATIONAL HISTORIC SITE
Rte. 12A, Cornish, N.H.
In the late 19th century, sculptor Augustus Saint-Gaudens bought an old New England tavern and transformed it into a gracious family home landscaped with formal gardens. Many examples of his work can be seen today on tours of the house, gardens, and studios.

STRAWBERY BANKE
Marcy and Hancock Sts., Portsmouth, N.H.
On a 10-acre site bearing Portsmouth's original name, some 40 historic buildings can be visited, including the functioning shops of a cooper, a boat builder, a weaver, a potter, and other craftspeople. Houses ranging from a humble 17th-century home to an elaborate 1811 mansion have been restored, furnished, and landscaped to represent changes in architecture and home life over the course of 350 years.

WENTWORTH-COOLIDGE MANSION
Little Harbor Rd., Portsmouth, N.H.
Henry Wadsworth Longfellow described Benning Wentworth's house as "a goodly place, where it was good to be." The governor of New Hampshire from 1740 to 1767, Wentworth built his home in stages by joining older structures and attaching additions. Rambling and eccentric, it is still "a goodly place," and one of the few colonial governors' homes to remain unchanged from the 18th century.

NEW JERSEY

EDISON NATIONAL HISTORIC SITE
Main St. and Lakeside Ave., West Orange, N.J.
This memorial to Thomas Edison includes the inventor's laboratory complex and, nearby, the Victorian mansion that was once his home. Both are replete with original equipment and furnishings, recalling the genius who invented such everyday miracles as the phonograph and the first practical incandescent light bulb.

GREAT FALLS HISTORIC DISTRICT
Paterson Museum, 2 Market St., Paterson, N.J.
Conceived by Alexander Hamilton and powered by the Great Falls of the Passaic River, America's first planned industrial complex flourished here for more than a century. Many of the old mills, including one that houses the Paterson Museum, can be seen on walking tours.

HISTORIC BATSTO
Rte. 542, Batsto, N.J.
This iron- and glass-making center prospered from 1766 until just after the Civil War. Now restored, the village's gristmill, sawmill, ironmaster's mansion, and other structures recall life during the early days of the Industrial Revolution.

MORRISTOWN NATIONAL HISTORICAL PARK
230 Morris Ave., Morristown, N.J.
The park preserves the sites where George Washington and his army spent two bitter winters. The complex includes the Ford Mansion, which served as Washington's headquarters; the place where his men built a small fort; and Jockey Hollow, the encampment where the troops spent the winter in log huts.

WATERLOO VILLAGE
Waterloo Rd., Stanhope, N.J.
Once an iron-making center and then a canal port, this hamlet includes more than 20 restored buildings where costumed craftspeople bring the past to life.

WHEATON VILLAGE
Tenth and G Sts., Millville, N.J.
The centerpiece of this re-created glass-making community is a working 1888 glass factory that features daily demonstrations. More than 7,000 items in the Museum of American Glass tell the story of glass-making in America.

NEW MEXICO

ACOMA PUEBLO
Rte. 23, Acoma, N. Mex.
Perched atop a mesa, Acoma Pueblo was founded sometime between the 7th and 12th centuries and is thought to be the oldest continuously occupied settlement in the country. It includes the Church of San Esteban del Rey, the largest of New Mexico's old missions.

CHACO CULTURE NATIONAL HISTORICAL PARK
Rte. 57, south of Blanco Trading Post, N. Mex.
The ruins here date from the 11th and 12th centuries. Pueblo Bonito, the largest of 12 pueblos in the complex, boasted some 800 rooms and is dotted with several kivas — below-ground-level rooms used for ceremonies.

KIT CARSON HOUSE
Kit Carson Rd., Taos, N. Mex.
Hunter, trapper, Indian agent, and guide, Christopher "Kit" Carson bought this house as a wedding gift for his second wife in 1843. A typical southwestern adobe, it contains many original furnishings, and artifacts that recall Carson's legendary life as a mountain man.

LINCOLN STATE MONUMENT
Rte. 380, Lincoln, N. Mex.
The deceptively serene town of Lincoln was in 1878 the site of a quick and bloody "war" starring William Bonney — Billy the Kid. The courthouse where the Kid was jailed is now a museum, and an array of vintage adobes make this one of West's best preserved cow towns .

OLD TOWN ALBUQUERQUE
Visitor center, 300 Romero St. NW, Albuquerque, N. Mex.
In this historic district, Albuquerque's oldest plaza is surrounded by a mix of architecture that echoes the city's Spanish colonial origin and Victorian era growth. The Church of San Felipe de Neri dominates the square, which is enlivened by galleries and craft shops.

SANTA FE PLAZA

Bounded by Palace, Washington, and Lincoln Aves. and San Francisco St., Santa Fe, N. Mex.

Prominent in this charming old square is the Palace of the Governors, in continuous use since 1610 and now a museum. In the 1800's the plaza was the bustling terminus of the Santa Fe Trail. It remains lively today with concerts, fiestas, and an open-air market featuring local arts and crafts.

TAOS PUEBLO

North Pueblo Road, Taos, N. Mex.

Already well-established when the Spanish arrived in 1540, Taos Pueblo is the largest multi-storied pueblo building in America. Visitors can attend ceremonial dances in the plaza and shop for handmade textiles, jewelry, and pottery.

NEW YORK

ADIRONDACK MUSEUM

Blue Mountain Lake, N.Y.

The museum, in the heart of the Adirondack Mountains, celebrates the region's heritage with exhibits that range from an oldtime resort hotel to transportation displays — including an outstanding collection of boats — and examples of the area's distinctive twig furniture.

CHAUTAUQUA INSTITUTION HISTORIC DISTRICT

Rte. 394, Chautauqua, N.Y.

Established in 1874 as an educational retreat for Sunday school teachers, the Chautauqua gatherings quickly became a vehicle for general adult education. The lakeshore meeting ground is still in use, including the Amphitheater; Palestine Park, a scale model of the Holy Land; and the 1873 Atheneum Hotel.

ERIE CANAL MUSEUM

Erie Blvd. East, Syracuse, N.Y.

Housed in an 1850 building where canal boats were weighed and tolls assessed, the museum's exhibits offer an introduction to the Big Ditch that linked the Great Lakes with the Atlantic Coast.

GEORGE EASTMAN HOUSE

900 East Ave., Rochester, N.Y.

Photography mogul George Eastman's mansion is now home to the International Museum of Photography. Its collections include millions of prints, movie films, and more than 10,000 cameras.

HOME OF FRANKLIN D. ROOSEVELT

Rte. 9, Hyde Park, N.Y.

FDR was born in this spacious house overlooking the Hudson River. His books and papers, his desk from the White House, and many other belongings are maintained just as he left them. Nearby is Val-Kill, the cottage where Eleanor Roosevelt lived after Franklin's death.

NATIONAL BASEBALL HALL OF FAME AND MUSEUM

Main St., Cooperstown, N.Y.

A monument to the national pastime, the museum has displays on all aspects of baseball as well as a Hall of Fame honoring the all-time great players.

NEW YORK STOCK EXCHANGE

20 Broad St., New York, N.Y.

Exhibits here focus on the Exchange and its history, and a visitor's gallery overlooks the action on the trading floor.

OLANA

Rte. 9G, Hudson, N.Y.

The home of landscape painter Frederick Edwin Church was designed by the painter himself in a mix of styles that he called "personal Persian." Overlooking the Hudson River, the house and its grounds form a cohesive unit as perfectly executed as one of Church's paintings.

RADIO CITY MUSIC HALL

1260 Avenue of the Americas, New York, N.Y.

With 5,784 seats, this Art Deco showplace in the Rockefeller Center complex is the largest theater in the country.

SCHUYLER MANSION

32 Catherine St., Albany, N.Y.

In 1780 Alexander Hamilton married Betsy Schuyler in the elegant drawing room of this rose-brick mansion. The house has Federal furnishings and displays of family items.

STATUE OF LIBERTY NATIONAL MONUMENT

Liberty Island, N.Y. Accessible by ferry from Battery Park, Manhattan

A gift from France to the people of America, Lady Liberty has held her welcoming torch aloft in New York Harbor since 1886. Nearby Ellis Island, where millions of immigrants entered the United States, also is part of the national monument.

SUNNYSIDE

West Sunnyside Lane, Tarrytown, N.Y.

Washington Irving described his whimsical house as "a little, old-fashioned stone mansion all made up of gabled ends, and as full of angles and corners as an old cocked hat." The grounds and interior are no less enchanting, and some of his original furniture remains in place.

UNITED STATES MILITARY ACADEMY

Visitor center, Rte. 218, West Point, N.Y.

The academy, familiarly known as West Point, was established in 1802 and has educated some of our most famous military leaders. The academy's museum displays an excellent collection of weapons, uniforms, art, and other memorabilia.

VANDERBILT MANSION

Rte. 9, Hyde Park, N.Y.

One of the grandest of the grand estates of the Gilded Age, this 54-room Italian Renaissance mansion was completed in 1899 and is sumptuously outfitted with fine furnishings, many of which came from a château once owned by Napoleon.

NORTH CAROLINA

BILTMORE HOUSE AND GARDENS

Rte. 25, Asheville, N.C.

Designed in the style of a French château, G.W. Vanderbilt's 1895 Biltmore House has been called the "largest, grandest residential estate ever built in America." Many of its 250 rooms are filled with art treasures, and the parklike grounds, landscaped by Frederick Law Olmsted, include 17 acres of gardens.

EDENTON

Visitor center, North Broad St., Edenton, N.C.

One of North Carolina's most important colonial towns is also one of its loveliest, with some of its fine 18th-century homes and public buildings open to visitors.

HISTORIC BATH

Visitor center, Carteret St., Bath, N.C.

Chartered in 1705, North Carolina's oldest incorporated town was the home of several governors — and of Blackbeard the pirate. Many of Bath's original buildings have been restored and several, including the 18th-century St. Thomas Church, can be visited.

OCONALUFTEE INDIAN VILLAGE
Rte. 441 North, Cherokee, N.C.
This outdoor museum re-creates 18th-century Cherokee village life and features a seven-sided council house. The nearby Museum of the Cherokee Indian displays artifacts representing 10,000 years of Indian history.

OLD SALEM
Visitor center, Old Salem Rd., Winston-Salem, N.C.
Moravian settlers built a town here in the 18th century and prospered through the production of pottery, tinware, clocks, and other goods. Of some 50 brick and half-timber buildings that have been restored, 10 are open to the public and range from a bakery famous for its Lovefeast buns, to shops, houses, and the Home Moravian Church.

OLD TOWN BEAUFORT HISTORIC SITE
Turner St., off Rte. 70, Beaufort, N.C.
Many of this coastal town's earliest buildings have been moved to this five-block area, including a 1796 courthouse, a one-cell jail, an apothecary shop, a fisherman's cottage, and other residences.

TRYON PALACE
Off Rte. 17, New Bern, N.C.
Built for Royal Governor William Tryon and completed in 1770, Tryon Palace was North Carolina's first permanent capitol. Later abandoned and partially burned, it has been rebuilt in exacting detail. Now furnished and landscaped as it was in the 18th century, the mansion and its formal gardens offer visitors a glimpse of pre-Revolutionary grandeur.

WRIGHT BROTHERS NATIONAL MEMORIAL
U.S. Bypass 158, Kill Devil Hills, N.C.
Wilbur and Orville Wright's first successful powered flight took place here on December 17, 1903. The visitor center displays a replica of the orignal plane, and markers indicate the Wrights' take-off and landing spots on that historic day.

NORTH DAKOTA

BONANZAVILLE, U.S.A.
Off I-94, West Fargo, N. Dak.
Recalling the bonanza-farm era, this reconstructed pioneer village comprises some 40 buildings, including a town hall, a sod house, and a vintage barbershop.

CHATEAU DE MORES STATE HISTORIC SITE
Off I-94, Medora, N. Dak.
Marquis de Mores, a French nobleman, built this lavish home in the town he founded as the site of his meat packing plant. The house contains many of the marquis's original furnishings.

FORT ABRAHAM LINCOLN STATE PARK
Rte. 1806, Mandan, N. Dak.
It was from this fort that George Armstrong Custer set out on the campaign that ended with the Battle of the Little Big Horn. In addition to Custer's house and other fort buildings, the park showcases the reconstructed earthen lodges of a Mandan Indian village.

FORT TOTTEN STATE HISTORIC SITE
Rte. 57, Fort Totten, N. Dak.
Built for the protection of travelers, Fort Totten is one of the best-preserved military posts in the West. Sixteen of its brick buildings are still standing, including barracks, officers' quarters, and a hospital.

FORT UNION TRADING POST
Buford Rte., Williston, N. Dak.
Several buildings have been reconstructed at what was once the most important trading post on the northern plains. A museum displays relics from its past, and every summer trappers and mountain men dressed in buckskins reenact the traditional fur-traders' rendezvous.

OHIO

CAMPUS MARTIUS: THE MUSEUM OF THE NORTHWEST TERRITORY
601 Second St., Marietta, Ohio
The museum features the only surviving home from the first permanent settlement in the Northwest Territory, as well as the 1788 land office where settlers received their land grants.

CARILLON HISTORICAL PARK
2001 South Patterson Blvd., Dayton, Ohio
This 65-acre park illustrates the history of American transportation and includes such treasures as an authentic Concord coach, a 1905 Wright brothers airplane, and a 1912 Cadillac — the first car ever equipped with the self starter invented by Ohio native, Charles Kettering.

MALABAR FARM STATE PARK
4050 Bromfield Rd., Lucas, Ohio
The homestead of writer and experimental farmer Louis Bromfield is maintained as a model farm and nature center. Bromfield's home is filled with many original family furnishings.

McGUFFEY MUSEUM
Spring and Oak Sts., Oxford, Ohio
William Holmes McGuffey built this house in the 1830's and then set to work on the first of his McGuffey Readers, the books that would make him famous. Exhibits include his eight-sided desk, family items, and many editions of the Readers.

OHIO VILLAGE
I-71 at Seventeenth Ave., Columbus, Ohio
The 19th century comes to life in this recreated Ohio village where costumed guides use period tools and techniques to demonstrate farming and various crafts.

ROSCOE VILLAGE
Rte. 16, Coshocton, Ohio
Roscoe Village flourished in the mid-1800's as a port on the Ohio and Erie Canal. Now restored, it offers a look at life in Ohio's canal boat era.

SCHOENBRUNN VILLAGE
Rte. 250, New Philadelphia, Ohio
A cluster of log buildings have been reconstructed on the site of Ohio's first Moravian settlement, established in 1772. Interpreters introduce visitors to the Moravians' pacifist ideals and their life among the Delaware Indians.

SERPENT MOUND STATE MEMORIAL
Rte. 73, Locust Grove, Ohio
Built in the form of a serpent 20 feet wide and 1,348 feet long, this prehistoric earthwork is the largest snake effigy in Ameri-

ca. A museum has exhibits about the mound, and an observation tower permits views of its full length.

ZOAR VILLAGE
Visitor center, Main St., Zoar, Ohio
Centering on a garden planted to symbolize the biblical New Jerusalem, this town was founded by German separatists in 1817. The garden has been restored and the houses and shops around it now contain exhibits of furniture and handicrafts.

OKLAHOMA

CHEROKEE HERITAGE CENTER
Off Rte. 62, Tahlequah, Okla.
Cherokee culture and history are celebrated at two re-creations here: a 17th-century Indian village and a 19th-century rural town. Presentations of the "Trail of Tears" drama each summer recall the Cherokees' expulsion from their southern homeland in the 1830's.

HAR-BER VILLAGE
Har-ber Rd., Grove, Okla.
More than 100 buildings, from log cabins to a stage depot, make up this re-created 19th-century village. Displays include Belle Starr's piano, Indian artifacts, and antique dolls and farm tools.

INDIAN CITY, U.S.A.
Rte. 8, Anadarko, Okla.
Authentically reconstructed Indian villages, complete with tepees, earth lodges, and other dwellings, illustrate the life styles of several Indian tribes.

NATIONAL COWBOY HALL OF FAME AND WESTERN HERITAGE CENTER
1700 Northeast 63rd St., Oklahoma City, Okla.
In addition to exhibiting a major collection of Western art, this 32-acre complex features the Rodeo and Western Performers halls of fame. Visitors can also step back in time by strolling down a street known as the West of Yesterday.

PAWNEE BILL MANSION
Rte. 64, Pawnee, Okla.
Cowboy-showman Gordon William Lillie first rose to fame as Pawnee Bill with Buffalo Bill's Wild West Show in the 1880's. His rambling 1910 mansion is filled with exotic furnishings and a barn on his ranch displays costumes, billboards, and other mementos of his career.

SEQUOYAH'S HOME SITE
Rte. 101, Sallisaw, Okla.
This one-room 1829 cabin was the home of Sequoyah, the Cherokee Indian who invented an alphabet for the Cherokee language, an accomplishment that led to widespread literacy among his people.

SOD HOUSE
Rte. 8, between Aline and Cleo Springs, Okla.
Like many homesteaders on the plains, Marshall McCully built his home from sod. Today the 1894 dwelling, furnished turn-of-the-century style, is the only original soddy remaining in Oklahoma.

WILL ROGERS BIRTHPLACE
Off Rte. 88, Oologah, Okla.
The 1879 birthplace of cowboy-humorist Will Rogers is furnished as it was in his youth. Other Rogers memorabilia can be seen at the Will Rogers Memorial in nearby Claremore.

OREGON

AMERICAN ADVERTISING MUSEUM
9 NW Second Ave., Portland, Oreg.
From classic jingles to posters and print ads, this museum takes a fascinating look at more than 300 years of advertising.

COLUMBIA RIVER MARITIME MUSEUM
1792 Marine Dr., Astoria, Oreg.
Fishing, the fur trade, and early exploration on the Columbia River come to life in exhibits of nautical equipment, photographs, and boat models. Visitors can also board the *Columbia,* the last active lightship on the West Coast.

FORT CLATSOP NATIONAL MEMORIAL
Off Rte. 101, Astoria, Oreg.
After finally reaching the "western sea," the Lewis and Clark Expedition spent the winter of 1805-06 here, gearing up for the long trek home. Costumed guides demonstrate canoe building and other crafts at a reconstruction of their log fort.

McLOUGHLIN HOUSE NATIONAL HISTORIC SITE
713 Center St., Oregon City, Oreg.
Known as the Father of Oregon, John McLoughlin helped settlers put down roots here by lending them boats and supplies and offering protection from the Indians. His clapboard house, now refurbished, contains original furnishings.

OLD AURORA COLONY MUSEUM
Second and Liberty Sts., Aurora, Oreg.
Furnishings, tools, and quilts in the Ox Barn Museum recall the religious colony that settled here in 1856. Other reminders of a bygone life style include a log cabin, a wash house, an herb garden, and a collection of old buggies.

OREGON TRAIL INTERPRETIVE CENTER
Fifth and Washington Sts., Oregon City, Oreg.
Exhibits and an abundance of artifacts commemorate the 250,000 pioneers who journeyed west on the Oregon Trail.

PENNSYLVANIA

DRAKE WELL MUSEUM
Off Rte. 8, Titusville, Pa.
In 1859 Edwin L. Drake gave birth to a mighty industry by drilling the world's first oil well. The centerpiece at this museum is a replica of his derrick and engine house on the site of the original well.

ECKLEY MINER'S VILLAGE
Off Rte. 940, Eckley, Pa.
The restored and rebuilt structures here harken back to the time when industry was fueled by coal. Mine workers' houses and other facilities are open to visitors in this authentic company town.

EIGHTEENTH-CENTURY INDUSTRIAL AREA
459 Old York Road, Bethlehem, Pa.
More than 30 trades were practiced by the Moravians who settled in Bethlehem. Their 1762 waterworks, a tannery, and a gristmill have been restored, and guides in 18th-century garb demonstrate crafts.

EPHRATA CLOISTER
632 West Main St., Ephrata, Pa.
German mystics founded this community in 1732. Twelve buildings remain and fine

handiwork, including exquisite illuminated manuscripts, is on display.

FAIRMOUNT PARK
Extending northwest from Philadelphia Museum of Art, 26th St. and Benjamin Franklin Parkway, Philadelphia, Pa.
Once described as "the most beautiful place of the whole civilized world," the park began with the landscaping of the city's waterworks. The water station is still here, as is America's first zoo and several 18th-century mansions.

GETTYSBURG NATIONAL MILITARY PARK
Visitor center, Rte. 134, Gettysburg, Pa.
In July 1863, some of the bloodiest battles of the Civil War were fought here. Throughout the park's 3,000 acres, markers, monuments, and observation towers recall the progress of the fighting.

HOPEWELL FURNACE NATIONAL HISTORIC SITE
Rte. 345, Elverson, Pa.
During the Revolution, the ironworks here produced cannon and shot, and in its peak years from 1820 to 1840, up to seven tons of ore per day were smelted for the production of cast-iron stoves and other goods. Costumed artisans re-create the bustle of 19th-century ironmaking.

INDEPENDENCE NATIONAL HISTORICAL PARK
Visitor center, Third and Chestnut Sts., Philadelphia, Pa.
The sites here saw the birth of many of the actions and ideas that created the United States of America. The founding fathers met in Independence Hall in 1776 to sign the Declaration of Independence; in 1781 to ratify the Articles of Confederation; and again in 1787 to frame the Constitution. The house where Thomas Jefferson penned the Declaration has been reconstructed, and the Liberty Bell hangs in its own pavilion. An additional 23 sites complete this cradle of our country.

LANCASTER
Visitors' bureau, 501 Greenfield Rd., Lancaster, Pa.
Renowned as the heart of Pennsylvania Dutch Country, Lancaster features two authentic Amish sites — the Amish Farm and House and the Amish Homestead. Also here are the Fulton Opera House, named for Robert Fulton, inventor of the steamboat, and Wheatland, the home of President James Buchanan.

OLD ECONOMY VILLAGE
Fourteenth and Church Sts., Ambridge, Pa.
This utopian community, founded by German separatists in 1825, is beautifully preserved. Seventeen buildings remain, most notably the 25-room home of the community's founder; several members' dwellings; and the community garden.

PENNSYLVANIA FARM MUSEUM OF LANDIS VALLEY
2451 Kissel Hill Rd., Lancaster, Pa.
This cornucopia of more than 75,000 artifacts forms a vivid record of rural Pennsylvania from 1750 to 1900. More than 20 buildings house collections that range from farm vehicles to Dutch folk art.

PHILADELPHIA MUMMERS MUSEUM
Second St. and Washington Ave., Philadelphia, Pa.
Displays here include costumes, stringband memorabilia, and photographs and videotapes of past Mummers' Parades.

VALLEY FORGE NATIONAL HISTORICAL PARK
Valley Forge, Pa.
Washington and his troops spent the winter of 1777-78 at this 3,000-acre encampment. Washington's headquarters is still here, as is the parade ground where Baron von Steuben turned raw recruits into a disciplined fighting force.

WASHINGTON CROSSING HISTORIC PARK
Rte. 32, Washington Crossing, Pa.
From this landing on Christmas night 1776, George Washington led a surprise raid on the Hessian forces massed across the Delaware River in Trenton, New Jersey.

RHODE ISLAND

JAMESTOWN
Off Rte. 138, Conanicut Island, R.I.
Much of Jamestown was burned by the British at the start of the Revolutionary War, but some of its 18th-century homes remain. The island also has a historic lighthouse and a 1787 windmill.

JOHN BROWN HOUSE
52 Power St., Providence, R.I.
Built in 1786 by John Brown, a wealthy merchant, this 12-room mansion has been called the finest house in New England.

NEWPORT HISTORIC DISTRICT NATIONAL HISTORIC LANDMARK
Newport Historical Society Museum, 82 Touro St., Newport, R.I.
An important pre-Revolutionary seaport, Newport boasts some of the best 18th-century structures in the country. Among those open for tours are the elegant Hunter mansion; the 1690's Wanton-Lyman Hazard House ; and the arcaded Brick Market. Walking tours of the district are offered by the Historical Society.

NEWPORT MANSIONS
Preservation Society of Newport County, 118 Mill St., Newport, R.I.
Newport was the turn-of-the-century summer playground of wealthy Americans, who built palatial oceanside estates here. Among the most extravagant are the Breakers, Marble House, and Mrs. Caroline Astor's Beechwood Mansion, where actors play Mrs. Astor's servants and guests in reenactments of the high life as it was lived around 1890.

SLATER MILL HISTORIC SITE
Roosevelt Ave., Pawtucket, R.I.
The first American textile factory driven by water power, the 1793 Slater Mill is part of a complex of riverside buildings that show the change from handspinning and weaving to mechanization.

TOURO SYNAGOGUE
85 Touro St., Newport, R.I.
Dedicated in 1763, Touro Synagogue is the oldest in America and is still in use. The lofty, classical interior is marked by 12 columns symbolizing the tribes of Israel, and a 450-year-old brass chandelier continues to cast its light on worshippers.

SOUTH CAROLINA

BEAUFORT HISTORIC DISTRICT
Chamber of Commerce, 910 Bay St., Beaufort, S.C.
Once among the most prosperous towns in South Carolina, the state's second oldest city preserves its illustrious past in a

300-acre district comprising some 90 homes, public buildings, and gardens.

BOONE HALL PLANTATION
Off Rte. 17, six miles northeast of Charleston, S.C.
Still a working plantation, Boone Hall also offers a glimpse of plantation life in the past. Its reconstructed Georgian mansion is flanked by outbuildings that include nine brick slave cabins — one of the few "slave streets" remaining in the South.

CHARLESTON HISTORIC DISTRICT
Visitor center, 85 Calhoun St., Charleston, S.C.
First laid out in 1673, Charleston evolved into one of America's handsomest cities. The historic district includes 73 pre-Revolutionary buildings and over 750 more that were built prior to 1840. Many are open to the public. The city's architectural highlights can also be viewed from horse-drawn carriages.

CHARLES TOWNE LANDING 1670
1500 Old Town Rd., Charleston, S.C.
The original 1670 settlement of Charles Towne has been re-created at this 200-acre park. Interpreters reenact colonial life in a little town complete with shops and houses, a 17th-century trading ketch, and a garden of historic crops.

DRAYTON HALL
Rte. 61, Charleston, S.C.
Visitors can take a true step back in time by strolling through Drayton Hall, an 18th-century plantation house that has remained untouched by modern paints or plumbing. It is shown unfurnished so that interior architectural details can be fully appreciated. The property also includes the 300-year old Magnolia Plantation and Gardens with dazzling displays of azaleas and camellias.

MIDDLETON PLACE
Rte. 61, Charleston, S.C.
As soon as Henry Middleton completed building his home in 1741, he went to work creating 65 acres of gardens that remain the oldest landscaped gardens in the United States. The house was partially burned during the Civil War, but has since been restored and is now furnished to reflect Middleton family life between 1741 and 1865.

SOUTH DAKOTA

CRAZY HORSE MEMORIAL
Off Rte. 16/385, Custer, S. Dak.
Taller than the Washington Monument and still being carved from the granite of Thunderhead Mountain, the world's largest statue depicts the legendary Sioux warrior Crazy Horse. Also here is the sculptor's studio-home and the Indian Museum of North America.

DEADWOOD HISTORIC DISTRICT
Chamber of Commerce, 735 Main St., Deadwood, S. Dak.
Gold diggers by the thousands descended on Deadwood after gold was discovered here in 1875. A treasury of late 19th-century buildings recall the heyday of the town that attracted such characters as Calamity Jane and Wild Bill Hickok.

HOMESTAKE GOLD MINE
Main St., Lead, S. Dak.
With 1,000 miles of tunnels, Homestake is the largest underground gold mine in the Western Hemisphere. Visitors can tour the milling plant and other surface facilities to see how ore is processed into gold.

LAURA INGALLS WILDER MEMORIAL
Visitor center, 105 Olivet St., De Smet, S. Dak.
After several attempts at homesteading, the Ingalls family settled in De Smet, the "Little Town on the Prairie" that Laura Ingalls Wilder made famous in six of her beloved books. Still here is the tiny frame house where they spent their first winter, and the house that Pa Ingalls later built.

MOUNT RUSHMORE NATIONAL MEMORIAL
Visitor center, Rte. 244, Keystone, S. Dak.
Sculptor Gutzon Borglum spent 14 years at Mount Rushmore, creating his 60-foot-high likenesses of presidents Washington, Jefferson, Lincoln, and Theodore Roosevelt. A visitor center documents the monument's construction, and Borglum's studio contains the five-foot scale models from which he worked.

PRAIRIE VILLAGE
Rte. 81, Madison, S. Dak.
In addition to dozens of restored 19th-century structures, this re-created town displays a vast collection of old farm equipment, a steam carousel, and a railroad car that was equipped as a church-on-wheels to bring religion to the frontier.

TENNESSEE

BEALE STREET
Visitor center, 207 Beale St., Memphis, Tenn.
Part of a seven-block entertainment district restored to look as it did in the 1920's, Beale Street is the place where the blues were born. Musician W.C. Handy, who wrote such classics as "Memphis Blues" and "St. Louis Blues," is honored with a statue in Handy Park.

BELLE MEADE
Rte 70S, Nashville, Tenn.
Belle Meade's fame as a Thoroughbred horse farm in the 19th century is remembered there today. Horse paintings and trophies are shown in the Greek Revival house and an extensive collection of horse-drawn carriages is displayed in the combined carriage house and stable.

CROCKETT TAVERN MUSEUM
2002 Morningside Dr., Morristown, Tenn.
Davy Crockett and his family moved to Morristown when he was seven, and the town has memorialized its best-known citizen with a reconstruction of the tavern-inn that was his boyhood home.

THE HERMITAGE
Off Rte. 45, Hermitage, Tenn.
Begun in 1819, this pillared mansion was the home of Andrew and Rachel Jackson. It still is furnished much as it was in their day, and a museum at the visitor center displays many family mementos.

HISTORIC RUGBY
Rte. 52, Rugby, Tenn.
This charming rural hamlet was founded in 1880 by English social reformer Thomas Hughes. Though his would-be utopia died out within two decades, many of its buildings are still standing and several, including the library, the school, and Hughes's own home, are open to visitors.

JACK DANIEL'S DISTILLERY
Rte. 55, Lynchburg, Tenn.
America's oldest registered distillery was founded here by Jack Daniel in 1866. Vis-

itors can see how the sour-mash whiskey is made, or stop in at the office, which is still set up with its original furnishings.

MUSEUM OF APPALACHIA
Off I-75, Norris, Tenn.
More than 30 log cabins and other buildings from the hills of Appalachia have been assembled on this 70-acre site. All are fully furnished with the accoutrements of everyday life to create the look and feel of a true mountain village.

THE PARTHENON
Centennial Park, Nashville, Tenn.
This exact replica of the Parthenon in Athens, Greece, was originally built for the Tennessee Centennial in 1897 and now houses art exhibits.

ROCKY MOUNT
Rte. 11E, north of Johnson City, Tenn.
Built in 1770, this sturdy two-story log house was for a time the territorial capitol. Costumed guides nowadays enliven tours of the restored home with demonstrations of threshing, spinning, and other traditional crafts.

TEXAS

THE ALAMO
Alamo Plaza, San Antonio, Tex.
The mission church where Jim Bowie and Davy Crockett died in the fight for Texas independence still stands as a shrine to all the heroes who defended it.

FORT DAVIS NATIONAL HISTORIC SITE
Rtes. 17 and 118, Fort Davis, Tex.
The tidy limestone and adobe buildings of this fort, one of the largest in the West, recall the dangers of life on the Texas frontier. In summer the grounds are filled with the re-created sights and sounds of the daily retreat parade.

JUDGE ROY BEAN VISITOR CENTER
Loop 25, off Rte. 90, Langtry, Tex.
Relying on a law book, instinct, and a pair of six-shooters, Justice of the Peace Roy Bean, the self-proclaimed Law West of the Pecos, handed down judgements in this courtroom-saloon.

RANCHING HERITAGE CENTER
Fourth St. and Indiana Ave., Lubbock, Tex.
A hillside dugout, a log cabin, a Victorian home, blacksmith shops, bunkhouses, and windmills are among the more than 30 authentic structures here that recall nearly a century of ranching history.

SAM HOUSTON MEMORIAL MUSEUM
Rte. 75, Huntsville, Tex.
Sam Houston, the hero who led Texas to independence, lived here at Woodland Home and died in the nearby Steamboat House, which actually resembles a paddle wheeler. Also on the grounds is a museum with mementos of his life.

SAN ANTONIO MISSIONS NATIONAL HISTORICAL PARK
Park headquarters, 2202 Roosevelt Ave., San Antonio, Tex.
Four Spanish colonial missions remain along the Mission Trail. Mission San Jose′, the finest, features a magnificent baroque church with carved stone ornamentation. Colorful frescoes are still visible in Mission Concepción. Elsewhere, portions of an impressive aqueduct system can still be seen.

SAN JACINTO BATTLEGROUND STATE HISTORICAL PARK
Off Rte. 225, east of Houston, Tex.
The Texas Revolution ended here when Sam Houston and his small, ill-equipped army launched a surprise attack on the troops of Mexican General Santa Anna. A 570-foot monument topped by a Texas Lone Star dominates the battlefield.

STRAND HISTORIC DISTRICT
Visitor center, 2016 Strand, Galveston, Tex.
More than 50 restored buildings in Galveston's historic district recall the heyday of this once-thriving port whose main commercial street was known as the Wall Street of the Southwest.

TEXAS RANGER HALL OF FAME AND MUSEUM
I-35 and University Parks Blvd., Waco, Tex.
Firearms, dioramas, wax figures, and paintings recall the colorful history of the Texas Rangers — the fast-riding, sharp-shooting patrollers who kept order on the Texas frontier.

UTAH

BEEHIVE HOUSE
67 East South Temple St., Salt Lake City, Utah
A wooden beehive, the Mormon symbol of industry, caps the cupola of this elegant Greek Revival structure, the home of Mormon leader Brigham Young. Mark Twain and U. S. Grant were among the many illustrious visitors to the house, which is filled with original furnishings.

GOLDEN SPIKE NATIONAL HISTORIC SITE
Off Rte. 83, Promontory Summit, Utah
One of the great engineering feats of the 19th-century was completed here on May 10, 1869, when the last spike was driven for the tracks of America's first transcontinental railway. Working replicas of the two engines that met at the gap in the rails commemorate the event.

PIONEER TRAIL STATE PARK
Visitor center, 2601 Sunnyside Ave., Salt Lake City, Utah
The park's huge "This is the Place" monument recalls Brigham Young's words when he first laid eyes on the Great Salt Lake Valley at the end of the long trail that Mormon pioneers had traveled en route to their new home. A village with authentic 19th-century buildings and costumed artisans reminds us of the rigors, and rewards, of pioneer life.

RONALD V. JENSEN LIVING HISTORICAL FARM
Rte. 89/91, Wellsville, Utah
Complete with livestock, this re-created Mormon farm features orchards, meadows, and more than a dozen authentic old structures, including a farmhouse, barn, root cellar, and smokehouse.

TEMPLE SQUARE
Visitor centers, South Temple and North Temple Sts., Salt Lake City, Utah
Dominating the 10-acre square at the spiritual heart of the city is the Salt Lake Temple, which took 40 years to build and can be entered only by Mormons in good standing. Also here is the Tabernacle, home of the Mormon Tabernacle Choir; the huge assembly Hall; and the Log Cabin, the city's oldest house.

VERMONT

BILLINGS FARM AND MUSEUM
Rte. 12, Woodstock, Vt.
On a working dairy farm, rural life of the 1890's is recalled in four barns filled with exhibits and at frequent demonstrations of cheesemaking, icecutting, and other country chores.

COOLIDGE HOMESTEAD
Rte. 100A, Plymouth Notch, Vt.
Following the death of Warren G. Harding in August 1923, Calvin Coolidge here took the oath of office as America's 30th president. Also nearby are his birthplace and simple grave.

HILDENE
Rte. 7A South, Manchester, Vt.
Built in 1904, the 24-room summer home of Robert Todd Lincoln, Abraham Lincoln's son, contains original furnishings, a 1,000-pipe organ, and personal items, including one of Abe's stovepipe hats.

MORGAN HORSE FARM
Off Rte. 23, Middlebury, Vt.
The Morgan horse, the first true American breed, originated here. Visitors can watch the daily workouts and training of the small but sturdy animals.

NEW ENGLAND MAPLE MUSEUM
Rte. 7, Pittsford, Vt.
A vast collection of maple-sugaring artifacts is displayed here, the art of maple-sugaring is demonstrated, and samples of the "sweet water" are available.

SHELBURNE FARMS
Off Rte. 7, Shelburne, Vt.
Sound agricultural practices are emphasized at demonstrations on this country estate that was built in the 1880's and is noted for its huge, handsome barns.

SHELBURNE MUSEUM
Rte 7, Shelburne, Vt.
Nearly 40 historic structures have been brought here from throughout New England — among them, homes of various periods, a general store, and a jail. On display in these and other buildings is an enormous collection of Americana, from dolls, carriages, and quilts to a hand-carved model circus. The museum also boasts a two-lane covered bridge and an authentic paddle wheel steamboat.

VIRGINIA

ALEXANDRIA HISTORIC DISTRICT
Visitor center, 221 King St., Alexandria, Va.
This lovely old city's 100-block historic district is awash with its distinguished past, including such sites as Robert E. Lee's boyhood home; the 1792 Stabler-Leadbeater Apothecary Shop; the 1724 Ramsay House, home of the town's first postmaster; and Gadsby's Tavern, patronized by George Washington.

BERKELEY PLANTATION
Rte. 5, Charles City, Va.
Two presidents — Benjamin Harrison and William Henry Harrison — lived here in the three-story brick plantation house on the James River. The land is still worked, and visitors are welcomed to tour the restored house and grounds.

BOOKER T. WASHINGTON NATIONAL MONUMENT
Rte. 122, 20 miles southeast of Roanoke, Va.
Booker T. Washington, the founder of Tuskegee Institute, was born a slave on this farm in 1856. The cabin he lived in has been reconstructed and the visitor center has exhibits relating to his life.

COLONIAL WILLIAMSBURG
Visitor center, Colonial Pkwy., Williamsburg, Va.
For 80 years, beginning in 1699, Williamsburg was Virginia's colonial capital. An ongoing restoration of this important American town now covers 170 acres, with some 90 acres of gardens and more than 85 restored 18th-century homes, shops, and public buildings. Also here is the Abby Aldrich Rockefeller Folk Art Center, with one of the world's finest collections of American folk art.

FREDERICKSBURG
Visitor center, 706 Caroline St., Fredericksburg, Va.
George Washington's boyhood hometown boasts many historic landmarks. Among those open to the public are the James Monroe Museum and Memorial Library, the 1761 Hugh Mercer Apothecary Shop, the Mary Washington House, and the Fredericksburg Area Museum and Cultural Center.

GUNSTON HALL
Rte. 242, Lorton, Va.
George Mason, author of the Virginia Declaration of Rights, farmed and raised his family on this plantation overlooking the Potomac River. He also built one of the most stylish houses of the mid-1700's. It has been restored and contains many Mason family heirlooms.

JAMESTOWN
Visitor center, off Colonial Pkwy., Jamestown Island, Va.
Only one structure — the Old Church Tower, built in 1640 — remains at Jamestown, the first permanent English settlement in North America. Nearby, however, the little village has been reconstructed as a living-history museum where visitors can watch craftsmen working, farmers plowing, and housewives cooking daily meals.

MONTICELLO
Rte. 53, Charlottesville, Va.
Thomas Jefferson spent 40 years perfecting Monticello, his magnificent hilltop estate. Everything seen there today — from the choice of plantings to the gracious architecture and inventive furniture designs — reflects the taste and genius of that great American.

MOUNT VERNON
Mt. Vernon Memorial Hwy., Mt. Vernon, Va.
George Washington was never able to spend as much time at Mount Vernon as he would have liked. But he did make his mark on the property, enlarging and modifying the house by his own design, and farming the land he so dearly loved. The mansion today is filled with family treasures and the grounds include his gardens, outbuildings, and a museum of memorabilia.

SCOTCHTOWN
Off Rte. 54, 10 miles morthwest of Ashland, Va.
Scotchtown was already more than 50 years old when orator Patrick Henry bought it in 1771. Among the many artifacts to be seen in the large brick house is Henry's ink-stained writing desk.

STRATFORD HALL
Rte. 214, Stratford, Va.
Thomas Lee built Stratford Hall in the 1730's and it was later the home of Light

Horse Harry Lee and Robert E. Lee. Appropriately furnished as a Lee homestead-museum, it is one of Virginia's grandest early houses.

YORKTOWN BATTLEFIELD
Visitor center, Colonial Pkwy., Yorktown, Va.
The site of the last major siege in the Revolutionary War is now a historical park. Visitors can wander the battlefields to see the Victory Monument and the Yorktown National Cemetery; visit Moore House, where the British signed the Articles of Capitulation; and examine artifacts from the battle at the Yorktown Victory Center.

WASHINGTON

CHELAN HISTORICAL MUSEUM
600 Cottage Ave., Cashmere, Wash.
The collection of Indian artifacts here chronicles some 9,000 years of life on the Pacific Coast and is one of the best in the Northwest. The museum also features a reconstructed pioneer village that brings the day-to-day experience of late-19th-century settlers vibrantly to life.

FORT CANBY STATE PARK
Off Rte. 101, Ilwaco, Wash.
The park's Lewis and Clark Interpretive Center displays artifacts collected on the explorers' 8,000-mile expedition. Also here are two lighthouses and an exhibit on the history of the fort, one of the oldest in the state.

FORT NISQUALLY
North 54th and Pearl Sts., Tacoma, Wash.
This reconstruction of a fort established by the Hudson's Bay Company contains the oldest structure in Washington — a granary built in 1843. Living history demonstrations and reenactments of the traders' and trappers' annual rendezvous delight visitors today.

MUSEUM OF FLIGHT
9404 East Marginal Way South, Seattle, Wash.
Two collections here explore the world of flight. In the Red Barn — the original Boeing plant from about 1910 — are exhibits on the history of flight from the 13th century to the late 1930's. The Great Gallery contains more than 40 contemporary aircraft, among them an Apollo command module, and an Aerocar, the first FAA-certified flying automobile.

PIONEER SQUARE HISTORIC DISTRICT
Visitor center, 117 South Main St., Seattle, Wash.
When much of Seattle was destroyed by fire in 1889, a new central city of brick and stone rose literally above the damaged storefronts that remained in place beneath new streets and sidewalks. Above- and below-ground walking tours provide a fascinating before-and-after look at this phoenix-like reincarnation.

SAN JUAN ISLAND NATIONAL HISTORICAL PARK
Visitor center, Friday Harbor, Wash.
The park contains remnants of two military camps, one British and one American, on the site of the notorious 1859 Pig War — actually a protracted joint occupation of the island sparked by the accidental shooting of a pig and focused on the ambiguity of a treaty that left the island's ownership in dispute. The benign conflict was eventually decided in favor of the United States.

WEST VIRGINIA

GRAVE CREEK MOUND NATIONAL HISTORIC LANDMARK
801 Jefferson Ave., Moundsville, W. Va.
Some 2,000 years ago Indians built a 69-foot-high burial mound here — one of the largest of its kind. A museum exhibits artifacts excavated from the site.

HARPERS FERRY NATIONAL HISTORICAL PARK
Visitor center, Shenandoah St., Harpers Ferry, W. Va.
Located at the confluence of the Potomac and Shenandoah rivers, Harpers Ferry was an early manufacturing center. But it was abolitionist John Brown's raid on the the arsenal and his subsequent hanging that made it a town America would never forget. The park encompasses part of the old town, where many buildings have been restored, including the engine house where Brown hid from authorities.

JEFFERSON COUNTY COURTHOUSE
George and Washington Sts., Charles Town, W. Va.
Abolitionist John Brown was tried and convicted of treason here in 1859. Nearby the Jefferson County Museum exhibits items that belonged to Brown as well as Civil War artifacts.

LEWISBURG
Visitor center, 105 Church St., W. Va.
Among the more than 60 historic buildings in this town's 236-acre historic district are a 1770 log barracks built by the British and the 1796 Old Stone Presbyterian Church, the oldest church in continuous use west of the Alleghenies.

PRICKETTS FORT STATE PARK
Off I-79, Fairmont, W. Va.
In a reconstruction of the stockaded fort where local families used to find refuge from Indian attacks, costumed guides now give demonstrations of 18th-century crafts and militia exercises.

WEST VIRGINIA INDEPENDENCE HALL
1528 Market St., Wheeling, W. Va.
It was in this Renaissance Revival structure, originally built as an Ohio River customs house, that representatives drafted West Virginia's Declaration of Independence from Virginia, thus making West Virginia the only state to be formed by breaking away from another state.

WISCONSIN

CIRCUS WORLD MUSEUM
426 Water St., Baraboo, Wis.
The town where the five Ringling brothers staged their first extravaganza now host's a 43-acre museum at the circus's former winter quarters. Exhibits trace the history of circuses and include the world's largest collection of circus wagons.

LITTLE NORWAY
Off Rte. 18-151, Blue Mounds, Wis.
A bit of Norway seems truly to have been transplanted to this 1856 pioneer homestead, which includes several charming log houses, barns, and outbuildings. But the showpiece here is a superbly crafted replica of a 12th-century Norwegian church filled with Norwegian antiques.

MADELINE ISLAND HISTORICAL MUSEUM

La Pointe, Wis.

Lake Superior's Madeline Island once was the home of Ojibwa Indians and a fur trading center. Four log buildings mark the site of the fur company that operated here from 1816 to 1847. The largest, the fur warehouse, is now a museum exhibiting Indian artifacts, missionary documents, and antique fur-trade and logging gear.

OLD WADE HOUSE

Rte. 23, Greenbush, Wis.

A welcome stop on the road west, the Wade House opened as an inn in 1851. From taproom to ballroom, the three-story building still contains many original furnishings and provides a look at the activities of a busy 19th-century hostelry. Also here is a museum with about 100 horse-drawn vehicles.

OLD WORLD WISCONSIN

Rte. 67, Eagle, Wis.

Wisconsin's pioneer past is recalled at this outdoor museum where buildings from throughout the state have been set up as the working farms of 16 different ethnic groups. Building styles and farming techniques date from the mid-19th century to the early 20th century.

PENDARVIS

114 Shake Rag St., Mineral Point, Wis.

Cornish workers who came to this lead-mining town in the early 19th century built houses just as they had in their native England. A street of their unusual log and cut-limestone homes has been restored and furnished with vintage household goods. Visitors can also take a look inside the Merry Christmas mine.

STONEFIELD

Off Rte. 133, Cassville, Wis.

The farm once owned by Wisconsin's first governor now boasts a farm museum and an entire village that re-creates rural life of the 1890's. Still humming with activity are the newspaper office, general store, meat market, post office, and many other sites.

WYOMING

BUFFALO BILL HISTORICAL CENTER

720 Sheridan Ave., Cody, Wyo.

This large and comprehensive complex has a museum filled with artifacts of the Plains Indians; another that traces the history of firearms; a third showcasing Western art; and the Buffalo Bill Museum featuring some 5,000 items related to Buffalo Bill Cody and the Wild West. Cody's boyhood home has also been relocated here.

FORT BRIDGER STATE HISTORIC SITE

Rte. 30, Fort Bridger, Wyo.

Originally opened in 1842 as a trading post by mountain man Jim Bridger, the fort here later saw service as a Pony Express station and as an army post. A museum now occupies the remaining buildings, with exhibits that highlight local Indian and pioneer history.

FORT LARAMIE NATIONAL HISTORIC SITE

Off Rte. 26, Fort Laramie, Wyo.

A onetime fur-trading post that later was taken over by the army, Fort Laramie also contributed to the settlement of the West by serving as a traveler's rest, stagecoach stop, and telegraph station. Some of the buildings have been restored, and in summer costumed guides bring the frontier encampment to life with re-enactments of military routines.

GRAND ENCAMPMENT MUSEUM

Seventh St. and Barnett Ave., Encampment, Wyo.

Fourteen buildings in the pioneer village here recall the area's past as an Indian encampment and copper-mining center. The village includes, among others, a sod-roofed stagecoach stop, a two-story outhouse, and collections of pioneer and Indian memorabilia.

SOUTH PASS CITY STATE HISTORIC SITE

Off Rte. 28, 32 miles south of Lander, Wyo.

In the 1860's South Pass City boomed briefly during a gold rush, but by 1875 it was a ghost town. Some two dozen of its buildings have been restored, permitting visitors to take a look inside miners' cabins, an authentic Western saloon, a Masonic lodge, and the oldest jail still standing in Wyoming.

TRAIL END HISTORIC CENTER

400 South Clarendon Ave., Sheridan, Wyo.

John Kendrick started out as a cowpuncher on cattle drives, and ultimately became a Wyoming governor and U.S. Senator. But he also became the owner of a huge cattle ranch and built this fine mansion for his home. The house is still furnished as it was at the turn of the century and offers a glimpse into the life of a true citizen of the West.

YELLOWSTONE NATIONAL PARK

Northwest corner of Wyoming. Six visitor centers at various locations

With more than 2 million acres, some 300 geysers, and a staggering array of wildlife, Yellowstone is a natural wonder of the first order. But it was also the world's first national park, and so represents the birth of a unique new concept that eventually spread to countries everywhere. The history of America's national park system is recalled at Yellowstone's Explorer's Museum.

Photo Credits

2-3 *background* Lee Boltin; 2 *top to bottom left* The Bettman Archive; The Bridgeman Art Library/Art Resource, N.Y.; Culver Pictures. 3 *top left* Chun Y. Lai/Esto; *bottom left* Viesti Associates, Inc.; *top right* Charles Phelps Cushing/H. Armstrong Roberts; *bottom right* The Cousley Historical Collections, photographed by James A. McInnis. 4 *bottom* The Bettman Archive; 5 *top* Culver Pictures. 8-9 *background* Stockphotos/The Image Bank; 8 *top to bottom left* The Bettman Archive; UPI/Bettman; *top to bottom right* H. Armstrong Roberts; Culver Pictures. 9. *top* The Bettmann Archive. .10-11 *(all)* New York State Historical Association, Cooperstown. 12 J. L. G. Ferris; Archives of 76, Bay Village, Ohio. 14 From the Hallmark Historical Collection, Hallmark Cards, Inc. 15 *left* Brown Brothers; *right* From the Hallmark Historical Collection, Hallmark Cards, Inc. 16 *top left* Lyman Allyn Art Museum, New London, Connecticut; *top right* Charles H. Phillips; *bottom (both)* Schecter Lee/Esto. 17 *top left* Courtesy, Winterthur Museum; *top right* Schecter Lee/Esto; *right (scrimshaw courtship scene)* New Bedford Whaling Museum; *bottom* Schecter Lee/Esto. 18 *left* The Granger Collection, New York; *right* The Bettmann Archive. 19 From the Collection of the Tennessee State Museum, Nashville, Tennessee. Photo courtesy of Robert M. Hicklin Jr., Inc., Spartanburg, South Carolina. 20 *top* Collection of the Maryland Historical Society, Baltimore; *bottom* The Granger Collection, New York. 21 Reuters/Bettmann Newsphotos. 22 Howard Giske/Museum of History & Industry. 23 *top* "Caught in the Act," by Tompkins Harrison Matteson; Collection, Vassar College Art Gallery, Poughkeepsie, New York; gift of Matthew Vassar; *bottom* Courtesy of the American Antiquarian Society. 24 Courtesy of The New-York Historical Society, New York City. 25 *(both)* Culver Pictures. 26 *left (top to bottom)* Culver Pictures; *right* Gift of Maxim Karolik for the Karolik Collection of American Paintings, 1815-1865; Courtesy, Museum of Fine Arts, Boston. 27 *top and middle* From the Bella C. Landauer Collection, courtesy of The New-York Historical Society, New York City; *bottom* The Bettmann Archive. 28 *(both)* The Bettmann Archive. 29 *top* Courtesy, The Winterthur Library Printed Book and Periodical Collection; *bottom* The Bettmann Archive. 30 *top* Henry Ford Museum & Greenfield Village; *bottom* Lionel, Inc. 31 *top left* Schecter Lee/Esto; *top right* Courtesy Essex Institute, Salem, Massachusetts; *bottom* Lionel, Inc. 32 The Bettmann Archive. 33 *middle* Nevada Historical Society; *bottom* UPI/Bettmann. 34 Library of Congress. 35 *top* Library of Congress; *bottom left* Culver Pictures; *bottom right* The Bettmann Archive. 37 *top* Reprinted by permission of the estate of Morton Roberts; *bottom* Jerry Howard/ Positive Images. 38 Collection of the Museum of American Folk Art, New York; Gift of Eva and Morris Feld Folk Art Acquisition Fund, 1981.12.8. 39 *top left* From the collection of the Kentucky Historical Society; *top right* John Gary Brown; *middle* Collection of the Museum of American Folk Art, New York; Museum of American Folk Art Purchase, 1981.12.27; *bottom* Courtesy The Strong Museum, Rochester, New York © 1992. 40 Smithsonian Institution. 41 *top* Cornell Capa/Life Magazine © 1950; Time Warner Inc.; *bottom* New York State Historical Association, Cooperstown. 42-43 *background* David Frazier/The Stock Market. 42 *top to bottom left* Brown Brothers; Camerique/H. Armstrong Roberts; UPI/Bettmann; *top right* The Bettman Archive; *bottom right* Brown Brothers; 43 *left* Culver Pictures 44 *left* Smithsonian Institution; *right* The Bettmann Archive. 45 The Library Company of Philadelphia. 46 From the collection of Mrs. Frances P. Garvan, Museum of the City of New York. 47 *top* National Archives; *bottom* From the Landauer Collection, courtesy of The New-York Historical Society, New York City. 48 *upper right and middle* Culver Pictures; *bottom* UPI/Bettmann. 49 *left* The Cousley Historical Collections, photographed by James A. McInnis; *right* UPI/Bettmann Newsphotos. 50 Culver Pictures. 51 *right* New York Public Library Picture Collection; *bottom* AP/Wide World Photos. 52 *top left (Cracker Jack prizes)* Wesley Johnson; *top middle*: From "Cracker Jack Prizes" by Alex Jaramillo; courtesy Abbeville Press; *top right* Wesley Johnson; *bottom far left (both)* James A. McInnis; *bottom left* Nabisco Inc. 53 *top (both)* George A. Hormel & Co. 54 *top left* Borden, Inc.; *bottom left* Culver Pictures; *middle* Michael Hostovich; *right* Nabisco Inc. 55 *top* From the collection of Dr. Ray Broekel, Chocolate and Candy Bar Historian; *left* From the collection of Dr. Ray Broekel, Chocolate and Candy Bar Historian, photographed by James A. McInnis; *far right top to bottom* Quaker Oats Company; Nabisco Inc., Chiquita Brands International. 56 Culver Pictures. 57 *top* Library of Congress; *bottom left* Courtesy of The New-York Historical Society, New York City; *bottom right* The Coca-Cola Company. 58 *top* The Bettmann Archive; *middle* Museum of the City of New York; *bottom* Library of Congress. 59 Brown Brothers. 60-61 *top left* Lesley Poling-Kempes; from the collection of Margaret Becker Crist; *middle left* University of Arizona Library, Special Collections Department; *bottom and inset* The Byron Collection/Museum of the City of New York; *top right* Brown Brothers. 62 *top* Richard J.S. Gutman Collection; *bottom* Thomas J. Lipton, Inc. 63 *top* Tombrock Corporation, Stamford, CT; Photo courtesy of Venturi, Scott Brown and Associates, Inc.; left Courtesy of The New York-Historical Society, New York City; *bottom* Collection of Whitney Museum of American Art, New York; gift of the artist and gift of Gertrude Vanderbilt Whitney. 64 *top* Library of Congress; *bottom left* Department of Special Collections, University Research Library, UCLA; *bottom right* Library of Congress. 65 *top left* Postcard from the John Baeder Collection; *top right* Photograph from "California Crazy" by Jim Heimann and Rip Georges ©1980. Published by Chronicle Books; *middle right* John Margolies/Esto; *bottom* Delmar Watson Photography. 66 *top* The John Work Garrett Library, Milton S. Eisenhower Library; The Johns Hopkins University; *bottom* The Toledo Museum of Art, Toledo, Ohio; Purchased with funds from the Florence Scott Libbey Bequest in Memory of her Father, Maurice A. Scott. 67 *top* Courtesy, Colorado Historical Society; *bottom* Abby Aldrich Rockefeller Folk Art Center. 68 *left* The Bettmann Archive; *top right* The Bettmann Archive; *inset* Culver Pictures. 69 *top left* The Bettmann Archive; *top right and middle* Courtesy of The New-York Historical Society, New York City; *bottom* From the collection of Mr. & Mrs. Austin O. Furst, Jr.; courtesy of Christie's, New York. 70-71 *background* Tim Bieber/The Image Bank. 70 *upper left* National Baseball Library, Cooperstown, NY; *bottom left* Free Library of Philadelphia, Print and Picture Department; *right* Culver Pictures. 71 *top* Martin & Osa Johnson Safari Museum. 72 *top (both)* Lake County (IL) Museum/Curt Teich Postcard Archives; *bottom* Culver Pictures. 73 *(north entrance plan)* Thomas Jefferson Papers, Manuscripts Division, Special Collections Department, University of Virginia Library; *top right* The Corporation for Jefferson's Poplar Forest. 74 From the collections of Justine Hommel, photographed by Lee Ferris. 75 *top* Collection of Mr. and Mrs. Raymond J. Horowitz; *bottom* National Museum of American Art, Washington, D.C./Art Resource, N.Y. 76 *top* Pioneer Museum; *bottom* The Broadmoor Hotel, Colorado. 77 *top* Haynes Foundation Collection, Montana Historical Society, Helena, MT; *right inset* Montana Historical Society, Helena, MT. 78 *left* Lake County (IL) Museum/Curt Teich Postcard Archives; *right* Brown Brothers. 79 AP/Wide World Photos. 80 *top to bottom* Culver Pictures; The Denver Public Library, Western History Department; Collection of David Woodworth; The Bettmann Archive. 81 *top* Culver Pictures; *middle left* Library of Congress; *middle right* The Bettmann Archive; *bottom* Yosemite National Park. 82 *top left* The Granger Collection, New York; *top right* William Manns Zoo; *lower left* The Bettmann Archive; 82-83 *(zebra)* William Manns Zoo; 83 *top right* Brown Brothers; *lower left to right* The Bettmann Archive; Tony Orlando; The Bettmann Archive. 84 *inset* Culver Pictures; *bottom* Brooklyn Public Library, Brooklyn Collection. 85 *top right and middle left* Brown Brothers; *bottom right* New York Public Library Picture Collection. 86 *(both)* Minnesota Historical Society. 87 San Francisco Public Library. 88 Culver Pictures. 89 The Granger Collection, New York; *inset* The Bettmann Archive. 90 *top* Culver Pictures; *bottom* Historic Hudson Valley, Tarrytown, New York. 91 *top center* New York Public Library Picture Collection; *top far right* Museum of the City of New York, The Theater Collection; *lower right* Courtesy of The New-York Historical Society, New York City. 92 *middle* The Bettmann Archive; *bottom* Courtesy of The New-York Historical Society, New York City. 93 *top* The Bettmann Archive; *bottom (music score)* The Bettmann Archive; *bottom right* Culver Pictures. 94 *top* Culver Pictures; *bottom* New York Public Library Picture Collection. 95 *(all)* Culver Pictures. 96 The Metropolitan Museum of Art, Fletcher Fund, 1925 (25.97.5); *bottom* James A. McInnis. 97 *top* Kaz Tsuruta; *bottom* UPI/Bettmann Newsphotos. 98 *top* Jack Zehrt; *upper left and bottom left* Culver Pictures; *bottom center* The Walt Disney Company. 99 *top right* Culver Pictures; *middle* Martin & Osa Johnson Safari Museum; *bottom right* Culver Pictures. 100 *top* The Bettmann Archive; *bottom* National Baseball Hall of Fame. 101 *top* UPI/Bettmann; *lower left* Brown Brothers; *bottom left* UPI/Bettmann; *lower right* Culver Pictures. 102 *top left* The Bettman Archive; *top right* Brown Brothers; *middle left* From the Bella C. Landauer Collection, 1855; courtesy of The New-York Historical Society, New York City; *bottom* Culver Pictures. 103 American Heritage Magazine. 104 *(both)* Mummer's Museum. 105 *left* Culver Pictures; *right* Plimouth Plantation. 106 *top* James A. McInnis; *middle* Arizona Photographic Associates, Inc.; *bottom* Brown Brothers. 107 *(both)* Culver Pictures. 108-109 *background* H. Armstrong Roberts. 108 *top left* FPG International; *bottom left* Culver Pictures. 109 *top & bottom left* Culver Pictures; *top right* FPG International; *remainder* UPI/Bettmann Newsphotos 110 *top left* New York Public Library; *bottom* The Connecticut Historical Society. 110-111 New Bedford Whaling Museum. 111 *bottom* Clarence P. Hornung/American Design. 112 *upper left* Library of Congress; *bottom* The Bettmann Archive. 113 *top and middle* The Bettmann Archive; *lower right* Library of Congress. 114 *left* Culver Pictures; *right* Brown Brothers. 115 *left* Illustration by Bill Shortridge, based on a photo courtesy of Library of Congress; *top right* Culver Pictures; *bottom center* Culver Pictures; *bottom right* Library of Congress. 116 *top and middle left* Culver Pictures. 117 *top* UPI/Bettmann; *bottom* Charles Atlas, Ltd. 118 *top left* John Margolies; *top right and bottom* Culver Pictures. 119 *top left and right* Library of Congress; *bottom left* Brown Brothers; *bottom right* John Margolies. 120 Culver Pictures. 121 *top* AP/Wide World Photos; *middle left and right* The Bettmann Archive; bottom S.E. Feist/U.S. Patent Office. 122 *top to bottom* San Francisco Academy of Comic Art; San Francisco Academy of Comic Art; The Granger Collection, New York; Culver Pictures. 123 *upper left* Culver Pictures; *top right* AP/Wide World Photos; *bottom* Library of Congress. 124 The Bettmann Archive. 125 *top right* Steven Mays; *middle right* Brown Brothers; *bottom left* Library of Congress. 126 *top left* Culver Pictures; *bottom left* New York Public Library Picture Collection; *center* Brown Brothers; *bottom right* The Bettmann Archive. 127 *top* The Bettmann Archive; *bottom left* Culver Pictures; *bottom right* From the Landauer Collection; courtesy of The New-York Historical Society, New York City. 128 *top left and right* Colonial Williamsburg Foundation; *center* Milo Reproductions; *bottom left* Culver Pictures. 129 *top* Betty Williams Studio; *middle right* New York Public Library Picture Collection; *bottom left* The Limited; *bottom right* Jantzen Archive. 130 *top and middle* Levi Strauss; *bottom* The Cousley Historical Collections. 132 *top* New York Public Library Picture Collection; *bottom* Dover Publications, Inc. 133 *(both)* Photofest. 134 *top left* Saxon White; *lower right* New York Public Library Picture Collection. 135 *top* San Francisco Academy of Comic Art; *bottom left* Joseph J. Pennell Collection; University of Kansas Library; *lower right* New York Public Library Picture Collection. 136 *top* The Bettmann Archive; *bottom left* National Archives; *bottom right* The Bettmann Archive. 137 *top* Culver Pictures; *lower right* Niagara County Historical Society. 138-139 *background* Alvis Upitis/The Image Bank 138 *(all)* Culver Pictures. 139 *top to bottom left* The Bettman Archive; Culver Pictures; The Bettman Archive. 140 *top left* Neil Shigley; (ad) New York Public Library Picture Collection. 141 The Thomas Gilcrease Institute of American History and Art, Tulsa, Oklahoma. 142 *top* Western History Collections, University of Oklahoma; *bottom* Nevada Historical Society. 143 *top to bottom* The Kansas State Historical Society; State Historical Society of North Dakota; The Denver Public Library, Western History Department; *bottom (both)* Brown Brothers. 144 *top* Historic Hudson Valley; *middle left* The Bettmann Archive. 145 Nebraska State Historical Society. 146 New York Public Library Picture Collection. 147 *top* Culver Pictures; *middle* The Frank Lloyd Wright Home and Studio Foundation; *bottom* Smithsonian Institution. 148 Gift of Miss Grace M. Mayer; courtesy Museum of the City of New York. 148-149 *bottom* Brown Brothers. 149 *top* Brown Brothers; *middle* Pennsylvania Dutch Visitors Bureau; *lower right* Kansas State Historical Society. 150 *upper left and middle* New York Public Library Picture Collection; *bottom (both)* Arents Collections, The New York Public Library; Astor, Lenox and Tilden Foundations. 151 *top* The Cousley Historical Collections; photographed by James A. McInnis; *lower right (both)* Smithsonian Institution. 152 *top (both)* Richard Nowitz. 153 *top* Paul Jensen. *lower left* Collection of S. George Ellsworth; *lower right* Clifton James/Dover Books, 1963 154 *top* New York Public Library Picture Collection; 154-155 *bottom* Shelburne Museum, Shelburne, Vermont/ photographed by Ken Burris. 155 *top* The Cousley Historical Collections; photographed by James A. McInnis. 156 *far left* The Cousley Historical Collections; photographed by James A. McInnis; bottom Vassar College Library, Poughkeepsie, New York. 157 *middle and bottom* Stanford University Libraries; *right* The Cousley Historical Collections; photographed by James A. McInnis. 158 *top* Harvard University Archives; *bottom* U.S. Military Academy Archives. 159 *top* Brown Brothers; *lower left* Brown Brothers; *lower right* Oberlin College Archives, Oberlin, Ohio; *bottom right* Library of Congress. 160 *top* Museum of the City of New York; *lower left and bottom inset* From the collections of Henry Ford Museum & Greenfield Village. 161 *top* Brown Brothers; *inset* University of Iowa Libraries, Redpath Bureau Collection. *middle left and right* Smith Library, Chautauqua Historical Collection. 162 The Chicago Public Library, Special Collections Division. 163 *top* By permission of the Houghton Library, Harvard University; *bottom* Washington County Free Library. 164 *bottom left* The Pennsylvania Academy of the Fine Arts, Philadelphia; Gift of Mrs. Sarah Harrison (The Joseph Harrison, Jr. Collection); *middle right* The Pennsylvania Academy of the Fine Arts, Philadelphia; Bequest of Charles Coleman Sellers. 165 *lower left* American Philosophical Society. 166-167 *background* Willard Clay. 166 *upper left* The Bettman Archive; *bottom* James Jerome Hill Reference Library; *upper right* From the Solomon D. Butcher Collection; courtesy Nebraska State Historical Society. 167 *upper left* From the Solomon D. Butcher Collection; courtesy Nebraska State Historical Society; *lower left* The Bettman Archive. 168-169 *(all)* The Historical Society of York County. 170 *top* The Bettmann Archive; bottom Culver Pictures. 171 *top* Ken Stevens/Unicorn Stock Photos; *upper right* Specialist Publishing Company; *middle left* Windmill Publishing Company. 172 *top* Shelburne Museum; *bottom* Gotham Book Mart & Gallery, Inc. 173 *top far right* Carl Sacks/American Heritage Society; *top* Ellwood House; bottom Stock Montage, Inc. 174 Louis Mauer Currier & Ives; Museum of the City of New York, The Harry T. Peters Collection. 175 *top* Norfolk Historical Museum; *bottom* Lake County (IL) Museum/Curt Teich Postcard Archives. 177 *(all)* W. Atlee Burpee & Co. 178 *(both)* Warshaw Collection, Smithsonian Institution. 179 *top and bottom right* Welch's Corporate Communications; *middle left* Culver Pictures. 180 *top* Library of Congress; *bottom* Rome Historical Society, New York. 181 *top* U.S. Department of Commerce Patents and Trademarks Division; *bottom* The Bettmann Archive. 182 *top right* W.D. Weiss; *middle left* Library of Congress; *bottom* Smithsonian Institution. 183 *bottom left* Brian Vanden Brink; *upper right* International Harvester; *lower right* Library of Congress. 184 The Bettmann Archive. 185 Library of Congress. 186 *top left* Brown Brothers; *top right* New York State Historical Association, Cooperstown, NY; *bottom* Library of Congress. 187 *top* Courtesy of the Sioux City Public Museum; *lower left* Culver Pictures. 188 *top* Colonial Williamsburg Foundation; *bottom* Vermont Historical Society. 189 Library of Congress. 190-191 (all) Viesti Associates, Inc. 192 New York State Museum. 193 The Bettmann Archive. 194 *upper left* The Bettmann Archive; *bottom* Harvard Theatre Collection. 195 *left* University of Oklahoma Library; *right* Library of Congress. 196-197 *background* H. Armstrong Roberts. 196 *upper left* Culver Pictures; *lower left* The Bettman Archive; *upper and lower right* Byron Collection/Museum of the City of New York. 197 *(all)* Brown Brothers.198 *top left* The Kiplinger Collection; *top right* New York Public Library. 199 *top* Museum of American Textile History; bottom Bruce Torrence Historical Collection. 200 *(both)* Marc Wanamaker/Bison Archives. 201 *top left* Danbury Scott-Fanton Museum & Historical

Society; *lower right* New York Public Library. 202 *top* Collection of Whitney Museum of American Art, NY; *bottom (both)* Museum of the City of New York. 203 *middle right* Metropolitan Board of Parks & Recreation, Nashville, TN; *bottom* Library of Congress. 204 *bottom* Missouri Botanical Gardens Archive, St. Louis, MO. 205 *(both)* Zoological Society of San Diego. 206 The Metropolitan Museum of Art; The Edward W.C. Arnold Collection of NY Prints, Maps & Pictures/Bequest of Edward W.C. Arnold, 1954. 207 *top* Library of Congress; *bottom* Hudson River Museum, Yonkers, NY. 208 Collection of Mr. & Mrs. Scheven Lorillard. 209 *(both)* Western Reserve Historical Society. 210 *upper left* Marshall Field Archive; *lower left* Collection of Brian McGinty. 211 *top* American Heritage; *bottom (plan)* Western Reserve Historical Society of Cleveland. 212 *top left* Frank Lloyd Wright Foundation; *upper center* Brown Brothers; *lower right* The Granger Collection, New York. 213 *upper right* Rebecca R. Shannon from "The City That Never Was."; *bottom* Avery Library/Columbia University. 214 Collection of Mr. & Mrs Scheven Lorillard. 215 *top left* The Bettmann Archive; *lower right* Lee Friedlander; *bottom right (inset)* Hamilton Library/Tulane University. 216 *upper left* The Bettmann Archive; *bottom* Museum of the City of New York/J. Clarence Davies Collection; *lower left (inset)* Theatre Collection/ Museum of the City of NY. 217 F.O. Bailey Antiquarians. 218 Courtesy of the Cincinnati Historical Society. 219 *upper right* Staten Island Historical Society; *middle left* "NY In The Nineteenth Century" by John Grafton/Dover Books; *bottom left* The Bettmann Archive; bottom right Library of Congress. 220 *top left* Franklin Institute Science Museum; *bottom* Courtesy CIGNA Museum & Art Collection, Philadelphia. 221 *top* Culver Pictures; *lower right* Historical Pictures. 222 *upper left* Courtesy of The New-York Historical Society, New York City; *bottom* The Bettmann Archive. 223 *top left* Brown Brothers; *middle right* Culver Pictures. 224 *top right* American Heritage; *middle left* Library of Congress; *bottom right* American Heritage. 225 *(both)* Virginia State Library. 226-227 *background* Tom Bean/The Stock Market. 226 *top* Bureau of Agricultural Economics/National Archives; *lower left* The Bettmann Archive; *right* Culver Pictures. 227 *upper left* The Bettmann Archive; *lower left* Culver Pictures. 228 The Thomas Gilcrease Institute of American History and Art, Tulsa, Oklahoma. 229 top Walters Art Gallery, Baltimore; *bottom* New York Public Library Picture Collection. 230 *(all)* Joslyn Art Museum, Omaha, Nebraska. 231 *(all except middle right)* Joslyn Art Museum, Omaha, Nebraska; *middle right* The Thomas Gilcrease Institute of American History and Art, Tulsa, Oklahoma. 232 *top* Massachussetts Historical Society. 232-233 *bottom* Coe Collection of Western Americana, Yale University. 234 *lower left* Library of Congress; *bottom left* California Historical Society, San Francisco/San Marino. 235 *top and bottom left* Courtesy Huntington Library, San Marino, California; *top to bottom right* (all) Courtesy of American Heritage. 236 *(all)* Loyola University Press, Chicago. 237 *top* The Thomas Gilcrease Institute of American History and Art, Tulsa, Oklahoma; *lower right* Library of Congress; *bottom right* Courtesy Buffalo Bill Historical Center, Cody, Wyoming; photographed by Lucille Warters. 238 *upper left* From the Collections of the Research Libraries of The New York Public Library; *bottom* Library of Congress. 239 *(both)* Library of Congress. 240 Remington Art Museum, Ogdensburg, New York. 241 *top* The Thomas Gilcrease Institute of American History and Art, Tulsa, Oklahoma; *bottom* Library of Congress. 242 *middle* Library of Congress; *bottom left* Dallas Historical Society. 243 UPI/Bettmann Newsphotos. 244. *top left* The Thomas Gilcrease Institute of American History and Art, Tulsa, Oklahoma; *bottom* The Center for American History, The University of Texas at Austin. 245 The Thomas Gilcrease Institute of American History and Art, Tulsa, Oklahoma. 244-245 top *(background)* Courtesy Buffalo Bill Historical Center, Cody, Wyoming. 246 *top* Yale University Library; *lower left* Historical Society of North Dakota; *bottom (inset)* Courtesy Picture Collection of the State Historical Society of North Dakota. 247 The Thomas Gilcrease Institute of American History and Art, Tulsa, Oklahoma. 248 *top* Collection of Mr. and Mrs. W.D. Weiss; courtesy of the Buffalo Bill Historical Center, Cody, Wyoming; *bottom* Collection of David R. Phillips, Chicago. 249 *lower center* Archives and Manuscripts Division, Oklahoma Historical Society; *bottom right* Culver Pictures. 250 *top* The Granger Collection, New York; middle *left* UPI/Bettmann; bottom The Bettmann Archive. 251 *upper left* UPI/Bettmann; *middle right* The Granger Collection, New York; *bottom right* Century Magazine; courtesy of the New York Public Library. 250-251 *bottom center* Colorado Historical Society. 252 *top right* Bryan Peterson/The Stock Market; *middle* Culver Pictures; *lower right* The Bettmann Archive. 253 *middle right* The Granger Collection, New York; *bottom* The Edward Mulligan Collection; courtesy of the University of Alaska Archives, Fairbanks. 254 *upper center* Coe Collection; Yale University Library; far left The Bettmann Archive. 255 *top* Library of Congress; *bottom* California State Library; *far right top to bottom both* Ted Mahieu/The Stock Market. 256 The Henry E. Huntington Library and Art Gallery. 257 *top right* Saint Joseph Museum, Missouri; *middle right* Brown Brothers; *bottom left* The Granger Collection, New York. 258 *top* Library of Congress; *bottom right* The Harvard Theater Collection, Cambridge, MA. 259 Nevada Historical Society. 260 Courtesy of the California Historical Society. 261 *top* Collection of Case and Draper, Photographers; courtesy Alaska State Library; *bottom* Denver Public Library, Western History Department. 262 *background* Joel Glenn/The Image Bank. 262 *upper left* Brown Brothers; *lower left* The Bettman Archive; *upper right* UPI/Bettman; 263 *upper left* Culver Pictures; *bottom* Brown Brothers. 264 *top right* As presented in Scientific American, August, 1846; *lower right* U.S. Department of Commerce, Patent and Trademarks Division; *lower left* As presented in American Mechanic, June, 1842 265 *top* From the Collection of the Minnesota Historical Society; *middle* Presented in American Mechanic, May, 1842; *bottom* Richard Cheek. 266 *top* The Granger Collection, New York; *bottom* Curt Teich Postcard Archives, Lake County, (IL) Museum. 267 *upper right* Smithsonian Institution; National Museum of American History, Warshaw Collection of Business Americana; *lower left and bottom right* U.S. Department of Commerce, Patent Office. 268 *top left and right* The Connecticut Historical Society, Hartford, CT. *bottom* New York Public Library 269 *top* The Bettman Archive; *middle* Culver Pictures; *bottom* Jim Bean, Inc., Courtesy the New York Public Library Picture Collection. 270 *(both)* Warshaw Collection, National Museum of American History, Smithsonian Institution. 271 The Procter and Gamble Company, Cincinnati, Ohio. 272 *top and inset* Porter/Novelli, Chicago, Illinois. 273 *top* The Bettmann Archive; *bottom* Johnson & Johnson. 274 *bottom* The Bettmann Archive; *far left top to bottom (all)* University of Illinois Library, Champagne, IL. 275 *top left and right* National Museum of American History, Ayer Collection; Smithsonian Institution; *bottom right* National Museum of American History, 3M Company Collection; Smithsonian Institution. 276 *top left* Culver Pictures; *bottom left (both)* Peabody Museum of Salem; gift of Miss Sarah A. Cheever. 277 *top* Library of Congress. 276-277 *bottom* Peabody Museum of Salem. 278 *(all)* The Mary Lea Shane Archives of the Lick Observatory; The University Library, University of California, Santa Cruz, CA. 279 *bottom left* The Granger Collection, New York; *far right top to bottom (all)* Curt Teich Postcard Archives, Lake County (IL) Museum. 280-81 *top* The Food Marketing Institute, Washington, DC; 280 *bottom left* The Curtis Publishing Company, *bottom center (inset)* The Smithsonian Institution. 281 R. Kord/H. Armstrong Roberts. 282 *top* Avon Products, Inc.; *middle and bottom* Gerber Products Company, Freemont, Michigan. 283 Alfred Eisenstaedt/Life Magazine, December 13, 1937. 284 UPI/Bettmann. 285 *top* UPI/Bettmann; *middle left* Collection of Carla Davidson; *middle right* New York Public Library; *bottom* Brown Brothers. 286 *(both)* The Greystone Society. 287 *top* Brown Brothers; bottom Hagley Museum, Wilmington, Delaware. 288 *top left and middle left* Rebus Inc.; *top right* Culver Pictures; *bottom left and bottom center* National Cash Register Corporation. 289 *top* Archive Photos; *far right* The Arizona Republic and The Phoenix Gazette; *bottom* UPI/Bettmann. 290 *upper left and bottom* The Bettmann Archive; upper right New York Public Library. 291 *(both)* The Granger Collection, New York. 292 *(both)* The Bettmann Archive. 293 *top left* The Granger Collection, New York; *top right* Wadsworth Atheneum, Hartford, CT; *bottom right* UPI/Bettmann. 294-95 *background* Alvis Upitis/The Image Bank. 294 *bottom* Culver Pictures; *upper right* The Bettman Archive; *bottom right* The Granger Collection, New York; 295 *upper left* The Bettman Archive; *bottom left* Culver Pictures. 296-297 *top* Courtesy of the New Hampshire Historical Society, Concord; 296 *bottom* The Granger Collection, New York. 297 *top right* The Bettmann Archive; *lower right* Brown Brothers. 298 *upper left* Brown Brothers; *lower right* The Bettmann Archive. 299 *top and middle* Brown Brothers; *bottom* Library of Congress. 300 *(both)* Culver Pictures. 301 *top left* Buckminster Fuller Institute; *upper center* UPI/Bettmann; *bottom* Brown Brothers. 302 *top left* Brown Brothers; *middle right* The Bettman Archive; *bottom left* The Bettmann Archive; 303 *upper right* Brown Brothers; *lower right* The Bettman Archive; *bottom* AP/Wide World Photos. 304 *top left* National Automotive History Collection, Detroit Public Library; *top right* Lake County (IL) Museum/Curt Teich Postcard Archives. 305 *top* Brown Brothers; *bottom (both)* AP/Wide World Photos. 306 *far left* Collection of Douglas A. Yorke, Jr.; *bottom* Motorbooks International, Osceola, Wisconsin. 307 *top* Shell Oil Company; *middle* Texaco Inc.; *bottom* American Petroleum Institute. 308 *(both)* The Granger Collection, New York. 309 *(both)* Florida Collection/Monroe County Public Library, Key West, FL. 310 *top right* Library of Congress; *upper left* The Granger Collection, New York; *bottom* Southern Pacific. 311 *upper left* The Bettmann Archive; *bottom* The Granger Collection, New York. 312 *top* The Bettmann Archive; *bottom* Union Pacific Railroad Museum Collection. 313 New York Central Railroad. 314 *top and bottom left* Library of Congress. 315 *top right* The Bettmann Archive; *bottom right* National Hobo Association, Los Angeles, CA. 314-315 *top* Painting by Drummond Mansfield; courtesy of the artist. 316 *(both)* The Bettmann Archive. 317 *top left* The Mariners' Museum, Newport News, VA; *middle right* Peabody & Essex Museum, Salem, MA; *bottom right (inset)* Painting by Mr. Carl G. Evers, Southbury, CT. 318 *upper left* From "Tales of The Mississippi," by A. Heritage, Jr. and L.B. Book; *middle right* Library of Congress; *bottom* Joan and Thomas Gandy Collection; courtesy Myrtle Bank Galleries, Mississippi. 319 *top* State Historical Society of Missouri; *bottom right* Lake County (IL) Museum/ Curt Teich Postcard Archives. 320 *left* Smithsonian Institution; *bottom right* Culver Pictures. 321 *bottom right* U.S. Coast Guard; *lower right* (inset) Brown Brothers. 322 *upper left* The Bettmann Archive; *top right* Library of Congress; *bottom* UPI/Bettmann. 323 *top right* New York Public Library; *middle right (inset)* National Air and Space Museum/Smithsonian Institution; *bottom* Culver Pictures. 324 *top right, middle and bottom left* National Air and Space Museum/Smithsonian Institution; *lower right* Culver Pictures. 325 *top* UPI/Bettmann; *bottom* William Underwood Collection. 326 *top* National Air and Space Museum/Smithsonian Institution; *lower left* William Simon. 327 *top right* National Air and Space Museum/Smithsonian Institution; *upper center (inset)* Library of Congress; *lower right* United Airlines. 326-327 *bottom* United Airlines. 328 *top right* The Glenn H. Curtiss Museum, Hammondsport, New York; *middle left* UPI/Bettmann; *bottom left* Brown Brothers. 329 *top right* National Air and Space Museum/ Smithsonian Institution; *bottom both* Norman Bel Geddes Collection; courtesy of the University of Texas at Austin. 330-331 *background* R.Krubner/H. Armstrong Roberts. 330 *top left* The Granger Collection, New York; *top to bottom right* H. Armstrong Roberts; The Bettman Archive; AP/Wide world Photos. 331 *top* Culver Pictures. 332 *upper right* Culver Pictures; *middle left* Connecticut Historical Society; *bottom* Courtesy Boston Museum of Fine Arts; William Wilkins Warren Fund. 333 *top left* H. Armstrong Roberts; *(inset)* Wide World Photos; *bottom* National Archives. 334 *top* The Granger Collection, New York; *bottom* Courtesy of The New-York Historical Society, New York City. 335 *(both)* Culver Pictures. 336 *upper left* The Bettmann Archive; bottom left Culver Pictures. 337 *middle* Collection of Lee and Rally Dennis, Portsmouth, NH; 336-337 *bottom center* The Bettman Archive 338 *top left* The Granger Collection, New York; *lower center (portrait)* Wide World; Photos; *lower center* Culver Pictures. 339 *top right* Ripley Entertainment; *middle* New York Public Library Picture Collection/Ripley Enterprises; *bottom* Culver Pictures. 340 *upper left* The Granger Collection, New York; *lower center* New York Public Library Picture Collection; *bottom left to right* King Features; King Features; NANCY reprinted by permission of UFS, Inc. 341 *top and upper center* King Features; *far right* Henry Groskinsky; *lower center* The Smithsonian Institution; *bottom left to right* Newspaper Feature Service; New York Public Library Picture Collection; Chicago Tribune; King Features. 342 *(both)* Culver Pictures. 343 *top (both)* Culver Pictures; *bottom* Curtis Publishing; courtesy New York Public Library Picture Collection. 344 *top right* The Bettmann Archive; *upper center* The Buffalo Bill Historical Society; *bottom* Mercantile Library. 345 *top left* Mercantile Library; *middle left* New York Public Library Picture Collection; *middle right* The Granger Collection, New York; *bottom* Charles Phillips. 346 *top right* Culver Pictures; *lower left* Library of Congress. 347 *top right* From International Photographer, 1933; *bottom* Denver Public Library. 348 *top* Museum of the City of New York; Harry T. Peters Collection; *bottom* H. Armstrong Roberts. 349 *top* Artkraft Strauss; *bottom left* Buffalo and Erie County Historical Society, Buffalo, NY; *bottom right* Brown Brothers. 350-351 *(top row) from left to right* Collection of H. Thomas Steele; Collection of Ewald Van Elkan; Collection of Ewald Van Elkan; Collection of H. Thomas Steele; Collection of H. Thomas Steele; *(middle row) all except second from left* Collection of H. Thomas Steele; *second from left* Collection of Ewald Van Elkan; *(bottom row) all except third from left* H. Thomas Steele; *third from left* Collection of Ewald Van Elkan. 352 *top* International Museum of Photography at George Eastman House; *bottom* Chicago Historical Society. 353 *top left* The Bettmann Archive; upper right ("Photography Reduced to Three Motions") Eastman Kodak Company; *upper right* International Museum of Photography at George Eastman House. 352-353 *middle* (train) Chicago Historical Society. 354 *upper left* International Museum of Photography at George Eastman House; *top right* Library of Congress; *lower left* Oakland Museum, Oakland CA; *bottom right* Edward L. Bafford Photography Collection; University of Maryland, Baltimore County Library. 355 *top (both)* From the Archives and Collections of The International Center of Photography; *bottom left* Museum of the City of New York; *bottom right* The George Arents Research Library for Special Collection; Syracuse University. 356 *top left* The Granger Collection, New York; *lower left* California State Library; 357 *lower left (inset)* UPI/Bettmann; *bottom right* National Postal Museum/Smithsonian Institution. 356-357 *top center* National Archives, U.S. Signal Corps #111-SC-10630. 358 *from top to bottom* Curt Teich Postcard Archives, Lake County (IL) Museum; New York Public Library Picture Collection; Collection of Romy Charlesworth; New York Public Library Picture Collection; The Bettmann Archive; *bottom far right* Viesti Associates, Inc. 359 *top left* The Cousley Collection; *top right* Postmaster's Advocate; *bottom left* Smithsonian Institution; *bottom right* Library of Congress. 360 *top left* John Ripley; *middle right* The Granger Collection, New York; *bottom left* The Marnon Collection, Minneapolis, MN. 361 *middle* American Telephone & Telegraph Company; *bottom right* Sy Seidman/Culver Pictures. 362 *top left* Library of Congress; *top right* Wide World Photos; *bottom* The Granger Collection, New York. 363 *top* © 1993 Florists' Transworld Delivery Association (FTD ®). Reprinted with permission from "Since 1910: A History of FTD"; *bottom* Wide World Photos. 364 *top and inset* The Bettmann Archive; *bottom left* The Kansas City Star; *bottom left* Library of Congress. 365 *top* Culver Pictures; *bottom* The Bettmann Archive. 366 *top and bottom right* Culver Pictures; *lower left* Everett Collection. 367 *(both)* UPI/Bettmann.

Efforts have been made to contact the holder of the copyright for each picture. In several cases these sources have been untraceable, for which we offer our apologies.

Art Credits

Sylvia Bokor: 36, 57 *upper left*, 267 *bottom right*. Dominic A. Colacchio (handcoloring): 94 *top right*. Jill Enfield (handcoloring): 81 *center left*, 85 *top*, 93 *top*, 95 *bottom*, 118 *bottom*, 124, 127 *bottom*, 134 *top*, 136 *top*, 137 *bottom*, 184, 199 *bottom*, 200 *bottom*, 255 *bottom*, 278 *center, left*, 292, 298 *top*, 318 *center*, 323 *bottom*, 342 *bottom*. Ann Mancaruso (handcoloring): 57, 61, 68-9. Chuck Schmidt (handlettering) 26, 67, 151, 176, 214, 253, 287, 313, 316. Neil Shigley: 13,165 *top right*. (spot art)-22, 32, 50, 53, 94, 100, 106, 116, 120, 140, 146, 162, 171, 176, 192, 204, 206, 207, 228, 233, 240, 259, 264, 266, 271, 284,296, 308, 316, 334 *top left*, 346 *top left*. Bill Shortridge: 115 *center*, 135, 242-3 *bottom*, 315 *box art*. Robert Villani: 73 *left*.

INDEX

Page numbers in **bold** type refer to illustrations.

K

L

M

N

P

T – U

Page numbers in **bold** type refer to illustrations.